Suicidology

Suicidology

Essays in Honor of Edwin S. Shneidman

Edited by
Antoon A. Leenaars

Consulting Editors
**Alan L. Berman, Pamela Cantor,
Robert E. Litman, and Ronald W. Maris**

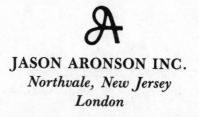

JASON ARONSON INC.
Northvale, New Jersey
London

This book was set in 10-point Baskerville by Lind Graphics of Upper Saddle River, New Jersey, and printed and bound by Haddon Craftsmen of Scranton, Pennsylvania.

10 9 8 7 6 5 4 3 2 1

Library of Congress Cataloging-in-Publication Data

Suicidology : essays in honor of Edwin S. Shneidman / edited by Antoon
    A. Leenaars ; consulting editors, Alan L. Berman . . . [et al.].
        p.   cm.
    Includes bibliographical references and index.
    ISBN 0-87668-571-8
    1. Suicide.   2. Shneidman, Edwin S. — Bibliography.   I. Shneidman,
Edwin S.   II. Leenaars, Antoon A.   III. Berman, Alan L. (Alan Lee),
1943-
    [DNLM: 1. Suicide — prevention & control.   HV 6545]
RC569.S943   1993
616.85′8445 — dc20
DNLM/DLC
for Library of Congress   93-12028

Manufactured in the United States of America. Jason Aronson Inc. offers books and cassettes. For information and catalog write to Jason Aronson Inc., 230 Livingston Street, Northvale, New Jersey 07647.

To
Edwin S. Shneidman
Father of Suicidology
from
his friends and colleagues
on the occasion of his seventy-fifth birthday
May 13, 1993

CONTENTS

Many people make significant contributions to established fields of knowledge. But few are vouchsafed the rare opportunity to create a new discipline, to name it, to shape it, to contribute to it, and, most importantly, to catalyze other competent investigators to invest in it. This book is dedicated to Edwin Shneidman, the father of contemporary suicidology.

Shneidman began his career in suicidology after his discovery of a collection of several hundred suicide notes at the Los Angeles Medical Examiner's vault while on an errand from the Veterans Administration hospital in which he was working. The decisive moment of his suicidological life was not when he came across the notes but rather a few minutes later, when he had a glimmering that the vast potential value of the notes could be immeasurably increased if he did *not* read them, but rather compared them blindly, in a controlled experiment, with simulated suicide notes, elicited from matched nonsuicidal persons. John Stuart Mill's Method of Difference came to his side and handed Shneidman a scientific career. The Chronology at the end of the volume gives some indication of the development of his career in suicidology.

Shneidman describes himself as "a would be student who has been struggling all his life to be a scholar and a scientist." That explains exactly his interest and his obsession. Thematic windows to his life are Herman Melville and literature *and* Henry A. Murray and psychology. Melville was certainly a scholar who seems to have aspired to be a scientist and a philosopher. Murray and, I would add, Shneidman are first rate in all three: scholar, scientist, and clinician.

There is an intellectual permissiveness to study phenomena in natural and laboratory settings. In this respect, Shneidman resembles Murray, who steadfastly opposed reductionism, whether positivistic behaviorism or biological nosology. Suicide is a multifaceted event, and suicidology is the study of psychological, biological, cultural, sociological, interpersonal, intrapsychic, logical, conscious and unconscious, and philosophical elements in the suicidal event. The field of suicidology encourages both nomothetic (statistical) as well as idiographic (intensive case study) approaches to knowledge.

The essays in this *Festschrift* represent the breadth of Shneidman's interests and reflect the range and significance of the discipline he founded. They are written by his friends and colleagues to honor him on his seventy-fifth birthday.

Antoon A. Leenaars

CONTRIBUTORS

Nancy H. Allen received her M.P.H. degree from the University of California, Berkeley. She was Assistant Chief of the Bureau of Health Education for the California Department of Public Health. She joined Dr. Shneidman in the Laboratory for the Study of Life-Threatening Behavior at the University of California, Los Angeles Center for Health Sciences in 1973. She is a past president of the American Association of Suicidology and the author of *Homicide: Perspectives on Prevention.*

Margaret P. Battin, Ph.D., is professor of philosophy and adjunct professor of internal medicine at the University of Utah. She holds an M.F.A. in Fiction Writing and a Ph.D. in Philosophy, both from the University of California at Irvine. She has authored or edited eight books, including a study of philosophical issues in suicide. In recent years, she has been engaged in research on active euthanasia and assisted suicide in the Netherlands and Germany. Her next book, *The Least Worst Death,* will be published in 1993.

Alan L. Berman, who took his Ph.D. from The Catholic University of America, taught at American University for twenty-two years. In 1991 he was appointed Director of the National Center for the Study and Prevention of Suicide at the Washington School of Psychiatry in Washington, D.C., where he also maintains a private practice at the Washington Psychological Center. He is a past president of the American Association of Suicidology. His published works include *Adolescent Suicide: Assessment and Intervention, Suicide: Prevention Case Consultations,* and *Assessment and Prediction of Suicide.*

Pamela Cantor, Ph.D., is a lecturer in psychology in the Department of Psychiatry, Harvard Medical School; co-director of the Harvard Medical School Symposium on Suicide; and lecturer in psychiatry at The Cambridge

Hospital of Harvard University. She maintains an active private practice and her research and teaching in suicidology have focused on youth suicide. She is a former president of the American Association of Suicidology.

Norman L. Farberow, Ph.D., was co-founder and co-director with Shneidman of the Los Angeles Suicide Prevention Center and of V.A. Central Research Unit for the Study of Unpredicted Deaths in Los Angeles. He is both a past president of the American Association of Suicidology and of the International Association for Suicide Prevention. Dr. Farberow is presently directing the LASPC's Survivors After Suicide program, and continues to document his research on bereavement in spouses of elderly suicides. With two colleagues he is currently preparing a book on children in disaster.

Calvin J. Frederick, Ph.D., is adjunct professor in the Department of Psychiatry and Biobehavioral Sciences at the University of California, Los Angeles, and chief of Psychology Services at the Department of Veterans Affairs Medical Center, West Los Angeles. From 1968–1972 he was deputy chief of the Center for Studies of Suicide Prevention with Dr. Shneidman at the National Institute of Mental Health where he later became chief of Emergency Mental Health and Disaster Assistance. The primary focus of his work continues in the realm of psychic trauma and emergency mental health.

Milton Greenblatt, M.D., is professor emeritus and vice chairman, Department of Psychiatry and Biobehavioral Sciences, Neuropsychiatric Institute, University of California, Los Angeles School of Medicine, and Chief of Psychiatry, Los Angeles County Olive View/UCLA Medical Center, Sylmar, California. Dr. Greenblatt received his M.D. degree *cum laude* from Tufts School of Medicine in 1939. His numerous publications include twenty-five books and monographs, mainly in the field of psychiatric administration, and social and community psychiatry.

Mamoru Iga, Ph.D., is professor emeritus of sociology at California State University at Northridge. Born in Japan, Professor Iga was educated in Japan and in the United States. He is author of *The Thorn in the Chrysanthemum: Suicide and Economic Success in Japan.* He was a Fellow in the 1960s of the Los Angeles Suicide Prevention Centre and continues his association with Shneidman to this day.

Douglas Jacobs, M.D., has been on the faculty of Harvard Medical School for twenty years where he is assistant clinical professor of psychiatry. He has edited two books on suicide, *Suicide: Understanding and Response: Harvard Medical School Perspectives* and *Suicide and Clinical Practice.* He was the founder of the Harvard Medical School Suicide Symposium. He is currently project director of National Depression Screening Day. He maintains an active clinical practice and serves as a consultant in medicolegal cases when there has been a question or outcome of suicide.

Jack Kamerman received his Ph.D. from New York University. He is associate professor of sociology at Kean College in Union, New Jersey. He has written on the sociology of death and the sociology of music. He is actively researching the lives of the survivors left behind by the ninety-three New York City policemen who killed themselves between 1934 and 1940. He is author of the forthcoming book, *The Illegacy of Suicide.*

Marci E. Klein, M.A., Ed.M. received a masters degree in education at Harvard University in 1986. She is currently completing her doctorate in clinical psychology at the University of Michigan–Ann Arbor. Her dissertation research is on the relationship between socioeconomic variables and depressive symptomatology in homeless mothers. She has collaborated with Dr. Jacobs on psychological autopsies and research on suicide.

Antoon A. Leenaars, Ph.D., C.Psych. is a psychologist in private practice in Windsor, Ontario. His published works include *Suicide Notes, Suicide Prevention in Schools, Life-span Perspectives of Suicide,* and *Suicide and the Older Adult.* He is currently co-editing a volume on the treatment of suicidal people. He is first past president of the Canadian Association for Suicide Prevention and active in the American Association of Suicidology and the International Association for Suicide Prevention. He began his association with Dr. Shneidman in the studies of suicide notes.

Robert E. Litman, M.D., Ph.D., is a clinical professor of psychiatry in the Department of Psychiatry and Biobehavioral Sciences, University of California, Los Angeles School of Medicine. He received his M.D. from the University of Minnesota, and a Ph.D. in Psychoanalysis from the Southern California Psychoanalytic Institute. He is a past president of the American Association of Suicidology. His association with Dr. Shneidman began in the 1950s with the inception of the Suicide Prevention Center in Los Angeles, where he was chief psychiatrist, and continues to this day.

John T. Maltsberger, M.D., lecturer on psychiatry at the Harvard Medical School, has studied and written about suicide since he was a senior resident at the Massachusetts Mental Health Center in Boston. He is a member of the faculty of the Boston Psychoanalytic Society and Institute, and a senior consultant at McLean Hospital in Boston. He is a past president of the American Association of Suicidology, author of *Suicide Risk,* co-editor of *Assessment and Prediction of Suicide,* and co-editor of a forthcoming volume on the treatment of suicidal people.

Ronald W. Maris received his Ph.D. from the University of Illinois (Urbana). After teaching at Dartmouth, he took a post-doctoral fellowship in psychiatry at the Johns Hopkins University School of Medicine, where he remained to direct their M.D.–Ph.D. program in the Behavioral Sciences. Since 1973 he has been a professor at the University of South Carolina, director of its Center for the Study of Suicide, and editor of the journal, *Suicide and Life-Threatening Behavior.* He is a past president of the American Association of Suicidology.

Jerome A. Motto, M.D., is professor emeritus of psychiatry at the University of California, San Francisco. He received his M.D. from that institution in 1951 and has served on its faculty in the Department of Psychiatry since 1956. He is a past president of the American Association of Suicidology and active in the International Association for Suicide Prevention.

Caroline C. Murray, Ed.D., took her doctorate in education and psychology at Boston University in 1967. She continued at Boston University as co-director of the Boston University Psychoeducational Clinic before her appointment as lecturer on psychology in the Department of Psychiatry, Harvard Medical School, where she worked with the Trauma Clinic at Massachusetts Mental Health Center and with inner city schools. She, and her late husband, Dr. Henry A. Murray, have been closely associated with Dr. Shneidman for years.

Robert J. Myatt, Ph.D., is visiting assistant professor and director of the Social Skills Training Program, Department of Psychiatry and Biobehavioral Sciences, Neuropsychiatric Institute, University of California, Los Angeles School of Medicine, and director of the Adolescent Suicide Research and Intervention Program (ASRIP), Department of Adolescent Psychiatry, Los Angeles County Olive View/UCLA Medical Center, Sylmar, California.

Hershel Parker, Ph.D. is H. Fletcher Brown Professor of American Romanticism at the University of Delaware. His Ph.D. was from Northwestern University. Author of *Flawed Texts and Verbal Icons* (1984) and *Reading Billy Budd* (1990), he is associate general editor of the Northwestern-Newberry Edition of *The Writings of Herman Melville,* of which twelve volumes have appeared. He began his association with Dr. Shneidman through their mutual interest in Melville.

Cynthia R. Pfeffer, M.D., is professor of clinical psychiatry at Cornell Medical College and chief of the Child Psychiatry Inpatient Unit at the New York Hospital-Westchester Division. She is author of the book, *The Suicidal Child* and a former president of the American Association of Suicidology. Aside from an active clinical practice, Dr. Pfeffer researches suicide in children.

Fritz C. Redlich, M.D., is professor emeritus of psychiatry at the Department of Psychiatry and Biobehavioral Sciences, Neuropsychiatric Institute, University of California at Los Angeles School of Medicine. Dr. Redlich is former chairman of the Department of Psychiatry and former dean of the School of Medicine at Yale University. He is currently writing a biography of Adolf Hitler emphasizing the medical aspects of the dictator's life.

Jean-Pierre Soubrier, M.D., graduated from Paris University. He is currently professor at the Medical College of Paris Hospitals and chief of the Infirmerie Psychiatrique since 1980, a traditional (since 1872) department of emergency psychiatry. He began his association with Shneidman when he came to the United States as a Fulbright Research Fellow at the Los Angeles Suicide Prevention Center in 1965. He founded, in 1969, the Groupment d'Etudes et de Prevention du Suicide (France) and has been active in the American Association of Suicidology and the International Association for Suicide Prevention.

Yoshitomo Takahashi took his M.D. from Kanazawa University School of Medicine. When he was assistant professor of psychiatry at Yamanashi Medical College, he was given an opportunity by the Fulbright Commission to study suicide prevention programs and psychotherapy for the dying patient under Professor Shneidman's guidance at the Neuropsychiatric Institute, University of California at Los Angeles between 1987 and 1988. He is presently vice-councilor of the Research Department of Psychopathology, Tokyo Institute of Psychiatry.

Louis Jolyon West, M.D., is professor of psychiatry, Department of Psychiatry and Biobehavioral Sciences, Neuropsychiatric Institute, University of California at Los Angeles School of Medicine. He is the former chairman of the Department (1969–1989) and director of that Institute. He is responsible for bringing Dr. Shneidman back to UCLA. Dr. West is an authority on brainwashing, cults, and violence.

Shirley L. Zimmerman, Ph.D., ACSW, professor of family social science at the University of Minnesota, teaches courses on family policy, including family policy research. She has written numerous articles related to that topic and is also the author of *Understanding Family Policy: Theoretical Orientations* published in 1988 and *Family Policies and Family Well-being: The Role of Political Culture,* published in 1992.

HISTORY, DEVELOPMENT, AND PUBLIC POLICY
Part I

We are celebrating both Edwin Shneidman's seventy-fifth birthday and contemporary suicidology's forty-fifth year. The first systematic experiments of suicide notes in 1949 started a new field of study. Part I of this volume outlines suicidology's history and development and provides some comments on public policy. It consists of four chapters: an outline of the evolution of contemporary suicidology as a professional career; a look at the precontemporary suicidology of one hundred years ago; an examination of the definition of suicide; and an examination of the political culture, public policy choices, and unmet needs that makes the point that advocacy in suicidology is needed in the future to meet the needs of vulnerable people seeking a solution to their problems.

1: THE EVOLUTION OF SUICIDOLOGY

Ronald W. Maris

The word *suicide* was first used by either Walter Charleton (1651) or Sir Thomas Browne (1642) (see Shneidman 1985). Shneidman himself begins his original definition of suicide as "the human act of self-inflicted, self-intended cessation" (Shneidman 1973); his most recent definition ends: "currently in the Western world, suicide is a conscious act of self-induced annihilation, best understood as a multidimensional malaise in a needful individual who defines an issue for which the suicide is perceived as the best solution" (Shneidman 1985, p. 203). For a more extensive review of the word *suicide* see my entry in the *Encyclopedia of Human Biology* (Maris 1991).

Suicidology, on the other hand, has been defined as "the study of suicide and its prevention" (Simpson and Weiner 1989, p. 145). The partial entry is as follows:

> **suicidology** The study of suicide and its prevention. Hence **suicidologist.**
>
> [**1929** W. A. Bongar in **Psychiatrish-Jurridish Geselschap** 9 Feb. 3 . . . the **suicidologie** . . . zou men haar kunnen noemen . . . **1964** E. S. Shneidman in **Contemp. Psychol.** IX. 371/2, I thank Louis Dublin, the Grand Old Man of **Suicidology**, for this book because in it he has given us all new clues to suicide. **1967 — Bull. Suicidology** July 7/2 The 10-point program for suicide prevention here outlined is a mutual enterprise whose successful development depends on the active interest, support, and activities of **'suicidologists'. 1969 Nature** 4 Oct. 12/2 The Johns Hopkins University in collaboration with the National Institutes of Mental Health has established a course in **'suicidology'** . . . **1976** E. S. Shneidman Suicidology 7 **Suicidology** is defined as the scientific study of suicidal phenomena.

A *suicidologist* can be defined as a professional who studies suicide. On March 20, 1968, in Chicago, Shneidman founded the American Association of Suicidology dedicated to the development of suicidology and the training of suicidologists (Shneidman 1991). In the remainder of this chapter I shall (as Dr. Shneidman might say) explicate the concept of suicidology, review the subdisciplines or domains of suicidology, examine past and current suicidology training programs, then conclude with considerations of the needs, problems, and prospects of suicidology. In a nutshell we shall examine both the prospects and products of Dr. Shneidman's dream for suicidology. The reader is well advised to review Dr. Shneidman's own autobiographical account of suicidological history (Walker 1991).

Although objectivity and comprehensiveness are my aims, no doubt someone's program, course, publication, perspective, idea, may have been omitted inadvertently or perhaps even misstated. I apologize in advance for these possible shortcomings. Also, any unreferenced opinions or interpretations expressed are solely my own.

THE CONCEPT EXPLICATED

Suicidology is akin to psychology or sociology. That is, it is the science of self-destructive behaviors, thoughts, feelings, and so forth, in the same way that psychology is the science that deals with the mind and mental process, feelings, desires, and so forth. Probably to many suicidology sounds alien, but no doubt so did psychology and sociology at first. Suicidology is unlike psychology in that suicidology has usually included not just the study of suicide, but also its prevention. In a sense suicidology is like internal medicine. An internist might well say, "You have a lump in your breast" or "You have a mass in your prostate— *a surgeon ought to take a look at it*" (Edwin Shneidman, personal communication). Not to add the suggested clinical intervention would be highly inappropriate. Nevertheless, there are some suicidologists who claim that the concept of suicidology does not logically entail suicide prevention (e.g., see Battin 1991).

Shneidman's original concept of suicidology envisioned university departments, Masters and Ph.D. degree programs, basic textbooks (see Perlin 1975), internships, residencies, postdoctoral fellowships (like the Johns Hopkins University Medical School program described below), a professional journal (viz., *Suicide and Life-Threatening Behavior*), annual scientific conferences (e.g., the American Association of Suicidology—in its twenty-fifth year as of 1992), tenure, professional titles, and licenses (as suicidologists), board certification, a research and training grant section at the National Institutes of Mental Health, paraprofessional certification, and so forth—all in the aborning field of suicidology.

Although emphatically (according to Shneidman) not reducible to medicine or psychiatry, suicidology probably should be a psychosocial specialty within medical schools. Shneidman has always regarded suicidology as a clinical discipline, but not a biological, chemical, neurological, laboratory research discipline. Shneidman contends that suicidology is always "personology" (1985). That is, suicides occur one at a time in a pained, perturbed, stressed individual human being who intends to cease living. The American Association of

Suicidology has always had suicide prevention and crisis intervention center institutional members, and suicidological education has usually included supervised clinical field placements.

Suicidology has always been an *interdisciplinary* discipline, a source of both its strength and many problems. For example, Blumenthal and Kupfer (1990) see suicidal behaviors as being divided into five overlapping domains: biology, psychiatry, family history and genetics, psychosocial life events, and personality and psychology (Cf., Maris, Berman, Maltsberger, et al. 1992, Shneidman 1985). Shneidman has always insisted that suicidology is not reducible to any one of its domains. For example, suicidology is not just the study of brain neurochemistry, nor suicide prevention simply the dispensing of antidepressant medication. My own view is that suicidology ought to be conceived of as a *biopsychosocial* discipline. Incredibly important basic research is now being done by research psychiatrists and neuropharmacologists like J. John Mann at the University of Pittsburgh and Michael Stanley at Columbia University. Suicidology may not be reducible to biology, but neither can it afford to ignore it.

THE SUBDISCIPLINES OF SUICIDOLOGY

Suicidology has subdisciplines rooted or based in, and assumes prior education, training, experience, and/or licensing in, one or more of the following professional fields:

medicine, psychiatry
psychology
social science (sociology, anthropology, economics)
public health, biostatistics, epidemiology
nursing, especially psychiatric nursing
social work, family studies
psychoanalysis
criminology, criminal justice
law, forensic sciences
biology, genetics, endocrinology
neuropharmacology, brain studies
philosophy, ethics
education, counseling
religion, theology
government, politics
drama, theater, literature

These areas or subdisciplines of suicidology could be extended or refined almost indefinitely.

Some of the above specialties traditionally have been regarded as more basic to suicidology than others—psychiatry, for instance, and to a lesser degree, psychology and nursing. The law tends more easily to recognize psychiatrists as

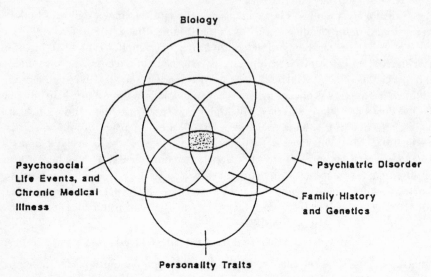

OVERLAP MODEL
(Five Domains)

FIGURE 1-1. Overlap Model for Suicidal Behavior From *Suicide Over the Life-Cycle,* edited by S. J. Blumenthal and D. J. Kupfer, p. 693. Copyright © American Psychiatric Press. Reproduced by permission. Washington, DC: American Psychiatric Press, 1990.

suicidologists or suicide experts. Any psychiatrist is usually accepted as a suicide expert in court by most judges, but non-MD (mainly psychology Ph.D.s) suicidologists sometimes are not recognized as suicide experts or are seen to have a very limited range of justifiable opinions (e.g., excluding not only psychotropic medication but sometimes even mental disorder diagnosis, as Figure 1-1 suggests), even though psychiatrists often cannot name a single citation on suicide and have never conducted or published any suicide research at all.

The list of subdisciplines of suicidology above suggests types of courses in a suicidology curriculum, degree programs, departments, or even chapters in a suicidology textbook (a definitive one has yet to be written). Suicidology requires many subdisciplines because the etiology of suicide is complex and multifaceted. It follows that suicidology and most suicidologists are often generalists. Of course, one could also argue that suicidology itself is general but that suicidologists should be specialized.

SUICIDOLOGY TRAINING

So how does one become a suicidologist? Are there training programs where an aspiring suicidologist could go study? What form, length, focus, degrees, and so forth do suicidology programs have? Are there any jobs for suicidologists?

The Johns Hopkins University Medical School Program

While there are not now, nor have there ever been, any university suicidology departments, M.A., or Ph.D. programs, at one time there was a full-year postdoctoral fellowship program at the prestigious Johns Hopkins University School of Medicine in Baltimore (Maris et al. 1973). As a part of his dream for suicidology, Dr. Edwin Shneidman, in concert with Drs. Seymour Perlin and Chester Schmidt of the Psychiatry Department of the Johns Hopkins Medical School created (in May 1967) the first postgraduate fellowship in suicidology. Johns Hopkins received a grant of $1 million from the Center for Studies of Suicide Prevention at the National Institutes of Mental Health for a five-year training program (the last two years, 1970 and 1971, were actually completed at Saint Elizabeth's Hospital in Washington, D.C., under the direction of Harvey L. P. Resnik, M.D. The Saint Elizabeth's suicidology program opened training to some students with only a B.A. or B.S. degree).

The main idea was that suicidologists-to-be would have already completed either a Ph.D., M.A., M.D., M.S.W., or R.N. degree and have had a minimum of three years postgraduate experience. Between 1967 and 1969 twenty-one students were trained: three from medicine, four from psychology, five from sociology, five from religion, three from nursing, and one from social work (roughly the same number of students and fields continued during the St. Elizabeth's years, 1969–1971). Included were graduates Daniel Lettieri, Carol Huffine, Pamela Cantor, Lee Ann Hoff, Bill Swanson, and Ronald Maris — just to mention a few.

The suicidology fellowship program at Hopkins was designed somewhat like a medical internship or condensed psychiatric residency training program. Academic courses included crisis intervention, principles of suicide prevention, sociology of suicide, biostatistics, psychology of suicide, depression and aggression, children and adolescents, epidemiology, a clinical case conference, a research seminar, an acute treatment clinic in the emergency room, a medical examiner's practicum (all the fellows were deputized and did psychological autopsies), law and suicide (including a moot court at the University of Maryland Law School), religious and philosophical perspectives, epidemiology of mental illness, and a supervised clinical field placement at a suicide prevention or crisis intervention center somewhere in the United States (e.g., Los Angeles, San Francisco, Buffalo, Gainesville, Seattle, etc.).

Several of the graduates of the Hopkins/Saint Elizabeth's suicidology programs went on to become distinguished suicidologists, directors at the NIMH, authors of important books and articles on suicide and suicide prevention, respected clinicians, directors of major suicide prevention centers, presidents and prize winners in the American Association of Suicidology, and so forth. Unfortunately, the Hopkins/St. Elizabeth's suicidology program was discontinued after only five years as a combined result of Dr. Shneidman's leaving the NIMH, shifts in funding priorities, new political emphases, and training money shortages. Today no such suicidology training program exists anywhere, even though there are about six hundred suicide prevention/crisis intervention centers in operation in the United States and a persistent demand for training from both academics and clinicians.

Thus, if you want to become a suicidologist today, in essence you have to put together your own training program, find your own study money, select your own reading list (although the American Association of Suicidology helps out here), fund much of your own research (since the NIMH offers relatively few grants in suicide research these days [see Moscicki 1991]), prove your own credentials and certification, and maybe create your own job (if not your own salary). To say that suicidologists face an uphill climb is an understatement!

Washington School of Psychiatry Certificate
Training Program in the Assessment and Treatment
of the Suicidal Patient

Almost twenty-five years after the Hopkins/St. Elizabeth's suicidology postgraduate fellowships a new certificate training program in suicidology is attempting to get started at the Washington School of Psychiatry under the directorship of Alan L. Berman, Ph.D. Like the Hopkins program, the Washington certificate program is for postgraduate education. Unlike the Hopkins program it is only for one hundred hours a year over five long weekends (Thursday to Sunday) and does not offer paid fellowships (which are probably the key to successful training in any subject).

The certificate program of the new National Center for the Study and Prevention of Suicide (the agency within the Washington School that offers the training) states its general program and objectives as follows:

> Suicidal behavior is the most frequently encountered mental health emergency for the mental health professional. Recent surveys have found that the average psychiatrist has a 50% chance of having a patient suicide; the corresponding odds for a psychologist are almost one in four. One increasingly untoward consequence of these patient deaths is the threat of litigation alleging malpractice on the part of the treating clinician. One significant explanation for these realities is that the typical mental health professional is seriously undertrained to deal with the suicidal patient. Given this, it is imperative that clinicians receive extensive training in the current practice of assessing and treating suicidal patients. Inaugurated in June, 1991 and continuing over four long weekends through the calendar year, the certificate program entails 100 hours of training with a renowned national faculty.

For 1991–1992 the faculty and curriculum of the certificate program included (in chronological order for each of the five weekends):

Ronald Maris, Ph.D. Lectures on the developmental career of the suicidal patient, empirical overview of suicide assessment and prediction, the ethics of suicide and suicide intervention, psychoanalytic thought on suicide.

John T. Maltsberger, M.D. The formulation of suicide risk, transference/

countertransference and the suicidal patient, and the psychotherapy of the borderline patient.

Bryan Tanney, M.D. Mental disorders and suicide, biological therapies, the decision to hospitalize, voluntary and involuntary commitment, losing a patient to suicide, working with ambivalence, inpatient care.

Cynthia Pfeffer, M.D., Alan Berman, Ph.D., and Joseph Richman, Ph.D. Life-span issues, the suicidal child, the suicidal adolescent, geriatric suicide, family therapy of the suicidal patient, humor in the treatment of the suicidal patient.

Alan Berman, Ph.D. and David A. Jobes, Ph.D. Psychotherapy and suicidal patients, cognitive-behavioral vs. psychodynamic treatments, working with survivors, malpractice, prevention, and community consultation.

Given the economic recession and the lack of fellowship funding for its students the Washington certificate program got off to a less than impressive start. Ten full-year registrants were needed to offer the certificate. Unfortunately, not enough students signed up, so the first weekend and the certificate program were cancelled for 1991–1992. However, the other four weekend programs were still offered and Dr. Berman hopes to initiate the suicide certificate program in future years. In spite of its initial problems this suicidology program remains one of the best prospects for sorely needed training.

Dr. Shneidman was probably right that if suicidology is ever going to become legitimate as a profession, specialty area, or scientific discipline, there will have to be at least one-year (ideally two- to three-year) postgraduate training programs like the Hopkins/St. Elizabeth's/Washington School programs—ideally leading to some kind of board certification. These fellowships will need to be funded by the federal government. Suicidology also needs more scientific journal articles; basic textbooks; competent paid M.D./Ph.D. faculty members; a few major universities and medical schools to house and care for the programs continuously over many years; a solid clinical suicidal patient component; a quality scientific suicide journal like *Suicide and Life-Threatening Behavior;* and, ultimately, more federal money for basic suicide research and training. Given the trend toward specialization in most professions and the fact that suicide is the eighth leading cause of death (and keeps moving up), there is no reason why Shneidman's dream could not be realized. Suicidology is a legitimate enterprise. It just needs to be developed, funded better, and made more substantive.

University-Based Courses

In contrast to full-year suicidology training programs several university suicidologists offer courses on suicide. These university courses range from a few sessions up to one semester in academic departments of psychology, psychiatry, sociology, nursing, social work, public health, criminal justice, and so forth. For example, suicide courses either are or have been offered by David Phillips

(University of California at San Diego), Lee Ann Hoff (Northeastern University), Antoon Leenaars (University of Windsor), David Lester (Richard Stockton State College), David Jobes (Catholic University), John McIntosh (University of Indiana at South Bend), Bryan Tanney (University of Calgary Medical School), Alan Berman (American University), Stephen Stack (Wayne State), and several others (including some I am no doubt unaware of).

Since no systematic surveys of suicidology courses have been done, I present my own course at the University of South Carolina as one example. The course is offered every semester in the College of Liberal Arts and Sciences and is entitled "The Social-Psychology of Suicide." It covers the following topics: definitions, types, taxonomies, commonalities and variations, history, art, epidemiology (especially, age, sex, race, marital status, occupation, and SES), suicide methods, lethality, motives and notes, life-span issues (children, adolescents, middle-aged, and elderly), social relations, work, the economy, marriage, sexuality, aggression, mental disorders, depression and affective disorders, the schizophrenias, alcoholism and substance abuse, biology, genetics, and neurochemistry, physical illness, religion, culture, ethnicity, mass suicide and contagion, ethical issues, euthanasia, rational suicide, treatment, crisis intervention, suicide prevention, postvention, survivors, legal cases, jail and prison suicides, life insurance, and malpractice. As a survey course the consideration of these topics tends to be brief and general.

For textbooks I have most recently used Blumenthal and Kupfer's *Suicide Over the Lifespan* (1990) and Jacobs and Brown's *Suicide: Understanding and Responding* (1989). In addition students are expected to do several exercises or practica. These include keeping a diary on suicide for the semester, reporting in detail on one case study and supplemental reading, visiting a local crisis intervention center, seeing three films on suicide, watching some videotapes of suicide cases, doing a data exercise, reporting on humor and suicide, and reading a play (*'Night Mother*). University suicide courses tend to be one of two main types: academic, religious, or philosophical vs. clinical, assessment, treatment, prevention, crisis focused.

American Association of Suicidology

The American Association of Suicidology (AAS) is dedicated to the understanding and prevention of suicide as a means of promoting human well-being. The AAS tends to be an applied, clinical, prevention-focused organization. Its emphasis is on crisis intervention, telephone referrals and evaluations, and volunteer training. The AAS even offers certification of individual crisis workers and crisis centers. With Guilford Publications, AAS publishes a quarterly scientific journal, *Suicide & Life-Threatening Behavior,* founded by Dr. Shneidman. There are also annual scientific conferences, a preconference suicidology update workshop, a survivors conference, a quarterly newsletter (including suicide prevention information and research abstracts) called *Newslink,* a national suicide information center in Denver, and a summer suicidology training institute in Aspen, Colorado.

In its third year in 1992, the Aspen summer suicide institute mainly offers continuing education credits for therapists and clinicians. It meets for five days in July of each year. The very best faculty in the United States offers intensive courses in adolescent and adult suicide assessment, biological therapy, forensic suicidology, and other relevant topics. Recent faculty members have included Paula Clayton, M.D., John T. Maltsberger, M.D., David Clark, Ph.D., Bryan Tanney, M.D., Morton Silverman, M.D., Alan Berman, Ph.D., Pamela Cantor, Ph.D., Ronald Maris, Ph.D., Barry Garfinkel, M.D., Marsha Linehan, Ph.D., and Robert Litman, M.D.

The Calgary University Medical School, 1982-1992

Starting in 1982 and continuing until the present, the University of Calgary (Alberta, Canada) has been a mainstay in suicidology education, training, and research. The prime movers in Calgary have been the late Sebastian K. Littmann, M.D., Bryan L. Tanney, M.D., Richard Ramsey, D.S.W., Menno Boldt, Ph.D., Christopher Bagley, Ph.D., Roger Tierney, Ph.D., Gayle Belsher, Ph.D., Philomena McKensie, Ph.D., and probably the world's only provincial suicidologist (in Edmonton), Ronald J. Dyck, Ph.D. I first became aware of the Calgary group in 1982 when a suicide prevention workshop was held there (October 26–29) with invited consultants Bryan Barraclough, M.D., Norman Farberow, Ph.D., Norman Kreitman, M.D., Daniel Lettieri, Ph.D., Peter Sainsbury, M.D., and me.

Calgary continues to sponsor annual research conferences each spring, to invite Killam Fellows (similar to the United States Fulbright Fellowships) to teach and write and conduct suicide research, to operate a Suicide Information and Education Centre (SIEC), which provides a computer literature and abstract search on suicide publications, and run a popular school-based suicide prevention training program. A suicide research center has been planned for years in Calgary, but has never really gotten the funding it needs to get started.

Other Suicidology Programs

There are also a host of other professional associations and special conventions, congresses, state and national conferences, and so forth that promote suicidology. The American Suicide Foundation (ASF), Herbert Hendin, M.D., director, is a New York City-based mainly psychiatric association, which focuses on funding small (under $10,000) suicide research grants. The International Association for Suicide Prevention (IASP), David Lester, Ph.D., 1991–1992, president, is the European counterpart to the American Association of Suicidology. It holds annual conferences and publishes a suicide prevention journal called *Crisis*. The International Academy for Suicide Research (IASR), Rene Diekstra, Ph.D., president, is a new organization based in Europe which is in effect the research component of IASP. It plans to publish its own journal, *Archives of Suicidal Behavior,* and has ties with the World Health Organization. The Canadian Association for Suicide Prevention (CASP), Antoon Leenaars, Ph.D., 1991–1992 president, is the Canadian equivalent of the AAS. Of course, there are several other national suicide prevention associations too numerous to mention throughout the world. Finally, there are special-topic state conferences on suicide and suicide prevention each year and state suicide prevention associations.

SUICIDE PREVENTION AND CRISIS INTERVENTION CENTERS

Since there are now over six hundred suicide prevention or crisis centers in the United States, a large part of suicidology is concerned with training and certifying volunteers and paraprofessionals and the institutions they staff. Suicide Prevention Centers started in the United States with the Los Angeles Suicide Prevention Center in about 1958 (see Shneidman and Farberow 1965). Suicide prevention centers are usually twenty-four-hour telephone evaluation, short-term crisis counseling, and clinical referral organizations, staffed mainly by nonprofessionals. Some centers (especially those based in hospitals or medical centers) actually provide crisis therapy to their clients in person (as opposed to on the phone). In the late 1960s and early 1970s there were major centers in Buffalo, Detroit, Gainesville, Los Angeles, San Francisco, and Seattle, among others. Gainesville has continued, and excellent current crisis centers (obviously not an exhaustive list) are also found in Florida's Duchess and Tompkins counties; New York; Hennepin County, Minneapolis; Nashville; Contact Pittsburgh; and St. Louis, Missouri.

The American Association of Suicidology examines and certifies both individuals (since 1988, with about seventy individuals certified by 1991) and crisis intervention centers (since 1976, about sixty certified by 1991). Training in crisis intervention (volunteers) involves about thirty to forty hours in knowledge, skills, and attitudes related to the following topics: telephone crisis intervention role playing and feedback; crisis intervention and suicide prevention principles; suicide lethality assessment; issues of grief, death, mourning, loss, and separation; victimization (rape, sexual, and physical abuse); psychopathology overview of *DSM-III-R,* Axis II type behaviors; analogies of suicide to natural disaster; and information referral. The American Association of Suicidology certification examiners also provide reading lists, site visits, exams, and ultimately individual and crisis center certification. In my view the American Association of Suicidology also eventually needs to expand the volunteer certification program to professional suicidology board certification. But clearly right now many of the pieces in the puzzle of professional suicidology certification are missing.

SPECIALIZED DISCIPLINARY SUICIDOLOGY

Since most suicide training, research, and practice takes place in the context of specific academic disciplines, a few of the major disciplinary programs merit review (with apologies to any I do not review here).

Psychiatry

There have been several psychiatric suicidology research and training programs at:

> Calgary (B. Tanney et al.)
> Cambridge (D. Jacobs, M. T. Tsuang, et al.)
> Chicago (J. Fawcett et al.)
> Los Angeles (R. Litman et al.)
> New York (D. Shaffer et al., M. Stanley et al., C. Pfeffer, H. van Praag et al.)
> Philadelphia (A. Beck et al.)
> Pittsburgh (J. Mann, D. Brent, D. Kupfer, et al.)
> San Francisco (Jerome Motto et al.)
> St. Louis (G. Murphy, E. Robins, et al.)
> Washington, D.C./NIMH (M. Linnoila, A. Roy, F. Goodwin, S. Blumenthal, G. Brown)

Most of these suicidology programs derive from basic research grant teams with suicide training piggybacked onto the research. The common products have been scientific articles, mainly in the *Archives of General Psychiatry* and the *American Journal of Psychiatry,* with a few research monographs, technical psychopharmacology and neurology papers, and research conferences.

Douglas Jacobs of Harvard held a series of suicide symposia in the 1980s eventuating in the book *Suicide: Understanding and Responding: Harvard Medical School Perspectives* (Jacobs and Brown 1989). Jacobs also has a new book called *Suicide and Clinical Practice* (1991) and recently has focused on forensic aspects of suicide. The Harvard conferences have expanded into a two day meeting over the past six years under the direction of Pamela Cantor. Another promising university psychiatric suicide center is at the Western Psychiatric Institute and Clinic in Pittsburgh. In June 1992, Pittsburgh sponsored an international suicide conference involving several of the leading suicide researchers in the world. J. Mann and David Brent have also been active on NIMH suicide research grant review committees and Mann edited the *Psychiatry Annual Review* update on suicide with Michael Stanley (1988). Of course, Aaron Beck and his colleagues at Pennsylvania have carried on basic longitudinal suicide research now for over twenty years.

Psychology

We know from Bongar and Harmatz (1989, 1991) that only about 40 percent of all graduate psychology Ph.D. programs offer any training in suicidology or suicide prevention at all, even though psychologists have about a 20 percent lifetime risk of losing a patient to suicide. The cities with the most active suicidology programs in psychology (usually a combination of clinical, research, and short academic courses) have been:

Boston (P. Cantor)
Calgary (G. Belsher)
Chicago (D. Clark)
Fort Collins, Colorado (S. Canetto)
Los Angeles (N. Farberow, E. Shneidman, et al.)
Pomona, New Jersey (D. Lester)
San Francisco (C. Huffine)
Seattle (M. Linehan)
South Bend, Indiana (J. McIntosh)
Topeka (J. Eyman)
Urbana/Champaign (R. Felner)
Washington, D.C. (A. Berman, D. Jobes)
Windsor, Ontario (A. Leenaars)

The Washington, D.C. programs of Alan Berman have been described above, as have the considerable pioneering work of Shneidman and Farberow. David Lester has been another very productive psychologist. Lester, a prolific publisher, has been president of the International Association for Suicide Prevention and edits valuable case histories of famous suicides under the rubric of "The Pavese Society." Pamela Cantor has been president of the National Committee on Youth Suicide Prevention and has written and narrated the film "Young People In Crisis. . . ." Most of the work in psychology is ad hominem and ad hoc, rather than institutionalized. David Clark at Rush-Presbyterian Hospital in Chicago also has been doing important funded research work on suicide.

Sociology

At least since Durkheim's *Suicide* (1897) many well-known sociologists have done major research and publication on suicide (see Maris 1989, 1991). These include James Short, Jr., Jack P. Gibbs, Jack Douglas, Ronald Maris, David Phillips, Stephen Stack, Ira Wasserman, and Bernice Pescosolido. However, most of this work has been nonclinical and limited to social factors (especially to imitation, contagion, and suicide). Only Breed, Goffman, Garfinkel, and Maris have done much applied clinical sociology.

The University of South Carolina has a fairly unique center for the study of suicide. The Center edits the journal, *Suicide and Life-Threatening Behavior* (the official publication of the American Association of Suicidology), offers courses on suicide, consults on forensic cases, conducts basic research on suicide (especially Garrison in Epidemiology, Geller in Psychiatry, and Maris in Sociology), provides public service information, and offers some training in suicidology. For example, one could pursue an M.A. or a Ph.D. at South Carolina with a special focus in suicidology.

David Phillips (of the University of California, San Diego) has done important sustained sociological research on contagion, modeling, and suicide (Phillips and Cartensen 1986 and Phillips, Lesyna, and Paight [in press]), as have Stephen Stack at Wayne State and Ira Wasserman at Eastern Michigan.

Nursing

Typically nurses in suicidology have been active in developing concepts and procedures of suicide risk assessment, crisis intervention, and therapy with survivors of suicide. For example, the sections on hospitals' policy and procedure manuals on suicide assessment, levels of suicide precaution, and suicide attempt interventions usually have been written by nurses. One thinks of Hoff's *People in Crisis* (1978), Valente and Hatton's *Suicide: Assessment and Intervention* (1984), and Dunne-Maxim and colleagues' survivor book, *Suicide and Its Aftermath* (1987). Similar important work in suicidology has been done by social workers and public health workers.

Forensic Sciences

After the fact, when one is investigating a possible or known suicide death, suicidology usually involves the forensic sciences. Such procedures can include knowledge and practice of both physical and psychological autopsies (Clark and Horton-Deutsch 1992). Professional forensic associations include the American Academy of Forensic Sciences (AAFS), the American Academy of Psychiatry and Law, and so on. The AAFS has subdisciplinary sections of criminalistics, general forensic sciences, jurisprudence, odontology (dental), pathology/biology, physical anthropology, psychiatry and behavioral science, questioned documents, and toxicology. The American Academy of Forensic Sciences publishes a very substantial bimonthly journal, entitled *Journal of Forensic Sciences*. Suicidologists are often called to be expert witnesses or consultants in contested life insurance cases, malpractice cases, jail and prison suicides, and workmen's compensation cases. For a basic statement of issues in forensic suicidology see Maris (1992).

NEEDS, PROBLEMS, AND PROSPECTS

Although suicidology has come a long way since the 1960s, it has yet to reach its full promise. There are currently no suicidology departments in universities, no degree programs, internships, residency training, or professional certification in suicidology. In fact there is not even a good basic suicidology textbook.

The Stagnation of Suicidology

Suicidology has become stagnant as a joint result of personology, politics, and the economy. Of course, all movements founded in charismatic leadership are precarious. In a very real sense Edwin Shneidman *was* suicidology for a long time. That is simply too big a burden for any one person. For example, when Dr. Shneidman left the NIMH to return to UCLA, funding for basic research and training in suicidology suffered a near fatal blow. Of course, the NIMH remains, but suicide research is underfunded and tends to be restricted to generic epidemiology, psychiatry, and biology — with few special funds set aside for suicide.

Early suicidological founders had many turf battles. They fought over who would control what, which areas and subdisciplines would be emphasized, and whether suicidology was mainly a biological/medical/body/brain specialty or more of a psychological/social/mind specialty.

Some contend that suicidology was republicanized (of course, a polemical term). Put another way, the conservative, right-wing politics of Nixon, Ford, Reagan, and Bush and their appointed federal officials have done suicidology (and lots of other things) in. When Shneidman created suicidology and founded the American Association of Suicidology, the Hopkins Medical School postdoctoral program, the NIMH Center for the Study of Suicide, the journal *Suicide and Life-Threatening Behavior,* and so forth, Democrats were in the White House (viz., JFK in 1961–1963 and LBJ from 1963–1969). The Democrats (other things being equal) traditionally have been more supportive of new programs and especially of the social and behavioral sciences.

Since 1969, four out of five U.S. presidents have been Republicans (viz., Nixon, 1969–1974; Ford, 1974–1977; Reagan, 1981–1989; and Bush, 1989–1993). Only Democrat Jimmy Carter intervened for four years (1977–1981). We have yet to see the impact of the Clinton presidency, but at least there is hope. Republicans traditionally have supported the medicalization or biologizing of mental disorders, psychiatry, and suicidology. At the risk of being simplistic and reductionistic, the development of suicidology as a professional specialty has not been helped much by the federal Republican leadership of the last twenty years. Although they are complicated issues with many sides, one could also raise questions about the federal government not following up adequately on recommendations made in the 1989 *Task Force on Youth Suicide* or the Violence Panel's recommendations for gun control.

Also for the last several years the U.S. economy has been in a recession. This has meant less research and training monies for the social and behavioral sciences (not to mention for suicidology), especially during Reagan's tenure as president. The late 1980s and early 1990s have been a time of retrenchment, a return to the basics — not a time for expansion into exotic subspecialties like suicidology.

Research and Training Grants in Suicidology

If suicidology is going to continue to develop, there needs to be more money for basic suicide research and training at the federal level. It also has to be acknowledged that suicidology is an interdisciplinary science. It is very difficult for suicidology to evolve properly when there is so little federal money for suicide, when it is given to a handful of senior research teams at prestige universities, and it is channeled into a few medical specialties.

In the fall of 1988 I was asked to be on an NIMH committee (with Jan Fawcett, David Kupfer, J. John Mann, George Murphy, Robert Hirschfeld, Lewis Judd, Darrel Reiger, Eve Moscicki, and Arlene Hegg) to review NIMH's funding and set priorities in the area of suicide research. Part of that consultation included a review of past NIMH funding of suicide research, 1986 to 1988.

Several conclusions were obvious to me. (1) There was very little federal money being allocated to suicide research at all (roughly $1 to $1.5 million per year). (2) Most of that money went to a few senior research teams (e.g., in 1986 80 percent of NIMH's suicide research money went to the teams of D. Shaffer, M. Stanley, or J. Mann). (3) Almost all the research NIMH funded went to medical researchers (viz., 90 percent). (4) Only 10 percent of NIMH suicide monies went to social or behavioral science researchers (e.g., M. Linehan or S. Stack). (5) Special topic (RFA) type research was overrepresented (especially that on adolescents). One certainly could not waltz into a research grant review committee with any old topic and expect to get funded, even if their proposal were outstanding. (6) New suicide research grants to nonestablished researchers outside medical institutions were very difficult (almost impossible) to obtain. Also, new suicide researchers were in fact often students of established researchers with prior funding. (7) Priority scores for research funding had gotten extremely competitive.

The inflated priority score problem deserves some elaboration. ADAMHA's (Alcohol, Drug Abuse, Mental Health Administration) priority scores (see Table 1-1) are as follows: After a study review committee (usually about twelve people) considered a research proposal each member (three reviewers read each proposal in detail and lead a discussion of it) rated the grant proposal from 1 to 5 (using decimals as well) and averaged their scores (there was also a percentile ranking of each proposal among all proposals evaluated, usually a minimum of twenty at one time). In 1990 I was told that to have a chance at funding, a research grant application would have to have an average priority score of about 1.2 (i.e., 120) or lower. When you add to this dismal picture the need to fund continuing research projects, very little new money, indeed, is available for suicide research. NIMH project officers are put in the awkward position of soliciting new research grant proposals knowing full well that almost none of them will ever be funded.

TABLE 1-1.

ADAMHA PRIORITY SCORE DESCRIPTORS

Descriptors	Priority Score Range	Cumulative Distribution
Outstanding	1.0–1.5	5%
Excellent	1.5–2.0	15%
Very Good	2.0–2.5	30%
Good	2.5–3.0	50%
Satisfactory	3.0–3.5	70%
Fair	3.5–4.0	85%
Marginal	4.0–5.0	100%

Training and center grants in suicide are usually tied to basic research grants. An institution typically does not get an NIMH training or center grant unless it has had several prior research (RO1) grants (presumably to demonstrate its competence to do the training). Also, training grants tend to be money only for student stipends (fellowships, internships, assistantships, residencies, etc.) plus about 5 percent overhead. Thus, there is little money to pay faculty, buy equipment, travel, and so forth—and, thus, little inducement to do training. These problems make the prospects for future suicidological training dim. And unless there is at least money for student stipends, most suicidology training programs will likely fail.

The Volunteerization of American Suicidology

Suicidology in the United States has strong ties with volunteers and paraprofessionals (McGee 1974), rooted in the British Samaritan movement (Varah 1974). One of the central fixtures of American suicidology is the hot-line telephone volunteer at a crisis center empathetically listening to a caller, then making a referral.

While this marriage of volunteers and professionals in American suicidology has been mutually productive, it has also been a troubled marriage verging on divorce for many years. For example, ever since the founding of the American Association of Suicidology there have been conflicts over the name *suicidology* (should it be the American Association of Suicidology and Crisis Intervention?), over how important the scientific journal *Suicide and Life-Threatening Behavior* is, whether or not nonprofessionals should be president and officers of the AAS, what the program content and emphases ought to be at the annual AAS meeting, and so forth.

I am convinced that the fairly recent American Suicide Foundation (an organization largely devoted to psychiatric research on suicide) and the even newer International Academy for Suicide Research are in part responses to conflicts of professional suicidology with volunteerism and over applied clinical issues. Somehow if suicidology is to continue to evolve as originally envisioned, professional–volunteer discord has got to be resolved.

Prevention versus Understanding

Strictly speaking suicidology is the scientific study of suicide. The pure understanding of suicide does not in itself dictate that suicide should be prevented. In fact the emphasis (nay, insistence) of the American Association of Suicidology, International Association for Suicide Prevention, and of most suicidologists on suicide prevention has hamstrung the scientific development of suicidology, has given it a kind of irrational, even lunatic, fringe. To argue that suicidology includes suicide prevention (almost by definition) is biased. It also means that in the eyes of most academics, suicidology is intellectually tainted by religious and moral zealots and dogmatism. Surely, we should be able to understand suicide without always and in all circumstances rushing to prevent it. In fact for most suicidologists suicide prevention almost always comes first, and the science of suicide is secondary. Try to imagine a university department with such premises! No wonder that suicidology is not very respectable.

I attended a suicidology board meeting recently in which a philosopher (prodded by a board response to Derek Humphry's book, *Final Exit* [1991]) argued to a group of suicidologists that suicidology does not logically entail suicide prevention. The suggestion was apparently so heretical and offensive (like "there is no God") that a discussion was never even initiated. Of course, a discussion in a busy meeting likely would have been unproductive and pointless, but I found it interesting and mildly depressing that suicidologists could not even bring themselves to address this crucial issue. I also contend that such rigid, irrational emotional behavior is a very bad sign for the future development of suicidology as a science.

For some, suicide prevention is merely pragmatic window dressing to get public support or money. Admittedly, it is hard to be "for" suicide and get support. Of course, such a position is dishonest. It may also misread public sentiment, given all the recent interest in living wills, the right to die, the Hemlock society (which at last count has fifty seven thousand American members), physician-assisted death, and so forth.

Biology versus the Behavioral Sciences

Dr. Shneidman has insisted that although the suicidological pie has many disciplinary sectors, with none reducible to any other (1985), still suicidology is personology. Among others things he means that the focus of suicidological attention properly ought to be on the conscious mind, not on the body (e.g., not on the synaptic cleft, neuroreceptors, brain chemistry, neurotransmitters, hormones, genetics, and the like). As we have seen, much of modern psychiatry disputes Shneidman's claim. The medical establishment seems to be investing very heavily in Prozac (fluoxetine HCl), Clozaril (clozapine), and other psychopharmacological research (e.g., in the case of suicide, the low level of 5-HIAA in cerebral spinal fluid).

There is much that is good in biology for suicidology. Caveats are appropriate, but psychology is not more central to suicidology than, say, neuropharmacology. Suicide runs the danger of appearing reductionistic, clinically mystical, and unscientific. Suicidology needs to be as scientific as it possibly can be. Psychopharmacology, epidemiology, biostatistics, endocrinology, genetics, neurology, and so forth, are absolutely basic sciences in the study of suicide.

CONCLUSIONS AND THE FUTURE

Suicidology started in earnest in the United States about 1958 with Edwin Shneidman's discovery of the Los Angeles Medical Examiner's dusty collection of suicide notes. Today there are over six hundred suicide prevention and crisis intervention centers in America; a twenty-one year old scientific journal on suicide; a professional and volunteer suicidological association entering its twenty-fifth year; thousands of books and journal articles on suicide; volunteer and center certification procedures; suicide courses, centers, and research institutes; some important basic suicide research, research funding, and research conferences; and several dedicated, trained professional suicidologists.

Thus, one should not be too gloomy in assessing the progress of suicidology. Of course, in the future we need more basic research monies and professional training for suicide. Whether suicidology should become a separate subdiscipline, department, area for professional board certification, and so forth, continues to be debatable. However, suicide itself is obviously not going to go away. If anything, suicide keeps moving up the ladder of leading causes of death. Usually, any individual suicide is a premature tragic ending to a troubled life, a desperate, unnecessary resolution. To be sure, death comes to us all, but suicide is nothing to celebrate.

REFERENCES

Alcohol, Drug Abuse, and Mental Health Administration (1989). *Report of the secretary's task force on youth suicide.* Volumes 1–4. DHHS Pub. No. (ADM) 89–1621. Washington, DC: US Government Printing Office.

Battin, M. P. (1991). Rational suicide: how can we respond to a request for help? *Crisis* 12:73–79.

Blumenthal, S. J., and Kupfer, D. J., eds. (1990). *Suicide Over the Life-Cycle: Risk Factors, Assessment, and Treatment of Suicidal Patients.* Washington, DC: American Psychiatric Press.

Bongar, B., and Harmatz, M. (1989). Graduate training in clinical psychology and the study of suicide. *Professional Psychology: Research and Practice* 20:209–273.

―――― (1991). Clinical psychology graduate education in the study of suicide: availability, resources, importance. *Suicide and Life-Threatening Behavior* 21:231–244.

Clark, D. C., and Horton-Deutsch, S. L. (1992). Assessment in absentia: the value of the psychological autopsy method for studying antecedents of suicide and predicting future suicides. In *Assessment and Prediction of Suicide,* ed. R. W. Maris, A. L. Berman, J. T. Maltsberger, and R. I. Yufit, pp. 144–182. New York: Guilford.

Dunne, E. J., McIntosh, J. L., and Dunne-Maxim, K., eds. (1987). *Suicide and Its Aftermath*. New York: W. W. Norton.

Durkheim, E. (1897). *Suicide*. Glencoe, IL: The Free Press, 1951.

Hoff, L. A. (1978). *People in Crisis*. Menlo Park, CA: Addison-Wesley.

Humphry, D. (1991). *Final Exit: The Practicalities of Self-Deliverance and Assisted Suicide for the Dying*. Eugene, OR: The Hemlock Society.

Jacobs, D. (1991). *Suicide and Clinical Practice*. Washington, DC: American Psychiatric Press.

Jacobs, D., and Brown, H. N., eds. (1989). *Suicide: Understanding and Responding. Harvard Medical School Perspectives*. Madison, CT: International Universities Press.

Mann, J. J., and Stanley, M., eds. (1988). Suicide. In *Review of Psychiatry*, vol. 7, ed. A. J. Frances and R. E. Hales, pp. 285-426. Washington, DC: American Psychiatric Press.

Maris, R. W. (1989). The social relations of suicide. In *Suicide: Understanding and Responding*, ed. D. Jacobs and H. N. Brown, pp. 87-128. Madison, CT: International Universities Press.

_____ (1991). Suicide. In *Encyclopedia of Human Biology*, vol. 7, ed. R. Dulbecco, pp. 327-335. San Diego, CA: Academic.

_____ (1992). Forensic suicidology. In *Dangerous Intersections*, ed. B. Bongar and M. Harmatz, pp. 235-252. New York: Oxford University Press.

Maris, R. W., Berman, A. L., Maltsberger, J. T., and Yufit, R. I., eds. (1992). *Assessment and Prediction of Suicide*. New York: Guilford.

Maris, R. W., Dorpat, T. L., Berkley, C., et al. (1973). Education and training in suicidology for the seventies. In *Suicide Prevention in the 70s*, ed. H. L. P. Resnik and B. C. Hawthorne, pp. 23-44. Rockville, MD: National Institute of Mental Health.

Maxim, E. J., McIntosh, J. L., and Maxim, K. D., eds. (1987). *Suicide and Its Aftermath: Understanding and Counseling Survivors*. New York: W. W. Norton.

McGee, R. (1974). *Crisis Intervention in the Community*. Baltimore: University Park Press.

Moscicki, E. (1991). National Institute of Mental Health, Suicide Research Program. 5600 Fishers Lane, Rockville, MD, 20857. Mimeographed.

National Institute of Mental Health Suicide Research Program (1991). Mimeographed. NIMH. 5600 Fishers Lane, Rockville, MD, 20857.

Perlin, S. (1975). *A Handbook for the Study of Suicide*. New York: Oxford University Press.

Phillips, D. P., and Cartensen, L. L. (1986). Clustering of teenage suicide after television news stories about suicide. *New England Journal of Medicine* 315:685-689.

Phillips, D. P., Lesyna, K., and Paight, D. J. (in press). In *Assessment and Prediction of Suicide*, ed. R. W. Maris, A. L. Berman, T. L. Maltsberger, and R. I. Yufit, pp. 499-519. New York: Guilford.

Shneidman, E. S. (1973). Suicide. In *Encyclopaedia Britannica*. Chicago: William Benton.

_____ (1985). *Definition of Suicide*. New York: Wiley.

_____ (1991). A life in death. In *The History of Clinical Psychology in Autobiography*, ed. C. E. Walker, pp. 225-292. Pacific Groves, CA: Brooks/Cole.

Shneidman, E. S., and Farberow, N. L. (1965). The LA SPC: A demonstration of public health feasibilities. *American Journal of Public Health* 55:21-26.

Simpson, J. A., and Weiner, E. S. C., eds. (1989). Suicidology. In *The Oxford English Dictionary*, p. 145. Oxford, England: Clarendon.

Valente, S., and Hatton, C. (1984). *Suicide: Assessment and Intervention*. Norwalk, CT: Appleton, Century, Croft.

Varah, C. (1974). *The Samaritans*. New York: Macmillan.

2: LOOKING BACK

Jerome A. Motto

The admonition is often repeated that history can provide a valuable perspective on contemporary questions. In the study of suicide and suicide prevention this is probably as true as it is elsewhere. Yet much of the early work in this field is not easily retrieved, or it appeared in a form that was not readily adapted to inclusion in the several bibliographies on suicide that have appeared during the twentieth century (Farberow 1969, Farberow and Shneidman 1961, Rost 1927). The breadth of the field poses a formidable challenge as well, encompassing as it does such diverse disciplines as psychology, sociology, medicine, law, religion, ethics, and philosophy.

To probe for a sample of what may be learned from earlier efforts in the study of suicide, an examination was carried out of the reports presented in the major American journal of a single discipline during the period 1844–1900, specifically, the *American Journal of Insanity,* the first psychiatric journal in the United States, which began publication in 1844 and has continued to the present (since 1911 as the *American Journal of Psychiatry*) as the primary voice of psychiatry in this country. Though clearly an American publication, it was customary for the editor to report items of interest in European journals, primarily from England, France, and Germany, as well as items from other U.S. journals and newspapers. The *American Journal of Insanity* began as a quarterly publication in July 1844, edited by the officers of the New York State Lunatic Asylum at Utica and printed at the asylum where Dr. Amariah Brigham served as medical superintendent and editor in chief.

The time period 1844–1900, roughly the last half of the nineteenth century, provides a one hundred year perspective from the vantage point of a like period in the twentieth century, during which most of our current thinking about suicide and suicide prevention has developed. A crude measure of progress might be the extent of contrast that can be seen between the information and attitudes that characterize these century-apart periods, though skeptics might argue that change is not necessarily progress.

The reports group themselves into three general categories: epidemiological, psychological-clinical, and ethical-philosophical-legal.

EPIDEMIOLOGY

The January 1845 issue provides the first epidemiological discussion of suicide in the form of a letter to the editor from E. K. Hunt, M.D., who gleaned information about 184 suicides from a newspaper, the *New York Mercury,* over the period of one year. While acknowledging the limitations of his data, he points out the familiar association of suicide with males, warm months of the year, the use of readily available means (especially hanging and drowning), and the preference of males for firearms.

In addressing the causes to which suicides were attributed, the interesting point is made that the stresses which lead to suicide are the same as those leading to insanity, the latter emerging if those stresses are permitted to operate on the mind for a considerable time. Contemporary psychiatry has little to say about suicide representing an aborted psychosis, but it remains a pertinent point.

The editor comments on the high probability of underreporting of suicides, a familiar theme in present-day thinking, and provides the annual number of suicides for the City of New York from 1805 to 1843, with population figures every five years. The reader is thus left to calculate the rates for him/herself, which vary from 34.3/100,000 in 1805 to 5.0/100,000 in 1815. Remarkably, this 85 percent decrease over a ten-year period is not commented on.

Another way of expressing rates is provided in the editor's table of suicides in eleven chief capitals of Europe, expressed as one suicide per number of persons in the populace. For example, Paris in 1836 reported 341 suicides or 1 in 2,700 persons, while London in 1834 reported 42 suicides or 1 in 27,000, and Palermo in 1831 listed only two suicides, or 1 in 180,000.

The next fifteen years saw attention primarily to data from the state of New York, with three reports detailing the incidence of suicide by age, gender, marital status, method, cause, and county. Of interest is the frequent attribution of cause to what we would now call the precipitating event, such as "pecuniary embarrassment," "disappointment in love," "after dispute with wife," or "after receiving a disagreeable Valentine." Other still familiar categories include such typologies as "insanity" (psychosis), "melancholy" (depression), and "despair." The editor is prone to add comments and comparison data, such as his observation in an April 1849 report that the most frequent method of suicide is hanging, not only in New York state, but in England and France as well.

In January 1860, the editor calls attention to an October 1859 article in *Winslow's Journal of Psychological Medicine,* in which "suicide fields" are mapped in England and Wales, delineating areas of increased suicide. These are seen to be related to proximity to population centers and to be consistent for the five years examined. The technique is reminiscent of similar mapping carried out much later in the United States in Seattle, Pittsburgh, and Minneapolis (Schmid 1933). No correlation could be found with age, sex, marital status, occupation, socio-economic status, lunacy, or drunkenness, leading to the deduction that "the average number of suicides decreases as the average amount of ignorance increases" (p. 360), an interpretation supported by a thirteen-year study of suicide and instruction in France. Dr. Brigham observes that "if this be a correct inference, . . . that education tends directly to produce suicide, we must indeed believe that the present systems of mental culture are in the greatest degree deficient" (p. 360). A recent systematic study of risk factors (Motto et al. 1985), is consonant with the observation that "risk increases with education" (p. 682), but any causal relationship seems farfetched. The Winslow study, for the first time in this journal, reports suicide rates in terms used at present, noting that in England and Wales during 1856, 1857, and 1858, both men and women averaged 6.8 suicides in every 100,000 of population.

In 1862 the South German Psychiatrical Society offered a prize for the best essay on the question, "What are the causes of the greatly increased number of suicides in modern times, and what are the means of preventing the same?" Editor in Chief Brigham reports that one entry, by a Dr. Salomons, argues that suicide rates had in fact decreased, that impressions to the contrary were a result of statistics obtained from large cities, and that suicide is a sure and certain accompaniment of political, industrial, and intellectual centralization. The essay did not win a prize, but shed some interesting light on the question addressed.

From the 1860s through the 1890s seven brief epidemiological items are reported, all—with two exceptions—gleaned from European journals by the editor in chief. Suicides in Bavaria were analyzed in the *Social Science Review* in traditional categories (age, sex, religion, urban/rural, month, etc.) with findings in 1863 much like the present, including the propensity of males for more violent death. Notable exceptions included highest rates in married persons, and hanging and drowning as the most frequent methods, with women preferring the latter.

Suicides in Prussia during 1880 likewise showed no unusual characteristics, except that specific notice is taken of the risk inherent in delirium tremens. Seventy suicides (sixty-nine men, one woman) were attributed to this common phenomenon, a causal relationship that is sometimes overlooked to this day, especially when alcohol withdrawal occurs in a setting where suicide risk is not routinely assessed.

A brief review of suicides in New York state in 1883 provided two notable observations. More Germans than any other national group were counted, totalling seventy, and for the first time in this journal, firearms were listed as the most frequent method.

In 1886 the *Lancet* is quoted in reporting a paper read before the Statistical Society of London on suicide in England and Wales for the period 1858–1883. It was notable in pointing out that physicians were high on the list as regards frequency "taking nearly equal rank with innkeepers and spirit, wine, and beer dealers" (vol. 42, p. 544). On the bottom of the list were miners, with clergymen very near them.

Later in 1886 (vol. 43, p. 268) the *Lancet* is again drawn on, quoting from a Russian newspaper *(Novosti)* that suicide had increased from 1.7/100,000 to 3.0/100,000, and that Saint Petersburg had more suicides than any other capital of Europe except Paris. Special concern was expressed that so many youngsters aged 8 to 16 were engaging in suicidal behavior. This theme has its obvious modern-day counterpart in the prominent role of youth suicide in contemporary suicide prevention efforts. Apparently overlooking this report, the *Lancet* is quoted yet again in 1895 to the effect that Professor Sidorski of the University of Kiev had collected statistics concerning the frequency of suicide in the different nations of Europe. Contrary to the *Novosti* data, his report indicated that "during the last thirty years the suicide rate has remained stationary in Russia, while in all other European countries it has increased 30 or 40 percent" (vol. 52, p. 268).

It seems clear that while the numbers have changed and the style of presenting data has become more precise and detailed, the nature and pertinence of epidemiological information is not notably different now from a century ago. Amariah Brigham's admonition in 1845 must still be taken seriously: "statistics of this kind must be very imperfect . . . the number given (is) probably far short of those actually committed" (vol. 1, p. 233).

PSYCHOLOGICAL AND CLINICAL OBSERVATIONS

Recognition and Treatment of Suicidal Persons

In Volume 1 of the *American Journal of Insanity* (January 1845), an article whose author is not identified provides six cases illustrating the importance of early treatment in preventing suicide. It is prefaced by the still-familiar observation that at inquest it is so often the case that friends or family members confirm that clues to the impending suicide were noticed but not acted on.

The first clue mentioned is the broad observation that if any area of a person's life shows "a striking change in character or conduct, there is reason for the apprehension of dangerous results" (p. 243). More specifically if a person becomes reserved or melancholy, loses affection for family and business, withdraws from social contacts, becomes indecisive, and sleeps poorly, "there is indication that immediate action may be necessary," as the person "is fast approaching that point where reason is often overwhelmed, or is exercised but to justify the act of self-destruction" (p. 244).

A clearer or more valid guideline for recognizing that a suicidal state may be present could hardly be offered. The writer bypasses the step of asking the person about suicidal ideas, however, and moves directly to what to do. Specifically, "the only security that such persons have is the constant care of a judicious friend, or what is still better for their recovery, a residence in a well-directed Lunatic Asylum . . . for usually such persons need medical treatment" (p. 244). In equally direct language, "the important truth to be inculcated is, that persons who have exhibited the above symptoms are insane; and for their own personal safety, as well as the safety of others, need restraint and appropriate treatment. The lives of others are sometimes in jeopardy, as the suicidal often fancy that the crime of murder is less heinous than that of suicide, and therefore seek death as the penalty of the former" (p. 244).

We may wince at the language used, but there is no denying that this statement is as applicable to suicidal persons today as it was in 1845. From a health care worker's standpoint it is even more compelling, in that increased legal vulnerability as well as clinical care is dictated in large measure by the ideas expressed.

The treatment provided to the six suicidal patients, all of whom exhibited severe mood and/or thought disturbance as well as suicidal behaviors on admission to the New York State Lunatic Asylum at Utica, is presented. They were given a supportive setting in the form of stress-alleviating "circumstances and associates" (hospital environment and staff). Any physical disorder was corrected, and "exercise, labor, and amusements" such as "milieu therapy" (p. 249) were encouraged—in short, all that would characterize a modern psychiatric hospital ward. But beyond this, descriptions of nineteenth-century psychiatric treatment bear little resemblance to current practice. The most common biological and pharmacological approaches involved the use of such agents as laxatives, tonics, iron carbonate, extract of conium, tincture of bark, wine, and morphine sulfate (to produce sleep), all in combination with warm baths.

While in the hospital, all suicidal patients were provided "constant watchfulness both night and day" (p. 248) and were not allowed access to sharp instruments or other potential suicide means. "Anything likely to tempt them, or to make them think of committing the act" (p. 249) was removed from their room. Knives and forks were counted after each meal. At night special care was taken to provide rooms that were suicide proof, and "the watchman is directed to give especial attention to them" (p. 249). With a few changes in terminology, a comparable suicide prevention program can be found in the policies and procedures manual of many contemporary psychiatric hospitals.

With obvious pride it is reported that all six suicidal patients were discharged from the hospital within two to four months perfectly well and that a one-year follow-up revealed no recurrence of emotional disorder.

A comment that is especially intriguing to a clinician is that in one case in which morphine sulfate was given to improve sleep, "the morphine in fact appeared to cure her, as for a short time it was omitted, and she became worse" (p. 246). This is not commented on further, but raises interesting questions regarding the potential of morphine for modifying mood, and the possible implications for treatment-resistant depression as well as for the problem of suicide in drug-abuse populations.

These questions are further stimulated by a discussion one year later in the January 1846 issue (vol. 2, p. 282), in which the editor in chief discusses the efficacy of opium in various clinical states. A remarkable case is described in which a manic patient attempted suicide by taking opium, and after a sound sleep awoke rational. The reader is advised that "persons afflicted with suicidal mania bear opium well, and in such cases it is very commonly prescribed in this country." In Europe, the legendary Esquirol is quoted as attesting to the value of opium in suicidal mania, to provide sleep. The import of sleep is reiterated in the caution that "in suicidal cases it is often important to keep up the effect of opium, and to take every precaution, as . . . depression returns as certainly as the effects of the opium cease; these patients are always thinking, and hence it is that sleep is so essential."

It seems that opium (and its derivatives) was the antidepressant of a century ago, and as is done today, if the agent doesn't suffice alone, it is combined with other available compounds to increase its efficacy. Thus favorable results are described by combining opium with vinegar, calomel, antimony, camphor, henbane, tartar emetic, or digitalis. We have no statistical data on the suicide-prevention value of these medicinal approaches, but it must be granted that current psychopharmacological agents are not well established as to effectiveness in this regard either. The psychiatric community and the pharmaceutical industry, in fact, are not free of contentions that the contrary effect may operate in some cases, especially with certain sedative and antidepressant compounds.

Another therapeutic approach long-since abandoned by medicine is called to our attention by the editor in chief's mention (vol. 1, January 1845) of a book review appearing in the French publication, *Annales Medico-Psychologique.* The review, by another legendary name, M. Brierre de Boismont, is of a volume entitled *Recherches statistiques sur le suicide,* published in Paris in 1844. The reviewer was prompted to recount an unusual clinical episode from this work, as follows:

> An English merchant, having met with pecuniary losses, became depressed and had a strong desire to destroy himself. His mind being well cultivated and naturally strong, he was enabled to strive against this desire. At length a great misfortune having thrown him into a state of great depression during the day, he said to his clerk that his head felt heavy and oppressed, and that he had a presentiment that something would happen before morning. The clerk advised him to consult a physician, but he thought it was unnecessary. In the middle of the night he awoke in extreme agitation. No language can describe his sensations. Self-destruction appeared to be his only resource. He arose, called his domestics and sent in great haste for a surgeon. As soon as the patient saw him enter, he cried, "Bleed me or I shall cut my throat." Accordingly, he was immediately bled. The blood had hardly begun to flow when the patient said, "Thank God, I am saved from self-destruction!" Since that time, he has not had a return of the symptoms mentioned. [p. 383]

The technique of bleeding, derived from the centuries-old humoral theory of illness, is mentioned from time to time in these nineteenth-century reports without elaboration as to rationale or effectiveness in suicidal states. Other than the dramatic anecdote above it is generally mentioned only in passing, for example (January 1845), regarding a twenty-year-old suicidal woman who "was bled and blistered and took cathartic medicines at home, but without any relief" (p. 248).

The closest contemporary parallel is the striking reduction in tension reported by some persons who persist in cutting themselves in a sublethal way. It has been considered characteristic of such persons that when they see the blood flowing, feelings of unreality diminish, they experience a gratifying sense of reassurance of being a living, feeling being, and they then proceed to an emergency room for repair of the laceration. Some use this experience to become expert at treating subsequent repeated cutting episodes themselves, in a way that minimizes scar formation.

Contagion by Imitation and Suggestibility

The awareness of suggestion as an influence in suicidal behavior is strongly represented in nineteenth-century psychiatry. In this regard, the editor in chief saw fit to include in volume 1 (January 1845), as the final paragraph of an epidemiological report, the following comment:

> That suicides are alarmingly frequent in this country is evident to all—and as a means of prevention, we respectfully suggest the propriety of not publishing the details of such occurrences. "No fact," says a late writer, "is better established in science, than that suicide is often committed from imitation. A single paragraph may suggest suicide to twenty persons. Some particulars of the act, or expressions, seize the imagination, and the disposition to repeat it, in a moment of morbid excitement, proves irresistible." In the justness of these remarks we concur, and commend them to the consideration of the conductors of the popular press. [p. 234]

Several years later (April 1849) the press is again entreated to exercise restraint, citing the death of an eight-year-old boy by hanging which could "without doubt, be attributed to a perversion of the natural instinct of imitation, caused by hearing the circumstances of a case of suicide narrated" (p. 308). A second case is noted in which a suicide, by the unusual method of cutting the femoral artery, followed very soon after another suicide by the same means. This sequence, it is suggested, "may be put down to the same cause, perverted imitation" (p. 309).

An interesting facet of nineteenth-century concerns about suicide contagion was reflected in Napoleon's famous order against suicide, reprinted in July 1845, in the *American Journal of Insanity*. It seems that the suicide of a French army grenadier was soon followed by a second suicide, and it was feared that the problem would assume an epidemic character. Bonaparte, with a view toward "putting a stop at once to the spread of what appeared to be a contagious malady" (p. 92) issued the following Order of the Day, dated at St. Cloud, 22 Floreal, an X (May 12, 1801):

The grenadier Groblin has committed suicide from a disappointment in love. He was in other respects a worthy man. This is the second event of the kind that has happened in this corps within a month. The First Consul directs that it shall be notified in the order of the day of the guard, that a soldier ought to know how to overcome the grief and melancholy of his passions; that there is as much true courage in bearing mental afflictions manfully as in remaining unmoved under the fire of a battery. To abandon oneself to grief without resisting, and to kill oneself in order to escape from it, is like abandoning the field of battle before being conquered.

Signed, Napoleon [p. 92]

The effect of this challenging statement is described as "truly magical" (p. 92) in that no further suicides occurred for a considerable time afterward. Credit for this outcome was attributed to Napoleon's great knowledge of human nature and his thorough insight into the character of the French soldier. Of course one wonders what would have happened in the absence of the order, but it is difficult to argue with a favorable outcome.

If we assume that Napoleon's statement did prevent an epidemic, do we have something to learn from this morsel of history? Has our society — or the suicide prevention community — appealed to the strength and courage of its youth with the confidence and vigor that Bonaparte conveyed in his simple statement? The same words would not be appropriate, but a nagging concern remains that a historical clue may be going unheeded.

BIOLOGICAL CAUSES OF SUICIDE

As an aside in an 1849 report of suicide statistics in New York (vol. 5), the editor comments on the familial and genetic influences believed to influence suicide at that time. He states without documentation that "the propensity to suicide is often transmitted from parents to children," and quotes M. Falret that "of all the forms of melancholy, that which tends to self-murder is most frequently hereditary" (p. 308). The latter provides an example in which all the female members of a family for three successive generations either attempted or committed suicide. M. Esquirol is mentioned as citing one case in which a father, son, and grandson all took their own lives, and another in which an entire sibship of seven brothers suicided when between the ages of thirty and forty. As though to temper his comments, the editor states that there are undoubtedly many persons who first think of suicide because of being aware that they "inherit a disposition to insanity, or from having a relative or friend commit the act" (p. 308). Current thinking would be in accord with Falret's view that depression has a genetic component, but would hold that the implication that suicidal behavior is genetically determined is still not demonstrated.

Reminiscent of some current observations of biological correlates of suicide, the editor reports in 1844 (Vol. 1) on a study by Dr. Kasloff, Professor of Anatomy in the University of Kiev. In the course of studying the cerebral circulation in cases of insanity, this researcher noted that the foramen lacerus posterius (the opening in the base of the skull for a major blood vessel to the brain), was very commonly contracted in the skulls of those who had committed suicide. An effort to confirm the finding in one case by another investigator resulted in the finding that "the foramen on the left side was so contracted it would not admit even a small probe, while that on the right easily admitted a large one." The editor (Dr. Brigham) asks, "But is not this frequently the case in those not insane? The circumstance is well worthy of investigation" (p. 82). This classic sequence, studying one biological characteristic only to discover that those who suicide form an apparent subgroup as regards that characteristic, has been dramatically replayed since the 1960s (Asberg et al. 1976, Bunney and Fawcett 1965). It is of interest that this report was in the first issue of the *American Journal of Insanity* (July 1844).

Even more suggestive of the current search for biological markers of suicide was a report by Dr. Alexander Haig summarized by the editor from the *Lancet* in 1896 (Vol. 52), entitled "Uricacidemia and Suicide." This paper suggests that some suicides may be due to "a depressed mental state caused by vascular blood tension from uric acid poisoning" (p. 582). Dr. Haig is quick to acknowledge that this is only one of the many possibilities of physical conditions leading to the mental state that induces suicide, "which has an infinite number of physical conditions that may be its primary causal factor. . . . The fact that we are so often unable to prevent suicide does not alter the fact that it may have as its remote cause even a comparatively slight physical derangement, too insignificant, perhaps, to attract attention" (p. 583). The current concept of a chemical imbalance to account for emotional disturbance is clearly foreshadowed.

Sociological Causes of Suicide

In 1884 (Vol. 41) a discussion of suicide as predominantly a desperate yearning to escape from unbearable psychic pain turns to an effort to understand the causes of such pain. Characteristically, only two categories of persons are considered, the sane ("intentionally conscious of what they are doing") and the insane ("either unconscious of their acts or perform them under hallucinations or delusions") (p. 255). The great majority of suicides are regarded as sane, hence the question, how can rational persons be vulnerable to such misery that suicide is seen as the only solution? The unnamed writer again summarized from *Lancet* (September 20, 1884), is unequivocal:

> The rate at which men and women live nowaday has something to do with this feeling. Boys and girls are men and women in their acquaintance with, and experience of, life and its so-called pleasures and sorrows, at an age when our grandparents were innocent children in the nursery. The young men of the day are *blasé* at two or three-and-twenty, the young women *ennuyée*. Life is played out before its meridian is reached, or the burden of responsibility is thrust upon the consciousness at a period when the mind can not in the nature of things be competent to cope with its weight and attendant difficulties. All this has been said before. There is not a new word or a new thought in it, and yet it is a very terrible

and pressing subject. We can not give it the go-by. "Forced" education commenced too early in life and pressed on too fast is helping to make existence increasingly difficult. We are running the two-year-old colts in a crippling race, and ruining the stock. If able and impartial observers would make it their business to ascertain the facts about suicide they would be doing a good and useful work. We believe, not without some data upon which to base our speculations, that suicide *is* increasing, and that the active cause of the evil is mind-weakness, the result of forced development and premature responsibility. Hasty and too early marriages, too anxious struggles for success in life, too hazardous ventures in business enterprise, the rush of undisciplined and untrained minds into the arena of intellectual strife, and, above all, that swinging of the self-consciousness — pendulum like — between excess in rigor of self-control and untempered license, which constitutes the inner experience of too many, are proximate causes of the breakdown or agony of distress which ends in suicide. The underlying cause is impatience, social, domestic, and personal, of the period of preparation which nature has ordained to stand on the threshold of life, but which the haste of "progress" treats as delay. It is not delay, but development: albeit this is a lesson rash energy has yet to learn from sober science. [p. 256]

The psychosocial issue of premature acculturation is still actively debated, as it probably has been through the ages. Progressively earlier exposure to such issues as divorce, sexuality/pregnancy/abortion, substance abuse, dating, and competitive educational pressures (gifted and talented programs, honors courses, advanced placement courses, college concerns in grade school) are considered legitimate concerns in contemporary efforts to understand increased suicide rates in young people. Does history simply remind us that there is nothing new under the sun?

Suicide and Mental Illness

The relationship of suicide to mental illness is considered in passing by comments scattered throughout the *Journal,* but only a few explore the nature of this relationship in a more systematic way. The first, in 1856 (Vol. 12), is a summary of an excerpt from A. Brierre de Boismont's "Du Suicide et de la Folie Suicide," published the same year in Paris. This renowned student of suicide makes it clear that, while those suffering from insanity are vulnerable to suicide, there are "circumstances in life in which suicide . . . can be readily accounted for by a state of mind far removed from insanity" (p. 351). Those who commit suicide "in full possession of reason" explain their act (by suicide notes) in terms of the stresses of everyday life, and "reason remains undisturbed," while the suicide of insane persons is "determined by hallucinations, illusions, and other morbid conditions" (p. 353) The *Journal* editor is in complete agreement, commenting that "Monsieur le Docteur Brierre de Boismont appears to be in the right when he defines this difference, which common sense, even, unaided by science, so readily establishes" (p. 351). Despite the unequivocal support for the validity of "rational suicide," debate has continued in American psychiatry — with diminishing intensity — to the present day.

A second report is provided in 1877 (vol. 34) in a review of the proceedings of the New England Psychological Society's June 26 quarterly meeting. The president, Dr. Tyler, read a paper on melancholia, choosing this topic because of "the great frequency of this form of insanity at the present time" (p. 98). There was a nearly unanimous feeling that the suicidal impulse is inherent in this form of illness and should be assumed in every case, even when denied by the patient and the family. One patient is recalled who, "no suicidal tendency having been observed or suspected during several months residence at the hospital, . . . having been removed for pecuniary reasons, committed suicide within a few days" (p. 99). Contemporary clinicians would generally concur with these views, though the frequency of the diagnosis has greatly diminished, and in facilities where electroconvulsive therapy is available the risk can be reduced relatively quickly. On the other hand, present-day psychiatrists are frequently prevented from using such measures in view of patients' "right to refuse treatment," a concept that was apparently unheard of a century ago.

In 1878 (vol. 34) the *Journal* provides a thirty-seven-page report by the Honorable O. H. Palmer, entitled "Suicide Not Evidence of Insanity," which was read before the Medico-Legal Society of New York. This scholarly work provides extensive historical, legal, and clinical documentation to support the thesis of the title. The focus is on the incentive to suicide provided by the life insurance system in this country combined with the erroneous belief of lay persons that suicide is by its nature the act of an insane person. There is an understandable desire of judges and juries to assuage the agony of a grieving family, especially at the expense of a wealthy and impersonal insurance company. But the invitation to "legalized fraud" by vitiating a suicide exclusion in a life insurance contract by finding every suicidal death to be due to "unsound mind" is a grave abuse of the system.

Three cases are meticulously documented in which the suicide was carefully planned as a means of providing for survivors, paying off debts, or achieving other well-defined goals. Intelligent juries "by sympathy and error" are said to have "robbed innocent policy-holders and rewarded rascality" and that "with a healthy and intelligent public opinion no such fraud could be consummated, nor outrage perpetrated" (p. 425).

Though national data on suicide were not kept at that time, it was clear to the speaker that "the suicidal mania is spreading beyond all precedent . . . the barriers to self-destruction seem to be giving way" (p. 461). Finally on a religious note, "destroy the faith of men in the Bible and the great truths it teaches, remove the restraints of religion and teach annihilation, and you will reap without the aid of insanity a harvest of suicides that will astonish the world" (p. 461).

No editorial comment is provided in the *Journal,* but we are reminded that of all the data gathered in the past half century, little if any has addressed the questions raised by the impassioned Mr. Palmer of a century ago. The most frequent litigation in psychiatry is said to involve suicide. Are we overlooking a lesson from the past?

LEGAL AND ETHICAL ISSUES

Nineteenth-century psychiatry was still very much influenced by religious concepts as regards the legal and ethical aspects of suicide, and generally seemed to regard it as a sign of moral weakness, or at least a form of mental weakness, as well as a felony. There were highly articulate arguments to the contrary, however, in the medical community. These arguments were presented in 1893 (vol. 49) from the *New York Times* for February 14 of that year, as follows:

> Suicide and the Law — Before the Society of Medical Jurisprudence last evening, meeting at the Academy of Medicine, 17 West Forty-third Street, S. B. Livingston read a paper on "Suicide and Recent Re-actionary Legislation." This treatise reviewed the manner in which suicide had been regarded by ancient and modern peoples and the various legal measures that had been resorted to prevent the act. The criminality of suicide, he said, became firmly established with the Christian era, being born of the belief that man's life is not his own. Mr. Livingston said he was forced to the conclusion, however, that no legislation had ever tended to prevent suicide. The theory of the old English common law, which has long been abandoned, was that suicide could be deterred by confiscating the estate left by the suicide and submitting the body to such disgrace as exposing it to public view and then burying it at the cross roads with a stake driven through it. The theory of the Penal Code of New York was that suicide would be deterred by punishing as felons those who attempted to take their lives and failed. This, he thought, had no other result than to make those who contemplated suicide surer of their method. Furthermore, he thought, the law was a dead letter, as he had never heard of the conviction of an attempted suicide under it. Dr. E. C. Spitzka, in the discussion which followed, said that he regarded laws to prevent suicide as relics of barbarism. Their absolute uselessness had been fully demonstrated, and they might work injustice. He corrected Mr. Livingston in his statement that an attempted suicide had never been punished under the New York law, by relating that just after the law was passed, in 1881, a poor longshoreman named Donohue, suffering from delirium tremens, had jumped into the river. He was fished out, and his being the first case after the passage of the law, he was sentenced to State prison and was there yet. No other attempt to convict had ever been made. [p. 626]

These views were destined to gain social acceptance, but it was not without a fight. The following year, 1894 (vol. 50), saw an equally forceful statement abstracted from the *Lancet* of September 9, 1893, titled "The Ethics of Suicide." This perspective focused on "the operation of moral forces," such that "the mind that connives at self-destruction" is not only unhealthy, but "in an even greater degree immoral, since, possessing within itself a sense of duty and of relationship with others in their lives, labors and attainments, it ignores all for the sake of a present gain of personal relief. No one can rid himself of this relationship without at the same time casting on others the burden of responsibility which he abandons" (p. 395).

The writer goes on to foreshadow a pressing issue of the 1990s by indicating disagreement with those who not only "go the length of excusing suicide" but are "even advocating the creation of facilities for its accomplishment" (p. 395). The inspirational tack is pursued with the exhortation that "the evil of suicide is not to be disguised by resorting to a lethal chamber or other permissive method—but by cherishing a sense of human fellowship and mutual duty—the divine order still prevails—for [everyone's] best interests. We have heard enough of the modern pessimism with its latest miserable canon of self-destruction. We could substitute for it the plain, old-fashioned but eminently wholesome and courageous precept, 'Never say die' " (p. 395). Such sentiments have considerable emotional force, and will probably be a significant factor in present-day appeals to society to move in permissive directions.

The specifics of a socially sanctioned assisted death are not addressed in detail with the exception of a historical note provided by O. H. Palmer in the 1878 paper referred to above. He points out that the first-century writer Valerius Maximus states that in the city of Marseilles "poisonous liquor was kept publicly that was given to such as exhibited themselves to the Senate, and procured its approval of the reasons which prompted them to get rid of life; that the Senate examined their reasons with care, and after deliberating whether the applicants were justified in wishing to leave the world, gave or refused its sanction accordingly" (p. 433). It is certainly of interest that in looking to history for approaches to current concerns, we find the most pertinent example not a century, but two millenia ago.

EPILOGUE

This exercise in looking back apparently provides us with no solutions to our late-twentieth-century dilemmas. Nor would that be a likely result were we to expand our scrutiny to the numerous other sources omitted from the present limited review. Yet one senses a benefit of a more diffuse nature—a greater awareness of the continuity of our struggles as individuals, as care givers, and as a society. An aura of connectedness to those who came before us seems to be generated, as well as an appreciation of their efforts in a period of relatively limited resources. If we achieve no more than a degree of enhanced humility in this age of advanced scientific development, the journey to one hundred years ago will have served us well.

REFERENCES

Asberg, M., Traskman, L., and Thoren, P. (1976). 5-HIAA in the cerebrospinal fluid: a biochemical suicide predictor? *Archives of General Psychiatry* 33:1193-1197.

Bunney, W., and Fawcett, J. (1965). Possibility of a biochemical test for suicide potential. *Archives of General Psychiatry* 13:232-239.

Farberow, N. (1969). Bibliography on suicide and suicide prevention. Public Health Service Publication No. 1979. Chevy Chase, MD: National Institute of Mental Health.

Farberow, N., and Shneidman, E. (1961). *The Cry for Help.* New York: McGraw-Hill.

Motto, J., Heilbron, D., and Juster, R. (1985). Development of a clinical instrument to estimate suicide risk. *American Journal of Psychiatry* 142:680-686.

Rost, H. (1927). *Bibliographie des Selbstmords.* Augsburg, Germany: Hass & Grabherr.

Schmid, C. (1933). Suicide in Minneapolis, Minnesota: 1928-32. *American Journal of Sociology* 39:30-48.

3: DEFINITIONS OF SUICIDE

Jean-Pierre Soubrier

A major issue in suicidology is the following: Do we have a common definition of suicide?

Suicide is a multidimensional phenomenon literally defined as "a crime against oneself." For many centuries suicide had been associated with crime and with its theological partner, sin. It is only since the early twentieth century that psychological, psychoanalytical, and cognitive theories about suicide have been introduced. Some authors, Stengel, for example (1964), have suggested that suicide be categorized according to different functions. Others, such as Farberow (1980), proposed to distinguish between self-destructive behaviors that are direct and those that are indirect.

Even within philosophy there are troubling complexities. A good example is the French writer, Albert Camus. In his *Myth of Sisyphus* (1942), there is a famous sentence: "There is only one serious philosophical problem: that is suicide." This sentence is usually cited in short. When we read Camus' book *Myth of Sisyphus*, we learn he wished to deliver a more dramatic message, apparently less permissive. Suicide was not a rationalization. For Camus, suicide was an absurd act of life and he asked how one can define an absurd act. Whether philosophical or psychological, defining suicide has been elusive.

A HISTORY OF THE DEFINITION OF SUICIDE

The word *suicide* was first introduced in the seventeenth century. Some authors cite Brown as the first person to have used the term around 1635. Others cite Philips in 1662 in the *New World of Words*. Anglo-Saxons say the word was given by Charleton in 1651. French culture and Latinists say suicide was first mentioned in the eighteenth century by either Abbé Prevot in 1734 or Abbé Desfontaines in 1737. Officially, the French Academy included the word in its dictionary in 1762 as "the murder of oneself."

Over the centuries, suicide had different meanings. Society had different attitudes toward it, corresponding to different moral laws. Socrates' suicide is one of the most famous examples. Socrates drank hemlock at the order of a Greek court. Was his death a sanction or an acting out provoked by Socrates himself at the old age of 70? As another example, early in the Catholic church, suicide was seen as a sacrifice by the Martyrs, but after the Council of Arles in 452, suicide was associated with sin and crime.

In France, Esquirol declared in 1838 that suicide was "an act only committed by mental patients in a moment of delusion." This declaration opened the discussion of suicide among scientists. Durkheim and Freud are the most noteworthy examples. Durkheim (1897), followed by Halbwachs (1930), insisted on the importance of social factors in suicide. Halbwachs (1930) stated "reasons for a suicide are in ourselves but also external to us." At the beginning of the twentieth century Freud (Friedman 1967) attempted to define suicide as a psychological act. In a famous symposium on suicide in 1910, Freud declared: "Suicide is a 180 degree self-murder." Elsewhere, Freud (1930) declared: "Suicide and war are different aspects of a unitary problem. They are expressions in human beings of instinctual destruction which in turn are interchangeable elements of the Death Instinct."

Suicide from the psychoanalytic perspective can be seen as acting out when the individual takes the risk to terminate his/her life. Shneidman calls it cessation. He writes: "Suicide is an intended act of self-inflicted cessation" (1985). From that perspective, suicide is an act of ending one's life whatever the fantasies, forms, attitudes, game, flirt between life and death in a risk-taking behavior. Suicide may then be defined as an act of life which may lead to one's death.

The French analyst Jacques Lacan called it "an outrage committed against one's life" (1969). Using Freudian concepts, we will say here that suicide is an act directed against oneself in the absence or inability to kill the other (significant other or whatever), in a moment of mourning of the self, whatever the impotency when facing or experiencing a death instinct or a paradoxical defense against anxiety. As an example, this is what a young survivor-patient said to me: "Suicide for me was a way to get out of an uncontrolled situation."

Karl Menninger in 1939 proposed in his book *Man Against Himself* to discuss suicide as three different types of wishes: the wish to die, the wish to kill, or the wish to kill oneself. He said: "Suicide is a murder but suicide is also a murder by the self." Although no explicit definition is given, the book contains important hypotheses in terms of which suicide might be understood. As an example, Menninger wrote: "No suicide is consummated unless in addition to this wish to kill and to be killed, the suicidal person also wishes to die."

A few years ago Chad Varah edited a book on the twenty-fifth anniversary of the Samaritans, *Answers to Suicide* (1978). In this book, he collected a variety of definitions of suicide from representatives of many different countries. Here is a sampling of their definitions:

Sarah Dastoor: (India)

I vengeful, killer, hate-inspired — so I die;
I guilty, sinner, trapped — escaping life;
I hoping rebirth, forgiveness divine — live again

Erwin Ringel: (Austria)

Suicide is the intentional tendency to take one's own life.

Jozef Hes: (Israel)

Fruit of illogical action resulting from "funnel" thinking, which prevents a person from perceiving alternatives to self-destruction.

Jerome Motto: (USA)

Suicide is self-inflicted, self-intentioned death.

Maria Luisa Gomezgil: (Mexico)

Alienation's last word.

Tadeusz Kielanowski: (Poland)

Suicide is the most tragic decision of a man who found nobody to hold out a hand to him.

Walter Hurst: (New Zealand)

The decision to commit suicide is more often prompted by a desire to stop living than by a wish to die. Suicide is a determined alternative to facing a problem that seems to be too big to handle alone.

Charles Bagg: (United Kingdom)

Suicide is the intentional act of taking one's life either as a result of mental illness (these illnesses frequently though not always causing distress to the individual carrying out the act) or as a result of various motivations which are not necessarily part of any designated mental illness but which outweigh the instinct to continue to live.

My own definition was: "Suicide is a final act of despair of which the result is not known, occurring after a battle between an unconscious death wish and a desire to live better, to love and be loved." In a footnote I stressed that it was my "definition of the day" and that it might vary from one day to another.

As can be seen, there are obviously different definitions. In 1991, in Boston, at the American Association of Suicidology meeting, I presented a paper discussing the many approaches to suicide phenomena, data from both a public poll and from interviews with psychiatrists. Peculiar results were revealed, such as:

"Only eighty-one percent of the psychiatrists agreed that professional evaluation is needed for every suicide attempt. Seventy-nine percent suggest hospitalization when there is a suicide risk. When asked if suicide is an abnormal or pathological act, the psychiatrists were unable to answer with unanimity: 54 percent thought that suicide is not a pathological act, 45 percent thought suicide is a pathological act and 1 percent expressed no opinion."

My conclusion (Soubrier 1990) was: Are we talking about the same phenomenon? Should we not define or redefine suicide? I concluded with the following: "It is necessary to encourage the participation of the various mental health professionals including psychiatrists in suicidology. This development should take place during the 1990s and we hope to eventually be able to redefine suicidal behavior."

At the same meeting, Berman and Maris (1991) declared: "Only recently have researchers focused on more primary and atheoretical questions such as that of operationally defining terms."

We have succeeded in destroying the taboo of suicide. Although it is impossible to review all the literature on suicide, it is noteworthy that a definition of suicide has been raised in studies of rational suicide.

It is important that the term suicide be used properly. For instance, the use of assisted suicide instead of the classical ethical terminology of assisting the death of someone at the end of life is regrettable. We should be careful about the term rational suicide. There is a danger of provocation to suicide among people who, in the last analysis, do not wish to die. In France, a law against provocation to suicide was passed in 1987. It condemns all assistance and help to suicide, including its promotion in publications and other media. If we are discussing suicide in too wide a philosophical angle, we are taking the dramatic risk of forgetting the *primum movens* of suicide thoughts, suicide being mainly an act of profound despair, a last call from one wishing to live better (Soubrier 1978).

Dr. Edwin Shneidman has brilliantly associated philosophy, psychology, semantics, and clinical experiences in defining suicide. In his books *Essays In Self-Destruction* (1967) and *Definition of Suicide* (1985) Shneidman discusses the problem of definition. In the former book, Shneidman wrote: "In relation to suicide — admittedly a somewhat intransigent topic — it seems evident that our current definitions (and our current conceptualizations) of suicide are not adequate. To put it another way, the definitions of suicide that we see in textbooks, use in clinical reports, read in newspapers, and hear in everyday talk are just not good enough to permit us to understand the events we wish to change. The basic need, in relation to suicide, is for a radical reconceptualization of the phenomenon of suicide. What is required is a new definition of suicide followed by a broadening of many clinical and social activities based on that new understanding." Further on, in this same book, Shneidman gives a personal definition, but one that concerns *only* the Western world, that is: "Currently in the Western world, suicide is a conscious act of self-induced annihilation, best understood as a multidimensional malaise in a needful individual who defines an issue for which the suicide is perceived as the best solution."

What about the other parts of the world?

And the question remains: Is this the last definition we should see, or only the latest in a long series of attempts to define the core event in our field?

THE MANY APPROACHES OF SUICIDE

Suicide has been defined differently by many different authors. Suicide has also been categorized according to various typologies or theories. Yet there are two main directions: social definition and mental/psychological definition. Although this view may be overly old-fashioned, it is interesting to see that the evolution of social and political ideas were of great help in the debate on this topic.

Suicide is also differently understood according to the location of the study. Religions and political regimes have contributed to different and even peculiar approaches to the problem of self-death. In former Communist Russia suicide was considered only as a capitalist vestige. Crime, prostitution, and unemployment were similarly viewed. Treatment of mental illness was, in fact, used for political reasons.

We can conclude here that suicide is also differently understood according to the place of study. The sentimental affective pain endured by relative survivors, for example, is largely different than in case of professionals, or of a district attorney or of an insurance company. Therefore, there is a difference in signification and meaning in our definitions of suicide.

SUICIDE AND ATTEMPTED SUICIDE

Is there a difference between those whose suicide is an act of behavior and those in whom suicide remains in thoughts and fantasies? In suicidological practice, we distinguish between the callers to a crisis line and the attempters who harm themselves and are seen in hospitals. Stengel (1964) proposed a fairly sharp distinction between suicide and attempted suicide. But, as Shneidman (1985) reports: "Suicidal acts are committed by suicidal individuals and parasuicidal acts are committed by parasuicidal individuals. Stengel was right in distinguishing between committed and attempted suicide and asserting that they are essentially separate events. He did not, however, go far enough in explicating the different psychological characteristics of individuals who are the principal actors in these two different dramas."

On this issue, Kreitman (1969) and his British colleagues have focused on the term *parasuicide*. Parasuicide refers to any apparently suicidal act or gesture not ending in or leading to death. From my view, (1) many parasuicides have finally died; (2) there is a risk of banalizing and minimizing a dramatic act of despair; (3) parasuicide can be compared to pseudo-suicide or somatocides; and (4) parasuicide will remain an ambiguous term. The fact is that Menninger (1939) had already approached this semantic possibility when he distinguished between chronic and acute suicides. Firestone (1988) more recently proposed the term *microsuicide,* referring to everyday life's minor suicidal attitudes such as: "self-damaging lifestyles or behavior patterns that are not necessarily undertaken with the ultimate aim of self-destruction."

CONCLUSION

For Camus (1942) the study of suicide was a philosophical reflection on absurdity. Is it not absurd to end one's own life? He stated: "If life is considered absurd why not decide one's death." Camus further wrote: "To kill oneself is in a way, like in a melodrama, to confess. To confess we are overtaken by life or we do not understand it." Although these ideas are important in defining suicide, we cannot rationalize suicide by only using philosophical statements because in practice, our goal is to understand, help individuals in despair whoever they are. It can be a person in a terminal condition, a chronic schizophrenic, or any person involved in religion or a political career, or simply human beings, all those who, in fact suffer and wish to live better, to live again (Soubrier 1981, Soubrier and Vedrinne 1981).

The French philosopher Landsberg (1951) in a posthumously published writing, declared: "Death is the great present–absent of human suicide behavior. It is the stake of the communication between suicide in individuals and its surrounding. Death gives its definition to suicide."

About suicide in general, Kubie (1967) declared: "But since suicide occurs at the end of many different roads, there is no one goal and no one warning. Once achieved, however, death is a single state which reduces all complexities to a single common denominator."

Every one of us has or will have different definitions of suicide. It will always be an act of despair occurring in a personal specific situation. Suicide ideation or attempt may be as well the last call for help or nothing but the blues. It is certainly the act of a temporary living human person.

REFERENCES

Berman, A., and Maris, R. (1991). Suicidal behaviors: towards consensus definitions. Proceedings from the 24th Annual Meeting American Association of Suicidology.

Camus, A. (1942). *Le Mythe De Sisyphe.* Paris: Gallimard.

Durkheim, E. (1897). *Le Suicide.* Paris: P.U.F.

Esquirol, E. (1838). *Des Maladies Mentales Considerees Sous Les Rapports Medicaux Hygieniques et Medicaux-Legaux.* Paris: J. B. Baillere.

Farberow, N. (1980). *The Many Faces of Suicide.* New York: McGraw-Hill.

Firestone, R. (1988). *Voice Therapy.* New York: Human Sciences Press.

Freud, S. (1930). New Introductory lectures on psycho-analysis. In *The Complete Psychological Work of Sigmund Freud,* ed. and trans. J. Strachey, vol. 22. London: Hogarth.

Friedman, P. (1967). *On Suicide.* New York: International Universities Press, 1910.

Halbwachs, M. (1930). *Les Causes du Suicide.* Paris: Alcan.

Kreitman, N. (1969). Parasuicide. *British Journal of Psychiatry* 115:746.

Kubie, L. (1967). In *Essays in Self-Destruction,* ed. E. Shneidman. New York: Science House.

Lacan, J. (1969). *Essai sur la Signification de la Mort. par Suicide.* Paris: Editions du Seuil.

Landsberg, P. L. (1951). *Essai sur l'Éxperience de la Mort.* Paris: Editions du Seuil.

Menninger, K. (1939). *Man Against Himself.* New York: Harcourt, Brace and World.

Shneidman, E. (1967). *Essays in Self Destruction.* New York: Science House.

—— (1985). *Definition of Suicide.* New York: Wiley.

Soubrier, J. P. (1978). What is the effect on the incidence of suicide of the removal of the most popular methods of committing it? In *Answers to Suicide,* ed. C. Varah, pp. 152–159. London: Constable.

—— (1981). Preface. In *Suicide et Conduites Suicidaires,* vol. I, pp. 11–14. Paris: Masson.

—— (1990). Beyond the scale: towards a new definition of suicide. In *Crisis II/I,* pp. 98–103. Toronto: Hogrefe.

Soubrier, J. P., and Vedrinne, J. (1981). *Depression and suicide. Proceedings from the 11th Meeting International Association for Suicide Prevention.* Paris: Pergamon.

Stengel, E. (1964). *Suicide and Attempted Suicide.* London: Pelican.

Varah, C., ed. (1978). *Answers to Suicide.* London: Constable.

4: POLITICAL CULTURE, POLICY CHOICES, AND UNMET NEEDS

Shirley L. Zimmerman

Those who monitor social trends may be struck by the increased frequency with which people have been resorting to suicide to solve their problems (Zimmerman 1990). Earlier analysis has shown that over a twenty-five-year period beginning with 1960, suicide rates in the United States have inched upwards (Zimmerman 1990), averaging 10.5 per 100,000 population for 1959–1961 (National Center for Health Statistics 1959–1961); 11.7 for 1969–1971 (National Center for Health Statistics 1969–71); 11.9 in 1980 (U.S. Bureau of Census 1983); and 12.3 in 1985 (National Center for Health Statistics 1987). In 1988, they stood at 12.4, but in 1986, they were as high as 12.8 per 100,000 population (National Center for Health Statistics 1988). In 1989, the last year for which such data were available at the time of this writing, the official national suicide rate was estimated to be 12.6 (National Center for Health Statistics 1990). Although national suicide rates have been higher at other times in the nation's history, the rate for 1986 was higher than for any other year since 1941 when the United States entered World War II (U.S. Bureau of the Census 1975). The year the rate was highest was in 1932, the cataclysmic year of the Great Depression, when it stood at 17.4. Because 1986 was not distinctive in terms of anything comparable to World War II or the Great Depression, one cannot help but contemplate the reasons for the creeping rise in suicide rates in this country.

To focus only on national trends, however, is to obscure the tremendous variation that exists in suicide rates within the United States among the fifty states. Over a twenty-five-year period, at four different time observations, 1960, 1970, 1980, and 1985, Nevada's suicide rates consistently ranked higher than

Author's note: The research on which this chapter is based was funded by the University of Minnesota, Agricultural Experiment Station, St. Paul, Minnesota. I would like especially to thank Cathy Schultz, whose assistance with the computer analysis was indispensable to the research.

other states, ranging from a low of 22.9 per 100,000 population in 1980 to a high of 27.0 in 1984. In 1985, Wyoming's suicide rate of 22.5 exceeded Nevada's by only .1. New Jersey ranked lowest among the fifty states in both 1969–1971 and 1980, 7.2 and 7.4 respectively, and second lowest in 1985 when New York ranked lowest with a rate of 6.8. In 1959–1961, Rhode Island ranked lowest with a rate of 6.4 followed by Mississippi whose rate was 6.5. Table 4–1 shows the ranking of each of the fifty states on suicide rates for each of these four time observations: 1960, 1970, 1980, and 1985. How to explain such variations among the states is the question addressed in this discussion. Its answer also may help to explain the over time variations observed in suicide phenomena as well.

SOCIAL INTEGRATION: DURKHEIM'S EXPLANATION OF SOCIETAL VARIATIONS IN SUICIDE RATES

Durkheim (1897) developed the concept of social integration to explain variations in the incidence of suicide in different societies. Durkheim viewed suicide as a statement about societal institutions that normatively function to bind individuals to each other and the larger community, marriage and family being two such institutions, social welfare another. Social welfare refers to societal measures for meeting the needs of individuals and families that the market does not provide for large segments of population (Titmuss 1968, Zimmerman 1987). By beginning with a macro set of assumptions about societal norms and institutions, Durkheim made the assumption that individuals not only react to such norms and institutions, but also create and sustain them (Munch and Smelser 1987). In so doing he provided a means for linking macro and micro levels of phenomena (Gerstein 1987), which is the focus of this discussion: the relationship between public policy choices and individual suicide events in the aggregate. Although sociologically speaking, suicide rates may be a measure of the strength in individuals' ties to societal institutions, in Shneidman's microlevel or psychological terms (1985, 1987), they also may be seen as an aggregated measure of the thwarted and frustrated needs of vulnerable individuals seeking a solution to their problems.

Public policy choices that refer to the collective decisions of governing bodies at all levels — federal, state, and local — also may be seen as a function of social integration. Such decisions reflect the consensus that legitimizes actions taken by political institutions to mediate connections between and among people so as to further their well-being (MacRae 1985). These actions go beyond the those of individuals and groups to help one another through their own private efforts. To the extent such consensus exists, governments are able to mediate such connections and, in so doing, promote not only the well-being of individuals, but also social integration. However, because those included in such networks of mutual aid and support typically receive more aid and cooperation than those who are not, integration affects the distribution of well-being when some people are excluded from them. Indeed, one of the meanings commonly

TABLE 4-1

STATE RANKINGS ON SUICIDE RATES AND PER CAPITA SPENDING FOR PUBLIC WELFARE: 1960, 1970, 1980, AND 1985[1]

(1 = LOWEST, 50 = HIGHEST)[2]

State	1959–1961 Suicide	1960 Public Welfare Expenditure	1969–1971 Suicide	1970 Public Welfare Expenditure	1980 Suicide	1980 Public Welfare Expenditure	1985 Suicide	1985 Public Welfare Expenditure
Alabama	10	40	8	34	18	21	9	8
Alaska	45	24	44	27	47	46	37	45
Arizona	37	25	46	4	48	1	45	5
Arkansas	4	41	7	26	22	20	33	24
California	48	45	48	50	41	45	41	46
Colorado	44	48	47	37	46	18	48	26
Connecticut	14	32	14	42	3	38	4	38
Delaware	32	19	31	29	26	27	6	21
Florida	42	13	38	5	44	2	44	3
Georgia	15	37	33	30	32	12	22	23
Hawaii	6	11	24	40	20	42	3	33
Idaho	41	15	43	10	36	9	34	4
Illinois	16	36	6	38	5	39	11	39
Indiana	28	2	21	1	9	7	16	15
Iowa	34	28	22	16	13	35	15	31
Kansas	31	23	18	22	12	26	18	19
Kentucky	24	26	25	33	34	29	27	29
Louisiana	5	49	9	43	27	24	28	30
Maine	38	35	36	39	31	40	39	43
Maryland	26	3	20	28	11	30	13	34
Massachusetts	7	44	4	49	2	48	5	47
Michigan	23	16	28	36	21	47	20	48
Minnesota	17	17	15	18	10	43	10	42

State								
Mississippi	2	38	5	20	4	25	8	16
Missouri	26	46	13	32	24	16	32	18
Montana	46	30	37	15	40	17	46	28
Nebraska	29	10	17	12	8	8	12	25
Nevada	50	12	50	11	50	4	49	1
New Hampshire	35	9	32	6	15	33	35	17
New Jersey	8	4	1	24	1	37	2	36
New Mexico	25	43	45	35	49	10	47	11
New York	19	21	3	48	6	50	1	50
North Carolina	20	6	27	8	19	15	25	7
North Dakota	9	33	23	17	14	19	23	32
Ohio	27	20	30	9	25	28	19	37
Oklahoma	13	50	11	47	35	32	42	27
Oregon	39	39	40	31	42	31	43	20
Pennsylvania	22	18	12	41	16	41	21	41
Rhode Island	1	42	2	46	17	49	7	49
South Carolina	3	5	19	3	7	6	17	6
South Dakota	12	27	10	14	33	23	14	10
Tennessee	18	14	34	13	28	13	24	13
Texas	11	22	26	19	29	5	36	2
Utah	21	29	39	21	37	11	29	22
Vermont	47	31	41	45	43	34	40	40
Virginia	40	1	35	2	39	22	31	9
Washington	43	47	42	44	38	36	38	35
West Virginia	33	34	16	23	30	14	30	14
Wisconsin	30	8	29	25	23	44	26	44
Wyoming	49	7	49	49	45	3	50	12

[1] Data Sources: U.S. Bureau of Census and National Center for Health Statistics.

[2] Spearman's rank order rho for state rankings on suicide rates and per capita spending for public welfare: 1960 = $-.11$, p = .22; 1970 = $-.26$, p = .03; 1980 = $-.35$, p = .01; 1985 = $-.35$; p = .01

associated with nonintegration is the exclusion of some individuals and groups from needed benefits and supports. For this reason, MacRae (1985) advises, any discussion of social integration must include its political as well as its social, psychological, and economic aspects.

It is the thesis of this discussion that suicide phenomena and public policy choices are a part of the same phenomena, and that one of the answers to the question, what accounts for the upward trend in suicide rates over the past decade and state variations in suicide rates, can be found in public policy choices and attitudes toward government's role in mediating connections between and among people so as to meet the needs of people, that is, in variations in states' political culture.

PUBLIC POLICY CHOICES AND TRENDS

With this is mind, it is instructive to review trends in federal and state spending choices for government social welfare programs between 1960 and 1985, a period of expansion, and then contraction, in the role of government in meeting people's needs. With the enactment of major federal legislation during the 1960s and early 1970s, government social programs in the United States expanded to include: the Aid to Families with Dependent Children Unemployed Parent (AFDC-UP) program in 1961, a program specifically aimed at keeping families with unemployed parents together; Medicaid, a medical assistance program for low income people, in 1965; Medicare, a medical insurance payment program for persons 65 years and older as part of the Social Security program, also in 1965; the Supplemental Security Income (SSI) program for elderly, blind, and disabled persons in 1973; Title XX social services in 1973; and child support enforcement services in 1975, among others. Through a series of court rulings, eligibility for such services also expanded during this period to include more people — in the manner reflective of social integration. As a consequence, relative to all other spending by the federal government, federal spending for such programs as social insurance, public assistance, health and medical programs, veterans' programs, and social services increased by 43 percent between 1960 and 1980, from 38 percent to 54.3 percent (U.S. Bureau of Census 1989).

Such expansion was followed by the enactment of the Omnibus Budget Reconciliation Act of 1981 (OBRA). OBRA not only tightened eligibility requirements for services and programs but also reduced federal funds for them as well, bringing further expansion of government's role in the social sphere in this country to a grinding halt. By 1985, the percentage of federal spending for social purposes had decreased from 54.3 percent in 1980 to 47.8 percent (U.S. Bureau of Census 1990). Whereas program expansion accounted for a 56 percent increase in federal social spending between 1970 and 1976, inflation accounted for a 13 percent increase in such spending between 1976 and 1982 (Bixby 1990). Since 1982, federal social spending has not increased in either relative or absolute terms, and was only 1.7 percent higher in 1987 than in 1986, not taking inflation into account; relative to the gross national product (GNP), it has been declining.

At the state level, spending for social purposes increased most sharply between 1960 and 1970 when it rose from 60 percent to 64 percent of all state and local spending. The sharpest decrease occurred between 1975 and 1980 when it dropped from 65.3 percent to 60.8 percent and then in 1985, to 59 percent. Relative to the GNP, state social spending was 7 percent less in 1985 than in 1975. Thus it would seem that decreases in social spending at both federal and state levels between 1980 and 1985 might have acted to compound each other for individuals and families seeking help with problems during this period and in the years that have followed.

STATE VARIATIONS: STATES' PER CAPITA SPENDING FOR PUBLIC WELFARE AND HOSPITALS

However, just as suicide rates vary over time and among the fifty states, so does spending for social purposes, reflecting variations in the extent to which a consensus exists about the role of government in promoting the well-being of individuals and families. In 1960, average state per capita expenditures for public welfare ranged from a low of $6.55 in Virginia to a high of $40.98 in Oklahoma; the national per capita average was $20.74 (U.S. Bureau of Census 1961). In 1970, the national per capita average was $65.24, but California, whose per capita spending on public welfare ranked highest that year, $129.76, spent twice as much as the national average and seven times more than the $18.77 of the lowest ranking state, Indiana (U.S. Bureau of Census 1971). In 1980, New York, which was the highest ranking state that year, spent $358.07 per capita for public welfare or over five times more than Arizona, the lowest ranking state, which spent $69.16, and almost twice as much as the national average, $195 (U.S. Bureau of Census 1981). By 1985, per capita public welfare expenditures averaged $282.71, New York again leading the way with per capita expenditures of $541.01, which again was almost twice as much as national average and four times more than the $125.42 of the nation's lowest ranking state, Nevada (U.S. Bureau of Census 1986). State spending for public welfare includes support and assistance to persons in financial or social need, such as cash assistance payments under the AFDC and SSI programs, burials, and other commodities and services, including social services for persons in financial need and vendor payments under medical assistance programs (U.S. Bureau of Census 1986). The latter refers to Medicaid which represents an increasingly larger share of all spending in this category, one-half in 1988 (Bixby 1991). A ranking of states on their per capita spending for public welfare is shown in Table 4-1 with state suicide rates. Table 4-1 also shows that the relationship between states' ranking on suicide rates and spending for public welfare has grown increasingly strong over time — in inverse direction.

State spending for hospitals similarly varies from state to state. Such spending includes the establishment and operation of hospital facilities, the provision of hospital care, and the support of other public or private hospitals. It does not include vendor payments for medical care which are administered as part of Medicaid under public welfare, as noted above. In 1960, average state per capita spending for hospitals was $9.85; it rose to $20.56 in 1970, $50.34 in 1980, and $67.12 in 1985. For these same years, such spending ranged in 1960 from a low of $3.72 in Arizona to a high of $17.55 in Delaware (U.S. Bureau of Census 1961); in 1970, from a low of $8.91, again in Arizona, to a high of $36.87 in New York (U.S. Bureau of Census 1971); in 1980, from $18.12 in Illinois to $101.78 in Rhode Island (U.S. Bureau of Census 1981); and in 1985, from a low of $17.90 in Nevada, less than what Illinois spent in 1980, to a high of $124.28 in New York (U.S. Bureau of Census 1986). Thus patterns may be discerned in states' spending for social purposes and the consensus that exists about government's role in fostering the well-being of state populations. Table 4–2 shows states' ranking on spending for hospitals in relation to their ranking on suicide rates. Not shown is the increasing strength in the relationship between states' spending for public welfare and hospitals between 1960 and 1970, from r = .07 to .45 following the enactment of Medicaid, after which the relationship between the two declined to r = .40 in 1980 to .38 in 1985.

MACRO AND MICRO LEVEL CONNECTIONS: THE RELATIONSHIP BETWEEN STATES' SPENDING FOR SOCIAL PURPOSES AND THEIR SUICIDE RATES

These patterns must be seen within the context of the New Federalism of the Reagan era and the so-called new paradigm of government's role in the Bush era. Both the New Federalism and the new paradigm emphasized state and local responsibility, voluntarism, and free-market approaches to social problems. This meant that with the pull-back of the federal government, individuals and families had to depend on the connections that the governments in the states in which they lived were able and willing to foster. Thus, it is not surprising that the relationship between states' per capita spending for public welfare and suicide rates increased in strength between 1960 and 1985, from r = .02 in 1960 to − .19 in 1970 to − .36 in 1980 to − .42 in 1985, given the contraction of the role of the federal government in countering the effects of observed state variations.

This relational pattern also pertains to states' spending for hospitals and suicide rates, correlations increasing from r = − .23 in 1960 to − .45 in 1970 to − .43 in 1980 to − .53 in 1985. Thus, states that spent less on public welfare and hospitals and did less to meet the needs of people had higher suicide rates. Although the relationship between states' spending for hospitals and suicide rates is stronger and more persistent over the observational period than it is between states' spending for public welfare and suicide rates, what is important in terms of this discussion is that both gained in strength during the 1980s when eligibility for social services tightened and cost containment policies in health care increasingly took hold. Without some alternative strategy in place to deal with the health and social needs of vulnerable people, such policies instead resulted in a number of dubious practices, one of them being "patient dumping," a means by which hospitals avoided the treatment of persons without obvious means of payment (Zimmerman 1990).

OTHER SOURCES OF STATE VARIATIONS IN SUICIDE RATES: STATES' DIVORCE RATES

Of course, states' policy choices are not the only factor that accounts for variations in states' suicide rates, and, indeed, are not even the prime factor. One of the most critical variables in explaining variations in states' suicide rates is their divorce rates. To the extent divorce represents a weakening of normative constraints on social interactions and behaviors (Munch and Smelser 1987), and the family as a social institution, divorce rates too may be viewed as a measure of social integration. Although a seemingly recent phenomenon, divorce rates have been rising in this country since at least the middle of the nineteenth century, beginning with the Civil War in 1862, increasing for a short time after every major war since then, especially after World Wars I and II (Cherlin 1981). After 1962, however, annual rates began to increase more dramatically, such that by the end of the 1970s, the period including the Vietnam War and the widespread dissent that attended it, they were well above what might have been expected, more marriages ending in divorce than in death at that time. Given the loosening of normative constraints on individual behavior in general and the general turmoil of the period, the rapid rise in divorce rates during this period should probably not be surprising.

More than doubling between 1960 and 1980, national divorce rates since then have stabilized or declined slightly (Zimmerman 1991). In 1960, they stood at 2.2 per 1000 population rising to 3.5 in 1970 and 5.2 in 1980. Between 1980 and 1985, they dropped to 5.0 per 1000 population; their peak years were 1979 and 1981 when they stood at 5.3 (National Center for Health Statistics 1990). Preliminary data show that in 1989, divorce rates declined even further, to 4.7, declining even in Nevada where divorce rates historically have ranked highest in the country. Even Nevada's divorce rate declined over this period from a high of 29.6 divorces in 1960 to 18.7 in 1970 to 17.3 in 1980 to 14.2 in 1985. One reason for Nevada's declining divorce rates is that by the late 1970s, almost all states had enacted some form of no-fault divorce legislation (Phillips 1988), allowing couples to dissolve unhappy marriages more easily in their own home states. Thus, as Nevada's divorce rates decreased, lowest ranking divorce rates began to increase: in New York, from .4 in 1960 to 1.4 per 1000 population in 1970; to 2.9 in Pennsylvania in 1980; to 3.4 in 1985 in both Pennsylvania and North Dakota. By 1989, lowest ranking rates had declined even further, to 2.6 per 1000 population in Massachusetts (National Center for Health Statistics 1990, U.S. Bureau of Census 1989), and highest ranking rates in Nevada to 14.1, reflective of declining trends more generally.

TABLE 4-2

STATE RANKINGS ON SUICIDE RATES AND PER CAPITA SPENDING FOR HOSPITALS: 1960, 1970, 1980, AND 1985[3]

(1 = LOWEST, 50 = HIGHEST)[4]

State	1959–1961 Suicide	1960 Hospital Expenditure	1969–1971 Suicide	1970 Hospital Expenditure	1980 Suicide	1980 Hospital Expenditure	1985 Suicide	1985 Hospital Expenditure
Alabama	10	13	8	9	18	40	9	45
Alaska	45	25	44	34	47	10	37	14
Arizona	37	1	46	1	48	4	45	1
Arkansas	4	16	7	13	22	15	33	17
California	48	28	48	12	41	14	41	16
Colorado	44	38	47	39	46	24	48	34
Connecticut	14	48	14	48	3	44	4	48
Delaware	32	50	31	46	26	26	6	26
Florida	42	15	38	6	44	6	44	3
Georgia	15	12	33	27	32	21	22	21
Hawaii	6	47	24	49	20	48	3	46
Idaho	41	14	43	2	36	1	34	2
Illinois	16	19	6	35	5	17	11	10
Indiana	28	24	21	14	9	13	16	13
Iowa	34	32	22	25	13	43	15	43
Kansas	31	37	18	40	12	30	18	35
Kentucky	24	4	25	8	34	19	27	9
Louisiana	5	45	9	44	27	46	28	49
Maine	38	34	36	22	31	3	39	6
Maryland	26	44	20	43	11	49	13	20
Massachusetts	7	46	4	45	2	31	5	44
Michigan	23	39	28	38	21	37	20	36
Minnesota	17	42	15	41	10	41	10	40

Mississippi	2	9	5	18	4	23	8	25
Missouri	26	17	13	30	24	28	32	22
Montana	46	26	37	16	40	7	46	7
Nebraska	29	33	17	33	8	33	12	33
Nevada	50	2	50	3	50	2	49	4
New Hampshire	35	35	32	20	15	16	35	11
New Jersey	8	18	1	29	1	42	2	30
New Mexico	25	3	45	7	49	38	47	41
New York	19	49	3	50	6	47	1	50
North Carolina	20	22	27	31	19	25	25	28
North Dakota	9	23	23	21	14	29	23	39
Ohio	27	29	30	5	25	27	19	31
Oklahoma	13	27	11	28	35	35	42	37
Oregon	39	41	40	26	42	34	43	32
Pennsylvania	22	36	12	42	16	32	21	29
Rhode Island	1	43	2	47	17	50	7	47
South Carolina	3	10	19	24	7	39	17	38
South Dakota	12	7	10	4	33	5	14	12
Tennessee	18	11	34	15	28	12	24	18
Texas	11	8	26	11	29	22	36	24
Utah	21	5	39	10	37	36	29	27
Vermont	47	31	41	19	43	20	40	8
Virginia	40	40	35	37	39	45	31	42
Washington	43	30	42	32	38	9	38	23
West Virginia	33	6	16	17	30	18	30	5
Wisconsin	30	21	29	36	23	11	26	15
Wyoming	49	20	49	23	45	8	50	19

[3]Data Sources: U.S. Bureau of Census and National Center for Health Statistics.

[4]Spearman's rank order rho for state rankings on suicide rates and per capita spending for hospitals: 1960 = −.01, p = .47; 1970 = −.40; p = .00; 1980 = −.50, p = .00; 1985 = −.51; p = .00.

The relationship between states' divorce and suicide rates has remained positive and strong over time, correlations between 1960 and 1985 ranging from r = .69 to .79 (Zimmerman 1992). Even when controlling for other variables that tap into other dimensions of social integration, such as states' rates of population change, unemployment, population density, racial composition, sex ratio, per capita income, and states' spending for public welfare or hospitals, the relationship between divorce and suicide remains strong and significant, ranging from beta = .50 to .56.

OTHER SOURCES OF VARIATION IN STATE SUICIDE RATES: POPULATION CHANGE AND DENSITY

The exception was in 1970 when state divorce rates were *not* predictive of state suicide rates. However, low population density and high rates of population were (beta = − .44 and .36 respectively). They also have something to do with social integration. High rates of population change are said to create a kind of "social churning" (Linsky and Straus 1986) that is highly disruptive of social and personal relationships. Newcomers may move on with the weather, and long-term residents may feel disinclined to adapt constantly to an ever-changing scene, contributing to the weakening of social commitment to others. Also, if the needs of newcomers for jobs, housing, hospital care, and other social services compete with those of longer-term residents, the situation is structured for social dissension and conflict, as in fact is the case in states such as Florida. Hence, although newcomers constitutionally can no longer be denied services or help on the basis of residency, in states characterized by high rates of population change, they may be viewed with hesitancy, and sometimes suspicion, circumscribing the nature of social interactions in ways that are conducive to social isolation and suicide. Some outsiders, indifferent to community mores and norms, may in fact behave in ways that invite such exclusion, fostering their own nonintegration so to speak ("After vagrant attack, Santa Monica decides generosity has limits," 1990). States having the highest rates of population change over the observational period were: Nevada, Florida, California, Alaska, and Texas (U.S. Bureau of Census 1989), California and Florida having the fastest growing populations in the country.

Low population density has implications for suicide because of the relative scarcity of opportunities for social interactions that could help to reinforce normative constraints on behaviors, or link individuals to societal institutions and the larger community. Low population density also places a constraint on the number of integrative and helping services that communities can provide. Between 1980 and 1987, rural areas alone suffered the loss of 163 hospitals (Doyle 1988). In the meantime, incidents of depression are reported to have doubled in many rural communities, and suicide has become the second leading cause of death among adolescents. Although mental health problems are reported to be growing faster in rural communities than in urban areas, rural services to address them are "totally inadequate" (Newlund 1990). Compounding the problem is the fact that people living in rural areas, especially men, are reticent about sharing their troubles with others and thus are reluctant to seek help from those agencies and services that do exist. States with the lowest population density in 1988 are: Alaska, Wyoming, Nevada, Montana, and North and South Dakota.

STATES' SPENDING FOR PUBLIC WELFARE AND HOSPITALS AS PREDICTORS OF THEIR SUICIDE RATES

Nonetheless, despite the ecological aspects of suicide that serve to undermine personal and social relationships such that many people are excluded from ties of mutual aid and support, policy choices of the 1980s served to exacerbate the problem. Although spending for public welfare was not predictive of state suicide rates in 1985, it was significant in predicting and accounting for half of the increased variation in state suicide rates that year—in inverse direction (beta = − .18) (Zimmerman 1992). This is important, given declining divorce rates and the fact that public welfare spending showed no predictive relationship to state suicide rates at earlier observations, once other variables were introduced into the equation. While the 3 percent increase in the variability of states' 1985 suicide rates attributable to state spending for public welfare may not seem like much, it highlights the widening disparities among the states in what governments do to meet the needs of people—and the consequences of these disparities.

The same can be said about states' spending for hospitals. Although showing no predictive relationship to state suicide rates in 1960 and 1970, such spending was inversely predictive of them in 1985, beta = − .23—even after controlling for the effects of states' divorce rates, population change rates, population density, per capita income, and racial composition. Such spending also was predictive of their increased variation in both 1980 and 1985, in a positive direction in 1980, and in a negative direction in 1985 (beta = .16 and − .14 respectively). The increased variability in states' suicide rates in 1985 represented a doubling over that of 1980, but in an opposite direction. Further, although the actual increase in state variability attributable to states' spending for hospitals was small, only 2 percent in 1985 and 1 percent in 1980, this represented 11 percent of the overall increased variation in states' suicide rates in 1980, and in 1985, one half of it. As may be remembered, during the early to mid-1980s, newspapers carried frequent accounts of suicides believed to be directly linked to the closing of state hospitals ("State hospital closing linked to suicides," 1982) and to the refusal of hospitals to readmit former patients whose insurance had run out. One study involving over five thousand patients suffering from a broad range of mental illnesses showed that severely mentally ill persons faced increased risk of early death in the first two years following discharge from a psychiatric hospital; suicide and accidents accounted for over two-thirds of these deaths ("Released mental patients' high risk of early death," *USA Today*, Jan. 4, 1985, Zimmerman 1990).

Critically ill and mentally disturbed persons are not the only ones who sometimes require hospital care. According to Lynch (1979), lonely people, whose numbers are rapidly increasing in the United States, often do too. For many lonely and isolated individuals, he says, a brief period of hospitalization is their only legitimate means of securing attention. Single, widowed, and divorced persons have far longer hospital stays than married persons with identical medical problems. Elliot (1986) also cites evidence suggesting that separated and divorced persons are at higher risk of admission to psychiatric hospitals than married persons (Ambrose et al. 1983). Divorced males are at particular risk (Robertson 1974).

Other studies also speak to the deleterious effects of social isolation on people. One recent study summarizing studies over the past twenty years in the United States, Finland, and Sweden reported that people who are isolated but healthy are twice as likely to die over the period of a decade as others in the same state of health, even after controlling for the effects of physical health, socioeconomic status, smoking, alcohol, exercise, obesity, race, life satisfaction, and health care. Those at greatest risk were the 10 to 20 percent at the extremes (House, Landis, and Umberson, 1988). These people reported that they do not have anyone with whom they can share their private feelings, and have contact with others less than once a week. Since Americans increasingly are less likely to live with others, to be married, to belong to social clubs or visit with friends than they were twenty to thirty years ago, the meaning of these findings is fairly obvious. For men, social isolation was found to be particularly devastating since the quality of their relationships tends to be of lower quality than women's. The cry of one young woman, "I'm sick, I'm sick, and I have no one," while being led away by the police after pushing another young woman off the subway platform onto the path of an oncoming train in New York City ("I'm sick, I'm sick, and I have no one," *New York Times,* Oct. 24, 1985) captures the essence of this research report. The woman had been released from the hospital's psychiatric services a month earlier after she had been found wandering the streets and diagnosed as dangerous to herself and others.

It is within this context that note is taken of the closing of an additional forty-eight and seventeen psychiatric and other specialty hospitals in 1987 (Tolchin 1989), and the several hundred additional hospitals that are projected to close in the future. It is also within this context that the consequences of increased variability in the role of governments in the fifty states in meeting the needs of people are observed. Such consequences manifest themselves not only in relation to suicide, but in relation to other phenomena as well: divorce rates, teen birthrates, and poverty rates (Zimmerman 1992).

POLITICAL CULTURE AS AN EXPLANATORY VARIABLE

As to what accounts for the widening differences among the states in what governments do to meet people's needs, it is necessary to consider a number of factors: their fiscal capacity as measured by their per capita income; available resources as measured by their per capita tax; constituent demand for services as measured by their divorce, teen birth, and unemployment rates, and also their sex ratio; together with their political culture. Political culture refers to the values and attitudes that people hold toward government and each other (Almond and Verba 1963, 1989, McClosky and Zaller 1984). The political culture of a nation or state generally refers to ways in which orientations toward political objects are distributed within a population. It has been observed that the political culture of the United States tends to be more individualistic than that of other countries (Inglehart 1990), consistent with the cultural traditions of its history and the dominance of individualism as a cultural theme. Individualism is a doctrine that justifies minimal government and lends support to utilitarianism as a particular theory of human behavior. This theory assumes that individuals derive pleasure from the acquisition and consumption of material goods and experience pain from economic loss, that they have needs that cause them to act in their own self-interest, and that the interests of all are served by individuals acting in their own self-interest with little government interference (Ball and Dagger 1990). Jeremy Bentham, a leading nineteenth-century proponent of utilitarianism, espoused the view that the greatest happiness for the greatest number of people could best be served by government's leaving people alone to pursue their own interests, a view with a familiar ring.

Individualism further holds that all individuals have an obligation to try to get ahead and equal opportunities for doing so, and that failure to do so is attributable to their own failings and inadequacies (Kahn 1969, Zimmerman 1988). However, because that which gives happiness is considered to be scarce, the pleasures of some individuals are expected to be gained at the expense of others' pain. The question "What's in it for me?" captures this brand of individualism best (Bellah et al. 1985).

Although the historical conditions of opportunity and mobility that prevailed during the eighteenth and nineteenth centuries in this country supported these value premises, for those who were unable to take advantage of such opportunities, either because they were too old, or were disabled, or too disadvantaged by circumstances, the doctrine of individualism was of little relevance (Kahn 1969, Zimmerman 1988). Here the Protestant Ethic came into play. The fates of such persons, along with society's failures, deviants, dropouts, and victims of catastrophe, were regarded as "acts of God," whose needs were to be met by personal charity and good deeds. As an act of free will and choice, charity not only exemplified the Puritan emphasis on moral worth, but also served as an expression of disdain and distrust for government as an institution. Reinforced by Poor Law traditions that early settlers brought to this country from Europe, such attitudes emphasized deterrence in seeking public help by demeaning and stigmatizing those who did.

The expectation was that natural networks of immediate and extended family and neighborhood would and should provide help to those who needed it.

Such networks, however, usually were comprised of persons similarly dispossessed and exploited, leading similarly fragmented and economically marginal lives in similarly demoralized neighborhoods. Thus, bonded by survival needs as much as by love and affection, these networks were seriously limited in the help they could offer (Wilensky and Lebeaux 1965), a situation that pertains to many families today. In practical terms, all of this meant that people were obliged to work hard and get ahead, that if they needed help, they should look first to their families, or, as a last resort, to charitable organizations in their own communities, but not to government.

In keeping with these cultural traditions, an individualistic political culture emphasizes that government is instituted for essentially utilitarian reasons to handle functions demanded by the people it was created to serve (Elazar 1984). Emphasizing the centrality of private over public concerns, the individualistic political culture places a premium on limiting community intervention—both governmental and nongovernmental—into private activities to the minimum necessary to keep the market in proper working order. In such a political culture, government action is largely restricted to the economic realm, its role being to encourage private initiative and widespread access to the marketplace. According to this formulation, it has a minimal role in mediating connections between and among people so as to further their well-being.

This kind of political culture is entirely consistent with both the New Federalism and the new paradigm of governmental relationships. However, just as states vary along other dimensions, they also vary in their political cultures, some states being more individualistic than others. Using the percentage of state populations voting for a Republican president as a measure of states' political cultures, states ranking highest and lowest on this measure over the study period were: Nebraska (62 percent) and Mississippi (25 percent) in 1960; Nebraska (60 percent) and Mississippi (14 percent) in 1968; Utah (73 percent) and Rhode Island (37 percent) in 1980; and Utah (75 percent) and Minnesota (49 percent) in 1984. Although some may raise questions about this measure of states' political cultures, numerous political polls show that Republicans more than Democrats tend to favor a smaller role for government in meeting the needs of people (McClosky and Zaller 1984). Ronald Reagan, it may be remembered, campaigned for the presidency in both 1980 and 1984 on a cut taxes, cut spending theme, not on doing more for people. George Bush campaigned for the presidency on the theme of "a thousand points of light" and voluntarism, not on the theme of a caring government.

The data are consistent with the thrust of this discussion. More individualistic states spent less for public welfare than less individualistic states $r = -.02$ in 1960, $-.20$ in 1970, $-.54$ in 1980, and $-.57$ in 1984. Although the bivariate relationships between states' political culture and their spending for hospitals were not as strong, their direction was inversely the same: $r = -.16$ for 1960, $-.19$ for 1970, $-.35$ in 1980, and $-.32$ in 1985. Thus, in general, it can be said that the relationship between states' political culture and spending for social purposes increased markedly in strength in inverse direction over the observational period.

This relationship persisted, even after controlling for states' per capita income; per capita taxes; unemployment, teen birth, and divorce rates; and states' sex ratio. The relationship between states' political cultures and their spending for such purposes was inversely predictive in 1970, 1980, and 1985, beta = − .33, − .28, and − .31, respectively. Political culture accounted for 15 percent of the variability in such spending in 1970, 11 percent in 1980, and *almost half* of it in 1985, or 32 percent. Analysis also showed that states' political culture was an underlying factor in the inverse relationship between states' spending for public welfare and their suicide rates. In short, the more individualistic their political culture, the less states do to meet the needs of people — and the higher their suicide rates; the less individualistic their political culture, the more states do to meet the needs of people — and the lower their suicide rates (Zimmerman 1992).

CONCLUSIONS

From this it may be concluded that one explanation for rising suicide rates in this country has to do with prevailing attitudes toward the role of government in meeting the needs of vulnerable people seeking a solution to their problems. Such attitudes not only fail to legitimize government's role in mediating connections between and among people in ways that address their problems, but as has been shown, they foster personal and social malaise in the process. Such attitudes, at the time of this writing, were reflected in a growing estrangement from government and politics in this country (Oreskes 1990) among people at all income levels, the wealthier one-fifth of the population as well as lower and middle class families (Reich 1991). George Bush was elected to the presidency in 1988 by only 27 percent of the electorate in what was the lowest turnout since 1924, and probably in United States history, attracting less than half of all eligible voters (Dolbeare 1990). Although the 1992 presidential election reversed a 30-year decline in voter participation rates with 55 percent of the electorate voting, the United States still ranks lowest among 24 democracies in the proportion of eligible voters who participate in national presidential elections.

Recent developments, however, could represent a reversal in trends of growing estrangement from government and politics and the problems of others. While the percentage of households contributing to charity declined by 20 percent between 1984 and 1988, from 89 to 71 percent (Goss 1988), and average contributions as a percentage of household incomes declined from 2.4 to 1.5 percent, philanthropic giving in 1991 increased 6.2 percent over 1990 (Teltsch 1992). Still, given the growth in the number of millionaires during the 1980s, this was far less than officials of many philanthropies had expected. Also, corporate giving, which in 1989 had not increased for three consecutive years (Teltsch 1989), continued to fall behind inflation in 1991. Further, because religious organizations continue to receive the lion's share of such contributions, many people continue to be excluded from these voluntary but private networks of mutual aid and support. This of course speaks to government's role in mediating connections that go beyond these "thousand points of light" of voluntary effort. Thus the estrangement of people from government and from the problems of others can be viewed as the other side of suicidal phenomena, illustrating what Durkheim observed so long ago, that people not only react to societal institutions and norms, but also create and sustain them. For this reason, rising suicide rates and increased interstate variations in suicide rates must be seen in relation to the larger socio-political-cultural context in which they occur. The more individualistic the political culture, the less governments do to address social problems and the greater such problems become. Whether 1992 represents a turning point in this regard remains to be seen.

REFERENCES

After vagrant attack, Santa Monica decides generosity has limits. (1990). *New York Times,* August 20, p. A10.

Almond, G., and Verba, S. (1963). *The Civic Culture.* Princeton, NJ: Princeton University Press.

_____ (1989). *The Civic Culture: Political Attitudes and Democracy in Five Nations.* Newbury Park, CA: Sage Publications.

Ambrose, P. Harper, J., and Pemberton, R. (1983). *Surviving Divorce: Men Beyond Marriage.* London: Harvester.

Ball, T., and Dagger, R. (1990). The "l-word": a short history of liberalism. *The Political Science Teacher* 3:1-9.

Bellah, R. N., Madsen, R., Sullivan, W. M., et al. (1985). *Habits of the Heart: Individualism and Commitment in American Culture.* New York: Harper & Row.

Bixby, A. K. (1990). Public welfare expenditures, fiscal years 1965-1987. *Social Security Bulletin* 53:10-16.

_____ (1991). Public social welfare expenditures, fiscal year 1988. *Social Security Bulletin* 54:2-16.

Cherlin, A. (1981). *Marriage, Divorce, and Remarriage.* Cambridge, MA: Harvard University Press.

Dolbeare, K. M. (1990). The decay of liberal democracy. *Policy Studies Review* 10:141-150.

Doyle, P. (1988). Hospital shortage growing: rural areas scrambling as financial woes force closings. *Minneapolis Star Tribune,* December 4, p. A 1.

Durkheim, E. (1897). *Suicide.* New York: The Free Press, 1966.

Elazar, D. (1984). *American Federalism: A View from the States.* New York: Harper & Row.

Elliot, F. R. (1986). *The Family: Change or Continuity?* Atlantic Highlands, NJ: Humanities International Press.

Gerstein, D. (1987). To unpack micro and macro: link small with large and part with whole. In *The Macro-Micro Link,* ed. J. S. Alexander, B. Giesen, R. Munch, and N. Smelser, pp. 86-111. Berkeley, CA: University of California Press.

Goss, K. A. (1988). In charitable giving, volunteers lead and the wealthy lag. *Chronicle of Philanthropy,* October 25, p. 1.

House, J. S., Landis, K. R., and Umberson, D. (1988). Social relationships and health. *Science* 241:540-545.

I'm sick, I'm sick and I have no one. (1985). *New York Times,* October 24, p. 26 Y.

Inglehart, R. (1990). *Culture Shift in Advanced Society.* Princeton, NJ: Princeton University Press.

Kahn, A. J. (1969). *Theory and Practice of Social Planning.* New York: Russell Sage Foundation.

Linsky, A., and Straus, M. (1986). *Social Stress in the United States: Links in Regional Patterns in Crime and Illness.* Cover, MA: Auburn House.

Lynch, J. J. (1979). *The Broken Heart.* New York: Basic Books.

MacRae, D., Jr. (1985). *Policy Indicators: Links between Social Science and Public Debate.* Chapel Hill, NC: University of North Carolina Press.

McClosky, H., and Zaller, J. (1984). *The American Ethos.* Cambridge, MA: Harvard University Press.

Munch, R., and Smelser, N. J. (1987). Relating the micro and macro. In *The Micro and Macro Link,* ed. J. C. Alexander, B. Giesen, R. Munch, and N. J. Smelser, pp. 356–388. Berkeley, CA: University of California Press.

National Center for Health Statistics (1959–1961). *Vital Statistics of the United States.* Vol. 1: *Mortality.* Washington, DC: U.S. Government Printing Office.

——— (1969–1971). *Vital Statistics of the United States.* Vol. 2: *Mortality.* Washington, DC: U.S. Government Printing Office.

——— (1987). *Advance Report of Final Mortality Statistics: 1985.* Monthly Vital Statistics Report (Vol. 36, No. 5), Supp., August. DHHS Publication No. PHS (87-1120). Hyattsville, MD: Public Health Service.

——— (1988). *Advance Report of Final Mortality Statistics, 1986.* Monthly Vital Statistics Report (Vol. 37, No. 6) Supp., September. DHHS Publication No. PHS (88-1120). Hyattsville, MD: Public Health Service.

——— (1990). *Annual Summary of Births, Marriages, Divorces, and Deaths: United States, 1989.* Monthly vital statistics report; vol. 38, no. 13. Hyattsville, MD: Public Health Service.

Newlund, S. (1990). Rural areas often lack resources to deal with suicide. *Star Tribune,* April 13, 7 Bw.

Oreskes, M. (1990). Alienation from government grows. *New York Times,* September 19, A 15.

Phillips, R. (1988). *Putting Asunder: A History of Divorce in Western Society.* New York: Cambridge University Press.

Reich, R. (1991). *The Work of Nations: Preparing Ourselves for 21st Century Capitalism.* New York: Alfred A. Knopf.

Released mental patients' high risk of early death. (1985). *USA Today,* January 4, p. 2D.

Robertson, N. C. (1974). The relationship between marital status and the risk of psychiatric referral. *British Journal of Psychiatry* 124:191-202.

Shneidman, E. S. (1985). *Definition of Suicide.* New York: Wiley.

——— (1987). A psychological approach to suicide. In *Cataclysms, Crises and Catastrophes: Psychology in Action,* ed. G. R. VandenBos and B. K. Bryant, pp. 151-183. Washington, DC: American Psychological Association.

Teltsch, K. (1989). Americans donated $104 billion in '88. *New York Times,* June 7, 12 Y.

——— (1992). Philanthropic giving rose 6.2% in '91 study says. *The New York Times,* June 24, p. A 12.

Titmuss, R. (1968). *Commitment to Welfare.* New York: Pantheon.

Tolchin, M. (1989). Study assesses impact of 69 hospital closings. *New York Times,* May 13, 1 Y.

U.S. Bureau of Census. (1961). *State Government Finances in 1960.* Washington DC: U.S. Government Printing Office.

——— (1971). *State Government Finances in 1970.* Washington DC: U.S. Government Printing Office.

——— (1975). *Historical Statistics of the United States, Colonial Times to 1970.* Bicentennial Edition, Part 2. Washington, DC: U.S. Government Printing Office.

——— (1981). *State Government Finances in 1980.* Washington DC: U.S. Government Printing Office.

——— (1983). *County and City Data Book.* Washington, DC: U.S. Government Printing Office.

——— (1986). *State Government Finances in 1985.* Washington DC: U.S. Government Printing Office.

——— (1989). *Statistical Abstract of the United States, 1989.* (109th ed.) Washington, DC: U.S. Government Printing Office.

——— (1990). *Statistical Abstract of the United States, 1990.* (110th ed.) Washington, DC: U.S. Government Printing Office.

Wilensky, H., and Lebeaux, C. (1965). *Industrial Society and Social Welfare.* New York: The Free Press.

Zimmerman, S. L. (1987). States' public welfare expenditures as predictors of states' suicide rates. *Journal of Suicide and Life Threatening Behavior* 17:271-287.

_____ (1988). *Understanding Family Policy: Theoretical Approaches*. Newbury Park, CA: Sage.

_____ (1990). The connection between macro and micro levels: states' spending for hospitals and their suicide rates. *Journal of Suicide and Life Threatening Behavior* 20:31–55.

_____ (1991). The welfare state and family breakup: the mythical connection. *Family Relations* 40:139–147.

_____ (1992). *Family Policies and Family Well-being: The Role of Political Culture*. Newbury Park, CA: Sage.

TRAUMA, VIOLENCE,
AND TERRORISM
Part II

"Currently in the Western world, suicide is a conscious act of self-induced annihilation, best understood as a multidimensional malaise in a needful individual who defines an issue for which suicide is perceived as the best solution" (Edwin Shneidman).

To understand this "self-induced annihilation," it is useful to understand the related topics of trauma, violence, destruction, homicide, and terrorism. Part II presents four chapters: an explication of violence and the legacy of violence, speculation on the role of trauma and violence in subsequent suicidal behavior, a brief note on homicide with specific reference to elderly Anglo females, and considerations on terrorism and hostage taking.

5:   THE ROOTS AND LEGACY
OF VIOLENCE

Pamela Cantor

Ours is a very violent country. Every day an estimated 400,000 students bring a gun to school. Every thirty-six minutes a child is killed or nearly killed by a bullet. By the age of 18, our children have watched 15,000 televised murders, and it is impossible to calculate how many brutal killings they have witnessed when we take movies such as *Rambo, RoboCop,* and *Commando* into account.

American television and movies have almost become synonymous with blood and gore. Even our commercials evoke images of violence. A message on drug prevention I saw recently showed the viewer a bag of cocaine while a voice said, "This bag costs $1,000 on the street." In the next image, a dead teenager in a body bag was being loaded onto a truck headed for the morgue while the voice announced, "This bag costs only $4.95 on the street." Public service messages informing women where to go to protect themselves from violence show violence. And many of the commercials that do not actually show violence, such as NRA promotional ads, play upon our fears of violence: they hold the viewer at gun point while they make their point.

And now for the first time in history, our television has brought us war— live. We watched the Persian Gulf War as it unfolded, saw missiles explode, and beheld the damaged faces of American soldiers who had been brutalized by their Iraqi captors.

If any of this threatened to become too powerful for us to bear, we always had the option to hit the clicker and make it go away. But few did. It was not too much for most of us to tolerate. Indeed, it seemed that we could not get enough. As it was, the war coverage was barely graphic and fast paced enough to keep our attention. We clamored for CNN to bring on the real combat, sitting through the talky segments filled with Pentagon officials and analysts in the hopes that the action would improve.

How did our children react to the violence of the war with its real life, live killings? They were scared, like we were, but, like us, not so scared as to have to turn away. After all, they too, are used to this. They have been watching murders since they were very small.

My daughter's reaction was to cry when she heard of the first bombings in Tel Aviv and to say that she did not want to live in a world filled with such inhumanity. My son, who watches movies and television shows that I cannot stomach, said, "Oh, good, I won't have any homework tonight." He knew his teachers would find the outbreak of the war a more pressing concern.

His reaction, could be ascribed to any number of causes. He was scared, and the best way he could deal with overwhelming fear was by denial. He is young, and young children tend to think of themselves and of their own concerns before they think of others. It may be that he is still at the level of moral development where the value of human life is seen merely as instrumental, a means of satisfying the needs of the possessor, that he has yet to attain the highest level, at which life represents the universal human value of respect for every individual, regardless of who or what he is. But finally, it may simply be that he has seen too many killings, too many bombings, too many explosions, too many brutalities, even too many gas masks, for anything that happens on television to have any real emotional impact on him.

At first, he regarded the televised war as just another violent movie, and *Iraq, The Movie* did not compare well with *Commando* for its fast-paced brutalities. Either he felt it too much and was dealing with the tension that was palpable in our living room that night by denying the reality of it, making light of it, even cracking a joke, or he really did not feel it at all. Perhaps he was numb. Or, perhaps he actually enjoyed watching violence.

THE ROOTS OF VIOLENCE

There is something fascinating for us all about violence. Karl Menninger wrote: "The very word 'violence' has a disturbing, menacing quality, enhanced by the contrast of such gentle words as 'violin' and 'violet' and hinting in a partial pun at something 'vile.' In meaning it implies something dreadful, powerful, destructive or eruptive. It is something we abhor. Or do we? Its first effect is to startle, frighten, even horrify us. But we do not always run away from it. For violence also intrigues us. It is exciting. It is dramatic. Observing it and sometimes participating in it gives us acute pleasure" (Menninger 1968, p. 157). Menninger felt violence to be innate, a fact of human life.

An international committee of twenty scholars at the Sixth International Colloquium on Brain and Aggression disagree. They state that "it is scientifically incorrect to say that war or any other violent behavior is genetically programmed into our nature" (Seville Statement on Violence 1986, p. 1167). The scholars say that it is the interaction between genetic endowment and conditions of nurturance that determines personalities.

The debate between nature and nurture will continue, but what is no longer debatable is the fact that violence is an inescapable part of American life. The United States Department of Health and Human Services says that violent crimes have increased so dramatically in the past twenty years that we are now in the midst of an epidemic of violence. They have declared interpersonal violence a major health problem, giving its solution a priority equal to finding the cures for cancer and heart disease. According to the Centers for Disease Control, violence costs as many lives and claims as many deaths as do these two major physiological killers. They want to gather data on the incidence of violence, look for the origins of violent behaviors, and, ultimately, find ways to curb them.

This will be difficult because our society places a premium on violence. We teach our children that might makes right. We try to tell them about good and bad, and the dichotomy of friend and enemy, but we really believe that violence is effective. We teach that the only difference between the perpetrator and the victim is who strikes first. At the school my son previously attended, the headmaster told me that he had received a mandate from many of the boys' parents to "teach their boys how to kick ass so they could get along in the real world." This conflicted with his goals of trying to teach the values of compassion and respect.

We need to develop alternatives and reorder our priorities. We need to stop teaching that "the victim asked for it," or that "the victim does not really care." Remarkably enough, to many in our society, the idea that thinking and speaking are better alternatives to beatings or slaughter remains a novel one.

Recently, children in Chicago's South Side were asked about violence. Over one quarter of those interviewed said they had personally watched someone die a violent death. As victims, as witnesses, as passive onlookers, and often even as the perpetrators of violence, our children are exposed to an unprecedented barrage of violence.

They see violence because most violence occurs between friends, acquaintances, or family members. There are about 25,000 homicides a year—half are the result of domestic violence. The majority of the victims are between 20 and 39. This means that every year several thousand children witness an actual murder; most of the time the victim, and/or the perpetrator, is their parent.

In the United States there are every year an estimated 800,000 rapes. Forty percent of these rapes occur at home, and half the rape victims are, again, between 20 and 39 years of age. Young adults are thus the victims of 12,500 murders and 400,000 rapes each year. Further, if we estimate that about one fifth of the time a child is home when a murder or rape occurs, then, yearly, 82,000 children actually witness these brutal acts or are present in the immediate aftermath. Add to this the incidence of domestic violence, sexual assault, and child abuse, and the numbers become staggering.

Some theorists believe the pivotal clue to the epidemic of violence in our country is the rising incidence of child abuse. Teachers and friends do not always know when a child is being beaten until he comes to school with bruises on his body, and even then, well-meaning adults may try to look the other way. Children who are burned or beaten by their mothers or fathers do not want to talk, except to say that it was a mistake or an accident. They do not want to see their parents as bad; it is easier for them to see themselves as deserving of their punishment.

Being assaulted by a parent places children in an impossible situation: should they tell the truth or protect their parent? Should they accuse someone else, or accept the blame themselves? Some feel rage, some feel grief, some try hard not to feel anything at all. These youngsters become completely detached, dissociated from their feelings. Perhaps it is the only way they can survive.

Perhaps it is the only way all of us can survive. What happens to these abused youngsters is happening to all of us. Many of us are dissociating our feelings from what we see on the screen, on television, and from what we hear and read.

The other morning I sat down to breakfast and opened my newspaper. The headlines of the first three pages were as follows: "Mother sues in killing of son," "Two men indicted in '86 murder," "Father arraigned in baby girl's death," "Mother of slain teenager files suit," "Gas-station attendant killed in throat slashing robbery," "Teenager who survived October fatal assault is found shot to death," "Murder trial hears pathologist," "Spouse says he is suspect in killing," "Ten dollar debt led to fatal stabbing," and "Girl hit by car may also have been abducted." These are not headlines from a scandal sheet. They come from the front pages of the *Boston Globe*. I need to numb myself in order to enjoy my bran fiber and fruit while I survey the headlines. If I were not to develop some protective mechanisms I would surely be unable to function.

And because we have begun to become numb to the violence that surrounds us, television, music, and Hollywood producers know that to keep our attention, they have to provide more. More and more it seems that violence defines the world we live in, the world we are giving to our children.

Some children who grow up amidst the most extreme violence, poverty, or family trauma, survive. Linda Dusenbury, a researcher at Cornell Medical College, searched the literature for the common characteristics of such children and found three factors that came up again and again. The youngsters had a sense of control over their surroundings, a strong sense of personal identity, and, most important, they had one adult they were able to count on, someone who knew them and gave them a sense of personal optimism about their future. Psychologist Norman Garmezy (DeAngelis 1991), who studies *escapees,* children who come from difficult backgrounds and survive, says that they survive and develop resistance because they have one consistent adult they can identify with and who feels they count.

These escapees, unfortunately, are not the norm. Psychologist Raymon Lorion (DeAngelis 1991) of the University of Maryland says our "culture of violence" will soon be embedded in the minds of our children. William

Saltzmann (DeAngelis 1991), commenting on drug use and resistance to violence, says that carrying a gun is quickly becoming the new status symbol for inner-city youth. A Washington colleague tells me that weapons are outselling cigarettes in the D.C. area. Our children have developed a disturbing fatalism about their lives because of the brutality they see around them. Psychiatrist Carl Bell reports that children in Chicago frequently express the opinion: "it is clear that we are supposed to die. So . . . why not participate in violent activities?" (DeAngelis 1991, p. 26).

THE VICTIMS OF VIOLENCE

It appears that our society is becoming increasingly violent and that many of our children, teenagers, and young adults are witnessing violence and are the victims of violence. But is it clear that witnessing violence or being the victim of violence puts one at risk for inflicting harm on others or on oneself?

Psychiatrists Alice Miller (1983), Heinz Kohut (1971), and Donald Winnicott (1971) believe that children who have been exploited, beaten, taken advantage of, manipulated, neglected, or deceived without the intervention of a loving person, children who have been dissociated from their feelings of anger, despair, helplessness, or anxiety, will eventually express their pain in destructive acts against others — such as criminal acts or mass murder — or against themselves — in drug or alcohol addiction, prostitution, psychiatric disorders, or suicide.

I believe that too. I recently had a new patient walk into my office who had just been released from a psychiatric hospital. She had been placed there because she had tried to kill herself, for the fourth time.

As she told me her history her affect was flat and she showed little emotion the whole hour. She could not look me in the eye and kept avoiding any contact. Yet, as she talked, she was extremely pleasant and from time to time her eyes twinkled. When she got to her high-school years she became agitated and abruptly started to put on her gloves and move off the sofa, preparing to leave, even though it was fifteen minutes too soon. She could not tolerate the internal tension her recollections were generating.

She had lived at home with her mother and father for her first two years. As a youngster she remembers spending so much time alone in her crib that she hit and banged her head against the wall just to hear something. She determined that she could move the crib around the room by banging her head against the wall, thus causing the crib to bounce and lurch forward.

Her parents separated when she was in kindergarten, and her father moved out of state. Her mother would spend days just sitting in a room with the curtains drawn, doing nothing. She and her sisters learned to take care of themselves. Mom did not pay the electric bills, so much of their day they stayed in the dark, and a lot of the time there was no food, so they were hungry. Her mother, she said, was not very maternal.

Her mother's sister began to worry about the girls and told their father. One afternoon when the girls came home from school to make lunch, they were greeted by their father in his car. He pulled them in and drove away. They never saw their mother again. They do not know if she is alive. They do not care.

She lived with her father for a short time but within a few months she was sent north to live with her father's sister. A few years later she and her sister joined her father and his fiancée. She did not get along with her stepmother and when she was in eighth grade, she was sent to a state institution. She spent ninth grade there as well. Then she returned to her aunt.

Elavil, Tegretol, and Prozac numb the pain and let her sleep. No, she does not care that she never saw her mother again, and no, she does not care that she does not see her father much. He lives with his sister now, and they are two unhappy adults. She doesn't care much about anything. In fact, she is considering shock treatment because it may make her feel something, and it may make her less willing to die.

She has no feelings, she says, except she can't stand remembering. She would rather "shoot her brains out."

THE ORIGINS OF VIOLENCE

Like suicide, violence is often undertaken in an attempt to escape from mental illness, just as some mental illness is an escape from the desire to do violence. Sometimes suicide is committed to avoid committing murder. Sometimes murder is committed to avoid suicide. The choice is usually the one the individual sees as the lesser of the two evils at the time (Menninger 1968).

What are the origins of violent suicidal feelings? Biologically oriented theorists such as Plutchik and van Praag pose the hypothesis that the same aggressive impulses underlie both violent and suicidal behaviors. They base this theory, in part, on the frequency with which violence and suicide are associated with one another. About 30 percent of violent individuals have a history of self-destructive behaviors, while 10 to 20 percent of suicidal persons have a history of violent behaviors. Relatively little, however, is known about why some people exhibit violent behavior only, some are suicidal, and some both.

A review of the many studies on this issue points to a number of factors that appear to predict violence. These are the loss of a parent at an early age, medical and neurological problems in the immediate family, severe punishment by parents, and easy access to weapons (Climent et al. 1974).

Of equal importance is the number of variables that seem to correlate negatively with violence. They are depression (which appears to protect against violence but somehow does not protect against suicide), anxiety, previous outpatient psychiatric treatment (perhaps the patient knows how to call for help), a history of drug addiction (in contrast to a history of alcohol addiction, which appears to correlate with violent behavior), and a timid and trusting personality (perhaps violence is not for the fainthearted).

Thus it appears there are certain identifiable factors that increase the likelihood of violence and others that decrease it. The exact valence or strength of any one of these variables at any given moment may predict the probability of violence.

These studies are consistent in showing a high correlation between suicide and aggressive behavior. But the relationship is not a simple one. The psychoanalytic idea that suicide is aggression turned inward has some validity, but it does not help us understand why some violent people are suicidal and others are not (Plutchik and van Praag 1990).

Neurophysiological research has established the existence of brain structures that organize patterns of aggressive behaviors. These are the lateral hypothalamus, ventral tegmental areas, midbrain central gray area, and the central and anterior portions of the septum. Research has also shown that particular neurotransmitters are involved in the expression of aggression. For example, if we deprive an animal of all tryptophan, it becomes increasingly aggressive. The implication is that low serotonin levels are associated with violent behaviors.

Studies in behavioral genetics point to the fact that certain emotional characteristics are inherited. Aggressive behaviors have been shown to be heritable in mice and dogs (Fuller 1986, Plutchik and van Praag 1990). And the fact that thirteen hundred nonhuman species and sixty human cultures are cannibalistic, suggests that aggressive behaviors can serve a survival function (Polis 1981). However, we need to distinguish between aggressive behaviors that are adaptive and violence that is maladaptive. Street violence may well be adaptive, while suicide among young people is both maladaptive and tragic.

SUICIDE AND VIOLENCE

Certain variables correlate with suicide but not with violence; others correlate with violence but not with suicide. The correlates of suicide alone are depression, a feeling of hopelessness in coping with life's problems, and recent psychiatric symptoms. The correlates of violence alone are impulsivity, problems with the law, menstrual problems in women, and recent life stresses (Plutchik and van Praag 1990).

Roy and Linnoila (1990) emphasize the role of monoamines (serotonin, dopamine, and neuroepinephrine) in suicide. They suggest that biochemical abnormalities in monoamine metabolism influence behavior and vulnerability to violent self-destruction. Further, they say there are biological predictors of suicide.

Thus, it appears that violence has roots in society, in the family, and in biology. People who witness violence are at risk for violence. People who are victims of violence are at risk for violence. People who inherit a strong tendency toward aggressive behavior are at risk for violence. All of these individuals are at risk for suicide. Thus, there is a relationship between violence and suicide, but it is not a direct one since suicide can be, but does not have to be, a violent act.

One form of suicide, however, which is clearly violent is suicide by gunshot. Sixty-five percent of all teenage suicides are committed with a gun. When a youngster consumes alcohol and has a gun available, the risk for violence escalates rapidly. The child who uses a gun to kill himself is five times as likely to have been drinking before the shooting than the child who suicides but does not use a gun. Guns are not the reason for suicide, they are the means of suicide, and without the means many of these suicides would not occur. Guns allow little room for rescue. The connection between alcohol, guns, violence, and suicide seems very clear. One can only marvel at the fact that it remains unclear to the NRA.

In 1968 Karl Menninger wrote:

> The easy availability of these engines of destruction, even to children, mentally disturbed people, professional criminals, gangsters, and even high school girls is something to give one pause. The National Rifle Association and its allies have been able to kill scores of bills that have been introduced into Congress and state legislatures for corrective gun control since the death of President Kennedy. Americans still spend about two billion dollars on guns each year; in addition the federal government disposes of about one hundred thousand guns annually at bargain prices. This is a heavy burden on the control of instinctual restrictiveness. [pp. 184–185]

For every instance in which a gun is used for protection, it is used thirty-seven times to kill someone accidentally or by suicide.

THE LEGACY OF VIOLENCE

Violent crimes committed by young people have been on the rise since the 1980s. Our young people have also become the victims of violent crime at an ever-increasing rate. In fact, our teenagers, ages 16 to 19, have the highest victimization rate for violent crimes, excluding homicide. The rates for firearm deaths for females, teenage boys, and young adult males have been higher during the 1980s than at any time previously. Males between the ages of 15 and 34 are at highest risk for death due to firearm suicide and homicide. Children are being exposed to extreme violence at home. The rate of reported child abuse and neglect has increased nearly 70 percent during the 1980s. Suicides among teenagers have tripled during the same time period and doubled for children ages 10 to 14.

We need to keep our children from growing up with violence, to protect them from becoming victims of violence, to stop them from being violent toward others, to keep them from becoming violent toward themselves, to modify the interactions between genetic endowment and conditions of nurturing that determine violent personalities.

One intervention that has emerged is violence-prevention education. There is evidence that knowledge, attitudes, and behaviors can be affected through education. Programs designed to lower the incidence of assaultive behavior by teaching conflict resolution skills are in use in Boston high schools. These programs are designed to provide students with an understanding of the extent of the violence problem, their vulnerability to injury, the role of anger in violence, and strategies for nonviolent conflict resolution. The effectiveness of these programs in preventing violent injury, however, remains to be seen (Centers for Disease Control 1989).

What we do not have to wait to understand is that we cannot combat the problem of violence in terms of old-fashioned psychotherapy alone. We have to combine efforts with educators, sociologists, economists, and law-makers to plan prevention programs to stop the epidemic of violence threatening our children.

Aggression, it seems, is part of human and animal nature. Violence, properly modified, has its purpose, but uncontrolled violence has no purpose. Meeting violence with violence only perpetuates violence.

Sigmund Freud saw "the fateful question for the human species . . . [as] whether and to what extent their cultural development will succeed in mastering the disturbance of their communal life by the human instinct of aggression and self-destruction" (Freud 1961, p. 145), and we are still grappling with this question. It is painfully clear that ours is a violent society and that we are giving our children a legacy of violence. It is clear that being a victim of violence or witnessing violence puts a young person at risk for destructive and self-destructive behaviors. It appears that the origins of violence are found in our social structures, in our families, in our biology, and in our brains. The question of our survival and of the survival of our children depends on how soon we understand and how successfully we control our violence.

REFERENCES

Centers for Disease Control. (1989). Year 2000 health objectives for the nation: reduce violent and abusive behavior. *U.S. Department of Health and Human Services*, pp. 1–41.

Climent, C. E., Rollins, A., Ervin, F. R., and Plutchik, R. (1973). Epidemiological studies of women prisoners: medical and psychiatric variables related to violent behavior. *American Journal of Psychiatry* 130:985–990.

DeAngelis, T., ed. (1991). Living with violence: children suffer and cope. *American Psychological Association Monitor* 22:26–27.

Freud, S. (1961). Civilization and its discontents. In *The Complete Psychological Work of Sigmund Freud*, ed. and trans. J. Strachey. London: Hogarth. 1930.

Fuller, J. L. (1986). Genetics and emotions. In *The Biological Foundations of Emotions*, ed. R. Plutchik and H. Kelleman. New York: Academic.

Kohut, H. (1971). *The Analysis of Self*. New York: International Universities Press.

Menninger, K. (1968). *The Crime of Punishment*. New York: Viking.

Miller, A. (1983). *For Your Own Good: Hidden Cruelty in Child-Rearing and the Roots of Violence*. New York: Farrar, Straus & Giroux.

Polis, G. A. (1981). The evolution and dynamics of intraspecific predation. *The Review of Ecology and Systematics* 12:225–252.

Plutchik, R., and van Praag, H. (1990). Psychosocial correlates of suicide and violence risk. In *Violence and Suicidality: Perspectives in Clinical and Psychological Research,* ed. H. van Praag, R. Plutchik, and A. Apter. New York: Brunner/Mazel.

Roy, A., and Linnoila, M. (1990). Monoamines and suicidal behavior. In *Violence and Suicidality: Perspectives in Clinical and Psychological Research,* ed. H. van Praag, R. Plutchik, and A. Apter. New York: Brunner/Mazel.

Seville Statement on Violence. (1990). *American Psychologist* 45:1167–1168.

Winnicott, D. W. (1971). *Playing and Reality.* New York: Basic Books.

6: CHILDHOOD TRAUMA AND SUBSEQUENT SUICIDAL BEHAVIOR

Caroline C. Fish-Murray

DISASTER

Disaster is defined as a sudden, extraordinary misfortune, an unfortunate event, a calamity, a catastrophe, a cataclysm. It is usually unforeseen and ruinous (Webster 1950). Disasters have happened to mankind on a regular basis since the beginning of phylogenetic history and often strike some individuals frequently over their life span.

The question is debated whether a child's development is helped or hindered by encountering disasters. Once extreme stress disequilibrates the cognitive schemata of a child, is that child so warped by horror that he or she seeks to try to escape life, or does he or she cope with the circumstances and become adept at growing? To answer such questions we must look at the wide system of interacting factors involved. Evolution and genetics shape any child's reactions. A child lives, grows, and is bound by his or her historical and contextual surroundings, and now new evidence from neurobiology would indicate that the brains of children are unalterably changed in registering traumatic events (Edelman 1987, Squire 1987). A child's individual historical past, then, may also uniquely and ineradicably shape a child's character as he or she encounters these storms.

Author's note: Sections of this chapter were presented as the NAIM Foundation Meeting, Georgetown University, Center for Contemporary Arab Studies, October 10–12, 1990. All case illustrations have been altered to disguise patients' identities.

CHAPTER 6

EFFECT OF DISASTERS ON CHILDREN

Resiliency

When we observe children traumatized by wars, refugee camps, and burnt-out slums of our cities, when we encounter sexually and physically abused children, we expect terrible psychological sequelae, but more often than not we find mentally healthy children adapting to the demands put upon them. Studies on the resiliency of children indicate that being assailed by disaster is by no means detrimental to adaptive growth (Widom 1989b). Children can use terrorizing events to sharpen their ability to assess and cope. Their need for proaction becomes stronger than their need for reaction. They become active agents in dealing with bad situations (Garmezy and Rutter 1983). They acquire a belief in the efficacy of rational thought and self control.

Culture is critical in shaping behavior. In a recent study of a random sample of one thousand households in Site 2, a Cambodian refugee camp in Thailand, it was found that only 9 percent of the adults had Post Traumatic Stress Disorder (PTSD) as defined in the American Psychiatric Association: Diagnostic and Statistical Manual of Mental Disorders, Third Edition Revised, (*DSM-III-R* 1987) even though these people had suffered through the holocaust of Pol Pot, the flight through the jungles, the dangerous escape from the armies of Pol Pot, and the stringent conditions of the camp. The teenage cohort of this Cambodian population had no statistical evidence of PTSD even though they had lived through a long list of documented traumas throughout their childhood (Mollica, Donelan et al., Mollica, Fish-Murray et al.). The Cambodian population in general had symptomatology, but the effects of trauma seemed to be expressed differently from Western cultures.

Studies of children forty years after their escape from the prison camps and Holocaust in Europe noted that the children had grown up and led normal lives, even though they were desperately preoccupied with conforming to those around them. As adults, they had no history of severe psychological problems (Krell 1985). Another study found that child survivors of the camps had been difficult to deal with when young but as adults they had no suicides and only one person had a psychiatric hospital admission. Most of the adults affirmed life and were active, compassionate, and flexible if not "chameleon like" (Moskovitz 1985).

Milgram (1990) recently reported on research on the psychological state of children in Israel. He found that their anxiety levels were a function of ideological and ecological features of their communities and especially correlated with the expectancy and standards set by military personnel and mental health professionals. In general, the children, living in warlike conditions, were observed to be well adjusted without a significant number of symptoms, flexible in their thinking, and adapting in spite of the warlike atmosphere in which they lived. Milgram did find, however, that anxiety increased with the degree of loss experienced by individual children.

Obviously, suffering through multiple disasters does not necessarily translate into pathological symptoms and suicidal tendencies. We are just beginning to understand how disasters can help us to develop competence to deal with untoward circumstances (Cowen et al. 1990).

Negative Effects of Disasters

A small proportion of traumatized children, however, do develop defensive and maladaptive behaviors after enduring disasters. Research is accumulating that shows that such a child is at risk for suicidal thinking and behavior both in the short and long term. Children who endure an accumulation of disasters may have had an inadequate response at the outset and this initial reaction becomes fixated. As Shneidman (1985) has pointed out, adults contemplate suicide not because of one precipitating event but because of some life-long coping patterns.

It is interesting to find that the Cambodian teenagers who had shown no statistical evidence of PTSD had attempted suicide at a higher rate than their cohorts in the United States (Mollica, Donelan et al., unpublished data). Pfeffer (1989), in a review of the literature, found a correlation between early traumatic childhood sexual and physical abuse and attempted and completed suicide, including a correlation between violence and suicidal behavioral. This supports Widom's (1989b) link between adult aggressivity and early childhood abuse in a small proportion of abused children. Continuously maltreated children can develop severe anxiety, depression, withdrawal, and suicidal thinking and acting out (Solomon et al. 1988, Widom 1989a). Herman, Perry, and van der Kolk (1989) found that physical abuse in childhood was significantly correlated with self-mutilation and suicide attempts. These behaviors were increased and maintained by a lack of secure attachments. Others have found also that sexual and physical abuse in early childhood was a significant factor in the development of suicidal behavior (Bryer et al. 1987, Keele and Ivry 1990).

Whether the child is resilient or headed for pathology, the evidence has become convincing that there are probable correlative if not causal effects of trauma on later personality development. In devising appropriate measures for strengthening character or in guiding therapy we need to know more about the specific mechanisms involved (Cowen et al. 1990).

In this chapter, we will concentrate on the role of memory and logic as inseparable functions of the cognitive system critical to understanding the effect of trauma. Memory and logic and the mechanisms involved ensure either adaptive or maladaptive growth and are therefore central to preventive interventions and the therapeutic process. We will use theory, the implications of newly recognized structural mechanisms, and studies of traumatized patients to suggest possibilities for working with suicidal patients.

Several studies have shown that the degree and duration of trauma may not be the primary factors in disabling the victims of trauma but rather how adequately the affected children can understand what is happening to them and why. In other words, their healthy adaptation depends in part on the complexity of their cognitive structures and functions. If a traumatized person can alleviate the stress of trauma through meaningful interpretations of the events, as well as through consequent useful adaptive behaviors, he or she is considered "resilient."

Some generalizations on developmental logic for instance can help explain resiliency. Children use a different logic from adults and cannot interpret trauma as adults would. The full range of possibilities and alternatives cannot be conceived of by a child (Kagan 1983). If the child is living within the bounds of a close attachment and is able to preserve a remnant of surrounding social networks, he or she retains a sense of belongingness, a strong attachment to another human being, and a sense of cultural and historical purpose that prevent the development of behavioral symptoms indicating psychopathology (Baker 1990, Kinzie et al. 1986, Ressler et al. 1988, Steinglass et al. 1985). Rituals of the life cycle, rites of passage, specific cultural and religious practices, and daily routines keep the child steady in his or her growth and flexible in thinking (Frederick 1985, Mollica, Fish-Murray, et al.).

The child certainly registers and remembers terror, horror, grief, rage, but these strong emotions encoded by structures and operations of the cognitive system do not prove relevant when they are absorbed and negated by the strength of social supports. Trauma can slip out of working memory. Also children who are continuously assailed by traumatic events practice their coping skills which keep them alive and well, thus inoculating themselves against further negative effects. The amazing bounce, enthusiasm, and curiosity of many deprived inner-city children in the early grades of city schools is evidence of this. Mastery and a growing sense of competence are preferred and sought by children. They do not like being afraid. Children will often be extremely brave, if not daring, in the face of emergencies.

MEMORY'S ROLE IN ADAPTATION AND PATHOLOGY

Whether we are looking for mechanisms of resilience or pathology it is probably within the memory system that the boundary conditions defining the variables will be found. The explosion of knowledge in the field of memory is generating hypotheses for altering theory and creating novel practical applications. In concentrating on memory, we should never lose track of its inextricable linkage with all other cognitive functions such as perception, attention, the role of assimilation and accommodation, and the cognitive operations that appraise and organize incoming data resulting in the evolving schemata of logic. Memory is only one system within the larger cognitive system, which in turn is influenced by the general systems of existence. In concentrating on memory, we recognize that there are still many unsolved questions about how memories are temporally registered, stored, and retrieved (Polster et al. 1991).

Memory codes, stores, and retrieves information on what is happening and has happened, and makes it possible to project what will happen. William James once said the purpose of memory is to help us forget. We can't remember everything. We must code, classify, and simplify, see patterns and relationships. The brain has to decide what combination of stimuli lead to survival and adaptation. We remember by categories that bring order out of multiple stimuli from the environment (Rosenfield 1988). It is obvious that humans and all other animals on the phylogenetic scale develop appropriate perceptual and classificatory systems sensitive to their various environments and hold these in their memories. Recent work of Anderson (1991) has shown that human memory seems exquisitely tuned to the statistics of information presented in the environment. Neither animals or humans want to experience traumas. We are always on the alert to avoid them. We remember what they are and what works to keep away from them. We have acquired, over millennia, functions, structures, and biological mechanisms that help us avoid horrendous events and deal with terror and pain if we are afflicted.

Much of our reaction to disaster is unlearned. We are phylogenetically primed, for instance, to fight, flee, or freeze when we first encounter terror. It is not something we have been taught or learned in our individual life time. Once presented with terror, we must make the cognitive choice as to whether to approach, withdraw, or wait. Which of the three we choose will depend on what we are able to retrieve from our memory stores to shape our future path.

ENCODING

Individual Differences

A wide range of individual differences in remembering trauma always must be taken into consideration. Some of these differences are related to the encoding process. The encoding of memories is affected by states. What is remembered in one state may only be retrievable if one reenters the same state (van der Kolk 1989). Mood affects encoding as does temperament. Shy children react differently from others probably because their steady state arousal level is already high. The stability of heart rate is important in dealing with discrepant information (Kagan 1983). Shy children seem to need more structure to compensate for their tendency to withdraw during treatment than hyperactive, demanding children. Circadian rhythms play an important part in encoding memories (National Institute of Mental Health 1970). Some have found it worthwhile trying to recondition or unlearn deleterious experiences by doing therapy at the same time of day that traumatic events originally occurred. There can also be ethnic differences as well as genetic ones (Kagan 1983).

Following Gardner's (1983) lead and research, we can expect individuals to encode events with a preferred symbol system once the visual imprint is made. The visual system will be important initially. As therapy proceeds, it helps to establish which of the several intelligences, or domains, is dominant and to use the symbolic mode of that system for communication. If the person is verbal, then talking and writing should be the focus of therapy. If the person is more visually and spatially adept, drawings should be used. The patient will convey more in that medium than by words and will also transform experiences more rapidly as was demonstrated vividly by Greenburg (1987). Sometimes showing reactions through bodily acts such as in psychodrama, miming, or reenacting the trauma can refine and redirect communications efficiently (Boothby, personal communication). Does the patient prefer conceptualizing the significant aspects of his or her experiences in relation to others, to his or her own fate, or does he or she see the problem as one that could be solved in a scientific manner? Is he or she "seeing" the solutions or explaining them?

The Role of the Limbic System

Memories are set down primarily in the limbic system. Emotions are essential for memory. The greater the emotional arousal, the stronger the memory. We always conceptualize our feelings in extremely complex terms, which are based on cognitive structures and operations (Lakoff 1987). Therapists work with these cognitive structures, not with emotions per se. We are not so much trying to get the patient to get in touch with feelings, or to discuss how a patient feels about something, but to know what the patient thinks about these feelings (Lazarus 1991). How is he or she identifying them (a cognitive operation)? How does he or she know that despair is different from hope (negation, a cognitive operation)? What categories, what relationships, describe these emotions? Whatever the explanation, it will inevitably be couched in highly complicated and ornately ruled, developmentally based language.

Memory is clearly a highly complex system of structures and functions. Memory and learning differ according to which area of the brain is involved (Thompson et al. 1986). Disastrous events are initially perceptually registered by the right hemisphere, giving us an immediate gestalt of the situation (Squire 1987). We all recognize the significance of the visual in trauma (Brett and Ostroff 1985). We can see what happened as we go back over events. Although other domains can be useful in sorting out present problems, visual memories are the easiest to work with and the most prevalent at the outset of therapy (Johnson 1991). These initial mental images of horrifying events are necessary for further transformation of the experience. We use remembered imagery to orient, plan, and change environments, to rebuild our shattered world and predict our future path. Memories, then, provide us with perceptual and spatial understanding, the recognition of place. Our first orientation for safety is place. Short-term memories established in the hippocampus give us a sense of place and help us navigate through space (O'Keefe and Nadel 1978). Place should be central to discussions at the beginning of therapy. Where was the person when the disaster happened? Can this place be described? Once the original description is obtained, it can be compared to the place the person is presently in, and the relative safety and danger of each can be discussed.

Recent studies suggest that aversive events are registered primarily by the amygdala (Kapp et al. 1986, LeDoux 1989, Squire 1987). Le Doux (1989) conjectures that one reason traumatic memories may be difficult to change is because the amygdala has few connections with the neocortex. Its major circuitry and connections are with the hypothalamus. Extreme fears, therefore, may become conditioned in the early phylogenetic brain. Repetitive memory phenomena such as nightmares, flashbacks, and reenacting trauma without awareness tell us the memory is encoded, assimilated, but not accommodated by the neocortex. The cerebellum has long been implicated in processing conditioned responses (Keele and Ivry 1990). As Piaget (1962) noted, years ago, this results in dissociation of the events from the conscious mind. This freezing of traumatic memories may interfere with the ability to assign useful categories of meaning using higher cortical functions.

What researchers are suggesting is that there are two bases in the brain for two opposite poles of learning, habituation and sensitization (Bachevalier 1990, Johnson 1991, Schacter 1990). Memories of disaster may move immediately via the amygdala into conditioned memory leading to repetitive experiences and actual reenactments in inappropriate circumstances, whereas some of the initial encoding may move via the hippocampus to the more recently acquired and higher brain functions that lead to sensitization. The hippocampus is crucial in registering facts but not procedures (Johnson 1991, Polster et al. 1991, Squire 1987). It follows that these two modes of encoding might be better treated in contrasting ways. Patients who suffer from conditioned habituation such as repetitive phenomena of nightmares, flashbacks, and reenactments may be treated best with deconditioning techniques like flooding (Keane et al. 1989, Saigh 1986), the aim being to make memories conscious. Therapy for the highly sensitized patient might emphasize the cognitive processes such as modeling (accommodation), meditation, visualization, and associative techniques.

Edelman and Mountcastle (1982) hypothesize that the most used, or so-called primitive networks, are the strongest and most readily available in a terrorizing situation. They suggest that early associations with affective states are critical in distributing memories to storage. These often repeated associations continue to shape encoding of subsequent information. The early responses are probably associated with motor and sensory responses initially started in hypothalamic areas and the medial forebrain bundle. If trauma is chronic, the memory and its associated motor and sensory responses may also become fixed and overlearned in these primitive modules.

Since emotions are necessary for memory, and fear is the primary emotion evoked by disasters, whenever any new fear occurs, it can trigger off previously encoded fears that are similar to the new one being experienced. Traumatic events imbedded in the memory systems return whenever a tincture of threat appears, putting the patient into a mode of thinking and coping that is like a child's, that is, thinking is fixated at the developmental level at which the individual experienced the original disaster. Indexing capacities are greatly reduced under stress, thus interfering with short-term memory registration and consequently limiting the efficacy of long-term memory functions needed for coping procedures.

The hippocampus actually can be damaged by repeated traumas. The limbic region loses its efficiency on routing and association of events under threat. It "downshifts," that is, it shifts to automatic and overlearned thought processes (O'Keefe and Nadel 1978). New evidence from studies of Ornitz and Pynoos (1989) shows trauma induces a long-lasting brainstem dysfunction in children. If an adult, in the face of disaster, or even just a shade of fright, uses primitive, if not damaged, childish thought processes to register current events, that person can slip readily into correlative childish behaviors to deal with the situation. This entitles them to be called *borderline.* Among seventy-four patients diagnosed with personality and bipolar disorders, those who had attempted suicide tended to react to current stressors as a return of childhood trauma, neglect, and abandonment (Herman et al. 1989).

Knowing that a small proportion of the general population will be at risk for suicide because of early trauma, it is important at intake of a patient with suicidal tendencies to discover whether early trauma has shaped memory processes. A young college student presented at a hospital with depression, feelings of helplessness and hopelessness, and an admission of entertaining suicidal thoughts. She went through a routine intake. The girl had plainly done well in her life, but now in college had just been rejected by her lover. He had become angry and physically threatening. At the end of the intake the therapist asked, "How were you punished as a child?" She replied, "My mother was a policewoman. Whenever I did anything wrong, she handcuffed me to the radiator and beat me with her billy club." Consequently, this young woman was treated not only for depression and the pressing grief at the loss of her lover, but with an eye toward exploring how her early traumatic memories were affecting her present behavior. She seemed to be approaching new difficulties with childlike thinking, defending herself against her all-powerful, abusive mother. Like so many traumatized patients, she was using irrelevant memories to cope with relevant prospective problems.

STORAGE AND RETRIEVAL

After encoding by the limbic system, memories seem to go into a wide variety of subsystems or multiple memory systems. Storage occurs primarily by category inclusion (Lakoff 1987). These multimemory systems have been designated in the literature in a variety of ways: short-term/long-term; habit; procedural/ declarative; taxon/locale; working/reference; implicit/explicit; recognition/ recall; episodic/semantic; or retrospective/prospective. Registration and recon- struction of events depend on the development of trajectories of various structures and functions of the general cognitive systems. We have many more memories stored in these many different systems than we have sufficient probes to get at them. The therapist's job is to facilitate finding probes.

MEMORY: ITS DEVELOPMENTAL COURSE

Qualitative and quantitative changes occur in memory over the course of development (Bachevalier 1990, Diamond 1990, Gruber and Voneche 1977). As the child grows, cognitive structures and functions are constantly transforming increasingly complex interlocking hierarchies of schemata and parellel processing networks. Edelman (1987) suggests that in early childhood the memories of sensory data are registered in so-called primary neural networks. These processing units grow increasingly powerful and complex and lead to generalizing and abstract thinking by secondary repertoires of higher order neuronal groupings. These repertoires are altered by experience and can be activated by internal as well as external stimuli.

Schacter (1990) distinguishes between implicit and explicit memories. Implicit memories correspond to what used to be generically called the *unconscious,* where memories are stored but not available for explicit recall at will. Schacter argues that implicit memories are based on a structural description system, a subsystem of a perceptual representation system operating at a presemantic level.

When a patient presents with the dreadful statement that all is hopeless and he or she is helpless, both the patient and therapist should be aware of the developmental shifts in memory and logic that go inextricably together throughout development. All borderlines, for instance, are not alike. The reaction of a borderline to treatment depends on where he or she is on the developmental continuum, and treatment must be adapted to this developmental course (Noam 1986).

Specific stages of making and remembering meaning are well known. Cognitive operations used to code information appear at approximately predictable ages from infancy through adolescence depending on mylenization of the brain (Diamond 1990, Fish-Murray et al. 1987, Gruber and Voneche 1977). We register memories with cognitive frames that are available at the time we experience disasters. What is encoded in a child's memory is based on his capability in registering incoming data. These memory sorts depend on where a child is in its developmental course (Fish-Murray et al. 1987).

When we remember or decode information at a later period we use existing schemata (White and Pillemer 1979). During the reconstruction of events during therapy the patient's memories are reprocessed by the current schematas of the patient's neuronal organization. This changes the initial encoding, thus making our memories faulty and certainly different in organization and detail from the original encoding. There is no such thing as an exact replica in memory of what actually happened: "memory is a construct, not a videotape" (Johnson 1991).

Consequently what we consider vividly held memories can trick us. Many examples can be cited: Piaget's abduction that never happened (Gruber and Voneche 1977); Stephen J. Gould's (1990) delightful description of his childhood memory of Devils Tower, Wyoming, that did not match the reality on his return. The therapist needs to understand the developmental transformation of memory and logic in order to help the suicidal patient sort out distortions in memories. Sometimes having patients draw themselves as children and as they are now helps to elicit data useful in understanding their lives' trajectories, the influence of past memories, and current transformations of experiences.

Logic has always been the focus of cognitive behavioral therapy. What is seldom taken into account, however, is the level of logic used when encoding disasters, how it compares to the present developmental level of the logic of the patient, and why a particular stage-specific logic is being used to solve the problem. A simplistic idea of magical, or immature, thinking is applied but seldom are actual operations and their sequence examined. A child grows by naturally experimenting with and seeking new information and discoveries. The reawakening of this curiosity, action, and will falls in part to the therapist. The goal of therapy should be to challenge discrepancies in the patient's views by understanding the sequential developmental level of logic and operations of that patient. This keeps the problem comprehensible and challenging for the patient. Noam's (1986) work with borderlines exemplifies this approach.

Sensorimotor Logic and Memories

If a child is traumatized in the sensorimotor stage, memories will be remembered primarily through the child's actions. These body movements will eventually become internalized thought. There is no general memory, just memories specific to actions. The encoding is done primarily by the right hemisphere, so memories of proprioceptor sensations and visual and auditory memories dominate. The left hemisphere does not become the dominant hemisphere until after age 2 (Fox and Bell 1990). It would follow that primitive networks probably don't use many left hemisphere operations such as comparing, contrasting, and comprehending information analytically. Universal amnesia for early childhood is not due to anxiety, guilt, or repression but is a necessary component of the discontinuities in cognitive functioning and information coding and retrieving over time (Neisser 1982, White and Pillemer 1979).

A child traumatized at this stage will react to and remember what happened depending on how the child is treated by his or her caretaker and culture. Pathological symptoms will probably appear as somatic. Trauma is remembered and expressed in bodily actions: clinging, fighting, throwing up, blocked bowels, food refusals, periods of intense crying. Sleep will be disturbed and the child may cease to thrive. The chief risk is weakening attachment behavior. The child may become shallow, indiscriminate, and diffuse in his or her attachments (Ressler et al. 1988).

A girl at this stage observed an accident in which her mother was severely and agonizingly wounded. Although somber at the time of the accident, she appeared to be handling herself well while neighbors, police, and ambulance drivers dealt with the emergency. Forty-eight hours later she was hospitalized with a bowel block.

A sensorimotor-stage child was caught in a 130 MPH wind gust during a hurricane and lifted off his feet into the air. Whenever the wind blew thereafter, he would retreat to the center of the house and curl up into a ball. Now at 40 he won't fly because liftoff fills his whole body with terror.

An Argentinian girl, "disappeared" at 1, was returned to her mother at 10. When back in her own room at night, the girl reported smelling a nursing baby when she tried to sleep (Grandmothers of Plaza Mayo, Buenos Aires, personal communication). Another child as an infant was in her mother's arms when the mother committed suicide by throwing herself under an oncoming bus. At the last second of her life she threw the child out of harm's way. This child, now nearing adolescence, feels herself being thrown away, unwanted, and in constant danger.

If adult suicidal patients revert to using primitive neuronal networks according to this kind of bodily logic, acting out their thinking, the therapist should accept this as reasonable and build on the developmental continuum until the patient has returned to thinking at an age appropriate level. A child or a regressed adult needs the comfort of physical contact although this becomes a difficult ethical issue. A terrorized infant needs to be held, hugged, and stroked. With adults, even a hand on the shoulder or a pat on the back helps. Of greatest importance is reestablishing the primary need for a strong attachment figure, which, of course, the therapist tends to become.

Preoperational Logic and Memories

By 2, the child has reached what Kagan (1989) calls the period of "psychological victories" including "the maturation of at least five competences: recognition of the past, retrieval of prior schemata, inference, awareness of one's potentiality for action, and, finally, awareness of self as an entity with symbolic attributes" (p. 242).

With preoperational thinking, the memories encoded continue to be primarily visual, based on iconic signs, but verbal tags are coming more and more into play. What the child *sees* is what that object *is*. If you show a child a rock made of sponge and get the child to squash the sponge and then ask, "What is it really, a rock or a sponge?" the child will answer, "Rock," because that is what it looks like. The left hemisphere is now becoming dominant. Rudimentary analytic thought is becoming possible. Regressed patients, like preoperational children, have trouble differentiating between physical and psychological events. If they say, "I hate you," they usually mean, "I don't like what you are doing." They adjust material to fit whatever hypotheses they have come to. They tend to think natural events are caused by humans and they have no sense of permanence.

Children at this stage have a wide range of classification systems for memorizing. These systems are rigid, however. This ability to establish new classes adds immensely to the range of memories they can process. Nevertheless, memories remain primarily iconic. Logic is only intuitive. These children continue to understand practical space when identifying places of trauma but would not be able to draw you a map of where they were. When you ask them what happened you get a paratactic series of "and then . . . and then . . . and then . . . ," strings of events in temporal order but recounted with little sense of understanding of causality or purpose. What occurs simultaneously in space and time is believed to have a causal relationship.

Children see themselves at the center of the universe. The child feels that he or she is at the center of the world's operations and concludes that all power rests with him or her. If terrible things happen, the child is apt to think he or she must be responsible. It thus proves difficult for therapists who attempt to explain that disasters are not the child's fault. Children are insulted and lose faith in the therapist who tries to assure them that responsibility does not lie with them. It is not surprising to find highly intelligent adults who still feel that they were responsible for a parent's death even though that death was from cancer or being killed in a war. These childlike memories and reasonings exert a strong influence.

The cognitive operation of negation develops at approximately 2 years, the hallmark of the terrible twos. Having made the wonderful discovery that *no* is the opposite of *yes,* and that doing the opposite of parents' wishes brings immediate attention, the child delights in his new playground of opposites. Dichotomies are necessary for dialectic reasoning, so playing around with opposites should be encouraged both in the child and in the regressed patient.

When preoperational, primitive neuronal networks are called into use, classification systems are rigid. As far as the child is concerned the classes do not and will not change. Children grow angry if you try to enlighten them. If bombing comes at dawn, then bombings will always come at dawn no matter what you tell them. Regressed adults, too, believe nothing ever changes or should change. They believe they are forever hopelessly and helplessly stuck. Adults are equally outraged at a suggestion of change. Therapy should aim at thawing out these rigid classification systems and trying to establish superordinate classes.

A 2-year-old child was brought into the hospital unconscious with severe injuries inflicted by her mother's boyfriend. At 8 this child was dysfunctional at school and still stuck in the thinking of a 2-year-old. A consultant was called in to explore the range and cause of the child's retardation. The consultant quickly found that the child was using a system of identifying and classifying that was age appropriate to the time she was initially abused. When asked to describe men, for instance, she answered, "They are tall, mean, and hurt." This was a rigid category and could not be changed. Therapy consisted of increasing her range of classifications, including men. With guidance, she began to identify and include in her class of men short, kind, and gentle men. She started with opposites as a 2-year-old would, and then moved to seriating, that is, perceiving that her mother's boyfriend was meaner than the school principal. Continuing on the developmental path of logic, she quickly came to think like the 8-year-old she was. This child developed age-appropriate logic and school work in a short period of time thanks to the coordinated effort of an understanding teacher, foster parent, and therapist. She was happy and self-confident in her new role as student. This ability of the child to play and correct, to assimilate and accommodate, and to strengthen sequential cognitive operations made the question of retardation moot.

Children traumatized during this developmental stage and adults returning to it will probably show the somatic reactions of the sensorimotor stage. Children will demonstrate increased thumbsucking, bedwetting, and poor impulse control. Verbal ability tends to decline (Cichetti and Beeghly 1987). Temper tantrums are frequent as are increased startle responses and exaggerated normal fears. Fears of ghosts and witches and personalized dread abound. Prospective memory creates omens. There is a dread of physical punishment. Leaps of logic occur with mistaken conclusions. Blood is bad; therefore cutting yourself makes sense. It gets rid of bad blood. Such errors of logic are made by children and by adult borderline patients.

Individuals who think preoperationally are accused of lying a lot, but from their point of view they are not lying. They are usually speaking from different characters whom their personality includes. One character knows and believes one thing, but then the person shifts to being another character with new truths. There is as yet little sense of a superordinate self, only a succession of selves emerging like the serial "and then . . . and then . . . and then." "I am a policeman," says a little boy, approaching the dinner table. In a little while the mother says, "Policeman, eat your vegetables." The child replies with a disparaging look at his mother, "I'm not a policeman, I'm a knight in shining armor. I never eat vegetables." Similarly, a child will explain that it was his imaginary companion who did the bad thing, not him.

One can expect a child or regressed adult to express rage at his or her parents, caretakers, or significant others for letting bad things happen. Grownups are all-knowing, all powerful, and should therefore never let awful things happen. An adult who reverts to leveling this kind of rage at fellow adults is devastating and appears incomprehensible to all around.

The therapist dealing with this stage of logic will want to get at the where, what, how, and why questions, especially, "Why me?" The child or depressed suicidal patient wants to know, "Why did I act as I did?" "What will I do if another catastrophe happens?" A 4-year-old will ask you an endless number of "why?" questions, but the child is not looking for cause so much as trying to establish links among classes and finding out what is included in each class.

When dealing with preoperational logic the therapist should begin to explore domains to find which symbol system is the easiest for the person to use to communicate. Sometimes bodily action, miming, making faces, and so forth, will communicate more than words. Moving from bodily representation to visual/spatial descriptions and finally to verbal communication not only gives the patient a rerun of developmental memory progressions but also provides the therapist a clue as to which domain will best facilitate the patient's communication.

Literal interpretations, mistaken hypotheses, and erroneous inferences abound at this stage of development. If a mother calls home to her child and says, "I'll be late. I'm held up at the supermarket," the child thinks the mother is tied up by robbers and the police should be called. These literal inferences can be useful in treatment. A 4-year-old slept every night with his mother's deodorant bottle on his bedside table. When asked why, he answered, "Because it says 'Guaranteed 100% protection.' " All spooks and monsters were kept at bay. The safety of routine is important as it provides control over time and a practicing and remembering of competent behavior as one goes through the day.

Children at this stage of logic use animistic thinking to help them. A little day-care child, abandoned mistakenly in a school bus, staved off panic by handling and talking to his magic crystal that he kept in his pocket. Adults, after all, have been known to have pet rocks, good luck charms, and lucky numbers. Such items can be useful in therapy at a certain point in the developmental progression.

A therapist has to be aware not only of the structural stages in the developing logic of the child but of the child's ability to use and understand language. Before the age of about 4, the child has trouble understanding clauses or passive sentences. If an older person seeking help is thinking as a child, the therapist would be wise to keep his communications at the simplest level, sticking to short declarative sentences like a kindergarten teacher. They should also avoid euphemisms since these are difficult for the child or regressed adult to translate.

Concrete Operational Logic and Memories

The major personality organization of the child is laid down by approximately age 7. Actions are now well internalized into schemas in the multiple memory systems. The arrival of the operation of reversibility allows for conservation and is a critical shift at this stage. Children now know that an object or person, including himself, remains the same even if it changes in visual appearance or shape. Children now compose and decompose classes and make and remember new class inclusions. Now they can understand how means can be shifted to meet ends, and they achieve a much wider understanding of determinants of causality. Although they begin to play with possibility as an extension of the real, they still make many false inductions from class overinclusion. Classes are extended and differentiated but relationships are inadequate. There is a general increase in recall of relevant information, but little or no increase in recall of incidental information. Children at this stage love to collect, to make their classification systems concrete. They take mementos of traumatic events and play with interrelationships, similarities, and differences, thus shaping a new reality. A child watched his mother's life threatened when he was about 2. Attackers, strangling the mother, held a knife at her throat. The child was amnesic for the event but in kindergarten would unexpectedly try to strangle girl classmates. After therapy this acting out stopped and at about 9, the child began collecting knives to demonstrate the many different uses of knives and how they differ cross-culturally.

There is a wide range of sex differences at this time of life, but each sex uniformly hates the opposite sex. Consequently, a group of the same sex working together is an effective therapeutic intervention. This is the age of gangs. In forming groups it helps to keep this in mind. The members of a gang or a group want to know their boundaries, their place in the immediate scene, the rules of the game, and their range of power and control.

The ability to dissociate and self-hypnotize are at their height around age 8. After a major school bus accident, one of the 9-year-old boys who had been on the bus appeared bright and cheerful two days later. He remembered nothing of the event. His mother reported he was having violent nightmares for which he was amnesic. He had, however, seen himself on the evening news on television the night of the accident and remembered, with pride, the reporter who interviewed him as he lay on a gurney in the hospital emergency room. The reporter announced to the TV audience that the boy was not only brave but handsome. This visual, auditory memory was enough to aid the boy in retracting his steps to the ambulance that brought him to the hospital and finally to what happened in the accident. Of all the children (except those in critical condition in the hospital) he had had the worst experience of the lot. We can tentatively hypothesize that the experience was registered via the amygdala to the lower brain but could be retrieved because it was so recent and available through visual and auditory memories.

During this period of cognitive development, trauma usually leaves children at risk, withdrawn from parents, teachers, and peers. They are depressed, irritable, and restless. They have trouble concentrating. School work declines and they show disruptive behavior. Imaginative play is inhibited, thus restricting the assimilation of the traumatic information. These children are well aware of possible ways they might have dealt with troubles but did not, and consequently they experience guilt. They are swamped with action fantasies of rescue and revenge. They are terrified of a recurrence of events. They consciously rerun their memories as if to prepare for another catastrophe. They are given to risk-taking behavior as if their predictive memory had momentarily lapsed.

When dealing with this kind of logic and resulting behavior, it helps to seize the significant image, the core of the trauma, as it is symbolized by the child or adult, and tolerate idiosyncrasies. Now predictive memory can be trained and used to help the patient deal adequately with possibilities for the future. Their memories are useful in anticipating new fearful situations and how they can deal with them. They can begin to compare and contrast. They are comfortable saying, "I did this as a child. Now I would do things differently." They need to be helped in avoiding the urge to retreat from time and growing up. At this stage they need reassurance that expressing grief and rage is tolerated and expected. Appropriate healing rituals are useful, especially if routine can be stressed.

Formal Operational Logic and Memories

Once formal operational logic is achieved with a new understanding of propositional thinking and maintaining several possibilities simultaneously, therapy takes a new direction. With formal operational logic, the person can abstract, distance him- or herself from the present, run back and forth in time and history, become more realistic and less impulsive in thinking and behavior, and achieve a comprehension of the social contract. The therapist can play with "as if" logic. The operation of chance is now understood. Making sense out of disasters can be hypothetical and deductive. At this age the young like to think reflectively. The adolescent can distinguish between contingent and necessary and can understand relativity. They can subordinate the real for the possible.

Values begin to be based on thinking through many possible relationships. Adolescents of both sexes tend to remember relationships more than events and historical narratives, so the therapist can concentrate on these first. Ideal love combines with passion. The youth at this stage has a highly developed sense of control (Pillemer et al. 1991), but adolescents have been shown to have either an overestimation or underestimation of risk. As Eth and Pynoos (1985) have shown, adolescents tend to act out if under stress. Trauma makes adolescents easily lose that new-found sense of control.

At this age, the young person needs to concentrate on accommodation, that is, remembering and practicing solutions that work. Whether resilient or symptomatic, the young person is contemplating and playing with high ideals that are not yet tested. Consequently the individual can suffer from fear of failure and move rapidly into a state of disillusionment. Assimilation of ideals is at its height, but accommodation, or testing the ideals has not yet been tried sufficiently.

It is precisely this ability to see the grand future and feel a rush of inadequacy in achieving it that may be a factor in the high rate of suicide among teenagers. They just don't see how they can achieve their goals. The therapist has to let the adolescent keep those ideals intact but begin to think out pragmatic steps for arriving at future dreams. One of the reasons the rise of suicidal behavior comes at adolescence in two such divergent cultures as Cambodian and American may be because the logic develops in both cultures in the same way and the same rate. The Cambodian youth in the refugee camp may have a higher rate of suicide than their equivalent cohort in the United States because of the severely limited conditions of achieving any future life in war-torn Cambodia.

CONCLUSION

Disasters will continue to plague mankind, but we can be optimistic about their effect on children. Only a minimal proportion of those traumatized will be at risk for pathology. Part of this pathology will be a tendency toward suicidal behavior. This group responds well to therapy based on neurocognitive findings.

The brain is a complex functional system that we are just beginning to understand and correlate with behavioral manifestations. The literature suggests that there are structural changes in the brain following trauma. Trauma desynchronizes widely distributed neurocognitive networks, destabilizing the victim in thought and behavior. Cognitive research can help us identify memory processes that affect adaptation of individuals and reveal possible mechanisms of coping or pathological behavior.

We can now begin to think of ways to activate the cognitive modules used in memory. We need to be aware of encoding, storage, and retrieval possibilities. At this point in research, we are not seeking a one-to-one isomorphic relationship between neural networks of memory and behavior but are looking for the possibilities of coordination and linkage of networks in the brain and their simultaneous use in problem solving (Volkow and Tancred 1970).

How disasters are remembered and interpreted depends on the person's stage of logical development and the individual's domain preference for symbolic representation. The therapist can probe the range of logic the patient used in making sense of events. The therapist has to work harder than the patient in adjusting his or her own logic in order to challenge the patient's logic at one stage in advance of the patient's thinking. The therapist has to help the patient repair deficits in cognitive attribution, to shape coping strategies based on domain strengths, cognitive operations, and the expected sequence of organizing schemata.

We are remarkably adaptive animals. Evolution seems to have provided us with a brain that molds itself distinctly to each arising situation and the brain's plastic nature allows most of us to adjust to and survive the horrors we encounter.

REFERENCES

Anderson, J. R. (1991). Optimality and human memory. Open peer commentary. *Behavior and Brain Sciences* 14:215–216.

Bachevalier, J. (1990). Ontogenetic development of habit and memory formation. In *The Development and Neural Bases of Higher Cognitive Functions,* ed. A. Diamond, pp. 457–484. New York: New York Academy of Sciences.

Baker, A. M. (1990). The psychological impact of the Intifada on Palestinian children in the occupied West Bank and Gaza: an exploratory study. *American Journal of Orthopsychiatry* 60:496–505.

Boothby, N. Personal communication, November 30, 1989.

Brett, E. A., and Ostroff, R. (1985). Imagery and post traumatic stress disorder: an overview. *American Journal of Psychiatry* 142:417–424.

Bryer, J. B., Nelson, B. A., Miller, J. B., and Kroll, B. A. (1987). Childhood sexual and physical abuse as factors in adult psychiatric illness. *American Journal of Psychiatry* 144:1426–1430.

Cichetti, D., and Beeghly, M. (1987). *Symbolic Development in Maltreated Youngsters: An Organizational Perspective.* San Francisco: Jossey-Bass.

Cowen, E. L., Wyman, P. A., Work, W. C., and Parker, G. R. (1990). The Rochester Child Resilience Project: overview and summary of first year findings. *Development and Psychopathology* 2:193–212.

Diagnostic and Statistical Manual of Mental Disorders, Third Edition, Revised (1987). Washington, DC: American Psychiatric Press.

Diamond, A., ed. (1990). *The Development and Neural Bases of Higher Cognitive Functions.* New York: New York Academy of Sciences.

Edelman, G. M. (1987). *Neural Darwinism. The Theory of Neuronal Group Selection.* New York: Basic Books.

Edelman, G. M., and Mountcastle, V. B. (1982). *The Mindful Brain. Cortical Organization and the Group-Selective Theory of Higher Brain Function.* Cambridge, MA: M.I.T. Press.

Eth, S., and Pynoos, R. S., eds. (1985). *Post-traumatic Stress Disorder in Children.* Washington, DC: American Psychiatric Press.

Fish-Murray, C. C. (1990). Memory of trauma: place and path. Paper presented at the NAIM Foundation, Georgetown University Center for Contemporary Arab Studies, Washington, DC, October 10–12.

Fish-Murray, C. C., Koby E., and van der Kolk, B. A. (1987). The effect of abuse on children's thought. In *Psychological Trauma*, ed. B. A. van der Kolk, pp. 89–110. Washington, DC: American Psychiatric Press.

Fox, N. A., and Bell, M. A. (1990). Electrophysiological indices of frontal lobe development: relations to cognition and affective behavior in human infants over the first year of life. In *The Development and Neural Bases of Higher Cognitive Functions*, ed. A. Diamond, pp. 677–704. New York: New York Academy of Sciences.

Frederick, C. J. (1985). Children traumatized by catastrophic situations. In *Post-traumatic Stress Disorder in Children*, ed. S. Eth and R. S. Pynoos, pp. 73–99. Washington, DC: American Psychiatric Press.

Gardner, H. (1983). *Frames of Mind. The Theory of Multiple Intelligences.* New York: Basic Books.

Garmezy, N., and Rutter, M., eds. (1983). *Stress, Coping, and Development in Children.* New York: McGraw-Hill.

Gould, S. J. (1990). Muller Bros. moving & storage. *Natural History* 99:12–16.

Grandmothers of the Plaza Mayo, Buenos Aires, Argentina. Personal communication, May 1988.

Greenberg, M. S. (1987). Retrieval and integration of traumatic memories with the "painting cure." In *Pychological Trauma*, ed. B. A. van der Kolk, pp. 191–215. Washington, DC: American Psychiatric Press.

Gruber, H. E., and Voneche, J. J. (1977). *The Essential Piaget. An Interpretive Reference and Guide.* New York: Basic Books.

Herman, J. L., Perry, J. C., and van der Kolk, B. A. (1989). Childhood origins of self-destructive behavior. *American Journal of Psychiatry* 146:490–495.

Johnson, G. (1991). *In the Palaces of Memory: How We Build the Worlds Inside our Head.* New York: Alfred A. Knopf.

Kagan, J. (1983). Stress and coping in early development. In *Stress, Coping and Development in Children*, ed. N. Garmezy and M. Rutter, pp. 191–216. New York: McGraw-Hill.

———— (1989). *Unstable Ideas: Temperament, Cognition, and Self.* Cambridge, MA: Harvard University Press.

Kapp, B. S., Pascoe, J. P., and Bixler, M. A. (1984). The amygdala: a neuroanatomical systems approach to its contribution to aversive conditioning. In *Neuropsychology of Memory* ed. L. R. Squire and N. Butters, pp. 473–488. New York: Guilford.

Keane, T. M., Fairbank, J. A., Caddell, J. M., and Zimmering, R. T. (1989). Implosive (flooding) therapy reduces symptoms of PTSD in Vietnam combat veterans. *Behavior Therapy* 20:245–260.

Keele, S. W., and Ivry, R. (1990). Does the cerebellum provide a common computation for diverse tasks?: A timing hypothesis. In *The Development and Neural Bases of Higher Cognitive Functions*, ed. A. Diamond, pp. 179–211. New York: New York Academy of Sciences.

Kinzie, J. D., Sack, W. H., Angell, R. H., et al. (1986). The psychiatric effects of massive trauma on Cambodian children. Part 1: The children. *Journal of the American Academy of Child Psychiatry* 25:370–376.

Krell, R. (1985). Child survivors of the Holocaust forty years later. *Journal of Child Psychiatry* 24:378–380.

Lakoff, G. (1987). *Women, Fire and Dangerous Things: What Categories Reveal about the World.* Chicago: University of Chicago Press.

Lazarus, R. S. (1991). Progress on a cognitive-motivational-relational theory of emotion. *American Psychologist* 46:819–834.

Le Doux, J. E. (1989). Indelibility of subcortical emotional memories. *Journal of Cognitive Neuroscience* 1:238–243.

MacLean, P. D. (1969). The internal–external bonds of the memory process. *Journal of Nervous and Mental Diseases* 149:40–47.

Milgram, N. (1990). Childhood PTSD in Israel: a cross cultural frame of reference. Paper presented at American Psychological Association Meeting, August, Boston, MA.

Mollica, R., Donelan, K., Tor S., Lavelle, J., et al. *Repatriation and Disability: A Community Study of Health, Mental Health and Social Functioning of the Khmer Residents of Site Two. Vol. 1. Khmer Adults.* Working Document, Harvard Program in Refugee Trauma, Harvard School of Public Health and the World Federation for Mental Health.

Mollica R., Fish-Murray C., Donelan, K., et al. *Repatriation and Disability: A Community Study of Health, Mental Health, and Social Functioning of the Khmer Residents of Site Two. Vol. 2. Khmer Children (12–13 Years of Age).* Working Document, Harvard Program in Refugee Trauma, Harvard School of Public Health and the World Federation for Mental Health.

Moskovitz, S. (1985). Longitudinal follow-up of child survivors of the Holocaust. *Journal of Child Psychiatry* 24:401–407.

National Institute of Mental Health (1970). *Biological Rhythms in Psychiatry and Medicine.* Chevy Chase, MD: NIMH.

Neisser, U. (1982). *Memory Observed: Remembering in Natural Contexts.* New York: W. H. Freeman.

Noam, G. G. (1986). The theory of biography and transformation and the borderline personality disorders. Part 2: A developmental typology. *McLean Hospital Journal* 11:79–104.

O'Keefe, J., and Nadel, L. (1978). *The Hippocampus as a Cognitive Map.* Oxford, England: Clarendon.

Ornitz, E. M., and Pynoos, R. S. (1989). Startle modulation in children with PTSD. *American Journal of Psychiatry* 141:146–147.

Pfeffer, C. R., ed. (1989). *Suicide among Youth: Perspectives on Risk and Prevention.* Washington, DC: American Psychiatric Press.

Piaget, J. (1962). *Play, Dreams and Imitation in Childhood.* New York: Norton.

Pillemer, D. B., Krensky, L., Kleinman, S. N., et al. (1991). Chapters in narratives: evidence from oral histories of the first year in college. *Journal of Narrative and Life History* 1:3–14.

Polster, M. R., Nadel, L., and Schacter, D. L. (1991). Cognitive neuroscience analyses of memory: a historical perspective. *Journal of Cognitive Neuroscience* 3:95–116.

Putnam, F. W. (1990). Developmental antecedents of trauma-related syndromes: prospective data. Paper delivered at a conference on psychological trauma, Harvard Medical School, May, Boston, MA.

Ressler, E. M., Boothby, N., and Steinbrock, D. J. (1988). *Unaccompanied Children: Care and Protection in Wars, National Disasters and Refugee Movements.* New York: Oxford University Press.

Rosenfield, I. (1988). *The Invention of Memory: A New View of the Brain.* New York: Basic Books.

Saigh, P. A. (1986). In vitro flooding in the treatment of a 6-yr-old boy's posttraumatic stress disorder. *Behavioral Therapy* 24:685–688.

Schacter, D. L. (1990). Perceptual representation systems and implicit memory: toward a resolution of the multiple memory systems debate. In *The Development and Neural Bases of Higher Cognitive*

Functions, ed. A. Diamond, pp. 543–571. New York: New York Academy of Sciences.

Schacter, D. L., Cooper, L. A., Tharan, M., and Rubens, A. B. (1991). Preserved priming of novel objects in patients with memory disorders. *Journal of Cognitive Neuroscience* 3:117–130.

Shneidman, E. (1985). *Definition of Suicide.* New York: Wiley.

Solomon, Z., Mikulincer, M., and Flum, H. (1988). Negative life events, coping responses, and combat-related psychopathology: a prospective study. *Journal of Abnormal Psychology* 97:302–307.

Squire, L. R. (1987). *Memory and Brain.* New York: Oxford University Press.

Squire, L. R., and Butters, N. (1986). *Neuropsychology of Memory.* New York: Guilford.

Steinglass, P., De-Nour, A. K., and Shye, S. (1985). Factors influencing psychosocial adjustment to forced geographical relocation: the Israeli withdrawal from the Sinai. *American Journal of Orthopsychiatry* 55:513–529.

Thompson, R. F., Clark, G. A., Donegan, N. H., et al. (1986). Neuronal substrates of basic associative learning. In *Neuropsychology of Memory,* ed. L. A. Squire and N. Butters, pp. 424–442. New York: Guilford.

van der Kolk, B. A. (1989). The compulsion to repeat the trauma: reenactment, revictimization, and masochism. In *Treatment of Victims of Sexual Abuse,* ed. R. P. Kluft, pp. 389–411. Philadelphia: W. B. Saunders.

Volkow, N. D., and Tancred, L. R. (1970). Biological correlates of mental activity studied with PET. *American Journal of Psychiatry* 148:439–443.

Webster's New International Dictionary of the English Language, 2nd Ed., Unabridged (1950). Springfield, MA: G. & C. Merriam.

White, S. H., and Pillemer, D. B. (1979). Childhood amnesia and the development of a socially accessible memory system. In *Functional Disorders of Memory,* ed. J. Kihlstrom and F. Evans, pp. 29–73. Hillsdale, NJ: Lawrence Erlbaum Associates.

Widom, C. S. (1989a). Child abuse, neglect and adult behavior: research design and findings on criminality, violence and child abuse. *American Journal of Orthopsychiatry* 59:355–367.

——— (1989b). The cycle of violence. *Science* 244:160–166.

7: MURDER AMONG ELDERLY ANGLO FEMALES

Nancy H. Allen

A newspaper article reported another homicide of a Los Angeles senior citizen: a 93-year-old woman who was sexually assaulted, beaten, and suffocated. The motive appeared to be robbery. The assailant was unknown (*Los Angeles Times*, 1991).

My long-time interest in homicide among the elderly was stimulated when I examined the results of a research project, "The epidemiology of homicide in the city of Los Angeles 1970–1979," a collaborative study by the University of California at Los Angeles and the Centers for Disease Control (Loya et al. 1985). Among the Anglo population in Los Angeles during that ten-year span, the highest rate of homicide was among persons 65 years old and older. In this chapter, reference will be made to this study and another study, which I conducted, of murders among the elderly occurring in 1981. The records of each homicide victim were made available for review by the Los Angeles City Police Department. Individual cases were studied, looking at a variety of variables, such as clues to the homicide, the role that the victim played in her demise, risk factors, and prevention and intervention strategies that might have been used.

STATISTICAL DESCRIPTIONS

The murder rate of Anglos 65 years of age and over increased in California over 200 percent between 1960 and 1970 (Allen 1982). This pattern can be seen throughout the United States during that same time period (Allen 1980). An increase in homicide rates continued from 1970 to 1979. The homicide rate in Los Angeles almost doubled during that 10 year period, increasing 84 percent from 12.5 per 100,000 to 23.0 per 100,000. By 1980, homicide ranked as the fifth leading cause of death in Los Angeles, while for the United States as a whole in ranked eleventh (Loya et al. 1985).

Tables 7-1 and 7-2 show that Blacks and Hispanics are at the greatest risk of being victims of homicide. But when isolating Anglos, it is those 65 years and over who have the greatest overall rate. The total number of all Anglo homicide victims 65 years and over was 250, representing 20 percent of the total Anglo victims.

In my 1981 study of homicides in Los Angeles there were 979 homicides. Forty three, or 4.3 percent, were 65 years of age and over. The majority were victims of robbery, killed by a stranger or unknown assailant in their own home. Case histories will be presented on the eight Anglo females murdered that year. It should be noted that the Los Angeles data are in excess of recent national homicide statistics (Centers for Disease Control 1989), but it does have implications for education and prevention programs throughout the United States.

RISK FACTORS AND LETHALITY

Identifying high-risk groups has implications for prevention. An increased focus on education of persons at risk regarding techniques on how to avoid becoming a victim would be helpful. Potential victims can be made aware of their own dangerous behavior patterns and the gaps of knowledge that make them susceptible to being murdered (Allen 1980).

Older people are especially vulnerable to victimization. Frequently they are too weak to defend themselves, and are dependent on others for care and protection. Senior citizens often isolate themselves and refuse to use precautions against crime, reflecting their feelings of physical and social inadequacy, fear, and helplessness (Davis and Brody 1979).

There are health problems that progressively appear in the aging. These too contribute to susceptibility. For example, the older person may not hear approaching footsteps, a warning voice, or someone entering the home. Deterioration of vision contributes to difficulty in the identification of suspects. There are neuromuscular and skeletal changes. Normal signs of aging are often markedly visible in the frail elderly. These individuals are unable to move or turn quickly to escape assault and do not have the agility and power required to fight off an assailant (Davis and Brody 1979). Some elderly exhibit the beginning of senility; they become careless and forgetful about securing their homes. Doors may remain unlocked and windows open. This absent-minded behavior can be an invitation to a perpetrator. Clearly, gaining entrance to a residence may be the beginning of a possible homicide scenario.

HOMICIDE CASE HISTORIES
IN EIGHT ELDERLY ANGLO WOMEN

Case histories can demonstrate the homicide scenario, the circumstances of the murder, and thereby illuminate the steps that might be taken to prevent the event. The case histories are taken from the Los Angeles City Police Department records. The cases are Anglo women ranging in age from 74 to 88 years old.

TABLE 7-1

Homicide Rate by Race/Ethnicity and Age of Victim
City of Los Angeles, 1970-1979 (Centers for Disease Control)

Age Group	Anglo	Black	Hispanic	Other
<15	1.8	7.4	2.9	2.8
15-24	8.2	71.4	33.1	6.6
25-34	10.6	84.0	27.5	11.0
35-44	9.3	65.7	20.7	5.3
45-54	9.3	49.8	19.6	7.0
55-64	7.3	32.5	11.4	3.9
65+	11.2	19.8	10.5	8.5

Notes: Rates are per 100,000 population.

The term *homicide* refers to criminal homicide. Excluded are 216 homicides for which there were no data on the race/ethnicity or age of victim.

TABLE 7-2

Number and Rate of Homicide by Race/Ethnicity, Sex, and Age of Victim
City of Los Angeles, 1970-1979 (Centers for Disease Control)

Male

Age	Anglo No.	Anglo Rate	Black No.	Black Rate	Hispanic No.	Hispanic Rate	Other No.	Other Rate
<15	29	2.0	59	8.2	32	3.3	5	2.5
15-24	144	11.0	510	118.9	386	60.5	15	9.0
25-34	181	14.3	525	143.0	278	49.7	31	17.2
35-44	136	13.8	320	117.1	117	34.2	11	9.0
45-54	146	14.2	209	90.6	77	35.6	12	13.2
55-64	106	11.8	102	58.8	30	23.3	3	4.7
65+	136	15.9	53	38.4	18	17.3	8	12.7

Female

Age	Anglo No.	Anglo Rate	Black No.	Black Rate	Hispanic No.	Hispanic Rate	Other No.	Other Rate
<15	22	1.6	48	6.7	24	2.5	6	3.2
15-24	73	5.5	146	29.8	31	5.0	7	4.2
25-34	78	6.6	131	31.7	26	4.8	9	4.9
35-44	45	4.7	61	19.9	24	7.1	2	1.6
45-54	49	4.6	39	14.6	13	5.4	1	1.1
55-64	32	3.2	25	11.5	3	1.9	2	3.1
65+	114	8.3	18	8.2	9	5.9	3	4.6

Notes: Rates are per 100,000 population.

The term *homicide* refers to criminal homicide. Excluded are 230 homicides for which there were no data on the race/ethnicity, sex, or age of victim.

These victims were chosen because they were especially vulnerable, and the risk of their being victimized appeared to intensify with age. The natural handicaps of aging made them more obvious targets.

Case A and B

Mrs. A. age 88, lived with her sister Mrs. B., 82, in a run-down house in Hollywood. The police report noted the house was in need of repair and painting. It was obvious that many of the windows and doors could easily be entered. The sisters were awakened at approximately 10:00 P.M. by an unknown assailant who demanded money, jewelry, and keys to a car. Mrs. A. said she did not keep money in the house and that she had no jewelry and did not drive. The assailant beat Mrs. A. to death with her cane and raped her. Mrs. A.'s face was crushed, her jaw and nose were broken. The sister, Mrs. B., tried to help and was also beaten; she received multiple injuries to her face, head, arms, and hands. She was hospitalized and later died.

Mrs. A. had chronic arthritis and used a wheelchair, walker, and cane. The sisters lived in a two-story house where it was difficult for them to go up and down the stairs. This resulted in their common practice of leaving the back door unlocked when the groceries were to be delivered. The morning after the murder the grocery boy came inside and placed the box of groceries on the kitchen table. He heard a cry for help from Mrs. B., went upstairs, and called the police.

The most obvious risk factor in this case is the back door left open overnight. Another factor is the increasing vulnerability caused by the process of aging and by incapacitating diseases. An emergency call button might have helped. Mrs. B. lived long enough to be hospitalized and to talk with the homicide investigators. The perpetrator remains unknown.

Case C

When the police from the L.A.P.D. Wilshire division were called to Miss C.'s residence they found her in an upstairs bedroom dead from multiple stab wounds to her head and body. The suspect had forcibly entered the victim's residence through a front window, ransacked the house, stolen a gun, and killed the 86-year-old woman.

Further study of the victim's homicide file described the death in more detail. Miss C. was a retired schoolteacher, who had lived in her home for forty years. She lived alone and rarely admitted visitors. Neighbors reported she lived like a hermit and had recently become senile. She collected cans and newspapers.

A friend came to visit Miss C. and finding the front door ajar notified the Los Angeles Fire Department. They found the victim dead and notified the L. A. P. D. The police noted the suspect forcibly entered the victim's residence through a front window. Although the front door was open there were no signs of forced entry. The victim was found lying across her bed. There were stab wounds to her pubic area and blunt trauma to her head. A candle was found inserted in her rectum. Vaginal and anal slides were taken and found to be negative for seminal fluid and sperm. On the stairs there was a blood trail made after the victim was attacked. Finger prints and hand prints with blood smears were taken. The ransacking of the bedroom was evident. An empty .22 caliber box containing the serial number was found. There were many clues—not enough, however, to find the still unknown perpetrator.

Miss C. did own a handgun. Since it is reasonable to believe she kept the gun for self-protection, she may have been attacked by surprise. Her reported senility exacerbated her helplessness. The victim had signs of body decomposition. She apparently had been dead for two or three days before she was found. An older person living alone should have someone telephone at least daily to determine if he or she is all right. Senility, the natural handicap of aging, plus an old house in bad condition, made Miss C. a target for violence.

Case D

Seventy-six-year-old Mrs. D. was walking home from the neighborhood market in West Hollywood. She became apprehensive when she observed two men walking past her and she held her purse tighter by its leather straps. She was approached from behind and one assailant hit her over the head with an unknown object. The victim fell to the pavement and the second assailant grabbed her purse. They drove away. Paramedics were called and took Mrs. D. to the closest emergency hospital two blocks away. She was released from the hospital the next day into the care of her husband. Three days later she was readmitted to the hospital where she died as a result of the trauma to her head.

The vehicle involved in the suspect's escape had been involved in grand theft auto. Witnesses had taken the license number as it drove away. The car was found by the police and later identified by the witnesses. The police record noted the case was "closed." The implication is that the suspects were arrested, tried in a court of law, and sentenced. There was no information on this in the records reviewed.

Older women become increasingly vulnerable when carrying a purse. For many potential perpetrators it is an open invitation to robbery. Old habits are hard to break, but Mrs. D. would have been less obvious if she had carried her money in a pocket or moneybelt. Also, the assault may have been deterred if she had been accompanied by her husband. It is advisable not to walk alone.

Case E

Mrs. E., 82 years old, was last seen by a bank officer who reviewed her investments and accounts monthly. One month later the same bank officer became concerned. Telephone calls were not answered. The bank officer went to Mrs. E.'s home where there was no response. The police were notified. A search of the house gave no immediate clues and Mrs. E. was recorded as a missing person. Mrs. E. was described as a "very lonely person who would put up with almost anything to get attention." Her deceased husband left her a multi-million dollar estate.

Before her death Mrs. E. had spoken to a friend about a 38-year-old man who had befriended her and had been trying to take over her life and estate. She reported that he had asked her to marry him three times and she had refused. She had experienced fear as he had threatened to beat her. He told her not to sign anything without his permission. He owed her money and was stealing from her. Mrs. E. was warned by a friend that Mr. X. could end up killing her.

The day after Mrs. E. was last seen Mr. X. began fraudulently selling the victim's real estate and removing funds from her bank account. He contacted the bank and asked for $103,000 to purchase a car. By now he was a suspect. Three months later Mr. X.'s attorney contacted the investigating police officers and stated that the suspect told them he had discovered the victim dead in her residence and had thrown her body in the ocean, "somewhere between here and Catalina Island." The attorney reported his client had found Mrs. E. in her bedroom and thought she had died of "natural causes." Mr. X. also told his attorney he had too much to drink and did not remember exactly what happened. He did admit stealing from the victim but stated he did not kill her. He forged checks for over $250,000 and sold her property. He then left Los Angeles. Mrs. E.'s car was found in storage in Arizona. Mr. X. said she gave it to him to drive. The suspect was arrested in Texas and returned to Los Angeles where on October 14, 1981, the district attorney filed murder and forgery charges. Mr. X. is currently in a state prison serving a fifteen-years-to-life term for second degree murder. Mrs. E.'s body was never found.

The situation where younger men take advantage of wealthy, older, lonely women can be lethal. Lending money is a mistake. Mrs. E. should have taken the advice of her friend who warned her about being killed. She should have followed her own instincts regarding Mr. X.'s threats and reported him to the police. A restraining order could have been placed on him. Greed is a frequent motive for murder. The elderly are repeated targets due to their loneliness which contributes to their vulnerability.

Case F

On August 18, 1981, Jerry entered his 80-year-old mother's residence. He found her strangled and dead on the living-room floor, nude from the waist down. He covered her with a sheet and called the police. The death scene was secured and the sheet was removed. The victim's legs were apart, a piece of nylon hose was observed on the left foot, and a panty girdle was on her right foot. Later the police reported that sperm and seminal fluid were not detected from the microscopic slides. At the death scene, close to the victim's foot, material was found that could have been used as a ligature. Her dentures were found on the floor. Every room had been ransacked. The police were not able to determine how the suspect had gained entry into the house. There was an open window in every room and both doors were unlocked. It was the opinion of the investigating homicide officers that the perpetrator gained entry through the front door. Mrs. F. either left the door open or opened the door to the suspect. When the son first arrived the door was open and the screen door unlatched.

Mrs. F. had lived in this home for twenty-one years. A detention center for male inmates was close to her residence. There were two neighbors who had seen a possible inmate at the victim's front door. Mrs. F. lived alone, as her husband had died fourteen years earlier and her three children had lives of their own.

Mrs. F. had immigrated to the United States sixty years prior to her death. She was known to be a trusting and open person. Earlier in her lifetime people routinely left doors and windows unlocked. Some people, especially the elderly, still do. For safety's sake, doors and windows should be locked. It is advisable to have an observation peephole in solid doors that open to the outside.

Case G

It was 2 P.M. when Mrs. G., a 74-year-old widow, left her apartment and went to her car parked in the subterranean garage. She was on her way to the bank to deposit rent receipts. As she approached her car she activated the garage gate with her plastic key. The garage lighting was poor and she did not see her assailant. She sustained six heavy blows to her head and appeared to have died immediately. Her body was in the main aisle. Her purse had been turned over. Her keys were covered with her blood. While walking from her car another resident of the building discovered Mrs. G.'s body. The cause of death was reported as "blunt force trauma." No murder weapon was found. The motive appeared to be robbery. The case remains open and the assailant unknown.

Most of us feel safe when going to the bank in the middle of the afternoon. Some of us are not safe due to unsuspected circumstances. An assailant can gain easy entry into a garage. Many people have been robbed in their parking areas, but most are not murdered. The elderly are especially vulnerable. They appear to be trusting, and being attacked is not on their mind. If the garage had been well lighted, Mrs. G. might have visually surveyed the area. If she had seen someone who did not belong there she could have gone back to her apartment and telephoned the police. It also helps to carry a screech alarm when walking alone.

Case H

Mrs. H. was an 80-year-old widow who lived with her nephew and his wife. She was left alone when they went to work at 7:30 A.M. They returned one evening to find their aunt dead, killed by two gunshot wounds to her head. The .22 caliber semiautomatic, used to kill the victim, belonged to her nephew. The gun was found at the homicide scene and booked into police custody. Mrs. H. was found on the floor of the living-room hallway. A neighbor, questioned by the police, told them of two men who had been going door-to-door in the neighborhood asking if there was a car for sale. The residence was entered through an unlocked door. There was no sign of forced entry. Household property was stacked at the front door, apparently awaiting removal from the location (television sets, microwave oven, sterling silver, two .22 caliber guns, and more). Glove impressions with a small zigzag pattern were noted by the police. There was a suspect, who, while incarcerated at juvenile hall, had talked about shooting an old woman. When the homicide detectives discussed the case with this suspect they noted he was "apprehensive." No arrest has been made. The case remains open.

It is possible that Mrs. H. would not have been murdered if there had not been a gun in the house. Her first mistake was not locking the front door. She apparently was taking her routine afternoon nap and awakened during the burglary. She seems to have confronted the perpetrator.

In the eight case histories presented, the recorded motive was robbery. In two cases the perpetrator left a series of clues that led to arrest and incarceration. In the remaining cases the clues were insufficient to bring the suspects to trial.

PREVENTION, INTERVENTION, POSTVENTION, AND EDUCATION

Prevention, intervention, and postvention are enhanced through education. Prevention is the most complicated, complex, and costly method of stopping a murder, but it is essential. Prevention can be developed at many levels, ranging from the informed elderly, who practice safe behavior, to the use of appropriate hardware to secure the home environment. This process involves a change in attitude that will effect a change in behavior. Education is an important part in the entire process of facilitating change. Senior citizens could be made aware of services already available to them, for example: *Multipurpose Senior Centers,* which provide a full spectrum of senior services including information and referral and counseling; *Home Secure,* which offers free crime-prevention, installation of dead-bolt locks, peepholes, and more. For those on a limited income, *Emergency Alert Response System (EARS)* provides senior citizens with equipment that will permit them to remain in their home and delay costly institutionalization (Riddick 1989).

Intervention relates to the management of the homicidal crisis before the series of life-threatening events escalate. Intervention needs to focus on the reduction of tension in the potential perpetrator so that he does not act out his aggressive, antisocial impulses. Potential victims can play an important role by trying to remain calm and cooperative. It is extremely useful for the elderly to have an emergency button (often worn around the neck), which activates emergency assistance.

Postvention is help given after the homicide has occurred. The family needs special counseling to enable them to work with the multiple and complex problems the homicide introduces. Grief in the face of such violence takes on different proportions and meaning. The family is disrupted at many levels as grief is experienced differently with each member, some coping better than others. Divorce is not unusual. Most survivor/victims do not understand the criminal justice system and their rights as family survivors. It is important that public and mental health workers recognize the need for postvention help and offer appropriate education services.

When counseling the grieving survivor/victim of homicide, it is important to know the issues the therapist will be confronting in order to guide the bereavement through its often stormy course. The following example of a postventive counseling may clarify the special needs of survivors.

Janet, a 42-year-old mother of two, was referred to me by a colleague. Her 67-year-old mother, Mrs. Jones, had been found dead in the law office where she worked. Janet had been contacted by the police and advised to go to the coroner's office to identify her mother. She went and viewed her face. She then was asked to transfer the body to a mortuary for funeral arrangements. At the time that Janet identified her mother, the coroner said her mother had died from a heart attack. She picked up the personal belongings and noted that her mother's wallet, watch, and checkbook were missing. Janet went to her mother's residence and searched for the missing property without success. She then went to the law offices where Mrs. Jones was a senior partner. She went to her mother's private office and was shocked to find blood streaks on the wall, blood under the desk, and private papers scattered about. She still did not find the missing belongings. At this point she suspected that her mother had been murdered. She contacted the police officer who had informed her of Mrs. Jones' death. The police said they could do nothing since the coroner had determined death to be from natural causes.

Two months after the death Janet came to see me for counseling. She talked about her mother and her feelings about the loss. She said that one of Mrs. Jones' associates, John, had borrowed a large sum of money from her mother and had not been seen at the law offices since her mother's death. Further investigation by Janet revealed that John had been picked up by the police in another city. John was driving a stolen car; her mother's watch, charge cards, and checkbook were found when he was searched. He served a few months in jail for the car theft.

It seems inexplicable to me (and probably to the reader), given all these facts, that no one who examined the death scene or looked at the death report suspected foul play and called this to the coroner's attention. But the fact remains, the death was certified as a natural death.

Janet felt there could be no resolution to her bereavement until the truth about the real circumstances of her mother's death were known. We discussed an exhumation of Mrs. Jones. I telephoned a forensic pathologist/

coroner in another county, and he expressed interest in helping Janet. During this period we had numerous counseling sessions. Her marriage was deteriorating, her husband felt he wasn't receiving enough attention, and could not understand why Janet did not go on with her life as it was before her mother's death. As an aside, when marital problems start, it is important that the therapist meet with the spouse and interpret the grieving process and indicate how it varies with different individuals and with the circumstances surrounding the death.

The exhumation took place. The coroner from a northern California county performed a second autopsy and determined Mrs. Jones had a normal heart and did not die from a heart attack. This was substantiated by two cardiologists. Head and body bruises and a skull fracture were noted by the pathologist. Mrs. Jones' brain was missing and was never found. The mode of death was changed to homicide and a police investigation was initiated. During this painful process, Janet was hospitalized by her physician for depression. She has been hospitalized periodically over the past fifteen years for severe episodes of depression. She has also had coronary bypass surgery and has suffered other illnesses. Exacerbations of physical and mental health problems are frequently seen in survivor/victims of homicide.

Janet and I continued our counseling sessions throughout the police investigation and the sentencing of John. I attended the preliminary court hearing with Janet at which John declared he was not guilty. Subsequently I put Janet in touch with the county victim's assistance program and a support group.

Once the trial started I discussed the importance of her preparing an impact statement to be read by her at the time of sentencing. The impact statement is addressed to the presiding judge. It is a written description of the emotional, medical, and financial effects the murder has had on the survivor/victim and other members of the family. Janet felt unable to write such a document. I reminded her that she had described the impact on her life during our counseling sessions, such as the initial impact of the loss of her mother, the frustration of her treatment by the coroner and police, the cost of hiring a private investigator, hospitalization, exhumation, and her recent divorce. All had taken their toll. I watched Janet read her impact statement at the sentencing of John. It was an emotional presentation and seemed to have an influence on the judge.

John received the maximum sentence for second-degree murder. However, after he had served only two years in prison he was released on a legal technicality. Janet continues to need emotional and financial support. She has moved to another state and is living with one of her daughters.

In this case I acted as ombudsman by bridging contacts among the police, coroners, private investigators, Los Angeles county victim assistance program, and community support groups. The impact statement is a victim's right but most people are not aware of this right. It can make a difference in resolution and closure and reduces the intense anger the survivor has toward the perpetrator.

I try to explain to my patients that bereavement is like swimming a channel of rough waters. The counselor helps with words, direction, and encouragement, but the patient has to do the swimming. The therapist coaches, but the hard work of mourning is done by the survivor/victim. Healing has many low points and recovery is never complete (Allen 1991).

CONCLUSIONS AND RECOMMENDATIONS

The potential victim's innocent disregard for the practice of general safety should be noted and integrated into specialized education programs. There needs to be an increased focus on prevention education geared for the elderly, covering techniques on how to avoid becoming a victim. For example:

1. Keep and maintain a safe residence with solid-core, dead-bolt locked doors, a peephole in all doors leading to the outside, locked windows, and good lighting around the house and garage.
2. Lock car doors.
3. When possible do not walk alone.
4. Do not carry a purse: keep money in an inside pocket or moneybelt.
5. If in a dangerous situation, do not exacerbate the circumstances by confronting or in any way antagonizing the criminal. Give the criminal what he wants.
6. Have a help alarm installed with a button to activate police and paramedic response.
7. Carry a shriek alarm when walking outside the house.
8. Have a friend telephone at least once a day at a designated time.

Specialized education programs should be focused at locations such as senior citizen centers, churches, and doctors' offices, where the elderly can be reached and can assemble. Formal presentations should be made, discussion groups and informative pamphlets should be directed to the elderly. Information can be distributed through flyers put in mailings or distributed through home visitors such as the Visiting Nurse Association or Meals on Wheels.

Education is needed at many levels, starting with potential victims who need to be aware of their own personal characteristics and the gaps in knowledge that make them vulnerable. Health-care providers need to recognize homicide as one of the nation's major public health problems. There is a need for more comprehensive education to enable the health-care worker to take action toward prevention. The general public should be better informed regarding homicide among the elderly, how it might be prevented, and their role in effecting change. Volunteer workers are extremely useful in befriending the elderly directly or through a telephone service. This would provide a means of checking on the seniors' welfare and also reducing the hours of loneliness felt by many elderly persons.

Potential victims can be made aware of the behavior patterns and gaps of knowledge that make them susceptible to being murdered. Attitudinal changes must occur before behavioral changes can be achieved. Changes in attitude will result in a more accurate perception of possible threats. The elderly need to learn to be less trusting and to accept the fact that society has become more dangerous. A good education program can teach survival techniques and how to practice them. The elderly person should know how to engage in a life-style that is safe. Potential victims need to realize that in today's society they must accept and assume primary responsibility for their own safety.

Many of the principles of prevention, intervention, postvention, and education have applicability to all age groups. Not all homicides can be prevented. The point is, some can. An informed community will serve to save lives.

REFERENCES

Allen, N. (1980). *Homicide: Perspectives on Prevention.* New York: Human Sciences.

_____ (1981). Homicide prevention and intervention. *Suicide and Life-threatening Behavior* 11:167–179.

_____ (1982). Reflections on homicide: a public health perspective. In *The Human Side of Homicide,* ed. B. Danto, J. Bruhns, and A. Kutscher, pp. 21–49. New York: Columbia University Press.

_____ (1991). Survivor-victims of homicide: murder is only the beginning. In *Horrendous Death and Health Toward Action,* ed. D. Leviton, pp. 5–23. New York: Hemisphere.

Centers for Disease Control (1989). Homicide death rates per 100,000 for years 1981–1987 (pamphlet). Atlanta, GA: Centers for Disease Control.

Davis, L., and Brody, E. (1979). *Rape and Older Women: A Guide to Prevention and Protection.* Washington, DC: DHEW.

Logan, M. (1979). Crime against the elderly: cruel and unusual punishment. *Victimology* 4:129–131.

Loya, F., Allen, N., Vargas, L., et al. (1985). *The Epidemiology of Homicide in the City of Los Angeles, 1970–1979.* Atlanta, GA: Centers for Disease Control.

Riddick, G. (1989). *Glenda Riddick Presents the Resource Directory for Los Angeles County* pp. 231–252. Orange, CA: Resource Directory.

8:   TERRORISM AND
HOSTAGE TAKING

Calvin J. Frederick

Hostage taking, as one aspect of terrorism, has attracted a broad spectrum of participants and observers worldwide because of its dramatic, sometimes violent, psychosocial and political implications. Due to modern developments in transportation and telecommunications, preplanned instructions to execute terrorist acts can be transmitted in a matter of seconds. The spate of present-day terrorist activities has captured the interest of political scientists, government officials, corporate executives, academicians, seers, self-anointed experts, and the uninitiated as well as highly sophisticated revolutionaries. The latter groups often justify their motivations under the cloak of an avowed cause célèbre. To say that terrorism is a desperate act of desperate people, as some writers do, is to miss the point. It implies that persons engaging in terrorist acts do so because they are emotionally or mentally disturbed. Nothing could be further from the truth.

   I (Frederick 1987) found that those involved in group terrorism are rarely mentally ill in the conventional sense of the term, although they may have values markedly divergent from societal norms. In contrast, perpetrators of individual acts of terrorism, including hostage taking and homicide, are often severely disturbed. However, the organizers of group acts of terrorism are generally very intelligent, thoughtful planners. It is a mistake to view them otherwise. Illustratively, Saddam Hussein was frequently characterized as crazy, another Hitler. In fact, he was not. Such a notion underestimated his cunning and calloused capabilities. Hussein, for example, connived to release oil into the Persian Gulf and torched the oil fields in Kuwait, whereas, Hitler removed Lisa

   Author's note: This chapter was adapted and revised from a presentation given at the 99th Annual Meeting of the American Psychological Association in San Francisco, California, 19 August 1991.

Meitner and other noted physicists from working on an atomic bomb in order to develop a gun that would shoot around corners! The latter showed a foolish, irrational, childish thought process; the former acts, despicable though they may have been, were crafty, calculated, rational operations that reaped tangible results. It was another facet of the ancient and widely practiced scorched-earth policy.

From among the behavioral factors comprising the author's alliterative pattern, which are often characteristic of individuals who single-handedly commit terrorist crimes, one factor is missing in the case of Saddam Hussein. Although he could justifiably be regarded as *calculating, crafty, calloused* and *cruel,* he was not *crazy!* Our own biases, distortions, and misperceptions of past and present cultural images occur far more frequently than is commonly believed (Dunbar 1991, Laquer 1987, Shalann 1988).

AN HISTORICAL PERSPECTIVE

While terrorist acts invariably conjure up images that are largely negative, historically that has not always been the case. As the author has noted elsewhere (Frederick 1983, 1987, 1989), terrorism, not unlike the term *guerrilla,* which derives from the French word *guerre* (war), has both positive and negative connotations, depending upon where, when, how, and by whom it is used. One person's terrorism may be another's altruism. The term terrorism derives partly from Greek mythology. The chariot of Ares or Mars, the god of war, was drawn by two horses: Phobos (phobia, fear, *terror*) and Diemos (demon, dread). Moreover, it relates as well to the Latin *terrere* (to terrorize or frighten). As such, it implies the presence of danger or evil. During the French Reign of Terror under Robespierre in 1793–1794, the Jacobins described their terrorist activities in a very positive light. Despite the fact that this period of conflict covered the relatively brief time span of some seven months, it resulted in the deaths of more than nine thousand persons. Although historians and political scientists have addressed some of the political implications of such events, the attending psychopolitical data concerning primary victims and co-victim friends and family members have not been gathered and evaluated in any straightforward, systematic fashion. An effort to do so in a preliminary way is one of the foci of this chapter.

Stimuli evoking fear and anger elicit feelings and emotions more primitive than the realm of cognition, since biochemical responses are elicited as well. Reactions of body and mind, even if maladjustive, of necessity occur to protect the organism. Physiological responses in nature inevitably precede cognitive ones.

Fear is the basic physiological response mediated by the thoracico-lumbar section of the autonomic nervous system via adrenergic impulses to the vital organs. Thus, psychophysiological factors can merge with psychopolitical ones to become a tool used by terrorists, many of whom are knowledgeable, sophisticated, and well educated.

A distinction can be made between terror and terrorism. While terrorism may be viewed as an organized effort, terror is a psychological concept, a state of mind in the eye of the beholder. Some authors maintain that terror can occur without terrorism, although terror is an inherent aspect of terrorism. Broadly conceived, as Cline and Alexander (1986) noted, terrorism may be categorized as consisting of two types: (1) state-sponsored terrorism and (2) nongovernment personal terrorism. The former is often of a group variety but the latter is usually an individual act. Hostages held in Lebanon exemplify the former, while the holding of hostages by a lone gunman in the Van Cleef and Arpels Jewelry store in Beverly Hills illustrates the latter. Coercion, fear, and threat are employed to force compliance against the will of an adversary. State-sponsored terrorists use psychopolitical measures such as propaganda, forced prewritten videotapes, and the like to weaken the resolve of their victims and attempt to influence officials and family members. Power, revenge, and fear are paramount ingredients (Arnold and Kennedy 1988).

PSYCHOPOLITICAL ACTIONS OF KEY MIDDLE EAST TERRORIST ORGANIZATIONS

The examples that follow are taken from my sojourns to Central and South America, Yugoslavia, Ireland, and the Middle East. My primary sources have been hostages who were held in Beirut, Iran, Kuwait, Ireland, and Central America, and Asian refugees and family members.

Among the better known terrorist groups in the Middle East are the Islamic Jihad (Islamic Holy War), the Hesbollah (Party of Allah), and the Revolutionary Organization of Socialist Moslems, one of the groups controlled by Sabri al Banna (Abu Nidal). The Islamic Jihad has been responsible for holding such American hostages as Terry Anderson, Thomas Sutherland, David Jacobsen, and Father Lawrence Martin Jenco. The Hesbollah began a series of kidnappings in March of 1984, by taking Jeremy Levin, CNN Beirut chief, and U.S. Embassy Official William Buckley, who died due to apparent torture, neglect, and impoverished captivity.

Abu Nidal, who has received financial support from Syria, Libya, and Iraq, was responsible for the execution of British journalist Alec Collett, among others. It was the activity of one of Nidal's groups, the Revolutionary Organization of Socialist Moslems, which gave rise to many of the terrorist operations still prevailing at the present time. Contributing to these acts was the involvement of a member of Nidal's family. In June of 1982, Marwan al Banna, a relative of Abu Nidal, shot and crippled the Israeli Ambassador to Great Britain in London during an assassination attempt.

Marwan Al Banna was apprehended and is now serving a thirty-year sentence in Parkhurst prison in England. After fruitless efforts to persuade the British to free Marwan, in March of 1985 Abu Nidal's group kidnapped Alec Collett, a British journalist with the United Nations. Following the common practice of using hostages to make videotapes for the transmission of messages, Alec Collett apparently was hanged. A videotape of the hanging convinced Collett's family of his demise, although the body has never been returned.

Media interviews with the family of Marwan al Banna clearly set forth the psychological and political aspects of hostage taking. Responding to questions regarding terrorist acts, the mother was emphatic, "Marwan's mission was political. He was not an assassin. He did a patriotic act." Asked about the motives of Sabri al Banna (Abu Nidal), she replied, "Of course, he will not abandon my son. He is a gentleman with a good personality. His concern is the liberation of his fatherland." When questioned about the morality of kidnapping innocent people such as Alec Collett, she resorted to her own version of syllogistic logic. "Alec Collett is British. My son is in a British prison."

Abu Nidal came from a wealthy merchant family in Jaffa, but moved to Nablus in territory seized by Israel in 1967. There he lived in an area of squalor and deprivation, which is known to engender anger and resentment against Israel by most of these inhabitants. Such a dramatic degradation of relative wealth in status and property evoked a strong need for revenge. With support largely from Syria at the outset and later from Libya, he organized a variety of terrorist activities virtually worldwide, including bombings, hijackings, assassinations, and kidnappings. Generally regarded as the most effectively organized terrorist in the world, the subgroups under him motivated by his charisma and power, operate strictly under his command, each usually without any knowledge of the agenda of any other. Customarily, a specific assignment or target is planned in complete secrecy. Since others know nothing about the operation, it is extremely difficult to infiltrate these groups.

TERRORISM, TRAUMA, AND SELF-DESTRUCTION

Abu Nidal has had no trouble in securing hundreds of young volunteers willing to sacrifice themselves as suicidal surrogates, if necessary, for a cause célèbre. For the first time in life their egos become enhanced through identification with a powerful figure. Acts of terrorism are designed to evoke traumatic sequelae in varying degrees, both physically and psychologically (Frederick 1987, 1990). Terrorism makes use of coercion and fear by depriving victims of personal power over their own minds and bodies. Even in situations where treatment of victims is not overtly abusive, terrorism takes its toll and brings about changes in the recipients. Bombings and hostage taking, for example, invariably leave emotional, if not physical, scars. Individual differences, however, must be taken into account, acknowledged, and respected. Among the Beirut hostages, David Jacobsen details his experiences and observations in a cogent work about his reactions to treatment during and following captivity (Jacobsen and Astor 1991). Fortunately, he is a man of strong will who feels that he is remarkably free of any marked negative effects, either physical or mental.

In our discussions, Jacobsen has frequently affirmed that his fellow hostages were essentially men with solid strength of mind and purpose. He does note, however, that he was also changed by the experience. For example, he became much less compliant and accepting of conditions which he finds objectionable. Frank Reed (1991), on the other hand, has not equivocated in stating that he is "not an ex-hostage but still a hostage," experiencing survivor guilt and emotional scars. Individual coping responses will vary. Father Martin Jenco and others realize that while they cannot be the same again, they function well and hope to release themselves from hurt and anger through forgiveness. Under such degrading conditions man's inhumanity to man becomes the order of the day and cannot help but try men's souls.

My own personal experience has enhanced my understanding and appreciation of the essence of victimization. It has increased my awareness of and sensitivity to the initial intense feelings of exigency, the ubiquitous and debilitating effects of the stressors inherent in captivity and victimization. It has taught me the importance of eschewing the fatuous advice of putative experts into whose hands persons often fall. In particular, it has helped me to recognize the potentially damaging effects of being alone, how it can increase the intensity of one's primitive feelings, heighten anxiety, and contribute to depression. It is not surprising that some hostages have thought actively of suicide stemming from loss of hope and overwhelming despondency.

During a professional mission in an Eastern European country, I became quite ill with a virus of some sort. Entirely alone, I soon realized that no one else could help me. I continued to run a fever and grew weaker daily. A physician with whom I consulted was distant and informed me that there was very little he could do. No one was interested in trying to help me. I equated such apathy and lack of interest with negativism and covert hostility. I was alone; alone in an exiguously furnished room with dark gray walls, poorly lighted, even in the daytime. It was early December; the weather was bleak, cold, and foggy. As I looked out upon the cobblestone street beneath the window of my drab, dreary, dank room, I could see that it was beginning to snow. Virtually consumed with utter despair, I felt too weak and disheartened even to cry. My mind replayed various components of my mission, the locations I had recently been, people I had encountered, in an effort to recall what I might have done to bring it all about.

As I grew weaker, I became fearful that exposure to the cold, snowy weather might worsen my condition even more dramatically. Cognizant of the fact that I needed to provide myself with nutrition, I obtained a supply of food for a day or two from a small place about a kilometer away and forced myself to eat. With the thought that I might never return to the United States alive, I felt completely helpless, dehumanized, utterly stripped of any personal power or control over my own destiny! There were no viable, positive options. I was in the hands of fate.

Being alone heightens feelings of helplessness and exacerbates depression.

Under such conditions, there may be an increase in the likelihood of suicidal thoughts. Victims of hostage taking in both Iran and Beirut entertained such thoughts, which vary in time and place with the individual circumstances. While I am not so presumptuous as to equate my experience with those of these hostages, it did, indeed, resemble such experiences in terms of the elements that comprise true victimization and survival. Clinging to hope for the future, treasuring images of loved ones, and setting subgoals in one's immediate surroundings while engaging in physical and intellectual exercises serve to assist materially in aborting self-destructive thoughts and acts.

Unlike many North American hostages in Iran and Beirut, Joseph Cicippio (*Los Angeles Times* 1992) was alone, chained to a wall, during much of his captivity. The deleterious sequelae of such an ordeal are apt to be more intense and pervasive than when one is held in the company of others. Simple interaction of any kind with other humans is, in itself, sustaining. It is well known that suicide is more likely among widowed and single persons than among married persons or those living together. With regard to factors contributing to depression and suicide, even a bad relationship is often better than no relationship. Merely having someone with whom to interact undercuts the insidiousness of depression.

A major concern with regard to diagnosis, intervention, and treatment of traumatized persons is their vulnerability. Because of the widespread interest in Vietnam combat veterans, much information has been disseminated that is inapplicable to other traumatized individuals. For example, the stress of jungle combat is not to be equated with feelings experienced by a woman who has been raped. Different stressors evoke different responses among individuals in different cultures. Much of the difficulty encountered in treatment can be laid squarely at the doorstep of traditional confrontive therapy. Many platitudes have virtually become the aphorisms of the professional gentry. (For example, "you now need to get on with your life" and "you are not facing reality.") The folly of incorporating the platitudes of unskilled and inexperienced therapists into one's own head can be enormously destructive, creating major second wounds or gratuitous traumas. Some of the standard responses made by most therapists are insufferably arrogant.

PROTESTATIONS, PLATITUDES, AND PITFALLS

Frequent Comments of Victim/Survivors

He/she/they made me anxious, fearful, depressed.
They did this to me.
They tortured me.
I was brutalized emotionally and physically.
I did the best I could at the time, under the circumstances.
I was robbed of all self-respect and volition.

Common Responses of Intervenor/Therapist

You have to take responsibility for your own actions.
You are blaming other people for your responses.
He/she/they didn't do it to you; you let them do it to you.
You had choices.
Are you saying that you could not have responded differently?

Responses of this type have become inappropriately reified and are tantamount to revered aphorisms among many professionals. In actuality, comments by intervenors such as those noted above are insensitive and convey a lack of empathy and understanding. Such remarks are repugnant and engender lack of trust. They disavow reality and deprive victim/survivors of the validation of their feelings to which they are entitled. Victim/survivor responses are purposeful. They seek and need reassurance. Their self-images require support and reinforcement:

Whatever you felt or did was all right!
Anything you feel now is all right!
You have survived!
Nobody can destroy you!
You are worthwhile, solid, and good!
Anything can be addressed and dealt with now because you have survived!

Post Traumatic Stress Disorder (PTSD) per se should not be regarded as pathological or abnormal but rather as adaptive, as responses that are to be expected. The organism must adapt mentally and physically to extreme stressors, by whatever means it can. Indications of at least mild PTSD appear in most hostages. Open expression of emotions is natural, whereas blunting of emotions is not and may be a precursor to a more serious disturbance. There are, in fact, normal responses to normal situations, normal responses to abnormal situations, abnormal responses to normal situations, and abnormal responses to abnormal situations. Each should be assessed and reviewed in its proper perspective.

Although a few of these subjects have contemplated and abortively attempted suicide due to despair and increasing loss of hope, none actually did so. Factors contributing to the lack of completed suicides include regard for surviving family members and friends, basic ego strength, and a prevailing taboo against self-destruction.

Survivors of terrorist acts with whom I have had contact have reported a range of physical injuries. Their experiences included: placement in darkened, cramped quarters devoid of heat, water, or toilet facilities; attachment of electric wires to the fingers and genitalia; confinement in a cell with only a hole in the floor clogged with feces, and no toilet paper, thereby necessitating wiping with one's hands; hanging by the wrists from an iron gate; rape; application of poles behind the knees and under the crotch followed by increased pressure to elicit pain and cut off blood circulation; beatings upon the body, head, and feet; and burnings with cigarettes.

It is a common practice for captives to be blindfolded, or for captives and/or captors to be hooded, in order to protect against recognition. The very thought of terrorism evokes negative emotional responses varying from apprehension to intense anxiety. Nevertheless, emotional defenses can manifest themselves so as to diminish the impact of traumatic events. Religious beliefs, maintaining hope, future planning, and mental and physical exercise can all be employed with profit.

Hostages, as has been noted, are customarily well-adjusted, high-achieving persons who have been seized precisely because of their accomplishments and visibility. They are no different from other successful, competent persons in the everyday world of business and academia. Differences exist principally in the sphere of personality. With respect to sensory deprivation, it appears to matter little whether an individual is primarily introversive or outgoing prior to capture and internment. Being deprived of accustomed levels of interaction with others does not appear to affect one person significantly more than another. However, an individual's response to sensory deprivation is affected by whether he is alone or has companions with whom to interact. An executive member of the Rossi family, owners of the Martini and Rossi corporation, who was held hostage in Italy, told the author that being placed in a hole in the ground alone was particularly stressful due to lack of human contact. Being with other hostages allows for displacement and ventilation of anger and fear away from the captors who could inflict severe punishment or death. While some hostages made unsuccessful attempts to escape, many were convinced that they would be killed after such attempts, the case of Jeremy Levin notwithstanding. A paradigm illustrating key aspects affecting the perceptions and behavior of hostages pre- and post-capture follows:

[Prior to capture]   [Captivity]   [Post release]
Normal stimulation → Sensory deprivation → Overstimulation = Disequilibrium

The extent to which the factors of normal sensory stimulation, sensory depri- vation, and overstimulation after release are manifest contributes to the degree of emotional and bodily disequilibrium experienced following release for varying periods of time. The organism is stressed by reduced stimuli and later flooded with stimuli beyond its capacity to handle or respond in a primitive fight or flight manner. No viable options exist. This paradigm assumes that the subjects are normal functioning, well-adjusted adults prior to capture. It further assumes the absence of premorbid vulnerability and previous traumatic experiences, which could account for maladjustive reactions. While it is important to acknowledge that most hostages from the developed countries are essentially normal, intelli- gent adults, it constitutes a disservice to all concerned not to recognize and accept the essence of this paradigm.

From among the various hostages with whom I have worked and interacted it has become clear that their responses are governed by such factors as: (a) premorbid vulnerability, (b) coping style, (c) intensity and severity of the experience, (d) duration, and (e) age. Defenses and coping styles are an individual matter. Responses that are effective for some are not useful for others. None should be viewed as right or wrong. It is debatable whether "forgiveness of thine enemies" serves as an efficacious means of coping over time, particularly in the absence of expressed anger. Professor Leo Eitinger (1983), the distinguished investigator of the Holocaust and a surviving victim himself, informed me that those who resisted the so-called Stockholm Syndrome fared better in the long run than subjects who experienced it. Unexpectedly perhaps, duration, per se, has less predictive value than age. Paralyzing reactions can develop from a single, relatively short-term experience (Leopold and Dillon 1963). In large measure, how each individual perceives of himself determines the degree of mental difficulty which he encounters during and after a terrorist experience. Older, more mature persons do not seem as likely to develop disabling negative reactions as younger persons. Life experience and rich, positive memories which are often present in older persons, but comprise a less prominent part of a younger person's repertoire, can serve as a solid buffer against the encroachment of debilitating anxiety and subsequent depression. Post Traumatic Stress Disorder, to a greater or lesser extent, is one of several disturbances that may accompany a terrorist experience. Various reactions during and following such an experience are, in themselves, normal and likely to occur. They are natural expressions of the total being, the totality of mind and body, attempting to adapt, adjust, and right itself. It is a matter of simple prudence to be mindful of the possibility that some unsettling reactions may appear, which, if ongoing and severe, may require the assistance of skilled professionals.

Although not inevitable, severe cases are likely to require a combination of deconditioning procedures and specific psychotherapeutic methods designed to focus upon the particular issues of individual involvement. Unfortunately, few persons are experienced in treating hostage traumas. While one's life can never be the same as it was previously, of course, the trauma need not become a disabling or dysfunctional experience and, curiously, may produce an outcome of positive growth.

MEDIA COVERAGE

Bombings, skyjacking, assassinations, and hostage taking are terrorist methods frequently employed to capture media attention. Bombings, which are the most common, are relatively easy to carry out with little likelihood of getting caught. Moreover, the perpetrators have no responsibility for guarding and feeding their captives. While bombings account for 70 percent of all terrorist acts, the psychopolitical components of hostage taking receive more intense and prolonged attention. As Livingstone and Arnold (1988) maintain, media coverage is a virtual sine qua non for modern terrorist activities. Coverage is extensive: governments are put on the defensive and held blameworthy while the process continues over time. The propaganda value of hostage taking is enormous. Government leaders come under pressure from family members, friends, the general public, and the media. The media responds to public pressure and the public's right to know, to put it in familiar terms. Furthermore, when the media in one country discloses information, others follow competitively. Hence, for the most part, freedom of the press prevails at any cost.

Although attempts have been made to cover up certain acts of violence and humiliation, they are ultimately revealed by the media. For example, violence has been apparent on both sides of the Palestinian/Israeli issue. Following the stabbing death by his own people of a Palestinian who collaborated with the Israelis, the homes of the two young Arabs involved, each worth over 100,000 pounds, were razed to the ground by the Israelis. This was done even though one of the assassins had already been prosecuted and sentenced to prison for life. The details were revealed by the media.

Due to widespread public interest and persistent pressure upon government officials to address the matter, directors of the printed media, television, and radio avidly follow developments. It becomes high drama and makes stimulating reading, viewing, and listening. Countless hours are devoted to kidnapping because it sells and is guaranteed to capture both public and official attention.

FAMILY MEMBERS AND FRIENDS AS CO-VICTIMS

There is little doubt that family members and close friends of the hostages are co-victims of any hostage crisis. Father Jenco told the author that his family suffered far worse than he did during his captivity. The uncertainty and ongoing lack of knowledge day after day precipitate intense anxiety for family and friends. Reliable information is guarded and inconsistent. The Department of State, for reasons of its own, customarily provides limited information, which proves unsatisfying to relatives who are anxious and depressed. Effective mutual support is often forthcoming from other families and associates.

Penelope Laingen, wife of former U.S. Ambassador to Iran Bruce Laingen, organized a Family Liaison Action Group (FLAG) comprised of hostage family members in order to coordinate their efforts. It provided emotional and moral support and functioned as a pressure group to push officials in the United States and abroad to bring about the release of the hostages. During periods of anxiety, restless activity, which might otherwise be counterproductive, can often be channeled into constructive effort as demonstrated by such a group as FLAG. Professionals, too, ought to be experienced and familiar with these issues. Insensitivity, although inadvertent, can cause gratuitous emotional traumas. Family members rejected stress-reduction procedures offered by mental-health professionals. Participants sensed an implicit arrogance in this approach, feeling that the leaders assumed that something was wrong with them emotionally or mentally. It is important for intervenors to know their boundaries and subjects, irrespective of their status — whether they be professional, paraprofessional, or volunteers. I have prepared intervention techniques for crisis contact staff, which can be adapted for use with a number of trauma victims and family co-victims. Comprehending the essence of the six basic components of these techniques can be invaluable. Moreover, their essence often prevails cross-culturally.

PEOPLE AS BARGAINING UNITS IN PSYCHOPOLITICS

Holding Sheik Obeid, a Shiite Moslem leader, gave Israel enormous bargaining power. His capture provided the greatest amount of leverage with which to negotiate their demands.

His capture can be compared to that of Terry Anderson, held by the fundamentalist group Islamic Jihad. I accurately predicted that Anderson would be the last North American hostage to be released. As an Associated Press employee, Anderson's hostage status provided invaluable bargaining power and media coverage for the Shiite position. This is the primary reason why the groups involved were reluctant to release either Obeid or Anderson early in the process. In the minds of many officials, this psychopolitical ploy needs to be abandoned in order to make any substantial progress toward lasting hostage resolution.

Penelope Laingen apprised me of her belief that hostage taking is likely to continue until we devalue the worth of the hostages. As long as it is known that a single American life is invaluable, terrorists will be inclined to use such a ploy in attempting to gain their objectives. Terrorism per se, however, is unlikely to end. Various forms of terrorism are apt to continue, the release of the North American hostages notwithstanding. Terrorism remains an ever-present means of psychopolitical action.

A softening of the hard lines previously taken by Iran and Syria, in particular, was due largely to the following factors: a) the impact of the Persian Gulf War, b) a decline in power and support from the Soviet Union, and c) the belief that the United States is less dependent upon the Middle East for petroleum. Former Secretary of State Henry Kissinger has underscored the importance of not allowing ourselves as a nation to be held hostage to conflicts between other nations, for example, Arabs and Israelis. The same principle holds for Northern Ireland and Great Britain and the conflicts existing in Central and South America. While such a posture may suggest isolationism, it has merit, since the United States can still exert its influence as mediator. Kissinger, along with others, has maintained that Israel would have to give up some of the territory under its rule before a real resolution can be obtained in the Palestinian/Israeli problem.

France has consistently avoided becoming involved in the conflicts of other countries. In 1978, for example, a young Arab terrorist was sentenced to fifteen years in prison for murder, but was released in half the time. French officials admitted that the release was not effected on legal grounds, but was done for political reasons, to allow the heat of emotions to cool down and relieve tension that would impede progress if unabated. Failure to resolve Palestinian conflicts has been due to lack of such an approach by other nations, according to the French position. They contend that their approach is good political psychology and permits them to pursue viable political solutions.

CHARACTERISTICS OF HOSTAGES

Do kidnappings of hostages occur at random? Could anyone be taken hostage? Are such kidnappings predictable? To some extent, these unsettling questions become the concern of most persons in the Western world. By and large, kidnappings do not occur randomly. It is highly improbable that state-sponsored terrorists would kidnap someone they did not know about and who would be unlikely to serve their psychopolitical purposes. While it is possible that anyone could become the victim of a bombing in an airport or other such place where crowds gather, the chances are low when compared with other accidents that might befall the average American or any citizen of another developed country. Kidnappings are, indeed, partly predictable (Arnold and Kennedy, 1988) since certain common characteristics are usually present, as shown by the hostages in the Middle East. Some of the pertinent factors that correlate with victims of hostage taking are as follows:

1. They have all been communicators with access to broad dissemination of knowledge and information (media or university affiliation, clergy).
2. They are prominent members of the private sector and occasionally the diplomatic core (influential in business or government).
3. They are usually males who have no obvious infirmity (require minimal care).
4. They have had a continuing presence in the area where they were kidnapped, for instance, the Middle East (known contact with and importance for the local gentry).

SIX BASIC AXIOMS FOR COMMUNICATION WITH
TRAUMATIZED PERSONS

1. Introduction

A natural, pleasant demeanor is of paramount importance. Maintaining eye contact with a smile during the introduction facilitates communication. Health workers and officials should explain who they are and the nature of their function. One should not be left to wonder about such matters. Nurturance of self-esteem can be enhanced by using name prefixes, that is, Mr., Mrs., Ms., or appropriate military rank if applicable. It is best at the outset to avoid speaking on a first-name basis unless given permission to do so. Otherwise, interchange can be viewed as intrusive and denigrating.

2. Rapport

Efforts to establish rapport must never be disingenuous. This can be enhanced from the beginning by (a) expressing regret that the incident happened, (b) showing relief that the person is likely to be all right after all, (c) providing reassurance that the victim was not blameworthy, (d) affirming that continuing support is available, and (e) confidence building by mutual sharing, promoting a partnership.

3. Acceptance

All persons need permission to feel whatever they feel. Any feeling must be accepted (anxiety, anger, fear, hostility, moodiness). Some people need to focus upon bodily complaints initially. Individuals must be allowed to hold onto what is important at the time. It is useless, if not harmful, to tell victims to try to put traumatic events out of their minds. They cannot. In point of fact, it may be viewed as insensitive, arrogant, and intrusive to say, "I know how you feel" or "I understand." Indeed, another person does not!

4. Gratuitous Traumas

Minimizing injuries and experiences should be avoided. Both direct and inadvertent, gratuitous remarks or acts can be perceived as demeaning and may reinforce an already bruised and damaged self-image. Always be respectful.

5. Coping

It is useful to ascertain coping style — withdrawing, relying upon faith, acting self-assured, and so forth. Any coping method can be helpful. We do not have the right to establish another person's coping behavior, transgress boundaries, or arbitrarily intervene. In the Moslem world, for instance, one is forbidden to touch an Arab woman, even if she is in the act of falling and subject to possible injury.

6. Reassurance

Attitudes and feelings need to be normalized and universalized. Pressure is frequently relieved by articulating this process, actually saying, "Many people who have experienced what you did have similar feelings." It is often fruitful to mention the value of comparing and sharing feelings with others who have had similar experiences. Many innocent remarks are well intentioned, but as the saying goes, "The road to Hell is paved with good intentions!" The FBI and CIA are two agencies that appear to be quite skilled at confidence building by sharing information, thereby giving the hostage/victim a feeling of being an in-group member of a team.

Former Beirut hostage David Jacobsen has characterized the 1970s as the decade of aircraft highjackings, the 1980s as the decade of hostage taking, and the 1990s as the decade of political terrorism (Jacobsen and Astor 1992). I concur with his view that modern technology in the 1990s can be turned into a political instrument used to disrupt the mental health of our country. He notes that monumental chaos may result from computer viruses in the world of finance and big business. The counterfeiting of official documents is a reality and could infect large populations via bank records, birth certificates, college degrees, and so forth, to say nothing of counterfeiting money. Iran, Libya, Iraq, and Syria, for example, are quite capable of very sophisticated technological procedures.

PSYCHOPOLITICAL AND CROSS-CULTURAL CONFLICT RESOLUTION

The psychopolitical differences cross-culturally between East and West are profound and clearly manifest in conflict resolution. In Egypt, Professor Mohammed Chalaan first called my attention to the amusing but cogent story of Mulla Nasruddin (also called Goha). When asked to arbitrate between the positions of conflicting parties he listened to the first present his position. "You are right," Goha replied. Then, after hearing the adversary present his views, Goha said, "You are right." A third party then questioned Goha, "How can both parties be right?" he asked. "You are right," Goha responded. This story exemplies the differences between the Middle East and the West. In the Western world this vignette is apt to be disregarded as ridiculous and confusing. Nevertheless, it serves to illustrate further the difficulty with dualistic or dichotomous thinking, so common in the Western world.

In the West we see only the oppressor and the oppressed, the wrongdoer and the one who is wronged. Goha's concept was not confused, but a step toward integration, accommodating both sides. It was a respectful, face-saving process, which could promote further discussion. In categorical thinking freedom from oppression often leads to role reversal with the oppressor becoming the oppressed. At the outset, if one views both parties as victims of an untenable situation or relationship that can be changed, there is hope for a peaceful resolution.

While the Intifada has incorporated elements of modern Western culture — in their views of sex roles and parenting, for instance — many cultural differences persist. There is nothing culturally determined about political freedom, however. True political freedom is inherently nonviolent. Violence begets violence. Oppression inevitably suffers from its own violence. In Newton's Third Law of Motion we find a paradigm in physics for this political truth: "For every action force there is an equal and opposite reaction force." The talion principle provides for the discharge of energy, but does not encompass the human condition: it fails to provide a long-term solution.

Severe punishment merely suppresses unacceptable behavior through fear;

it does not extinguish it. Putative obedience and forced compliance make destructive bed partners. They will return to plague the oppressor. As a case in point, it is in their own best interest that the Israelis and Arabs become coparticipants against oppression and violence. In large measure, the Israelis and the Palestinian Arabs have each been their own worst enemies.

It is difficult for Westerners to comprehend the meaning and importance of faith for those in the Middle East. If one asks them to define the term operationally, they cannot; yet, it is one of the most important landmarks along the pathway to love, mercy, friendliness, and respect. Faith is important in the prevention and treatment of suffering. They believe that when this powerful element is allowed to play its role without bias, it will move science toward truly fruitful endeavors. In this regard, my good friend and colleague Dr. Gamal Abou el Azayem, former president of the World Federation for Mental Health, often quotes from the Koran as follows: "Good actions are healing, while offensive ones are destructive. One must try to keep the constructive ones and overlook enmity. This will cause your adversary to change his inimical attitude to a respectful one. No one will be granted such a rank, except those who exercise patience and restraint."

Faith, in relation to all aspects of life and death, is an integral part of the lives of people in the undeveloped and developing countries of the world. In the Middle East, for example, faith is timeless and far more pervasive than in the United States. The incorporation of religious beliefs is of inestimable value to entire communities as well as to persons on an individual basis, young and old alike.

Severe trauma, depression, death — all require Faith Therapy according to Middle Eastern psychologists and psychiatrists. Suicide is forbidden in the Islamic faith, Orthodox Judaism, the Roman Catholic Church, and virtually all orthodox religions. Such persons are not entitled to receive any last rites. Only God can take a life. For it is God alone who giveth and who taketh away. In the event that such a person can be declared insane, however, last rites may be given, since the individual was not in possession of his/her mental faculties.

During one of my trips to the Middle East I learned of a tragic school bus accident, which occupied the attention of professional colleagues (Azayem 1989, Hashem 1989). The bus carrying one hundred primary school children was struck and demolished by a train. Death and physical injuries were widespread. Forty children were killed while twenty others were injured. Initial psychological and psychiatric assessments were made of forty-five surviving youngsters. Seventy one percent suffered major physical injury requiring surgical or orthopedic intervention. Sixteen percent had loss of consciousness of more than twelve hours. The entire school was comprised of only three hundred children in a small community of five thousand persons. Most prevalent symptoms were anxiety (56 percent), attachment to mother (66 percent) and insomnia (40 percent); yet, no severe Post Traumatic Stress Disorder was found. Moreover, these responses were thought to be temporary. When I asked my colleagues how they could account for such a lack of stronger reactions, they replied simply, "We do not look at death the way you do." What was done to alleviate symptoms? How was faith operationalized to effect ameliorations? I was informed that many stories were told to the children to clarify the meaning of death. For example, a chicken lost by a child was found again in paradise, thus constituting a form of rebirth or faith therapy. Faith is an essential component of most treatment and virtually all psychotherapy throughout the Middle East.

The late President Anwar Sadat of Egypt (1978), speaking of his own Post Traumatic Stress following 31 months of imprisonment, described his debilitating psychological symptoms in terms that emphasized the importance of faith and love of God (Allah). He noted how this sustained him and helped ameliorate his symptoms. "I felt I lived in His love, that love was a law of life. In love—nay, being itself—becomes possible; without love being comes to an end. . . . Love is a homa safeguard against all pitfalls. Whoever lives in love, must have spiritual fecundity. . . . Love is the only force capable of pulling down the barriers which may stand between matter and spirit, between the visible and the invisible, between the individual and God" (pp. 86–87).

In the absence of such beliefs it is likely that Sadat would not have been able to actualize his potential in becoming perhaps the greatest president in Egypt's history.

The Arabs have a phrase that speaks volumes: "In Chalah, Bukrah, Malesh," which, in homely American parlance, means something like: "Not to worry, Allah will handle it." Cultural differences do make a difference!

REFERENCES

A captive no more? (1992). *Los Angeles Times,* June 28, 1992, pp. E1.

Arnold, T. E., and Kennedy, M. (1988). *Terrorism: the New Warfare.* New York: Walker.

Azayem, A. G. A. (1989). Community action to cope with crisis. In *Mental Health Services to Victims of Community Violence,* ed. G. A. El Azayem, A. Saleem, and S. Dunbar, pp. 111–114. Cairo, Egypt: Gamal Abou El Azayem Mental Health Centre.

Cline, R. S., and Alexander, Y. (1986). *Terrorism as State-sponsored Covert Warfare.* Fairfax, VA: Hero.

Dunbar, S. S. (1991). Report on the mental health of Palestinians in the West Bank and Gaza Strip. Cairo, Egypt, and Cyprus, Greece: The Palestinian Red Crescent Society.

Eitinger, L. (1983). Psychological consequences of war disturbances. In *Helping Victims of Violence: Proceedings of a Working Conference on the Psychosocial Consequences of Violence,* ed. H. A. Van Guens, pp. 47–56. The Hague, Netherlands: Ministry of Welfare, Health, and Cultural Affairs.

Frederick, C. J. (1983). Violence and disaster: immediate and long-term consequences. In *Helping Victims of Violence: Proceedings of a Working Conference on the Psychosocial Consequences of Violence,* ed. H. A. Van Guens, pp. 32–46. The Hague, Netherlands: Ministry of Welfare, Health, and Cultural Affairs.

———— (1987). Psychic trauma in victims of crime and terrorism. In *Cataclysms, Crises and Catastrophes,* Master Lecture Series, vol. 8, ed. G. R. VandenBos and B. K. Bryant, pp. 55–108. Washington, DC: American Psychological Association.

———— (1989). Diagnosis of post traumatic stress disorders in children and adults. In *Mental Health Services to Victims of Community Violence,* ed. G. A. El Azayem, A. Salem, and S. Dunbar, pp. 99–110. Cairo, Egypt: Gamal Abou El Azayem Mental Health Centre.

_____ (1990). Resourcefulness in coping with severe trauma: the case of the hostages. In *Learned Resourcefulness,* ed. M. Rosenbaum, pp. 218–228. New York: Springer.

Hashem, A. H. (1989). Psychiatric morbidity among the children of Abou Seer. In *Mental Health Services to Victims of Community Violence,* ed. G. A. El Azayem, A. Saleem, and S. Dunbar, pp. 115–119. Cairo, Egypt: Gamal Abou El Azayem Mental Health Centre.

Jacobsen, D., with Astor, G. (1991). *Hostage: My Nightmare in Beirut.* New York: Donald Fine.

Laingen, P. (1987). The hostages: family, media and government. The human side of terrorism. Paper presented at the conference on terrorism, University of Maryland Center for International Development and Conflict Management, the International Society of Political Psychology, and the Association of American Foreign Service Women, Washington, DC, March.

Laquer, W. (1987). *The Age of Terrorism.* Boston: Little, Brown.

Leopold, R. L., and Dillon, H. (1963). Psycho-anatomy of disaster. *American Journal of Psychiatry* 119:913–921.

Livingstone, N. C., and Arnold, T. E. (1988). *Beyond the Contra Crisis.* Lexington, MA: Lexington Books. D.C. Health.

Reed, F. (1991). CBS Sunday Morning, October 20.

Sadat, A. (1978). In *Search of Identity.* London: Collins.

Shalaan, M. (1989). Current cultural and cross-cultural practices in conflict resolution. In *Mental Health Services to Victims of Community Violence,* ed. G. A. Azayem, A. Saleem, and S. Dunbar, pp. 21–42. Cairo, Egypt: Gamal Abou El Azayem Mental Health Centre.

PSYCHOLOGICAL
DIMENSIONS OF SUICIDE
Part III

The psychological dimensions of suicide are, to use Shneidman's arborial image, the trunk of suicide. At the core of every conscious decision to end one's life are causes and motivations rooted in the personal history of the individual. Some of these are accessible to that individual and form the basis of his or her conscious decision. There are yet others of which that individual remains unaware or only partially aware; these are often the more powerful causes. Part III illustrates how the tools and theories of psychology can help us to begin to make sense of an act and a choice that often seem bereft of logic and of sense. It consists of two chapters: a study of the unconscious processes, and an explication of the confusions of the body, self, and others in suicidal states.

9: UNCONSCIOUS PROCESSES

Antoon A. Leenaars

Whatever else suicide is, it is a *conscious* act. It is a conscious act of self-induced annihilation. This is not to say that there are no vital unconscious elements in the total scenario. In other words, "it is meant to indicate that, by definition, suicide can occur only when an individual has some conscious mediation or, better, some conscious intention to stop his or her own life. There is always an element of some awareness and conscious intentionality in suicide (Shneidman 1985, p. 204)." On the other hand, the driving force is an *unconscious process*. By definition, one must be conscious of the act to kill oneself, but the conscious aspect of the human mind is only one part of the act. The unconscious is a vast domain and a key to our understanding.

THE UNCONSCIOUS

Consciousness (including at the precise moment that I decide to kill myself) is composed only of what I am aware of at that moment. Consciousness is, indeed, important in understanding a complicated human act like suicide. Yet, there is much more. We have long known that there are many thoughts and feelings connected with what we do.

The unconscious is probably one of Freud's most important concepts (Ellenberger 1970, Fenichel 1954, Heidbreder 1933). Its appeal probably lies in its usefulness for explaining a variety of phenomena, from dreams to slips of the tongue to the writing of suicide notes. One can show that these phenomena are related and emanate from the unconscious mind.

Freud first began to postulate the unconscious from his work with his patients while studying with Breuer in the 1880's. Freud was most interested in symptoms due to hysteria such as functional blindness and glove anesthesia. One of Breuer's patients, Anna O., had been especially significant to Freud. She was a young woman whose hysterical symptoms had developed out of a childhood experience. As Freud said, "I do not want to feel any painful sensation is the first and final motive of defense" (Fenichel 1954 p. 161). Symptoms—and I would add suicide—can be seen as a defense (or a solution) to pain. In treatment the patient became aware of the root of her pain. Breuer and Freud's interpretation was that an original experience had aroused a pain that had been prevented from expressing itself in a normal fashion. Rather, the pain became expressed in a symptom. The symptom, thus, was not physical nor conscious in origin.

Freud postulated that for many of his patients' symptoms—expressions of pain—there were no physical determinants and no conscious reasons. The person, for example, suffering from hysterical blindness had not decided to be blind. Freud's patient could describe essential details about the blindness, yet, was unaware of critical aspects.

Thus, Freud (1915) wrote:

> The assumption of the existence of something mental that is unconscious is necessary and legitimate. It is necessary because the data of conscious have a very large number of gaps in them; both in healthy and in sick people, psychical acts often occur which can be explained only by presupposing other acts, of which, nevertheless, consciousness affords no evidence. At any given moment consciousness includes only a small content, so that the greater part of what we call conscious knowledge must be for very considerable periods of time, in a state of latency, that is to say, of being psychically unconscious. The assumption of an unconscious is, moreover, a perfectly legitimate one, inasmuch as postulating it, we are not departing a single step from our customary and generally accepted mode of thinking. [p. 166]

What one knows about one's behavior provides only a fragmentary aspect of the total personality. This is not to say that it is insignificant, only that it is not the driving force behind behavior. The unconscious is the driving force. The unconscious is active, dynamic, and personal. In a sense, Freud here anthropomorphizes all of mental life. He describes the unconscious as if it were distinctly personal, as personal as the people we meet in everyday life.

In order to understand human acts, including suicide, one must be conversant with the concept of the unconscious. Suicidology would be overly barren without it. Suicidologists can learn much about suicide by focusing on the unconscious processes.

A SERENDIPITOUS FINDING

A series of studies spanning the last 14 years (Leenaars 1979, 1985, 1986, 1987, 1988a,b,c; 1989a,b, 1990, Leenaars and Balance 1981, 1984a,b,c; Leenaars et al. 1985) introduced an empirical approach to suicide notes that presented a method for their theoretical analysis. Essentially, this method (Leenaars 1988a, Leenaars and Balance 1984a) calls for the notes to be treated as an archival source and subjected to the scrutiny of control hypotheses, following an ex post facto research design (Kerlinger 1964). Suicide notes are recast in different theoretical contexts (hypotheses, theories, models, etc.) for which lines of evidence of each of these positions can then be pursued in the data, utilizing Carnap's logical and empirical procedure (1959) for such investigations. These positivistic procedures call for the translation of theoretical formulations into observable (specific) *protocol sentences* in order to test the formulations. The protocol sentences are the meaning of the theory as they are matched empirically, by independent judges, with the actual data. Next, conclusions are developed from the verified protocol sentences to facilitate model building and test construction.

To date, the theories of ten suicidologists have been investigated (Leenaars 1988a), specifically, those of Adler, Binswanger, Freud, Jung, Menninger, Kelly, Murray, Shneidman, Sullivan, and Zilboorg. (Certainly these views do not represent all of the psychological variables that might prompt someone to commit suicide; yet, these individuals are generally recognized as having given us a rich history of theory about suicide). A specific series of studies (Leenaars 1987, Leenaars et al. 1985) on Shneidman's formulations of suicide revealed that important unconscious processes were present in over half of the suicide notes studied, regardless of age and sex. It was also found that unconscious processes were significantly more frequently observed in genuine suicide notes than simulated suicide notes (Leenaars 1986). The specific protocol sentence, or classification, derived from Shneidman's work (1980, 1981, 1985) was: In the suicide note, the person's communication appears to have unconscious psychodynamic implications. Very few variables to date have been observed to be so critical in suicide notes.

It is most pertinent that independent clinical judges had made these observations with substantial interjudge reliability. It was also shown that the judges were able to obtain an overall average (presence or absence) score-rescore agreement significantly greater than chance would allow. Thus, some aspects of reliability have been documented about the scoring of unconscious processes in suicide notes.

A serendipitous observation emerged from a cluster analysis (Leenaars 1986, 1987). The unconscious forces were grouped with a set of protocol sentences labelled *relations*. Specifically, the protocol sentence was grouped with a dyadic event, a calamitous relationship, the withdrawal of a key significant other person, expressions of love and hate toward a person, an ambivalent attitude toward a person, the perception of another person as dooming one to death, and the feeling of hopelessness and helplessness about establishing meaningful relations. It appeared that the unconscious processes were most associated with these relational aspects of suicide, whether with a person or some other ideal (e.g., freedom, health).

Regrettably, however, when the judges were asked what the unconscious process might be and how they reached their conclusion, no agreement was reached. One judge cited concepts and decision rules based on psychoanalytic defense mechanisms, whereas the other cited concepts and rules that were generally derived from Shneidman's work. Of course, theorists themselves tend to disagree generally about such concepts. Freud cited intense identification with a lost or rejecting object *and* aggression turned inward as the critical variables. Shneidman would cite intense (unbearable) psychological pain, with accompanying constriction, hopelessness, push for egression, and so forth, probably sparked underneath by dramatically frustrated psychological needs that are critical in the individual's makeup. Other suicidologists, that is, Jung, Menninger, Murray, Zilboorg, and so forth, cite other notions. It is hence understandable that individuals would respond in different ways to these exceedingly complex issues.

Elements of the unconscious are not as readily observed as manifest content. This, of course, was true in the case of Anna O. Further procedures were needed, such as providing more structured classification or operational definitions about the nature of the latent (i.e., unconscious) content and decision rules or guidelines for assigning a vote to the classification.

A STUDY: AN INTRODUCTION

Dreams have often been subjected to latent analysis. Since both dreams and suicide notes can be seen as a response, as it were, to the blank card of the Thematic Apperception Test, both are amenable to the rules of thematic interpretation in general. The primary difficulty in conducting research on latent concepts is that observation and interpretation tend to be subjective (Kerlinger 1974). After all, unconscious processes cannot be assessed directly (Freud 1915), but only through analysis of the distorted manifest content. Freud (1917) proposed that the wishes, needs, motivations, and so forth that are related to psychological conflict are frequently repressed into the unconscious and, subsequently, expressed in dreams and, although the mental processes are different in some ways (Freud 1901, 1917), in everyday life (e.g., verbal expressions, writings). These expressions are, however, *distorted*. However, the unconscious forces can be assessed *indirectly* by way of these verbal and associative distortions (Freud 1916). Based on this perspective, Foulkes (1978) attempted to develop *objective* general principles to describe the types of distortions that commonly occur in the manifest content of dreams; these principles can equally be applied to suicide notes and other thematic material. Foulkes' Scoring System for Latent Structure (1978) is an objective and explicit scoring system. He proposed that unconscious forces are presented in linguistic form in psychologically meaningful units, namely subject-verb-object relationships. Table 9-1 presents a summary of Foulkes' scoring classifications. As an analysis technique, Foulkes' Scoring System is unique and innovative because it attempts to establish a reasonable and orderly set of rules for the analysis of latent content.

Foulkes' scoring system for the interpretation of the latent content in these personal documents was used in a study of suicide notes (Leenaars and McLister 1989, McLister 1985, McLister and Leenaars 1988) to examine genuine suicide

TABLE 9-1

Foulkes' Scoring Classifications

Classifications	Examples
Interactive Verbs:	
Moving Toward	loving, wanting, needing, accepting, liking, helping
Moving From	withdrawing, disconnecting, disenfranchising, detaching from
Moving Against	being aggressive toward, rejecting dominating, controlling, exploiting
Creating	discovering, nurturing, inventing
Associative Verbs:	
With	associated with
Equivalence	being identical to
Means	acting as the means/medium
Nouns:	
Father	father, older man
Mother	mother, older woman
Parent	scored when sex of parent is unknown
Sibling	brother, sister
Spouse	spouse, peer of opposite sex in long-term relationship
Peer Male	males of approximately same age
Peer Female	females of approximately same age
Children	males/females of younger age
Ego	self
Symbolic	animals, material objects, thoughts

Author's note: This table is based on material from the work of David Foulkes and is used here with Dr. Foulkes' permission.

notes and simulated suicide notes (as control data). Based on previous research it was predicted that unconscious forces would be present in the statements of the genuine suicide notes more frequently than in the simulated notes, that is, more distortions would be identified in genuine notes according to established operational definitions.

A STUDY: THE METHOD

Two independent raters with graduate training in psychology served as the judges. The judges were blind to the purpose of the study. As suggested by Leenaars (1986) and recommended by Foulkes (1978), judges received considerable instructions in the scoring system and were trained on a large sample of suicide notes (N = 63). The judges' scoring agreement reached at least 90 percent on all classifications before initiating the study.

The judges were then asked to score Shneidman and Farberow's (1957) 33 genuine and 33 simulated suicide notes. Shneidman and Farberow had randomly obtained (with the cooperation of the Los Angeles County's Coroner's office) the 33 genuine notes from a sample of 721 suicide notes and had subsequently obtained the 33 simulated notes from independent, nonsuicidal individuals who were matched by sex, age, and occupation. The judges were unaware of the use of simulated notes as control data.

As recommended by Foulkes (1978), the judges scored the suicide notes independently and, subsequently, met to reconcile their scoring to minimize deviation from the scoring rules. The reconciled scores were employed in the data analysis.

The judges read Foulkes' (1978) description of the rules for the Scoring System for Latent Structure. Every sentence in a note is scored on the basis of explicit rules — not intuition, theoretical tenets, or the like — with relationships as the conceptual unit of analysis. Every sentence is scored for subject (noun), verb (interactive or associative) and object (noun). The rules are briefly summarized below.

Verbs are scored as either interactive or associative (See Table 9-1). Interactive statements are scored for subject-verb-object relationships, using the verb categories: *moving toward, moving from, moving against,* and *creating.* Associative statements are scored when nouns are linked by relationships defined as *with, equivalence,* and *means.* Interactive verbs can be modified. Modifications that enhance the intensity of the relationship are scored " + " and those that diminish the intensity of the relationships are scored " – ".

Foulkes lists the various noun categories (See Table 9-1). Any reference to the self is scored as *Ego.* Nouns are scored using various categories. For example, persons of the same generation as the Ego are scored as *sibling, spouse, peer male,* or *peer female,* depending on their sex and relationship to Ego. Nouns can be modified. Nouns described in terms that are positive or enhance their adequacy are scored " + " and nouns described in terms that are negative or diminish their adequacy are scored " – ".

The decision rules for scoring Ego are described by Foulkes (1978). Every interactive statement is considered to be a self-statement, so either the subject or the object must be scored as Ego. Ego may be the subject or the object in a statement, but may not be both. Thus, the scoring system requires that the writer of the note "is located in, at least, one pole of every scored interactive relationship" (Foulkes 1978). This assumption is based on Freud's statement that "dreams are completely egotistical." A similar assumption has been made about the other forms of expression (Freud 1916) and can be readily applied to suicide notes. Ego is either stated directly in a note or can be inserted into the context by being represented in a note in several ways and/or times through *identification* with extraneous persons (and/or other objects). Other things being equal, since the suicidal person is the author of the note, he/she is the subject of each sentence. The principle is called *active voice,* that is, the subject is Ego (although this can be "modified by 'identification' rules which align Ego with persons of like age and sex" [Foulkes 1978]). If the object of the sentence is clearly the writer, the object is scored as Ego. Ego can be scored only once in each sentence, even in sentences like "I hate myself." The latter, reflexive type sentences are scored as modifying Ego (in this case, with a " – ") but do not constitute interactive statements. When neither the subject nor the object is explicitly described as Ego in a note, decision rules are applied to infer Ego. The primary identifications are by active voice, by sex, and by age. More complex rules are also provided when statements describe, for example, third persons and symbolic interactions. All interactive statements that cannot be scored directly from the text but call for decision rules to be applied constitute one type of distortion.

Foulkes, following Freud's dictum that associations or contextual data are given a priority if available, also explains that under certain circumstances, associative statements lead to a transformation of interactive statements. Nouns in interactive statements can be replaced (transformed) with nouns that have been linked to them in associative statements. For example, if in a note the person writes "I hate x" and "x goes with spouse," then one can conclude: "I hate spouse." Associative sentences are exempt from the rule that Ego must be scored in each sentence; that is, third person sentences can occur, following Freud's conclusion that associations, and so forth—unlike dreams—are not always ego-cathected (nor significant). The example above illustrates the exemption. When associative statements result in transformations of interactive statements, it implies that a distortion has occurred (although different from distortions related solely to interactive statements). Thus, there are two types of distortions scored in the system. One related to associative transformations and the other related to cases in which interactive statements cannot be scored directly from the text.

The scoring rules are only summarized here and are described in detail by Foulkes (1978).

A STUDY: THE RESULTS

Following Foulkes' rules of analysis (1978), the results indicated that genuine and simulated suicide notes did not differ in distortions related to associative transformations. In the interactive statement only 7.87 percent of the genuine notes and 5.42 percent of the simulated notes contained such transformations. This finding is likely related to the fact that free associations cannot be obtained for suicide notes as they can for dreams and that this type of distortion is generally dependent on associations. Subsequent references to distortions refer to cases in which interactive statements could *not* be scored directly from the text. It was here that a significant finding was observed: genuine suicide notes contained significantly more distortions than the simulated notes.

Of the genuine suicide notes, twenty-one contained distortions—almost two-thirds of the notes—and distortions were associated with 25.2 percent of the interactive statements. Of the simulated suicide notes, twelve contained distortions—about one-third of the notes—and distortions were associated with 11.82 percent of the interactive statements. A large proportion of the distortions in both the genuine (86.40 percent) and simulated (80.77 percent) notes involved the employment of the decision rules to determine whether the Ego should be scored in the position of subject or object of an interactive relationship between two third persons or between a third person and an object.

No differences were found in the frequency with which each interactive verb (moving toward, moving from, and moving against) was noted in genuine and simulated notes. Moving toward was scored most frequently, accounting for 67.45 percent of the interactive statements in the genuine notes.

As specified in the scoring rules, Ego was scored as the subject or object in 100 percent of the interactive statements. Spouse was the next most frequently employed noun; relationship between Ego and spouse accounted for 57.22 percent of the interactive statements in the genuine notes. Analysis indicated that only father and spouse were significantly more often scored in genuine notes. Spouse was employed in thirty-two genuine notes (although this, in part, is likely reflective of the fact that Shneidman and Farberow's notes were written only by married individuals).

A STUDY: CONCLUSIONS

The procedures outlined thus appeared to have been useful in research on the unconscious processes in suicide notes and would very likely be so with other clinical material that is thematic in nature. Even if one does not accept the psychoanalytic assumptions in this paper, one is still confronted with the fact that blind to the hypotheses judges scored latent content (i.e., distortions) more frequently in genuine notes than in simulated ones. Although further validity studies of Foulkes' system are warranted, the procedures in this study subjected the investigation of unconscious psychodynamic forces in suicide notes to the first reported structured, objective analysis in the literature. The fact that both studies — one with clinical judgments and the other with operational definitions — report similar findings and that Foulkes' system can be applied to dream reports, suicide notes, and, likely, other thematic material, begin to add some support to the idea that the distortions as operationally defined may well measure what they purport to measure.

SPECULATIONS ON THE UNCONSCIOUS

An obvious concern is the following: Are we, indeed, measuring what we are purporting to be measuring? It may well be, as some would argue, that we are simply measuring the confusion associated with the mental state that precedes suicide. The suicidal person may simply be unaware (unconscious) of aspects of the information processing. However, such a concern goes against Freud's (1916) suggestion that distortions (as well as displacements, bizarreness, etc.) measure the *dynamic unconscious*. The focus in this view — implied in Foulkes' system — is on repressed unconscious processes (e.g. wishes, needs). As Eagle (1987) has noted, this is an issue of markedly different theoretical tenets, that is, different conceptions of the unconscious. The ideas in this paper are largely based on a number of tenets of psychoanalytic psychology. It accepts the distinction between manifest and latent. It accepts that latent implications (i.e., unconscious processes) are important in understanding a suicidal person. It accepts that there are procedures for inferring the latent implications from the manifest content in suicide notes. For example, it implies that distortions are symptomatic of unconscious forces. In contrast, the more cognitive-behavioral view would hold that the person is *only* unaware (unconscious) of processes that influence behavior, such as what would occur when the suicidal person decides to end one's life due to mental constriction, unbearable pain, hopelessness-helplessness, and so forth. I do not mean to suggest that such processes espoused by the cognitive view do not occur; rather, I believe that both, and other processes as well (e.g., biological [including neuropsychological], socio-cultural, philosophical), occur in an individual who defines an issue for which suicide is perceived as the best solution. My point is that it is possible to understand suicide notes and, by implication, suicide from a perspective that includes consideration of unconscious forces. Further analysis incorporating the thoughts and observations of various diverse theorists on latent content is needed, although a critical contingency of such investigations, as in all studies of completed suicide, will be the availability of adequate data (e.g., associations) (Maris 1981). If we could put the suicide notes in the context of their authors' lives, we could make greater use of associations, and so forth, to understand the event.

The results support the observation that genuine suicide notes contain more unconscious implications than simulated notes. The second, more formal, study substantiated the finding of an earlier one by utilizing an objective scoring system. Significantly more distortions were found in the interactive statements of individuals who wrote genuine suicide notes than matched individuals who wrote simulated suicide notes. Distortions are reflections of latent content (Foulkes 1978, Freud 1916). Genuine suicide notes more often called for decision rules to be applied about the latent meaning in the interactive statements. A large proportion (86.4 percent) of the distortions involved deciding whether the Ego should be scored in the position of object or subject of an interactive relationship between two third persons or between a third person and an object. One possible interpretation of these findings is that the manifest content of a suicide note may not be identical with all of the writer's wishes, needs, and so on. By analyzing the latent content, we may be able to uncover some of these underlying forces. For example, it may be assumed, from my perspective, that attachments are very important in suicide although I would add that the concept of attachment is an extremely complicated one.

Suicide is often interpersonal in nature (Freud 1920). I recently suggested that unconscious processes are related to this interpersonal aspect of suicide (Leenaars 1986). Freud (1920) speculated on the latent interpretation of what leads someone to kill himself: "Probably no one finds the mental energy required to kill himself unless, in the first place, in doing so he is at the same time killing an object with whom he had identified himself and, in the second place, is turning against himself a death wish which had been directed against someone else" (p. 162).

The suicidal person has had to develop a strong identification with another person (or, as Zilboorg [1936] has shown, some other ideal). Attachment, based upon an important emotional tie with another person, is for Freud (1921) the meaning of identification; the person (or other ideal) does not merely exist outside, he becomes introjected into one's own personality. The attachment is deep within one's unconscious. As Litman (1967) noted, our "ego is made up in large part of identifications" (p. 333). These identifications are especially associated with our earliest attachments (e.g., parents) and significant people (e.g., spouse, child). With loss, rejection, and so forth, the energy (libido) in this attachment is withdrawn, but the person continues to exhibit an overly painful attachment. As Fenichel (1954) noted, "the loss is so complete that there is no hope of regaining it. One is hopeless . . . and helpless" (p. 400). The importance of attachment is articulated by Freud in his analysis of Anna O. and Dora, a patient who had been suicidal. In both it was the relationship to the father that was so painful and critical in their development. The loss does not need, I believe, to be actual. It may be fantasized, like the attachment itself. Our research has substantiated that it is the attachment that is the basic unconscious process in suicide, not the death wish. Although aggressive wishes, whether directed inward or outward, occur in some suicides, it is primarily identification that is the key in most suicides. Suicide is more an outcome of frustrated attachment needs (wishes) than of aggressive wishes. The loss of the attachment, often experienced as abandonment, at both the more obvious manifest level and the deeper latent level, fuels the pain that becomes unbearable: No love, no life.

The dynamics in suicide, I believe, are thus related to key significant others (e.g., father, mother), although ideals may serve as the object of attachment. Further, the need in these relations is often one of moving toward (attention, approval, gratitude, affection, love, sex, etc.) rather than moving against or moving away. According to Horney (1950), from whom Foulkes developed his schema for interactive verbs, such a person evaluates his life according to how much he "is liked, needed, wanted, or accepted." This type of person is self-effacing and has a continual wish (or need) for attachment—"attention, approval, gratitude, affection, love, sex." To be loved is to be safe. This type of person will sacrifice all to be loved. Horney writes: "While curtailed in any pursuit on his own behalf, he is not only free to do things for others but, according to his *inner dictates*, should be the ultimate helpfulness, generosity, considerateness, understanding, sympathy, love, and sacrifice. In fact, love and sacrifice in his mind are closely intertwined: he should sacrifice everything for love—love is sacrifice" (Horney, 1950, p. 220; italics added). Although other needs may be present, it is the need for attachment, within a historical context, that is central in most suicide.

Freud himself associated suicide and love; indeed, his only overt suicide threats, years before his suicide, occurred during his engagement to his wife-to-be, Martha Bernays (Litman 1967). According to Jones (1953–1957), Freud had decided to commit suicide if he lost Martha. In a letter to Martha, Freud wrote: "I have long since resolved on a decision, the thought of which is in no way painful, in the event of my losing you. That we should lose each other by parting is quite out of the question. You would have to become a different person, and of myself, I am quite sure. You have no idea how fond I am of you, and hope I shall never have to show it" (Jones 1953–1957). Freud was quite attached to Martha and, as his history revealed, to some ideals (e.g., health).

It is equally noteworthy that Karl Menninger, when asked recently (Jacobs and Brown 1989) if he would change any aspect of his triad of motives in suicide—to kill, to be killed, to die—stated: "I think there is one more unconscious motive to add to the triad. I think some love gets into suicide motivation" (p. 484).

It is likely that as a group, suicidal individuals are, in fact, quite pathological in their love. In his analysis of Freud's speculations on suicide, Litman (1967) writes: "Freud often referred to certain dangerous ways of loving, in which the ego is 'overwhelmed' by the object. Typically, the psychic representations of the self and other are fused and the other is experienced as essential for survival" (p. 340).

We term such attachments "symbiotic" and it is likely that "symbiotic love is a potential precursor of suicide" (Litman 1967). Some suicide notes, not all, exhibit such unhealthy love. For many, it is simply the loss that they cannot bear. The loss is so complete that there is no hope of living. The pain is unbearable.

Suicide occurs in a needful individual. "It is difficult to conceptualize an individual committing suicide apart from that individual seeking to satisfy certain inner felt needs; . . . there can never be a needless suicide; . . . it focally involves the attempt to fulfill some urgently felt psychological needs. Operationally, these heightened unmet needs make up, in a large part, what the suicidal person feels (and *reports*). . . ." (Shneidman 1985, pp. 208–209, italics added). If we let the unconscious speak through the suicidal person's own report, the suicide note, we learn that the suicidal person is not so much withdrawing, detaching from, disconnecting, disenfranchising himself, nor even being aggressive toward, rejecting, dominating, controlling, or exploiting so much as loving, needing, wanting, liking, accepting. In the suicidal person, love and sacrifice are closely intertwined. A person sacrifices everything for love . . . love is one of the driving forces in suicide.

AN IDIOGRAPHIC ILLUSTRATION

On arrival, contacted Deputy Smith, who directed writer to the bathroom where victim was observed lying on the floor, head resting on a pillow, toward the north, feet pointed toward the south. Victim was dressed in a green housecoat; was cold to the touch, rigor mortis having started to set in. On the pillow it was noted there was a stain, caused by purge from victim's mouth. Photographs of the scene were taken.

Deputy Smith turned over to the undersigned a small bottle with the label bearing "prescription No. XXX, Dr. Joe, Mrs. Natalie _____ , one capsule at bedtime, dated _____ ; Sam's pharmacy, telephone 000–0000, _____ , _____ ." This bottle was empty. Also a small plastic container was received from Deputy Smith, with label inside the cover reading, No. XXXX, one tablet 4 times daily, regularly, Mrs. Natalie _____ , , Jane's pharmacy _____ , telephone 000–0000, Dr. Ed; this container had 30 white tablets, " _____ " printed on one side and a line on the other side. Also at this time, notes, reading as follows, were turned over to the writer, by Deputy Smith.

By way of concluding this essay, I would like to present the case of Natalie, a 39-year-old woman who killed herself. What is instructive about this case for suicidology is that in addition to her suicide notes, there exist over one hundred separate documents. They include the following: early school records, teachers' notes to her parents, physicians' reports, school evaluations, college records, several psychological tests, numerous questionnaires that she had completed, and dozens of letters and other miscellaneous personal documents. These documents and other records provide us with the associations that are lacking for most suicide notes. They allow us a clearer glimpse of a life that ended in suicide, including the processes of the conscious and unconscious mind. A full account of the case has been presented by Shneidman (1980).

Let me begin with Natalie's five suicide notes cited verbatim:

1. To her adult friend:

Rosalyn—Get Eastern Steel Co. Tell them and they will find Bob right away. Papa is at his business. Betty is at the Smiths. Would you ask Helene to keep her until her Daddy comes—so she won't know until he comes for her. You have been so good—I love you. Please keep in touch with Betty. Natalie.

2. To her elder daughter:

Betty, Go over to Rosalyn's right away. Get in touch with Papa.

3. To her ex-husband, from whom she was recently divorced:

Bob—I'm making all kinds of mistakes with our girls. They have to have a leader and everyday the job seems more enormous. You couldn't have been a better Daddy to Nancy and they do love you. Nancy misses you so and she doesn't know what's the matter. I know you've built a whole new life for yourself but make room for the girls and keep them with you. Take them where you go. It's only for just a few years. Betty is almost ready to stand on her own two feet. But Nancy needs you desperately. Nancy needs help. She really thinks you didn't love her, and she's got to be made to do her part for her own self-respect. Nancy hasn't been hurt much yet—but ah! the future if they keep on the way I've been going lately. Barbara sounds warm and friendly and relaxed and I pray to God she will understand just a little and be good to my girls. They need two happy people—not a sick mixed-up mother. There will be a little money to help with extras. It had better go that way than for more pills and more doctor bills. I wish to God it had been different but be happy—but please—stay by your girls. And just one thing—be kind to Papa. He's done everything he could to try to help me. He loves the girls dearly and it's right that they should see him often. Natalie

Bob — This afternoon Betty and Nancy had such a horrible fight it scares me. Do you suppose Gladys and Orville would take Betty for this school year? She should be away from Nancy for a little while — in a calm atmosphere.

4. To her stepfather:

Papa — No one could have been more kind or generous than you have been to me. I know you couldn't understand this — and forgive me. The lawyer had copy of my will. Everything equal — the few personal things I have of value — the bracelet to Nancy and my wedding ring to Betty. But I would like Betty to have Nana's diamond — have them appraised and give Betty and Nancy each half of the diamonds in the band. Please have somebody come in and clean. Have Bob take the girls away immediately. I don't want them to have to stay around. You're so good Papa dear —

5. To her two children:

My dearest ones — You two have been the most wonderful things in my life. Try to forgive me for what I've done — your father would be so much better for you. It will be harder for you for awhile — but so much easier in the long run. I'm getting you all mixed up. Respect and love are almost the same. Remember that — and the most important thing is to respect yourself. The only way you can do that is by doing your share and learning to stand on your own two feet. Betty, try to remember the happy times — and be good to Nancy. Promise me you will look after your sister's welfare. I love you very much — but I can't face what the future will bring.

In her notes, Natalie seems pushed, weary, harried, and beaten by life. Her personal documents clearly give evidence of trauma; even her everyday life was described as too "enormous." She noted that life was too painful. She wanted immediate relief. She wanted to depart from her distress. To her children she wrote, "I can't face what the future will bring." For her, suicide had adjustive value. It provided relief from intolerable suffering.

Natalie's father had reported to the police: "that approximately two weeks ago, victim told him that she was going to commit suicide. He said he talked her out of the notion at that time, and did not figure she would make any further attempt on her life. He further said victim had been in ill health since her divorce and had been treated by a psychologist, address unknown; also that the victim had filed a will which is currently in the possession of her attorney."

To put the situation into the appropriate historical context (something that a suicide note does not provide but may be essential in understanding the suicidal person), the following brief synopsis of Natalie's life is provided from the documents: Natalie's birth and early years were noted as normal. When Natalie was six, her mother wrote to a friend: "I have tried to use a lot of common sense and have answered every question to the best of my ability because she is an understanding child and will listen to reason. I have not had to stimulate a desire to learn because she always wanted to know everything her older playmates knew and she would try to learn voluntarily." She had a brother, who was eight years older than she. Later she would say about him that "he could never make a living."

When Natalie was 6 years old, in the first grade, she was given an individual intelligence test, scoring in the extremely superior category. Curiously, one of the few items that she missed on the test was this one: "Yesterday the police found the body of a girl cut into 18 pieces. They believe that she killed herself. What is foolish about that?" Her nonprophetic answer was: "She wouldn't kill herself."

A very important event occurred in Natalie's life when she was 7: her father deserted the family. It is noteworthy that Natalie became quite irritable after the desertion. Later in her life she noted, with obvious sadness, that "my father never came to see me except once."

A characteristic of Natalie's that is worth remarking about that started to develop at this time was her irritability. It would be a marker of her personality. Her personal documents from the very beginning — with a hiatus during most of her teen years — until her death are full of references to this characteristic. Before the age of 7, Natalie's family doctor described her as nervous. Records, notably after her father's desertion, are replete with words like "somewhat irritable," "very irritable," and "mental characteristic is irritability." School records, except in high school, concurred. The psychologist who administered Natalie the IQ test at age 6 noted that she fatigued quickly. Natalie's mother in the early years denied the problem. There were numerous medical tests, all reporting that there was no physical basis for the irritability.

A few years after the father's desertion, Natalie's mother remarried; the marriage had a very positive influence on Natalie and her family. When Natalie was 13, her stepfather was described as "devoted," encouraging Natalie at home, school, and elsewhere. It is, in fact, noteworthy that after Natalie's death, her children lived with her stepfather.

The records of her childhood are interesting. Natalie's mother saw Natalie at this time as understanding, competent, and having a stimulating desire to learn. Her mother also saw her as egotistical and vain, which was in sharp contrast to teachers' reports. At school, Natalie was seen as decidedly modest. By age 10, her mother noted that Natalie had overcome these problems.

At age 12 there were several items of interest. She suffered from numerous headaches and had corrective eyeglasses prescribed, but she continued to report troubled eyestrain. She experienced her menarche; she was a straight-A student (in the seventh grade) and indicated that she wanted to go to college. A hearing loss had been diagnosed earlier. It was now assessed to have increased and she was somewhat sensitive about it; she would not admit this difficulty to any of her teachers. One teacher reported that although Natalie was extremely bright, she "shrinks from opportunities for leadership." During these years, school records are, however, generally positive. Natalie was described as well liked, as having many friends, and as belonging to many clubs. At this time, Natalie wanted to be a dancer; however, this vocational choice was discouraged by her parents. For Natalie, this was quite painful and became a dream never realized.

She finished high school and went on to college for three years but did not graduate. At the age of twenty-five, having been, in her own words, "an unsuccessful secretary," her "ultimate goal [was to] be a successful homemaker." She married and in the next two years lived in five different cities due to frequent moves related to her husband's employment. Understandably, she wrote that "it is hard to develop interests in any one place and then have to leave them." She hoped to settle down. She became pregnant almost immediately after getting married. Natalie's life revolved around her husband, seeing her husband as having a profound influence on her life. The frequent moves, however, became seen, especially in the later years of the marriage, as an irritating factor. Her own aspirations were neglected. She wrote: "I feel that I haven't made the most of my opportunities."

There are a number of other letters about her relationships over the years. Here are a few excerpts:

> My marriage is my career. Being a housewife and a mother, . . . but I married because I wasn't a success in my career . . . and all my friends were getting married — I'm not a good housekeeper, but I genuinely like homemaking — cooking, sewing, etc., and I would rather do it than anything else I know of.

> Neither my husband and I were prepared for marriage. Just being married, moving around and taking care of my little girls have been as much as I can do.

Nevertheless, in the same letter she adds that her husband and she are "quite compatible."

Natalie's twenties were marked by irritability. She herself often remarked about her constant irritability. She wrote, "I let small things upset me," and elsewhere, "fatigue is my biggest problem."

There is a gap in the records for five years. By age 30 she had two children and reported a "great tendency to worry and extreme nervousness." Her marriage was not peaceful. Her husband was drinking rather heavily. In her letters, there are frequent remarks like "my husband drinks" and "after being very drunk." There was a dramatic change in her own physical and psychological state. She reported that she was "too tired even to wash the windows."

Her irritability became quite painful in her thirties. She wrote: "great tendency to worry and extreme nervousness." She describes herself as "chronically worn out and tired." She was well aware that there was no physical basis for her symptoms, recognizing "that I had neurotic tendencies." Often the pain was overpowering (unbearable?). She longed for relief, a solution. She wrote, "in my heart I've never doubted that I can be a happy, relaxed, useful human being." The relief never came.

In the later years of her life, it was especially the strain with her husband that was unsatisfying and frustrating. Here is part of a letter she sent her favorite teacher, written when she was about 35:

> Until I was 25 I didn't know there were such things as problems in this world, but since then with the exception of my two lovely children and my perfect relationship with my mother, I've had just one struggle after another, made one blunder after another. My husband and I bicker constantly. I've wanted to divorce him a thousand times and still I know that is not the solution. We were both raised in

broken homes and we both love our children too much. He comes home drunk at night far too often. He can't afford it. He refuses to look at the bills and says "Why haven't you saved money?" I have no one to talk to. I feel like I'm cornered. . . . My mother's youngest brother and my nearest neighbor both committed suicide in one month [about a year before].

Natalie's children were very important to her during these years; yet, even here, there was a strain. Here is a letter regarding her relationship with her children:

Our little ones are nice, but the eldest still bites her fingernails and fights constantly with her younger sister. She is the result of my selfishness. . . . Well, I've poured out my heart and I'm a little ashamed. In my heart I've never doubted that I can be a happy, relaxed, useful human being, but it's taking such a long time to get there.

Her children were, however, a critical attachment; she worried about them in her marriage. Often she was critical of herself as a mother. For example, she wrote: "A successful woman has happy, well-adjusted children."

When Natalie was 39, she and her husband separated because of "his violent temper, his selfishness and his drinking." Yet, the separation was like their marriage, painfully ambivalent. Both stayed in the marriage for the children. One month after they separated, they tried a reconciliation, only to separate again. Natalie stated during the reconciliation that she was determined to make her marriage work. In a letter to her teacher, she wrote:

Three months ago I asked my husband for a divorce and told him I definitely didn't love him anymore because of his violent temper, selfishness and drinking. He wouldn't cooperate in giving me an uncontested divorce. He was going to try to disprove my points and ask for partial custody of the children. I was awarded $300 a month to support the children. After three months of being alone I began to realize something that is so obvious it seems ridiculous. In spite of everything—he was the father of my children, a good Daddy, and I needed him desperately—I had always felt that I was a little better than he and that with my own small properties I'd be much better off without him. This wrong attitude of mine undoubtedly caused a lot of the temper, etc. My step-father, who had little use for my husband was living with us the year before our separation and I was constantly in a stew to keep them both happy. But my loyalty should go to my husband. I'm not saying our problems are solved—but two people fighting against instead of for one another can never be successful.

It would appear that her life with her husband was in many ways a recapitulation of her attachment to her father, strikingly ambivalent and painful.

Nine months after the above letter she was divorced. Four months after the divorce was final (and her ex-husband had already remarried), she was dead. At the end, Natalie was frantic to achieve a satisfying relationship, "the feeling of childhood love." This love was expressed in one of her suicide notes to her stepfather: "You're so good Papa dear." But to her own father there was no note. Shneidman (1980) summarized the relationships thus:

In her suicide she reenacted her own earlier life drama—the yearning for her parents to be together—and in this misdirected symbolic sacrifice, instead of giving her children a (seemingly) united home, she, in the most traumatic way possible, deprived them of their own mother. Her aspirations—to be her father's favorite, to be accepted and not abandoned, to care for and not reject her own children (as she had been rejected and not cared for), to be symbolically reunited with her father in a happy home, to sacrifice herself so that some of the problems of her children might be solved—were no better realized in her death than they were in her life. [p. 66]

To return to the event, two weeks before her death Natalie's father reported (see above) that Natalie had told him that she was going to kill herself. He reported that it was because the divorce, the loss of her husband, was so painful. Although this is likely true, I wonder what occurred at that moment. I suspect that it was critical. It was a *moving toward* event. Was it one more painful rejection? A loss? Was it one more event that tapped the pain in her unconscious? What happened to Natalie at a conscious level? Unconscious? Regrettably we will be left somewhat in darkness.

To analyze the latent meaning of Natalie's suicide, let me now return to one of Natalie's notes. Table 9-2 presents a note scored by Foulkes' system. From the analysis we learn that Natalie was deeply attached to her father. The distortions in her notes relate to him. Natalie was aware of some vital aspects of her act, as her notes show, but not all. The original attachment had likely aroused unbearable pain. The pain could not be expressed. A driving force, I believe, behind Natalie's death was her need for attachment to her father.

Given my focus on interpersonal relations, what is clearly evident from the documents related to Natalie's life is that her relationships were disturbing. She had experienced considerable loss and rejection in her attachments, not only from her ex-husband but also (and deeper) from her father. The identification has, I suspect, many similarities in terms of its development as those of Anna O. and Dora. In a letter about her troubled life, Natalie said this about her father: "I adored my father from afar. Our occasional meetings were unsatisfactory— my father is a very brilliant man—however, he has little use for me—he lives 20 minutes away but has been in our home only once for a few minutes in the past two years." Elsewhere she wrote: "I adored my father from afar. Our occasional meetings were very unpleasant but it was a very shallow relationship." Natalie clearly identifies with her father in these words; she is and wants to be attached to him. Her relationship with her father, as with her ex-husband, was, however, under a constant strain—her wishes, needs, and so forth, were unsatisfied and frustrated.

Natalie's personal documents are filled with overpowering pain. She was frantic. Pitiful forlornness, deprivation, distress, and grief were all evident in her "emotional intoxication." Feelings (and ideas) of vengefulness and aggression toward herself appear to be evident—especially submission. Her note to her husband is manifestly a painful mea culpa. She takes all the blame. She punishes herself. She is passive, fearing aggression and violence. All of the feelings are

TABLE 9-2 AN ILLUSTRATION OF A SUICIDE NOTE SCORED BY FOULKES' SYSTEM

Text	Scoring	Distortion
Bob—I'm making all kinds of mistakes with our girls	Ego (+) moving against (+) children [Ego with (+) children] [Spouse with (+) children]	
They have to have a leader and everyday the job seems more enormous	(−) Ego (−) creating (+) children [(−) Ego creating (+) children ((−) means (+) children]	
You couldn't have been a better Daddy to Nancy and they do love you—	[(+) Spouse with child] Ego (+) moving toward spouse	(+) children to ego
Nancy misses you so and she doesn't know what's the matter	(−) Ego (+) moving toward spouse	Child to ego
I know you've built a whole new life for yourself	Spouse (−) creating (+) ego	Life to ego
but make room for the girls	Spouse moving toward (+) ego	(+) Children to ego
and keep them with you—	[Spouse (+) with (+) children]	
Take them where you go—	[Spouse (−) with (+) children]	
It's only for just a few years—Betty is almost ready to stand on her own two feet—	(−) Ego moving from spouse	Child to ego
But Nancy needs you desperately.	(+) Ego (−) moving toward spouse	Child to ego
Nancy needs help [from you]	Spouse (−) moving toward ego [Spouse (−) moving toward ego (child ((−) means child)]	Child to ego
She really thinks you didn't love her and she's got to be made to do her part for her own self-respect	Spouse (−) moving toward (−) ego	Child to ego
Nancy hasn't been hurt much yet—	Ego (−) moving against child	
but ah! the future if they keep on the way I've been going lately—	Ego (−) moving against child	

(continued)

TABLE 9–2 (*continued*)

Text	Scoring	Distortion
Barbara sounds warm and friendly and relaxed and I pray to God	Ego moving toward father	God to father
she will understand [me] just a little	[(+) peer female (−) with ego]	
and be good to my girls—	Peer female moving toward (−) ego	
	Ego moving toward (+) spouse	(+) Children to ego
	(+) Children moving toward	
They need two happy people—	(+) ego	Peer female to ego
not a sick mixed-up mother—	(+) Children (−) moving toward (−) ego	
	[Money (+, −) with extras]	
There will be a little money to help with the extras	[Money with (+) child]	
It had better go that way	[Extras with (+) child]	
than for more pills and more doctor bills.	[Money (−) with (+) pill]	
	[Money (−) with (−) father]	
I wish to God	Ego moving toward father	God to father
It had been different but be happy—but please—stay by your girls—	[Spouse with (+) children]	
And just one thing—be kind to Papa—	Ego moving toward father	Spouse to ego
		Father-in-law to father
He's done everything he could to try to help		Father-in-law to father
me—	Father (+, −) moving toward ego	father
	Father (+) moving toward ego	(+) Children to ego
He loves the girls dearly		
		Father-in-law to father
and it's right		
that they should see him often—	Ego (+) moving toward father	(+) Children to ego
		Father-in-law to father
Natalie		father

expressed overtly in her final letters. It is easy to detect the anger toward her ex-husband and her father. She also exhibited love, concern, and so forth, toward others (her stepfather, her children). Our latent analysis would suggest that a primary attachment—love—was toward her father. She so desperately needed to be loved by him and to love him. Her notes and other documents are marked by ambivalence—love and hate. At the end, Natalie was boxed in, passive, rejected, and especially helpless and hopeless; yet, it is affection, approval, love, and the like that are so central in her notes. She needed to move toward people. For example, she writes, "I pray to God," which, if one accepts the premises in this paper, translates: "I move toward my father." As another example, she writes, "He's done everything he could to try to help me," which means: "My father — albeit both positive and negative — moves toward me." There are a number of expressions in her notes like these. The unbearable pain is, I suspect, associated with unconscious processes of identification with her ex-husband and (at a deeper level) her father.

All this discussion about Natalie's father does not imply that her mother was not an important attachment. I merely wish to emphasize the loss/rejection — the pain — in her moving toward her father. Indeed, love for and from her mother was always central to Natalie's life. Natalie's mother died at age 67. (It is likely that this is why there is no reference to her in Natalie's notes.) Natalie was then 36, a period in her life when her pain began to be increasingly overpowering. She wrote at that time, "I love her more than anyone else on earth." And elsewhere she described her attachment to her mother as "my perfect relationship with my mother." Natalie's attachment to her mother cannot be overstated. She once wrote about her mother: "My mother was overly generous toward me and wanted to make up for my not having a father." One can only wonder what the loss of this "perfect" attachment meant to Natalie both consciously and unconsciously. Remember, Natalie herself died only a few years later at age 39. By way of a suicidological footnote, it is worth remarking that around this time her favorite book was Karl Menninger's *Man Against Himself*.

As can be gleaned from Natalie's notes, Natalie was not only figuratively overcome by her pain but also by her perception and ideas. Her notes are full of permutations and combinations of grief-provoking content (despite the ever-present thrust of ambivalence). She believed that her life was hard, futile. She was preoccupied with ideas such as the following: "I can't face what the future brings." She said that she was "making all kinds of mistakes." She clearly believed, with flawless logic from her perspective, that once she was dead it would be "so much easier" for her children, her ex-husband, herself — everybody. She comes close to stating the following prototypical sentences: "Everyone will be much better off when I'm dead. Everything will be much better when I'm dead." She would sacrifice everything for love.

Natalie's suicide, from my perspective, is much less logical than she believed. Here, for example, is some of Shneidman's (1980) analysis of the content in her notes in relation to cognition:

> Natalie's suicide note to her children is filled with contradictions and inconsistencies. (We remember that when she was tested as a child, the psychologist called her extremely logical.) In the suicide note, the implicit logical arguments flow back and forth, between assertion and counterassertion, never with any resolution. Here are some examples: She says, in effect, you will stay with your father, you should love

your father, I know that you cannot love your father but at least you must respect him. She then almost free-associates to the word "respect" and argues, rather lamely, that love and respect are almost the same anyway, and in case that argument is not persuasive (which it is not), then one should, at least, respect one's self. The logic wanders; yet for Natalie, the logic made sense: It is her argument about *her* father.

Another sad example: She says to her children, You must stand on your own two feet, but she also implies that the point of her removing herself from their lives is so that they can be reunited with their father — as, probably, she unconsciously yearns to be reunited with her father.

To tell one's children in a suicide note to remember the happy times certainly has some contradictory element in it, on the very face of it. I love you so much, she says, but the end result of her actions is to make them orphans. She adds, I can't face what the future will bring, but she then takes her life largely because of the haunting, inescapable past. And finally, there is her statement, "I'm getting you all mixed up," which obviously betokens the confusion not in their minds but in her own. [pp. 66–67]

One wonders about what the unconscious is expressing here.

One can conclude that Natalie was emotionally perturbed; but it would not be accurate, based on her personal documents, to call her weak or not adequately developed. Natalie's history, however, does attest to the fact that she had difficulties developing constructive and loving attachments. She had suffered defeat which, at the time of her death, she felt she could not overcome. The active withdrawal by key significant others — notably, at an unconscious level, the desertion of her father, but likely as well the death of her mother — plunged Natalie into despair, grief, hopelessness, and helplessness. She was not able to go on; she described herself as "a sick mixed-up mother." Indeed, her notes suggest that she was figuratively "drugged" by overpowering emotions and constricted perceptions. Her history was full of these "mixed-up" states, which one of her doctors described as "neurotic tendencies." From Freud's perspective these symptoms had developed out of childhood experiences. Life, in fact, she said, "seems so enormous."

In her mid-thirties, a medical doctor had noted that Natalie was on "the verge of a nervous breakdown." She went to see a therapist. About this treatment, she wrote, "my tension symptoms are so chronic and severe that they must have their origin in my childhood." Regrettably, the therapist's notes are unavailable. Did Natalie gain some insight into the rejection by her father? The attachment to her mother? Her husband failed to support her in her treatment, seeing Natalie's problem as exaggerated and therapy as "plain silly."

She was often strikingly ambivalent about treatment. In one occasion, she wrote: "I feel now that a psychologist is the last thing in the world I need to see. Now I am just capable of furnishing (earning) part of our monthly needs and being a wise mother to my girls." She saw herself as hopeless and helpless, not knowing "the rudiments of daily living." Life was painful, "the slightest response is a strain."

We know from the police report that at the time of her death Natalie was seeing a psychologist three times a week. One can conclude that at some time her pain in her conscious *and* unconscious mind became *unbearable*. Suicide became the only solution.

In the end, Natalie appeared to have been so preoccupied with her trauma that she was unaware of how to adjust and she chose cessation. We would here follow Shneidman's belief that each individual tends to die as he or she has lived, especially as he or she has previously reacted in periods of threat, stress, failure, challenge, shock, and loss. Her history, as shown through the looking glass of personal documents, was so important in her conscious choice of death. Yet, it is likely that her unconscious dynamics — to be loved, to love — were the major determinants of her suicide. In many ways, Natalie's case is paradigmatic. Suicide is complex, more complicated than the suicidal person's conscious mind had been aware. Deep is the pain. Love even deeper than aggression.

REFERENCES

Carnap, R. (1959). Psychology in physical language. In *Logical Positivism,* ed. A. Ayer, trans. G. Shick, pp. 165–198. New York: Free Press, 1931.

Eagle, M. (1987). Revisioning the unconscious. *Canadian Psychology* 28:113–116.

Ellenberger, H. (1970). *The Discovery of the Unconscious.* New York: Basic Books

Fenichel, O. (1954). *The Psychoanalytic Theory of Neurosis.* New York: W. W. Norton.

Foulkes, D. (1978). *A Grammar of Dreams.* New York: Basic Books.

Freud, S. (1901). The psychopathology of everyday life. *Standard Edition* 6:1–310, 1974.

_____ (1915). The unconscious. *Standard Edition* 14:159–215, 1974.

_____ (1916). Dreams. *Standard Edition* 15:83–228, 1974.

_____ (1917). General theory of neurosis. *Standard Edition* 16:243–483, 1974.

_____ (1920). A case of homosexuality in a woman. *Standard Edition* 18:147–172, 1974.

_____ (1921). Group psychology and the analysis of the ego. *Standard Edition* 18:67–147, 1974.

Heidbreder, E. (1933). *Seven Psychologies.* New York: Century.

Horney, K. (1950). *Neurosis and Human Growth.* New York: W. W. Norton.

Jacobs, D., and Brown, H. (1989). *Suicide: Understanding and Responding.* Madison, CT: International Universities Press.

Jones, E. (1953–1957). *The Life and Work of Sigmund Freud.* New York: Basic Books.

Kerlinger, F. N. (1964). *Foundations of Behavioral Research.* New York: Holt, Rinehart and Winston.

Leenaars, A. (1979). A study of the manifest content of suicide notes from three different theoretical perspectives: L. Binswanger, S. Freud, and G. Kelly. Unpublished Ph.D. dissertation. Windsor, Canada.

_____ (1985). Freud's and Shneidman's formulations of suicide investigated through suicide notes. *Suicide Notes and Other Personal Documents in Psychological Science.* Symposium conducted at the meeting of the American Psychological Association, Los Angeles, CA.

_____ (1986). A brief note on the latent content in suicide notes. *Psychological Reports* 59:640–642.

_____ (1987). An empirical investigation of Shneidman's formulations regarding suicide: age and sex. *Suicide and Life-Threatening Behavior* 17:233–250.

_____ (1988a). *Suicide Notes.* New York: Human Sciences.

_____ (1988b). Are women's suicides really different from men's? *Women and Health* 18:17–33.

_____ (1988c). The suicide notes of women. In *Why Women Kill Themselves,* ed. D. Lester. Springfield, IL: Charles C Thomas.

——— (1988d). A thematic guide to suicide prediction: a proposal. Paper presented at the American Association of Suicidology Conference, Washington, DC, April.

——— (1989a). Suicide across the adult life span: an archival study. *Crisis* 10:132–151.

——— (1989b). Are young adults' suicides psychologically different from those of other adults? *Suicide and Life-Threatening Behavior* 19:249–263.

——— (1990). Do the psychological characteristics of the suicidal individual make a difference in the method chosen for suicide? *Canadian Journal of Behavioural Science* 22:385–392.

Leenaars, A., and Balance, W. (1981). A predictive approach to the study of manifest content in suicide notes. *Journal of Clinical Psychology* 37:50–52.

——— (1984a). A logical empirical approach to the study of the manifest content in suicide notes. *Canadian Journal of Behavioural Science* 16:248–256.

——— (1984b). A predictive approach to Freud's formulations regarding suicide. *Suicide and Life-Threatening Behavior* 14:275–283.

——— (1984c). A predictive approach to suicide notes of young and old people from Freud's formulations regarding suicide. *Journal of Clinical Psychology* 40:1362–1364.

Leenaars, A., Balance, W., Wenckstern, S., and Rudzinski, D. (1985). An empirical investigation of Shneidman's formulations regarding suicide. *Suicide and Life-Threatening Behavior* 15:184–195.

Leenaars, A., and McLister, B. (1989). An empirical investigation of the latent content in suicide notes. Paper presented at Amarical Association of Suicidology Conference, San Diego, CA, April.

Litman, R. (1967). Sigmund Freud on suicide. In *Essays in Self-Destruction,* ed. E. Shneidman, pp. 324–344. New York: Jason Aronson.

Maris, R. (1981). *Pathways to Suicide.* Baltimore, MD: Johns Hopkins Press.

McLister, B. (1985). *Content Analysis of Genuine and Simulated Suicide Notes Using Foulkes' Scoring System of Latent Structure.* Unpublished Ph. D. dissertation. Windsor, Canada.

McLister, B., and Leenaars, A., (1988). An empirical investigation of the latent content of suicide notes. *Psychological Reports* 63:238.

Shneidman, E. S. (1980). *Voices of Death.* New York: Harper & Row.

——— (1981). *Suicide Thoughts and Reflections: 1960–1980.* New York: Human Sciences.

——— (1985). *Definition of Suicide.* New York: Wiley.

Shneidman, E. S., and Farberow, N., eds. (1957). *Clues to Suicide.* New York: McGraw-Hill.

Zilboorg, G. (1936). Suicide among civilized and primitive races. *American Journal of Psychiatry* 92:1347–1369.

10: CONFUSIONS OF THE BODY, THE SELF, AND OTHERS IN SUICIDAL STATES

John T. Maltsberger

Continuing experience with suicidal patients across the diagnostic spectrum challenges the clinician's synthetic curiosity. What have these patients in common? Suicide, protean in form, one of the greatest challenges in psychiatry, has its commonalities. Shneidman (1985) has led the way in the search for interconnecting ties. I have observed that in case after case suicidal people do not trust their bodies, do not like them, and do not feel at home in them.

Wishing to show how this is true I have prepared this chapter. Because the range of body–self disturbances is broad and I wish to survey them before examining as precisely as I can what disturbances in the self-representation are found in suicide, the reader may find me discursive. I offer it nevertheless in the hope that others may find what I have written helpful in suicide-risk assessment, and that empirical researchers may be stimulated by it. In the nexi and interstices of this text I hope they may find opportunities for further investigation.

Suicidal patients are restless tenants of their bodies. Most of us are so much at home in our own flesh that the integration of mind and body into the self is never questioned. The more introspective among us may sometimes briefly puzzle about what is the essential self, and what is ancillary. Whether the body is of the self's essence has been discussed by philosophers before Plato and since. Children, conceiving their feces to be part of themselves, may be terrified at the prospect of parting with them. Primitive people, feeling there is something of the self's essence in a snippet of hair or a fingernail paring, fear that such disjecta may fall into the hands of an enemy. In the minds of some primitives, to be photographed is to surrender the soul to the photographer, a magician who imprisons it in film.

What are the boundaries of the self? Most of us include our bodies in the images of ourselves, defining self as skin and what is within it. Others extend their boundaries to include clothing or adornments, and various extensions of space outside the skin. Many patients who suffer from borderline personality disorders seem unsure of where self leaves off and others begin, injuring their skin to make sure, as though visual perception of their physical bounds was not enough, and physical pain at the boundary itself was necessary for sure definition. Others stare restlessly into the mirror to see whether their bodies cohere (Elkisch 1957). Jung (1931) believed that for most, the body is a place of safety in which we feel secure from the outside world. For many suicidal patients, however, the body is no such haven. It may be experienced as a prison house in which one is helplessly confined, escape from which is passionately desired. It may be experienced as a crowded tenement where others press in. It may be experienced as a frightening place swarming with vermin, or an alien chamber into which evil spirits or monsters penetrate and crowd out the self. It may be experienced not as a part of the self at all, or, if it is, not experienced as essential self, but as a disposable self-part, escape from which is not lethal, at least to the essential self, which is mental.

THE PANORAMA OF BODY-SELF DISTURBANCES IN SUICIDAL PATIENTS

Many psychopathological phenomena illustrate disturbed relationships between the body and the rest of the self; many of them imply a heightened risk for suicide or suicide attempts when patients can endure their suffering no longer and try to escape the confines of the physical self from which the suffering seems to arise (see Table 10-1).

Hypochondriasis is an example of a comparatively benign disturbance of self and body relatedness. The patient who complains of debilitating aches and pains in the absence of physical pathology is to be found in every consulting room. Sometimes psychoanalytic investigation will show that the organ or organ system of which the hypochondriac patient complains is identified with somebody else, commonly enough with a person who is dead. This is familiar in cases of pathological grief.

Others are preoccupied with imaginary defects in their physical appearance, isolating themselves from others because they are falsely convinced that some bodily idiosyncrasy, minor or imaginary, renders them socially revolting. These patients suffer from body dysmorphic disorder (Phillips 1991); they are often depressed; they may sometimes become psychotic. Freud's "Wolf Man," dysmorphophobic (uneasy and uncomfortable about his body appearance) for many years, developed a late life monomaniacal preoccupation with his nose (Gardiner 1971). Hypochondriasis, body dysmorphic disorder, and somatic delusions of illness are all commonly encountered in patients with major depressive illnesses. They accompany and contribute to suicide.

TABLE 10-1. BODY–SELF DISTURBANCES

Body as Troublesome
  Hypochondriasis
  Dysmorphophobia and body dysmorphic disorder
  Somatic delusions of ailment
Body as Defective
  Unreal
  Empty or hollow
  Missing an essential part
    A viscus
    The penis (Koro)
    The soul (Shlemiel, Dracula)
  Dead (Cotard syndrome)
  Body as impersonated (cf. Capgras syndrome)
Body as Inhabited by Others
  Delusions of infestation (Ekbom syndrome)
  Multiple Personality Disorder
  Possession
  Werewolf delusions
  Delusions and hallucinations of invasion by others
Body as Divisible
  Doubles
  Partial autoscopic phenomena
  Mirror phenomena
Body as Escapable
  Suicide

Sometimes the worry that something may be wrong with one's body may rise to the level of a delusion of illness. This phenomenon is familiar in melancholia; that patients with profound depressions may be convinced that they suffer from cancer, AIDS, or, in former times, syphilis, is a clinical commonplace.

Body dysmorphic disorders, dysmorphophobia, hypochondriasis, and somatic delusions all imply disturbances in the body scheme. Psychoanalytic study of many of these patients suggests that destructive, hostile impulses disavowed by the patient may be split off and assigned to a part of the body, or to the body in general, which has become unconsciously identified with another person (Asch 1966, Freud 1915, Rosenfeld, D. 1984, Rosenfeld, H. 1965).

Fears or convictions of illness, deformity, or ugliness are the first level of uneasy relationships between the body and the self. There are other ways in which patients may believe something is seriously wrong with themselves physically. Those suffering from borderline personality disorders, for instance, often tell us that they feel unreal. Close examination usually shows that the feeling of unreality refers not so much to the patient's total self, but to the body.

Others tell us they feel empty. Emptiness complaints are almost always referred to the bodily self, and most of the time, the patients who say such things are speaking metaphorically. This is not always the case, however; questioning sometimes shows a patient is convinced a viscus is missing. Others will confidently assert that somewhere in the trunk or abdomen there lies an actual empty hole from which emanates the most painful affects. Like their hypochondriacal brothers and sisters, these patients suffer from body–self disturbances. They cannot muster a subjective sense of personal cohesion (Lichtenberg 1975). The incapacity to maintain a consistent sense of self-cohesion over extended periods is likely to give rise to the complaint of emptiness, a kind of suffering closely akin to the sense of nothingness, or aloneness. Some theorists attribute this disturbance to the failure of the developing child to form adequate good introjects, which afford the possibility of self-soothing (Adler and Buie 1979). Others attribute it to the defensive denial of the introjected bad mother. The intolerable fear of emptiness and aloneness arises from the "uncontrolled, unencapsulated, freed, bad and empty object starving, like the self, within," according to Singer (1977, p. 478). This formulation suggests that the destructive introject is experienced physically and is localized in the mental representation of the patient's body. Painful affects of this kind can precipitate suicide (Maltsberger 1986).

Though I am unaware of any psychodynamic studies to prove the point, it seems likely that similar self-object confusions may lie at the root of Koro. In Koro, a syndrome occurring primarily in South China, men sometimes develop the conviction that the penis is retracting into the abdomen and is about to disappear. Chinese folklore holds that the genitalia of both men and women are influenced by both the Yin (masculine) and Yang (feminine) principles. When the masculine principle is too much depleted and the feminine dominates, Koro occurs, they say. In Western terms, destabilization of self-regard in males can often be related to unstable paternal-masculine identification and ambivalent maternal introjections, from which hostile attitudes toward the body-self arise. Koro-like clinical phenomena have been described in Westerners, including depersonalization of the genitalia (Rubin 1982).

Other convictions of body–self deprivations appear in folklore. The character Shlemiel from E.T.A. Hoffman's *Tales* sells his soul and because of this loses his reflection in the mirror. Folklore tells us that vampires, the living dead, have no mirror reflection. We meet this clinically—patients who see their doubles always report that the double casts no shadow (Damas-Mora et al. 1980). In Cotard's syndrome the patient's nihilistic delusions sometimes take the form that the body is dead (Cotard 1882).

One patient in my experience suffered from a transient paranoid illusion about her body. The patient's basic difficulty was borderline personality disorder, and, like most with this diagnosis, she was plagued with feelings of depersonalization and derealization, to relieve which she repeatedly lacerated her arms. The following exchange (which I was fortunate enough to record verbatim) took place between us as I tried to understand why she cut herself.

> When you cut yourself . . . is it a feeling you have that it is really you, yourself?
>
> It doesn't hurt . . . I mean, I can feel that it is sort of attached; it doesn't always feel like it is mine.
>
> Does it ever feel like it could be somebody else?
>
> Not like it is the person there, but it doesn't feel like it's mine. Sometimes it even looks like it is mine, but it doesn't—it's almost like a good copy, but it's not quite the same. You know, it is different.
>
> Not really you?
>
> Yeah, it's like somebody pretending to be you. It doesn't quite feel right, it isn't right, it is just slightly off. It is almost like a negative that just— that is just slightly off. And I know it.
>
> And who would the somebody be?
>
> I don't know.
>
> You couldn't name the person. If I count to three?
>
> . . . I don't imagine it as anybody, like, that I know. You know, I don't think it is my mother . . . I never thought that. But I think somebody is trying to play tricks on me.
>
> So you show them? You stop the trick? [It's as though you say,] "I'm on to you and I'll attack you"?
>
> Yeah. . . . It feels swollen somehow, numb. . . . That's why it doesn't feel like it is really mine because it has a strange kind of feeling when I touch it. Like it is an imitation arm. And even when I bleed it doesn't even hurt. It is interesting . . . it is interesting. It is actually very, very interesting. . . . I feel the warm blood. That always feels kind of nice. It is just interesting.

The detached, alienated attitude toward the body-self, so striking in this patient's description of the "imitation body," is reflected in much of the work of the brilliant, morbid poet, Sylvia Plath. In "Cut," a poem inspired by the slicing off of the tip of her thumb, she describes the thumb impersonally, as somebody else, namely, a pilgrim scalped by Indians (Plath 1961).

In Capgras's syndrome (Enoch et al. 1967), the patient suffers from the delusion that imposters have been substituted for those whom the patient knows; although the imposters look identical, or nearly identical, to the originals, the patient "knows" they are not the same, but doubles. The patient just described had no illusions that others around her were doubles, or imposters, but she plainly believed that her body was. On this basis in attacking her arm she attacked not herself, but a double. But because her mental self was contained within the physical shell of the double, her experience differed somewhat from that of those who attack ordinary doubles. Ordinary doubles, as we shall see, are experienced as bodily duplicates outside the boundaries of the physical self.

Another class of patients experience their bodies as inhabited or invaded by others. Fantasies and delusions of infestation are clinically very common. A 30-year-old schoolteacher in the grips of a bipolar illness of the mixed type, asked to describe to me the nature of the mental pain that had driven her to attempt to escape the locked ward in which she was confined, in order to shoot herself, said that she felt helplessly paralyzed while a thousand worms crawled through her abdomen biting and chewing. Another patient complained that an ape had got into her uterus and was crouched inside her eating away at her vitals. Delusions of infestation of this sort are sometimes referred to as Ekbom's syndrome (Ekbom 1938, Hopkinson 1970).

In multiple personality disorder the body-self seems to be inhabited not by one mental self but by a variety of mental selves. Sometimes two or more of the multiple personalities are bitter enemies, and attacks on the common body occur as one strikes out against the other, who seems to be closer to the bodily self. Indeed, suicide and suicide attempts are very common in this group of patients. There may be personalities in the multiple complex who seem especially closely associated with the bodily self, inasmuch as their role is to protect the body from injury, sometimes protecting it from the onslaughts of the others (Putnam 1989). Three out of four patients with this diagnosis are believed to have made at least one serious suicide attempt (Putnam et al. 1986).

The literature on demonic possession is extensive, but the basic phenomenon involves the seizure of the subject's body-self by some seemingly alien force, perhaps a malignant spiritual entity, or, in contemporary cinema, by an invader from interstellar space. The mental self of the host is suppressed in these circumstances and cannot return until the invader is cast out, by priestly intervention, or some other agency from outside the self. Freud understood such states as arising from the splitting off of bad or reprehensible wishes from the conscious self, their repression, and their reemergence into consciousness where they are experienced as alien (Freud 1923b).

Closely related to states of possession are those cases in which the patient believes he is transformed into an animal or monster and either behaves accordingly or fears he may. (Keck et al. 1988, Surawitz and Banta 1975). A patient in my experience had suffered bitterly at the hands of his violent, sadistic father, a victim of Huntington's chorea. He hated his father bitterly. When the patient himself developed early signs of Huntington's chorea in middle life, he was horrified that he would become a brute like his father, became delusionally convinced that he was turning into a werewolf, and became acutely suicidal. In this case the werewolf delusion clearly arose from an identification with the hated father, centered on the patient's body as the expected source of violent impulses and vicious behavior. In destroying his body he wanted to destroy the violent father who threatened to reappear in it and take it over.

Some patients suffer from bizarre complex auditory and visual hallucinations in which their bodies become confused with those of others (Havens 1962). The following case is that of a 39-year-old Australian who shot himself to get rid of a hallucinated second head, but survived to describe his experience. He was quite clear that the second head was not vividly fantasied. He perceived it visually. He also could hear it talking to him in insulting ways.

> He described a second head on his shoulder. He believed that the head belonged to his wife's gynaecologist, and described previously having felt that his wife was having an affair with this gynaecologist, prior to her death. He described being able to see the second head when he went to bed at night, and stated that it had been trying to dominate his normal head. . . . "The other head kept trying to dominate my normal head; I would not let it. It kept trying to say to me I would lose, and I said bull-shit. 'I am the king pin here,' it said and it kept going on like that for about three weeks and finally I got jack of it, and I decided to shoot my other head off."
>
> He stated that he fired six shots, the first at the second head, which he then decided was hanging by a thread, and then another one through the roof his mouth. He then fired four more shots. . . . He said that he felt good at that stage, and that the other head was not felt any more. Then he passed out. Prior to shooting himself, he had considered using an axe to remove the phantom head. [Ames 1984, p. 193]

Up to this point the discussion of self-body boundaries has presumed fragile but more or less preserved integrity of a single coherent body self. Let us now turn our attention to another group of phenomena that imply body splits: autoscopic phenomena. The phenomenon of the double occurs in suicide. Some patients report that the self is experienced as either partially or completely dimorphic. All patients who report derealization or depersonalization experiences should be asked about this. It is not at all uncommon to learn that they experience themselves hovering outside their bodies, usually slightly above them, looking down at themselves. Some of them will hallucinate their double.

The splitting of the self as a psychopathological phenomenon had of course been recognized by ancient writers and is implicit in the older literature concerning possession, double personalities, and the like. Scientific description and study of splitting phenomena (especially fugues and depersonalization) was an extensive French enterprise in the nineteenth century; Freud was introduced to them as a student of Charcot and Janet in Paris (Charcot 1889, Ellenberger 1970, Janet 1889). What he learned there led to the development of psychoanalysis and seminated his theory of the unconscious. Body-self splitting had captured the popular imagination under the influence of Anton Mesmer, and inspired more than one of Poe's stories (Poe 1839, 1845).

In one of them, "William Wilson," we read of a double who persecutes the protagonist past all endurance. When Wilson can endure it no more he engages his double in a duel, stabs him with his sword, and then turns to a large mirror nearby to discover that he has mortally wounded himself as well. As he dies, he hears the voice of the double declare, "You have conquered, and I yield. Yet, henceforward art thou also dead . . . and, in my death, see by this image, which is thine own, how utterly thou hast murdered thyself" (Poe 1839, pp. 356–357). This tale recapitulates many legends and stories in which the appearance of a double foretells the imminent death of the person to whom it appears. The phenomenon is even a part of the English language. Though the etymology of the word *fetch* is uncertain, it is probably Old English and derives from the north of England and Ireland. It signifies a wraith or apparition in the form of a double of a living person, the appearance of which is a harbinger of that person's death.

Doubles are not phenomena of folklore and literature only, but have been fully described in the psychopathological literature. Doubling occurs in suicide (Lukianowicz 1958, Todd and Dewhurst 1963). Characteristically the double will appear suddenly and without warning, although sometimes there is a preliminary sense of a "presence," usually behind the patient, before it appears. It is usually situated in the visual space in front of the patient, just beyond arm's reach or farther away. The double often seems to imitate the patient's movements and facial expressions, though occasionally it may only stare. Most often it fades away and disappears if the patient tries to touch it. It is most often gray or misty, semi-transparent, or jellylike. Though sometimes the double may seem to be solid, it does not cast a shadow. When confronted with the double, patients are likely to feel that their real bodies are cold, unreal, and automatic, whereas the double seems the more alive and real. The experience is accompanied by anxiety, discomfort, and sadness. Some patients say the double feels sad, cold, or weary. Sometimes it seems critical and hostile, and sometimes it seems to be in agony (Damas-Mora 1980, Todd and Dewhurst 1963).

Todd and Dewhurst (1955) discuss the phenomenon of doubling as the result of splitting of the body image with projection of the split-off portion in the form of a visual hallucination. Though the body image may be completely divided with projection of all its components, sometimes only one component, or less than all, will be projected. Sometimes only a face or an arm will be seen. Sometimes the double is silent, but it may also speak in the patient's own voice, so that auditory hallucination is a part of the process. Lukianowicz (1958) has reviewed the panorama of autoscopic phenomena in psychiatry.

Phenomena of the mirror are closely related to autoscopic experiences of the double. Freud described a personal experience of a transient illusion of his double which is a common experience in normal people. Catching sight of his reflection in the mirror on the back of a door in a railway compartment, Freud at first thought he was seeing a rather unpleasant old man fumbling his way into the wrong place by mistake. Only after a moment did he realize he was looking at his own reflection (Freud 1919).

Virginia Woolf, another victim of suicide, did not like to look at her reflection in the mirror. To look gave rise to feelings of shame. In an autobiographical note she relates her dysmorphophobia to sexual abuse at the hands of her half-brother, Gerald Duckworth, and recounts the following experience:

> Let me add a dream; for it may refer to the incident of the looking-glass. I dreamt that I was looking in a glass when a horrible face — the face of an animal — suddenly showed over my shoulder. I cannot be sure if this was a dream, or if it happened. Was I looking in the glass one day when something in the background moved, and

seemed to me alive? I cannot be sure. But I have always remembered the other face in the glass, whether it was a dream or a fact, and that it frightened me. [Woolf 1976, p. 69]

BODY IMAGE DISTURBANCES AND SELF-FRAGMENTATION

The destabilization of Virginia Woolf's body image implied in her memory of the beast in the mirror may remind us how frequently patients who suffer from borderline personality disorders report sexual and physical abuse in childhood. These patients report sexual abuse as often as 71 percent of the time according to some authors; physical abuse other than sexual is found in 42 percent. A control group of depressed patients reported sexual abuse in 22 percent, physical abuse in 33 percent (Ogata et al. 1990). Others confirm these reports of a very high incidence of abuse (Gunderson 1990). Stone, like many others, concludes that sexual abuse is a powerful causative factor in borderline disorder. Refining his conclusion, he comments: "It is probably nearer the truth to say that incest and severe parental abuse alter the recipient's nervous system to become less capable of modulation and more prone to immediate uncontrolled responses . . ." (Stone 1990, p. 145). Patients suffering from multiple personality disorder, a group closely akin to borderline personality disorder, and frequently co-morbid for it, give equivalently common reports of abusive treatment in childhood (Putnam 1989).

That these patients are very disturbed in their body attitudes is well known, as the foregoing discussion implies. But the nature of the body–self difficulties they experience has only been studied in a superficial way. It is not unreasonable to assume that the abuse these patients suffer in the course of development interferes with the development and integration of a stable body image, and that it is a causative factor in the kinds of splitting and body distortion that I believe contribute to suicide (Stolorow 1975). Indeed, Stone (1990) reports that borderline patients abused in childhood are more likely to suicide than those not abused. It is not out of the question that the impulsiveness borderline patients exhibit is the consequence of the disturbed body self, but I am not aware of any empirical studies that would prove or disprove this hypothesis.

An important current in psychoanalytic thought, one that seems to be gathering increased force with the passing of time, is the development of the theory of the mental representation of the body and its integration with the rest of the self. Since Freud much effort has been expended in the elaboration of such terms as self, self-image, self-imago, body-self, body image, body schema, and self-representation. The development of this line of thought cannot be reviewed here, but some important contributions merit notice.

Shortly before Freud (1915) noticed that it was possible for the ego to treat itself as an object and developed the implications of that observation for melancholia, and, by implication, suicide, Head and Holmes (1911–1912) pointed out that there existed in the mind what they called a *body image* (body-scheme, *image de soi*), a plastic model of the bodily self built up from perpetually changing alterations of perceptual change, especially perceptions of the body's position in space and perceptions of movement (proprioception and proprioceptive change). In France, Lhermitte took up the idea and expanded it to include in the term body-image many more aspects of the physical self than simply postural ones. It was he who first suggested that the body image is very gradually built up during infancy by the interaction and integration of a variety of childhood experiences, including painful stimuli, visual impressions, play, and "libidinous factors." He asserted that some years pass before the body-image stabilizes into what might be called an adult pattern (Critchley 1950).

Paul Schilder psychologized the body-image, discussing it in *The Image and Appearance of the Human Body* (1950) not only in terms of neurological-postural terms, but also in terms of libido theory, unconscious forces, and in terms of ego defense. In many respects his work foreshadowed this discussion inasmuch as he directed attention to disturbances of body image in schizophrenic and other patients with sadomasochistic attitudes, specifically offering the opinion that feelings of body disintegration reflect the turning of hostility against the self. (Fisher 1990).

Since Schilder's work Kohut (1971) has elaborated a self-psychology that has stimulated the development of new themes in psychoanalysis and psychotherapy in general, but has particularly invited the clarification of such terms as *self* and *ego*. Before Kohut's work appeared Hartmann (1950) had pointed out the ambiguities in Freud's use of the word *ego*. Originally Freud used the term to refer to the totality of the mental self in a plastic, loosely defined way. With the passing of time he more often used it to refer to a specific agency, or group of agencies, of the mind. After 1923 he was much more inclined to restrict the term to denote a mental system of the mind, part of the familiar tripartite mental machinery of ego, superego, and id.

The reader will permit me some definitions at this juncture so that the terminological murk which surrounds such terms as *body-image* (it has been used in many differing and confusing ways) can be avoided.

By *self* I denote the whole person of an individual, including the body and body parts, as well as the psychic organization and its parts (Hartmann 1950). The term *ego* is used to refer to a system of the mental apparatus concerned with such mental mechanisms as perception, memory, the mechanisms of defense, reality testing, and the maintenance of a coherent mental sense of the self, including the bodily self. The ego is also the seat of consciousness and what has been called the *representational world*.

The representational world is the arena within the mind wherein representations of the self and other people (objects) move and interact. Sandler and Rosenblatt (1962) compare it to a stage-set in a theater. "The characters on the stage represent the . . . various objects, as well as the [subject] himself. . . . The theater, which contains the stage, would correspond to aspects of the ego, and various functions such as scene shifting, raising or lowering the curtain, and all the machinery auxiliary to the actual stage production would correspond to those ego functions of which we are not normally aware. . . . The characters on this stage correspond, in this model, to self- and object-representations" (p. 134).

Hartmann (1950) has defined the *self-representation* as the unconscious, preconscious, and conscious endopsychic representations of the bodily and mental self in the system ego. Similarly, an *object-representation* is the unconscious, preconscious, and conscious endopsychic representation of the bodily and mental other in the system ego of the subject.

BODY ALIENATION IN SUICIDAL PATIENTS

Faulty development of the body-representation, or the incapacity to maintain a stable body-representation over time, was attributed to disturbances in the mother–child relationship in the first eighteen months of life, and to traumatization between the ages of 2 and 4, by Greenace (1953). That assertion is congruent with the empirical research that suggests a causal link between the development of borderline personality disorder and childhood abuse discussed above. Putnam (1989) believes that the extreme physical suffering to which so many patients with multiple personality disorder are subjected in childhood is intimately related to their adult self-fragmentation. Sadomasochistic fixations, so common in suicidal patients, are invited by overwhelming suffering in childhood. Child specialists have long appreciated that traumatized children may take indifferent, or even hateful, attitudes toward their bodies, often seeking out injury and suffering (Furman 1984).

The poor integration of the body into a stable self-representation was illustrated by a 43-year-old woman who originally consulted me in a bitterly angry, hopeless suicidal state. Hospital admission was narrowly averted. As her treatment unfolded it emerged that the patient had witnessed her sister's incestuous abuse from the age of 3, and that she herself had been subjected to repeated oral and vaginal incestuous assault from early childhood up to the time of adolescence, when she was strong enough to fight her father off. Memories of the abuse had been repressed at the beginning of the treatment, but were gradually recovered and substantially integrated through an extremely painful psychotherapeutic experience.

> When I think of how he abused me I could tear out my hair, I could rip up the blanket on the bed.
> I notice it is your head, hair — your body you think to attack when you remember. Why not him?
> What's the difference? What does a child of 3 know about anything? My body? It was my body that was doing the hurting, my body that was giving the pain. It was his. I learned to hate it early. That's where the hurting and the fear and the humiliation was. I was trapped by him and my body was his cage.

The same patient's disturbed self-representation is evident in a dream in which she murders her double. She reported that as she stepped through a doorway into a house another woman who was also herself raised a pistol, pointed it at her, and, grasping it with both hands, fired it at her. Her body flew into pieces.

The dream plainly demonstrates that the patient is able to treat herself as though she were another person. Her body-self appears here as split, emerging in the representational world both as self-representation and object-representation. The same confusion between self- and object-representations were clear in the suicidal fantasy she reported a few sessions after the dream.

The patient said she wanted to throw herself over a railroad bridge and die by smashing on top of a car pulled by a bullet-shaped locomotive rushing west. Her associations to this fantasy were that the bullet locomotive was her father's penis and that the train was the rest of his body. Its westerly direction was significant because the city in which the incest had taken place lay to the west of the patient's home. She said in some way the fantasy expressed the wish to send her body smashing into her father's corpse (he had died some years previously). The fantasy would seem to express the wish to rid herself of her hated body, which in her mind was the source of the pain her father inflicted, and which was part of him. She wanted to merge it with him as symbolized by the retreating train.

SELF-OBJECT CONFUSION IN THE LIGHT OF "MOURNING AND MELANCHOLIA"

It was in "Mourning and Melancholia" that Freud spelled out the idea that hatred for another turning in against the self produced depression. This idea dominated psychoanalytic thinking about suicide for many years. Hate turned against the self remains central to our understanding of suicide, and Freud's concept led Professor Shneidman (1976) to coin the aphorism: "Suicide is murder in the 180th degree."

At the heart of "Mourning and Melancholia" lies the ingenious clinical observation that the bitter complaints that the depressed patient directs against himself really fit somebody else much better:

> If one listens patiently to a melancholiac's many and various self-accusations, one cannot in the end avoid the impression that often the most violent of them are hardly at all applicable to the patient himself, but that with insignificant modifications they do fit someone else, someone whom the patient loves or has loved or should love. Every time one examines the facts this conjecture is confirmed. So we find the key to the clinical picture: we perceive that the self-reproaches are reproaches against a loved object which have been shifted away from it onto the patient's own ego. [p. 248]

"Mourning and Melancholia" was written eight years before Freud developed his tripartite, structural theory of the mind. The id-ego-superego theory had to wait for full exposition until 1923 when *The Ego and the Id* appeared. In the earlier essay Freud made no reference to the superego at all, but referred to "the critical agency of the ego," the conscience, as being involved in melancholia. He said there that in melancholia the ego is split, and that the critical agency takes the rest of the ego *as an object* which it scorns.

Freud's thinking in 1915 was still very much dominated by the libido theory. He wrote that the libido, or sexual energy, invested in the person who had been lost, was withdrawn and directed back into the self, or the ego. Libido invested in another, Freud called object-libido. Libido that had been invested in another, but that was withdrawn and directed back toward the self, he termed the libido of secondary narcissism. In the 1915 theory of melancholia we are told that as the object-libido is drawn back into the self an identification takes place between the ego and the lost object, and that at the same time there is an increase in the narcissistic investment of the ego. Because of the ego split, and because of the increased ego-investment with the libido of secondary narcissism, it becomes possible for the conscience to relate to the remainder of the ego in the way it would relate to somebody else. This is what Freud (1915) meant in the famous sentence, so often quoted: "Thus the shadow of the object fell upon the ego, and the latter could henceforth be judged by a special agency [the conscience] as though it were an object, the forsaken object. In this way an object-loss was transformed into an ego-loss and the conflict between the ego and the loved person into a cleavage between the critical activity of the ego and the ego as altered by identification" (p. 249).

Finally, Freud (1915) said that the ego can kill itself "only if it can treat itself as an object—if it is able to direct against itself the hostility which relates to an object, and which represents the ego's original reaction to objects in the external world" (p. 252).

This rehearsal of central points in "Mourning and Melancholia" is intended to show how Freud lay the groundwork for the contemporary understanding of so much narcissistic psychopathology. We already have here ego-splitting, a consequent instability in the sense of a self as discrete from objects, and difficulties in self-esteem regulation.

Freud's next great theoretical step was the elaboration of the structural theory in 1923, and we find a number of very significant new points in *The Ego and the Id* that bear on our understanding of melancholia. What he called the "critical activity" of the ego is now elevated to a separate system of the mind, the Superego, which itself derives from object relationships that have been abandoned, or at least partially abandoned, in childhood. Before this Freud had emphasized that the ego became identified with a lost object. Now he stresses that the critical function derives from past object-relationships as well.

The other point to emphasize here is Freud's depiction of the ego as dependent on the loving approval of the superego for its survival, much as the small child must depend on the parents to survive. He writes that

the fear of death in melancholia admits of one explanation: that the ego gives itself up because it feels itself hated and persecuted by the super-ego, instead of loved. To the ego, therefore, living means the same as being loved—being loved by the super-ego, which here again appears as the representative of the id. The super-ego fulfils the same function of protecting and saving that was fulfilled in earlier days by the father. . . . But, when the ego finds itself in an excessive real danger which it believes itself unable to overcome by its own strength, it is bound to draw the same conclusion. It sees itself deserted by all protecting forces and lets itself die. [p. 58]

There are certain differences in emphasis between these two versions of the relationship between self and conscience. In the earlier version we have conscience, the critical factor, turning on the self because the self, through identification, has become equated with a lost object. In the later version, we have the superego, derived from an old object-relationship, turning against the self and abandoning it when it is devalued and helpless.

I will now present two case examples, making use of suicide notes, which demonstrate how suicide occurs because the self has become confused with others. The first case is dynamically similar to the suicidal patient discussed before — the woman injured by incest who imagined throwing her body onto the passing train (her father); here the destruction of the bodily self amounted to murdering somebody else. In the second case, suicide occurs because an introjected object, exerting its effect through the patient's super-ego, turns against the self and kills it.

CONFUSIONS OF SELF- AND OBJECT-REPRESENTATIONS IN SUICIDE: THE BODY AS ESCAPABLE

Let us turn to the first case. A 23-year-old psychotic patient committed suicide while in the hospital. She addressed the following note to her psychiatrist who, before reading it, had not been aware that the patient was deluded:

These last few days were a deathlike existence. I am so tired I just want to sleep. My mind, oh, my mind, it's sick. I feel as if I am sinking and I can't call for any help but death. I don't seem to feel as though I want to die. It's like another person telling me what to do. I feel as though my mind isn't connected to my body, and it seems to refer to me as in 'you,' as in, 'Die, you fool, die.' I feel as though there are two of me, and the killer is winning. When my death comes, it won't be suicide. It's that someone has murdered me. While I am writing this letter, it's like the other part is laughing at me and calling me a fool for writing this nonsense, but it's how I feel, I know it must sound confusing to you, but this is the only way I can express myself. I wish I could have told you many of my confused feelings, but I feel as though you won't understand and believe me and then the other part takes over and goes into therapy for me. I want to destroy that part of me, but I cannot seem to separate myself in therapy to do it, while it's trying to kill me, I'll kill myself and take it with me. . . . I took those pills before, it was to kill the other part of me, but I really won't die, I'll just wake up and things will be different. That's how I feel tonight, that I'm not really going to die, and the other one is and I don't know how to explain that to you. I seem to be contradicting myself, but I am writing as I feel. . . . I have used the term Robot to you, it's like someone is hurt up in my head and is using my eyes as windows and controlling me and my actions.

This tormented patient (whose pain was compounded by the added discomfort of not being able to explain her confused inner state) plainly suffered from self-fragmentation and self–object confusion. The suicide note shows us her view of what is transpiring on the stage of her representational world. Because she suffered from a severe narcissistic disturbance she was unable to maintain a cohesive self-representation. Her fragmenting self-representation is confused with an object-representation of a mad robot.

With the help of this suicide note it is possible to infer various components of the self-representation that are in health well integrated into a stable, consistent whole with a positive affective coloring. These would include: 1.) The body-representation, a representation of the subject's own body. 2.) The intellectual representation, a representation of the patient's thinking self. 3.) The feeling-representation, a representation of the patient's own affective-instinctual self. 4.) The representation of the subjective sense of self. (Here is the depiction of oneself as consciously reflecting, feeling, acting, the self as the so-called observing ego, the self of decision making and action. This is the inner picture of the self as "me." For want of a better word I would refer to this section of the self-representation as the myself-executive-representation.) 5.) The judging-self representation. (This part is the representation of the patient's conscience, experienced as the moral sense.)

The suicide note illustrates clearly the failure of the integration of these self-components, and the intrusion into the self-sense of the robotic object-representation. Figure 10–1 is a graphic representation of the state of affairs in this case.

The patient's self-representation is split. On one side of the split is the patient's executive-representation, who seems to be writing the suicide note to her psychiatrist and trying to explain what she observes on her inner stage. Associated with the executive-representation is the representation of the intellectual-self, and also the representation of the affective-instinctual self. On the other side of the split is the patient's body-representation, and her conscience-representation. The conscience-representation here is identified with the robot, presumably arising from an ill-integrated introject of somebody else, and having, therefore, the quality of an object representation.

The executive-self perceives itself to be under attack from an inner persecutor who is attempting to kill it, and in self-defense decides to commit suicide for self-protection. Here we have a psychotic fantasy in which the executive-self plans an attack on the body-self. The body-representation of the patient, because it has become fused with the robot-representation, is not experienced as a part of the self. This suicide, as the patient tells us, is murder in self-defense: she is attempting to murder her insane conscience.

Self as Object

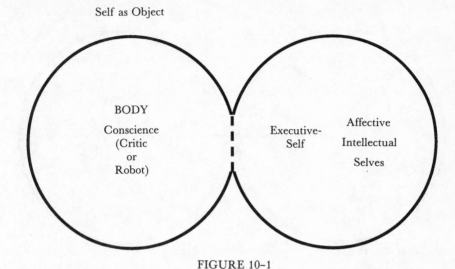

FIGURE 10-1

This case can clarify for us the fact that in seriously depressed patients the so-called "voice of conscience" is not subjectively experienced as very close to the core of the self. We have seen before that such patients may feel invaded by an inner critic who allows no peace of mind. This is in contrast to the subjective experience of ordinary people whose consciences are generally helpful, gently protesting against a fantasied act from time to time, somewhat reproachful for blunders, but basically friendly. In the serious depressions one might say that the conscience-representation is not well integrated with the rest of the self-representation, and that it is comparatively far from the myself-executive portion of the self-representation.

In paranoid cases the conscience-representation is not experienced as a part of the self at all, but is split off and fused with object representations. This is a representational portrayal of projection, and it is part of the phenomenon of persecutory delusions. This constellation is portrayed in Figure 10-2.

Some borderline patients in transient episodes of self-fragmentation will mutilate themselves because of similar fusions of object-representations with split-off body-representations. One of my patients repeatedly lacerated the skin of her abdomen when she was feeling depersonalized. She insisted that she hated her fat belly, even though in fact she was quite thin. In time she realized that the "fat belly" she was slicing was not her own, but her mother's. She did not experience her own abdominal skin as a self-part, but as an object-part. This is a situation similar to the configuration in Figure 10-1.

Strictly speaking, suicides of this type, in which the executive aspect of the self strikes out at a split-off part of the self, typically the body-representation, which has become fused with a menacing object-representation, do not appear to have been specifically foreshadowed in Freud. Closest to it, perhaps, is the

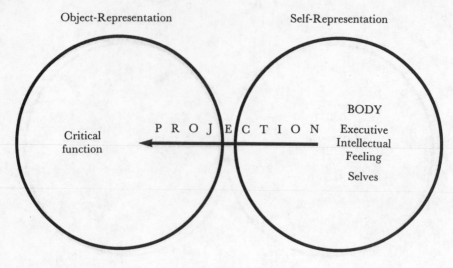

FIGURE 10-2

discussion in "Mourning and Melancholia" that describes an ego-splitting wherein the critical side of the split attacks the other side, which has become identified with an object. But in that schema the attack on the ego-as-object is not an attack in self-defense, because the ego-as-object portion of the split is not experienced as aggressive. It is experienced as bad, and the attack comes from the conscience side of the split.

Let us turn now to the second suicide note. This was written by a 41-year-old unmarried woman lawyer who had striven mightily to live up to her father's rigid perfectionism in every aspect of her life. Both her parents had achieved much. She had a somewhat distant relationship with her mother who was an undemonstrative person; her idealized father was everything. The family was deeply religious, and so was the patient. The father had demanded perfect performance academically, professionally, and socially from his children, and had greeted their failures with rages and sometimes with beatings. As a child the patient was the least rebellious, the most obedient, and the most adoring of her siblings — she had said of her father that he was, in her heart, "next to God." Sometimes when the father would fly into a rage at the patient's younger brothers the patient would offer herself to be punished in their places, and take a whipping.

After completing law school and working for some time in another city, the patient returned home and joined her father's law firm. She had done well in her previous practice, but following the death of a friend she became depressed. Shortly thereafter she was raped, and developed a melancholia which was inadequately treated with medicines. She began to drink excessively. Both her professional difficulties and the drinking enraged her father who did not conceal his scorn. After some months passed the patient committed suicide. Here is her note. It was dictated, and it rambles; the patient was drunk. She left it for her father. I have shortened it considerably and altered a number of details for purposes of confidentiality.

This is Sarah. I have said before that I don't know her anymore. I don't know her anymore. I want to have you forgive me since I can't forgive myself—oh, God, why have you abandoned me? I have prayed every day—miserable. . . . The summer was the toughest. The frights were back. I had pure panic attacks, hopelessness. I relied a lot my doctor. She helped me through the summer. I was OK for a month. And then it was back. I tried, God, I tried. You see, I'm a weak person and I'm tired now. I don't have the strength I used to have and I cannot become dependent. I have used my family too much and I have used my friends too much. Tell Frank Elliott [an older lawyer and a friend of the father who had been the patient's mentor] I'm sorry. He trusted me. He helped me. He was like a father to me. I disappointed him as much as I disappointed you. I have taken care of everything. I'm sorry I could not junk all the things in my house. God has abandoned me. I hope I have the strength to do this one last thing. I have been disapproved since I started practice. At law school I was respected. I don't know, but I wasn't good enough for them. I never was good enough, and so my life was bent on doing. And I could make it. I tried very hard. And then I was attacked. [The patient refers to the rape.]

I was screaming [after he] took hold of me. . . . He said it wasn't even good. I lived with it and for a long time I tried to push it out of my mind. I couldn't dress very well after that. I didn't care. I was dirty and nobody knew and could tell me differently. Oh! I have not been any good at work for a year. No future. So the only way out is for me to die. I left a list of things in my mind on a piece of paper. I loved tennis, I loved music, I loved building, I liked cleaning—I don't know, there are so many things I liked, but they don't have any meaning anymore and I've lost my way and life doesn't have meaning anymore. I calmed the shakes after a while and now they are back and I have no more strength. I used to be very strong but I have no strength. I'm tired. I'm oh so tired. I'm very disappointed with myself. I guess that's the biggest disappointment of all—to be disappointed with yourself. It leaves you nothing. Oh, I've spent a year in tears and it doesn't help. I need a little kindness to myself and I just can't give it. I have wanted to die for a year and now I know it is my destiny.

I don't think you'll ever know how black the world looks. I can't go on as Sarah anymore. She used to be sharp as a tack. I don't know Sarah anymore. I don't know her. I thought I did. I had ideals for her. I wanted to go to New York, work for the poor. It was my only desire. My dreams were about that, now my dreams are no more, they are all over. I can't wish anymore for that. I am too disappointed in myself. I have no more. I have nothing, it's hopeless.

I'll go to Mary and Joan's tonight and then I must do what I must do tomorrow. I know this is my fate. I have been trying to kill myself since Sunday and I had never gotten the courage, and I am trying to get the courage, and I ask that you forgive me. I can't ask God to forgive me anymore because He has abandoned me. I never prayed so hard. I just, I just needed somebody to say I was worthy. I can love you and I can't be loved. I don't know why, and now it's over. And I know what I must do. Good-bye, good-bye, good-bye, good-bye.

> I have disappointed myself so much. I have not lived up to my ideals in
> life. So when one has no more meaning to life then there's no more meaning
> to live it.

This case is of particular interest because it is so close dynamically to the
formulation in *The Ego and Id*. You will recall that Freud spoke of the ego giving
itself up because it feels itself hated and persecuted by the super-ego, instead of
loved, and allows itself to die.

One of the functions of the super-ego is to hold out before the self the ideals
and expectations which the self must achieve in order to win the approval of the
super-ego. The particular aspect of the super-ego that does this work is
commonly called the ego-ideal. In order to earn the approval of the ego-ideal, the
self-representation must be perceived on the stage of the inner world as
approximating the demands of the ego-ideal. When the demands are approxi-
mated a positive affective coloring of the self-representation results (Schafer
1960).

When the demands of the ego-ideal are not attained, the positive affective
coloring is absent, and the self-representation will be negatively colored through
the punitive function of the superego. Narcissistic equilibrium is impossible
unless the ego-ideal is satisfied.

The case of Sarah demonstrates a situation in which a somewhat obsessional
woman, by virtue of extremely hard work and excellent professional achievement, had been for some years only just able to satisfy the extraordinarily high
demands of her ego-ideal. The history shows beyond all doubt that her ego-ideal,
giving rise in her representational world to a picture of her ideal-self, was formed
almost point for point on the extreme demands of her father with whom she was
so extensively identified.

One of Sarah's father's moral principles was that worthwhile people never
get sick. He had made a Spartan point of dragging himself into the office for
years, even when running a high fever, because he was convinced that the strong
and the brave never admit to being sick, that they never give in to it. When
Sarah developed her depression and was unable to work, both she and her father,
the exterior and the interior father, saw it as a moral failure.

The particular aspect of Sarah's mind responsible for this judgment against
sickness was her ego-ideal. And the negative self-judgment that resulted gave
rise to increased depression, and increased depression gave rise to more negative
self-judgment. The shame and guilt that followed the rape were overwhelming
for the patient.

Sarah's failure to achieve full individuation as an adult is reflected in the
fact that although she had plainly introjected her father as the poisonous root of
her conscience, she had never been able to integrate into her super-ego system a
loving aspect of her father. In fact her father, though very perfectionistic and
demanding, and though prone to anger, was also very loving and valued his
daughter highly. She had to depend on her father as a real person for any
indication that she was worthwhile; her inner father, in the form of her

super-ego, was ready to reject almost all the time, for almost anything short of perfection. Her ego-ideal was therefore very deformed in at least two ways: it was impossibly unrealistic—only a goddess could have lived up to its expectations. And it was also very incomplete, lacking any loving aspect. This left the patient quite dependent on her exterior father for any positive indication of her worth and value as a person.

If you will look closely at the text of the suicide note I think that you will infer, as I do, that at the time the patient took her life lethal shifts had taken place in the configuration of her representational world, and her self-executive functions had been taken over by the object-representation of her father. (See Figure 10–3.)

"I don't think you'll ever know how black the world looks. I can't go on as Sarah anymore. She used to be sharp as a tack. I don't know Sarah anymore. I don't know her. I thought I did. I had ideals for her," the patient says. But is this the patient speaking, or is it the introject of her father which has invaded her self-representation? Who here is denying knowing Sarah anymore? Who is giving her up as not worth saving, a dirty, degraded creature not even able to fight off a depression by dint of will-power?

The father-conscience is declaring through the executive aspects of the patient's self-representation not only that Sarah is a hopeless failure and disappointment, but that Sarah is no longer knowable. The father-conscience is bidding Sarah good-bye, and the patient's split self-representation is prepared for suicide.

I would argue that the suicide proceeded as follows: the executive-self-representation had become identified with derivatives of the father-representation. Split off therefrom and under judgment was the representation of the depressed, professional Sarah, strongly negatively colored, not worth

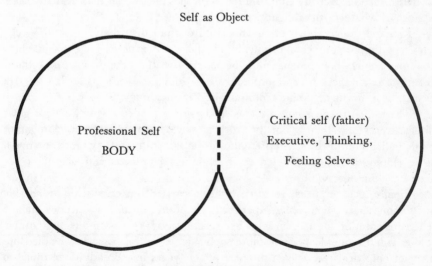

Self as Object

Professional Self
BODY

Critical self (father)
Executive, Thinking,
Feeling Selves

FIGURE 10–3

saving, deserving only the contempt and hatred that a traitor might earn for betraying a great cause.

CONCLUSION

Jacobson (1964, 1971) called attention to problems of separation and individuation in depression and psychosis, studied depersonalization from the psychoanalytic point of view, and observed that incomplete separation of the child's body-representation from the object-representation of the mother lay at the root of much psychopathology. When psychological individuation remains incomplete, the self-representation and object-representation of the mother are not fully distinguished, or, if they are, they are prone regressively to re-fuse under stress. The unstable, fluid, more or less fused self-object-representation that suicide-vulnerable patients carry lies at the heart of their self-destructive behavior.

Developmental theories that attempt to explain the etiology of psychotic, suicidal, or borderline states on the basis of phase-specific mother–child interactional breakdown are almost certainly inadequate. For many years the emphasis that Mahler (1971) and her followers placed on disturbances in the rapprochement subphase dominated clinical thinking. Contemporary students, basing their conclusions on empirical data and not so much on clinical impressions, now hold that for borderline patients, at least, multiple developmental phases are etiologically important. Gunderson (1984, 1990) identifies major emotional neglect through childhood, active parental withdrawal and inconsistency at critical developmental junctures, and physical and sexual abuse as important etiologically. Disturbed self-representations are ubiquitous in the borderline group. It is my clinical impression that the same is true in many cases of suicide, whatever the diagnosis.

Research may show us in the future that disturbances of the self-representation are universal in suicide. Further study is needed to show just how ubiquitous such phenomena may be. I suspect that the future may show disturbances of the self-representation are so universal in suicide that we will identify it as an intrapsychic "commonality" (Shneidman 1985).

These disturbances can alert us to the importance of searching for their clinical traces as we carry out the work of suicide risk assessment. Sometimes subtle indications of the self-representation's fragmentation may be an early sign of developing psychosis. Evidences of self-object confusion can alert us to the need for close observation.

Finally, the empirical research hitherto carried out on suicide vulnerable populations has given only superficial attention to the vicissitudes of the self-representation as it expresses itself clinically. We may hope that future studies will become deeper and more sophisticated in this respect. The development of empirical research in the past fifteen years has already done much to correct inaccurate former clinical assumptions. As it progresses our under-

standing of suicide may deepen and our ability to diagnose and treat this tragic
condition may grow keener.

REFERENCES

Adler, G., and Buie, D. H. (1979). Aloneness and borderline psychopathology: the possible
relevance of child developmental issues. *International Journal of Psycho-Analysis* 60:83-96.
Ames, D. (1984). Self shooting of a phantom head. *British Journal of Psychiatry* 145:193-194.
Asch, S. S. (1966). Depression: three clinical variations. *Psychoanalytic Study of the Child* 21:150-171.
New York: International Universities Press.
———— (1980). Suicide, and the hidden executioner. *International Review of Psycho-Analysis* 7:51-60.
Charcot, J. M. (1889). *Lecons due mardi a la Salpetriere.* Paris: Progres Medicale.
Cotard, J. (1882). Nihilistic delusions. In *Themes and Variations in European Psychiatry,* ed. S. R. Hirsch
and M. Shepherd, trans. M. Rohde, pp. 353-374. Bristol, England: John Wright, 1974.
Critchley, M. (1950). The body-image in neurology. *Lancet,* February 25, pp. 335-341.
Damas-Mora, J. M. R., Jenner, F. A., and Eacott, S. E. (1980). On heautoscopy or the
phenomenon of the double: case presentation and review of the literature. *British Journal of
Medical Psychology* 53:75-83.
Ekbom, K. (1938). Praeseniler dermat-zooenwahn. *Acta Psychiatrica Scandinavica* 13:227-259.
Elkisch, P. (1957). The psychological significance of the mirror. *Journal of the American Psychoanalytic
Association* 5:235-244.
Ellenberger, H. F. (1970). *The Discovery of the Unconscious.* New York: Basic Books.
Enoch, M. D., Trethowan, W. H., and Barker, J. C. (1967). *Some Uncommon Psychiatric Syndromes.*
Bristol, England: John Wright.
Fisher, S. (1990). The evolution of psychological concepts about the body. In *Body Images,
Development, Deviance and Change,* T. F. Cash and T. Pruzinsky, pp. 3-20. New York: Guilford.
Freud, S. (1915). Mourning and melancholia. *Standard Edition* 14:239-260.
———— (1919). The uncanny. *Standard Edition* 17:217-256.
———— (1923a). The ego and the id. *Standard Edition* 19:3-66.
———— (1923b). A seventeenth-century demonological neurosis. *Standard Edition* 19:67-105.
Furman, E. (1984). Some difficulties in assessing depression and suicide in childhood. In *Suicide in
the Young,* ed. H. S. Sudak, A. B. Ford, and N. B. Rushforth, pp. 245-258. Boston: John
Wright/PSG.
Gardiner, M. ed. (1971). *The Wolf Man.* New York: Basic Books.
Greenacre, P. (1953). Certain relationships between fetishism and faulty development of the body
image. *Psychoanalytic Study of the Child* 8:79-98. New York: International Universities Press.
Gunderson, J. (1984). *Borderline Personality Disorder.* Washington, DC: American Psychiatric Press.
———— (1990). New perspectives on becoming borderline. In *Family Environment and Borderline
Personality Disorder,* ed. P. S. Links, pp. 149-159. Washington, DC: American Psychiatric
Press.
Hartmann, H. (1950). Comments on the psychoanalytic theory of the ego. *Psychoanalytic Study of the
Child* 5:74-96. New York: International Universities Press.
Havens, L. (1962). The placement and movement of hallucinations in space: phenomenology and
theory. *International Journal of Psycho-Analysis* 43:426-435.
Head, H., and Holmes, G. (1911-1912). Sensory disturbances from cerebral lesions. *Brain*
34:102-254.
Hopkinson, G. (1970). Delusions of infestation. *Acta Psychiatrica Scandinavica* 46:111-119
Jacobson, E. (1964). *The Self and the Object World.* New York: International Universities Press.
———— (1971). *Depression.* Madison, CT: International Universities Press.
Janet, P. (1889). *L'automatisme Psychologique.* Paris: Alcan.
Jung, C. (1923). *Psychological Types.* Trans. H. G. Baynes. London: Pantheon.

———— (1931). *Psychology of the Unconscious.* Trans. B. M. Hinkle. New York: Dodd, Mead.

Keck, P. L., Pope, H. G., Hudson, J. I., et al. (1988). Lycanthropy, alive and well in the twentieth century. *Psychological Medicine* 18:113–120.

Kohut, H. (1971). *The Analysis of the Self.* New York: International Universities Press.

Kraepelin, E. (1904). Introduction: melancholia. In *Lectures on Clinical Psychiatry,* trans. T. Johnston, pp. 1–10. New York: Hafner, 1968.

Lichtenberg, J. D. (1975). The development of the sense of self. *Journal of the American Psychoanalytic Association* 23:453–454.

Lukianowicz, N. (1958). Autoscopic phenomena. *Archives of Neurology and Psychiatry* 80:199–220.

Mahler, M. (1971). A study of the separation-individuation process and its possible application to borderline phenomena in the psychoanalytic situation. *Psychoanalytic Study of the Child* 26:403–424. New Haven, CT: Yale University Press.

Maltsberger, J. T. (1986). *Suicide Risk: The Formulation of Clinical Judgment.* New York: New York University Press.

Maltsberger, J. T., and Buie, D. H. (1984). The devices of suicide: revenge, riddance, and rebirth. *International Review of Psycho-Analysis* 7:61–72.

Ogata, S. N., Silk, K. R., and Goodrich, S. (1990). The childhood experience of the borderline patient. In *Family Environment and Borderline Personality Disorder,* ed. P. S. Links, pp. 85–104. Washington, DC: American Psychiatric Press.

Phillips, K. A. (1991). Body dysphoric disorder: the distress of imagined ugliness. *American Journal of Psychiatry* 148:1138–1149.

Plath, S. (1966). *Ariel.* New York: Harper & Row.

Poe, E. A. (1839). William Wilson. In *Edgar Allan Poe: Poetry and Tales,* ed. P. F. Quinn, pp. 337–357. New York: The Library of America, 1984.

———— (1845). The facts in the case of M. Valdemar. In *Edgar Allan Poe: Poetry and Tales,* ed. P. F. Quinn, pp. 833–842. New York: The Library of America. 1984.

Putnam, F. W. (1989). *Diagnosis and Treatment of Multiple Personality Disorder.* New York: Guilford.

Putnam, F. W., Guroff, J. J., Silberman, E. K., et al. (1986). The clinical phenomenology of multiple personality disorder: a review of 100 recent cases. *Journal of Clinical Psychiatry* 47:285–293.

Rosenfeld, D. (1984). Hypochondrias, somatic delusion and body scheme in psychoanalytic practice. *International Journal of Psycho-Analysis* 65:377–387.

Rosenfeld, H. A. (1965). *Psychotic States.* New York: International Universities Press.

Rubin, R. T. (1982). Koro (Shook Yang), a culture-bound psychogenic syndrome. In *Extraordinary Disorders of Human Behavior,* ed. C. T. H. Friedmann and R. A. Faguet, pp. 155–172. New York: Plenum.

Sandler, J., and Rosenblatt, B. (1962). The concept of the representational world. *Psychoanalytic Study of the Child* 17:128–148. New York: International Universities Press.

Schafer, R. (1960). The loving and beloved superego in Freud's structural theory. *Psychoanalytic Study of the Child* 15:163–188. New York: International Universities Press.

Schilder, P. (1950). *The Image and Appearance of the Human Body.* New York: International Universities Press.

Shneidman, E. (1976). Some psychological reflections on the death of Malcolm Melville. *Suicide and Life-Threatening Behavior* 6:231–242.

———— (1985). *Definition of Suicide.* New York: Wiley.

Singer, M. (1977). The experience of emptiness in narcissistic and borderline states: II. The struggle for a sense of self and the potential for suicide. *International Review of Psycho-Analysis* 4:471–479.

Stolorow, R. D. (1975). Toward a functional definition of narcissism. *International Journal of Psycho-Analysis* 56:179–185.

Stone, M. H. (1990). Abuse and abusiveness in borderline personality disorder. In *Family Environment and Borderline Personality Disorder,* ed. P. S. Links, pp. 131–148. Washington, DC: American Psychiatric Press.

Surawicz, F. G., and Banta, R. (1975). Lycanthropy revisited. *Canadian Psychiatric Association Journal* 20:537–542.

Todd, J., and Dewhurst, K. (1955). The double: its psycho-pathology and psycho-physiology. *Journal of Nervous and Mental Disease* 122:47–55.

——— (1963). The significance of the doppelganger (hallucinatory double) in folk-lore and neuro-psychiatry. *The Practitioner* 188:377–382.

Woolf, V. (1976). *Moments of Being: Unpublished Autobiographical Writings.* Ed. J. Schulkind. New York: Harcourt Brace Jovanovich.

SUICIDE IN
YOUNG PEOPLE
Part IV

Suicide occurs in the lives of many people of various ages. For a long time, children were considered to be uniquely immune to suicide. Thanks to the findings of suicidology, suicidal behavior in children began to be recognized. Adolescent suicide, on the other hand, has been documented for centuries. Although by virtue of the human quality, the psychological pain of being a child, an adolescent, or an adult has a number of important psychological characteristics in common, life-span studies, and especially investigation of youth suicide, are at the forefront of contemporary conceptualizations about suicide. Part IV presents a chapter on suicidal children, which identifies these youngsters as having serious developmental problems, and a review of current perspectives on adolescent suicidal behavior including some comments on future directions for study.

11: SUICIDAL CHILDREN

Cynthia R. Pfeffer

For quite a long time, children, in contrast to adolescents or adults, have been considered to be uniquely immune from risk of suicidal behavior. This notion was based principally on the belief that childhood is in large measure a blissful state free from the effects of intense problems. Other more scientific arguments were that children do not have the developmental maturity to conceptualize or implement suicidal acts.

In the late 1960s, some descriptive reports (Ackerly 1967, Lukianowicz 1968, Mattsson et al. 1969, Morrison and Collier 1969, Sabbath 1969, Shaw and Schelkun 1965, Toolan 1962) of childhood suicidal behavior were published. Mattsson, Seese, and Hawkins (1969) observed that among suicidal children referred for psychiatric care, 40 percent had symptoms of depression. Toolan (1962) concurred by noting that depression is a significant factor in childhood suicidal behavior. Ackerly (1967) broadened the concern about emotional disturbance and proposed that children who threaten or attempt suicide show serious signs of emotional disturbance. Morrison and Collier (1969) pointed out that childhood suicidal behavior represents an acute emotional distress that stems from long-standing problems. Lukianowicz (1968) emphasized that one of the most enduring problems for suicidal children involves problems in relations with parents. Sabbath (1969) provided the dramatic psychodynamic formulation that suicidal children believe that they are expendable to their families. Such children perceive themselves blameworthy for family problems and, as a result, they feel hopeless and wish to die.

These early reports represent the beginnings of new levels of knowledge about children and suicide. These reports were published before improved research techniques and intense observation of clinical samples of children were utilized in the development of empirical, epidemiologically based studies of childhood psychopathology. These reports were also published before the rapid increase of youth suicidal behavior that began in the early 1970s. These reports serve as precursors and important bases for current knowledge of risk for childhood suicidal behavior.

OVERVIEW

The significance of suicidal behavior in children who are less than 12–14 years old as an important developmental problem can be validated in a number of ways. The focus of this chapter will be to present issues that highlight the complexity and multifaceted aspects of suicidal behavior in children. It will identify issues that specifically present in suicidal children and issues that are important to suicidal individuals in general, and that are observable among suicidal children. Finally, this chapter will suggest that while there is a commonality to suicidal behavior along the life cycle, differences in character- istics of suicidal behavior are derived from the phase of development in which the suicidal behavior is expressed.

THE SUICIDAL CHILD

Descriptions of suicidal behaviors point out the varied motivations, situations, methods, and emotional states associated with children's suicidal ideas and acts. These are illustrated below:

> Andrea was a 6-year-old child whose suicidal behavior was motivated by her wishes to join her dead father in heaven. Andrea was hospitalized in a child psychiatry inpatient unit after she ran into the street in front of a moving truck. This behavior followed an increasing series of accidents in which she sustained minor burns. Andrea admitted that she ran into the street so that she would be hit by a car. She wanted to die because, she said, "I miss my Daddy." [Pfeffer 1986]

This brief description illustrates the definite suicidal intent that very young children experience. It also points out the importance of bereavement as a specific type of family loss that may precipitate childhood suicidal states. In fact, bereavement, especially among children who have lost a parent or sibling to suicide, may be an important risk factor for childhood suicidal tendencies (Ness and Pfeffer 1990).

> Sarah, a 7-year-old child with learning disabilities was admitted to a child psychiatry day treatment program after she expressed repeated ideas of wishing to kill herself. She said that she wanted to drown herself, take pills, or strangle herself. Three months before, she was evaluated at school because she appeared to have difficulty concentrating in class and was unable to read or do math. She was a shy child who was liked by many children. [Pfeffer 1986]

Chronic constitutional or neuropsychological problems may be associated with a chronic vulnerability to suicidal behavior. Added stress which may impair self-esteem and create humiliation may be the immediate precipitants of a child's acute suicidal state, as was illustrated by Sarah's situation. She carefully planned numerous ways of hurting herself; very young children do have the capability to plan and implement suicidal acts.

Martin was 11 years old when he was psychiatrically hospitalized after he ingested six Valium stolen from his mother. He had become increasingly unhappy, showed a marked decline in school performance, and was less obedient with his parents. These changes became evident after his parents divorced.

Andrew was 10 years old when he was psychiatrically hospitalized after he threatened to jump out the third floor window of his apartment. This suicidal threat occurred during a fight with his mother when she reprimanded him for not going to school. Andrew wanted to die because he had "too many problems." [Pfeffer 1986]

The examples of Martin and Andrew point out that lethal suicidal acts are threatened or enacted by children. A common precipitant involves family problems especially concerning parental discord or parent–child conflicts. These types of stresses may be developmentally specific to children who contemplate or carry out suicidal acts.

Each example highlights that children have a definite intent to cause self-harm or death. Such goals represent the suicidal nature of these children's wishes. Although young children may not fully conceptualize the process or finality of death, a concept of death is all that is necessary in defining a child's self-harmful intent as suicidal. As development proceeds into young adolescence, children can understand death in more mature terms and the definition of suicide for such youngsters implies a clearer concept of the finality of death. The modification of the definition of suicidal behavior for young children lends a developmental perspective to understanding suicidal behavior.

EPIDEMIOLOGY AND MEASUREMENT OF CHILDHOOD SUICIDAL BEHAVIOR

Perhaps one reason that suicidal behavior in children had been minimized as a significant developmental problem is that it is the rarest form of suicide among all ages. In 1988, compared to 30,407 suicides for a rate of 12.4 per 100,000 among the population in the United States, 243 children, age 5–14 committed suicide. This is a rate of 0.7 per 100,000 (National Center for Health Statistics 1990). More boys committed suicide than girls—a trend that is consistent for all ages. Suicide among 5–14 year olds is the sixth leading cause of death in this age group and is preceded by accidents, malignant neoplasms, congenital anomalies, homicide, and heart disease. There were a total of 8,925 deaths for a rate of 25.8

per 100,000 among 5-14 year olds in 1988. Almost 3 percent of these deaths were due to suicide. More whites commit suicide than nonwhites — a characteristic of childhood suicide consistent with that of other ages. Although children use a variety of methods to commit suicide, firearms is the single most common method used. In 1988, the rate of suicide by firearms was 0.8 per 100,000 population for 10-14 year olds compared to a rate of 0.5 per 100,000 in 1979 (Fingerhut et al. 1991). The rate of nonfirearm suicides in 1988 for 10-14 year olds was 0.7 per 100,000 population.

Although the rate of suicide for 5-14 year olds is low, the rate of nonfatal suicidal behaviors identified in clinical and community samples is appreciable and shows a variation specific to the type of sample studied. For example, Pfeffer and colleagues (1986) reported that there was an increasing prevalence of suicidal ideation and attempts from 12 percent in community samples to 25 percent for psychiatric outpatient samples to 79 percent for psychiatric inpatient samples. With regard to suicide attempts in children, approximately 1 percent of community samples, 1 percent in psychiatric outpatient samples, and 33 percent in psychiatric inpatient samples report recent suicide attempts. Although there is no national data for suicide attempts, other reports corroborate that nonfatal suicidal behavior in children is a serious problem of psychiatric morbidity.

It may be that the rates of fatal and nonfatal suicidal behavior in children are underestimated, not only because there may be a lack of uniform agreement about the definition or classification of suicidal behavior in young children but also because there may be great variation in reporting such behavior. Validation of this has been suggested by studies of the degree of agreement in reporting suicidal behavior in children and adolescents. Pfeffer and colleagues (1991) reported that there was only modest agreement among parents and children in reporting suicidal states of the children. Similar results have been noted in other studies (Walker et al. 1990) and it appears that when there are discrepancies between parent and child reports, the children report more suicidal behavior than parents. These findings are especially important in suicide prevention efforts where early recognition is an important aspect of preventing suicidal behavior. An implication of these results is that it is essential to interview a child who may be a risk for suicidal behavior and not depend only on reports from other people.

Interviewing children about their suicidal states should be comprehensive and specific. Important areas to cover include a child's suicidal fantasies or ideas and actions, a child's concepts of what would happen if he or she carried out a suicidal act, the circumstances at the time of the child's suicidal behavior, a child's previous experiences with suicidal behavior, and motivations for suicidal behaviors (Pfeffer 1986).

Clinicians and researchers who wish to systematically rate the type, severity, and frequency of children's suicidal tendencies can use standard research instruments such as the Spectrum of Suicidal Behavior Scale (Pfeffer 1986) which classifies suicidal behavior along a five-point scale ranging from nonsuicidal behavior to suicidal ideation to suicidal threat to mild suicide attempt to serious suicide attempt to suicide. The Kiddie-Schedule of Affective Disorders and Schizophrenia, another standard research instrument, includes four scales to rate suicidal behavior (Chambers et al. 1985). One scale rates suicidal tendencies that range from degrees of ideation to suicide attempt. Another scale rates number of suicide attempts. A third scale rates seriousness of suicide intent and another scale measures degree of medical lethality of suicidal act. These four scales are highly correlated with each other (Robbins and Alessi 1985) and correlated with the Spectrum of Suicidal Behavior Scale (Pfeffer 1991). This suggests that there is overlap among these scales for the specific aspects that each scale measures.

An important issue for suicidal behavior is whether there is an overlap or continuity in different manifestations of suicidal behavior. For example, are there similarities to suicidal ideation, suicide attempts, and suicide? Controversy exists about this but there is increasing evidence to suggest that among children, there is a continuous spectrum of suicidal behaviors. Pfeffer and colleagues (1982) reported that among child psychiatric inpatients there was a positive correlation between the spectrum of suicidal behavior and the severity of depression and other psychopathology. Brent and associates (1986, 1988) also suggested a continuous spectrum of suicidal behavior in two different studies. One (Brent et al. 1986) reported a positive correlation between severity of suicidal tendencies and degree of depressive symptoms in children and adolescents. The other study (Brent et al. 1988) compared adolescent suicide victims with adolescent psychiatric inpatients who reported suicidal ideation and attempt. The results, suggesting that there is a continuity between suicide attempts and suicide, were that there was a similarly high rate of affective disorder in the adolescent's and family histories of affective and antisocial disorders and suicide. However, these results were not conclusive in that the suicide victims had more prevalent bipolar disorders, affective disorders with co-occurrence of other disorders, less previous psychiatric intervention, and more availability of firearms in the home. Carlson and Cantwell (1982), in contrast, proposed that children and adolescents who attempt suicide are different from those who contemplate suicide because although severity of suicidal ideation was positively associated with degree of depressive symptoms, those who attempted suicide were less likely to be depressed but had nonaffective types of psychopathology.

These studies emphasize that further work is needed to clarify this issue. Until this occurs, studies should clearly describe the methods used and define the nature of suicidal behavior to be evaluated. Furthermore, various approaches should be used to study suicidal behavior using categorical as well as continuous ratings of suicidal behavior.

RISK FACTORS ASSOCIATED WITH SUICIDAL BEHAVIOR IN CHILDREN

There is a paucity of research on suicide in children younger than 14 years old. This is mainly due to the low incidence of suicide in this group of children and the difficulty of conducting studies of suicide. Three studies (Corder and Haizlip 1984, Hoberman and Garfinkel 1988, Shaffer 1974) address this age group most specifically. These reports suggest that children who commit suicide are afflicted with psychiatric problems, most often involving symptoms of affective and antisocial disorders. Common circumstances precipitating suicide were humiliating experiences resulting from disciplinary crises in the home or school, loss of special role within the family system, and problems living with psychiatrically disturbed relatives who often exhibit psychotic, depressive, and suicidal symptoms. These studies suggest that children who commit suicide are psychiatrically disturbed and often experience severe stresses in their environments.

Studies of factors of children who contemplate or attempt suicide reveal a complex interaction. Pfeffer (1986) proposed that recent problems related to the child's current emotional state, current aspects of interpersonal relations, current level of adaptive functioning, past developmental experiences, as well as a past history of suicidal behavior are risk factor categories for childhood suicidal behavior. Pfeffer (1986) proposed that suicidal behavior in children is an episodic phenomenon that has an onset and offset which can be identified and tracked over time. When risk factors occur, the likelihood of an onset of an episode of suicidal ideation or acts is enhanced.

More specifically, research suggests that children at risk for suicidal behavior have psychopathology (Pfeffer et al. 1986, 1988, 1991) and are not normal children experiencing stresses of life. Other researchers (Kienhorst 1987, Myers et al. 1985) concur with these premises. Risk factors noted to be associated with suicidal ideas or attempts in samples of children obtained from the general community and psychiatric inpatient and outpatient services are symptoms of general psychopathology with a specific emphasis on mood and conduct disorders, violence, preoccupations with death, poor impulse control, ego defense mechanisms that involve displacement of feelings and ideas to others, and parental suicidal behavior. Kienhorst and colleagues 1987 and Myers and colleagues 1985 emphasize discordant family environments as strong risk factors for childhood suicidal behavior.

Stress endured by suicidal children has been observed to be greater and more chronic than in comparison children who are not suicidal but are depressed or suffering from other psychiatric disorders (Cohen-Sandler et al. 1982b). Such stress may involve particular family events such as death, birth, illness, divorce, and moves of relatives. Chronic mental illness in parents is a particular type of intense stress (Friedman and Corn 1985). Perhaps the most severe form of stress is physical or sexual abuse of the child and is a particularly strong family risk factor for childhood suicidal behavior (Rosenthal and Rosenthal 1984). Discord within the family and other environmental stresses promote intensely dysphoric feelings for children who sometimes feel so hopeless and helpless that they contemplate or enact suicidal behavior. Depression and hopelessness are strong risk factors for suicidal behavior of such children, although hopelessness is a stronger predictor than depression (Kazdin et al. 1983). Asarnow, Carlson, and

Guthrie (1987) evaluated self-concepts, coping strategies, hopelessness, and perceptions of family environments of suicidal and depressed children. Suicidal children perceived their families to be highly conflicted, out of control, and low on cohesiveness. Such children were less apt to use effective coping strategies to deal with such family stress. Depression among such children intensified cognitive perceptions of hopelessness and helplessness.

Family problems, as risk factors for suicidal behavior, may be among the most important risk factors for children. These problems may be less significant during other stages of development when autonomy and coping skills are highly developed. Children are naturally dependent on their families for basic sustenance, emotional support, and other aspects of socialization. As a result, it is critical to evaluate the family system of children at risk for suicidal behavior and to intervene to arrest imbalances in interfamilial relationships.

Pfeffer (1981) suggested that family constellations of suicidal children lack boundaries among the generations so that parents are conflicted about their roles as parents; have severe conflicts among the spouses often leading to family breakup, abusive and violent interactions, and suicide attempts; have parental feelings that are projected onto the children who are not perceived as developmentally needing parental support; have symbiotic parent–child relationships with intense, unchangeable dependency relationships and inflexibility in the entire family system. Children enduring such family experiences feel trapped, helpless, hopeless, isolated, and unable to effect any relief except by contemplating or carrying out suicidal acts. Interventions for such children involve a major emphasis on working with the parents in addition to treatment of the child who may require support from the family in order to relieve the intensity of stress.

Finally, not all suicidal children are alike with respect to their risk factors for suicidal behavior. Pfeffer and colleagues (1983) suggested that subtypes exist that are based on symptoms of violence and suicidal behavior. Children who were suicidal with minimal levels of externally directed violence were predominantly depressed, had low levels of antisocial tendencies, had good reality testing, and had parents who reported suicidal behavior. Those children who reported suicidal and violent behavior showed symptoms of depression, high levels of antisocial symptoms, lower levels of reality testing, and parents who reported suicidal and assaultive tendencies. Other subtypes of suicidal children may exist but studies have not been conducted to evaluate this. For example, some children may be vulnerable to suicidal tendencies because certain biological mechanisms may have alterations in functioning. Pfeffer and colleagues (1991) recently reported that children with persistently high levels of plasma cortisol have a greater likelihood of reporting suicidal behavior. This finding was independent of psychiatric diagnosis of the child. Other issues, such as genetic factors, which have been reported among suicidal adults, may be a basis for subtyping suicidal children. The associations between childhood suicidal behavior and family history of suicidal behavior have not been reliably identified.

OUTCOME OF SUICIDAL CHILDREN

Only a few systematic follow-up studies of suicidal children exist. Cohen-Sandler, Berman, and King (1982a) followed up seventy-six child psychiatric inpatients during a 5-month to 3-year period after discharge from the hospital. The sample included twenty children who reported suicidal behavior before hospital admission. One child died in a boating "accident" during the follow-up period. During the follow-up period, suicidal children were as well adjusted as the other former psychiatric inpatients. However, the suicidal children more frequently received treatment during the follow-up period away from their homes. Four (20 percent) of the initially suicidal inpatients reported suicidal behavior in the follow-up period.

Pfeffer has been conducting one of the most comprehensive prospective follow-up studies of suicidal children. A 2-year follow-up assessment of children who were initially selected from the general community revealed that among the eight children who reported suicidal behavior at the time of initial assessment, 50 percent reported suicidal ideation or acts at the 2-year follow-up assessment (Pfeffer et al. 1988). This result suggested that there is a short-term stability to children's suicidal states. Suicidal tendencies at the time of follow up were associated with depression, death preoccupations, aggressive symptoms, signs of psychopathology, and ego defenses of denial, reaction formation, and projection.

Most recently, Pfeffer and associates (1991) reported on a 6–8 year follow up of children who were initially psychiatrically hospitalized and the community sample noted above. At the initial assessment, eighty-four (79.2 percent) of the inpatients reported suicidal ideation or attempts within 6 months of the initial assessment. These children were considered to be at high risk for future suicidal behavior. During the 6–8 year follow-up period, no child died but significantly more suicidal inpatients (23.2 percent) than community controls (6.3 percent) attempted suicide at least once in the follow-up period. The strongest risk factor for these repeated suicide attempts during the follow-up period were the presence of a mood disorder in the follow-up period. More specifically, having a chronic depressive disorder and a previous history of suicidal behavior highly predicted the occurrence of a suicide attempt in the follow-up period. Furthermore, 50 percent of the youngsters who reported a suicide attempt in the follow-up period reported more than one suicide attempt during this time. Based on the results of this study, Pfeffer and colleagues (1991) proposed that suicidal children grow up but experience excessive degrees of chronic psychiatric morbidity and repeated episodes of suicide attempts during follow up. Thus, while few suicidal children commit suicide, suicidal behavior at an early age predicts highly pathological outcomes; therefore, childhood suicidal behavior is a serious developmental problem.

SUMMARY AND CONCLUSION

This chapter, personally dedicated to Ed Shneidman with special regard to his pioneering work in identifying perturbing mechanisms leading to the intense, painful state of suicidal people and to his endeavors to understand the long-term courses of people at risk for suicidal behavior, discussed factors that validate that young children who reported suicidal tendencies have serious lasting developmental problems. Such children are at risk for repeated suicidal episodes. They suffer from serious psychiatric disorders such as intense depressive states and disturbances of conduct. They grow up in an intensely stressful environmental milieu beset by extreme family discord, violence, mental disturbances, and suicidal behavior. Hopelessness and inability to cope adequately are forces responsible for a child succumbing to suicidal impulses.

One of the most important unsettled issues is how to prevent childhood suicidal behavior and its associated morbidity. While early identification of vulnerable children is necessary, interventions need to be offered that effectively decrease risk factors for suicidal behavior. To date, there have been no systematic studies evaluating efficacy of psychosocial or biological interventions for suicidal children. Concerted research efforts are needed and evaluation of current clinical procedures with suicidal children is warranted. Perhaps some day it will be possible to conceive of the possibility that all children grow up and none are suicidal.

REFERENCES

Ackerly, W. C. (1967). Latency-age children who threaten or attempt to kill themselves. *Journal of the American Academy of Child Psychiatry* 6:242–261.

Asarnow, J. R., Carlson G. A., and Guthrie, D. (1987). Coping strategies, self-perceptions, hopelessness, and perceived family environments in depressed and suicidal children. *Journal of Consulting and Clinical Psychology* 55:361–366.

Brent D. A., Kalas R., Edelbrock C., et al. (1986). Psychopathology and its relationship to suicidal ideation in childhood and adolescence. *Journal of the American Academy of Child Psychiatry* 25:666–673.

Brent D. A, Perper J. A., Goldstein C. E., et al. (1988). Risk factors for adolescent suicide: a comparison of adolescent suicide victims with suicidal inpatients. *Archives of General Psychiatry* 45:581–588.

Carlson C. A., and Cantwell D. P. (1982). Suicidal behavior and depression in children and adolescents. *Journal of the American Academy of Child Psychiatry* 21:361–368.

Chambers W. J., Puig-Antich J., Hirsch M., et al. (1985). The assessment of affective disorders in children and adolescents by semi-structured interview: test-retest reliability of the Schedule for Affective Disorders and Schizophrenia for School-age Children—present episode version. *Archives of General Psychiatry* 42:696–702.

Cohen-Sandler, R., Berman, A. L., and King, R. A. (1982a). A follow-up study of hospitalized suicidal children. *Journal of the American Academy of Child Psychiatry* 21:398–403.

———— (1982b). Life stress and symptomatology: determinants of suicidal behavior in children. *Journal of the American Academy of Child Psychiatry* 21:178–186.

Corder, B. F., and Haizlip, T. M. (1984). Environmental and personality similarities in case histories of suicide and self-poisoning by children under ten. *Suicide and Life-Threatening Behavior* 141:59–66.

Fingerhut, L. A., Kleinman, J. C., Godfrey, E., and Rosenberg, H. (1991). Firearm mortality among children, youth, and young adults 1–34 years of age. Trends and current status: United States, 1979–1988. Monthly vital statistics report: Volume 39, number 11, supp. Hyattsville, MD. National Center for Health Statistics.

Friedman, R. C., and Corn, R. (1985). Follow-up five years after attempted suicide at age 7. *American Journal of Psychotherapy* 39:108–113.

Hoberman, H. M., and Garfinkel, B. D. (1988). Completed suicide in children and adolescents. *Journal of the American Academy of Child and Adolescent Psychiatry* 27:689–695.

Kazdin A. E., French N. H., Unis A. S., et al. (1983). Hopelessness, depression, and suicidal intent among psychiatrically disturbed inpatient children. *Journal of Consulting and Clinical Psychology* 51:504–510.

Kienhorst C. W. M., Wolters W. H. G., Diekstra R. F. W., et al. (1987). A study of the frequency of suicidal behavior in children, age 5–14. *Journal of Child Psychology and Psychiatry* 28:153–165.

Lukianowitz, N. C. (1968). Attempted suicide in children. *Acta Psychiatrica Scandinavica* 44:415–435.

Mattsson, A., Seese, L. R., and Hawkins, J. W. (1969). Suicidal behavior as a child psychiatric emergency. *Archives of General Psychiatry* 20:100–109.

Morrison, G. C., and Collier, J. C. (1969). Family treatment approaches to suicidal children and adolescents. *Journal of the American Academy of Child Psychiatry* 8:140–155.

Myers K. M., Burke P., and McCauley, E. (1985). Suicidal behavior by hospitalized preadolescent children on a psychiatric unit. *Journal of the American Academy of Child Psychiatry* 24:474–480.

National Center for Health Statistics (1990). Advance report of final mortality statistics, 1988. Monthly vital statistics report, volume 39, number 7, suppl. Hyattsville, MD. Public Health Service.

Ness, D. E., and Pfeffer, C. R. (1990). Sequelae of bereavement as a result of suicide. *American Journal of Psychiatry* 147:279–285.

Pfeffer, C. R. (1981). The family system of suicidal children. *American Journal of Psychotherapy* 35:330–341.

—— (1986). *The Suicidal Child.* New York: Guilford.

—— (1991). Measurement of suicidality in high-risk children. In *Our Children: Our Future: CME Syllabus and Proceedings Summary.* American Psychiatric Association, May 11–16, New Orleans, LA.

Pfeffer, C. R., Klerman, G. L., Hurt, S. W., et al. (1991). Suicidal children grow up: demographic and clinical risk factors for adolescent suicide attempts. *Journal of the American Academy of Child and Adolescent Psychiatry* 30:609–616.

Pfeffer, C. R., Lipkins, R., Plutchik, R., et al. (1988). Normal children at risk for suicidal behavior: a two-year follow-up study. *Journal of the American Academy of Child and Adolescent Psychiatry* 27:34–41.

Pfeffer C. R., Plutchik, R., and Mizruchi, M. S. (1983). Suicidal and assaultive behavior in children: classification, measurement, and interrelations. *American Journal of Psychiatry* 140:154–157.

Pfeffer, C. R., Plutchik, R., Mizruchi, M. S., and Lipkins, R. (1986). Suicidal behavior in child psychiatric inpatients and outpatients and in nonpatients. *American Journal of Psychiatry* 143:733–738.

Pfeffer, C. R., Solomon, G., Plutchik, R., et al. (1982). Suicidal behavior in latency-age psychiatric inpatients: a replication and cross-validation. *Journal of the American Academy of Child Psychiatry* 21:564–569.

Pfeffer, C. R., Stokes, P., and Shindledecker, R. (1991). Suicidal behavior and hypothalamic-pituitary adrenocortical axis indices in child psychiatric inpatients. *Biological Psychiatry* 29:909–917.

Robbins, D. R., and Alessi, N. E. (1985). Depressive symptoms and suicidal behavior in adolescents. *American Journal of Psychiatry* 142:588–592.

Rosenthal, P. A., and Rosenthal, S. (1984). Suicidal behavior by pre-school children. *American Journal of Psychiatry* 141:520–525.

Sabbath, J. C. (1969). The suicidal adolescent. *Journal of the American Academy of Child Psychiatry* 8:272–289.

Shaffer, D. (1974). Suicide in childhood and early adolescence. *Journal of Child Psychology and Psychiatry* 15:275–291.

Shaw, C. R., and Schelkun, R. F. (1965). Suicidal behavior in children. *Psychiatry* 28:158–168.

Toolan, J. M. (1962). Depression in children and adolescents. *American Journal of Orthopsychiatry* 33:404–415.

Walker, M., Moreau, D., and Weissman, M. M. (1990). Parents' awareness of children's suicide attempts. *American Journal of Psychiatry* 147:1364–1366.

12: ADOLESCENT SUICIDAL BEHAVIOR

Robert J. Myatt and Milton Greenblatt

"To me it seems that youth is like spring, an over-praised season — delightful if it happen to be a favored one, but in practice very rarely favored and more remarkable, as a general rule, for biting east winds than genial breezes."

Samuel Butler (1835–1902)

HISTORICAL PERSPECTIVE

In discussing the history of youth suicide, Pfeffer (1986) noted that suicide had been a topic for discussion in literature and music long before clinical manuscripts began emphasizing the subject. *Hamlet* by Shakespeare, *Moby Dick* by Melville, *Romeo and Juliet* by Shakespeare, *Hedda Gabler* by Ibsen, *The Counterfeiters* by André Gide, *Jude the Obscure* by Hardy, and *Phantom of the Opera* by Gaston Leroux are just a few literary works that address the topic of suicidality.

Pfeffer (1986) relates that the history of the formal, scientific study of suicidal children began in the nineteenth century when the first psychiatric descriptions of suicidal children appeared in European journals. It was the psychoanalysts who presented much of the early theoretical examination of childhood suicide.

Sigmund Freud suggested that the most significant influence on suicidal behavior was conflict with significant others and proposed that a major precipitating factor of childhood suicide was incest. From a psychoanalytic perspective, Freud loosely developed a hypothetical model of suicide, that involved conflict between Eros (the drive toward love and life) and Thanatos (the drive toward destruction and death). For the suicidal person, an intrapsychic imbalance with Thanatos achieving more significant representation and influence in the individual's libido leads to the suicidal behavior. This model was never fully developed or explicated by Freud and neither empirical attention nor support has evolved.

THE PREVALENCE OF ADOLESCENT SUICIDE

Youth suicide has increasingly become a topic of national concern as witness the following disturbing statistics. Within the past decade, suicide has become the second leading cause of death in adolescence (behind accidents). In 1988 (the most recent year for which national suicide statistics are available), 4,929 young people in the United States between the ages of 15 and 24 committed suicide. This translates into approximately 13.5 suicides per day and roughly one successful suicide by a young person every 2 hours. In the United States, suicides by adolescents have doubled in the past decade and tripled in the past 2 decades (Figures 12-1-12-6).

Perhaps even more alarming, the suicide rate among adolescents has continued to increase while that among the population at large has remained relatively stable. In the early 1970s, the rise in suicide among the 15-24 age group was nearly eight times the increase among the general population (Alcohol, Drug Abuse, and Mental Health Administration 1989).

In 1988, 2,059 adolescents between the ages of 15 and 19 (Figures 12-1-12-3) and 2,870 young adults between the ages of 20 and 24 (Figures 12-4-12-6) reportedly committed suicide in the United States, accounting for approximately 20 percent of all reported suicides in the country. (This was a rate of 13.2 per 100,000 [National Center for Health Statistics 1991]). However, when the number of attempted suicides is also taken into account, the dimensions of this tragedy are magnified. Compared to the 4,929 adolescent suicides committed in 1988, it was estimated that there were at least 1,000,000 adolescent suicide attempts. In 1990, the Centers For Disease Control estimated that 276,000 high school students made at least one suicide attempt requiring

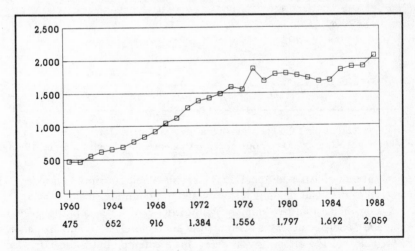

FIGURE 12-1. Suicide Deaths in the United States, 15-19 Year Olds, 1960-1988. Data Source: National Center for Health Statistics (1991).

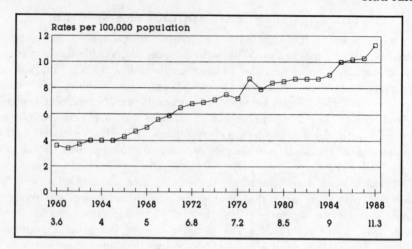

FIGURE 12-2. Suicide Rates in the United States, 15-19 Year Olds, 1960-1988. Data Source: National Center for Health Statistics (1991).

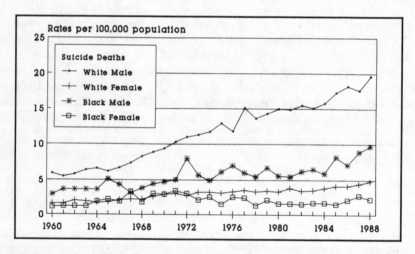

FIGURE 12-3. Ethnic Composition of Suicide Rates in the United States for 15-19 Year Olds, 1960-1988. Data Source: National Center for Health Statistics (1991).

medical attention. An additional 27.3 percent of all students in grades 9-12 reported that they had thought seriously about attempting suicide.

It is estimated that five million living Americans, of whom approximately 1 million are adolescents, have attempted to kill themselves. There are generally three female suicide attempts for every male attempt but almost five male completions for every female completion (National Center for Health Statistics, 1991). It has been suggested that each suicide directly affects at least six other

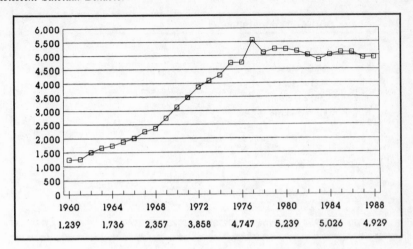

FIGURE 12-4. Suicide Deaths in the United States, 15–24 Year Olds, 1960–1988.
Data Source: National Center for Health Statistics (1991).

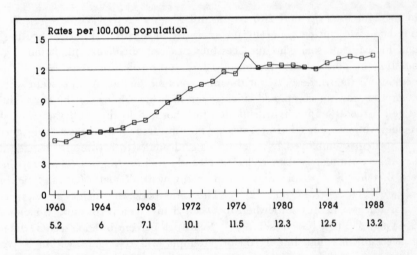

FIGURE 12-5. Suicide Rates in the United States, 15–35 Year Olds, 1960–1988.
Data Source: National Center for Health Statistics (1991).

people. As a result, by 1988 an estimated 3.1 million people in the U.S. were directly affected by suicide and this number increases by approximately 200,000 each ensuing year.

A critical distinction must be made between actual suicide and attempted suicide. Although there is obviously an overlap between the two populations (one must attempt suicide in order to commit suicide), there are major differences besides the obvious fact that one is successful and the other is not. For example,

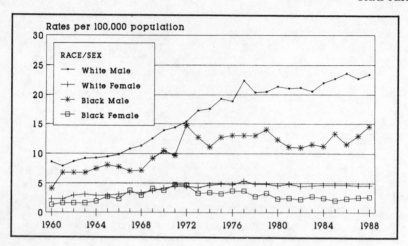

FIGURE 12-6. Suicide Rates in the United States, 15–24 Year Olds, 1960–1988.
Data Source: National Center for Health Statistics (1991).

the methods used by these two groups differ significantly. People who successfully complete suicide generally use more lethal means, primarily shooting or hanging. Most persons who unsuccessfully attempt suicide use inhalation of gas, ingestion of poison, cutting, or overdoses of medications—all less efficient methods. Drug overdose, by far the most common method in adolescent suicide attempt, is rare in completed suicide, for most overdoses can be successfully treated if the attempter is transported to a hospital in time. Of the successful suicides who use drugs, barbiturates are the most frequently ingested substances.

Strategies employed by adolescents and adults to accomplish suicide are remarkably similar as data collected recently in Los Angeles (a metropolitan area that has a relatively high suicide rate) by the Chief Medical Examiner indicate (Figures 12-7 and 12-8). The ratio between suicide attempts and actual suicides ranges somewhere between 8 to 1 (Farberow and Shneidman 1961) and 350 to 1 (Garfinkel 1989). Nearly 15 percent of adolescents who are unsuccessful in their initial suicide attempts will try again within 3 years following the first attempt (Hawton and Catalan 1987). Adolescents often use the same method of attempting suicide during subsequent episodes although a percentage will graduate to a more lethal approach as they continue their suicidal behavior.

Accurate data on adolescent suicide attempts are more difficult to compile than data on committed suicides. A national system for gathering and organizing statistics in this area does not exist. The few studies available primarily examine emergency room admissions, the experiences of private practitioners, or inpatient psychiatric programs. The principal mechanisms employed to estimate rates of attempted suicide in young adults is still by extrapolation from data on completed suicide.

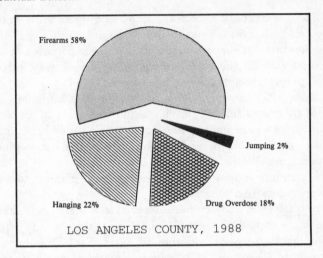

FIGURE 12-7. Suicide Methods for 15-24 Year Olds in Los Angeles County, 1988. Data Source: Los Angeles County Dept. of Chief Medical Examiner (1991).

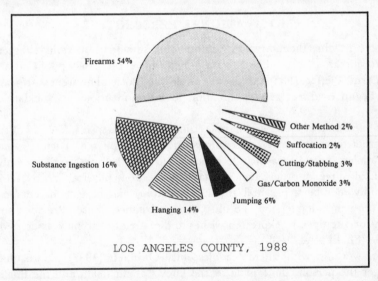

FIGURE 12-8. Suicide Methods for All Ages in Los Angeles County, 1988. Data Source: Los Angeles County Dept. of Chief Medical Examiner (1991).

STATISTICAL PERSPECTIVE

Available statistics on suicide are considered by many experts to be underestimates (Farmer 1988, Hawton and Osborn 1981, Shneidman 1981, Sudak et al. 1984, Weissman and Worden 1974). Because of legal, social, and religious proscriptions, many committed suicides go unreported. Toolan (1981) indicates that even more committed suicides go unreported for children and adolescents than for adults. As might be expected, parents and significant others are often reluctant to deal with a youth's suicide due to the overwhelming grief and sense of responsibility that this engenders. Unfortunately, as parents and other adults protect themselves from the horror of the adolescent suicidal behavior, they promote and perpetuate ignorance of adolescent suicidality.

Shneidman (1980) ascertained that suicide notes are left in only about 12 to 15 percent of completed suicides, leaving authorities and families with the task of determining motivation and intention surrounding deaths in which a note was not available. Left to their own devices, many people prefer to conclude that the death was accidental. While accidents are the leading cause of death in young people, it is currently impossible to determine how many of these so-called accidents were unreported suicides.

O'Carroll (1989), in a paper discussing suicide mortality data, states that the true suicide rate may be between 1.2 and 3.8 times the officially reported rate. He also notes that the correct certification of suicide has been estimated to range from 26 percent to 71 percent. Thus, determining the true rate of occurrence of suicide is a daunting task (Farmer 1988, Moscicki 1989, O'Carroll 1989).

MOTIVATIONAL PERSPECTIVE

Only recently has the motivation behind youth suicide been examined intensely. Recent media reports about youth suicide have increased public awareness and alarm (Pfeffer 1986). As a result of elevated societal awareness, researchers have begun to direct greater attention to the motivations of suicidal adolescents.

Shneidman (1980, 1967) has determined from extensive analyses of suicide notes that there are many reasons given for killing oneself. Factors associated with adolescent suicides include exposure to suicide by a family member or friend; affective disorders such as major depression; physical and sexual abuse by family members; parental absence, rejection, and neglect; parents' psychiatric problems, aggression, hostility, and substance abuse. Previous suicidal threats or attempts, or expressed wishes to die, are also strongly associated with suicide (Shafii et al. 1985).

In working with suicidal adolescents, Quinnett (1987) reports that the younger the person, the less he or she knows about death and the finality of death. Music, television, and motion picture presentations have made suicide less abhorrent and brought it more within the range of common parlance. He postulates that many adolescents perceive suicide as a fashionable and impermanent approach to major life problems. These same teens also presume that if suicide does not resolve the life stressor/problem, then a different strategy can be introduced down the line. Younger suicide attempters are less able to appreciate the significance and irrevocable nature of suicide. Pokorny (1968) notes that suicide is a "final common pathway of many diverse forces and circumstances, typically a summation of predisposing and precipitating factors culminating in an act of desperation."

DIAGNOSTIC PERSPECTIVE

A plethora of clinical syndromes has been associated with suicide. It is difficult to specify exactly the relationship between clinical categories and suicide rates, although the most common psychiatric diagnoses are depressive illness (accounting for about half of those persons who commit suicide), chronic alcoholism (accounting for between one-fifth and one-quarter), and a significant but smaller number classed as schizophrenic (Miles 1977). Psychiatric illness is a factor in the majority of cases (Rich et al. 1986). Pokorny (1983) reports that patients admitted to an inpatient psychiatric service have a suicide rate that approaches nine times that in the general population of the same age and sex.

In the 15–24 age group, the principal diagnoses associated with suicide are affective disorder (Apter et al. 1988, Asarnow et al. 1987, Cole 1989, Garfinkel 1989, Kazdin et al. 1983, Minkoff et al. 1973, Neimeyer 1983, Robbins and Alessi 1985, Rotheram-Borus and Trautman 1988, Toolan 1981, Wetzel et al. 1980), conduct disorder (Brent et al. 1986), borderline personality disorder (Crumley 1979, Friedman et al. 1983), and substance abuse (Brent et al. 1988, Murphy 1988). Substance abuse accounted for half the diagnoses applied in one major study of suicide (Fowler et al. 1986). Anxiety disorders, obsessive-compulsive disorders, and somatic disorders have all been observed in suicidal adolescents. These diagnoses may occur alone or in combinations.

Marttunen and colleagues (1991) state that comorbidity (the presence of two or more diagnosable conditions) in adolescents is associated with greater frequency of suicidal behavior. Patients diagnosed with both an affective disorder and borderline personality disorder have been reported at higher risk for suicidal behavior than other diagnoses (Friedman et al. 1983, Robbins and Alessi 1985). Welner, Welner, and Fishman (1979) have also reported that former psychiatric patients suffering from Bipolar Affective Disorder with psychotic features are at particularly high risk for suicide.

Most psychological autopsy studies indicate that individuals who suicide have had symptoms of at least one psychiatric disorder at the time of their death (Brent 1989). Rich and associates (1988) sum up the literature on psychiatric diagnosis and suicide: by stating that virtually everyone who suicides suffers from a psychiatric disorder.

PSYCHOBIOLOGICAL PERSPECTIVE

The biological correlates of suicidal behavior are coming under increasing scrutiny (Gross-Isseroff et al. 1989, Krieger 1970, Lidberg et al. 1985, Mann et al. 1989, Mann et al. 1986, Nemeroff et al. 1988).

Bunney and Fawcett (1965) were two early researchers who suggested that a biological marker for suicidal behavior existed. Their research found high levels of urinary 17-hydroxycortico-steroids in suicidal depressed patients. However, Levy and Hensen (1969) reported that urinary tests failed to be useful as a predictor of suicidality.

Roy and colleagues (1986) determined that depressed patients who had attempted suicide had significantly lower levels of CSF homovanillic acid (CSF HVA)—a serotonin metabolite—and a lower CSF homovanillic acid to CSF 5-Hydroxyindoleacetic acid (CSF 5-HIAA) ratio than patients who had not attempted suicide. The most frequently replicated finding in the biological suicide research has been the presence of low concentrations of 5-HIAA in the cerebrospinal fluid of depressed and suicidal adults (Asberg et al. 1986). These findings are yet to be replicated with adolescents or children. Plasma and CSF studies of suicidality are still too few to warrant steadfast conclusions.

Gross-Isseroff and colleagues (1989) utilized autoradiographic analysis of the postmortem brain tissue of suicides and found reduced binding of tritiated prazosin in brain sections compared to matched control subjects. This finding suggests a functional noradrenergic abnormality in the central nervous system of suicidal individuals.

Dorovini-Zis and Zis (1987) found that adrenal weight was significantly higher in victims of violent suicide than in subjects that died of other causes. The authors theorize that there is a relationship between depression, hypertrophy of the adrenal cortex, and suicide.

A study by Struve, Klein, and Saraf (1972) indicated that in adults, there is a positive, significant association between paroxysmal EEGs and 1) suicide ideation alone, 2) suicide ideation plus attempts, and 3) assaultive-destructive behavior without a suicidal component. This line of research has not been further pursued.

Stanley and Stanley (1989) note that many of the postmortem studies that have examined suicidality yield inconsistent results due to factors such as extensive postmortem delay, death by overdose or carbon monoxide poisoning, selection of varying brain sections for dissection and analysis, and lack of age-matched control groups. In addition, they note that levels of monoamines and their metabolites can be significantly influenced by uncontrolled factors such as the suicide's diet, alcohol use, and illicit substance use.

The presence of a genetically determined correlate to suicidality has received support in the literature according to a review by Roy (1986). Suicide rates are significantly higher in the families of completed suicides (Murphy and Wetzel 1982, Roy 1983a, Shaffer 1974) and twin studies have indicated a significantly higher concordance rate for self-destructive behavior in monozygotic versus dizygotic twins (Roy 1986, Tsuang 1977). Other large-scale genetic studies such as the Copenhagen Adoption Study (Schulsinger et al. 1979), the Iowa-500 study (Tsuang 1978), and the Amish Study (Egeland and Hostetter 1983, Egeland and Sussex 1985) have suggested genetic involvement in suicide. Mann, DeMeo, Keilp, and McBride (1989) point out that a benefit of determining a genetically based correlate for suicide would be to produce a detectable biological trait that is the phenotypic expression of that genotype.

At the present time, further research is necessary to determine the relationship of various biological markers and suicidality as well as to develop a clearer understanding of the specific emotional and behavioral manifestations of these markers.

PSYCHOSOCIAL PERSPECTIVE

Many studies during the past two decades have attempted to identify personality characteristics, stressors, life situations, and events related to suicidal behavior. Unfortunately, the literature is not consistent, nor definitive, in presenting the attributes and conditions that precipitate self-destructive actions.

Age, sex, marital status, socioeconomic status, and other demographic characteristics have been examined (Farmer 1988, Kennedy and Kreitman 1973, Kreitman and Casey 1988, Taylor and Wicks 1980, Weissman and Worden 1974). Personality characteristics such as depression (Cole 1989, Kazdin et al. 1983, Neimeyer 1983, Robbins and Alessi 1985, Rotheram-Borus and Trautman 1988, Wetzel et al. 1980), hopelessness (Beck et al. 1985, Brent 1987, Cole 1989, Holden et al. 1989, Kashani et al. 1989, Kazdin et al. 1983, Kazdin et al. 1986, Rotheram-Borus and Trautman 1988), poor problem-solving ability (Krarup et al. 1991, Levenson and Neuringer 1971, Schotte and Clum 1987, Schotte et al. 1990), lack of interpersonal effectiveness (Cole 1989), as well as family conflict (Pfeffer 1981, Wade 1987, Walker and Mehr 1983), excessive levels of life stress (Cohen-Sandler et al. 1982, Orbach 1984, Rich et al. 1988, Sands and Dixon 1986), substance abuse (Murphy 1988), temperament (Benfield et al. 1988), intropunitiveness (Goldberg and Sakinofsky 1988), and serious emotional disturbance (Brent et al. 1986, Friedman et al. 1983, Kuperman et al. 1988, Tardiff and Sweillam 1980) have also received attention.

Based on the current literature, a psychosocial/social-behavioral approach to understanding adolescent self-destructive behavior appears to be most heuristic (Figure 12-9). Adolescent suicide never occurs in the absence of powerful social influences and stressors. Though ultimately suicide is usually a

✓ SKILL DEFICITS (never learned, poor modeling, punishment, etc.)

✓ INTERPERSONAL FAILURE (particularly salient during school years)

✓ "LEARNED HELPLESSNESS"/NEGATIVE COGNITIONS/ FEELINGS OF INADEQUACY (lowering of self–esteem)

✓ HOPELESSNESS

✓ FURTHER REDUCTION IN SOCIAL BEHAVIOR AND REINFORCERS

✓ ISOLATION AND DEPRESSION

✓ SUICIDAL IDEATION/BEHAVIOR

FIGURE 12-9. Social-Skills Deficits/Depression/Suicidality Model

solitary action, its genesis is primarily social in nature. It is important to qualify this assertion with the proviso that the authors perceive that suicide will inevitably be understood best from a diathesis-stress model. This type of model assumes that a genetic/physiological/biochemical diathesis predisposing to suicidal behavior through exposure to salient psychosocial stressors will yield the greatest potential for comprehending and treating adolescent suicidal behavior.

SUICIDAL BEHAVIOR AND PSYCHOTIC PROCESS

Myatt, Caccavale, and Hussey (in press) in a study examining the correlates of suicidal behavior in one hundred adolescents psychiatrically hospitalized at the Adolescent Suicide Research and Intervention Program (Department of Adolescent Psychiatry, Olive View Medical Center) have obtained preliminary data that indicate that suicidal adolescents demonstrate significantly higher levels of psychotic symptomatology than do adolescents who have been hospitalized for reasons other than suicidal behavior or same-age adolescents in the community. Based on these data, we suggest that adolescents who engage in suicidal behavior may be suffering from a low-grade psychotic disorder that precipitates the self-destructive ideation and behavior. Since formal thought disorder has not been hypothesized to be a primary factor in adult or adolescent suicides, the possibility of psychotic process in adolescent suicidal behavior has not been investigated extensively.

Suicide notes accompanying several adolescent suicide attempts offer additional support for this hypothesis. For example, a 17-year-old boy hospitalized at the Adolescent Suicide Research and Intervention Program wrote the following note:

> I sit here in total isolation for I have been alienated from the general population. I see half a sun and it still blinds me for I want total darkness to surround me. What do I do now? I cannot live. I cannot die. Please God help me. I dream of white horses running through green meadows. I hate this for I shall live for black knights and capital punishment. I cannot stay here in what you peasants call life. Please God wake me. The castle on the mountain and the King's on the right for his knight will slay the evil seven-headed dragon. The dragon does not deserve to wear crowns. Therefore I must kill the dragon myself and dwell in my Father's kingdom for eternity.

There was no evidence of (and the patient denied) alcoholism or illicit substance abuse at the time of the note. He was not diagnosed as schizophrenic and within a short time after admission to the hospital and the introduction of a low-dose neuroleptic, his psychotic symptomatology decreased dramatically along with his suicidality.

Analysis of adult suicide notes, such as those presented by Shneidman (1980) in *Voices of Death,* offer similar evidence of a psychotic process underlying suicidal behavior. Shneidman and other thanatologists have developed constructs such as *perturbation, constriction,* and *tunnel vision* to describe the intense agitation that precedes a suicide attempt. It seems equally plausible to propose that a psychotic process, percolated by depression, hopelessness, and psychosocial stressors, is the condition on which suicidal behavior is predicated.

Jorgensen and Mortensen (1990) note that studies of mortality risk following psychosis have been sparse and inconclusive. Their research indicates that first-admitted patients with reactive psychosis have a higher mortality risk than the general population. They also report that this excess mortality is highest for patients of young age and in the first years following the psychotic episode. Anderson and Laerum (1980) relate similar findings, and reference to the relationship between psychosis and mortality can be found in the literature dating back to 1962 (Astrup et al. 1962).

In addition, Braunig (1989) reports an unusually high incidence of suicidality in corticosteroid-induced psychoses and suggested that this phenomenon may be related to corticosteroid-induced lowering of brain serotonin levels. He further remarks that patients with low serotonin metabolism could be predisposed to psychosis and suicidal behavior.

A benefit from conceptualizing the antecedent(s) of suicidal behavior in terms more akin to *DSM-III-R* formulary is that specific treatment strategies are more clearly indicated. In our clinical experience, the introduction of a low-dose neuroleptic to augment the antidepressant medication regimen that is usually in place has been very fruitful. The addition of the low-dose neuroleptic appears to address the confusion, obsessive thoughts, bizarre ideation, constricted worldview, illogical thinking, loosening of associations, and occasional hallucinations presented by these adolescents.

Relieving the depression through antidepressant medication without addressing a covert psychotic process may explain why amelioration of the depressive symptomatology alone does not necessarily resolve the suicidality and in some cases, actually appears to precipitate the suicide attempt. In these cases, it would be theorized that although the individual has more energy and mobility, he is thereby better able to act upon disorganized, irrational, and self-destructive ideation. It also would explain why the suicide methodology and events surrounding the suicide attempt are often so disorganized and illogical. Much effort has gone into explaining and rationalizing the clearly irrational behavior of suicide attempters. It could be advantageous to investigate the premise that the illogical force driving suicidal behavior may be psychosis.

SUICIDE CLUSTERS/CONTAGION

For adolescents, suicide appears to have the potential to be contagious (Bollen and Phillips 1982, Brent et al. 1989, Coleman 1987, Gould and Shaffer 1986, Gould et al. 1989, Robbins and Conroy 1983, Wodarski and Harris 1987). Brent and colleagues (1989) report that at an urban high school in Pittsburgh two students committed suicide within a 4-day period following which seven students attempted suicide (within 18 days of the initial suicides) and an additional twenty-three students developed suicidal ideation. This phenomenon has been referred to as *suicide clusters* and *suicide contagion* (Coleman 1987).

It has been reported that adolescents who kill themselves after a much publicized suicide are frequently those who perceive themselves as contending with similar life circumstances and situations. Preliminary research indicates that adolescents who commit or attempt suicide in the contagion have either contemplated or attempted suicide in the past (Small and Nicholi 1982). The publicized suicide appears to offer the at-risk young adult a stimulus for his or her own suicidal behavior. It is important to note that suicide clusters appear to be an adolescent/young adult phenomenon and are not as well demonstrated in older age groups (Phillips and Carstensen 1986). Adolescents and young adults appear to be easily influenced by the news and entertainment media that often romanticize, sentimentalize, and sensationalize teenage death (Coleman 1987).

ASSESSMENT OF ADOLESCENT SUICIDAL BEHAVIOR

A review of the literature indicates very little agreement on how suicide intent, lethality, and behavior should be evaluated and measured. Smith and colleagues (1984) emphasize that a clear differentiation needs to be made between lethality (the degree to which the individual's suicidal behavior jeopardizes his or her life) and intent (the degree to which the individual perceived that his or her suicidal efforts would result in death). An individual may have a high degree of intent, yet unknowingly select a method with a low degree of lethality. On the other hand, the individual may have a low degree of intent motivating his or her behavior, yet inadvertently select a mode of highly lethal suicidal behavior. For both dimensions, little agreement as to appropriate evaluation exists.

Most mental health practitioners have advocated relying on clinical judgment for assessing suicidality. This method generally does not involve objective, specific criteria. Using clinical judgment alone to evaluate suicidal behavior is marred by being dependent on subjective impressions that are often varied and inconsistent (Hengeveld et al. 1988).

Various scales to measure suicide intent and suicide lethality have been developed (Neuringer 1974). The Suicide Intent Scale (Beck et al. 1974) and the Index of Potential Suicide (Zung 1974) have demonstrated promise as screening tools. The Risk-Rescue Rating Scale (Weisman and Worden 1974), devised as an index of lethality, examines the ratio of risk (the likelihood that the suicidal behavior enacted will result in death) and rescue (the likelihood that the individual will be discovered/rescued). Smith, Conroy, and Ehler (1984) constructed the Lethality of Suicide Attempt Rating Scale in an effort to evaluate objectively the severity of suicidal behavior. Carlson and Cantwell (1982) have advocated utilizing the Children's Depression Inventory (CDI) along with a semistructured interview to evaluate depression and suicidality.

In addition to evaluating suicide intent and lethality, many efforts have been made, as noted above, to ascertain the correlates of suicidal behavior (Asarnow et al. 1987, Droogas et al. 1982, Kashani et al. 1989, Kazdin et al. 1983, Toolan 1981, Wade 1987). The theory here would be that by identifying the exact *suicide correlate equation,* researchers and clinicians would conceivably be able to predict suicidality in a cookbook fashion. Unfortunately, the divination of a recipe for suicide has not been effected.

In a fashion similar to the predicament once faced by depression researchers, acknowledging the prevalence of suicidal phenomena among children and adolescents has left researchers and clinicians in a position of trying to extrapolate the adult suicide literature to a younger population with limited understanding of how much application is appropriate (Sands and Dixon 1986). It is very likely that (similar to the phenomenon of depression) developmental factors are an important subset of variables in outlining the parameters of adolescent suicidal behavior (Pallis et al. 1982). Thus it is quite possible that adult suicide measures will have inconsistent and limited utility in assessing adolescent suicide risk and behavior. While the adult suicide literature is helpful in identifying broad issues in suicide assessment, researchers would be well advised to make efforts to develop assessment tools that are specific to suicidal youth.

Pfeffer (1989) notes that with the realization that youth suicidal behavior has multiple determinants, evaluation of risk must involve many parameters and their multilevel interactions. Instruments, scales, and procedures to evaluate and intervene with suicidal adolescents must be developed and improved. Precipitate, fragmentary, incomplete, and erroneous assessments of suicidal adolescents engender the grave potential to mislead the treatment professionals and to bring about dire consequences.

TREATMENT OF ADOLESCENT SUICIDAL BEHAVIOR

Pfeffer (1988) notes that there are few empirical studies assessing the effectiveness of treating suicidal adolescents. Most information about psychotherapeutic intervention with suicidality has come from the publication of case studies. Turgay (1989) states that a critical gap exists in the literature regarding treatment, management, and prevention issues.

Brent and Kolko (1990) identify four broad treatment strategies for intervention with suicidal adolescents on an outpatient basis: 1) maintenance of a no-suicide contract, 2) availability of 24-hour clinical back-up, 3) steps to maintain compliance, and 4) removal of firearms from the home of the at-risk adolescent. They further note that treatment of the suicidal adolescent should proceed on three levels: 1) treatment of the underlying psychiatric illness, 2) remediation of social- and problem-solving deficits, and 3) family psychoeducation and conflict resolution.

The three significant modes of intervention strategies germane to a successful outcome of decreasing suicidal intent and behavior outlined by Pfeffer (1990) include: (1) a psychotherapeutic-cognitive approach, (2) an environmental-stabilizing approach, and (3) psychopharmacotherapy. When these interventions are used together, they appear to provide the most powerful impact on inhibiting suicidal behavior (Pfeffer 1990).

A cognitive approach to psychotherapy directs attention to the adolescent's coping mechanisms, specifically on reality orientation, impulse control, and perceptions of life circumstances. Often the suicidal adolescent has endured a significant number of lifelong and recent life stresses. These stresses might involve loss of parents or relatives, residential instability, birth of siblings, and family unemployment or illness.

Judicious use of psychopharmacology to help stabilize the suicidal adolescent is an important addition to the other components of treatment. Antidepressants, neuroleptics, and other psychoactive agents titrated to appropriate clinical levels can be very effective. At present, there does not exist a single medication of choice for adolescent suicidality, hence treatment must be individualized.

Based on the premise that the ability to relate well to others is essential to good mental health and success in the home, classroom, and job, social-skills development programming is clearly indicated. Schinke and Gilchrist (1984) propose such a broad-based program under the title of *life skills counseling*.

In most cases, family therapy is indicated. The suicidal adolescent and other family members can work with the therapist to identify mutual concerns, current factors increasing stress, prevailing family coping strategies, and to evaluate interventions that would be most effective in overcoming problems and alleviating stress.

If the adolescent has made a suicide attempt, or if the severity of his or her suicidal ideation seems to indicate that a suicidal attempt is imminent, the adolescent is put on a 72-hour hold and admitted to an acute care psychiatric facility. Crisis intervention temporarily alleviates the adolescent's suicidal action by providing an immediate, monitored, safe environment. However, without continued direct therapeutic intervention, the adolescent will often return to an acutely suicidal state. This is particularly likely if the psychosocial stressors that contributed to the initial suicidal behavior remain unchanged.

In 1989, the Department of Health and Human Services released an important report on youth suicide, which conveyed that public awareness is essential in preventing suicide and that early intervention is critical. Public education should be directed to identification of suicidal behavior and sources of help for the at-risk person. Suicidal acts are more likely to be prevented among adolescents if risk factors associated with suicidal intent are identified as early as possible by family and community members so that treatment can begin immediately.

CURRENT ISSUES, FUTURE DIRECTIONS

The suicidal adolescent population is a grievous problem more substantial today than ever before. It is more than a hypothesis to assert that understanding adolescent suicide and developing more effective forms of intervention are critical professional, ethical, and societal goals. The condition of being dangerous to oneself isolates adolescents from crucial socializing, developmental, and educational forces. Adolescents need a stable peer group, secure family life, consistent extrafamilial adults to serve as objects of identification, as well as a regular school program with numerous healthy academic and extracurricular influences. Many adolescents admitted to inpatient psychiatric facilities due to suicidality have already been hospitalized two, three, or even six times on previous occasions with a subsequent profound disruption of their critical, formative years.

Unfortunately, according to the Secretary's Task Force on Youth Suicide (Alcohol, Drug Abuse, and Mental Health Administration 1989), far too little effort has been expended on research regarding the assessment and treatment of adolescent suicidal behavior. The majority of texts and research regarding this topic has been accomplished during the past 2 decades. Most suicide research in the past has focused on adults.

It is likely that society's conceptualization of childhood and adolescence as developmental stages unsullied by the tragedies of suicide has led to a myopic evaluation of this phenomena. It is only during recent years that the public has acknowledged that children and adolescents do, in fact, take their own lives and that this is developing into a matter of national and international importance.

The recent bestseller, *Final Exit: The Practicalities of Self-Deliverance and Assisted Suicide For the Dying* (Humphry 1991), has achieved great notoriety and some say has prompted a rash of inquiries and purchases by those preoccupied with self-destruction.

Mental health professionals have always relied on the fact that children and adolescents tend to be rather unsophisticated and inaccurate regarding suicide methodology. This proviso is in jeopardy at the present time due to the current widespread notoriety and availability of a cookbook for what the author refers to as *self-deliverance*. While Humphry has defended the book as useful for terminally ill adults who do not want to continue persevering when death is a painful, foregone conclusion, he has not addressed the gravity of making a suicide cookbook available at nationwide booksellers where any distraught teenager with $16.95 can learn explicit strategies for successful self-destruction. The publicity, extensive media coverage, and hyperbole surrounding the release of this book appear to underscore the current national fascination with suicide and death while also emphasizing the fact that we, as a society, are in many ways woefully inept at understanding and handling these topics.

At present, there is a pressing need for developing formal programs of research to evaluate the correlates and components of suicidal behavior. Hospital-based programs, which have access to large numbers of suicidal adolescents, are uniquely qualified to examine these issues. Pfeffer and her team of researchers have utilized this format to conduct relevant, exploratory research of this nature. She has installed one of the few programs in the nation that is consistently examining the phenomenon of child and adolescent suicide. It is clear that similar programs need to be established throughout the country so that a maximum amount of this type of critical information can be obtained, integrated, and published. Furthermore, by establishing these initial programs and demonstrating that they can be instituted and maintained, other institutions will be encouraged to broaden the base of adolescent suicide research by doing likewise.

Arnold (1983), in his book on adolescent alienation, relays a quotation from the Danish theologian and psychologist Kierkegaard: "Every theorist lives in a shack beside the castle that he's built with his language." It is imperative that mental health professionals in the field struggling to develop elaborate theoretical models of adolescent suicidal behavior assessment and remediation, do not end up building castles that neither they themselves nor their audiences can live in or utilize. True improvement in the state of the art will not only be appealing in a conceptually elegant sense, but also must be heuristic, relevant, and realistic.

Our society hypothesizes that childhood and adolescence should be relatively carefree, lighthearted periods. Unfortunately, this must in many cases be considered a misconception on the part of the adults in the youth's social environment and, as Butler so eloquently observed, is often the exception rather than the rule.

REFERENCES

Alcohol, Drug Abuse, and Mental Health Administration (1989). *Report of the secretary's task force on youth suicide. Vols. 1–4.* (DHHS Pub. No. ADM 89-1621). Washington, DC: Superintendent of Documents, U.S. Government Printing Office.

Anderson, J., and Laerum, H. (1980). Psychogenic psychoses: a retrospective study with special reference to clinical course and prognosis. *Acta Psychiatrica Scandinavica* 62:331–342.

Apter, A., Bleich, A., and Tyano, S. (1988). Affective and psychotic psychopathology in hospitalized adolescents. *Journal of the American Academy of Child and Adolescent Psychiatry* 27:116–120.

Arnold, L. E. (1983). *Preventing Adolescent Alienation.* Lexington, MA: D.C. Health.

Asarnow, J. R., Carlson, G. A., and Guthrie, D. (1987). Coping strategies, self-perceptions, hopelessness, and perceived family environments in depressed and suicidal children. *Journal of Consulting and Clinical Psychology* 55:361–366.

Asberg, M., Nordstrom, P., and Traskman-Bendz, L. (1986). Cerebrospinal fluid studies in suicide: an overview. In *Psychobiology of Suicidal Behavior,* ed. J. J. Mann and M. Stanley. New York: Annals of the New York Academy of Sciences.

Astrup, C., Fossum, A., and Holmboe, R. (1962). *Prognosis in Functional Psychoses.* Springfield, IL: Charles C Thomas.

Beck, A. T., Steer, R., Kovacs, M., and Garrison, B. (1985). Hopelessness and eventual suicide: a 10-year prospective study of patients hospitalized with suicidal ideation. *American Journal of Psychiatry* 142:559–563.

Beck, R. W., Morris, J. B., and Beck, A. T. (1974). Cross-validation of the Suicide Intent Scale. *Psychological Reports* 34:445–446.

Benfield, C. Y., Palmer, D. J., Pfefferbaum, B., and Stowe, M. L. (1988). A comparison of depressed and nondepressed disturbed children on measures of attributional style, hopelessness, life stress, and temperament. *Journal of Abnormal Child Psychology* 16:397–410.

Bollen, K. A., and Phillips, D. P. (1982). Imitative suicides: a national study of the effects of television news stories. *American Sociological Review* 47:802–809.

Braunig, P. (1989). Suicidality and corticosteroid-induced psychosis. *Biological Psychiatry* 26:209–210.

Brent, D. A. (1987). Correlates of medical lethality of suicide attempts in children and adolescents. *Journal of the American Academy of Child Psychiatry* 26:87–89.

Brent, D. A., Kalas, R., Edelbrock, C., et al. (1986). Psychopathology and its relationship to suicidal ideation in childhood and adolescence. *Journal of the American Academy of Child Psychiatry* 25:666-673.

Brent, D. A., Kerr, M. M., Goldstein, C., et al. (1989). An outbreak of suicide and suicidal behavior in a high school. *Journal of the American Academy of Child and Adolescent Psychiatry* 28:918-924.

Brent, D. A., and Kolko, D. J. (1990). Suicide and suicidal behavior in children and adolescents. In *Psychiatric Disorders in Children and Adolescents,* ed. B. D. Garfinkel, G. A. Carlson, and E. B. Weller, Philadelphia: W.B. Saunders.

Brent, D. A., Perper, J. A., Goldstein, C. E., et al. (1988). Risk factors for adolescent suicide: a comparison of adolescent suicide victims with suicidal inpatients. *Archives of General Psychiatry* 45:581-588.

Bunney, W. E., Jr., and Fawcett, J. A. (1965). Possibility of a biochemical test for suicidal potential. *Archives of General Psychiatry* 13:232-239.

Carlson, G. A., and Cantwell, D. P. (1982). Suicidal behavior and depression in children and adolescents. *Journal of the American Academy of Child Psychiatry* 21:361-368.

Centers For Disease Control (1991). Attempted suicide among high school students—United States, 1990. *Journal of the American Medical Association* 266:1911-1912.

Cohen-Sandler, R., Berman, A. L., and King, R. A. (1982). Life stress and symptomatology: determinants of suicidal behavior in children. *Journal of the American Academy of Child Psychiatry* 43:962-965.

Cole, D. A. (1989). Psychopathology of adolescent suicide: hopelessness, coping beliefs, and depression. *Journal of Abnormal Psychology* 98:248-255.

Coleman, L. (1987). *Suicide Clusters.* Boston: Faber & Faber.

Crumley, F. E. (1979). Adolescent suicide attempts and borderline personality disorder: clinical features. *Journal of the American Medical Association* 241:2404-2407.

Dorovini-Zis, K., and Zis, A. P. (1987). Increased adrenal weight in victims of violent suicide. *American Journal of Psychiatry* 144:1214-1215.

Droogas, A., Siiter, R., and O'Connell, A. N. (1982). Effects of personal and situational factors on attitudes toward suicide. *Omega* 13:127-144.

Egeland, J. A., and Hostetter, A. M. (1983). Amish study. Part 1: Affective disorders among the Amish, 1976-1980. *American Journal of Psychiatry* 140:56-60.

Egeland, J. A., and Sussex, J. N. (1985). Suicide and family loading for affective disorders. *Journal of the American Medical Association* 254:915-918.

Farberow, N. L., and Shneidman, E. S. (1961). *The Cry for Help.* New York: McGraw-Hill.

Farmer, R. D. (1988). Assessing the epidemiology of suicide and parasuicide. *British Journal of Psychiatry* 153:16-20.

Fowler, R. C., Rich, C. L., and Young, D. (1986). San Diego suicide study. Part 2: Substance abuse in young cases. *Archives of General Psychiatry* 43:962-965.

Friedman, R. C., Aronoff, M. S., Clarkin, J. F., et al. (1983). History of suicidal behavior in depressed and borderline inpatients. *American Journal of Psychiatry* 140:1023-1026.

Garfinkel, B. D. (1989). Depression and suicide among adolescents. Paper presented at Treatment of Adolescents with Alcohol, Drug Abuse, and Mental Health Problems Conference; Alcohol, Drug Abuse, and Mental Health Administration; Arlington, VA.

Goldberg, J., and Sakinofsky, I. (1988). Intropunitiveness and parasuicide: prediction of interview response. *British Journal of Psychiatry* 153:801-804.

Gould, M. S., and Shaffer, D. (1986). The impact of suicide in television movies: evidence of imitation. *New England Journal of Medicine* 315:690-694.

Gould, M. S., Wallenstein, S., and Davidson, L. (1989). Suicide clusters: a critical review. *Suicide and Life-Threatening Behavior* 19:17-29.

Gross-Isseroff, R., Israeli, M., and Biegon, A. (1989). Autoradiographic analysis of tritiated imipramine binding in the human brain post mortem: effects of suicide. *Archives of General Psychiatry* 46:237-241.

Hawton, K., and Catalan, J. (1987). *Attempted Suicide: A Practical Guide to its Nature and Management.* Oxford, England: Oxford University Press.

Hawton, K., and Osborn, M. (1981). Suicide and attempted suicide in children and adolescents. In *Advances in Clinical Child Psychology,* vol. 4, ed. B. Lahey and A. Kazdin. New York: Plenum.

Hengeveld, M. W., Kerkhof, A. J., and Van der Wal, J. (1988). Evaluation of psychiatric consultations with suicide attempters. *Acta Psychiatrica Scandinavica* 77:283-289.

Holden, R. R., Mendonca, J. D., and Serin, R. C. (1989). Suicide, hopelessness, and social desirability: a test of an interactive model. *Journal of Consulting and Clinical Psychology* 57:500-504.

Humphry, D. (1991). *Final Exit: The Practicalities of Self-Deliverance and Assisted Suicide for the Dying.* Eugene, OR: The Hemlock Society.

Jorgensen, P., and Mortensen, P. B. (1990). Reactive psychosis and mortality. *Acta Psychiatrica Scandinavica* 81:277-279.

Kashani, J. H., Reid, J. C., and Rosenberg, T. K. (1989). Levels of hopelessness in children and adolescents: a developmental perspective. *Journal of Consulting and Clinical Psychology* 57:496-499.

Kazdin, A. E., French, N. H., Unis, A. S., et al. (1983). Hopelessness, depression, and suicidal intent among psychiatrically disturbed inpatient children. *Journal of Consulting and Clinical Psychology* 51:504-510.

Kazdin, A. E., Rodgers, A., and Colbus, D. (1986). The Hopelessness Scale For Children: psychometric characteristics and concurrent validity. *Journal of Consulting and Clinical Psychology* 54:241-245.

Kennedy, P., and Kreitman, N. (1973). An epidemiological survey of parasuicide ("attempted suicide") in general practice. *British Journal of Psychiatry* 123:23-34.

Krarup, G., Nielsen, B., Rask, P., and Petersen, P. (1991). Childhood experiences and repeated suicidal behavior. *Acta Psychiatrica Scandinavica* 83:16-19.

Kreitman, N., and Casey, P. (1988). Repetition of parasuicide: an epidemiological and clinical study. *British Journal of Psychiatry* 153:792-800.

Krieger, G. (1970). Biochemical predictors of suicide. *Diseases of the Nervous System* 31:478-482.

Kuperman, S., Black, D. W., and Burns, T. L. (1988). Excess mortality among formerly hospitalized child psychiatric patients. *Archives of General Psychiatry* 45:277-282.

Levenson, M., and Neuringer, C. (1971). Problem-solving behavior in suicidal adolescents. *Journal of Consulting and Clinical Psychology* 37:433-436.

Levy, B., and Hensen, E. (1969). Failure of the urinary test for suicidal potential. *Archives of General Psychiatry* 20:415-418.

Lidberg, L., Tuck, J. R., Asberg, M., et al. (1985). Homicide, suicide, and CSF5-HIAA. *Acta Psychiatrica Scandinavia* 71:230-236.

Mann, J. J., DeMeo, M. D., Keilp, J. G., and McBride, P. A. (1989). Biological correlates of suicidal behavior in youth. In *Suicide among Youth: Perspectives on Risk and Prevention,* ed. C. R. Pfeffer. Washington, DC: American Psychiatric Press.

Mann, J. J., Stanley, M., McBride, A., and McEwen, B. S. (1986). Increased serotonin and B-adrenergic receptor binding in the frontal cortices of suicide victims. *Archives of General Psychiatry* 20:100-109.

Marttunen, M. J., Aro, H. M., Henriksson, M. M., and Lonnqvist, J. K. (1991). Mental disorders in adolescent suicide: *DSM-III-R* Axes I and II diagnoses in suicides among 13 to 19 year olds in Finland. *Archives of General Psychiatry* 48:834-838.

Miles, D. (1977). Conditions predisposing to suicide: a review. *Journal of Nervous Mental Disorders* 164:231-246.

Minkoff, K., Bergman, E., Beck, A. T., and Beck, R. (1973). Hopelessness, depression, and attempted suicide. *American Journal of Psychiatry* 130:455-487.

Moscicki, E. K. (1989). Epidemiological surveys for studying suicidal behavior. *Suicide and Life-Threatening Behavior* 19:131-146.

Murphy, G. E. (1988). Suicide and substance abuse. *Archives of General Psychiatry* 45:593-594.

Murphy, G. E., and Wetzel, R. D. (1982). Family history of suicidal behavior among suicide attempters. *Journal of Nervous Mental Disorders* 170:86–90.

Myatt, R. J., Caccavale, J., and Hussey, S. (in press). *Adolescent Suicidal Behavior and Psychotic Symptomatology.* Manuscript submitted for publication.

Neimeyer, R. A. (1983). Toward a personal construct conceptualization of depression and suicide. *Death Education* 7:127–173.

Nemeroff, C. B., Owens, M. J., Bissette, G., et al. (1988). Reduced corticotropin releasing factor binding sites in the frontal cortex of suicide victims. *Archives of General Psychiatry* 45:577–579.

Neuringer, C., ed. (1974). *Psychological Assessment of Suicidal Risk.* Springfield, IL: Charles C Thomas.

O'Carroll, P. (1989). Validity and reliability of suicide mortality data. *Suicide and Life-Threatening Behavior* 19:1–16.

Orbach, I. (1984). Personality characteristics, life circumstances, and dynamics of suicidal children. *Death Education* 8:37–52.

Pallis, D. J., Barraclough, B. M., Levy, A. B., et al. (1982). Estimating suicide risk among attempted suicides. *British Journal of Psychiatry* 141:37–44.

Pfeffer, C. R. (1981). The family system of suicidal children. *American Journal of Psychotherapy* 353:330–341.

—— (1986). *The Suicidal Child.* New York: Guilford.

—— (1988). Clinical dilemmas in the prevention of adolescent suicidal behavior. *Adolescent Psychiatry* 15:407–421.

—— (1989). Assessment of suicidal children and adolescents. *Psychiatric Clinics of North America* 12:861–872.

—— (1990). Clinical perspectives on treatment of suicidal behavior among children and adolescents. *Psychiatric Annals* 20:143–150.

Phillips, D. P., and Carstensen, L. L. (1986). Clustering of teenage suicides after television news stories about suicide. *New England Journal of Medicine* 315:685–689.

Pokorny, A. D. (1968). Myths about suicide. In *Suicidal Behaviors,* ed. H. L. P. Resnik. Boston: Little, Brown.

—— (1983). Prediction of suicide in psychiatric patients: report of a prospective study. *Archives of General Psychiatry* 40:249–257.

Quinnett, P. G. (1987). *Suicide: The Forever Decision.* New York: Continuum.

Rich, C. L., Fowler, R. C., Fogarty, L. A., and Young, D. (1988). San Diego suicide study: relationships between diagnoses and stressors. *Archives of General Psychiatry* 45:589–592.

Rich, C. L., Young, D., and Fowler, R. C. (1986). San Diego suicide study. *Archives of General Psychiatry* 43:577–582.

Robbins, D. R., and Alessi, N. E. (1985). Depressive symptoms and suicidal behavior in adolescents. *American Journal of Psychiatry* 142:588–592.

Robbins, D., and Conroy, R. C. (1983). A cluster of adolescent suicide attempts: is suicide contagious? *Journal of Adolescent Health Care* 3:253–255.

Rotheram-Borus, M. J., and Trautman, P. D. (1988). Hopelessness, depression, and suicidal intent among adolescent suicide attempters. *Journal of the American Academy of Child and Adolescent Psychiatry* 27:700–704.

Roy, A. (1983a). Family history of suicide. *Archives of General Psychiatry* 40:971–974.

—— (1983b). Suicide in depressives. *Comprehensive Psychiatry* 24:487–491.

—— (1986). Genetics of suicide. In *Psychobiology of Suicidal Behavior,* ed. J. J. Mann and M. Stanley. New York: Annals of the New York Academy of Science.

Sands, R. G., and Dixon, S. L. (1986). Adolescent crisis and suicidal behavior: dynamics and treatment. *Child and Adolescent Social Work* 3:109–122.

Schinke, S. P., and Gilchrist, L. D. (1984). *Life Skills Counseling with Adolescents.* Baltimore: University Park.

Schulsinger, R., Kety, S., Rosenthal, D., and Wender, P. (1979). A family study of suicide. In *Origins, Prevention, and Treatment of Affective Disorders,* M. Schou and E. Stromgren. New York: Academic.

Schotte, D. E., and Clum, G. A. (1987). Problem-solving skills in suicidal psychiatric patients. *Journal of Consulting and Clinical Psychology* 55:49–54.

Schotte, D. E., Cools, J., and Payvar, S. (1990). Problem-solving deficits in suicidal patients: trait vulnerability or state phenomenon? *Journal of Consulting and Clinical Psychology* 58:562–564.

Shaffer, D. (1974). Suicide in childhood and early adolescence. *Journal of Child Psychology and Psychiatry* 15:275–291.

Shafii, M., Carrigan, S., Whittinghill, J. R., and Derrick, A. (1985). Psychological autopsy of completed suicide in children and adolescents. *American Journal of Psychiatry* 142:1061–1064.

Shneidman, E. S. (1967). *Essays in Self-Destruction.* New York: Science House.

———— (1980). *Voices of Death.* New York: Harper & Row.

———— (1981). *Suicide Thoughts and Reflections, 1960–1980.* New York: Human Sciences.

———— (1985). *Definition of Suicide.* New York: Wiley.

Small, G. W., and Nicholi, A. M. (1982). Mass hysteria among school children. *Archives of General Psychiatry* 39:721–724.

Smith, K., Conroy, R. W., and Ehler, B. D. (1984). Lethality of Suicide Attempt Rating Scale. *Suicide and Life-Threatening Behavior* 14:215–242.

Stanley, M., and Stanley, B. (1989). Biochemical studies in suicide victims: current findings and future implications. *Suicide and Life-Threatening Behavior* 19:30–42.

Struve, F. A., Klein, D. F., and Saraf, K. R. (1972). Electroencephalographic correlates of suicide ideation and attempts. *Archives of General Psychiatry* 37:164–169.

Sudak, H. S., Ford, A. B., and Rushforth, N. B. (1984). Adolescent suicide: an overview. *American Journal of Psychotherapy* 38:350–362.

Tardiff, K., and Sweillam, A. (1980). Assault, suicide, and mental illness. *Archives of General Psychiatry* 37:164–169.

Taylor, M. C., and Wicks, J. W. (1980). The choice of weapons: a study of methods of suicide by sex, race, and region. *Suicide and Life-Threatening Behavior* 10:142–151.

Toolan, J. M. (1981). Depression and suicide in children: an overview. *American Journal of Psychotherapy* 35:311–322.

Tsuang, M. T. (1977). Genetic factors in suicide. *Diseases of the Nervous System* 38:498–501.

———— (1978). Suicide in schizophrenia, manics, depressives, and surgical controls: a comparison with general population suicide mortality. *Archives of General Psychiatry* 35:153–155.

Turgay, A. (1989). An integrative treatment approach to child and adolescent suicidal behavior. *Psychiatric Clinics of North America* 12:971–985.

Wade, N. L. (1987). Suicide as a resolution of separation-individuation among adolescent girls. *Adolescence* 22:169–177.

Walker, B. A., and Mehr, M. (1983). Adolescent suicide—a family crisis: a model for effective intervention by family therapists. *Adolescence* 18:285–292.

Weisman, A., and Worden, J. W. (1974). Risk-rescue rating in suicide assessment. In *The Prediction of Suicide,* ed. A. T. Beck, H. L. Resnik, and D. Lettieri. New York, Charles.

Welner, A., Welner, Z., and Fishman, R. (1979). Psychiatric inpatients: eight-to-ten year follow-up. *Archives of General Psychiatry* 36:689–700.

Wetzel, R. D., Margulies, T., and Davis, R. (1980). Hopelessness, depression, and suicide intent. *Journal of Consulting and Clinical Psychology* 41:159–160.

Wodarski, J. S., and Harris, P. (1987). Adolescent suicide: a review of influences and the means for prevention. *Social Work* 32:477–484.

Zung, W. W. (1974). The Index of Potential Suicide (IPS): a rating scale for suicide prevention. In *The Prediction of Suicide,* ed. A. T. Beck, H. L. Resnick, and D. Lettieri. Bowie, MD: Charles.

THE PSYCHOLOGICAL
AUTOPSY
Part V

Various approaches to knowledge are encouraged in suicidology. The study of suicide notes is one avenue; another, which also has its origin at the beginning of contemporary suicidology, is the *psychological autopsy*. Shneidman, in collaboration with the Los Angeles Suicide Prevention Center and the Los Angeles Medical Examiner's offices, coined the term. It refers to a set of procedures, including systematic interviews of survivors, whose primary purpose is to establish the mode of death of the decedent. Part V consists of three chapters: a review of literature, exemplified by two cases; an outline of the psychological autopsy in forensic suicidology; and an explication of a suicide videotape, addressing the question, "When someone commits suicide, who is responsible?"

13: THE EXPANDING ROLE OF PSYCHOLOGICAL AUTOPSIES

Douglas Jacobs and Marci Ellyn Klein

INTRODUCTION

It was Edwin Shneidman, in collaboration with the Los Angeles Suicide Prevention Center and the Los Angeles Medical Examiner's Office, who coined the term *psychological autopsy* to refer to a procedure used to classify equivocal deaths. The method entails reconstructing a biography of the deceased person through psychological information gathered from personal documents; from police, medical, and coroner records; and from interviews with family, friends, co-workers, school associates, and physicians (Litman 1989). While the psychological autopsy has traditionally been used as a technique for gathering data, since its development in the late 1950s it has been become recognized as a valuable tool for therapeutic and other purposes as well.

Indeed, the literature describes at least six purposes of psychological autopsies. Psychological autopsies, for example, are currently used to: (1) determine the mode of death; (2) determine a person's intention to die through retrospective reconstruction; (3) determine why a person would choose suicide in terms of their motivation, personal philosophy, and psychodynamics; (4) determine why a person would suicide at a particular time by analyzing the temporal precipitants; (5) serve as a research tool to aid in the understanding and prevention of suicide; and (6) serve as a therapeutic tool to aid the survivors of suicide.

In this chapter, we will first review some of the traditional ways in which psychological autopsies have been used, and then propose two new ways in which we have found the psychological autopsy technique to be helpful. In one, a psychological autopsy which we conducted was admitted as evidence in a criminal case in which a mother was accused of contributing to the suicide of her teenage daughter. In the second, a psychological autopsy which we conducted was used as a basis for congressional testimony regarding whether a naval crewman on the USS-Iowa was both suicidal and homicidal at the time of the shipboard explosion. In both of these cases, the admission of the psychological autopsy as evidence in a judicial and legislative arena, respectively, was considered to be precedent-setting and, as such, raised issues which we feel warrant discussion.

TRADITIONAL USES OF PSYCHOLOGICAL AUTOPSIES

Use of Psychological Autopsies in Coroner's Reports

A primary function of coroners is to determine modes of deaths—that is, whether the manner of death is natural, accidental, homicidal, suicidal, or unable to be determined. While certification of death is thought to have important social, legal, and research implications, the determination is often difficult to make, and this is especially the case when it comes to differentiating suicides from accidents. Indeed, two-thirds of those who suicide reportedly do not leave notes (O'Carroll 1989). Thus, in 1958, the chief medical examiner of the Los Angeles coroner's office asked a team of psychologists and psychiatrists, including Litman, Faberow, and Shneidman, to assist him in evaluating the equivocal cases. Their efforts to clarify situations in which the cause of death could be established, but the mode of death was not immediately clear, became known as psychological autopsies (Shneidman 1981).

Equivocal suicides, as originally defined by Litman and his colleagues (1963), are "cases in which suicide is a possibility but in which there could be more than one interpretation and therefore, the decision is uncertain and doubtful (p. 102). Suicide, according to these same authors, should involve a "direct connection between a deceased's intention, his self-destructive action, and his subsequent death" (Litman et al. 1963, p. 102). Uncertainty about the correct certification is purported to exist "when the victim's intention is ambivalent, with coexisting wishes both to live and to die, or when the self-destructive action is in itself inconclusive, or when death follows the action after a considerable delay" (Litman et al. 1963, p. 102). The psychological autopsy technique focuses on what is usually the missing element," according to Curphey (1968), "namely the *intention* of the deceased in relation to his own death" (p. 41).

The psychological autopsy method is based on the assumption that "most suicide victims communicate their intentions and the role of the psychologist or psychiatrist is to find the clues left behind. Interviews with survivors are conducted. Medical records are studied, along with notes, diaries and letters left behind by the victim" (Scanlon 1987). Clark and Fawcett (1992), who reviewed the literature on community-based psychological autopsy studies, found that indeed there was direct communication of suicidal intent to significant others in the weeks prior to the suicide in two-thirds of completed suicides. It should be noted, however, that these family members and friends of the suicide victim may not have recognized the gravity of the communication at the time that it was relayed (Clark and Fawcett 1992, Robins et al. 1959).

Determining the mode of death is ubiquitously considered important. Indeed, suicide mortality data has been used since the well-known work of the sociologist Emile Durkheim in the nineteenth century to assess the magnitude of the problem of suicide; to identify particular groups at risk for suicide; and to generate and test hypotheses about the etiology of suicide. Suicide mortality data has also been used to evaluate the effectiveness of suicide prevention efforts and to measure the general mental health of communities (O'Carroll 1989). Even so, there are strong doubts regarding the reliability and validity of suicide statistics in the United States and abroad as a result of the widely varying methods currently used to report and classify suicidal deaths, and the fact that in many places, as Curphey (1968) points out, "problems of certification are resolved on superficial or incomplete evidence or on impressions and preconceived opinions rather than on the objective accumulation of all the possible facts, including histological, toxicological, and *psychological data* . . ." (p. 44). O'Carroll (1989), of the Centers for Disease Control in Atlanta, who reviewed the literature regarding the validity and reliability of suicide statistics, found that while there is general agreement that suicides are likely to be undercounted both for structural and sociocultural reasons, there is not much agreement as to the degree to which true suicides are undercounted. O'Carroll's (1989) estimate is that the sensitivity with which medical examiners certify true suicides varies from approximately 55 percent to 99 percent, though specificity is good.

In Los Angeles, about one in five hundred deaths each year is classified an equivocal suicide (Litman et al. 1963), and between sixty and sixty-five of these equivocal cases are referred each year to the Los Angeles Suicide Prevention Center for psychological autopsies by the coroner's office, who have had a contract with each other since the early 1960s (Litman 1989). However, there is reportedly only one other jurisdiction outside of Los Angeles that routinely relies on psychological autopsies in equivocal cases (Jobes et al. 1986). One reason for the infrequent use of the psychological autopsy technique may be the limited training and exposure that coroners (who are often politically appointed, legally or medically trained) receive in the psychological aspects of equivocal deaths (Jobes 1986). Curphy (1961), when he was chief medical examiner-coroner in Los Angeles, noted that "social scientists with special skills in human behavior can offer [coroners] much valuable assistance" since "both the pathologist and the lay investigator lack sufficient training in the field of human behavior to be able to estimate with any fair degree of accuracy the mental processes of the victim likely to lead to suicidal death" (Shneidman 1981, p. 329). Thus, because of the circumscribed use of psychological autopsies, "too many certificates of death fall within the category of fictitious accuracy" (Curphey 1968, p. 44).

However, it is clear that if psychological autopsies are to be implemented more frequently, it needs to be demonstrated that psychological autopsies actually have an impact on coroners' determination of death in equivocal cases.

Jobes and colleagues (1986) were the first researchers to attempt to evaluate empirically the effect of psychological information on coroners' determinations of manner of death in equivocal cases. In their study, 195 coroners serving as subjects reviewed either *typical* cases of death (i.e., cases in which the manner of death was not difficult to certify) or *equivocal* cases of death with or without psychological autopsies. The psychological autopsies were standardized in this study to provide similar information in all cases, and included the decedent's demographics, lifestyle, personality features, and a psychological interpretation of death. Jobes and colleagues' (1986) findings suggested not only that psychological information has a statistically significant impact on coroners' determinations of manner of death in equivocal cases involving single cars, children, autoerotic hanging, and psychosis, but also in some previously classified typical cases involving Russian roulette and psychotic deaths as well. When Litman (1989) compared coroners' original opinions of "probable suicide," or alternatively "probable accident," with the final opinions of the Los Angeles Suicide Prevention Center, he too found that the original opinion was contradicted in about 5 percent of the cases.

Moreover, Jobes and his colleagues (1986) found that coroners have a response bias against labeling certain deaths, particularly Russian Roulette[1] and psychotic deaths, as suicides. These empirical findings are important insofar as O'Carroll (1989) has argued in his aforementioned article on the reliability and validity of suicide mortality data that: "When official statistics are interpreted with a degree of caution and an understanding of source and direction of biases likely to affect published rates, however, it seems unlikely major conclusions based on these statistics will be in error" (p. 14). In this same vein, Litman (1989) also found significant bias in the Los Angeles studies in favor of excluding gunshot deaths and including ingestion deaths in equivocal cases. In fact, as Shneidman (1981) and Curphey (1968) pointed out, drug-related deaths can be among the most equivocal as to mode of death, and especially so when they involve ingestion of barbiturates and/or tranquilizers. As a related aside, Litman and his Los Angeles colleagues, who had conducted a psychological autopsy of Marilyn Monroe's drug-related death, concluded that the actress "probably committed suicide" (Scanlon 1987).

Thus, descriptive case studies have often been used to show the utility of psychological autopsies for certifying the manner of death in equivocal cases (Litman et al. 1963). Shneidman (1981) reports that "between 5 and 20% of all deaths that need to be certified are not clear as to the correct or appropriate mode" (p. 326), and that the drug ingestion deaths can be among the most equivocal cases. Suicidologists are considered to be helpful to the coroner's office by suggesting ways of differentiating suicides from other modes of death and by helping to educate the coroner's staff in the interpretation of these standards

---

[1]It is interesting to note that Litman, in a 1987 article, strongly argues that "death by Russian roulette is known and predictable" and that he would term death by such means as suicide (p. 90).

(Litman 1989). Psychological autopsies "serve to increase the accuracy of certification (which is in the best interests of the overall mental health concerns of the community)" (Shneidman 1981, p. 333). Thus, as Weisman (1967) opines, the major contribution of psychological autopsies "has been to introduce the psychosocial context into decisions about the cause of death" since the "examination of post-mortem remains can tell only what lesions the patient died *with* not what he died *from*" (p. 18).

The utility of psychological autopsies for determining mode of death has also received some empirical support. Jobes and his colleagues' (1986) study, for example, provided some validation of the use of psychological autopsies in equivocal cases, as well as in cases involving psychotic and Russian-Roulette deaths.

Use of Psychological Autopsy Studies in Research

Litman (1989) reviewed five-hundred equivocal cases, which had been referred to the Los Angeles Suicide Prevention Center between July 1977 and May 1985. The purpose of this research study was to identify those factors used in making the determination of whether an equivocal death was an accidental death or a suicide. He found that significant factors included life-style, recent stress, suicidal communications, previous self-destructive behaviors, history of depression, and special efforts to procure the method of death and to secure privacy as well as physical evidence (e.g., large amounts of drugs in the blood).

The psychological autopsy technique is reported to have been used for research on suicide even before the term was ever coined. The first psychological autopsy is thought to have been a community-based research study reported by Robins and his colleagues in 1959 of 134 cases of completed suicide in St. Louis. While there have only been a handful of large-scale community-based studies of suicide using psychological autopsies as a research technique (Clark and Horton 1990), these studies have yielded a great deal of data regarding the characteristics and factors common to the histories of suicide completers. For example, suicide completers have been found to be twice as likely to be male as female, to almost always qualify for a psychiatric diagnosis,[2] and more often than not to communicate intent (Clark and Horton 1990). These risk factors have enabled clinicians, families, and others to better predict the signs of suicidality and to seek treatment sooner than they otherwise would.

Sanborn and colleagues (1974) also used the psychological autopsy technique in their study of possible risk factors for suicide. Specifically, they focused on the relationships between occupational status and related variables and suicide in a sample that consisted of the twenty-two suicides that occurred between March 1968 and March 1970 in two counties in New Hampshire.

---

[2]About half of suicides are preceded by major affective disorder with one or more episodes (Litman 1987).

Psychological autopsies were reportedly utilized by these authors to discover information of a psychosocial nature, which was unattainable from the usual sources, such as the type of person the victim was and what he wanted from life; whether there was a significant change in his behavior toward the end; what he hated, feared, or cherished in life; and what was the victim's attitude toward life and death. The findings from Sanborn and colleagues' (1974) psychological autopsy study indicated that the prototypical suicidal individual is either not currently working or working and frustrated, is experiencing acute stress and frustration in life areas apart from work, has experienced a major change in his occupational status within the past 12 months, and has an alcohol problem. While these researchers did not conduct psychological autopsies of a control group of nonsuicidal deaths, they did compare their findings whenever possible to available epidemiological data. For example, they reported that 50 percent of their sample of completed suicides had histories of chronic heavy drinking as compared to the national norm of one adult in twenty-five being alcoholic.

Shneidman (1971) reanalyzed Terman's well-known, longitudinal study of intellectually gifted male children to determine if prodromal clues for suicide could be found in this data too. Terman's data consisted of, for example, a developmental record, health history, medical examination, home and family background, school history, character-trait ratings, personality evaluations by parents and teachers, interest tests, and school achievement tests. Thirty cases were selected for Shneidman's (1971) study, including five suicides, ten natural deaths, and fifteen persons who were still living. The latter two subgroups were matched with the five suicides in terms of age, occupational level, and father's occupational level.[3] While Shneidman was blind to the classifications (suicide, natural death, or living) of the cases, he did know the total numbers of cases in each subgroup, a small limitation of this study. The cases were analyzed in terms of two basic continua—perturbation (i.e., how upset the individual is) and lethality (i.e., how likely it is that he will take his own life in the immediate future)—by means of both a Meyerian *life chart* and a psychological autopsy. The method was able to predict four of the five cases who had committed suicide, which is an excellent validation of the utility of Shneidman's procedure insofar as the chance probability of this occurring is reportedly one in 1,131.

While the ideal procedure for conducting psychological autopsies is to interview close survivors of the decedent, Shneidman (1971) was limited in this study to an examination of folder materials. His findings, however, were

---

[3]Shneidman's decision to control for occupational level was an interesting, though unexplained, choice insofar as there is data suggesting that there may be a correlation between socioeconomic status, which includes such variables as occupation and status, and suicide. The direction of the relationship between these variables, however, is not yet clear. Ellis and Allen (1961), for example, found the suicide rate to be directly related to social status, with people in the professions killing themselves more frequently than unskilled laborers; Maris (1969), however, found the suicide rate to be inversely related to social status. (See Sanborn and colleagues [1974] for a brief review of the literature.)

striking, and suggested that discernible early clues to suicide may indeed be found in longitudinal case-history data. In fact, "among those who committed suicide in their fifties—the pattern of life consistent with this outcome seemed clearly discernible *by the time they were in their late twenties*" (Shneidman 1971a, p. 36). The prodromal clues to suicide in this gifted sample were deemed to be instability (e.g., chronic as well as a recent downhill course); trauma in early childhood, adolescence, or adulthood (e.g., acute rejection by one or both parents, lack of family psychological support, separation or divorce of parents, rejection by wife) and personality controls (negative inner controls of default). In addition, the behavior of significant others as well as a burning out of the individual's drive and affect (the very style of living which was thought to be in itself a substitute for overt suicide) were also noted to be important factors affecting outcome. While there is no reason to believe that Shneidman's (1971) findings would not generalize to others, further research needs to be done to demonstrate the applicability of these prodromal clues to suicide in individuals who are not extremely bright, or Caucasian, or male.

In addition, it should be noted that the psychological autopsy method has been used in comparisons of male driver fatalities with completed male suicides. Shaffer and his colleagues (1972), in their study at Johns Hopkins School of Medicine, found that male suicides were seen as more negative, helpless, suspicious, anxious, withdrawn, nervous, bizarre, and depressed than driver fatalities by informants. Indeed, the male suicides not only exhibited significantly more psychopathological symptoms, but were also reported to create greater dissatisfaction in informants with socially expected as well as free-time activities (Shaffer et al. 1972). Shaffer and his colleagues, in this 1972 paper, also advocated the use of the Katz Adjustment Scales—R forms, a standardized instrument, to increase the reliability and validity of the psychological autopsy studies. Other researchers, such as Rudestam (1979), also stressed the value of incorporating quantitative measures and standardized interviews and assessments into psychological autopsy studies.

Thus, psychological autopsies can have, as Shneidman (1981) stated, "the heuristic function of providing the serious investigator with clues that he may then use to assess lethal intent in living persons" (p. 333). Psychological autopsy studies, for example, have indicated that being male or alcoholic; or having a history of past suicide attempts, depression or other symptoms of psychopathology; as well as instability, trauma, and/or a nonsupportive spouse put one at increased risk for suicide in adulthood.

Use of Psychological Autopsies for Research on Childhood and Adolescent Suicide

There is research indicating that young children, like adults, can have suicidal thoughts and carry out suicidal actions (Litman 1987, Pfeffer 1984). Indeed, a series of studies by Pfeffer and her colleagues beginning in 1979 have found, for example, a 75 percent prevalence rate of suicidal behavior in psychiatric inpatients aged 6 to 12, a 33 percent prevalence rate of suicidal behavior in psychiatric outpatients, and even a 12 percent rate of suicidal ideation and behaviors in school children with no psychiatric history (Pfeffer 1984, Pfeffer et al. 1979, 1980, 1982). Suicide in preteenage children though is generally rare since self-destructive behaviors in children are usually not fatal since children, because of developmental and cognitive constraints, often lack the ability to form and carry out suicidal plans. As Litman (1987) reports, "experience indicates that a person must have a certain minimal degree of intact volition and thinking ability, and understanding of cause and effect, in order to produce fatal self-inflicted injuries" (p. 91). In this same vein, Pfeffer et al. (1980) found that psychiatrically hospitalized children with suicidal ideation are more verbal and have higher IQ scores than nonsuicidal child psychiatric inpatients.

As in adults, there is hesitancy on the part of individuals in both the medical and wider community to label deaths in children and adolescents as suicides.[4] Part of this clearly arises from the fact that there is generally a low risk of suicide in children and adolescents compared to other age groups; but it is also likely related to the psychoanalytic tradition that has for years theoretically argued over the presence of depression in children, along with the stigma and taboo ubiquitously attached to suicide — which, according to Litman (1965), is considered "a grave social wrong by the prevailing religious, legal, social, and medical ethics" (p. 570). Indeed, O'Carroll (1989), in his consideration of the reliability and validity of suicide mortality data, reported that "at least some true suicides are incorrectly certified, sometimes deliberately, in response to a variety of factors that influence coroners and medical examiners to avoid certifying deaths as due to suicide. These factors may be sociocultural (Douglas 1967), religious, financial (Litman et al. 1963), or political" (p. 7). While, as in adults, some argue that the suicide rate in children and adolescents is a gross underestimate of the actual rate of suicide in these populations, all would agree, however, that the rate of suicide in children and adolescents has increased dramatically over the years. A conservative estimate reported by Shafii and his colleagues (1988) based on statistics from the Centers for Disease Control is that more than fifteen-hundred children and adolescents under 19 years of age commit suicide every year in the United States.

Thus, there is much literature to suggest that suicide has increased dramatically among children and adolescents. Some estimate that the rate of suicide in adolescents in particular has increased by as much as 72 percent in 2 decades (Curran 1987) and by 300 percent in 3 decades (Brent, Perper, and Allman 1987, Frederick 1978, Shaffer and Fisher 1981). In fact, suicide has

---

[4]Interestingly, Litman (1989) found that equivocal deaths are somewhat younger than the cases classified as nonequivocal suicides by the Los Angeles Suicide Prevention Center, and one might wonder to what extent this is due to hesitancy to classify deaths where there is suicidal intent and actions in children and adolescents as suicides.

recently been ranked as the leading cause of death among adolescents over the age of 15 (Brent, Perper, and Allman 1987). Brent and colleagues (1987), who reviewed death certificates and coroners reports of 10- to 19-year-old residents of Allegheny County who committed suicide between the years 1960 to 1983, proposed that the epidemic increase in the suicide rate among youth may be related to both the increase in the prevalence of alcohol abuse and the association between alcohol intoxication and suicide by firearms. Yet there is still relatively little known about the phenomenon of suicide in childhood and adolescence since many of the studies that have investigated the factors contributing to suicide in these age groups are rife with methodological difficulties, including such problems as lack of control groups and follow-up studies (Shafii et al. 1985, Stanley and Barter 1970).

The psychological autopsy technique, though, has recently been applied to studies of completed suicide in children and adolescents with promising results. Shafii and his colleagues (1985) at the University of Louisville School of Medicine, for example, used the psychological autopsy technique to explore systematically the psychological factors contributing to suicide in children and adolescents. The psychological autopsies these researchers conducted consisted of interviewing family, relatives, friends, and significant others of twenty children and adolescents aged 12–19 years who had committed suicide and twenty matched-pair control subjects who were friends of the suicide victims using a 109-item psychological profile of suicide that had been developed specifically for this purpose. Their findings indicated that suicide victims were more likely than controls to have expressed suicidal ideation and to have had a history of suicide threats, suicide attempts, drug or alcohol abuse, antisocial behavior, or inhibited personality. In addition, exposure to suicide in family and friends as well as a parental history of emotional problems and absence or abusiveness were significant factors. Interestingly, Shafii and his colleagues (1985) did not find significant differences between the victims and control subjects in terms of broken homes, overcrowded living conditions, parental dependency on drugs or alcohol, demanding parents, poor academic performance, being behind age appropriate grade level, or being a school dropout.

In a later article, Shafii and colleagues (1988) reported on their results from psychological autopsies on twenty-one children and adolescents aged 11–19 years who committed suicide and a matched-pair control group. Their primary interest in this study was to explore whether suicide in children and adolescents results from serious emotional disorders or, alternatively, from isolated impulsive acts in response to a personal crisis in otherwise healthy individuals. In their study, they found that in almost all cases suicide was the final outcome of a serious psychiatric disorder. Indeed, *DSM-II-R* criteria for postmortem diagnosis revealed that 95 percent of the suicide victims as compared to 48 percent of the controls had at least one diagnosable mental disorder; 81 percent of the suicide victims had co-morbidity as compared to 29 percent of the controls; 76 percent of the suicide victims versus 24 percent of the controls had a primary or secondary diagnosis of major depression and/or dysthymic disorder; and 62 percent of suicide victims versus 29 percent of controls had a primary or secondary diagnosis of alcohol or drug abuse. While all these findings were statistically significant, there were no statistically significant differences found in this study between the suicide victims and the controls in terms of the presence of either personality or physical disorders.

Shafii and his colleagues' (1985) research is important insofar as it is a first attempt to address one of the primary criticisms of the use of the psychological autopsy technique. This is, as Shaffer and colleagues (1972) have pointed out, that: "Implicit in this approach is the need to explain phenomenon on a plausible, causal, usually psychodynamic basis. Unfortunately, the plausibility of any such explanation is no guarantee of its validity. Indeed, one might question whether similar dynamics might frequently be uncovered in the backgrounds of persons whose lives were not terminated." Shafii and his colleagues' efforts are among the first to attempt to increase reliability and validity of information concerning psychosocial and personality characteristics and level of personal adjustment of suicide completers by comparing psychological autopsies of adolescent suicides with those of a control group. Brent and his colleagues (1988a) in Pittsburgh also utilized a control group, that of adolescent suicidal inpatients, in their psychological autopsy study of adolescent suicide completers. Both of these studies, however, point out the difficulty in finding an adequate control group for adolescent suicide victims; matched-pair controls, for example, may reflect the tendency of the victim to befriend another emotionally troubled person.

The methodological issues that tend to arise in psychological autopsy studies are basically due to the retrospective nature of the instrument. The mood associated with bereavement at the time of the interview as well as the time lag between deaths and interviews are two of the factors that have been hypothesized to influence the quality of information reported. However, Brent (1989), on the basis of data derived from the psychological autopsy of twenty-seven adolescent suicides, found no association between time lag and parental reporting of psychiatric symptomatology in the suicide victim within a range of 2–6 months. Researchers worried that informants could either exaggerate the presence of psychiatric symptomatology due to guilt or, alternatively, minimize the victim's psychiatric problems due to idealization. Brent (1989) negates these concerns by finding that similarities exist between the reporting of depressive symptoms in depressed completers and depressed patients, as well as the fact that the review of psychological autopsy studies showed the presence of psychiatric disorder in 90 percent of suicide victims. In addition, Brent and his colleagues (1988b) found that whether or not parents of suicide victims were noted to have an affective disorder at the time of the interview had no impact on the information given during the interview.

Brent and his colleagues (1988a,b) chose adolescent suicidal inpatients as control group for their study of adolescent completed suicide. The choice of suicidal adolescent inpatients, as Shafii and his colleagues (1988) point out, may be confounded by the large overlap between attempters and completers as well as the fact that the suicide attempters have been hospitalized and thus are a self-selected and treated population being compared to a nonselected suicide group. But like Shafii and his colleagues' (1985) earlier psychological autopsy study, the choice of a control group in this study was also based on the assumption that variables that discriminate between suicide victims and a control group are likely to be the risk factors for completed suicide.

In particular, Brent and his colleagues (1988a) compared psychological autopsies of twenty-seven adolescent suicide victims with fifty-six suicidal psychiatric inpatients. The fifty-six suicidal psychiatric inpatients included eighteen inpatients who seriously considered suicide and thirty-eight inpatients who actually attempted suicide. The findings from this study indicated that, along with suicidal intent, the risk factors for completed suicide include: 1) a diagnosis of bipolar disorder; 2) affective disorder with co-morbidity; 3) lack of previous mental health treatment; and 4) the availability of firearms in the homes. Indeed, this was the first study to demonstrate that the availability of guns is much greater in the homes of suicide completers than in the homes of a comparable at-risk group. Moreover, as Brent and his colleagues (1988a) stress, their "data suggest that restriction of accessibility of firearms by altering the method of storage is not likely to be as effective as removing all firearms from the home" (p. 587).

Thus, psychological autopsy studies of adolescent suicide, such as those completed by Brent and his colleagues in Pittsburgh and Shafii and his colleagues in Louisville, have served to identify risk factors for suicide that not only aid suicide assessment, but that also suggest interventions like the removal of all firearms from the home. Moreover, what was perhaps most striking about Brent's (1989) findings was that no differences between the suicide completers and psychiatric inpatient controls were found in terms of psychiatric diagnosis, frequency of common stressors like losses and disciplinary problems, history of psychiatric illness prior to the current episode, history of suicidal threats or attempts, family history of psychiatric illness or suicide, or frequency of exposure to models of suicide (Clark and Horton 1990). This latter finding suggests that suicidal inpatients are at extremely high risk for suicide since they so closely resemble completed suicidal victims — much more so than did the matched-pair controls in Shafii and his colleagues' (1985, 1988) study. This is an extremely important finding since one issue that has been related to suicide intervention is the question of whether adolescents who attempt suicide are similar to those who commit suicide, or, more generally, the question of whether there is a continuum of suicidal behavior that ranges from nonsuicidal behavior to suicidal ideas, suicidal acts, and suicide (Pfeffer 1988). Brent's (1989) psychological autopsy findings when put together with Shafii and his colleagues' (1985, 1988) psychological autopsy findings indicate that the answer to this question may be yes.

Use of Psychological Autopsies for Geriatric Research

Kastenbaum (1970), in an eloquent commentary, wrote: "Ordinarily, the death of an elderly man serves to confirm our implicit trust in the pecking order of death. We have no desire to inquire further to challenge this comfort" (p. 34). However, this complicity is problematic insofar as epidemiological studies have consistently found a higher rate of suicide in the elderly in the United States than in any other age group (National Center for Health Statistics 1988).

Clark and Horton's (1990) report that the psychological autopsy method has not been applied to research studies on elderly suicides. While we challenge Clark and Horton's (1990) claim that psychological autopsy studies have not been applied at all to studies of elderly suicide, since in the present review we did find a few circumscribed cases in which researchers utilized the method to understand suicide in the elderly, we do concede that psychological autopsy studies of elderly suicides are exceedingly rare. This is perhaps due to the commonly held belief that interviews of survivors of elderly suicides will be difficult or impossible to conduct since elderly individuals who suicide are purported to be socially isolated prior to death. A recent study by Younger, Clark, Ohmig, and Stein, however, does not substantiate this assumption, finding instead that most elderly individuals who suicide were married at the time of their death and had had frequent contact with two or more informants during the weeks prior to their deaths (Clark and Horton 1990). As Clark and Horton (1990) report, this evidence suggests that "informant-based psychological autopsy studies of elderly suicides are feasible" and may indeed be "necessary before research in this field can be expected to progress in the same manner as has been true in other age groups" (Clark and Horton 1990 p. 10; see also Osgood and McIntosh 1986).

Sanborn and colleagues (1974), as part of their psychological autopsy study assessing the relationships between occupation-related variables and suicide in New Hampshire, did indeed compare suicide completers over the age of 65 with those under the age of 65. The elderly individuals were found to have experienced their inability to cope with stresses for a shorter period of time than the younger individuals, indicating perhaps that the problems elderly individuals face are qualitatively different from the problems that the younger generation faces. Sanborn and his colleagues' (1974) study, however, included twenty-two suicide cases, only four of which were over 65. Miller (1977), as an offshoot of a study examining the problem of suicide among white males in Arizona aged 60 and older, also conducted and published a psychological autopsy of a geriatric suicide, which he presented in the form of a single case study. These two studies may have been excluded by Clark and Horton's (1990) review since they did not satisfy their specified criteria that psychological autopsy studies "include sample sizes of 60 or more completed cases" (p. 25). Both Sanborn and his colleagues' study as well as Miller's study were enlightening. Miller's psychological autopsy study, for example, brought increased insight into the motivations of a suicide (e.g., why this elderly individual suicided at this particular time) to a survivor whose grieving was felt to have been unnecessarily prolonged by her inability to understand the motivations associated with her father's suicide.

In their 1968 monograph, Weisman and Kastenbaum detail their findings from psychological autopsies of eighty patient deaths in a geriatric hospital. This research on a geriatric population was not a study of suicide in particular, but of the terminal phase of life. The psychological autopsies that these authors conducted consisted of a multidisciplinary casework conference designed to gather and correlate medical, social, and psychiatric information about a patient during the final period of his life. The scope of the autopsy in their study extended in particular from the circumstances leading to the hospitalization and the patient's institutional adjustment and relationships to the precipitating medical, social, and psychological events that initiated the terminal illness. The study also dealt with each patient's social, ethnic, occupational, and economic background; his attitude toward hospitalization; the medical diagnosis on admission; as well as a review of his hospital course emphasizing, for example, how the patient got along with others.

Weisman and Kastenbaum (1968) see these psychological autopsies as an alternative version of the psychological autopsies originally developed by Shneidman and his colleagues (Shneidman and Faberow 1961) insofar as their purpose was not to establish the intentionality of victims of accidents, illnesses, poisoning, and other fatalities, but rather to reconstruct "the final days and weeks of life by bringing together every available observation, fact, and opinion about a recently deceased person in an effort to understand the psychosocial components of death" (Weisman and Kastenbaum 1968, p. 1). This type of psychological autopsy is based on the premise that there is a connection between the psychology of an individual and the time of his death (Shneidman 1981). In a later paper, Shneidman (1981) expresses support for this use of psychological autopsies, stating: "When a death, usually a natural death, is protracted, the individual dying gradually over a period of time, the psychological autopsy helps to illumine the sociopsychological reasons why he died as that time" (p. 327).

It should be noted that Weisman and Kastenbaum's (1968) work was done at a time when there were relatively few attempts to study systematically the social and emotional processes of dying, and consequently relatively little was known about what happened to elderly individuals as they pass through the terminal phase of life. The psychological autopsy was seen by these authors as a method to assess "ways in which a community integrates or isolates the dying, accepts or sloughs off responsibility, hastens or delays the advent of death" (Weisman and Kastenbaum 1968, p. 3), and to learn how individuals within the community should care for the dying. Their findings offered a challenge to what were then existing theories of aging—suggesting, for example, that, generally, elderly individuals do not progressively lose contact with or interest in reality nor do they fear death. Weisman and Kastenbaum's (1968) psychological autopsies served as a basis and support for contemporary theories of aging and dying, of which Kubler-Ross' (1969) theory is perhaps the most famous, and revealed avenues for both potential research on and treatment of dying individuals.

Uses of Psychological Autopsies in Clinical Work

While Weisman and Kastenbaum (1968) had primarily instituted the use of psychological autopsies in a geriatric hospital for the research purpose of studying the terminal phase of life, they also found psychological autopsies to be of therapeutic benefit to hospital staff. In their 1968 monograph, they write: "It has been noted that even having a weekly conference to discuss a recently deceased patient may have a salutary effect on the staff" (p. 57). These authors also report that the psychological autopsies conducted in this geriatric setting not only helped improve communication with terminal patients insofar as the staff had to report and justify procedures at the weekly conference, but that the procedure also alerted staff members to alternative ways to reach patients who had until then seemed inaccessible.

Weisman (1967) also discussed the potential benefit of psychological autopsies in *premortem* clinical investigations of potential suicides. He proposed that modifications of the psychological autopsy that they developed for studying the terminal phase of life in aged patients could be combined with the therapeutic consultation and introduced in general hospitals to improve assessments of suicidal risk. The rationale for this is the assumption that suicide actually "belongs to the larger problem of pre-terminal illness" insofar as it is "only one of the many ways in which imminent or inevitable death is confronted" (Weisman 1967, p. 23). This was an interesting new use of the psychological autopsy insofar as the term psychological autopsy had been coined to connote its postmortem and scientific content (Curphey 1968).

Shneidman and Farberow (1961), Curphey (1961, 1967), as well as Litman and his colleagues (1963) had suggested early on that psychological autopsies could also be of potential therapeutic benefit. Though all these authors felt that the primary purpose of their psychological autopsies was investigative, Litman and his colleagues (1963), for example, observed that psychological autopsies were therapeutic in twelve of fourteen cases in which survivors had initially demonstrated great difficulty in accepting the idea of possible suicide. Sanborn and Sanborn (1976), of the Departments of Community Medicine and Psychiatry at Dartmouth Medical School, however, were the first authors of a number to focus almost exclusively on the validity of using psychological autopsies for therapeutic purposes.

Sanborn and Sanborn (1976) reasoned that psychological autopsies could be helpful to survivors of suicide as a therapeutic tool through which counseling, information, and referral could be brought to them directly. There is a great deal of research showing that the aftermath of suicide can leave survivors with unresolved emotional turmoil and potential psychopathology. Cain and Fast (1966b), who are still on the clinical psychology faculty at the University of

Michigan-Ann Arbor, for example, found that surviving spouses are often cut off from community support due to the stigma and taboo of suicide, and that this can engender in the surviving spouse an inappropriate sense of shame and guilt, which can in turn prevent the working through of the mourning process. Cain and Fast (1966a) also found that children of a suicide experience guilt, blame, separation problems, a deep sense of loss, misconceptions, and anger over desertion, as well as necessitated realignments in family dynamics following the loss. Indeed, diagnostic assessments of children of suicides showed that these children felt responsible for the suicide, and that they had a higher incidence of psychopathology than children of nonsuicides (Cain and Fast 1966a).

Sanborn and Sanborn, through the use of case histories, illustrate how psychological autopsies can be used for preventative purposes. They found that survivors, as Cain and Fast (1966b) have suggested, do indeed feel a lack of community support and communication insofar as the interviewers were often the first person outside of the immediate family and various officials with whom the survivors had talked. In addition, the survivors were found to have many unresolved and contradictory feelings, such as guilt, anger, and relief, which they were able to discuss with the interviewer. Litman and his colleagues (1963) too had earlier reported that their "interviews nearly always reduced guilt in survivors and made it easier for them to accept the death of a victim" (p. 927). In addition, survivors were reported often to need practical information regarding social security, insurance policies, and wills, and the interviewers were in a key position to give information, or alternatively to suggest referral to an appropriate therapist or agency when indicated. Curphey (1961) noted that the Los Angeles Coroner's Office had in a few cases even referred distraught survivors to members of the team for supportive interviews even when the specific mode of death was not in doubt.

In addition, it has been argued that the major need in suicide intervention is better techniques to identify potential suicides. Hospitals continue to report suicides by patients both in the hospital and on passes, which have resulted in a concomitant increase in the number of psychiatric malpractice suits. Clark and Horton (1990), based on a review of psychological autopsy studies, reported that about 30 percent of suicides occur either while the subject was in the hospital or within 12 months of psychiatric hospital discharge. The psychological autopsy has also been reported in the literature to be a useful framework for both investigating and dealing with the suicide of a hospitalized patient. As Neill and colleagues (1974) remark: "Without it, all too frequently many questions surrounding the suicide would remain unanswered, and the insights gained would be lost to staff and future patients" (p. 36).

Thus, while Weisman (1967) advocated the use of premortem psychological autopsies to improve assessment of suicidal risk in hospital settings, Krieger (1968) was the first to write about the use of postmortem psychological autopsies in hospital suicides, based on his experience conducting thirty-seven psychological autopsies of hospital suicides at the Veterans Administration hospital in Palo

Alto between January 1964 and January 1968. Krieger (1968) was also interested in detailing staff reactions to a hospital suicide based on this experience, and speculated that the psychological reaction to a suicide may correlate with the frequency of suicide on a unit though he did not have actual data to support this. It should be noted, however, that Krieger (1968) stressed that his purpose in conducting psychological autopsies of hospital suicides was "administrative rather than therapeutic" insofar as "there was no exploration of the staff's personal dynamics" (p. 43).

Salmon and colleagues (1982) cited another use of conducting psychological autopsies of patients who suicide in nonpsychiatric hospitals, pointing out that it can assist in the early recognition and prevention of suicidal behavior in medical-surgical patients in general hospitals. A retrospective examination of the suicide of one such patient by these authors, for example, called attention to the psychiatric facets of advanced respiratory disease. Based on this psychological autopsy and a review of the sparse literature on this topic, Salmon and his colleagues (1982) posited that medical-surgical patients with advanced physical illnesses and compromised or inadequate social support may be at high risk for suicide.

Salmon and his colleagues from Minnesota's (1982) paper was not the first psychological autopsy study to suggest an association between physical illness and suicide. As Clark and Horton-Deutsch (1990) point out, Beskow (1979) reported that severe crippling diseases, such as cancer, tuberculosis, and diseases of the nervous system, were more common in suicide completers in Sweden and Chynoweth and his colleagues (1980) found that the association between physical illness and suicide is not an artifact of the aging process. Another Swedish community-based psychological autopsy study published by Hagnell and Rorsman (1978, 1979, 1980), however, found that subjects who suicided were no more likely than controls to manifest a physical illness during their last year of life, but that they more commonly manifested a negative and uncooperative attitude toward hospital treatment and were more likely to refuse medical help. Clark and Horton-Deutsch (1990) concluded from a review of psychological autopsy studies that only about 2 percent to 3 percent of suicide victims had been struggling with a terminal illness at the time of their death.

While the above researchers proposed that psychological autopsies can be of use in both psychiatric and general hospital settings, Litman's (1965) article also seemed to allude to the role that psychological autopsies could potentially play in outpatient settings as well. As part of the psychological autopsies that he collaborated on as head of the Suicide Prevention Center in Los Angeles, Litman interviewed hundreds of psychotherapists in attempts to reconstruct the life situation and attitude of the deceased and, in a 1965 article, reported on the psychological reactions of two hundred psychotherapists whose patients had committed suicide. Specifically, Litman (1965) observed that their reactions to the suicide of a patient seemed, not surprisingly, to vary in relation to the intensity of their relationship to the deceased. His qualitative findings suggested, as did Krieger's (1968), that the reactions of therapists to suicide can cover a wide range, from denial, grief, guilt, depression, and personal inadequacy, to anger. However, as Maltsberger (1992) pointed out in a chapter that also focused on the implications of patient suicide for the surviving psychotherapist, Litman did not follow this up with a systematic study of the more lasting effects of suicide on the therapist.

Litman, though, did propose in this 1965 article that one technique that appeared to be helpful in working through a therapist's pain was to review the case and present it to colleagues with the object of learning from it. While Litman (1965) did not say so outright in this early article, this mechanism for working through an outpatient suicide could ideally be a psychological autopsy. Maltsberger (1992), too, reported that along with ward meetings, support groups, and conferences with experienced supervisors, psychological autopsies are "useful and necessary" in preventing and managing pathologic reactions to patient suicides. This latter point by Maltsberger was based on one earlier made by Shneidman (1969).

Thus, psychological autopsies can aid in the understanding and investigation of suicides in both hospital and outpatient settings. Indeed, Sanborn and Sanborn (1976) advocate the integration of the technique into community mental-health programs and crisis outreach efforts, as well as its use as a framework for research and evaluation. It should be noted that Shneidman (1967, 1971b, 1973) termed the therapeutic work with survivors as *postvention*. Psychological autopsies used for clinical and postvention purposes often take more time than psychological autopsies used for other purposes, though the resultant data is purported to be richer in clinical and psychosocial material.

Use of Psychological Autopsies for Historical or Literary Purposes

In a paper presented at a meeting of the Melville Society in December of 1975, and subsequently published in the Winter 1976 issue of *Suicide and Life-Threatening Behavior,* Shneidman presented his findings from a psychological autopsy of Malcolm Melville, the son of the author of *Moby Dick,* Herman Melville. Malcolm Melville died in September of 1887 of a pistol shot wound to his right temporal region. While historically the mode of Malcolm Melville's death had been classified as equivocal, a psychological autopsy of the available material at the Los Angeles Suicide Prevention Center in 1973 (which could be considered a blind study in the sense that the participants thought that they were evaluating an open case) found Melville's death to be a "probable suicide." This finding was based on evidence of psychological abuse by his father as well as of a psychological state of isolated desperation. Indeed, the psychological autopsy concluded that Malcolm Melville likely felt unwanted by his father and thought he was better off dead.

In this tradition, psychological autopsies of other famous individuals have been conducted, such as Deikel's (1974) psychological autopsy of Lenny Bruce, which was used to determine the role that the comedian played in his own demise. Psychological autopsies have also been conducted of fictional characters, like that reported by Eisen (1980) on Seymour Glass, a character who is repeatedly encountered in J. D. Salinger's fiction. The psychological autopsies of both Lenny Bruce and Seymour Glass were written by students at the University of California-Los Angeles and utilized several basic principles of Shneidman's psychological autopsy as a framework for investigation. For example, Eisen (1980) included details of death, historical information related to the victim's marriage and previous suicide attempts, assessment of the victim's level of perturbation, description of the victim's personality and life-style, and assessment of intention and lethality.

Interestingly, Eisen's (1980) foray is a good illustration of the expansion of the use of the psychological autopsy to clarify and evaluate deaths that are unequivocally suicidal. As Shneidman (1981) writes: "When the mode of death is, by all reasonable measures, clear and unequivocal — suicide, for example, — the psychological autopsy can serve to account for the reasons for the act or to discover what led to it" (p. 327). This latter point will become important when we discuss our use of the psychological autopsy in the case of Tina Mancini. In this case, the mode of death was clear — Tina shot herself in the head with a .357 Magnum.

Use of Psychological Autopsies in Legal Cases

Litman (1984, 1987), in a series of articles, has explored, as well as advocated, the use of psychological autopsies in clarifying *intention* in suicide. Indeed, as Shneidman (1981) notes, "in essence the psychological autopsy is nothing less than a thorough retrospective investigation of the *intention* of the decedent" (p. 326). In legal and other cases, for example, Litman (1987) finds psychological autopsies extremely helpful in judging whether self-destructive acts are intentional insofar as, in a psychological autopsy, the history, life-style, stresses, communications, and behaviors of a decedent are reviewed, with special attention to the last days and hours of a person's life. The certification of suicide, according to Litman (1987), requires that "the person understood that the self-destructive act would end his or her physical existence" (p. 86).

Psychological autopsies have been used in legal cases involving life-insurance claims. In most insurance policies, there is a clause stating that death benefits will not be paid during the first 2 years after a policy is bought if the death is deemed a suicide. Courts are thus sometimes asked to decide whether insurance benefits should be paid after a death, and this will depend on determining whether the "preponderance of evidence"[5] does or does not support

---

[5]While the court-ordered decision guideline for classifying mode of death is generally "a preponderance of evidence," Litman (1989), however, argues that in practice the assembled evidence is often used to construct a "most credible" scenario to explain the death (p. 638).

suicidal intention. In addition, psychological autopsies have been used to settle estate questions, such as whether a gift is in contemplation of death under section 2035 of the 1954 Internal Revenue Code (Dregne 1982). Attorneys representing the Howard Hughes estate, for example, asked Raymond Fowler, who was then incoming president of the American Psychological Association, to conduct a psychological autopsy of Howard Hughes because the billionaire's will was being contested and they felt that it was important to know what his mental state was at various periods in his life (Bass, *The Boston Globe,* December 7, 1987). Finally, psychological autopsies have been used in medical malpractice cases, such as when a psychiatrist is sued because a patient whom they had been treating committed suicide. In our work on medical malpractice cases, we have often relied on the modifications of the psychological autopsy technique.

The legal guidelines concerning who is responsible and who is financially liable for a suicide death are, according to Litman (1987), undergoing transition. For example, while the relationship between insanity and suicide has been argued both philosophically and legally, it is now generally agreed that the capacity to have intent to commit suicide is lost due to mental disorders only under special and unique circumstances (Litman 1987). Furthermore, the Michigan courts have recently had to deal with the issue of who is responsible for a suicide in the case of Dr. Kevorkian, who is known in many circles as Dr. Death, the well-known advocate of physician-assisted suicide. Charges were brought against Dr. Kevorkian and subsequently dropped in several of his physician-assisted suicides. There are many ethical considerations that will have to be addressed as Michigan explores changes in state laws. In the following case of a mother who was convicted of contributing to the suicide of her teenage daughter by subjecting her to emotional abuse, which included forcing her to work as a stripper, we will also confront issues related to who is ultimately responsible for a suicidal death.

Use of Psychological Autopsies in Criminal Cases

The psychological autopsy has been traditionally used in criminal defense cases to demonstrate that defendants were in imminent danger, acted upon that belief, and used appropriate means to ensure their safety and the safety of those around them (Lichter 1981). Arizona, in fact, was the first state to admit a psychological autopsy as evidence in a criminal case to demonstrate self-defense (Dregne 1982). In one of these Arizona cases, a woman killed her unarmed husband at close range with a shotgun after announcing her intention to do so to neighbors. The psychiatric autopsy revealed that her husband was a sadistic, paranoid psychopath who beat his wife and threatened their family. The jury's verdict of voluntary manslaughter as opposed to first-degree murder in this case was noted by Lichter (1981) to reflect its reliance on the psychiatric autopsy.

Psychiatric autopsy is a term coined by Otto Bendheim. Bendheim (1979) differentiates the psychiatric autopsy from the psychological autopsy in that it takes into account medical data such as toxicology, pharmacology, and anatomical pathology in evaluating the life of the deceased. The psychiatric autopsy, according to Bendheim (1979), is "the psychiatric analysis of the deceased person, with full consideration of his genetic and environmental background, his personal experiences, all documents which he may have left behind, either written by himself or others pertaining to him, but also contributions and statements, so-called oral history, by friends, relatives, acquaintances, and witnesses." However, Litman had stated that the difference between psychiatric autopsies and psychological autopsies is "semantic." Both "psychological and psychiatric autopsies create a biography with emphasis on a particular time period, reconstructing the state of mind of someone who is now dead," according to Litman (Scanlon 1987, p. D2). We tend to agree, and have chosen to continue to use the term psychological autopsy which Shneidman had coined to refer to such evolving versions of the procedure.

The use of psychological autopsies in criminal cases, however, is not without its controversial aspects. Criminal cases differ from civil cases in that the standard of proof is "beyond a reasonable doubt" rather than "the preponderance of evidence." Some argue, for example, that the use of psychological autopsies in criminal cases is unnecessary, overly prejudicial, or based on hearsay elements. Because it is prepared in anticipation of litigation, based on third-party information, and usually excludes examination of the subject in question, the procedure when applied to legal cases raises important issues of admissability (Lichter 1981). We will address some of these issues in the following case examples.

TWO NEW USES OF PSYCHOLOGICAL AUTOPSIES

Psychological Autopsy of Tina Mancini

In this section, we will first discuss issues surrounding the admission of a psychological autopsy that we conducted as evidence for the prosecution in a 1987 criminal case in Florida. This case was precedent-setting in that it was the first time that a psychological autopsy had been used by the prosecution in a criminal case, and that a mother had been accused and convicted of contributing to the suicide of her daughter. Because of this as well as the fact that the details of the case were, as Shneidman has so euphemistically put, "of a mildly salacious nature," the case received a great deal of media attention.

Traditionally, as Lichter (1981) has stated, "defense counsel and defense psychiatrists have praised the psychiatric autopsy and prosecutors have criticized its use harshly" (p. 633). In this case, the reverse was true: it was the defense attorney who strongly objected to the admission of our psychological autopsy as evidence. The defense attorney, along with others such as David Clark (1988) of Rush-Presbyterian Hospital in Chicago, questioned the place of the psychological autopsy in criminal prosecution. It was argued vehemently, for example, that the psychological autopsy method yielded tentative research diagnoses rather than clinical diagnoses, that it failed to meet the legal *Frye* test whereby it is necessary to show that evidence is widely accepted as valid within a field of specialty, and that it may be inappropriate for a mental-health professional to testify directly to the issue of criminal guilt or responsibility. Clearly, these psychological and legal issues are of concern to suicidologists, and will be discussed in more detail in the case of Tina Mancini.

Tina Mancini was the middle of three children. Her parents were divorced when Tina was 3. Her father moved to California; Tina had little contact with him. Tina's mother remarried a man who was known to be a transvestite and ultimately had a sex-change operation. The grandfather was distressed at this and became very involved with Tina and her brother, Rico. Rico went to live with the father in California because of the unstable home environment. This second marriage did not last long; shortly thereafter, Theresa Jackson, Tina's mother, married for a third time.

Tina manifested her difficulties at the age of 13 when she made a suicide attempt. She took approximately seventy pills and called a friend who subsequently called the police. She was admitted to a pediatric unit at a local hospital, where she stayed 3 days. She was seen in consultation by a psychiatrist who deferred diagnosis, recommending family treatment, which the mother subsequently refused. Her friends were later to testify at depositions that the basis for this suicide attempt was that the mother "called the daughter a slut."

The turmoil in Tina's life began to escalate. During the fall of 1984, Tina dropped out of school. Tina had been an A student, but in the fall her grades began slipping. In the ensuing 6 months, tension mounted at home. In the summer of 1985, she and her brothers attempted to run away from home. However, their attempts were unsuccessful and they were brought back by the police. Three days following one run-away incident, Tina called the police to come to the house because she and her mother were fighting. When the police arrived on the scene they felt it was best to have Tina stay at a friend's house for the night. The police offered intervention to Tina and her mother. However, the mother became angry, claiming that the police always sided with her daughter. The mother refused follow-up, and Tina did not call the police again for assistance.

A week after this incident in August 1985, the mother's current husband called the police stating that he was frightened of his wife's violence after he had asked for a divorce. The police investigated and confiscated a handgun owned by the mother. On that occasion, the police asked Tina if she would like to spend the night away from home. Tina had replied to the police officer, "No. She'll be over it by then." What struck the police officer reporting this incident was that someone had, "just threatened her [Tina] with a gun and it was an ordinary thing to her." The apparent reason for the nonchalance was that the mother frequently terrorized Tina with a gun, holding it to her head with the trigger cocked.

In September of 1985, Theresa Jackson was separated, ultimately to divorce for the third time. Chaos seemed to reign following the divorce. Tina's two brothers were in and out of the house. In January of 1986, Theresa Jackson "allowed" her daughter to work at a topless nightclub. The mother obtained the grandfather's notary public stamp and forged Tina's birth certificate so that Tina could work. Tina felt powerless to do anything about this. The mother, filled with admiration, drove her daughter to work. She took $200 a week for rent and $100 a week for driving from her daughter's earnings. The actual rent for the apartment was $465 per month. At least Tina was making a "contribution."

Tina did well at her new job. The mother "allowed" her to work at a second club starting in March of 1986. Tina told her friends how she wanted to stop working, but felt she could not do anything about it. She secretly started to accumulate money. At this point in time, the brothers were living away from home and Tina and her mother were alone, fighting constantly.

On the day of her death, Tina and her mother got into a violent argument about Tina's work. This was reported by the brother who witnessed the argument. Even though Tina was making a lot of money and enjoyed the dancing, she found the work humiliating. Tina had pleaded with her mother to let her stop dancing at the nightclubs. The mother said, "No. You will have to continue working. In fact, you'll have to work more than ever and if you don't I will go to the clubs and report that you are under age." Tina was confused at this point. What would happen if she were found to be under age? After the mother left that day, Tina called her friend to learn whether it would be possible to live with her. She told her friend that she had $2000 for a car and thus could move in. The friend stated that her mother was afraid of Tina's mother. She knew that Tina's mother would come after her, that the police would become involved, and that Tina would have to be sent back home. Her friend reluctantly and sadly told Tina, "I'm sorry, you can't stay with us." A half hour later, on March 24, 1986, Tina Mancini fatally shot herself with a .357 magnum.

Tina's mother was subsequently accused by two relatives, her own father and son, Tina's grandfather and brother, respectively, of compelling the daughter to work as a nude dancer, committing forgery by doctoring the girl's birth certificate, verbally abusing the girl, and not seeking treatment for the girl after a prior suicide attempt. After a police investigation, the mother was charged and prosecuted. In October of 1987, the judge heard arguments about whether to allow a psychiatrist, the author of this paper (D. J.) to testify for the prosecution as to why the daughter may have taken her life based on a psychological autopsy. The judge ultimately accepted the testimony in court, and the jury ultimately found the mother guilty on charges of forgery, procuring sexual performance by a child, and child abuse. Theresa Jackson was sentenced to one year in prison for forgery; two years of house arrest for procuring sexual performance of a minor; and three years of probation, on the condition that she continue to receive outpatient therapy at a mental-health clinic for aggravated child abuse (i.e., for driving her teenage daughter to suicide by forcing her to dance nude in a nightclub).

Theresa Jackson appealed the conviction, arguing primarily that the psychological autopsy is an unreliable technique and not generally accepted in the field of psychiatry, and thus should not have been admitted as evidence in a criminal trial. On December 13, 1989, the appellate court, however, ruled to uphold the conviction in this case, on the basis that there was no merit to the arguments raised.

Discussion of Tina Mancini Case

In the few precedents where psychological autopsies were utilized in criminal cases, the experts had always used the procedure in their testimony for the defense — to help clarify in the traditional sense whether a death was due to accident or suicide (Clark 1988). In the Mancini case, however, the mode of death was not under scrutiny. Tina had suicided — that is, no one doubted that she clearly intended to end her life when she shot herself in the mouth. Instead, the question that the psychological autopsy in this case was used to answer was whether the abuse from Tina's mother was a significant contributory factor in her suicide. The psychological autopsy that we conducted concluded that it indeed had been. That is, our reconstruction of Tina's life based on a review of all available material indicated that had it not been for this young girl's being the victim of an exploitive relationship with her mother and thus feeling powerless and hopeless, she would not have suicided at the particular time she did. Interestingly, Shaffer (1974) noted that the suicides of the thirty young adolescent victims in his study were also provoked by an immediate family or peer crisis.

Thus, the question in this case was not whether the abusive relationship was the *sole cause* of the daughter's suicide, but rather whether it was a *significant contributory factor*. This is an important distinction, which we feel needs clarification. Suicide is clearly a multidetermined act. As Leston Havens eloquently wrote in a special article entitled "The Anatomy of a Suicide" for a 1965 issue of the *New England Journal of Medicine:* "Suicide is the final common pathway of diverse circumstances, of an interdependent network rather than an isolated cause, a knot of circumstances tightening around a single time and place, with the result, sign, symptom, trait or act" (p. 401). A psychological autopsy is a retrospective analysis of what went on in a person's life to cause him to commit suicide. Some factors are more relevant than others, and we felt that the aggravated child abuse by the mother, which included, for example, such atrocities as forcing her daughter to dance nude, subjecting her to verbal abuse, and failing to seek treatment for her following an earlier suicide attempt, in this case significantly contributed to Tina's suicide.

We addressed the issue of causation from a clinical standpoint. In our approach to the suicidal person, we generally rely on four models. 1) The *empirical model,* developed by Clark and Fawcett (1992), which can be used to establish a psychiatric diagnosis and substance-abuse history and to examine the symptom profile of an individual within a diagnostic group to help determine when the person is at risk. 2) The *architectural model,* developed by Mack (1989), a systems approach, which takes into account eight separate factors including predisposition, personality development, community context, the clinical situation, and family history. It is a comprehensive view, which also includes issues related to the development of self-esteem. 3) The *psychodynamic model,* developed by Buie and Maltsberger (1989), which sees the suicide-vulnerable individuals as having deficiencies in ego development, and focuses not only on self-worth, but also on whether a person can use external resources, as well as their relationship to death. 4) The *psychological model,* developed by Shneidman (1989), which lists the ten commonalities of suicide, including such factors as hopelessness, the role of escape, psychological pain, and the constriction of thought that leads one to see no options. (See Figure 13-1.)

Shneidman's approach to a suicidal person was central to our formulation of this case. Shneidman has shown that people who had committed suicide ranked at the top on three scales, measuring "psychological pain," "perception of options," and "decisiveness." At the top of this scale, a person feels unbearable psychological pain. Tina Mancini, for example, felt this kind of pain in having

---

THE 10 COMMONALITIES OF SUICIDE

1. The common purpose is to seek a solution.
2. The common goal is cessation of consciousness.
3. The common stimulus is intolerable psychological pain.
4. The common stressor is frustrated psychological needs.
5. The common emotion is hopelessness–helplessness.
6. The common internal attitude is ambivalence.
7. The common cognitive state is constriction.
8. The common action is egression.
9. The common interpersonal act is communication of intention.
10. The common consistency is with lifelong coping patterns.

FIGURE 13-1.   The Ten Commonalities of Suicide. Shneidman, E. S. (1989). Overview: A multidimensional approach to suicide. In Jacobs, D. G., Brown, H. M. *Suicide, Understanding, and Responding: Harvard Medical School Perspectives.* Madison, CT: International Universities Press, p. 16.

to obey her mother's orders to dance nude. With respect to perceived options, people who kill themselves believe that they have no other options. Tina Mancini, for example, had tried unsuccessfully to get away from her mother (e.g., running away, moving in with a friend) and felt she had no alternative but to kill herself. Finally, with respect to decisiveness, at the top of this scale are people who feel they must act immediately. Tina Mancini likely felt that she could no longer live with the pain and the humiliation she felt.

Menninger (1938) had also theorized that there are three motives for suicide. His triadic model of suicide included the wish to kill (revenge), to be killed (guilt), and to die (escape). Using this model, one can formulate the Mancini case in the following way. Tina had feelings of murderous rage and revenge toward her mother, which she expressed symbolically in her use of her mother's gun to kill herself. Tina also felt degraded by nude dancing, and the guilt associated with this likely intensified her self-destructive impulses. In addition, Tina felt trapped. She ultimately felt forced to participate in nude dancing to bring home money to support her mother, whom she resented supporting. When she tried to stop working as a stripper, her mother would not let her, and this is the psychological straightjacket in which Tina must have found herself. She felt she had no choice. People always look for avenues to escape pain, and in Tina Mancini's case, the way out was suicide.

In addition, the psychological autopsy that we conducted revealed that Tina Mancini was a psychologically vulnerable teenager with a history that included a previous suicide attempt, an unstable home environment, dropping out of school, and being the victim of sexual exploitation. Thus, she possessed a number of what have been considered by some, and articulated quite well by Pfeffer (1988), to be risk factors for completed suicide. For example, Shaffer (1974) reported that approximately 46 percent of thirty young suicide victims had evidence of previous suicidal behavior, which, as you will recall, is in line with Shafii and his colleagues' (1985) finding that 40 percent of adolescent suicide victims had previous suicidal attempts compared to 6 percent of matched-pair teenagers who did not commit suicide (Pfeffer 1988). In addition, Cohen-Sandler and colleagues (1982) found that suicidal youngsters have more family stresses, such as parental separation, death, and divorce, than nonsuicidal depressed youngsters or youngsters with other forms of psychopathology. Moreover, the factors that distinguished adolescents who showed repeat suicidal acts from those who were never suicidal or were only suicidal at the time of initial assessment in Stanley and Barter's (1970) study were, among other things, having poor school records. And finally, Pfeffer and colleagues (1985) identified sexual abuse as one of a number of environmental factors associated with suicidal acts in two hundred adolescents who were psychiatrically hospitalized.

It should be noted, however, that the above risk factors for adolescent suicide are not seen as incontrovertible. Shafii and his colleagues (1985), as you will remember, did *not* find more evidence of broken homes, poor academic performance, or being a school dropout in the histories of adolescent suicide victims than in the histories of matched-pair controls, though there is a possibility that these findings may be due to the tendency of suicide victims to befriend other emotionally troubled individuals. In addition, Clark and Fawcett's (1992) review of community-based psychological autopsy studies suggested that 60 percent of all patients who commit suicide had never made a prior suicide attempt in their lifetime; and those who have made a nonfatal suicide attempt, according to Clark and Fawcett (1992), have only about a 7–10 percent risk for dying by suicide.

Another factor in this case is that Tina did not receive follow-up psychiatric treatment after a serious suicide attempt. While it is unclear whether this is a manifestation of a long-standing tendency not to accept help on Tina's behalf, it is important to mention that an unwillingness to accept help is considered by some, including Litman (1987), also to be "a crucial factor" in completed suicides. Interestingly and discouragingly, Goldacre and Hawton (1985) found that about 9.5 percent of 2492 adolescents aged 12–20 who had taken overdoses repeated a suicidal act with 2.8 years of initial admission (Pfeffer 1988). Mattson and colleagues (1969) reported that about 50 percent of seventy-five adolescents evaluated in an emergency service for suicidal behavior did not follow-up on the recommendation for additional intervention. Taylor and Stansfield (1984) reported similar results: only twenty-eight of fifty adolescents who took over-doses (like Tina did) kept an appointment for psychiatric treatment (Pfeffer 1988). Indeed, Pfeffer (1988) reports that the most important factors associated with whether the youngster went for treatment in Taylor and Stanfield's study (1984) were parental attitudes and the parent's cultural background. In the Mancini case, the prosecution contended that the aggravated child-abuse charge was partially based on the mother's failure to seek treatment for her daughter after an earlier suicide attempt. This mother's noncompliance with treatment recommendations for her daughter was negligent and also contributed to the suicide.

In addition, Tina had access to a firearm in the home, and used it as the method for suicide. At the trial, the author (D. J.) testified that "the fact that she chose a violent, lethal method indicates that she had reached the final straw, that she was not placing herself in a position of rescue" (see appellate ruling transcript, p. 8). Nearly 60 percent of all completed suicides are reportedly done by firearms (Cantor 1992). Brent and his colleagues' (1987) studies of completed suicide in adolescents in Pittsburgh, as you will also remember from our review of the literature on the use of psychological autopsies in a research on adolescent suicide, were the first to show that one of the primary differences between suicide completers and suicide attempters is the presence of a firearm in the home. Pfeffer classifies possession of firearms as a sociocultural risk factor in the United States insofar as in the last several decades it has become culturally accepted in some communities in the United States to own firearms. As Pfeffer (1988) writes, "not only has there been an increase of firearms in the household, but also efforts to control gun sales have been significantly opposed" (p. 415).

Regardless, the presence of a firearm in the family home in this case increased Tina's risk for suicide. In fact, given the knowledge of Tina's previous suicide attempt, Tina's mother's failure to remove firearms from the home, or at the very least to limit their accessibility, was clearly negligence.

Thus, our psychological autopsy revealed that aggravated child abuse by the mother was the significant contributory factor in Tina's suicide: that is, had it not been for the exploitative relationship with her mother, Tina would not have suicided at that particular time. The trial jury as well as the appellate court agreed. Now, it was not unheard of within the legal system to convict someone for causing the mental anguish that leads to suicide. In a 1932 legal case, *Stephenson v. State,* for example, the Indiana Supreme Court upheld a murder conviction for a man who kidnapped a woman acquaintance, attempted to rape her, and failed to seek immediate medical attention for her when she took poison. The woman died after the defendant took her home (Moss 1988). Tina Mancini's case was precedent-setting to the extent that it was the first time that a mother was convicted of contributing to the suicide of her daughter.

And because this was the first time that child-abuse charges had been brought against a parent after a child's suicide, some feared that this case would also set a precedent for inquiry into the family life of teens who commit suicide. The Washington Post even quoted one individual as stating: "The Florida ruling smacks of medieval church law, whereby family survivors after a suicide were treated as accessories to both a sin and a crime" (Colburn 1988, p. 13). However, we feel that this is a special case. This woman had clearly abused her daughter, and one of the consequences of that was suicide. Tina's mother exploited her sexually, creating an environment that made her feel that her only worth was the amount of money that she was bringing in from dancing. Tina lived in an extremely poor psychological environment, filled with humiliation and abuse, and felt that there was no way out. While there is always the possibility that there will be inappropriate applications of this precedent, we have faith in the legal system and hope that the outcome of this case will serve not to blame the victims but rather to direct much needed attention toward the rights of children. Perhaps the judge in the case of *State of Florida v. Theresa Jackson* put it best:

> The tragedy in this case reminded me of a wise jurist's remarks to a bar association that we have to be shocked before we respond to a societal need. All of Dr. Jacobs' testimony should shock us enough to be so concerned about our individual self-worth that we do something about it — for ourselves and our families. Finally, I wanted future readers of this opinion to remember the victim, the defendant, the needlessness of what occurred here and, in my view, our obligations to ourselves to learn from it. [District Court of Appeal State of Florida, Fourth District, Case No. 88-0264]

This was cited as one of the reasons why he did not believe that the trial court had abused its discretion in admitting the psychological autopsy as evidence in this criminal case.

The psychological autopsy in the Mancini case attempted to reconstruct

Tina's mental state at the time of her death by examining the school, hospital, and employment records, police incident reports, a custody dispute, as well as by reading pretrial depositions taken of her family, friends, and co-workers. Some have argued, including the defense attorney in this case, that in reconstructing a suicidal individual's mental state, a psychiatrist or psychologist must conduct face to face interviews with everyone who knew the suicide victim, including the suicide victim himself. That is, how can one know the state of mind of someone one has never met? While one can never know with 100 percent certainty what is going on in someone's mind, Tina Mancini's mind was the mind of a suicidal person.

Some have even argued that the definition of a psychological autopsy study itself necessitates direct interviewing. Clark and Horton, for example, strongly articulated this view in a 1990 chapter. These authors even contend that psychological autopsies used for purposes of mortality conferences in hospitals or for legal purposes are *not* psychological autopsy studies but should instead be called *suicide postmortem conferences, clinical audits,* or *case reviews.* In addition, they argue that psychological autopsy studies should not rely on depositions, since they are elicited in the context of an adversarial examination, the expert is unfamiliar with the interview skills of the deposer, and informants are not interviewed in a standardized fashion and thus are difficult to compare against previous psychological autopsy studies. Clark and Horton (1990) further posit that the only situation in which forensic case review takes the form of psychological autopsy study is when the expert "undertakes a preliminary case review together with the opposing legal parties to identify all potential knowledgeable informants and then undertakes structured interviews with identified informants independent of the deposition process" (p. 169). While this process may be the ideal, it will be extremely difficult to invoke in practice given today's legal system.

In fact, researchers have even noted that one of the primary problems in conducting psychological autopsies of children and adolescents is the difficulty of obtaining parental cooperation for interviewing themselves or their friends and family. This difficulty has also been reported by Herzog and Resnick (1968) as well as Cantor (1975). Interestingly, less than 10 percent of families of completed suicide in children and adolescents who Cantor approached for one study responded to the questionnaires, and many of those who responded left unanswered questions (See Shafii et al. 1985). While in research studies or therapeutic work informants should most certainly be interviewed, they are rarely interviewed in hospital cases or civil suits for a variety of reasons.

We do not agree that a psychological autopsy necessitates direct interviewing. As you will remember, there are many published psychological autopsies in which direct interviews were not conducted by the author for various reasons, including the fact that one case is of an individual who died in the late 1800s and one is of a fictional character. Deikel (1974) reports that he attempted to interview survivors and significant acquaintances of Lenny Bruce, but that all interviews were canceled. In the Mancini case, we felt that we had enough information available on which to base an opinion.

In cases in which direct interviews are not conducted, however, care should be taken to ensure that information obtained for the psychological autopsy is reliable. Deikel (1974), for example, detailed the procedures he employed to increase the reliability of information on Mr. Bruce, which included excluding opinions and reactions of individuals not acquainted with the comedian, excluding sensational and extreme information, ensuring that facts had been verified by an alternative source, and including only material written before the comedian's death in August 1966. In criminal cases, it is not the role of the expert to determine whether the information has a basis in fact. That is up to the state to prove, for the defense to rebut, and the jury to decide. The expert's role is not to question the charges, but to question and then determine, within the limit of his or her expertise, the mind of the suicidal victim, which we feel is in the domain of suicidologists relying on the psychological autopsy technique. As the author (D. J.) stated at the trial:

> I decided that, had it not been for this young girl's being the victim of an exploitive relationship with her mother, feeling powerless and hopeless, she would not have suicided at the time that she did. My role was not to question the charges, but to question and then determine the mind of a suicide victim, which I feel confident within my expertise to do (Jacobs 1987, 918–919).

In the Mancini case, the expert testimony was also called last so that it discussed facts already in evidence.

Litman, one of the pioneers of the psychological autopsy technique, responded in one media report that he feels that doing psychological autopsies on the basis of documentary evidence is not at all unusual or alarming. He stated: "Police reports and other sources of information compiled shortly after a death are often in many cases more helpful than are personal interviews conducted months after the fact, when witnesses have had a chance to forget—and conceivably alter or embellish—the facts." In addition, from a clinical point of view, psychological autopsies of suicide victims with whom the person conducting the psychological autopsy has had no prior contact removes the vagueness of the interpersonal relationship between the psychiatrist and examinee. As such, psychological autopsies may actually be more objective and less controversial than the analysis of living patients (Lichter 1981).

An ideal addition to the psychological autopsy would be to call the mental-health professional who saw the patient in the days or weeks preceding his suicide to the stand in the trial, and to incorporate his opinions into the psychological autopsy. In most cases of completed suicide, however, the decedent had not had contact with a mental-health professional in the period immediately prior to his or her suicidal death, and the decedent is no longer available to be interviewed. Indeed, as Clark and Fawcett (1992) report from their review of community-based psychological autopsy studies, half or more of all persons who die by suicide had never seen a mental-health professional in their lives.[6] Thus, mental-health professionals are forced to rely on retrospective techniques to reconstruct the state of mind of the deceased.

Thus, the psychological autopsy has been found by researchers, such as Brent and his colleagues (1988b), as well as by the legal system to be a reliable and valid method to reconstruct the state of mind of a decedent who suicided. As the 1989 appellate ruling in the case of *Theresa Jackson v. State of Florida* states:

> The expert psychiatrist specialized in suicidology and, for purposes of this trial, performed a psychological autopsy on the appellant's seventeen-year-old daughter who had committed suicide in March of 1986. His testimony explained that a psychological autopsy is a retrospective look at an individual's suicide to try to determine what led that person to choose death over life. In order to make that determination, in this case, the expert reviewed the child's school records, the police records surrounding the case, including all of the state's evidence and all of the defendant's statements and medical records, an incident report from an earlier suicide attempt by the child and various testimony from the witnesses appearing at this trial. However he admitted that he did not personally interview any of the witnesses who appeared at trial nor did he ever meet or interview the suicide victim. His opinion, bounded by reasonable psychiatric certainty, was that the nature of the relationship between the defendant and her daughter was a substantial contributing factor in the daughter's decision to commit suicide.
>
> Having reviewed the record, we are satisfied that the state presented sufficient evidence to establish that the psychological autopsy is accepted in the field of psychiatry as a method of evaluation for use in cases involving suicide and that the trial judge acted within his discretion in admitting this evidence at trial. Sections 90.402; 90.403; 90.704; Fla. Stat. (1987).
>
> With regard to the concerns of the defense that the psychological autopsy was not established as reliable before it was admitted as evidence, we note that such opinions are subjective and therefore the issue of reliability is best left to the jury. Further, we perceive no distinction between the admission of the expert's opinion in this case and, for example, admitting psychiatric opinion evidence to establish a defendant's sanity at the time of committing an 'offense or to prove the competency of an individual at the time of executing a will. See *Morgan v. State,* 527, So.2d. 272 (Fla. 1202), *United States vs. Edwards,* 819 F.2d 262 (11th Cir. 1987); see also *Krusa v. State,* 483 So.2d. 1383 (Fla. 4th DCA 1986); *Terry v. State,* 467 So.2d 761 (Fla. 4th DCA 1985); In re *Estate of Hammermann,* 387 So.2d 409 (Fla. 4th DCA 1980).
>
> There being no merit to the other arguments raised, we affirm the judgment of conviction.

Psychological Autopsy of Gunner's Mate 2nd Class Clayton Hartwig

On April 19, 1989, the Navy battleship the U.S.S. Iowa exploded off the coast of Puerto Rico killing forty-seven sailors and causing fifteen to twenty million

---

[6]Though Clark and Fawcett's (1992) review of community-based psychological autopsy studies did find that about 50 percent of those who committed suicide saw a physician in the 6 months prior to death, 80 percent of whom saw a physician in the last month of death, unfortunately, these physicians, as Clark and Fawcett (1992) point out, may not always be in a position to screen for acute psychiatric illness, let alone suicide risk.

dollars worth of damage. No eyewitnesses survived. The Navy investigation of the incident focused on the culpability of 24-year-old gunner's mate 2nd class Clayton M. Hartwig, who was captain of the middle gun and died in the explosion. Their controversial conclusion, based on an FBI psychological profile of Clayton Hartwig, was that the shipboard explosion was an act of suicide. Hartwig was thought to be a troubled homosexual who took his own life.

In order for the Navy to be able to state this, however, we felt that they needed to show that Clayton Hartwig was not only suicidal, but that he was also homicidal at the time of the shipboard explosion. In this case, unlike in the aforementioned Mancini case, there was no conclusive evidence as to the mode of death, and thus we conducted a psychological autopsy of Clayton Hartwig to determine the mode of death. The results of this psychological autopsy were summarized in a report which the author (D. J.) submitted and testified to before Congress during its review of the Navy investigation of the U.S.S. Iowa explosion, in December 1989. The findings of this psychological autopsy will be discussed below. A Navy investigative team had previously found the explosion was caused by a man "who *intended* to die that morning."

The Navy tried to make the case that Clayton Hartwig had a suicidal profile. They described him as an individual who was "shy, a loner, interested in weapons, spending time in his room." That he had homosexual tendencies and wrote voluminous letters, and consequently had low self-esteem. Our psychological autopsy revealed that while it is true that Clayton Hartwig did not have many friends, he did form intense relationships with several individuals throughout his lifetime. He formed an intense relationship with the Navy. He had a long-standing interest in learning about weapons. None of these together, or alone, is indicative of suicide potential.

Indeed, there did not appear to be a basis for concluding in particular that Clayton Hartwig had low self-esteem. Self-esteem is determined in part by how a person feels about how he is measuring up to his goals. This is referred to in the psychiatric literature as ego-ideal (Mack and Hickler 1981). Low self-esteem results when there is a wide gulf between the perceived self and the ideal self. As for Clayton Hartwig, he hoped to achieve his ego-ideal, his ideal self, by joining the Navy and becoming a Navy man. Other young people likewise emulate rock stars, scientists, or sports heroes. In order for the Navy to prove its theory of murder/suicide, it would have to prove that Clayton Hartwig's ego-ideal was shattered, that he suffered a significant betrayal by the Navy, and that he would want to destroy the very object that he idealized.

As noted above, the psychological motives for suicide include: the wish to die (to escape), the wish to kill (to aggress against another), and the wish to be killed (to appease guilt) (Menninger 1938). Suicide can be brought on by real or imagined loss with a precipitous fall in self-esteem. The person can then develop a state of intolerable psychological pain, feel helpless and hopeless, and seeing no other way out may "choose" suicide as a solution to his problem, as did Mancini.

However, this decision typically develops over time and most frequently in a person with a major mental disturbance.

The review of Hartwig's letters and reports of the interviews with shipmates and his family did not reveal a major psychiatric disorder. This is an important point insofar as in the overwhelming majority of circumstances, suicide is a pathologic behavior occurring in a mentally disturbed person. Indeed, an episode of psychiatric illness has been found by researchers to almost invariably be present in the weeks or months before suicide. Based on a review of community-based psychological autopsy studies, Clark and Fawcett (1992), for example, found that 93 percent to 95 percent of all cases of completed suicide qualify for one or more *DSM-III-R* diagnosis. Indeed, these researchers found that major depression can be reliably diagnosed in 40 percent to 50 percent of suicide victims; alcoholism, especially chronic alcoholism, can be reliably diagnosed in 20 percent of suicide victims; and chronic schizophrenia appears in about 10 percent of suicide victims. In this case, there was no evidence of substance abuse. In addition, while the available material did not conclusively rule out the existence of a psychotic or depressive disorder, we thought that these diagnoses were highly unlikely based upon the observations of his fellow navy men, his letters, and phone calls.

Another question our psychological autopsy addressed was whether Clayton Hartwig had any predispositions to suicide. That is, were suicide risk factors present? He was male, he had availability and knowledge of weapons, and he was not afraid of death. There are conflicting reports as to whether he had a history of previous suicidal ideations or behaviors. Suicidal ideation, as noted by Shneidman, is measured in terms of a person's intent and lethality. Is there a persistence of thoughts of death? Does a person have a specific plan to kill him- or herself? Are there deterrents to suicide? The Navy's report of their investigation stated that there was a history of a past suicide attempt with a knife when Clayton Hartwig was in late adolescence. However, the friend who had supposedly observed this suicide attempt had later retracted this testimony. Thus, the basic issue as to whether Clayton Hartwig was previously suicidal is undecided.

Moreover, there is implication on the part of the Navy investigative team that because Clayton Hartwig may have had suicidal ideation and/or behavior he was likely to suicide. The association between suicidal ideation, attempted suicide, and completed suicide is complicated. In a recent study conducted by the National Institute of Mental Health, 4 percent of persons without any discernible psychiatric disorder were found to have suicidal ideation as opposed to 30 percent with a psychiatric disorder (Moscicki and Regier, 1987). Of those with suicidal ideation, approximately 50 percent may go on to make a suicide attempt. Furthermore, it is known that only 10 percent of people who make suicide attempts go on to kill themselves at a rate of about 1 percent per year. Thus, there is not direct association between ideation, attempts, and completed suicide, and researchers have even argued over whether there is continuum among these symptoms. The Navy seems to place a great deal of weight on Clayton Hartwig's past suicidal behavior. In our opinion, this determination is not only inconclusive, but the connection of this to their formulation of suicide is inappropriate.

Another potential predisposition proposed by the Navy was Clayton Hartwig's "dark side." Clayton Hartwig, however, was a romantic. He was able to express his emotional feelings in the written word. This does not make him pathologic. This does not make him a suicide risk. How common is it for sailors to write letters? Adolescents and young adults are known to keep journals and diaries as they struggle to develop their own identity. Moreover, what use did the Navy make of the letters of Clayton Hartwig? It is likely that these letters serve as the most reliable indicator of Clayton Hartwig's mental state in the weeks before the day of his death. While Clayton Hartwig could have been deceptive in these letters, this was not consistent with his personality as we saw it.

The mental state of a suicidal person seems to include at least several of the following: turmoil, hopelessness, helplessness, anger, frustration, depression, psychosis, or confusion. We did not find any evidence of these characteristics in the letters. In fact, what is remarkable about the letters is their structural similarity. The letters to his friends are all written in similar linguistic style and neatness. The bottom of each page is carefully numbered. He dates and times each letter in standard military time and signs it in the same characteristic way, occasionally adding a P.S. Moreover, the letters are replete with statements about the future and hopefulness. To one friend, for example, someone with whom he had been angry, he states in a letter of March 19 that he is going to be over in London for 2 to 3 years and "I probably won't be able to come home during that time so before I go over I am going to take thirty days leave. I'd like to come down and see you during that time." This was written approximately 1 month before the alleged suicide. This statement regarding plans for the future would be inconsistent with the psychological characteristics of a suicidal person.

The last letter written by Clayton Hartwig was dated 16 April 1989. The Navy reported that this letter was perceived by the friend to be very different in focus when compared to the others. The letter seemed to be self-centered and the closing was different in focus from all the others. The only difference that we found, however, was that it was signed "love always" instead of just "love." Moreover, in the letter he does inquire of his friend: "So what's new with you? Passing your classes? At least you'll be home for the summer soon anyway." These passages indicate an interest in the other person. He ends the letter with the statement, "Well, I guess I'll close for now. Take care and write soon okay?" This statement would be unlikely to come from someone who was planning to kill himself 2 days later.

Clayton Hartwig and Kendall Truitt, a 21-year-old Gunner's Mate 3rd class who survived the explosion, had an intense relationship. Truitt had also been the focus of the Navy investigation into the incident because he was the beneficiary of $50,000 double indemnity policy that Hartwig had taken out on his life shortly before the Iowa's 1987–1988 deployment in the Persian Gulf. From the correspondence between them it is clear that Hartwig and Truitt shared intimate emotions. Hartwig was aware that he could be criticized for being close to Truitt, and that he could be subject to being labeled a "fag," which may have had implications for the military, which bars homosexuals. There was no evidence from the material that we reviewed that there was any overt homosexuality, which is an important point. Furthermore, there is no evidence in the general literature to state that there is a higher incidence of suicide among homosexuals. Clayton Hartwig had a reaction to Kendall Truitt getting married. We did not find evidence in the material that this reaction reached the point of murderous rage. They purchased insurance policies for each other. If Hartwig felt murderous rage toward Truitt, it is doubtful that he would have kept the policy in effect at the time of his death. Moreover, murder/suicide most frequently occurs in psychotic conditions, and there was definitely no evidence of psychotic behavior in this case.

Finally, the description of the interview with the last person to have spent any meaningful time with Clayton Hartwig was critical to our formulation. Hartwig did not specifically mention suicide on the morning of the nineteenth. He did seem somewhat quiet and withdrawn, but his behavior was not extreme. He did not mention suicide on April 19; there was no communication of suicidal intent. Thus, even to the end, there was no dramatic change in his behavior. Litman (1987) reports that only a "minority of suicides (I estimate 15%) occur rather suddenly and impulsively when people feel themselves to be in crisis and when they are under great stress or provocation" (p. 89). While "[o]ften in these cases, there have been few premonitory clues revealed to other persons about what was going to happen," "[i]n most suicides a person has been considering suicide for some time and has communicated clues to other persons" (p. 89).

There are pitfalls in conducting a posthumous determination of suicidal tendencies and behavior. Inferences have to be made from observations by people not trained to understand psychology. Due to the complexity of suicide, there is never a simple explanation. While it is possible to develop a suicidal state overnight, in the majority of situations there are certain consistencies that develop over time. We did not find evidence in the interviews and the letters of Clayton Hartwig that is consistent with a suicidal state. It was essential to the Navy's case to be able to prove that Clayton Hartwig was suffering from a number of stressors that would have affected his mental state and caused a precipitous suicide. Although one cannot conclusively rule out an underlying psychiatric disturbance or an acute undetected psychological state precipitating suicide, one cannot prove beyond a reasonable doubt — the standard in criminal cases — that Hartwig committed suicide/homicide; nor can one show that the preponderance of evidence, the standard in civil cases, weighed in favor of a suicidal/homicidal death. Both of these issues are relevant to this case.

CONCLUSION

Originally, psychological autopsies were used to determine mode of death in equivocal cases, and specifically to discriminate between suicides and accidents.

Since that time, it has been applied to research studies discriminating male driver fatalities from suicide (Shafer 1972) and to see whether aircraft accident victims were actually suicides (Jones, 1977). Not only can psychological autopsies assess intention and imputed lethality, but they can also introduce the psychodynamics of death into the death certificate. As Shneidman (1981) so eloquently concluded: "In this way, we might again permit the certification of death to reflect accurately our best current understanding of man" (p. 340).

While initially psychological autopsies were used only in suicide cases, recognizing the general utility of psychological autopsies has led to a more general application of psychological autopsies to studies of the mental states of dying patients (Kastenbaum 1977) and studies of a suicide's effect on the family (Rudestam 1977). Psychological autopsies have been used to identify and treat potential suicides and individuals unsuccessful in suicide attempts in hospital and other settings (Krieger 1968, Salmon et al. 1982) as well as the survivors of suicides (Sanborn and Sanborn 1976). They have also been used to clarify history and to better understand literature (Deikel 1974, Eisen 1980, Shneidman 1976). Psychological autopsies have also been found relevant in several areas of litigation (Dregne 1982, Lichter 1981).

In this chapter, we have discussed the applicability of the psychological autopsy technique to two new realms, criminal prosecution and congressional testimony. We showed, moreover, that in these two cases not only can psychological autopsies be used to determine the mode of death, but also to reconstruct the psychological state of a suicidal person and to elucidate contributing factors. While the use of the psychological autopsies in criminal cases has received its share of controversy, we feel that with appropriate safeguards it can be extremely helpful to the judicial system. As Shneidman states: "The key to every suicide is psychological pain. Therefore, the psychological autopsy which tries to explain what psychological needs were blocked or thwarted is quite absolutely relevant," whether a case involves civil or criminal charges.

REFERENCES

Appellate decision. (1989). *Theresa Jackson v. State of Florida.* In the District Court of Appeal of the State of Florida, fourth District, Case No. 88-0264.

Bass, A. (1987). Experts debate value of "autopsy" on suicide's mind. *The Boston Globe,* December 7th, pp. 49–50.

Bendheim, O. (1979). The psychiatric autopsy: its legal application. *Bulletin of the American Academy of Psychiatry and Law* 7:400–404.

Beskow, J. (1979). Suicide and mental disorder in Swedish men. *Acta Psychiatric Scandinavica* 277:(Suppl)1–138.

Brent, D. A. (1989). The psychological autopsy: methodological considerations for the study of adolescent suicide. *Suicide and Life-Threatening Behavior* 19:43–57.

Brent, D. A., Perper, J. A., and Allman, C. J. (1987). Alcohol, firearms, and suicide among youth: temporal trends in Allegheny County, Pennsylvania, 1960–1983. *Journal of the American Medical Association* 257:3369–3372.

Brent, D. A., Perper, J. A., Goldstein, C. E., et al. (1988a). Risk factors for adolescent suicide: a comparison of adolescent suicide victims with suicidal inpatients. *Archives of General Psychiatry* 45:581–588.

Brent, D. A., Perper, J. A., Kolko, D. J., and Zelenak, J. P. (1988b). The psychological autopsy: methodological considerations for the study of adolescent suicide. *Journal of the American Academy of Child and Adolescent Psychiatry* 27:362–366.

Buie, D., and Maltsberger, J. (1989). The psychological vulnerability to suicide. In *Suicide, Understanding, and Responding: Harvard Medical School Perspectives,* ed. D. G. Jacobs and H. M. Brown, pp. 59–72. Madison, CT: International Universities Press.

Cain, A., and Fast, I. (1966a). Children's reactions of parental suicide. *American Journal of Orthopsychiatry* 36:873–881.

—— (1966b). The legacy of suicide: observations of the pathogenic impact of suicide on marital partners. *Psychiatry* 29:406–411.

Cantor, P. (1975). The effects of youthful suicide on the family. *Psychiatric Opinion* 12:6–11.

—— (1992). Environmental, educational, and psychological interventions in suicidal adolescents. In *Suicide and Clinical Practice,* ed. D. Jacobs, pp. 131–146. Washington, DC: American Psychiatric Press.

Chynoweth, R., Topnge, J., and Armstrong, J. (1980). Suicide in Brisbane—a retrospective psychosocial study. *Australia and New Zealand Journal of Psychiatry* 14:37–45.

Clark, D. C. (1988). Psychological autopsy in the courtroom. *Suicide Research Digest* 2:3–4.

Clark, D. C., and Fawcett, J. (1992). An empirically based model of suicidal risk assessment for patients with affective disorders. In *Suicide and Clinical Practice,* ed. D. Jacobs, pp. 55–74. Washington, DC: American Psychiatric Press.

Clark, D. C., and Horton-Deutsch, S. (1992). Assessment in absentia: the value of the psychological autopsy method for studying antecedents of suicide and predicting future suicides. In *Assessment and Prediction of Suicide,* ed. R. Maris, A. Berman, J. Maltsberger, and R. Yufit, pp. 144–182. New York: Guilford.

Cohen-Sandler, R., Berman, A. L., and King, R. A. (1982). Life stress and symptomatology: determinants of suicidal behavior in children. *Journal of the American Academy of Child Psychiatry,* 21:178–186.

Colburn, D. (1988). Psychological autopsy in the courtroom: pinpointing the cause of a suicide is an emotionally charged endeavor. *Washington Post,* April 19, p. 13.

Curphey, T. (1961). The role of the social scientist in the medicolegal certification of death from suicide. In *The Cry for Help,* ed. N. Farberow and E. Shneidman. New York: McGraw-Hill.

—— (1967). The forensic pathologist and the multidisciplinary approach to death. In *Essays in Self-Destruction,* ed. E. Shneidman. New York: International Science Press.

—— (1968). The psychological autopsy: the role of the forensic pathologist in the multidisciplinary approach to death. *Bulletin of Suicidology,* 4:39–45.

Curran, D. K. (1987). *Adolescent Suicidal Behavior.* Washington, DC: Harper & Row.

Deikel, S. M. (1974). The life and death of Lenny Bruce: a psychological autopsy. *Life-Threatening Behavior* 4:176–192.

Douglas, J. (1967). *The Social Meanings of Suicide.* Princeton, NJ: Princeton University Press.

Dregne, N. (1982). Psychological autopsy: a new tool for criminal defense attorneys? *Arizona Law Review* 2:421–439.

Eisen, G. S. (1980). The suicide of Seymour Glass. *Suicide and Life-Threatening Behavior* 10:51–60.

Ellis, E. R., and Allen, G. N. (1961). *Traitor Within: Our Suicide Problem.* New York: Doubleday.

Frederick, C. (1978). Current trends in suicidal behavior in the United States. *American Journal of Psychotherapy* 32:172–200.

Goldacre, M., and Hawton, K. (1985). Repetition of self-poisoning and subsequent death in adolescents who take overdoses. *British Journal of Psychiatry* 146:395–398.

Hagnell, O., and Rorsman, B. (1978). Suicide and endogenous depression with somatic symptoms in the Lundby study. *Neuropsychobiology* 4:180–187.

—— (1979). Suicide in the Lundby study: a comparative investigation of clinical aspects. *Neuropsychobiology* 5:61–73.

—— (1980). Suicide in the Lundby study: a controlled prospective investigation of stressful life events. *Neuropsychobiology* 6:319–332.

Havens, L. L. (1965). The anatomy of a suicide. *The New England Journal of Medicine* 272:401–406.

Herzog, A., and Resnick, H. (1968). Clinical study of parental response to adolescent death by suicide with recommendations for approaching survivors. In *Proceedings of the 4th International Conference for Suicide Prevention,* ed. N. Garberay. Los Angeles: International Association for Suicide Prevention.

Jacobs, D. G. (1987). In Proceedings *State of Florida,* plaintiff v. *Theresa Jackson,* defendant. In the Circuit Court of the 17th Judicial Circuit. Case No. 86–6502. pp. 601–920.

–––––– (1989). Psychological profile of Clayton Hartwig. In *Review of Navy Investigation of U.S.S. IOWA Explosion.* Joint Hearings before the investigations subcommittee and the defense policy panel of the Committee of Armed Services House of representatives. One Hundred First Congress. Hearings held December 12, 13, and 21, 1989.

Jobes, D. A., Berman, A. L., and Josselson, A. R. (1986). The impact of psychological autopsies on medical examiners' determination of manner of death. *Journal of Forensic Sciences* 31:1, 177–189.

Jones, D. R., (1977) Suicide by aircraft: a case report. *Aviation, Space, and Environmental Medicine* 48:454–459.

Kastenbaum, R. (1970). Psychological autopsy: a case commentary. *Bulletin of Suicidology* 7:33–35.

–––––– (1977). The mental life of dying geriatric patients. *Gerontologist* 7:97–98.

Krieger, G. (1968). Psychological autopsies of hospital suicides. *Hospital and Community Psychiatry* 19:42–44.

Kübler-Ross, E. (1969). *On Death and Dying.* New York: Macmillan.

Lichter, D. (1981). Diagnosing the dead: the admissibility of the psychiatric autopsy. *American Criminal Law Review* 18:617–635.

Litman, R. E. (1965). When patients commit suicide. *American Journal of Psychotherapy* 19:570–576.

–––––– (1984). Psychological autopsies in court. *Suicide and Life-Threatening Behavior* 14:88–95.

–––––– (1987). Mental disorders and suicidal ideation. *Suicide and Life-Threatening Behavior* 17:85–92.

–––––– (1989). 500 psychological autopsies. *Journal of Forensic Sciences* 34:638–646.

Litman, R., Curphey, T., Shneidman, E., et al. (1963). Investigations of equivocal suicides. *Journal of the American Medical Association* 184:924–929.

Mack, J. E. (1989). Adolescent suicide: an architectural model. In *Suicide, Understanding, and Responding: Harvard Medical School Perspectives,* ed. D. G. Jacobs and H. M. Brown, pp. 221–238. Madison, CT: International Universities Press.

Mack, J. E., and Hickler, H. (1981). *Vivienne: The Life and Suicide of an Adolescent Girl.* Boston: Little, Brown.

Maltsberger, J. T. (1992). The implications of patient suicide for the surviving psychotherapist. In *Suicide and Clinical Practice,* ed. D. Jacobs, pp. 169–182. Washington, DC: American Psychiatric Press.

Maris, R. W. (1969). *Social Forces in Urban Suicide.* Homewood, IL: Dorsey.

Mattson, A., Seese, L., and Hawkins, J. (1969). Suicidal behavior as a child psychiatric emergency. *Archives of General Psychiatry* 20:100–109.

Menninger, K. (1938). *Man Against Himself.* New York: Harcourt, Brace, and World.

Miller, M. (1977). A psychological autopsy of a geriatric suicide. *Journal of Geriatric Psychiatry* 10:229–242.

Moscicki, E. K., and Regier, D. A. (1987). *Reduction in the Suicide Rate in Young People: Progress Review.* Division of Clinical Research, National Institute of Mental Health, Rockville, MD 20857.

Moss, D. C. (1988). Psychological autopsy touted. *ABA Journal,* February 1, p. 34.

National Center for Health Statistics (1988). *NCHS Monthly Vital Statistics Report* 37, (6 Suppl.).

Neill, K., Benensohn, H. S., Farber, A. N., and Resnik, H. L. P. (1974). The psychological autopsy: a technique for investigating a hospital suicide. *Hospital and Community Psychiatry* 25:33–36.

O'Carroll, P. W. (1989). A consideration of the validity and reliability of suicide mortality data. *Suicide and Life-Threatening Behavior* 19:1–16.

Osgood, N., and McIntosh, J. (1986). *Suicide in the Elderly: An Annotated Bibliography and Review*. New York: Greenwood.

Pfeffer, C. R. (1984). Clinical aspects of childhood suicidal behavior. *Pediatric Annals* 13:56–61.

_____ (1988). Clinical dilemmas in the prevention of adolescent suicidal behavior. *Annals of the American Society for Adolescent Psychiatry* 15:407–421.

Pfeffer, C. R., Conte, H. R., Plutchik, R. et al. (1979). Suicidal behavior in latency-age children. An empirical study. *Journal of the American Academy of Child Psychiatry* 18:679–692.

_____ (1980). Suicidal behavior in latency-age children: an empirical study: an outpatient population. *Journal of the American Academy of Child Psychiatry* 19:703–710.

Pfeffer, C., Newcorn, J., Kaplan, G., et al. (1985). Suicidal behavior in adolescent psychiatric inpatients. Paper presented to the Annual Meeting of the American Psychiatric Association, Dallas, Texas.

Pfeffer, C. R., Solomon, G., Plutchik, R., et al. (1982). Suicidal behavior in latency-age psychiatric inpatients: a replication and cross validation. *Journal of the American Academy of Child Psychiatry* 21:564–569.

Review of Navy Investigation of U.S.S. IOWA Explosion. Joint hearings before the investigations subcommittee and the defense policy panel of the Committee of Armed Services, House of Representatives. One Hundred First Congress. Hearings held December 12, 13, and 21, 1989.

Robin, E., Murphy, G., Wilkinson, R., et al. (1959). Some clinical considerations in the prevention of suicide based on a study of 134 successful suicides. *American Journal of Public Health* 49:888–899.

Rudestam, K. E. (1977). Physical and psychological responses to suicide in the family, *Journal of Consulting and Clinical Psychology* 45:162–170.

_____ (1979). Some notes on conducting a psychological autopsy. *Suicide and Life-Threatening Behavior* 9:141–144.

Salmon, J. A., Hajek, P. T., Rachut, E., et al. (1982). Mortality conference: suicide of an "appropriately" depressed medical patient. *General Hospital Psychiatry* 4:307–313.

Sanborn, D. E., and Sanborn, C. J. (1976). The psychological autopsy as a therapeutic tool. *Diseases of the Nervous System* 37:4–8.

Sanborn, D. E., Sanborn, C. J., and Cimbolic, P. (1974). Occupation and suicide: a study of two counties in New Hampshire. *Diseases of the Nervous System* 35:7–12.

Scanlon, C. (1987). Evidence of a new kind. *St. Petersburg Times,* December 1, pp. D1, 2.

Shaffer, D. (1974). Suicide in childhood and early adolescence. *Journal of Child psychology and Psychiatry* 15:275–291.

Shaffer, J. W., and Fisher, P. (1981). The epidemiology of suicide in children and young adolescents. *Journal of the American Academy of Child Psychiatry* 20:545–561.

Shaffer, J. W., Perlin, S., Schmidt, C. W., and Himmelfarb, M. (1972). Assessment in absentia: new directions in the psychological autopsy. *Hopkins Medical Journal* 130:308–316.

Shafii, M., Carrigan, S., Whittinghill, J. R., and Derrick, A. (1985). Psychological autopsy of completed suicide in children and adolescents. *American Journal of Psychiatry* 142:1061–1064.

Shafii, M., Stelz-Lenarsky, J., Derrick, A. M., et al. (1988). Comorbidity of mental disorders in the post-mortem diagnosis of completed suicide in children and adolescents. *Journal of Affective Disorders* 15:227–233.

Shneidman, E. (1967). Sleep and self-destruction: a phenomenological study. In *Essays in Self-Destruction*. New York: Science House.

_____ (1969). Suicide, lethality, and the psychological autopsy. *International Psychiatric Clinics* 6:225–250.

_____ (1971a). Perturbation and lethality as precursors of suicide in a gifted group. *Life-Threatening Behavior* 1:23–45.

_____ (1971b). Prevention, intervention, and postvention of suicide. *Annals of Internal Medicine* 75:453–458.

_____ (1973). *Deaths of Man*. New York: Quadrangle.

_____ (1976). Some psychological reflections on the death of Malcolm Melville. *Suicide and Life-Threatening Behavior* 6:231–242.

_____ (1981). The psychological autopsy. *Suicide and Life-Threatening Behavior* 11:325–340.

_____ (1985). *Definition of Suicide.* New York: Wiley.

_____ (1989). Overview: a multidimensional approach to suicide. In *Suicide, Understanding, and Responding: Harvard Medical School Perspectives,* ed. D. G. Jacobs and H. M. Brown, pp. 1–30. Madison, CT: International Universities Press.

Shneidman, E., and Farberow, N. (1961). Sample investigation of equivocal suicide deaths. In *The Cry for Help,* ed. N. Farberow and E. Shneidman. New York: McGraw-Hill.

Stanley, E. J., and Barter, J. T. (1970). Adolescent suicide behavior. *American Journal of Orthopsychiatry* 40:87–96.

Taylor, E., and Stansfeld, S. (1984). Children who poison themselves: prediction of attendance for treatment. *British Journal of Psychiatry* 145:132–135.

Weisman, A. D. (1967). The psychological autopsy and the potential suicide. *Bulletin of Suicidology* 2:15–24.

Weisman, A. D., and Kastenbaum, R. (1968). The psychological autopsy: a study of the terminal phase of life. *Community Mental Health Journal,* Monograph 4:1–59.

Alan L. Berman

INTRODUCTION

The psychological autopsy is a postmortem investigative procedure that helps ascertain the decedent's role in his or her own demise. Through interviews with knowledgeable informants, the decedent's background, personal relationships, habits, character, and coping patterns are reconstructed. From this reconstruction the relationship between an individual's life-style and death-style may be established (Brent 1989, Clark and Horton-Deutsch 1992). As a postdictive analysis, the psychological autopsy is speculative. It provides a probabilistic statement, a best-bet conclusion, giving a logical understanding of the interaction between the person and events leading to that person's death.

The psychological autopsy owes its birth to the pioneering early works of Zilboorg and Robins between 1940 and the mid-1950s (Clark and Horton-Deutsch 1992). Its development, however, was nurtured out of the frustration of a medical examiner (Theodore Curphey), the expertise of three behavioral scientists (Edwin Shneidman, Norman Farberow, and Robert Litman), and the wedding of their interests. The term, coined by Shneidman (1951), came to be applied in the early 1960s to a set of procedures "of gently done systematic inquiries of survivors" (Shneidman 1991, p. 253) designed to clarify the intention of the decedent, therefore the decedent's role in effecting his or her death. Thus, the primary purpose of the psychological autopsy was to establish the *manner of death* (e.g., suicide vs. accidental) to as high a degree of certainty as possible in cases deemed equivocal.

In 1981, Shneidman wrote that the psychological autopsy helped answer two other questions[1] as well: Why did the individual do it? and Why did the death occur at this time? That is, reasons, motivations, dynamics, predisposing conditions, and precipitating events could be elucidated and understood. This, of course, is what suicidology is all about — the study and understanding of suicide. In this new context the study of suicide was simply broadened to apply to equivocal deaths, that is, deaths that *possibly* were suicides. By means of the developing procedures of the psychological autopsy, suicides could now be better distinguished, differentiated, and understood relative to other manners of death, most notably accidents.

FORENSIC SUICIDOLOGY

Given its birth into the world of forensic pathology, it was, perhaps, only a matter of time before the psychological autopsy would find itself brought into the courtroom. The certification of manner of death determined by the coroner or medical examiner is an opinion. Should a litigant have reason to challenge that opinion, it would ultimately be in the courtroom (and the preliminary procedures of discovery), where alternative opinions are presented and argued, that such a challenge would take place. Decisions assigning responsibility for a death and, if applicable, penalties for that liability are the province of the court. When we introduce the study of suicide to the home of legal argumentation and decision, we create the emerging field of forensic suicidology.

This union between suicidology and the law typically involves two broad types of cases, those of *parens patriae,* or custodial caretaking, and those of *contested life insurance claims.* In some cases, both of these issues pertain.

Parens Patriae

Society typically assigns blame for every death, either to God (natural and accidental death) or man (homicide and suicide) (Litman 1980). Where the responsibility for a death can be attributed to human negligence, punishments are called for. Where once the suicide him- or herself was punished through forfeiture of property, degradation of the corpse, and so forth, modern legal thinking has shifted from blaming the victim (now seen as suffering from mental disorder) to extending compassionate concern for survivors and conferring responsibility on those in custodial and caretaking roles of protecting the potential suicide from conditions predisposing self-harm or from actual self-harm behavior.

Within this category of litigation, there are any number of types of potentially negligent caretakers. The law simply asks whether the caretaker or

---

[1]In addition to these purposes, Shneidman noted that the interviews, conducted in a skillful and compassionate manner, had therapeutic value to survivors, that is, they allowed for catharsis, receiving support, and a signaling of further need for bereavement counseling.

custodian's negligence was a proximate cause of (a link in the chain leading to) the suicide. The most common types of cases involve the following:

1. Employers: For example, workmen's compensation or FELA cases. The typical claim here is that an employer was responsible and, therefore, liable for the unsafe working conditions that led to an injury, followed by mental distress or deterioration, and ultimately suicide.

Case Example: A lifelong railroad employee injured his back when attempting to pick up a greasy coupling. After months of pain and unsuccessful physical treatments, he became increasingly despondent and resumed an earlier habit of alcohol abuse. Now believing he would never be able to work again, he shot himself in the head. His wife sued the railroad for not ensuring safe working conditions specifying regulations requiring no greasy couplings on the job site.

2. Therapists and Treatment Institutions: Malpractice cases allege that the practitioner and/or employing hospital, clinic, and so forth practiced below the standard of care, that is, that opined level of care expected of the reasonable and prudent average practitioner. In hospital settings, this typically involves violations of the psychiatry unit's policy and procedures (e.g., the implementation of orders or the failure to safeguard the environment). In outpatient settings, the typical complaint focuses on the failure to assess and treat appropriately, including questions of the need for hospitalization and/or medication.

Case Example: A psychiatry inpatient with a history of seven suicide attempts in 18 months showed signs of increasing distress, panic, and head banging as her planned discharge approached. Ordered into seclusion and restraints for two consecutive nights and removed to the open ward during the days, the patient hanged herself in the late afternoon after a family meeting with her husband regarding her discharge. The husband sued the hospital and treatment team for not keeping her on a 24-hour suicide watch.

3. Product Manufacturers: Those who produce products for human use have a responsibility to ensure the safety of that product and its user. For example, liability is potentially attributed to pharmaceutical houses whose medications have been implicated in causing suicides. As one illustration, a recent report (Teicher et al. 1990) about the widely prescribed antidepressant fluoxetine being implicated in the suicides of patients taking it have led to a spate of suits against its manufacturer (Lilly-Dista) and psychiatrists prescribing it. As another illustration, well-publicized suits have been instituted against record and television broadcasting companies alleging that their songs and movies precipitated suicidal deaths.

Case Example: A successful attorney, feeling increasing work pressure, began suffering from insomnia. He was prescribed the drug triazolam to help him sleep. While under the care of his treating physician, his behavior grew increasingly agitated, until he awakened early one morning, went to his office at 5:00 A.M., overturned his furniture, trashed his files, and jumped through the fifth-story window. He survived his jump and, after a nearly complete recovery, sued the drug's manufacturer, alleging his suicide attempt was caused by the drug.

4. Penal Institutions: Jails and prisons have custodial responsibilities toward those held by or sentenced to them. The typical jail suicide, for example, is that of a young male arrested for a misdemeanor committed while drunk. The risk of his suicide is greatest in the first 24 hours of incarceration. When jail personnel fail to learn of an inmate's history, evaluate the propensity toward suicide, or monitor appropriately an evaluated risk, surviving family members become potential litigants.

Case Example: A 19-year-old male was arrested for vandalizing cars during a drunken spree through city streets. Brought to the city jail, he was booked and placed alone in a small cell. His behavior was agitated and verbally abusive. When a guard went to check on him after his tirade had presumably been calmed by sleep, he was found hanging by a bedsheet. The jail and the city were sued by his family for negligence.

5. Family Members: As, perhaps, a wave of the future, parents and spouses may be held criminally liable for creating conditions later seen to be a proximate cause of a suicide of a family member. In one widely publicized case in Florida, a teenage girl's mother was charged with compelling her daughter to be a nude dancer in order to earn money for the family. Her daughter's suicide was alleged to have been a result of her humiliation and rage as a consequence of her mother's punitive control.

Case Example: A manic-depressive male with a history of suicide attempts married a woman he met while living in a group home after being hospitalized during his early adulthood. Increasingly, she managed his affairs and soon dominated his every behavior. In addition she dispensed his medications to him, keeping him constantly overmedicated. Meanwhile, she allegedly took up with another man, spending most of every day away from the home with him and spending large amounts of her husband's inherited wealth on herself. When he was found dead by self-inflicted gunshot wound, his parents initiated suit against his wife, charging her with abusive disregard for his well-being.

Contested Life Insurance[2]

Suicide poses a special problem for life insurance contracts. On the one hand, it is presumed that in suicide the time of death is in the hands of the insured. Thus

---

[2]For an excellent review of issues regarding the investigation of suicide in insurance claims cases the reader is referred to Nolan (1988).

insurance companies consider that the applicant for life insurance has an unfair advantage in their actuarial bet. To hedge that bet, insurance contracts typically include an exclusionary clause, denying payment of benefits, for example, if the death is by suicide within 2 years of the date the policy went into effect. On the other hand, one of the objectives of the potential decedent is the monetary protection of his or her family irrespective of the prematurity of or intention in his or her death. Families have every reason to believe that the decedent who died within the time frame of an exclusionary clause neither intended to die nor made application for death benefits expecting to defraud the insurance company.

If denied benefits, the estate of the insured thus may take the insurance company to court. Under a suicide exclusion clause, the insurance company has the burden to prove, as an affirmative defense, that the death was a suicide. The majority (N = 27) of the states in the United States have some form of presumption of law against suicide; this presumption applies whenever the manner of death is unclear (equivocal). As noted above, the certification of a death as a suicide by a coroner or medical examiner is not legal proof of how one died; it is simply one opinion to be considered by the court in deciding this type of contract dispute.

As one of these considered opinions, a conclusion derived by a suicidologist employing psychological autopsy procedures to answer the question of the decedent's intent increasingly has been of value. This opinion, based on a thorough investigation of the factual record, death site, and biography of the decedent, especially noting the decedent's activities proximate to termination, is helped by the expert's reliance on operational criteria for classifying suicide (Rosenberg et al. 1988).

The method of death establishes, in part, certain working hypotheses in the investigation of equivocal, especially unwitnessed, deaths. For example, adult deaths by self-inflicted gunshot wound rarely are considered to be accidents. In contrast, motor vehicle and pedestrian deaths rarely are initially considered to be suicides. Yet, in the former case the decedent's history of gun use and death-site clues may implicate an accidental death, and in the latter case the automobile indeed may be used as a lethal weapon in an intended death. In contrast, the manner of death in unwitnessed drownings and falls or jumps from heights, in particular, rarely can be determined simply on the basis of physical evidence alone. It is here that psychological data can provide valuable clues as to the mind of the decedent, giving evidence of why the decedent was at the death site.

Case Example: A 47-year-old, twice divorced woman died from drowning with contributing shark bites while on a vacation cruise. Toxicological analyses revealed a blood alcohol level of 0.13 percent. The night before her death she broke 13 months of abstinence by drinking with fellow passengers; she was reported to be still unsteady on her feet the following afternoon. This binge ended the most prolonged period of sobriety in her adult life, one during which she had been described as happy and stable.

Prior to this she had a long history of mood swings, alcoholism, and suicide attempts.

Her entry into the water was unwitnessed, although there were several reports that she cried for help once immersed. At the foot of the ship's railing where she went overboard was found her purse, on top of which was a piece of paper listing her cabin number written in her hand.

What is suggested as an accidental fall into the water under the influence of alcohol, upon further investigation, has all the trappings of an intended death. She had recently taken out new life insurance. Preceding this by a few weeks a significant relationship with a man had ended abruptly. Her decision to end sobriety did not occur without reason, most probably initially as a way to numb her pain and return to the comfort of a lifelong habit. However, there can be little doubt that alcohol potentiated her depression and that she continued to drink well into the next day. The carefully placed handwritten note at the site can only be interpreted as a suicide note, a final instruction as to her identity should she not be discovered missing for some time. Also, site investigation revealed that the ship's railing was more than waist high, making it unlikely she accidentally fell over. What she could not have anticipated were the sharks that attacked soon after she entered the water. Her cries for help at that time were most probably precipitated by this unexpected and gruesome consequence of her suicidal act.

Within this framework it is the intent of this chapter to illustrate the forensic application of the psychological autopsy using cases of deaths by asphyxiation by drowning. As noted below, suicide by drowning is both relatively rare and difficult to determine. Given these considerations, two extensive cases will be presented as examples of the two general classes of forensic cases discussed above.

Asphyxiation by Drowning

Atkinson (1978) argues that drowning is probably the most equivocal of all manners of death. Morphological criteria provide no evidence for determining how a body came to be in the water. An individual can slip, fall, jump, or be pushed into the water.[3]

A body recovered after a brief period of immersion in water will show few external signs of the cause of death. Internally, there will be nonspecific evidence of anoxia, pulmonary congestion, and massive pulmonary edema, this resulting in a mushroom of white froth externally at the mouth and nares (Hendrix 1972). If there is sufficient time lapse between death and autopsy, decomposition and

---

[3]A good example of the difficulties faced in this regard by a coroner can be found in Noguchi's (1983) discussion of the 1981 drowning death of actress Natalie Wood.

destruction of the body by scavenger fish make even the identification of the body difficult.

No reliable test permitting the unequivocal diagnosis of drowning exists. Even the presence of a cadaveric spasm or instantaneous rigor is inconclusive in this regard (Spitz and Fisher 1980). This violent muscular reaction causes the person to grip tightly anything being held at the time of death. As a drowning person literally may "grasp at straws" (weeds, wood, etc.), the evidence "in hand" may show that at least the person was alive after entering the water.

Overall, the great majority of deaths by drowning are accidental. Statistically, the annual incidence of unintentional (accidental) drowning averages about ten times that of intentional (suicidal) drownings. The melodrama of a depressed person walking off into the ocean is much more common in film than in real life, as is the underworld disposal of a body on the ocean's floor with feet set in concrete.

The majority of accidental drownings are of victims under the age of 24. They occur attendant to swimming or water sports during the summer months. Additionally, they usually are witnessed. Evidence at the scene corroborates the unintentional manner of death. The body is dressed appropriately, that is, in bathing suit; on-site evidence—fishing gear, for example—describes an intent other than suicide; environmental conditions—a treacherous undertow—describe why a good swimmer failed to stay afloat.

When a body is dressed inappropriately or when clothing is found neatly folded on land or a structure adjacent to the water, the possibility of a suicide must be considered. Similarly, when environmental conditions were not hazardous to a good swimmer's skills, intentional death is suspected. Particularly when a body is recovered in shallow water, where self-rescue is considered easily accomplished, the possibility of suicide is high. One would expect to find either anatomical or toxicologic evidence to otherwise explain the failure of the self-preservation instinct. Thus, adult drownings in bathtubs most often must be considered to be suicidal.

The following two cases illustrate the use of the psychological autopsy in equivocal deaths by drowning. In each case the autopsy provided significant input to forensic cases as described above.

Contested Insurance: The Case of Paul Artis

Paul Artis was 50 years old, married with two children. His body was found, fully clothed and face down, in 4 feet of water in an inlet one-half mile from his home. Attached to his waist was a rope; at its other end was a styrofoam raft. Toxicological analyses revealed a blood alcohol level of 0.11 percent. There was no evidence of external injury to the body. The medical examiner certified his death to be a suicide. When life insurance benefits were denied, his wife sued.

History   Paul was an only child whose mother died in childbirth. His father, who raised him, died 10 years prior to his own death. The family was poor, but Paul's childhood was reported to have been happy. After earning a graduate degree in engineering, Paul married his childhood sweetheart at the age of 25. Four children were born of this union (ages 18–24 at the time of his death). Again, others described Paul as happy in this marriage, but an extramarital affair led to its dissolution. Five years prior to the drowning, he married his lover, fathered a daughter and adopted his new wife's daughter (at the time of the drowning, aged 2 and 12, respectively). When this new family bought a new home by the water 3 years before his death, Paul had to change jobs, losing both status and title. The home was in an isolated area. The couple was reported to have made few friends.

Paul had no prior history of suicidal behavior, no family history of suicide, and was not accident prone. He rarely drank. He was a good swimmer.

Proximal Events   Two months prior to the drowning, Paul was arrested and charged with two offenses of second degree rape of his step-daughter and her 11-year-old girlfriend. Later he would claim that he felt uncared for by his wife; lacking a sexual relationship with her, he turned to his physically precocious step-daughter for what he termed "tender love." On his initiation, this relationship soon turned sexual, lasting for over a year. His step-daughter later stated that she had been frightened, in the first place because she had been raped by her natural father when she was 5, and because her father had threatened to kill himself "if you tell."

After sleeping overnight at the house, his step-daughter's girlfriend unexpectedly found Paul lying on top of his step-daughter. Frightened as well, she agreed to have sex with him. Her involvement lasted for 3 months, ending only after an argument between the girls led to the friend telling her parents what had been going on.

When Paul learned of her disclosure, he stated to his step-daughter that he "would have to go to jail for about 50 years," "he would rather kill himself," and that the girls "would have to go to reform school." Upon his arrest, the step-daughter told the police: "I don't want to see him get hurt. I love him very much and he loves me."

Upon learning of his arrest, Mrs. Artis first denied its plausibility and later took the blame "for not being a good wife." She defended her husband, stating it was "a natural occurrence," that "no harm had been done," and that "if it weren't for society's intolerance and rigid rules, there would be no problem."

Paul felt it was "unreasonable" that he had been arrested and charged. He stated that the girlfriend was sexually experienced and had asked to be involved because she came "from a family without love." To his attorney he expressed anxiety about his case in court, embarrassment for his family, and fear about losing his job. He felt panicked that he would not survive jail. Planning an insanity defense, Paul's attorney referred him for a psychiatric evaluation. He was diagnosed as having a narcissistic personality disorder and poor social judgment. Paul's attorney immediately petitioned the court's permission to seek a second evaluation.

Over the next several weeks the Artises made plans should Paul be sentenced to jail. Six weeks before his death a large loan was secured from his credit union in order to consolidate debts. A premium for life insurance to cover the loan was paid at this time. They further agreed they would sell the house and that Mrs. Artis would return to live with her mother to save money until Paul was released. It was for the purpose of increasing the value of their property that Mrs. Artis believed her husband had gone to repair the pier on the night before he was found dead. The pier had sustained damage during the winter freeze.

Final 24 hours   On the morning before his death, Paul left home before 8:00 A.M. to meet with his attorney and, then, to go to work. Around 2:00 P.M. his wife called him as was her custom. She later reported she noticed nothing out of the ordinary in his voice or in the content of this call. She then left around 2:30 P.M. to shop and take her daughter to after-school activities. At 3:00 P.M. Paul told his boss that he wasn't feeling well. He was given the rest of the day off. The drive home took approximately 45 minutes. Paul telephoned his attorney about 4:30 P.M. and was told that their request for a second psychiatric evaluation had been denied, meaning therefore that the original insanity plea would probably be withdrawn. Paul again expressed his anxiety about going to prison. He was last seen by a neighbor chopping wood around 5:30 P.M.

When his wife returned home later that night, Paul was nowhere to be found. The oven had been left on and an uncooked TV dinner had been left on top of the stove. On the dining-room table were her husband's wallet, key ring, glasses, and watch. Searching frantically for him to no avail, she grew worried and called the police. She informed them that it was unusual for him to leave the house for any period of time without leaving her a note.

Paul's body was found late the following afternoon. The coroner estimated the time of death as somewhere between 5:30 P.M. and 8:00 A.M. Police reports indicated a water depth of only 2 feet extending 50 feet beyond the end of the pier. The pier itself was at such a height that had Paul been standing on the raft in order to repair the pier, he still would not have been able to reach it. Furthermore, no tools were found on or about the pier. Thus the police doubted his wife's assumption about why he had gone to the pier the night of his disappearance.

Manner of Death Determination   The null hypothesis posed by equivocal deaths is that each of four manners of death is equally possible. In the case of Paul Artis, the coroner's autopsy had ruled out death by natural causes; the police investigation gave no reason to suspect homicide. Thus we must test the research hypothesis most typically found in cases of equivocal death, that of accidental (unintentional) versus suicidal (intentional) death.

That Paul Artis's death could have been an accident is a plausible interpretation of the available data. The pier, indeed, was in disrepair. He had motive to be there. It is possible he intended merely to spend but a few minutes inspecting the pier, preparatory to later repair, while waiting for the oven to preheat for his TV dinner. This would explain his not leaving a note for his wife. He may have left his personal belongings on the dining room table, emptying his pockets to protect against the possibility of an accidental fall into the water. He was not prone to incur unintentional injuries. His characterological carefulness may also be attested to by the rope tied around his waist, particularly given that he had had a few drinks. He had no history of suicidal behavior and had shown concern for the long-term future in discussions with his wife. Thus, in spite of his caution, he may have tragically misjudged the effects of alcohol, slipped from the pier or raft, knocked himself unconscious, and drowned in shallow water.

On the other hand, there was no sign of external injury that could have rendered him unconscious or otherwise unable to rescue himself in spite of having been drinking. He drowned in but 2 feet of water. No tools were found on or near the pier.

Paul had a careful, well-planned life-style. He had helped his wife take care of the future in expectation of his absence. Again, he was not prone to accidental behavior; nor was he an excessive risk-taker. He had more than sufficient motive to suicide. His world had been his job and his family. He was now anxious about his job, embarrassed for his family, and fearful for his life if sent to prison. He had threatened suicide. On the day of his disappearance, he learned from his attorney that his only defense against serving time was now in severe jeopardy. Feigning illness at work (he told his wife nothing of feeling sick an hour earlier and was well enough to chop wood two hours later), he came home and drank, somewhat out of character and probably to screw up his courage to carry out his decision to suicide. That he had recently taken a consolidated debt loan that was covered by a life insurance policy suggests he would have reason to attempt to disguise his death as an accident.

On the basis of the psychological autopsy the determination that Paul Artis's death was suicidal was supported. In consideration, however, of the family's pain and suffering (and in lieu of future court costs), the insurance company agreed to a compromise settlement.

In the following case, extensive observational, historical, and psychological information is provided and summarized for the reader. The same data, viewed by experts for both plaintiff and defendant, leads not surprisingly to markedly different interpretations. Their opposing views provide a unique view to the human variables of interpretation and opinion involved in these forensic procedures. I leave the reader to arrive at his or her independent conclusions regarding the determination of manner of death. As is common to many of these forensic cases, the litigation initiated by the parents against the custodial caretaker provided no satisfaction in ruling for one or the other side. This case ended in a settlement and a sealed file — no bottom-line dollar figure was publicly announced even to the expert witnesses involved (a not uncommon occurrence!). In so doing, settlement neither implies nor admits guilt on the part of the defendant.

Parens Patriae: The Case of Bobby Severn

> Dear Mom,
>   This place is the pits. It is no fun. If it wasn't for the cost of it, I would get thrown out on purpose. I mean only a couple of changes of clothes for 2 weeks sucks! Also my councelors [sic] are assholes (excuse my language). We hike about 5 miles a day. And with packs weighing about 35 pounds. The food is also raunchy. It is so boring I would rather be sitting at home doing nothing. The bugs are terrible. I would rather be eaten alive. I am never going to make it through the solo hike [not a hike but a 24-hour solo wilderness experience] for 2 days by myself. We have to sleep in holes and deep under plastic to not get wet. We don't even have toilet paper. Tell . . . I said Hi and I probably won't be able to write her. I also probably won't be able to write you back but I'll try. I miss you and everyone so much. I love you. Bye Bye.
>   Love,
>   Bobby

By the thirteenth day of a 15-day Wilderness Adventure trip Bobby's patience had worn thin. Although he had mastered a solo hike, his homesickness and negative attitude had been evident to both of his counselors and the twenty-one other campers throughout the camping experience. No kid wanted to be on this trip; most had been told it would build character. Just what a 14-year-old wants!

Bobby's job, this day, was to be navigator. He had map-reading skills and was to lead the group to the evening bivouac by a mountainous lake. Sometime in the early afternoon the group arrived at a four-way intersection. Bobby became confused and was teased by several kids. A sensitive kid, he got angry and bolted from the group. When his counselors and the others caught up with him, he was at a nearby lodge calling home long distance, first to his mother who wasn't to return from a business trip until that evening, then to his grandmother and brother. He was crying so hard his brother told him that he would have his dad call him right back. When his dad called, Bobby insisted he be picked up right away and taken home. His father patiently told him that it was a 300-mile trip, that the experience would be ending in only 2 more days, and that he would pick him up as arranged on day 15, but would indeed try to come earlier than planned that day. Bobby calmed somewhat and rejoined the group.

That afternoon the group went belaying. Some of the boys remembered that Bobby "did not participate" and "was not actively involved." A counselor recalled he was "cooperative and interested."

By evening's meal his behavior was noticeably different. Other campers later recalled him to appear disoriented and confused, describing him as "strange," "weird," and "spaced out." At dinnertime he was asking where things were that were right in front of him, tripping over things, and shaking so hard he neither could hold nor prevent spilling food from his bowl. He couldn't remember the name of a camper he knew well. Two boys recalled that he fell, placing his hand near the embers of the campfire and showed no response. A little later, when ready to go to sleep, his counselors had to help him get his boots off. It had rained the night before and it was cold (in high 30s) by bedtime. The sleeping bags were damp and cold. The campers huddled close to each other in their tent for warmth. The counselors slept apart from the boys in a tent about 50 feet away. At 10:30 P.M. one camper was awakened by the sound of someone throwing up. Around 12:45 A.M. everyone was awakened by a boy's voice coming from offshore. He was yelling for help and retching, but because it was foggy, no one could be seen. The counselors yelled back, but got no response. A quick head count revealed that Bobby was missing; the counselors quickly got in a canoe and paddled out. By now the voice had quieted. No one was found. The state police were summoned and an onshore search was mounted. At daybreak divers entered the lake and found Bobby's body fully clothed about 100 feet offshore in about 10 to 12 feet of water.

An autopsy was performed at the County Hospital and the cause of death was determined to be asphyxiation due to freshwater drowning.

An investigation of the "Incident at Carver Lake" ordered by the Board of Directors of Wilderness Adventures reported the following:

1. Bobby had been regularly seeing a counselor because of "poor academic performance" for the past 2 years. It was on the counselor's recommendation that Bobby was enrolled in the course.
2. There was no indication of substance use. Bobby was not taking prescribed medications.
3. The descriptions of Bobby's behavior at the evening meal are consistent with explanations of "acting out, confusion, or hypothermia among other causes." The reported incident of burning his hand was not corroborated on autopsy as no lesions were found.
4. No other "student" showed evidence of hypothermia. Air temperature was between 35 and 39 degrees that night.

5. Bobby was known to be a strong swimmer.

6. After Bobby's father called him back that afternoon, his father spoke to one of the counselors, and closed by saying: "Keep an eye on him." When his grandmother was informed by phone of his death, her first words were: "It wasn't suicide, was it?" (Later she denied that she said this.)

7. Police stated that Bobby's sleeping bag was "soaking wet," an observation "emphatically denied" by the trip's counselors.

8. Interviews with Bobby's parents revealed the picture of a "quiet, introverted boy who had difficulty expressing his feelings, was very attached to his mother, and aloof from his peers. He had occasional spells of temper tantrums, but no history of confusion, depression, substance abuse, or suicide attempt. His mother saw him as a coward and easily frightened, very unlikely to roam out of the lean-to at night."

Family History   Bobby was the youngest of three children (sister, 21; brother, 19) born to Dr. & Mrs. Severn. Developmental history was uneventful, his physical growth average for his age. His parents' marriage of 20 years ended in separation 4 years prior to Bobby's death. The divorce papers were finally signed just before he left for this trip. After years of marital conflict, his father, a dermatologist, began having a series of affairs and was discovered by his wife in bed with another woman at Bobby's grandmother's house. Bobby's parents immediately separated. Bobby responded with signs of depressive withdrawal and violent temper outbursts. A long-standing sibling rivalry with his brother worsened. In one incident he picked up a kitchen knife during an argument with his brother and threatened to kill him (2 years prior to the drowning).

He was particularly angry at his father, but avoided him after the separation, as he was fearful of his father's anger. On the other hand, he clung dependently to his mother, fearful he would lose her. Until the age of 12 he often slept in his mother's bed. He did not express fears of the dark, nor did he sleepwalk. When he began showing signs of concentration difficulty and distractibility, his school performance declined. Over the next 2 years, he attended three different schools. He was referred for psychological evaluation and subsequently for therapy. He remained in therapy until the summer before camp. That summer, but for a vacation at the beach, Bobby was at home, played with his dog, and swam in a local pool. Within a few weeks of leaving for camp, the family moved and his maternal grandfather died.

A psychological evaluation conducted 18 months prior to his death revealed a Full Scale IQ of 116 with a Verbal IQ of 121 and Performance IQ of 108. This pattern was interpreted as "action oriented." He did relatively well on tasks requiring perceptions of details and judgment. The psychologist noted, "He [knows] what is going on in his world." His potential was seen as inhibited by emotional factors, including poor planning ability under stress and a diminished capacity for concentration.

Projective tests revealed an insecure, guarded boy with strong, unsatisfied dependency needs. He was described as emotionally withdrawn and drive-dominated, deriving satisfaction from fantasy. Furthermore, problems with underlying anger caused him anxiety for he feared aggression from others. Although he was seen as possibly acting out aggressively if provoked, he was more likely to be passive aggressive or passive resistant.

Feelings of rejection and abandonment characterized his relationship with his parents. He lacked trust and socialization skills. He was afraid of his father's violent anger and fantasized his father's death as retribution. Under conditions of stress, it was stated, Bobby was more likely to be preoccupied with idiosyncratic thinking, to deny, withdraw, and regress. These defenses, however, were not seen as working effectively, resulting in feelings of confusion and depression. "He has self-destructive tendencies and his reality ties may be tenuous."

He was diagnosed by his psychologist as having an Adjustment Disorder with mixed disturbances of emotions (depression, primary; anxiety, secondary) and conduct. During almost 2 years of treatment, he expressed no suicide ideation or behavior. He often, however, was described as withdrawn, unhappy, and angry, having little interest in and being resistant to learning. He was interested in tennis and swimming and had made the school swim team the year of the drowning.

There are several possible scenarios that may explain Bobby's death:

1. Depressed and hurt by his father's apparent rejection, Bobby acted out for attention. Feeling sick during the night he went into the woods to vomit, then screamed for attention. Getting none he went into the lake, waded out too far, developed laryngospasm, aspirated vomitus, panicked, could not stay afloat in his clothing, and could not save himself.
2. Becoming sick during the night, he left the lean-to to vomit, called for help, became lost, confused, or panicky, wandered into the lake. . . .
3. An acute psychotic reaction or illness could have precipitated some sort of organic brain syndrome. [The possibility of drug use or abuse had been ruled out upon toxicological analysis.]
4. Bobby deliberately crept out and waded into the lake with the intention of suiciding.

The expert witness for the plaintiff collapsed these scenarios into three working hypotheses posed to explain Bobby's death: His death was: (1) a suicide; (2) a suicide gesture gone awry, that is, death by misadventure; or (3) an accident, due to hypothermia and/or a dissociative episode or some other acute psychiatric event.

To support the first hypothesis, evidence for intentionality would be necessary. Although there are clearly some predisposing symptoms (depression and anxiety), there is no evidence of intent to suicide.

To support the second hypothesis, we would need evidence that Bobby had a history of attention-seeking behavior, manipulative behavior, or suicide gestures. We have none. Furthermore, as a skilled swimmer, it would be unlikely that he would have a "misadventure" in the water. If he were intent on manipulating attention, he would not have to go far out into the water (the slope of the lake was gradual, having only a 5 foot depth over 45 feet from the shoreline).

To support the third hypothesis, sufficient evidence of some interference in or to his self-preservation instinct would be needed. Here we might look for evidence of a dissociative episode or some other reason that he would lack awareness of where he was or that he might save himself by using automatic and well-developed aquatic skills. Normally, he was relatively aware of details in his environment (WISC-R, Picture Completion Scale). Normally, the cold air and water temperature would startle someone into awareness. Something interfered with the adaptive use of his ego and behavioral skills. Hypothermia could be one probable cause.

Is there evidence for suicide? He had a history of suicide ideation prior to the last two years of his life and one soft sign on testing (one — stem #63 — of 100 Sentence Completion responses; see Figure 14-1). He could be rageful and had evidence of losing control behaviorally — at home, but not in school or other settings. The knife incident, 2 years before his death, gives evidence of a breakthrough of aggression and episodic impulsivity. He was an anxious, fearful child who wished to escape and avoid.

Withdrawing for attention was a common method of coping. He did feel unloved and unnurtured; perhaps he had feelings of expendability. His therapeutic alliance was not strong; he was last seen in therapy 6 weeks prior to leaving for this trip. He had had multiple recent losses (move, school changes, death of grandfather) and had to deal with the temporary absence of his mother at a time of great upset (he was told, however, that she was to return that night).

---

59. While he was speaking to me I *butted in*

60. My mother always *yells.*

61. They didn't like him because *he was weird*

62. When they asked my opinion, *I didn't tell them*

63. Whenever he did poorly, he *tried to commit suicide*

64. He didn't study because *he knew he'd fail*

65. I lost out because *I didn't try*

66. In a group of people, I generally feel *fine*

FIGURE 14-1. Sentence Completion Scale

Is there evidence arguing against suicide? There is no evidence of intent or planfulness. There is evidence in his testing of the ability to control; he is attentive to detail and gives minimally impulsive responses. There is no past suicidal behavior; no history of using suicidal behavior as a manipulation of others; no profound hopelessness. Although there are signs of depression and so forth, he did not meet the diagnostic criteria for a Mood Disorder. Nor did he meet the criteria necessary to diagnose a Separation Anxiety Disorder. There is evidence, however, for chronic problems and a number of associated features of a Conduct Disorder (low self-esteem, poor frustration tolerance, temper outbursts, anxiety, depression, poor academic performance), although again, not sufficient evidence to meet the diagnostic criteria. The most probable, best fit diagnosis is that of Personality Disorder, Not Otherwise Specified.

There is no evidence of family pathology or suicidal behavior and no other known exposure to others who were suicidal. The losses recently sustained had occurred prior to this trip. In spite of these losses, he had successfully coped (but with great complaint) with the overall wilderness experience and, in particular, with the solo hike. If he had been on the verge of a psychotic break, one might expect it would have happened during the stressful isolation of the solo. There is no evidence of separation anxiety at or around the time of the hike — no fear of the dark, no regressive sleeping with mother, no night terrors, no nightmares.

There is no known history of sleepwalking, but some suggestion of a possible dissociative episode. He had a sense of himself as weird, his "Draw-A-Person" is split in two (see Figure 14-2) and to Card 14 of the TAT he responded: "About a boy who was asleep and he had a bad dream and he always sleepwalks when he has bad dreams. Once he sleepwalked and went out the window and fell to the ground and died."

Lastly, a counselor reported that he had been cooperative with belaying (after the telephone call to home). Drowning was incompatible with his competence as a swimmer.

The expert witness for the defendant viewed Bobby quite differently. According to this perspective, Bobby was an extremely vulnerable, emotionally fragile youngster who basically felt abandoned, rejected by his parents. He had little trust in those significant authority figures, nor in his therapist.

He experienced an intense stress in being sent away for the first time in his life to camp. He had just moved to a new home the month before his grandfather passed away. His parents had just finalized their divorce.

He had a very fragile ego. He was blocked in terms of expressing feelings, having tremendous anger inside, which periodically exploded in what appeared to be homicidal tendencies.

He suffered from separation anxiety, manifested by pervasive fears of being separated from his mother on whom he was overly dependent. Up to the age of 12 he slept with her. He lacked the support and nurturance of a

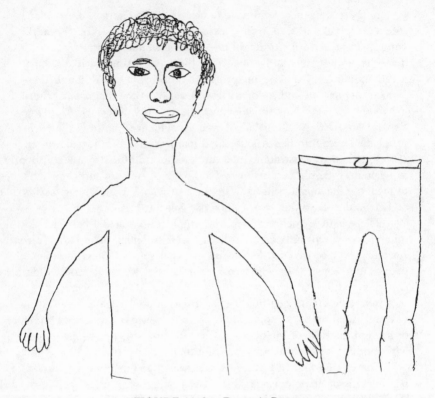

FIGURE 14-2.   Draw-A-Person

stable family. He had an unstable academic background having been in six
different schools by the seventh grade.

   He was placed in a situation grossly improper, given his vulnerabilities
and problems. This was a huge miscalculation. The therapy had reached an
impasse. Very little progress had been made in the whole course of therapy.
There never had been any trust developed. In fact, Bobby did poorer
academically, having failed a grade, after entering therapy.

   Over the 13 days of camp, he was becoming angrier and more
unhappy. He was frightened. On this day he had a panic attack. He called
home to his mother only to learn she was out of town. He spoke with his
father whom he feared. That night he manifested some unusual behaviors.
These were expressions of his inner preoccupation at the expense of being
aware of external stimuli. He was out of touch. It is probable that Bobby
had a panic attack (possibly a psychotic episode), feeling both tremendous
rage and anger at his parents. He acted impulsively to hurt them, hurt
himself, and escape from a situation he could not tolerate. In support of
this view his projective drawing (Figure 14-3) depicts a diver underwater
with a shark and a small fish, with the oxygen line clearly evident. Near
the diver on the ocean floor is a tombstone. That drawing shows his

FIGURE 14-3. Projective Drawing

impending drowning. Again, his sentence completion response (stem #63) is a second smoking gun. His Draw-A-Person reflects poor judgment and impulsivity.

The night of his death he was trying to say to his counselors, "You're not paying enough attention to me. I'm going to make sure you know I'm serious." He was in an acute psychiatric episode, put himself in a life-threatening situation that was miscalculated and went awry.

CONCLUSION

As should be apparent to the astute reader, the psychological autopsy is but a tool in the armamentarium of those expert in its use. Rather than ascertaining any cause–effect relationship, which the court ultimately must decide, it can only illuminate and suggest. What the psychological autopsy allows is polyperspective. It is an intensive single-case research study with multiple measures, both distal and proximal to the death event. The light it throws on its subject may be distorted both by the quality and veracity of its sources and by the prismatic lens of its interpreter. Nevertheless, it illuminates.

Suicidology has evolved as a true interdisciplinary field, thankfully because suicide belongs to no one discipline of study. Those of us who toil in that field are motivated in part by our need to go beyond the walls of our training, to maximize our understanding of a complex phenomenon using all the tools available to us. With the development of the psychological autopsy we have become at once forensic behavioral anthropological pathologists. No small accomplishment in the single generation since a frustrated county coroner called for some help and three behavioral scientists responded.

REFERENCES

Atkinson, J. M. (1978). *Discovering Suicide: Studies in the Social Organization of Sudden Death.* London: MacMillan.

Brent, D. A. (1989). The psychological autopsy: methodological considerations for the study of adolescent suicide. *Suicide and Life-Threatening Behavior* 19:43–57.

Clark, D. C., and Horton-Deutsch, S. L. (1992). Assessment *in absentia:* the value of the psychological autopsy method for studying antecedents in suicide and predicting future suicides. In *Assessment and Prediction of Suicide,* ed. R. W. Maris, A. L. Berman, J. T. Maltsberger, and R. I. Yufit, pp. 144–182. New York: Guilford.

Hendrix, R. C. (1972). *Investigation of Violent and Sudden Death.* Springfield, IL: Charles C Thomas.

Litman, R. E. (1980). Psycholegal aspects of suicide. In *Modern Legal Medicine,* ed. W. Curran, A. McGarry, and C. Petty, pp. 841–853. Philadelphia: F. A. Davis.

Noguchi, T. T. (1983). *Coroner.* New York: Simon and Schuster.

Nolan, J. L., ed. (1988). *The Suicide Case: Investigation and Trial of Insurance Claims.* Chicago: American Bar Association.

Rosenberg, M. L., Davidson, L. E., Smith, J. C., et al. (1988). Operational criteria for the determination of suicide. *Journal of Forensic Sciences* 33:1445–1456.

Shneidman, E. S., ed. (1951). *Thematic Test Analysis.* New York: Grune & Stratton.

_____ (1981). The psychological autopsy. *Suicide and Life-Threatening Behavior* 11:325–340.

_____ (1991). A life in death. In *The History of Clinical Psychology in Autobiography,* ed. C. E. Walker, pp. 225–292. Pacific Grove, CA: Brooks/Cole.

Spitz, W., and Fisher, R., eds. (1980). *Medicolegal Investigation of Death.* Springfield, IL: Charles C Thomas.

Teicher, M. H., Glod, C., and Cole, J. O. (1990). Emergence of intense suicidal preoccupation during fluoxetine treatment. *American Journal of Psychiatry* 147:207–210.

15: A VOICE OF DEATH

Robert E. Litman

Student: What is the optimal number of cases for research on suicide?
Dr. Shneidman: One.

The following is the case of a man who voiced his final thoughts—his suicide note—on videotape rather than on paper. It was the unexpected discovery of several hundred suicide notes in the vaults of a coroner's office more than 40 years ago that first attracted Edwin Shneidman's attention to suicide. His fascination with suicide notes, and other personal documents, has continued to the present time, with almost no lapse of interest (Shneidman 1980). With Dr. Shneidman we continue to ask, "What can we learn about suicide from suicide notes?" in whatever form they come as, in this case, in a videotape. I add another theme, of special interest to me: When someone commits suicide, who is responsible?

My first acquaintance with Conrad "Skip" Lahser was through his suicide videotape. I did not treat him or even talk to him before his death. This case report is based on interviews with people who knew Mr. Lahser, and with a painstaking review of various documents, including his school, army, business, and medical records. A biography of Mr. Lahser was created by a number of eminent suicidologists, including Alan Berman, Ronald Maris, H. L. P. Resnick, and myself, who were involved in the case because of ensuing litigation. Shneidman coined the term *psychological autopsy* for this method of research, and provided a complete description (Shneidman 1981). According to Shneidman, "The psychological autopsy is no less than a reconstruction of the motivations, philosophy, psychodynamics, and existential crises of the decedent" (Shneidman 1973a, p. 132)

LAHSER

By the time Skip Lahser, age 37 in 1980, came to work for the Central Telephone Company (Centel) in Killeen, Texas, some 50 miles from

Austin, he had a long history of repeated partial successes, each ending in failure from which he would rebound to try again. In college he did well at first, then dropped out, later to return and do well again, only to drop out once more just one quarter short of graduating; but he never returned. He started several small businesses, none of which ever showed any continuing profit and one of which ended in bankruptcy. He had two marriages, one child, two divorces. He had been in the army, had done well at first, and then was discharged as unsuitable for the service. His was a cyclic personality, probably a true manic-depressive. By the time he came to Centel he knew that he was unsuited for long range commitments, planning responsibility, or management. But he was a good salesman, with great enthusiasm, and an energetic personality that was attractive to both men and women.

In the Spring of 1982, the Company appointed him Directory (Yellow Pages) Manager for Killeen and vicinity, despite his protests that he was better suited for sales than management. By that summer he was noticeably irritable and excitable, extending himself to make contacts all over the State of Texas and beyond, looking to expand his local directory business. He submitted plans for Killeen to become the headquarters for the Directories of the entire Centel area (headquartered in Chicago). When these plans were not approved Skip was greatly upset, and fired questions at his supervisors: Why? One supervisor pointed out that Killeen is a long way from Chicago, maybe other Directory Managers were better able to offer entertainment and other perks to the high management of Centel. Another supervisor contributed what he later was to claim was a joke, "Maybe they are taking kickbacks up there."

With no other evidence than these comments, Skip contacted the enforcement division of the Federal Communications Commission (FCC). There he spoke with a government attorney, Mr. A., who assured him the conversation would be held in confidence. But in fact the attorney contacted Centel Headquarters and revealed the name of Lahser. They fired him immediately.

After he was fired, Skip traveled twice to Washington to meet with FCC officials and the Congressional Oversight Committee on Communications. Now he was armed with voluminous files he had taken from the Killeen office, claiming these substantiated his initial charges. He interviewed dozens of former and present Centel employees, collecting grievances from them. He began an intense media campaign against Centel with regular press conferences on radio talk shows, and interviews by CBS, ABC, NBC, and CNN. He had been fired in August of 1982, and this campaign continued full bore into January of 1983. Skip took his case to the Texas Employment Commission and won full unemployment benefits. On March 22, 1983, his attorneys filed a lawsuit for damages due to wrongful discharge, and planned to bring a class-action suit against the telephone company for malicious persecution of Lahser and other ex-employees. Lahser did not share their enthusiasm. About this time (March) he appeared depressed and discouraged in a T.V. interview.

In January 1983, the attorneys noticed that Skip seemed more nervous, and less confident, lacking his usual intensity. They referred him to a clinical psychologist, Dr. B., who thought he was depressed, and gave him a Minnesota Multiphasic Personality Inventory to fill out. Dr. B. referred Lahser on to Dr. C., a highly respected forensic psychiatrist in Austin, Texas. The psychiatrist saw Skip four times for a total of two and one half hours over the next 5 weeks, February 14 to March 21. Dr. C. encouraged Mr. Lahser in his struggle against the phone company. The diagnosis was Post Traumatic Stress Disorder. The doctor gave Skip an unknown number (later estimated at forty-five) of Triavil (4–50) samples at the last consultation (March 21, 1983). Apparently Skip did not take the medication, because these were the pills that he used to commit suicide.

On April 5, Mr. Lahser left Killeen for a scheduled appointment with Dr. C., but instead of going to the doctor's office, Skip went to a nearby hotel, made a 41-minute videotape, and then took the pills that killed him. His body was not found for almost 48 hours. The police found a loaded (unused) gun in his car.

The content of the tape is quite repetitive. For example, he describes three times his complicated differences with Centel, each time in almost the same words. The edited transcript, which follows, omits the repetitions. I have numbered the paragraphs for reference.

SKIP LAHSER'S VIDEOTAPE

1. This is April 5, 1983. It's about five o'clock in the afternoon. I am here in Austin at the Holiday Inn. My name is Skip Lahser. I am the former directory manager for a company now known as Wilco, Incorporated. Wilco is a subsidiary of Central Telephone Company of Texas and Centel out of Chicago. The actions which led up to my dismissal as directory manager were prompted because of a sincere belief that Central Telephone Company was acting contrary to the best interests of its stockholders, the division that I headed, and the general public. And when I say Central Telephone Company, excuse me, I am specifically referencing your officers of Centel, Mr. R., Mr. M., Mr. G., most assuredly Mr. L., who are all out of our corporate offices in Chicago. . . .

2. Well, in a perverted way the humor of all of this is that when I headed up Directory, I headed it up only because the telephone company through, first J., who is vice-president of sales, and Mr. B., who is regional vice-president of Wilco, begged, in fact, pleaded with me to take on the job. I'm not proud of the fact but in 1976 I had a bankruptcy in Houston and when I came with Centel in September of '80 I made it very clear at that time that I was not interested in any management responsibilities because I felt very bad over the bankruptcy that I personally had and felt that I just mentally and emotionally was not in a position to want or to be able to handle the responsibilities to be necessary in a management capacity with the telephone company. In the capacity as a sales rep, I didn't have to worry about

any politicking in the company, I could do my job, as long as I did my job well, which I knew I could and I did do well, that there would be no pressures or stress on me. Well, things didn't work out quite like we planned. The growth of the directory operation was something that was very important to a lot of people, not the least of which was J. and myself and Mr. L., in his way, and P. and all of the gals in comp. . . .

3. Now I need to digress here just for a second. The first thing is I am not going to presuppose that I am better than anybody else, but I do want to make one thing clear. Since I have been terminated by Centel, Centel has gone to great lengths to destroy my character, to discredit me, to promote confusion in the minds of different people as to what my real intentions are. My intentions the whole time I was with Directory, and now, have always been to tell the truth, to get the story told about irregularities that I feel are fundamentally improper and in the worst case scenario could be very, very damaging and destructive, not just to myself and friends of mine, but to the basic framework and fabric upon which this great country of ours is built.

4. I say this because my actions tonight are not actions of desperation or despair, though I guess there is a certain degree of that in it. They are more one of crying out — and there is an old expression I have heard years and years ago, and I guess it has taken on new significance, and that is: dying to get the story told. You know, an individual is placed in a very, very peculiar position when they have information which other people in a big company don't want to come out. If the individual comes forward to the media, the company says the individual is guilty of a big ego, of a desire to see their name in the headlines, of a desire to inflate and inflame the situation, and of a desire of setting up situations to their own best interest. And in their way of explaining the matter, the telephone company comes across as a very ornate company. I guess a big company comes across as a very level-headed, cool, methodical professional group of people. And the individual that has come forward is very quickly portrayed as a bit of an erratic, frustrated person who doesn't really know how to maintain his or her cool. I know because I have most recently been having these problems here with Central Telephone Company. On the one hand, if I don't do anything, the story doesn't come out. On the other hand, if I do something, they try to put me in a light as to suffer from delusions of grandeur myself. I guess there is a desire to see a story told and your name in print, but, not for reasons that they suggest, but because you realize that you have people that are having the opportunity to hear another side of the story. I am digressing here and I apologize. I don't mean to. It is just that there is so much to be said in such a short period of time and I really would like to have the nucleus of this problem understood.

5. There is one other thing I wanted to cover before I get more to this problem with Centel. This will be about my background in which I was very insecure and shy as a child. I did try to commit suicide when I was 23. I will be honest about that. I have never held that back from anybody. It was not a weakness — well, I guess it was out of weakness, too. I didn't like myself. What I tried to do was run into a bridge in a small car, but, I mean, 2 days before, after I had selected, prior to running into the bridge I had (inaudible) pardon me. This car wouldn't get up to too much speed without a steep grade. So, anyway, one night I had just had enough and went down the highway toward this particular embankment. They had put a guard rail up 2 days before and I can tell you personally that doesn't work. The incredible thing is . . . I will never forget sitting in that car after hitting the guard rail, dust and the debris was just kind of filtering around the car, and I sat there and just wailed because I felt so frustrated. And I looked at myself and I realized that, hey, your problems are caused because you

don't have control of yourself, of your actions, your destiny, and you need that control. What I did to try to gain the control is I would get up early in the morning before I went to work and think about what was going to happen during that day because I stuttered and I was, again, very insecure. It bothered me terribly. And I realize that in a situation things happen and repeat themselves, particularly unpleasant things. So the best way to eliminate that type of problem is to have a rebuttal, if you will, plan your action and stick to your plan, so to speak. At the end of the day I would sit down in a chair and view what had happened that day, and if something hadn't gone well, I would try to anticipate what I could have done differently to make the situation as I felt it should have been. This has worked well. The reason it has worked well is because it required a high degree of candor. I shall try and have tried to use that candor to explain what has happened here.

6. Something is fundamentally wrong when officers of a utility and in particular a telephone company feel that they can wiretap, without a court order, private telephone conversations; when they feel that they can lie before the Public Utilities Commission and get by with it; when they feel that they can distort and alter documents for their own personal slant on things and they can use company money for the purchase of private equipment, recreational or gardening equipment; when they feel they can intimidate and harass people with impunity. All of this has happened at Central Telephone Company. The villains are not very many. As a matter of fact, most of the people that work with Centel are very honest people. They are very interested and desirous to do a good job. . . .

7. Unfortunately when I took over as directory sales manager and then later as directory manager there was an awful lot of conflict and dissension. Conflict and dissension causes a lot of backbiting going on and the backbiting was encouraged because if people are going at each other they won't go at the company, number one; number two, the company uses that as a wedge to find out information on other people. People that work for them, people outside the company. And as they get this type of information they build a file and then if there is a problem with an employee they have a documented brief that is used to discredit and destroy a person. This is not something that just happens, this is something that is encouraged. The emphasizing of the person as a human being. When I took over as directory manager and, as my staff will tell you and particularly F. and K., they thought I was, to use a very common expression back then, a pure son of a bitch. . . .

8. In Directory we had some of the most beautiful people, and yet at that point and time I didn't see their beauty, and they didn't see the beauty of me either. The way I overcame the problem was that I asked them quite candidly, when I took over and I said, as my habit, I like to have meetings and I like to have people know what is going on. And I told them, I said look, do me a favor. Give me 90 days. If at the end of 90 days you are not happy with me or what we are doing, I'll give you recommendations or whatever is necessary, give you the time off to go find another job. I need your help right now. I think you will find if you work with me and give me a fair chance that I will give you a fair chance.

[Here Mr. Lahser looks sad, almost in tears]

9. You know, I have done very little in my life I am proud of. The Directory is something that I cherished. I had a family there. I had a relationship and an opportunity to be with friends and prove to people in this whole wide world. Good people. Honest people. Sincere people. People trying to do an honest job. I don't know exactly what I could have done different than I did. I don't try to paint rosy pictures. I don't try to be overly optimistic. I just don't understand how it is possible that a company, and in particular a utility company, can so abuse its people and get by with it. It is very difficult to know what to do at a time like this. In August I sent

one of a number of memos to my immediate supervisor, Mr. M. This was after Mr. M. had been told by Mr. W. that Mr. L. was on the take. But if you hear this you may say I don't remember saying that, but in your heart you know you did. We were outperforming everybody in the system — General Telephone, Donnelly, Barrett, the big boys — we were doing a better job than they were. And yet our own company was not letting us grow. C. told me that one of the reasons we were not being allowed to grow is because Mr. B. and Mr. M. had associations with these outside vendors, which they didn't want to break. I was confused and concerned because it didn't make sense that my own company didn't want us to grow. We were outperforming everybody else. We could draw sixty million dollars on the bottom line in 5 years, additional profits, which could reduce the cost of phone service to the general public, it could increase dividends to the stockholders of the company. We could make, bonuses. . . .

10. I guess what I am trying to tell you is there is a question here that I don't understand. Where do your loyalties lie? Do they lie to the company that pays you? Do they lie with the supervisors that make it possible for you to grow and prosper? Do they lie with the people that do the work and make it possible for you to make money so you can grow and succeed and so the company can pass the thing down to the stockholders in the form of dividends and the general public as a way of reduced costs? Do they lie with yourself? You know it is a real shame chivalry is not practiced anymore. There is nothing I would like better than to stand Mr. L. and Mr. B. in a suit of armor and get your swords and let's go at it. One right after the other. Either I survive or you survive. At least we get it over with. Someone survives. No one is surviving in this situation we are in now. The people that I care for, the people that are important to me, the people that feel special about me, are in a damnable position because if they come forward and talk could be accused of breaking the code of ethics, which is nothing more than a muzzle to keep you quiet. And yet if they don't come forward and talk, they are encouraging actions that are not direct or proper. And I don't like that either. . . .

11. Something needs to be done, ladies and gentlemen. I think I know, have some ideas anyhow, as to what it could be. Laws should be passed to make it possible for employees, particularly of the utility, to come before a tribunal, committee, or a group, and bring forward information that they have. If that information tends to suggest the officers of a company are acting contrary to the best interest of the public or to the stockholders of the company, then that board should be charged with seeking out the accuracy of this information. If it is found that the charges made by the individual are correct, the individual needs, should have their job protected under Texas law. Right now the individual can be fired. I didn't do anything wrong to the FCC. I was asking for help. I asked for information and the FCC took it upon themselves, at least Mr. A. did. I don't know why. Maybe Mr. A. can explain it to you. I don't know why . . . [Long pause]

12. As I sit here thinking about what to say, this probably is not coming across very well and if it isn't I apologize for that. There is so much to say and I feel so inadequate to say it. God, I wish this hadn't happened and yet I don't know what else I could have done. If it could be anything that I could be remembered for, I pray that it's that I did or tried to do a good job with one of the most fantastic groups of people in the world. Such fantastic people. I was very fortunate and I hope this makes it possible for you to succeed and prosper. I hope the story comes out. It needs to come out. God, it needs to come out. [Pause]

13. I say it again and I say in closing, something is fundamentally wrong when officers of the telephone company can without a court order wiretap, bug, and monitor private telephone conversations, when they can put a watch on a person 24

hours a day with impunity. When they can destroy an individual, something is wrong. Something is wrong when the people that are trying to do an honest job aren't allowed to do that job and yet are threatened when they do their job well. Who's to fight for the little guy? I don't know any more. I don't know. The FCC sure didn't. The SEC tried, at least they cared, they tried. They said they hadn't broken any laws or enough laws for us to get involved. The Public Utilities said, "Eh, nothing we can do." It is not regulated. It needs to be regulated. Please look into what I have said. Look into these charges. Let me be remembered for the accuracy or inaccuracy of what I have said. I'll live by that. Please tell the people I worked with how great they were. I love them all very much. That was the happiest days of my life being in Directory and I thank them. Thank you. [He is seen to lean forward and turn off the recorder.]

MORE LIFE HISTORY FROM THE PSYCHOLOGICAL AUTOPSY

Originally, Dr. Shneidman was fascinated with suicide notes as perhaps the best available way of understanding suicidal phenomenon. "I believed that it was possible to unlock the mysteries of suicidal phenomena by using suicide notes as the keys" (Shneidman 1980, p. 42). Perhaps he expected too much. There was a subsequent counterreaction recognizing the psychological constriction and narrow thinking of the presuicidal state. Dr. Shneidman (1973b) briefly wondered if suicide notes could hardly ever be illuminating or important psychological documents. These two almost opposite views were then synthesized into his present position. "I now believe that suicide notes by themselves are uniformly neither bountiful nor banal, but that they definitely can have a great deal of meaning under certain circumstances, specifically when they are put into the context of the detailed life history of the individual who both wrote the note and committed the act" (Shneidman, 1980, p. 43).

We can add more details about the life history of Skip Lahser derived from the psychological autopsy. Mr. Lahser, Sr., Skip's father, was an executive in the Boy Scouts of America. This meant that the family was shifted frequently from state to state and city to city. Skip was born in North Carolina, but lived successively in Virginia, Georgia, Maryland, Pennsylvania, New Jersey, upper New York State, and finally Pittsburgh, at which point Skip was old enough to leave home. His mother, who has been treated at least twice in hospitals for alcoholism, remembers Skip as a shy and somewhat unhappy child who was subject to blackouts. In 1965, when he was 22 years old, he married Elaine and started a small lighting business, which failed. He attended Clemson University and came very close to graduating. A daughter was born in 1966. This first divorce was in 1973. Elaine says "we were divorced because we wanted different things. I wanted a home, children, and a family life. He spent all of his time on his projects, his schemes, his work, 16 hours a day, and he was always angry at the people that tried to shaft him." Both the mother and the first wife said that the reason Skip was discharged from the military service was "blackouts."

Several of Skip's business ventures failed. Skip's father claimed he was owed $20,000.00 by Skip at the time of his death. There was a bankruptcy in 1977, which left Skip so depressed that he was unable to work for almost a year. Eventually he recovered his energy and remarried in 1978, only to be divorced again in 1981. He left Houston in 1980 under clouded working circumstances. His last employment had been with General Telephone Company (a competitor of Centel). Because he felt that company had mistreated him, he had turned in false disbursement statements and received bonuses he didn't deserve, and, in addition, he had destroyed some company records out of anger before he left. Later he felt guilty about having done this.

In Killeen Lahser met Joann, who became his fiancée. He moved in with her in the summer of 1982, then moved out in the fall, and later moved back, in the spring of 1983. She agreed entirely with Skip's claim that the telephone company had bugged their telephone, and had delegated agents to follow Skip around. When Alan Berman interviewed Joann, he reported her view that what precipitated Lahser's suicide was her emotional breakdown: filled with feelings of frustration and helplessness, she had dissolved into tears the night before he left Killeen for Austin. "I was his rock, his only support," she said, "and when I collapsed, he lost everything." His survivors agreed that Lahser had a very strong need to feel in control and not to be beaten. Dr. Berman could not agree with the psychiatrist's (Dr. C.) diagnosis of Post Traumatic Stress Reaction. More accurately, there were a number of stressful events spread out over time, a whole series, not one major blow.

Mr. Lahser filled out a self-reporting questionnaire when he first came to see the psychologist, Dr. B. He said his presenting complaints were confusion, rage, anxiety, frustration, and betrayal. He said this had been acute for the past 4 months, but had been in the background much longer than that. His personal data form emphasized an unhappy childhood with verbal abuse, many fears, stammering as a chronic problem, head banging at times, and suicide attempts. He said he had been introverted and shy. What he feared most about himself was his temper and the possibility of violence, also his instability and inability to see clearly and strive for future goals. He also feared "taking advantage of people who trust me." But he was most especially concerned about "my inability to control my emotions." On the questionnaire, Lahser reported suicidal ideas, memory problems, inability to relax, frequent anger and headaches. He said he used to feel that he had a sense of humor, but was now bothered by "my desire to get even." He says that his mother suffered from alcoholism, and that he has a sister who is retarded. What makes him particularly anxious is "my desire to strike out."

Dr. B. felt that Lahser was depressed, paranoid, hopeless, angry, fearful, feeling victimized, not psychotic, but skeptical about the possibility of psychiatric help. She felt his fears and ideas of persecution had some basis in reality, and certainly that his feeling of being betrayed was not inappropriate. She came to a quick decision early in February 1983 that Lahser needed more help than she could offer because of his depression, agitation, and suicidal ideas. She referred him on to the psychiatrist, Dr. C., for further evaluation and antidepressant medication. Unfortunately, in my opinion, Dr. C. was distracted by the forensic aspects of the case, and failed to pay attention to the patient's mental illness, and his need for standard psychiatric evaluation and treatment of the depression. Later Dr. C. testified that he had no memory of Dr. B.'s evaluation of depression and suicide risk, that he did not know there had been a Minnesota Multiphasic Test, and that it had never occurred to him that Lahser was potentially suicidal.

WHAT CAN WE LEARN

Student: Dr. Shneidman, do you really mean just one case?
Dr. Shneidman: Well, actually you would want four. One case provides 80 percent
of the information you need. Cases two and three tell you that
your first case was not an extremely deviant one. Case four is one
last check on the other three.

If this case had been presented at a Los Angeles Suicide Prevention Center staff conference in the 1980s, I would have focused on the psychiatric pathology, the manic-depressive history, and the obvious depression. I would have emphasized the need for a thorough mental-status examination, including a painstaking exploration of suicidal ideas, as part of the psychiatric evaluation. The prescription of lithium carbonate, combined with an antidepressant drug, carefully monitored, with frequent follow-up telephone calls, and weekly office visits, would have been appropriate treatment for Mr. Lahser, and might have prevented the suicide. Ed Shneidman would have agreed with me in part, I think, and disagreed quite emphatically with my narrow focus. His view of suicide is broader, more encyclopedic, and generally more phenomenological than mine. Quite recently he wrote to the *New England Journal of Medicine* to protest what he saw as an overemphasis on the diagnosis and treatment of affective disorders as the crux of suicide prevention. "The problem of suicide should be addressed directly, phenomenologically, without the intervention of the often obfuscating variable of psychiatric disorder" (Shneidman 1992a, p. 890).

His recent chapter (Shneidman 1992b) in a suicidology volume, gives information from three cases. For Dr. Shneidman, "It is possible to conceptualize the commonalities of these (and all other) suicides in terms of the basic and omnipresent elements of the suicidal scenario—a conspectus of suicide, as it were" (p. 51). He listed six fundamentals that combine to result in suicide. Number 1 is a sense of unbearable psychological pain. Number 6 is "a conscious decision that egression—leaving, exiting or stopping life—is the only (or at least the best possible) solution to the problem of unbearable pain" (p. 52). In a similar broad conceptualization, Shneidman has referred to what he sees as ten *commonalities* of suicide, which are the common psychological features in human self-destruction. These are summarized in Figure 15–1.

I am presenting Lahser's suicide as "case four." How does it illustrate Shneidman's commonalities?

I. The common purpose of suicide is to seek a solution.	VI. The common cognitive state in suicide is ambivalence.
II. The common goal of suicide is cessation of consciousness	VII. The common perceptual state in suicide is constriction.
III. The common stimulus in suicide is intolerable psychological pain.	III. The common action in suicide is egression.
IV. The common stressor in suicide is frustrated psychological needs.	IX. The common interpersonal act in suicide is communication of intention.
V. The common emotion in suicide is hopelessness-helplessness.	X. The common consistency in suicide is with lifelong coping patterns.

Note: From *Definition of Suicide* by E. S. Shneidman, 1985, pp. 121–149. New York: Wiley. Copyright © 1985 by Edwin S. Shneidman. Reprinted with permission.

FIGURE 15-1. The Ten Commonalities of Suicide

Skip Lahser's conscious motive for making his suicide videotape (and committing suicide) was to get the story told. "My actions tonight . . . are more one of crying out . . . dying to get the story told" (Paragraph 4). He is addressing himself not to his fiancée, his family, or the police, but to the television audience. "Something needs to be done ladies and gentlemen" (Paragraph 11). In fact, his death was widely publicized in Texas, and made into a minidocumentary by CNN. There is considerable ambivalence about living and dying. "Please look into what I have said. Look into these charges. Let me be remembered for the accuracy or inaccuracy of what I have said. I'll live by that" (Paragraph 13). He thinks of himself as fighting for the little person, victimized by the corrupt officials of Centel, whom he names. Earlier he had written for Dr. B. that what he feared the most was, "giving into his emotions," especially the wish to get even.

The most frequent expression found generally in suicide notes is "I love you." Skip did express love, but not specifically for his fiancée or for his daughter; he expresses his love for the people he worked with. He thinks of them as one of the most fantastic groups of people in the world. "I was very fortunate and I hope this makes it possible for you to succeed and prosper" (Paragraph 12).

Reviewing Shneidman's commonalities, it seems to me that Skip Lahser felt intolerable psychological pain because he was being ignored, and his fight for the little guys against the villains of Centel was being ignored. His perception of his life had become constricted into this narrow area of the struggle against his ex-employer. His emotion was hopelessness mixed with anger in defeat. To a large extent his suicide was his attempt to keep from feeling helpless and defeated. Surely he was ambivalent about dying, and in considerable degree he thought he might live. Actually there was, in fact, a good chance that he might be rescued because the drugs he ingested kill slowly. His purpose was to seek a solution to his major problem, which was that he had committed himself to leading a struggle against the phone company, and he now felt hopeless and helpless in that struggle, and he wanted out—that is, egression. In this, his suicide as egression was consistent with his lifelong coping pattern of egressing from situations that required struggle and commitment. It seems to me that cessation was more a means to the end of getting the story out, rather than a primary goal in itself. Of the ten Shneidman commonalities, this case demonstrated every one.

WHO IS RESPONSIBLE

What is responsible for the suicide of Mr. Lahser? His own genetic makeup, which left him vulnerable to emotional highs and lows? His childhood, where he felt insecure and low in self-esteem? His successive failures in life? Failures of nerve and of commitment? Failures of judgment?

The telephone company certainly is at fault. They promoted him into a position for which he was not suited, then fired him arbitrarily and improperly. And there probably was some persecution after he was discharged. Surely Mr. Lahser's confidence was betrayed by Mr. A. and the FCC. Were they responsible for his death? Could they be held financially liable?

What about the doctors? The psychologist, Dr. B., tested Skip, but did not have the MMPI interpreted by a standard computer program. I sent the data to two standard computer programs. Both of them made a diagnosis of hypomania with agitation, and recommended treatment with lithium carbonate. The psychiatrist, Dr. C., said he was unaware of any testing having been done on Mr. Lahser.

Dr. C. should have known better than to give out a package of antidepressant samples without noting with the patient the number of units, and giving the patient specific directions about how to take them and what to expect. It was negligent of Dr. C., not to monitor closely Mr. Lahser's use of these medications, watching for side effects, or for noncompliance. Dr. C. supported the efforts of Mr. Lahser to stir up official support for his investigations and charges against Centel even when Lahser became depressed. Was this good psychiatric judgment? Were the expectations of his attorneys, and his doctors, and his fiancée, that he continue to be strong and active and the leader of a popular crusade against the phone company too much for Mr. Lahser?

POSTSCRIPT

After Mr. Lahser's suicide his fiancée and his ex-wife, acting for his daughter, sued Centel and the FCC for millions. Centel sued the doctors claiming they were responsible for the death. Expert opinions were solicited by all parties. As is usual in such litigation, none of the parties wished to hazard everything on the unpredictable decision of a judge and jury, so a pretrial negotiated settlement was reached, and the actual dollar amount was veiled in secrecy. All of the attorneys said they were "happy" with the outcome.

278

REFERENCES

Shneidman, E. S. (1973a). *Deaths of Man.* New York: Quadrangle/New York Times Book Co.

———— (1973b). Suicide notes reconsidered. *Psychiatry* 36:379–395.

———— (1980). *Voices of Death.* New York: Harper & Row.

———— (1981). The psychological autopsy. *Suicide and Life-Threatening Behavior* 11:325–340.

———— (1985). *Definition of Suicide.* New York: Wiley.

———— (1992a). Rational suicide and psychiatric disorders. *New England Journal of Medicine* 326:889–890.

———— (1992b). A conspectus of the suicidal scenario. In *Assessment and Prediction of Suicide,* ed. R. W. Maris, A. L. Berman, J. T. Maltsberger, and R. I. Yufit, pp. 50–64. New York: Guilford.

HISTORICAL AND LITERARY STUDIES
Part VI

The intense personal study of suicidal lives has been explicitly supported by Allport, White, Murray, and Shneidman. Here, one is not limited by actual clinical cases but can also use historical figures and literary studies. This means we can study people who are long dead or even fictional. Part VI consists of two chapters: a careful study of the medical records of Adolf Hitler, and an examination of the subintentioned death of Herman Melville through newly found documents.

16: THE DEATH AND AUTOPSY OF ADOLF HITLER

Fritz C. Redlich

Edwin S. Shneidman brought to my attention a memorandum by Henry A. Murray, entitled "Analysis of the Personality of Adolf Hitler," with predictions of his future behavior and suggestions for dealing with him at the time and after Germany's surrender. The memorandum was written during the latter part of the war (Murray 1944). It is based on the work of Murray and other distinguished scholars, amongst them Ernst Kris and Bert Lewin. Murray predicted that Hitler would commit suicide. Nearly 30 years later, W. R. Langer, a psychoanalyst who was a staff member of the Office of Strategic Services (OSS) under Henry Murray, made a nearly identical statement (Langer 1972). Langer did not mention Murray or the OSS as a source.

SUICIDAL THREATS AND SUICIDE

Hitler spoke of suicide on four occasions, the first time after the failed putsch in November 1923. In great excitement, he wanted to shoot himself. According to his statement in *Mein Kampf,* he overcame his upset after he resolved to defend his comrades (Hitler 1924). On 16 September 1931, he threatened to kill himself after the death of his half-niece, Angela Raubal, Jr. (Geli), with whom he was in love. After one week he recovered sufficiently to continue his election campaign. The third time he expressed suicidal intentions was when the National Socialist Party threatened to split up in 1932. It seems these threats were cries for help and approval rather than announcements that he really would commit suicide. According to General Alfred Jodl, one of Hitler's close military staff members, Hitler realized during the winter of 1941–1942 that he might not win the war (Jodl 1965), but fought on with determination to be in an advantageous position when the war ended. What mattered to him was retaining his identity as a charismatic leader, even in the face of the major military reversals after 1942.

Author's note: This research has been supported by the Carnegie Foundation of New York.

Concomitant with thoughts of survival were thoughts of death. In January 1942, he severely criticized Field Marshall Paulus for surrendering at Stalingrad rather than committing suicide. After the attempt to assassinate him on 20 July 1944, Hitler had short bouts of depression. What kept him going was his anger against the Allies, the Jews, and his generals, whom he accused of incompetence and treachery. His two severe somatic illnesses, Parkinson's disease and temporal arteritis (Redlich [in press]), also contributed to his depressive moods. With some self-pity, he made a statement to the effect that a quick death would be a delivery from his suffering (Morell Diaries 1942).

During the last third of April 1945, Hitler began to think seriously of suicide. The thought did not come easily, and he wavered in his resolve almost to the end. His mistress (and later wife), Eva Braun, had joined him in the Reich Chancellery—allegedly against his will—to share his fate, whatever he decided to do. It is likely, however, that Hitler was relieved about her arrival, as he needed her to comfort him. He did not mention his suicidal intentions during a last birthday party on 20 April 1945. His associates tried to persuade him to leave his underground bunker in Berlin and move to his Alpine fortress in Bavaria, but Hitler decided to stay. The birthday party was not a happy occasion, in spite of all the champagne, which Hitler—a teetotaller—did not touch. On 21 April, he permitted his personal physician, Dr. Theodor Morell, to leave the chancellery. He was replaced by an SS physician, Dr. Ludwig Stumpfegger. It is unclear whether Hitler dismissed Morell because he had lost confidence in him, or whether it was a humanitarian act to evacuate his sick physician. Two days later, during a military conference, Hitler repeatedly broke out into uncontrolled rages, sobbed, and seemed desperate (Kriegstagbuch 1945). The Russians were already at the gates of Berlin in mid-April 1945, when he declared to General Koller that "now the Russians will suffer the bloodiest defeat" (Koller 1948). He believed he could split the Russians and the Western Allies in spite of their commitment to unconditional surrender, but almost simultaneously he declared that fighting made no sense any more. On the following day he recovered and decided to fight on. A message from Reichsmarschall Hermann Göhring arrived—it seems Göhring had heard of Hitler's breakdown—offering to take charge of all military and political matters, if Hitler so desired. The offer was not presumptuous in tone, but Hitler, instigated by his secretary, Martin Bormann, flew into a rage, stripped Göhring of his rank, and expelled him from the National Socialist Party (Reitsch 1945). On 28 April, in a severe, uncontrolled rage, Hitler also expelled Reichsführer SS Heinrich Himmler as a traitor after he learned that Himmler had tried to negotiate with the Allies behind his back (Hitler 1945). One matter of utmost importance to Hitler was loyalty; abandonment and treason by these two top persons was extremely stressful. Hitler's behavior during these days fluctuated, alternating between uncontrolled rages and, in general, composed and efficient behavior. Often, his orders did not reach his retreating and demoralized troops. In his bunker world he still had absolute authority. He peremptorily sentenced SS General Fegelein, Himmler's representative and Eva Braun's brother-in-law, to death for treason and cowardice, assuming that Fegelein had been Himmler's accomplice.

The definitive decision to commit suicide was probably made on 28 April 1945. He had given up. The official explanation for the double suicide was Hitler's desire to avoid the shame of flight and capitulation. An important motivation was his fear of falling, alive or dead, into Russian hands. He did not want to see his body vilified or fall into the hands of enemies who, for the amusement of their stirred up masses needed a new spectacle, arranged by the Jews (Hitler 1945). April 29, 1945 was a busy day for Hitler. He hardly slept, and continued to issue orders to resist to his military commanders. He dictated two wills. The first was a personal will in which, like any good *Bürger,* he bequeathed his belongings to family members and old associates. The second, the political will, was full of hatred, accusing the generals of treason and, most of all, blaming the Jews for unleashing the war. The last sentence: "Most of all I obligate the leadership of the nation to the most careful execution of racial laws and the pitiless resistance against the world poisoner of all peoples, international Jewry" (Hitler 1945).[1] On this day, Hitler also heard of Mussolini's death. The dictator and his mistress, Clara Petacci, were caught by partisans and shot before they reached the Swiss border. Their bodies were hanged upside down from girders on a construction site in Milan, the sort of desecration that Hitler feared. Also on 29 April, in a civil ceremony, Hitler married Eva Braun, who for many years had been his neglected mistress but had stood by him. Hitler was most concerned that his suicide not fail. He got advice on how to commit suicide from Professor Werner Haase, who at one time had been one of Hitler's personal surgeons *(Begleitarzt).* In April 1945, Haase was in charge of the lazarette in the Reich Chancellery. He experimentally poisoned two of Hitler's German shepherds with potassium cyanide and advised Hitler about a fail-safe method of committing suicide (Schenck 1985).

On April 30, Hitler had a last meal with his secretaries and his cook. Eva Braun joined him later when he gathered with a small group of his intimate associates in the conference room and said good-bye to them. He then went into his private chambers and instructed his valet, Heinz Linge, to enter the chambers after a while. Nobody knows precisely what happened in the chambers (Boldt 1973, Kempka 1975, Linge 1980, O'Donnel and Bahnsen 1977, Roper 1962, Schenk 1985). Some of the men in the conference room stated that they heard a shot, but others did not. When Linge entered and, shortly thereafter, Martin Bormann, General Hans Rattenhuber, and adjutant Otto Günsche, Hitler and Eva Braun were dead. Eva Braun had poisoned herself with potassium cyanide. About Hitler's method of suicide, no unanimous opinions were expressed, and later violent arguments between Russian and Western scholars erupted. The Western scholars assumed he shot himself, the Russians

---

[1]The two wills are impressive testimony to Hitler's ambivalences and split of personality: the petit bourgeois and the monstrous politician.

that he took poison. The truth could be established only much later. The corpses were carried out into the garden by men of Hitler's entourage at the Chancellery and burned in an open gasoline fire that could barely be started because of Russian artillery shelling. It burned for 8 hours. Then Hitler and Eva Braun were buried in a shallow bomb crater. Hitler's explicit wish had been that the cremation would result in the total destruction of the corpses and that no witnesses other than those involved in the task would be present; however, the corpses were not completely burned, and by chance three persons watched the grisly ceremony from a distance. On 5 May, the Russian troops entered the bunker and disinterred thirteen corpses, amongst them the corpses of Joseph and Magda Goebbels and their six children, who had been murdered by their parents. On 1 May 1945, the German radio announced that Hitler had died a hero's death fighting at the head of his troops to save Europe—perhaps the ultimate lie about the world's greatest liar.

HITLER'S AUTOPSY

A medical commission of the Russian intelligence service (SMERSH), consisting of pathologists and forensic experts, performed autopsies on the corpses found in the Chancellery garden. The first report of the autopsies, among them those of a man and a woman considered to be Adolf Hitler and Eva Braun Hitler, reached the West through a book by Lev Besymenski in 1968. A second, expanded edition, only in German translation, appeared in 1982 (Besymenski 1982). The Besymenski publications were received with suspicion and dismay by leading historians Hugh Trevor-Roper (1962) and Maser (1980), not only—as Besymenski assumed—because they had been published by Russians. Trevor-Roper and Maser were irritated with the delay and suspicious as to whether Adolf Hitler had been properly identified. Maser also challenged some of the Russian autopsy findings (Maser 1980). Besymenski replied that a 30-year waiting period in top-secret matters was usual. But why should such secrecy pertain to an autopsy report? Besymenski also gave an explanation that made little sense, explaining that by not publishing, the rise of usurpers could be prevented, and more of Hitler's henchmen would be caught if no definitive news of Hitler's death existed. Another explanation by Besymenski made more sense. The Russians were not sure they had found the right corpse. Besymenski claimed that their secrecy was to prevent any embarrassment over a false report. Stalin had been told about the autopsy by the Russian intelligence service (SMERSH) and in Potsdam in July 1945 expressed doubts about Hitler's death. According to Besymenski (1982), Stalin did not like the report and did not want it discussed in public—a possible explanation for the delay. Even the ranking Russian commander, Marshal G. K. Shukow, was not sure whether Hitler was dead (personal communication). In defense of Besymenski, it can be stated that the Russian journalist was given the reports of the pathologists, but had no chance to examine the organs and tissues. When new reports appeared, he reported them candidly.

Maser was particularly critical of the Russian findings and maintained that the Russians had autopsied the wrong corpse (Maser 1980). Maser did not believe the Russians had autopsied Hitler, because they found only one testicle, while he was convinced that Hitler was not monorchic (Maser 1980).

If one could know with certainty whether Hitler had one or two testicles, one could follow these strange arguments. Without such assurance, this line of argumentation makes no sense. On the other hand, Waite stated that he believed the Russians because they had stated that Hitler was monorchic (Waite 1977). Waite also contended that the members of the Russian autopsy team would not have risked their reputations by writing a fraudulent report. They may well have written an honest report, but a change dictated by Stalin and his bureaucrats, for whatever political reasons, certainly could have been possible. Waite's remark that there was no political or medical reason to state that Hitler suffered from monorchism is naive. Sexual denunciation and degradation is despicable, but it is widely used in politics. Rumors about Hitler's sexual malfunction were widespread. Allied soldiers sang a song belittling Hitler's and other National Socialist leaders' genitals, and one can assume that this was known to the Russian intelligence service (SMERSH), under whose auspices the autopsy was performed. It is possible that the Russian statement was politically motivated. My own view is that it is likely that Hitler had a genital deformity.

Maser was convinced that the Russian statements about Hitler's teeth — the main identifying point — were not based on autopsy findings, but rather on very prolonged interrogation of the dental assistant, Käthe Heusermann, and the dental technician, Fritz Echtermann, both of whom assisted Hitler's dentist, Professor Hugo Blaschke. Hence, the autopsy report must have been fraudulent. The feud over Hitler's teeth — "der Zank um die Zähne" — ended when Reidar F. Sognaess and Ferdinand Strom, two forensic dentists, examined all evidence pertaining to Hitler's teeth and furnished conclusive proof that the Russians performed an autopsy on Hitler's corpse (Sognaess and Strom 1969). Sognaess's data were obtained from X-ray pictures of Hitler's skull and teeth in American archives, from personal interviews with persons who were involved in dental treatment, and from the Russian autopsy report. From such evidence, Sognaess and Strom concluded that the autopsied person was Adolf Hitler. The Sognaess report was accepted by Western experts (Endriss 1975), and it can be safely assumed that the corpse the Russian commission autopsied was Adolf Hitler's.

What was not established with certainty was how Hitler died. In the first edition of his book, Besymenski stated that the Russians concluded that Hitler died by poison. They discredited the inconsistent statements of Linge and other German witnesses in the bunker who maintained that Hitler shot himself. They believed the inconsistency was part of a German plot to disguise the facts. The Russian insistence on the poison theory was interpreted as an attempt to downgrade Hitler (Fest 1975). One additional bit of evidence, revealed in Besymenski's second edition, provided a new variant of the story. A fragment of the parietal bone was found with clear evidence that Hitler shot himself. The

Russians assumed that the bullet entered the mouth, where glass splinters from the vial of cyanide were found. They still postulated that Hitler had poisoned himself, but that one of his followers rendered a coup de grace. In my view, a shot in the mouth by a bystander would have been most unlikely. Waite assumed, without any specific evidence, that it was Eva Braun who rendered the coup de grace (Waite 1977). Schenck asserted that Hitler bit down on the glass ampule while he simultaneously pulled the trigger of his revolver and shot himself through the right temple. This was the method of suicide that Walther Hewel used when he and Schenck fled the Chancellery and were caught by the Russians. Hewel told Schenck shortly before his death that Hitler gave him a cyanide capsule and told him to commit suicide by the prescribed method (Schenck 1985). The question can be raised as to whether Hitler's right hand was steady enough to carry out such an act. The Parkinson's tremor is a rest tremor and would not exclude this method. The most likely explanation is that Hitler placed a cyanide capsule in his mouth and the gun barrel at his right temple and pulled the trigger (Schenck 1985, 1989). This would have been, considering Hitler's tremor, a fail-safe method. Possibly, further data will be released when *glasnost* reaches the Russian Archive of the Great War.

The fact that Hitler is dead does not need any proof. Who would doubt it at the end of this century, when Hitler would be over 100 years old? The myths of Hitler's escape from the bunker are recognized for what they were — poor fiction. It is unlikely that a new myth about Hitler dwelling in the *Unterberg* near Salzburg or in the Kyffhäuser Mountains, like Emperor Barbarossa waiting to return to save the world, will arise. One also can be certain that the Russians performed the autopsy on the right corpse. The reflections about Hitler's method of suicide are strange. It does not behoove historians and clinicians to degrade a man for any reason, and particularly not on flimsy and peculiar evidence. No one needs to make Hitler any worse than he was. One should not fault Hitler for committing suicide one way or another, but only for committing suicide at such a late date. An earlier suicide or surrender would have saved millions of lives.

MOTIVATIONS FOR HITLER'S SUICIDE

Erich Fromm (1973) developed the concept of necrophilia, a characterological type of person with malignant aggression and destructive and self-destructive tendencies. According to Fromm, the necrophilic person is attracted to dead, putrid, and rotten matter. Fromm finds Hitler the prototype of necrophilia. Malignant aggression certainly was an important characteristic of Hitler. There is, however, no evidence of an attraction to decaying matter, unless, as Fromm did, one views Hitler's compulsive cleanliness as a reaction formation to the necrophilic. But such an assumption without detailed analytic data would be precarious, and it remains doubtful whether the necrophilia concept is valid and useful. It does not contribute anything to an understanding of Hitler's suicide, nor to his personality in general. No one doubts Hitler's malignant aggression, which is not elucidated by the necrophilia concept. Hitler did, however, have a strong affinity to death. He did not fear death. He glorified death—and also survival—in an apocalyptic, Wagnerian sense. He actually died in a dismal *Götterämmerung*. What he hoped for was a survival of his work in the "Reich of a Thousand Years." Nothing remained of it except a mess of world problems.

Suicide, since Sigmund Freud and Karl Menninger (1958), is viewed as a form of extreme self-destructiveness, in most cases a form of self-punishment for murderous impulses. Hitler had murderous and destructive impulses. At the end, he wanted to destroy the Jews, the Slavs, and Germany as well. Yet, I find very little evidence of conscious or preconscious self-punitive behavior. An explanation offered by Shneidman (1984) makes more sense: A person chooses to end his life when death is preferable to other solutions. Hitler could not stand to lose his precarious identity as a charismatic leader. More specifically, he could not stand being humiliated and vilified by the Russian victor. Death and disappearance from this world were preferable to an ignominious existence.

ADDENDUM

An important article about Hitler's death and autopsy has recently appeared: "Hitler's letzte Reise" (Hitler's last trip) in *Der Spiegel,* vol. 30, 1992. The article contains three items of interest:

1. Hitler's burnt corpse was disinterred nine times, moved to different locations in Germany, finally to Lefortowo Prison in Moscow where it was completely incinerated.

2. Lev Besymenski admitted that he based his report without any expression of doubt or protest on false and insufficient data, which he received from the Soviet authorities. (I suspected this.)

3. A second autopsy was done by Professor Semjonowski, who considered the first autopsy woefully inadequate. (I did too.) The second autopsy report lies still unpublished in a Moscow archive.

Lev Besymenski deserves praise for his courage. The Western world is well acquainted with major and minor confessions obtained under Josef Stalin and his KGB. Besymenski's confession is different. It is voluntary.

Glasnost has not reached some of the Soviet archives, and we still do not know the content of autopsy reports. I do not know why the Russian authorities continue to play games, but there is hope. The Russian Orthodox Church has become more powerful again in post-Bolshevik Russia, and a miracle might occur: the genuine reports may yet be published. Mother Russia needs miracles.

REFERENCES

Besymenski, L. (1982). *Der Tod des Adolph Hitler.* 2nd ed. Munich: Herbig.
Boldt, G. (1973). *The Last Ten Days.* Berlin: Coward McCann and Geoghegan.
Endriss, R. (1975). *Archiv fur Kriminologie* 156:95.

Fest, J. (1975). *Hitler.* (Trans. from German.) New York: Random House.

Fromm, E. (1973). *The Anatomy of Human Destructiveness.* New York: Holt, Rinehart and Winston.

Hitler, A. (1924). Sämtliche Aufzei Chnungen. In *Gesamte Aufzeichnungen, 1905–1924,* ed. E. Jackel and A. Kuhn, p. 1101. Stuttgart: Deutsche Verlagsanstalt, 1980.

———— (1945). *Political Testament. Part II.* Washington, DC: National Archives. (April 29, 1945).

Jodl, A. (1965). Notes dictated in Nuremberg Prison on 25 February, 1946. In *Hitler als militarischer Führer,* ed. P. Schramm, pp. 144–155. Frankfurt: Bernard und Graefe.

Kempka, E. (1975). *Die letzen Tage mit Adolf Hitler.* Preussisch Oldendorf: A. Schütz.

Koller, K. (1948). *Der letzte Monat.* Esslinger Bechtle, 1985.

Kriegstagbuch: (war diary) KTB/OKW. *Der Spiegel,* April 22, 1945, p. 1696.

Langer, W. (1972). *The Mind of Adolf Hitler.* New York: Basic Books.

Linge, H. (1980). *Bis zum Untergang.* Munich: Herbig.

Litman, R. (1967). Sigmund Freud on suicide. In *Essays in Self-Destruction,* ed. E. Shneidman, pp. 324–344. New York: Science House.

Maser, W. (1980). *Adolf Hitler.* Düsseldorf: Econ.

Menninger, K. (1958). *Man against Himself.* New York: Harcourt, Brace and World.

Morell Diaries (1942). Microfilm, T253–262. Washington, DC: National Archives (Modern Military Section), December 17.

Murray, H. (1944). Analysis of the Personality of Adolf Hitler. Unpublished OSS memorandum.

O'Donnel, J., and Bahnsen, U. (1977). *Die Katakombe.* Munich: Deutscher Taschenbuchverlag.

Redlich, F. C. (in press). A new diagnosis of Adolf Hitler. *General Archives of Internal Medicine.*

Reitsch, H. (1945). Statement. International Military Trial, NB 3734-PS.

Schenck, E. G. (1985). *Als Arzt in Hitler's Reichskanzlei.* Düsseldorf: Droste.

———— (1989). Patient Hitler. Düsseldorf: Droste.

Shneidman, E. (1984). Aphorisms of suicide and some implications for psychotherapy. *American Journal of Psychotherapy* 38:319–328.

Sognaess, R., and Strom, F. (1969). The odontological identification of Adolf Hitler. *Acta Odontological Scandinavia* 31:43.

Trevor-Roper, H. (1962). *The Last Days of Hitler.* New York: Collier.

Waite, R. (1977). *Adolf Hitler: The Psychopathic God.* New York: Basic Books.

17: NEW MELVILLE DOCUMENTS AND SUB-INTENTIONED DEATH

Hershel Parker

In September 1966, at the conference on Hawthorne and Melville at the Berkshire Athenaeum in Pittsfield, Massachusetts, Edwin S. Shneidman spoke on "The Deaths of Herman Melville" (Shneidman 1968). The thanatologist depicted himself as an intruding amateur among the professional literary critics, and in fact he was out of step with at least the younger Melvilleans present. They had been trained under the then fashionable literary approach, the New Criticism, to look at one work at a time, but Shneidman scanned all of Melville's fiction (and some of his poetry) for references to death. Rather than analyzing only passages regularly analyzed by previous critics, he pointed his dowsing finger at words no one had ever thought carried any particular force, such as this passage from *White-Jacket:*

> It is a good joke, for instance, and one often perpetrated on board ship, to stand talking to a man in a dark night-watch, and all the while be cutting the buttons from his coat. But once off, those buttons never grow on again. There is no spontaneous vegetation in buttons. [p. 38]

Unconcerned, as a psychologist, that the New Criticism had tabooed discussion of any connection between the majesty of words and a writer's personal life, Shneidman concluded from Melville's prose works and letters that along with "his many other ambiguities, Melville, with his great zest for life, was a death-intoxicated man" (p. 132).

Melville, in Shneidman's description, had endured anguish at coming too early to "the enigmatic and unanswerable issues that are more grim even than those of misery and death, namely, eternal and total cessation, naughtment, and annihilation" (p. 130). Loosed among the English professors, the thanatologist outdid them as a phrase-maker: "To answer a soul's need to deal with the issue of one's own annihilation before he is thirty-five is to tackle God's world at off-season, at hurricane time . . ." (p. 131). He tossed off provocative observations: "It is debatable whether *Moby-Dick* is as much about terminal death as it is about partial death, and especially about suicidal equivalents" (p. 123). He defined a category for death for people like Melville, *sub-intentioned* death, where "the decedent plays some, partial, covert, or unconscious role in hastening his own demise," and where the "objective evidence of the presence of these roles lie in such behavioral manifestations as, for example, poor judgment, imprudence, excessive risk taking, abuse of alcohol, misuse of drugs, neglect of self, self-destructive style of life, disregard of prescribed life-saving medical regimen, and so on" (p. 120). He described the choices open to the gifted and proud writer who suffers under "criticism, rejection, verbal abuse" (p. 135); in his reading, Melville's disdainful behavior toward his critics was a maneuver that exacts the cost of "the death of part of one's social and hence psychological self" (p. 136). He eloquently described Melville's years of "not being totally socially alive" as "a partial social death" (p. 122). This thanatologist with his odd charts quantifying and analyzing death in Melville's books proved himself a humane man and a sensitive reader—a true literary critic.

NEW MELVILLE DOCUMENTS

In its published form, "The Deaths of Herman Melville" has become a classic among those most devoted to Melville, but widely as he ranged for Melville's comments on death in 1966, Shneidman now would need to range much wider. Since the mid-1970s, and especially since the early 1980s, many new Melville documents bearing on death have been discovered. For example, among the newly recovered marginalia is Melville's comment on this passage from Edmund Spenser's "Colin Clout's Come Home Again":

> Who life doth loath, and longs death to behold
> Before he die, already dead with fears,
> And yet would live with heart halfe stonie cold,
> Let him to sea, and he shall see it there. [vol. 6, p. 195]

Melville wrote in the margin: "Absolute coinciding here between Spenser's conceit & another person's in connection with a very singular thought" (Leyda and Parker in press). Going to sea for Melville even in 1839 and 1841 may have been far from merely an expression of robust adventurism. In 1975, two astounding letters were published showing that by May 1867, Melville's wife for a long time had been thinking of leaving him (Kring and Carey 1975). Even her husband's family, we learned, had accepted her opinion that Melville was insane and had agreed to say nothing against her if she left him. These new documents cast miserable new light on a matter of enduring interest to Shneidman, the suicide of Melville's son Malcolm in September 1867, 4 months after the crisis seemed to pass.

In 1983, a treasure trove of Melville documents, part of Melville's sister Augusta's papers, was found in a barn near the former family property in

Gansevoort, New York, and promptly purchased by the New York Public Library—documents ranging from the eighteenth century up through 1863. (These documents will be in Leyda and Parker [in press].) Birth is occasionally celebrated in these papers (as in an exuberant letter Melville wrote to his brother Allan in February 1849, after the birth of his son Malcolm in Boston and Allan's daughter Maria in New York), but death permeates them—death in the womb for sister Helen's almost full-term son (married late because of the family poverty, she never bore a living child); death in babyhood of cousin Herman Gansevoort and niece Julia Melville; death in adolescence of a cousin doubly related, on both the Van Rensselaer and Douw sides; death in young adulthood of cousin Julia Melvill [*sic*] and brother Gansevoort Melville; and many, more timely, deaths of elderly uncles and aunts and cousins.

In 1990, I tracked down a smaller trove of documents among which were many letters dealing with the death of Sarah Morewood, Melville's neighbor and friend, and the Melvilles' part in easing her death and mourning her. (These papers descended through Melville's brother Allan's daughter "Milie"—the Maria of Melville's newly discovered 1849 letter—who married Sarah's son Willie.) In this little trove was a letter Augusta wrote Allan in May 1851, just after she had been released from copying duties on the whaling book. I quote it here for the first time: "So you had a flying visit from Herman? When does he make the longer one? That book of his, will create a great interest, I think. It is very fine." Several of the new documents confirm and sharpen what Shneidman said in 1966 about the degree to which Melville aided and abetted in his own aesthetic, social, or physical death—the degree to which he was what he called Ungar in his poem *Clarel*, "Oblivion's volunteer."

SUB-INTENTIONAL DEATH

Shneidman applied his concept of sub-intentioned death not only to Melville's bodily death in 1891 but to his career, and from new documents we know more now about how behavioral manifestations—such as poor judgment, imprudence, excessive risk taking—ended Melville's career as a popular writer. The deathblow to that career was suffered in 1852, although the death throes lasted 5 years. Melville's recklessness, we now know, was first of all financial. When Melville impulsively decided to move out of the New-York-City-Melville-clan house (purchased with money from his father-in-law, Lemuel Shaw, and from his brother Allan's mother-in-law) in order to finish his whaling book in the grandeur of the Berkshires, his father-in-law advanced him part of the purchase price for Arrowhead, Melville's name for the farm south of Pittsfield, and the previous owner, Dr. George Brewster, took a mortgage for the remainder. (Among Shaw's reasons was that he would be sure of seeing his daughter every fall when he came to hold court in nearby Lenox.) Melville had not waited to sell his half of the house in New York City (legally it was his, not his wife's), and after it remained unsold a few months his younger brother Allan (we now know from the Augusta papers) took it off his hands, at what must have been a bargain for Allan, in view of the fact that Melville felt he had to borrow $2,050 (an enormous sum) from "T. D. S." on 1 May 1851. Melville innocently thought that the fact that he was writing a great metaphysical whaling book meant that he would make money from it: he would quickly get out of debt to his publishers, the Harper brothers, pay off T. D. S. (T. D. Stewart [Barber 1977], who emerges in the Augusta papers as an old friend from Lansingburgh, New York), and then lead the life of a writer-farmer.

In comparison with most of his previous books, *Moby-Dick* did not sell fast when the Harpers published it in November 1851. Within 6 more weeks Melville had finished a new novel, which he probably thought would surely get him out of debt, since he implied in a letter to Nathaniel Hawthorne that it was going to be a better book than *Moby-Dick,* as much greater as the legendary Kraken was bigger than a whale. *Pierre,* when Melville finished it (about the last week of 1851), was estimated to make up 360 pages—short by Kraken standards. In it Melville relentlessly depicted the tragic consequences for Pierre Glendinning of growing to maturity in a household where sexual impulses were acknowledged only as aesthetic impulses and where basic family relationships were subtly perverted by anomalous role playing (in pleasantry Pierre's widowed mother pretended to be his sister and he pretended to be her brother but treated potential suitors as rivals). Accustomed to an atmosphere of dangerous idealism, Pierre, at the first crisis of his life, confuses sexual impulses with his highest idealistic impulse to act in imitation of Jesus. In this psychological novel Melville meticulously analyzed the supersubtle complexity of psychological processes, then asserted the autonomy of half-conscious processes over "consciously bidden and self-propelled thought" (p. 84). At the very least, the book as Melville originally wrote it must have been the greatest psychological novel yet written in English.

By 1851, Melville was deep in debt to the Harpers, even though they were paying him at the good rate of fifty cents on the dollar after their costs (Parker 1977). When he showed the manuscript of *Pierre* to the publishers in the first week of 1852 (the dating is partly from letters in the Augusta papers), the Harpers cautiously offered only twenty cents on the dollar after costs, a rate he must have felt as punitive, especially since it came just a few months after he had gone into debt to finance his burgeoning career. Knowing how deeply Melville had run into their debt when they were paying him fifty cents on the dollar, the Harpers must also have known how devastating he would find their new terms. When he signed the contract he was in effect accepting their judgment that his career was over. From our point of view, it seems that he should not have been without other options. For example, he could have returned resolutely to Pittsfield and put together a book designed to be as popular as *Typee,* the story of his experiences as a captive of a tribe of South Sea islanders. Then he could have hawked it from publisher to publisher until he found one who would give him his old terms, if not a better deal than he had ever had from the Harpers.

At any rate, once he had agreed to the terms of the contract for *Pierre,* any more time spent on it was time wasted.

It has been said that writing *Pierre* was a suicidal gesture on Melville's part; it wasn't — not until after he had *finished* it. His recklessness was not primarily in writing *Pierre* but in enlarging it, which he began to do a few days after the Harpers offered him a contract and he accepted it. (This dating of the enlargement is from a letter Allan Melville wrote the publisher on 21 January 1852. Jay Leyda referred to it in the 1951 *Log* but did not realize it dated the start of the enlargement. I printed it and showed its significance in 1977.) My guess is that before he accepted the contract, Melville went to his friend Evert Duyckinck with the manuscript, for only a few months before, in August 1851, Duyckinck had tried to persuade him to give the whaling book to Redfield, not to the Harpers. Perhaps Duyckinck told Melville that he could not possibly ask Redfield to publish a book that hinted at incest; perhaps, at this, Melville stalked away rigid with controlled anger. This confrontation is imaginary, but it fits the facts. We know how appalled Duyckinck was at *Pierre,* since he reviewed it when it was published the next year in a much longer form. And we know what happened in the first week of 1852, probably just after Melville accepted the Harpers' terms for the manuscript: he opened the manuscript to a convenient spot two-thirds or three-quarters through, and wrote into it a satirical portrait of Duyckinck, starting the addition with the staggering news that Pierre had been a juvenile author and now was going to become a professional writer. And we know that the friendship was overtly broken about this time, for Melville brusquely canceled his subscription to the Duyckinck brothers' *Literary World* in February, and then in April, after the Duyckincks continued to send him the magazine, he again asked them to stop sending it (in a note not available in 1966 but now in the possession of Dr. David Shneidman).

Any reader of the original manuscript and any reader of *Pierre* as published would have known perfectly well that young Pierre had not been a writer, for in Melville's comprehensive analysis of Pierre's psychological development he had said much about Pierre as an immature reader but not a word about Pierre as an immature writer. Melville did not bother to go back to revise the earlier parts of the manuscript to work the Pierre-as-writer theme into it. Here is the way he introduced the news that Pierre had been a writer:

> Among the various conflicting modes of writing history, there would seem to be two grand practical distinctions, under which all the rest must subordinately range. By the one mode, all contemporaneous circumstances, facts, and events must be set down contemporaneously; but the other, they are only to be set down as the general stream of the narrative shall dictate; for matters which are kindred in time, may be very irrelative in themselves. I elect neither of these; I am careless of either; both are well enough in their way; I write precisely as I please. [p. 244]

He may have intended to write only a few pages so as to get his anger at Duyckinck out of his system; whatever he first intended, he was drawn on into an elaborate interpolation about Pierre's premature struggle to write a great book—an elaboration that amounted to some 160 pages. Melville could not have imagined the consequences, beginning with his loss of an English publisher (which opened a black gap in his reputation with English readers—few of his English admirers knew any of *Pierre* or his short stories until the 1920s). Months later, in the late summer of 1852, came the savage reviews of *Pierre*, then the inexorable, though not immediate, loss of his career: he published no book of prose after 1857 although he lived until 1891. He had recklessly prided himself on yielding to that "certain something unmanageable" in "some of us scribblers" (this in a letter to his English publisher Richard Bentley, 5 June 1849, after the failure of *Mardi*), but he had never before so blatantly insulted his public. Declaring that he wrote precisely as he pleased was the single most suicidal public notice Melville ever gave, however little he may have understood it then in those terms.

No one can say what the consequences of Melville's publishing the short version of *Pierre* would have been. But the consequences of his writing it and his recklessness in enlarging it are worse than we ever thought, for the disastrous reception of *Pierre* probably had much to do with the destruction of the next book Melville wrote. Shneidman knew nothing of this part of the story, which I pieced together from letters in the Augusta papers in 1987. In 1990, in *American Literature,* I showed that Melville had written a book called *The Isle of the Cross,* a title no one had known and a book no one has read, although some canny scholars had suspected that Melville had completed the book his mother had reported in April 1853 as being nearly finished. (Others thought his mother was exaggerating, but her veracity is plain throughout the Augusta papers.) This book, which Melville completed on or just after 22 May 1853 and carried to New York to the Harpers in early June, almost surely was a fictionalized version of a story he had been told in 1852, just before *Pierre* was published, about a Nantucket woman who had rescued a sailor from drowning, nursed him to health, and married him, only to have him desert her and reappear, years later, as a bigamist. What interested Melville, apparently, was her long-suffering nature, and we now know that after attempts to persuade Hawthorne to write the story, Melville wrote it himself, very possibly using some notes on local color that Hawthorne had taken during a stay in the Isles of Shoals in the fall of 1852. Melville, in a letter to the Harpers in November 1853, referred to the work he "had been prevented from publishing." Why he was prevented from publishing it in June we do not know. Neither do we know how long he preserved it, although the November letter indicates that he still had it in his possession. We have every reason to think that Melville destroyed the entire book-length manuscript—a suicidal act performed after, perhaps very long after, Melville had unintendingly (or sub-intentionally?) induced the death of his career then helplessly witnessed the denunciations at its burial—the reviews of *Pierre*. At the age of 33, Melville began living a posthumous life. We have suspected all along that Melville probably immolated some of the poetry he wrote starting in the late 1850s and tried to publish in book form in 1860. What would Shneidman have said in "The Deaths of Herman Melville" if he had known Melville had destroyed an entire book, the product of several months of brooding and five or so months of intense labor, *The Isle of the Cross?*

ANNIHILATION

In elaborating a portrait of Melville as a "death-intoxicated man" at far too early a stage of life, Shneidman explained why death was "laden with more than ordinary anguish": "for Melville, death meant more than physical demise or even more — if one can imagine it — than psychological cessation; it meant complete, that it, eternal, annihilation. More than do or die, it was exult or never have been" (p. 133). Shneidman's discussion was built on a number of passages in Melville. One is "The Whiteness of the Whale," chapter 42 of *Moby-Dick,* in which Ishmael speaks of being stabbed "from behind with the thought of annihilation, when beholding the white depths of the milky way" (Leyda and Parker in press). Another is Hawthorne's report of Melville's telling him in Southport in 1856 that he had "pretty much made up his mind to be annihilated." This passage has been explicated variously. Lewis Mumford (1929) said it meant that "Melville would not commit suicide: that was a weak way out: but he might deliberately withdraw" (p. 263).

In 1983, Melville's unknown two-volume reading copy of Milton's poems turned up on the auction market, fetching $100,000 plus commissions. After more years of seclusion from scholars and another auction, the volumes are available at Princeton. Melville heavily marked the passage in Book 6 of *Paradise Lost* where Michael's sword cuts Satan, who then "first knew pain." The fallen angels bear Satan off:

> there they him laid
> Gnashing for anguish and despite and shame
> To find himself not matchless, and his pride
> Humble'd by such rebuke, so farr beneath
> His confidence to equal God in power,
> Yet soon he heal'd; for Spirits that live throughout
> Vital in every part, not as frail man
> In Entrailes, Heart or head, Liver or Reins,
> Cannot but by annihilating die. [ll. 339–347]

Instead of blood, an angel like Satan possesses a nectarous fluid, which heals up even grievous wounds very fast. A creature "vital" (full of life force) in "every part" can only die by total annihilation, not piecemeal from decay or damage to one organ or another. Although no scholar had seen Melville's marked copy of Milton until 1983, I had found and ignored a clue in 1962. Melville's brother made a speech at a Great Repeal Meeting in New York on 20 September 1843. On 29 September, the New York *Evening Post* quoted him as calling the cause of Repeal (of the union between England and Ireland):

> Vital in every part,
> And cannot but by annihilating die.

Gansevoort's application of Milton's words may be a little askew (American politicians wooing the Irish vote should not have equated the cause of repeal with Satan), but his allusion does suggest the possibility that the quotation was a familiar one in the Melville household, as many other literary allusions were. In the light of this new evidence of a special, specific poetic meaning for annihilation and its association with Satan, Shneidman might want to elaborate his conclusion to "The Deaths of Herman Melville," where he reviews Henry A. Murray's account of the stages of Melville's attitudes toward annihilation. In the Miltonic context, when Hawthorne records that "Melville, as he always does, began to reason of Providence and futurity," the notation that Melville had "pretty much made up his mind to be annihilated" may well mean that he was not looking forward to passive decline into nothingness but to resisting, up until the time when he would be utterly wiped out.

My final example from new material concerns *Clarel,* the 18,000-line poem Melville wrote (from about 1870 to 1875). Melville wrote *Clarel* at odd moments in his work week or on Sundays, and tried to keep even his family from knowing he was writing poetry again, but despite the secrecy the writing of the poem was life-affirming. At the peak of his intellectual powers and aesthetic control, although all but forgotten, Melville was writing a poem as ambitious as those being published in England by Tennyson, Browning, and Arnold, a great national poem, a pessimistic epic to fit the nation at the corrupt end of its first century. Joel Barlow had written the optimistic *The Vision of Columbus* (1787) and *The Columbiad* (1807); Melville was writing an *Anti-Columbiad,* in which the main American characters agreed that only "grudged thanks" were due to Columbus, and that the time had come to build fanes to Terminus, the god of limits, not to the god of opportunities. (The Northwestern-Newberry edition of *Clarel* was published in 1991, the centennial of Melville's death — in time for historians to use it in the Columbus quincentennial.) Melville's dying uncle, Peter Gansevoort, learned of the completed poem in 1875 and promised Melville the money to publish it. In 1876, after his uncle's death, Melville used the legacy to pay Putnam's to publish the poem. On 2 February 1876, the readying of the manuscript for printing and the initial proofreading had made his wife call it a "dreadful *incubus* of a *book*" on his shoulders "(I call it so because it has undermined all our happiness)" (Leyda and Parker in press). In the next months the proofreading put still more severe strains on the household.

A SUICIDE NOTE

Forewarned by the negative reception of his volume of Civil War poems in 1866, and now forearming himself, Melville prefaced *Clarel* with one of the saddest notes an author ever wrote: "I here dismiss the book — content beforehand with whatever future awaits it." This stoic bravado masked, in all likelihood, Melville's last reserves of his old rage for recognition. The reviewers almost all treated the book as a disastrous mistake on the part of the man who a lifetime before had been a popular prose writer but who had no talent at all for poetry. In the year after publication, denied critical recognition, his household still shaken by the half year of intense proofreading, Melville was reduced to a pathetic prideful contest with his cousin Kate Gansevoort, who wanted to give him the hundred dollars the book had cost him above the original sum of $1,200; the stubborn cousins passed the money back and forth, Kate determined to fulfill her father's wishes at the small cost of an additional hundred dollars, Melville knowing that the $1,200 had been wasted, as far as the world's opinion went, and wanting to save a rag of dignity.

On 27 March 1879, a little less than three years after publishing *Clarel*, someone at Putnam's summoned Melville to the office on Fifth Avenue near 23rd Street and informed him that the unsold copies of *Clarel* were creating a space problem. The copies were Melville's responsibility, since he had paid for the publication. He probably had the option of having them hauled a few blocks to his house on 26th Street. What could he do with two hundred sets of a poem that had "undermined" the fragile new "happiness" of the household? Stash them under the bed Malcolm had shot himself in? Probably Melville did not seriously consider claiming the books. Instead, taking a piece of Putnam stationery, he wrote this: "Please dispose of cases 2 & 3 ("Clarel") containing two hundred and twenty four copies, on my account, to paper-mill." (*Clarel*, p. 638) He was authorizing Putnam's to destroy all the surplus copies of *Clarel*—perhaps two-thirds of the entire edition. In the bitter depth of his lost reputation, a few dark years before British admirers began to write fan letters to him and to write articles about him, Melville became an accomplice in the murder of his own aesthetic and philosophical life. Putnam's, for its convenience, extracted from him the equivalent of a suicide note.

THE LIVES OF HERMAN MELVILLE

The new death-related documents I have quoted or alluded to will all be in the three- or four-volume edition of *The New Melville Log*, my expansion and revision of Jay Leyda's monumental two-volume documentary life of Melville. When it appears, we will need from Shneidman some supplemental meditations on the new death-related documents not only because many more documents will be available but also because the professional critics of Melville are no nearer talking about the author in relation to his works than they were in 1966. Now reader-response critics are locating literary meaning in themselves, not the author; now leading structuralists are declaring that their essays in theory are more interesting than novels and poems; now the New Historicists are writing what amounts to literary history without research. The situation is such that in the London *Times Literary Supplement* (15 November 1991) the former editor, John Gross, at last speaks out:

The body of theory that has accumulated over the past few years, taken as a whole, seems to me a monstrous excrescence, a vast distraction, a paltry substitute for the experience of literature itself. I believe that in time it will fade, but I am filled with a cold horror at the thought of how much further it could spread before it does.

Take "theory" to include criticism, and these words apply to most of what has been written on Melville since 1966. In Shneidman's "The Deaths of Herman Melville," knowledge of human psychology always enriches "the experience of literature itself." Shneidman saw Melville's life as almost unbearably tragic and saw the works he left to us as valuable altogether beyond reckoning. Until literary critics can acknowledge such pain and celebrate such achievements, Melville lovers will have to wait for amateurs such as Shneidman to say the right words about the new documents.

REFERENCES

Barber, P. (1977). Two new Melville letters. *American Literature* 49:418–421.
Kring, W. D., and Carey, J. S. (1975). Two discoveries concerning Herman Melville. *Proceedings of the Massachusetts Historical Society* 87:137–141.
Leyda, J. and Parker, H. (in press). *The New Melville Log: A Documentary Life of Herman Melville, 1819–1891.* (An expansion of *The Melville Log: A Documentary Life of Herman Melville, 1819–1891*, by Jay Leyda, 1951.) New York: Harcourt, Brace.
Melville, H. (1970). *White-Jacket.* Chicago: Northwestern University Press and the Newberry Library.
———— (1971). *Pierre.* Ed. H. Hayford, H. Parker, and G. Thomas Tanselle, Chicago: Northwestern University Press and the Newberry Library.
Mumford, L. (1929). Herman Melville. New York: Harcourt, Brace.
Parker, H. (1977). Contract: *Pierre,* by Herman Melville (ed. H. Hayford, H. Parker, and G. Thomas Tanselle). *Proof* 5:27–45.
Shneidman, E. S. (1968). The deaths of Herman Melville. In *Melville and Hawthorne in the Berkshires: A Symposium. Melville Annual 1966,* pp. 118–143. Kent, OH: Kent State University Press.
Spenser, E. (1787). *The Poetical Works of Edmund Spenser.* (8 vols.). London: J. Bell.

SUICIDE IN JAPAN
Part VII

Suicide is a multifaceted event and suicidology is a multidisciplinary enterprise. Much of our understanding, however—including our very definition—is culturally determined, based on perceptions that are distinctly Western. But suicide is not, of course, a uniquely Western phenomenon. In Part VII, we examine suicide in Japan, not only in an effort to understand the cultural elements of suicide, but also because Shneidman was himself instrumental in bringing contemporary suicide prevention to Japan in the 1960s. In what follows we find a personological and contextualistic view of Japanese suicide, and some perspectives on recent trends of suicide and its prevention in Japan.

18: JAPANESE SUICIDE

Mamoru Iga

In Japan, suicide has traditionally been an accepted, if not welcomed, way of solving a serious problem. One of the contributions made by Dr. Edwin S. Shneidman has been to place suicide in a personological and contextualist perspective (Murray 1938, Pepper 1961, Shneidman 1985). This perspective also facilitates our understanding of Japanese suicide and gives insight unattainable from the usual statistical correlational studies.

CONCERN WITH SUICIDE

Traditional Views of Suicide and Death in Japan

Suicide is not a sin in Japan; it is not punished by God. Suicide is not viewed as a social or national issue but a personal problem. Therefore, the Japanese government is little concerned with it. About half (44 percent) of the college students and 24 percent of high-school students surveyed in Kyoto in 1960 indicated such positive or uncritical attitudes toward suicide as: "Suicide is a matter of individual freedom"; "I feel sympathetic toward the suicide victim"; or "Society is to be blamed for suicide." There was a 24-percent rate of "No Response" (Kosaka and Usui 1966, p. 225). If not explicitly, the Japanese nevertheless regard suicide as an expression of sincerity *(makoto)*, which is the highest value in Japan. Suicide may be a sincere reaction to the sense of shame.

The Japanese attitude toward suicide is based on their views of death. For the Japanese, death does not generate a sense of fear and anxiety as much as it does in Westerners. This is so for several reasons. First, death is a philosophical concept based on the idea of *mujō* — the sense of eternal change and the ephemeral quality of all things, including human beings. Common among all schools of Buddhism is the belief that (1) all life is inevitably sorrowful, (2) sorrow is due to craving, (3) sorrow can only be stopped by the cessation of craving, and (4) this cessation can be accomplished only through a course of careful self-discipline and moral conduct.

The first three elements of this teaching were eagerly accepted by all classes of Japanese people during the period from the eleventh through thirteenth centuries, when people suffered from miserable living conditions as a result of earthquakes, storms, flood, famine, and rampant banditry. Unsound economic conditions caused widespread distress among the people, aggravated by incompetent, exploitive, and licentious leaders (Sansom 1943). A pessimistic view of life has continued as a strong undercurrent of Japanese life. Although the political system may have changed, mores do not change as rapidly as folkways do.

Second, death is welcome to many Japanese as an emancipation from the illusion and anguish that are seen as the substance of human life. In medieval times, many priests and their followers drowned themselves in the ocean, believing that they were going to *saiho jōdo* — Buddha Land, which was believed to exist at the western end of the earth (Kosaka and Usui 1966).

Third, death is viewed as conferring a sense of achievement, returning the soul to its natural habitat after the person has fulfilled his or her obligations and duties on earth.

Fourth, death for the group is considered to be the ultimate fulfillment of human potential. Since in Japan sincerity means selfless devotion to one's group or master, the highest form of sincerity is complete self-negation, that is, death. Death for love is also admired because it shows a selfless sincerity.

Fifth, death is perceived as beautiful. Dr. Shneidman told of having once sat next to a young chemical engineer on a bullet train in Japan. The young man said in English, "Cherry blossoms are blooming quickly and scattering at once. Better to come to fruition and die like the blossoms." The main themes of Japanese literature and drama are love and death. In both a person negates himself and does not know what he will get in return. The complete negation of the self and the sense of impermanence are the two things the Japanese consider to be the most beautiful. The perception of death as beautiful is promoted by mysticism, a characteristic of Japanese thinking.

Sixth, through death one can identify himself with the family. An individual's death means his continuing life (post-self) as a family member. This biological mode of immortality is epitomized by the notion of family continuity — of living on through one's sons and daughters and then through their sons and daughters, in an endless chain of biological attainment.

Finally, the belief that the deceased can communicate with family members at the *butsudan* (miniature household temple), and even become an *angel god* who watches over their welfare, makes death much easier to accept.

Religion and Philosophy

In addition to the teaching of sorrowful life, Buddhism had to adjust itself to Shintoism, the original religion in Japan. Shintoism is a complex of animism, shamanism, and ancestor worship. According to Takeshi Umehara at Kyoto University (1987), Shintoism is "the undercurrent of all systems of Japanese thoughts" (p. 3). Professor Shoichi Saeki of Tokyo University (1987) holds that Shintoism has served as the "ultimate source of the Japanese effort toward success" (p. 110). Shintoism developed the dependence on spirits and shamans for welfare.

As a consequence of its assimilation to Shintoism, Japanese Buddhism lost its original emphasis on individuality and rationalism. It stresses faith in supernatural deities, and its believers rely on external objects and their magical power (for example, Buddha or chanted Namu-Amidabutsu) for goal attainment and tension reduction. Shinran, the nonconforming founder of Shinshu, the largest denomination in Japan, denounced superstitions and rejected magics, but he emphasized faith over reason. Salvation is attained, he taught, only through chanting of Namu-Amidabutsu. His followers were more concerned with their salvation than with enlightenment. As a result, Japanese Buddhism heavily contributed to the fact that "even today the majority of Japanese are dominated by folk religion in its social, family, and individual life as well as its productive activities. Their daily lives require several kinds of rites, ceremonies, and their connected magic and taboo" (Hori 1968, p. 2). Thus, Japanese Buddhism tends to promote dependence and conformity, leading to pessimism about human capacity.

One of the unique aspects of Japanese culture is the coexistence of advanced technology with premodern religious beliefs. In 1981, some seven thousand Japanese companies built new office shrines for Inari (the fox), the patron deity of business prosperity (*Kashu Mainichi,* May 18, 1982). These premodern religious beliefs contribute to Japan's national solidarity.

Such coexistence provides many impediments to the outsider's understanding of Japan. The Japanese are often regarded as "inscrutable" by Westerners, as Richard Storry, the author of *A History of Modern Japan,* states (Riesman and Riesman 1967).

> If one travels east from Great Britain one comes eventually to Hong Kong, which seems extremely exotic in comparison; but the Japanese mentality is far more alien than the Chinese, for the Chinese can think philosophically and logically, and the Japanese cannot. The Japanese mentality is unique, a kind of end of the line in the East, and the more I study it the more I am baffled by it. [p. 10]

It may sound too harsh to say that the Japanese cannot think philosophically and logically. However, the traditional Chinese religion, Confucianism (in which Max Weber saw a functional equivalent of the Protestant ethic) is much more philosophical and logical than Shintoism. Shintoism is a system of mystical beliefs, magic, and rituals for pragmatic purposes. Shintoism, modified by Hobbesian statism, is called Nihonkyo, which may be "the strongest religion in the world, because it is so deeply ingrained in the core of the Japanese personality that they are not aware of it" (BenDasan 1971 p. 115).

The Japanese worldview generally is akin to Immanuel Kant's idea that history is the continuing process of culture, whereby the original animal nature of man becomes transformed into the distinctly human. Against Jean-Jacques Rousseau's optimistic view of human nature, Kant provided intellectual justification or rationalization of the subordination of the individual to fixed and ready-made universal principles. Reason and law are regarded as synonymous (Edman 1965). Georg Hegel is also close to Japanese hearts. His effort was to consecrate the Prussian states and to enshrine bureaucratic absolutism. Freedom in Japan is self-mastery, attained only by complete conformity to absolute rules.

Under the influence of German philosophies, Japanese philosophers attempted to combine Shintoism with Hobbesian statism. The effort to consecrate the state is the essence of the famous work, *Zen no Kenkyu (A Study of Good),* first published in 1911. Written by Kitaro Nishida, this book became a bible of Japanese nationalism, guiding the country throughout World War II. Nishida's special emphasis is that an individual's consciousness *(kojin no ishiki)* is part of the society's collective consciousness *(shakai no ishiki).* The society's consciousness is manifested in its culture — hence, the subordination of the individual to society. The traditional goal of Japanese socialization is to produce egoless conformers who blindly follow elitist bureaucrats.

As a whole, the difference between German and Japanese thinkings is that the latter is much less philosophical and more religious, stressing faith over reason. By comparing the Japanese language with Indian, Chinese, and Tibetan languages with reference to Buddhist concepts, Dean Hajime Nakamura of Tokyo University (1964) concluded that Japanese thinking is nonrational. It is nonlogical, lacking in consistency of meanings. Henry Kissinger (1989) wrote that because the Japanese are not inclined to discuss philosophical concepts (for example, what is man? what is good?), he could not know what they were going to do in world politics and global economy.

What is lacking in Japan is a humanistic tradition. Humanism, characterized generally by the emphases on the life, worth, and creativity of the individual human, is rooted in Hellenism and Hebraism. These traditions developed not only rationalism and idealistic individualism, but also respect for the individual. In contrast, Japanese culture regards people as children who need to be guided, as exemplified by Tenno ideology and the 1917 Imperial Rescript of Education.

Tenno ideology, which has been emphasized since the Meiji era (1868–1911), implies that Japan is the land of the gods, inhabited by a people uniquely superior in the world, who live together as a single family under the benevolent guidance of a divine emperor (Gluck 1985). The Rescript teaches that "our subjects ever united in loyalty and filial piety, . . . be filial to your parents, affectionate to your brothers and sisters; as husbands and wives be harmonious." Authoritarian familism is the underlying principle of Japanese education, which is characterized by *kanri kyōiku* (managed education) and *seikatsu shidō* (life guidance). This kind of education produces people who do not question why they think in a certain way and who do not comprehend how another thinks or why he thinks that way. Shichihei Yamamoto thinks that Japanese generally can empathize (put their own feelings into another) but not sympathize (feel the other's feelings). This is understandable because the Japanese generally behave according to their internalized role expectations rather than the goals of interpersonal communication.

Humanism in Japan, mostly interpreted as *ningenshugi* with a focus on human sentiments, is illustrated by *Manyōshū (Collection of Myriad Leaves)*, compiled in the eighth century. It is also applied to *jimmon shugi*, which stresses cultural refinement and creativity, represented by the elite writers and artists of Shirakaba-Ha in the 1930s. Japanese humanism, on the whole, emphasizes the harmony between man and Nature (Mutai 1975). This harmony is held to be attainable only through the subjugation of man to Nature and society, in accordance with *Nihonkyō* (worship of Japanese tradition).

Following Rousseau and John Dewey, I interpret humanism as the belief in man's ability to develop his potential (especially reason, love, and self-expression) through reasoning. Although science (the best method of reasoning) is often said to be value-free, it is rooted in humanism. Humanism provides ideals, or models, for scientists. Without the image of ideal health, medical science would not have made such progress as we see today. Suicide prevention is an act of humanism sui generis. The greatest problem of American social sciences and education seems to be in the confusion between two ideals: humanism (aiming at self-actualization and responsibility) and capitalism (self-profit and laissez-faire). The confusion is noticeable when we compare American education with Japanese education, which is directed solely by Nihonkyo.

Reason, love, and self-expression seem to be potentials peculiar to man. Reason is the conscious process by which the ego chooses from among alternatives the best means for attaining a certain goal under given conditions. The ability to initiate symbolic communication through self-expression is unique to man. So is love, especially self-love in Erich Fromm's sense, as indicated by concern with the love object's future welfare, the effort to understand that person, respect for the person's ability to solve his or her own problem, and by taking the responsibility to assist him or her in action if necessary.

Not only do these potentials distinguish humans from other forms of animals, but they are also necessary for the survival of the species. World peace is not possible without the development of these potentials by all peoples. For example, only reason enables people to examine their own culture (i.e., a system of conventions and prejudice). Without self-love (not narcissism) and concomitant security, and without such values as reciprocity, fairness, and suprasocietal justice, which are by-products of reason, love, and self-expression, men cannot cooperate with each other in constructive ways. Confucius, Shakyamuni Buddha, and Jesus Christ all stressed the importance of reason (wisdom), love (compassion), and honest self-expression. It can be assumed that an individual who has developed these potentials is less susceptible to the suicidal wish: his or her coping mechanism is more constructive. The lack of humanistic development in Japan underlies its traditional lack of concern with suicide.

According to Freudian concepts, which are typically humanistic, the ego is gradually differentiated from the id (instinctual processes) as a result of reality-perceiving. For the necessity of coping with reality, thought (reason) and reality-regulated strivings develop. However, Japanese socialization does not allow the development of reasoning as Western cultures do. Therefore, the Japanese ego, as a whole, develops more through reality-regulated strivings that are memorized from customs, than through reasoning. Thus, the Japanese ego is, relatively speaking, a bundle of feelings more than reasoning. This seems to be what Dr. Hayato Kawaii at Kyoto University means by his *jiga chuuku ron* (the theory of the central emptiness), whereby he characterizes the Japanese personality.

Authoritarian Familism

The accepting attitudes toward death and suicide reflect not only Japan's religion-philosophy but also its society. The country's incessant internal warfare ended when the Tokugawa Shogunate united it in 1600 and established a strict hierarchy of samurai, farmers, artisans, and merchants. Below merchants, there were outcasts. A member of the samurai class (about 6 percent of the total population) could kill commoners, if he felt offended by them. Nonsamurai were not allowed to own any weapons, including a knife longer than 1 foot.

Authoritarianism stresses the established social order, emphasizing faith, loyalty, and obedience on the part of social inferiors. It produces personalities characterized by dependence, tunnel vision, and a limited good mentality. This mentality is characterized by the attitude to regard everything good as limited in quantity. Such things are to be fought for and, once acquired, to be carefully guarded even by force. Such a perception is characterized by envy, jealousy, gossip, calumny, and invidious competition (Foster 1965). Japan's success today owes much to this competitive mentality.

Japanese leaders' authority is sustained by the "might is right" ideology, severe punishment of nonconformers, the collective responsibility principle, and an elaborate system of espionage. Yakuza, crime syndicate members, who control gay quarters, traditionally function as spies for the police. Today, such espionage has been mostly replaced by *sōgo kanshi* (mutual surveillance) (Sugimoto 1990) and *kōban* (the neighborhood police box), whereby detailed information on all residents of a neighborhood is collected by the government. Such methods are very effective because of strong informal sanctions, as exemplified by the case of a 17-year-old girl. Her family was ostracized when she wrote to a newspaper about a dishonest campaign in a village election. The power of informal sanction, with its intimidation tactic, is demonstrated in the following description of a local election (*"Tensei Jingo," Asahi Shimbun,* reprinted in *Kashu Mainichi,* April 25, 1987):

An election without alternatives to choose from is the primary characteristic of local Japanese politics. Occasionally, some opponent shows his intention to compete. Then, behind the scenes, local bosses induce those who have influence upon the person to dissuade him from running, on the grounds that in the contested situation it is obvious who votes for whom, and this disturbs the community peace. Anybody who disturbs the community harmony is an enemy to other people. So, the prospective candidate is told that if he wants to stay in the community, he should not run. Very few Japanese can defy such pressure, because to do so is tantamount to inviting ostracism, and can lead to suicide in that tightly knit community.

In Japan, especially in rural areas, who votes for whom is almost predetermined, because people vote on the basis of personal connection rather than on issues. Consequently, it is easy for the prospective candidate to count how many votes he would get. Such considerations discourage him from an "absurd" attempt to disturb the community. [p. 1]

Interacting with formal and informal social sanctions is personality, characterized by a lack of self-confidence, strong dependency need, suppressed aggression, and pessimism. The lack of self-confidence and dependency need are indicated by two studies conducted by Irwin Mahler. In one (1974), he uses Levinson's IPC Control Scale to compare a Japanese university sample of 109 women and 59 men with an American university sample of 61 women and 59 men who were attending Japanese universities. His finding was that the Japanese university students scored significantly lower on the "I" scale (occurrences are seen as controlled by the individual himself) than did the American students. The mean score on "C" (controlled by chance or fate) was significantly higher for Japanese students. Although there was no significant difference as a whole, on "P" (controlled by powerful others), Japanese women were found to perceive things as "being controlled by powerful others" to a much higher degree than did the Japanese men, American men, or American women.

In another study (1976), Mahler compared 345 Japanese university students (160 females and 185 males) with 75 American university students (37 females and 38 males) who were living in Japan, using of the Tennessee Self-Control Scale, in terms of self-feelings (identity, self-satisfaction, and behavior) and of self-description from an external frame of reference (the physical self, the moral self, the personal self, the family self, and the social self). The difference between the median scores of the two samples were significant in all categories at the .01 level of the test. Mahler concludes that the Japanese subject sees himself as "less adequate than the American subject sees himself" and is "a highly guarded and defensive individual who does not wish to reveal himself to others." The external locus of control and the lack of self-confidence point to dependency syndrome *(amae),* which Takeo Doi (1962) calls the key to understanding Japanese culture and personality.

Along with the dependency need, authoritarianism produces suppressed aggression. Ralph White and Ronald Lippitt (1953) found that authoritarian social relationships are associated with "much hostility and aggression, including aggression against scapegoats," "discontent that does not appear on the surface," "more dependence and less individuality than in a democratic situation," and "less group-mindedness and less friendliness" (p. 581). The first three clearly apply to Japan, but the last may not appear to do so, because Japanese are generally known for group-mindedness and friendliness. However, the apparent group-mindedness and friendliness may be defensive, more rooted in dependency need than in affection and mutual understanding.

Authoritarianism produces pessimism and mistrust. The Japanese premier's office compared Japanese and American youths from 18 through 24 years old. In contrast to 16 percent of American youth who thought that "Man is by nature evil," 33 percent of Japanese thought so. While only 10 percent of American youths "had no friend whom they could trust," 23 percent of Japanese said so. In contrast to 62 percent of the American subjects who were "satisfied with their society," only 26 percent of the Japanese felt this way. While 51 percent of the American youth believed that "their nation protects adequately their welfare and rights," only 11 percent of Japanese youth believed this (Kurihara 1981, p. 177).

A pessimistic view of social resources is strengthened by defensive egoism, as shown by the general indifference toward the poor and weak, which is quite marked among the Japanese. Shichihei Yamamoto even says that Japanese can bestow "kindness" upon others, but they cannot really "sympathize" (1990, p. 20). When Japanese do something good they seem to be more concerned with the reward than with behavior itself. I feel that even when Japanese are sympathetic to a victim, they usually are not confident of helping him, because they are not educated to be resourceful. Japanese people are aware of this inclination toward defensive egoism, which they call *shimaguni konjō* ("insular mentality"). Because of this inclination, they tend to view their equals as competitors rather than as friends. The projection of this attitude onto others makes people in trouble feel more pessimistic.

Ideally, Japanese authoritarianism is ameliorated by the familistic emphasis on cooperation for family goals and ties. The child-role persons are supposed to be protected by their parent-role persons. Therefore, in the ideal situation, Japanese authoritarianism is not as despotic as authoritarianism in other Asian countries. The Japanese leader is not generally a talented planner and organizer, as is the Western leader. He is a coordinator of the ideas and works that his subordinates provide, and his subordinates are relatively free in performing their tasks, as long as they are on good terms with the superior. The emphasis on family goals and ties not only softens but also strengthens authoritarian control, because the subordinates cannot resist the authority of their "parent," who is supposed to be always concerned with the child's welfare.

Traditionalism

Despite external pressures upon Japan to be democratized, the Japanese government makes great effort to maintain authoritarian familism. In order to catch up with Western powers, Japan has to learn technology from Western cultures, but, Japanese are "Westernized" in technology in order to maintain their tradition. Since Japanese history has not produced the value of the suprasocietal their concept of the ideal society is the established social order under the emperor; people should be happy playing their proper roles under governmental directions. Today the emperor may appear to be replaced by tradition as the object of worship, but the worship of their society as it is remains unchanged.

According to Professor Takeyoshi Kawashima at Tokyo University (1976) the Western legal system was adopted by the Japanese more than a century ago as a *tatemae* (front), for the purpose of rectifying the inequities of the extra-territorial rights imposed upon Japan by the Western powers. "Therefore, the Japanese leaders did not intend to adhere to the laws. Later at the expense of the masses the leaders made great effort to restore some premodern conditions of the Japanese economy for developing Japanese capitalism."

More recently, about the strength of Japanese traditionalism, Patrick L. Smith (1990) writes:

> The Fundamental Law of Education, which nominally replaced the Imperial Rescript of Education in 1947 (enacted under the pressure from American Occupational Forces) did not do much to free the educational system, which now produces generations of Japanese shockingly ignorant of the recent past, and far less open to outside ideas than local fashion and worldly habits might suggest. In conversations with visiting business executives, I am often tempted to define the emperor as the ultimate import-bearer.

The ignorance of the recent past (e.g., World War II) is to be expected from Japanese thinking, which is characterized by a lack of historical objectivity. Japanese history is the one that is written from their present-time point of view (Yamamoto 1987). In the Japanese mind, there is no historical fact, as separated from the perceiving mind. Japanese phenomenalism accepts "nothing but the concrete demonstration which can be seen by eyes and taken in hand" (Nakamura 1964).

The lack of historical objectivity is the other side of situational realism, with which Ruth Benedict (1946) characterized Japanese thinking. *Situational realism* is the tendency to regard the situation in which a person is placed as the only reality; accordingly, preceding situations in which he was involved in the past (i.e., "historical facts" to Westerners) are no longer real or factual. To them, history is not a series of facts against which the present is examined. Past events are interpreted by the present necessity. If the past is in conflict with the present convenience, the past must be changed. Such a view of the past appears to contradict traditionalism. Traditionalism, however, means that the worship of tradition is an attribute of the ego, which examines past incidents and changes them according to what the ego considers to be the most favorable past.

Traditionalism is also shown by the Japanese view of cultural relativism. In contrast to American thinkers who advocate the concept for preventing their own ethnocentrism, Japanese scholars welcome cultural relativism because it enables them not only to maintain their ethnocentrism but also to take advantage in trade competition. A Kyoto University professor of economics holds:

> When challenged by culture and practices outside the Western tradition, increasingly the impulse among Americans and Europeans is to condemn what is non-Western as unethical and unfair. It is against this background of rising anti-cultural relativism among European and American opinion leaders that trade conflicts have gained momentum. With such a philosophical conservatism on the loose, it might be unrealistic for us to expect the understanding of our culture, and our social structure and custom. [Van Wolferen 1989, p. 293]

Cultural relativism is generally accepted as ethical relativism, that is, each culture has its own ethical principle and should not be evaluated by the outsider from his own cultural point of view. Thus, American intellectuals tend to accept Japanese culture in toto, rather than study both positive and negative aspects of the culture (e.g., prejudice). If ethical relativism is correct, we should not criticize apartheid or Nazism. Some form of transcultural value seems to be necessary for world peace, and it seems to be accepted unconsciously by most American cultural relativists.

Another view of cultural relativism is more compatible with the concept of transcultural value, whereby any culture may be studied objectively. It is the Sapir-Whorf Hypothesis, that is, that a language, like the larger culture of a society, shapes its people's perception of the world. From this point of view, we have to explain Japanese behavior only in terms of Japanese culture, but "openness" should be, as Allan Bloom (1987) says, the "openness to study" rather than "openness to accept." Bloom continues, "Openness used to be the virtue that permeated us to seek the good by using reason . . . it now means accepting everything and denying reason's power. Science's latest attempt to grasp the human situation — cultural relativism, historicism, the fact-value distinction — are the suicide of science" (p. 38). The suicide of science means the suicide of democracy, because, as Dewey says, "democracy is the political manifestation of scientific method." (Archambault 1964, p. xvii)

On the grounds of ethical relativism, Japanese stress the idea of value-free science and statistical correlation studies because as long as Americans do not delve into motivation, the Japanese can enjoy their advantage in trade competition. Motivation is explained only through sensing the nuances of nomothetic (statistical, behavioral, cognitive) data. This sensing requires the understanding of value-orientation. Japan's basic advantage in trade conflict is the motivation of its people by Nihonkyo in contrast to American individualism, which turns on laissez-faire capitalism.

Accommodationism

The greatest concern of the Japanese government is social order under the emperor. The primary objective of Japanese education is to produce people of

"Japan spirit; Western skills" *(wakon yōsai)*. Their tradition of "Let people depend; don't let them know" *(yorashimu-beshi; shirashimu-bekarazu)* still dictates Japanese education. In their traditionalism, there is a mechanism that keeps change in nontechnical areas to the minimum. This mechanism is accommodationism, the combining of new and old ideas without attempting logical integration.

Accommodationism is what makes the Westerner's understanding of Japanese culture extremely difficult. The best example is the discrepancy between *tatemae* (what they say, e.g., democracy) and *honne* (what they feel and do, e.g., prejudice). *Tatemae* is shown when the Japanese wish to look good in the eyes of the social superior. Professor Jun Eto (1990) of the Tokyo Institute of Technology explains:

> When we speak to foreigners, often we still speak *tatemae* (false front). Sometimes we feel relatively relaxed, free to make any kind of comment or speech (i.e., *honne*), but in the face of criticism, we suddenly shrink and begin hiding ourselves (in *tatemae*). [*Newsweek,* April 2, 1990, p. 20]

The *tatemae–honne* discrepancy does occur among Americans, too, as shown, for example, by the expression, "off the record." Americans, however, tend to pride themselves on moral integrity. The agreement between speech and action is perceived to be an indication of maturity. In contrast, the mature Japanese is the one who moves between *tatemae* and *honne* freely, depending on the situation. It seems very difficult for Americans to understand that the discrepancy is normal in Japan. When Professor Hiroshi Wagatsuma (1987) of UCLA explained the *tatemae* and *honne* to Americans, their response was typified by the statement: "It is very strange that what a person says and what he does is so different. If the juxtaposition is true among Japanese people, they must be schizoid or hypocritic" (p. 137).

Although the *tatemae–honne* discrepancy appears similar to Leo Festinger's concept of cognitive dissonance, there is an important difference. According to Festinger, if there is a conflict between beliefs and the facts to which these beliefs pertain, and the facts cannot be adjusted to the beliefs, or the beliefs cannot be abandoned, the tendency is for people to isolate themselves from the facts. This cognitive dissonance functions as a psychological defense against frustration. In contrast, among the Japanese the juxtaposition of contradictory ideas does not constitute a psychological defense, because they are, for the most part, unaware of the contradiction between *tatemae* and *honne*. The Japanese are generally not concerned with the definition of abstract terms, such as democracy and authoritarianism, as their thinking is characterized by intuitionism.

When people are frustrated by a discrepancy between concepts and make an attempt to integrate them logically, the effort leads to psychological stress. Such stress is seen in the discrepancy between an ideal (e.g., transcendental value) and a reality, leading to social instability and then change. This is the source of Western civilization. The highest value in Japan, however, is not a transcendental value but the established social order and, therefore, the Japanese do not experience frustration from the discrepancy between a transcendental ideal and actual society.

Thus far we have seen that despite the Westernization of Japan, rationalism is not applied fully to social and behavioral problems. As a result of a lack of rationalistic and humanistic development, suicide has not been an object of rational inquiry. About ten years ago, when the International Congress of Suicide Prevention asked Dr. Kichinosuke Tatai, Japan's representative to WHO, about holding a conference in Japan, he replied that Japanese companies would not sponsor such a conference because they do not see its necessity.

Change

In the 1960s Japanese psychiatrists and psychologists visited the Los Angeles Suicide Prevention Center, which was headed by Edwin Shneidman, Norman Farberow, and Robert Litman. These people, especially Drs. Kenshiro Ohara and Hiroshi Inamura among others, became the core of Japanese efforts on suicide prevention, including translation of Shneidman and Farberow's publications. In 1965, Shneidman was invited to give lectures at Japanese universities and Farberow followed soon after. As a result, Japan's first suicide prevention center, called Inochi-no-Denwa, or Life Line, was opened in Tokyo under the direction of Reverend Yukio Saito in 1971. Subsequently, Professors Kanichiro Ishii and Teruchika Katsumata opened such centers in Osaka and Kumamoto, respectively.

In the beginning there was an apprehension that, because of their sense of shame, the Japanese would not reveal their troubles to strangers. However, Inochi-no-Danwa was accepted surprisingly well. In 1990, Inichi-no-Danwa was operating in thirty-three cities in Japan, with the following statistics:

Telephone counselors	4,748
trainees	1,050
Contributing members	19,752
Telephone calls in 1989 (per day)	157,573 (980)
Suicide calls in 1989 (per day)	9,313 (26)

EXPLANATION OF SUICIDE

Sociological studies of suicide place their primary focus on statistical correlation, for example, between suicide and social integration. The high suicide rate in Japan before World War II, as shown in Table 18–1, is explained in terms of high social integration under authoritarian familism conducive to altruistic and fatalistic suicides in Durkheimian terms. The extremely high suicide rates among Japanese females in comparison with American females (e.g., 16.0 vs. 6.9 in 1930 and 18.1 vs. 6.0 in 1980) indicate strong sexism. During war time, suicide rates are low. The high rates in 1955 and 1960 are attributed to a temporary anomie (declining social integration) caused by sudden prosperity thanks to the Korean War. Anomie produces a wide end–means discrepancy.

TABLE 18-1.

CHANGES IN SUICIDE RATES IN JAPAN AND THE UNITED STATES, BY SEX

	Japan				U. S.		
	Total	Male	Female		Total	Male	Female
1987	15.3	20.8	10.0				
1985	19.5	26.3	13.0				
1980	17.7	22.3	18.1	(1979)	12.1	18.5	6.0
1975	18.0	21.4	14.6		12.7	18.9	6.8
1970	15.3	17.3	13.3		11.5	16.7	6.5
1965	14.7	17.3	12.2		11.1	16.8	6.1
1960	21.6	25.1	18.2		10.6	16.5	4.9
1955	25.2	31.5	19.0		10.2	16.0	4.6
1950	19.6	24.1	15.3		11.4	17.8	5.1
1945	–	–	–		11.2	17.2	5.8
1940	13.7	16.5	11.0		14.4	21.9	6.8
1935	20.5	25.1	15.8		14.3	21.7	6.8
1930	21.6	27.2	16.0		15.6	24.1	6.9
1925	20.5	25.1	15.9		12.0	18.0	5.8
1920	19.0	23.3	14.7		10.2	14.5	5.7
1915	19.2	24.6	18.9		16.2	24.3	7.6
1910	19.1	24.0	14.0		15.4	23.0	7.2
1905	17.4	21.4	13.2		13.5	20.2	6.8
1901	17.7	21.8	18.5		10.4	15.5	5.3

Source: *Jisatsu Shibo Tokei* (Ministry of Welfare) 1984, p. 78. Keisatsu-cho, Hoanbu, Bohan Kikaku-ka. 1986, p. 6.

Recent rise in suicide rates may be attributed to increasing suicides among males of middle ages (Table 18-2). The rise for the 40–49 age group since 1982 is remarkable, especially in contrast to the decline of the rates for young people (aged 20–24). The rise is explained by Hiroshi Inamura (1990), first of all, in terms of the conflict between the still strong dependency need *(amae)* among the middle-aged males and the necessity of independence required to function in more democratic institutions (e.g., requirement of achievement necessary more for promotion than before). Second, the greater probability of isolation of middle-aged males from the close mother–child relationship, accentuated by work stress, illness, mental disorder, cultural views of life and death. Still the sense of shame and obligation, or the hatred of the ugliness of old age, seem to exert a strong influence upon the dissatisfied Japanese man. His isolation from his family members is largely due to long working hours and *tanshin funin*. *Tanshin funin*, which one in about every six workers in Japan experiences, is the transfer of a worker to a new place of work, where he sets up his residence alone while his wife and children stay in Tokyo, where schools are better for entrance examination purposes.

In addition to social integration, economic difficulty plays an important

TABLE 18-2.

CHANGE IN SUICIDE RATES FOR YOUTH AND MIDDLE AGE GROUPS IN JAPAN BY SEX

	All Ages		20–24		30–39		40–49	
	Male	Female	Male	Female	Male	Female	Male	Female
1987	—	—	20.8	10.0	—	—	—	—
1985	26.3	13.0	19.9	8.7	25.3	10.3	42.5	14.4
1984	27.9	13.2	22.4	9.5	28.0	11.1	46.3	14.2
1983	29.1	13.3	24.5	11.0	30.2	18.9	48.8	14.6
1982	23.4	12.6	22.9	9.9	26.0	11.7	37.1	13.3
1981	22.0	12.4	6.7	4.9	19.3	15.4	22.3	14.7
1980	22.8	18.1	7.6	5.7	20.0	14.8	21.1	14.3
1975	21.4	14.6	26.0	16.4	24.7	13.3	27.4	13.5
1970	17.3	13.3	18.8	16.2	18.8	11.9	17.3	11.5
1965	17.3	12.2	23.3	18.8	16.9	10.9	18.1	10.3
1960	25.1	18.2	58.7	44.0	20.8	17.5	21.2	14.7
1955	31.5	19.0	84.1	46.8	27.4	17.1	27.9	15.7
1950	24.1	15.3	44.0	27.8	23.4	15.3	28.4	16.7
1940	16.5	11.0	23.6	17.8	18.1	12.4	21.0	14.6
1930	27.2	16.0	44.3	31.3	28.7	17.5	41.3	18.4

Source: for 1980–1985: Keisatsu-cho Hoanbu Bohan Kikaku ka, 1986.
for 20–24 age group in 1930–1967: Kosaka and Usui, 1966, p. 33;
for 1930–1965: average of 30–34 and 35–39 groups and 40–44 and 45–49 groups:
Jisatsu Shibo Tokei, 1986, p. 22.

part in Japanese suicide. Much of the above-mentioned work stress and mental disorder among middle-aged males likely involve actual or expected economic difficulty. Table 18-3 indicates that higher suicide rates occur among those in occupations with low or unstable income: mining (130.5 for males; 611.8 for females) and agriculture and fishing (55.4 for males; 32.8 for females), followed by services (30.5 for males). In contrast, the lowest rates are found among those in professional-technical occupations (18.1 for males, 6.0 for females) and managerial fields (22.0 for males, 18.8 for females).

The importance of economic difficulty alone, however, does not sufficiently explain suicide, since such difficulty is perceived differently by individuals. The effort to find intervening factors between suicide and social structure is shown in Table 18-4. The focus is placed on institutional goals and means, perceived conditions, the degree and quality of social interaction, and psychological states.

The ultimate cause of suicide depends, of course, on the situation of the individual involved, with these three basic elements being common to all cases: (1) too wide an end–means discrepancy (e.g., between one's ego-ideal and self-concept), (2) rigid social conditions, and (3) a lack of alternative means from which to choose for problem solving or tension reduction. The objective of psychological autopsy (Shneidman 1981, Weisman 1974) is to gain insight into

TABLE 18-3.

Suicide and Occupation

	(1985)	
	Male	*Female*
Total	34.1	9.9
Professional; Technical	18.1	6.0
Managerial	22.0	18.8
Clerical	21.6	4.9
Sales	25.2	9.0
Agriculture; Fishing	55.4	22.8
Mining	130.5	611.8
Transportation; Communication	27.3	25.7
Craftsman	19.7	6.3
Hoan (Security)	19.7	91.3
Service	30.5	9.0

Source: Inamura, Hiroshi, *Chu-Kōnen no Jisatsu.* (Suicide of Middle-Aged and Old Japanese), Kyoto: Dohosha, 1990, p. 15.

the relationship among goals, means, conditions, social interaction, and personality of the individual concerned.

Social meaning, obtained by a definition of the situation, is one of the major interests in sociological tradition, as shown in the works of Max Weber (Protestant ethic), W. I. Thomas (definition of the situation), Charles Cooley (the looking-glass self), G. H. Mead (the social self), P. A. Sorokin (altruism), Talcott Parsons (action frame of reference), and others. With reference to suicide, Jack D. Douglas (1967) is concerned with the motivation that is inferred from suicidal definitions of the situation, for example, death for the purpose of a better post-self, for changing one's image in the mind of significant others, for achieving fellow feelings, or for getting revenge.

Shneidman (1980) focuses his attention on the ingredients of the definition of the situation, such as whether the personality of the individual involved is characterized by inimicality (acting against one's own adjustment and adaptation), perturbation (frightened, depressed, agitated reaction), constriction (tunnel vision), and the idea of death. He combines psychological inquiry with the sociological stress on meaning in a personological-contextualist perspective.

A case of *oyako shinju* (parent–child suicides in Japan; murder-suicide in the United States) involving a Japanese woman will be explained with reference to sociocultural factors that affect the individual's perception of conditions to adjust to, and of the range of social resources available.

In 1950, there were 316 *oyako shinju* reported in Japanese newspapers. During the period from 1946 to 1972, there were 288 mother–child/children, 55 father–child/children, and 49 parents–child/children suicides in the city of Tokyo alone (Inamura 1990). In the case of *shinju* that occurred in Oigawa in 1979, nine

TABLE 18-4.

PSYCHOCULTURAL COMPONENTS OF DURKHEIM'S TYPES OF SUICIDE

	Egoistic	Altruistic	Fatalistic	Anomic
A. Cultural regulation				
1. Goal	Self-oriented with a philosophical principle	Collectivism	Accommodation of individual goal to groupism	Self-profit-oriented
Means	Nonconformance	Conformance	Conformance	Inconsistency
B. Interactional cohesion:				
1. Social restraint (e.g. obligation)	Weak; effort to deny	Strong	Strong	Declining
2. Demands, self-expression	Self-oriented—high	Group goal—high	Low	High for self-profit
3. Meaningful communication	Low	High	Low	Declining
C. Psychological indications	Desire for meaning of life, obtainable only by social attachment (212); Nonconforming value vs. unconscious wish for sympathy (211); loss of the will to live; depression and melancholy (214)	Sense of obligation and the state of impersonality (223); mystical joy (233); shame and guilt	Excessive physical and moral despotism, sense of "future pitilessly blocked and passions violently choked" (276); resentment, fear, resignation	Wider goal—means discrepancy (246); sense of relative deprivation (253); inflated ego ideal and dependency; insecurity, greed, feverish imagination, disillusionment jealousy (253)

The numbers refer to pages in Emile Durkheim's Suicide: A Study in Sociology, 2nd ed., trans. J. A. Spaulding and G. Simpson Glencoe, IL: Free Press, 1958.

Source: M. Iga, The Thorn in the Chrysanthemum: Suicide and Economic Success in Modern Japan. Berkeley: University of California Press, 1986, p. 10.

persons died, including parents, a grown-up son, his wife, three grown-up daughters, and two small grandchildren.

In the United States, there were three cases of *oyako shinju,* involving Japanese women during the period from 1985 through 1989 (two took place in California and one in Hawaii). One of the California cases involved Fumiko K. She was a gentle woman and a devoted mother, but she walked into the Pacific Ocean off Santa Monica, taking her infant daughter and 4-year old son with her. They were pulled from the water by passers-by; she survived but the children died. Charged with murder, Fumiko told the police that she took them because she loved them. The tragedy occurred ten days after Fumiko learned that her husband, a Japanese-born restaurateur, had had a mistress for 3 years. The mistress telephoned to let Fumiko know that she was going to be divorced.

Fumiko's act, beyond most Americans' comprehension, made headlines in the United States. The incident raised such questions as why the prospect of being divorced led the woman to attempt suicide, how she could have killed the children because "she loved them," and why she had not become socialized to American attitudes toward divorce, infanticide, and social services, since she had lived in the United States for more than 14 years. I will attempt to answer these questions in terms of environmental and personality factors.

Social Resources and Isolation

The primary factor that would have affected Fumiko's decision to commit suicide was the threat of divorce. Divorce deprives most Japanese women of their future security almost entirely. There is very little government protection for the divorcée. There is strong prejudice against the female in employment, and especially against the divorcée. The divorcée is usually blamed for the marital failure on the grounds that she could not satisfy her husband's needs. Such prejudice makes it extremely difficult for a divorced woman in Japan to find respectable self-supporting employment. The employment most often available to her is part-time work in a subcontracting firm, which means a very low income or work in the entertainment business (such as waitress, hostess, barmaid, and so on), from which income is unstable. In many cases these women have to supplement their income by selling sexual favors. Further, the strong social stigma attached to the divorcée means that she is usually not welcome to move in with her parents. Japanese people are usually not well-to-do enough to welcome an additional member to the household, and housing is mostly too crowded.

Social resources that may be available for tension reduction and problem solving are limited for the Japanese divorcée. Japanese people are generally afraid of being involved in other people's trouble. They are not usually trained to be resourceful enough to help themselves, much less others. Fumiko would have carried this attitude to the United States, consequently assuming that all people are unreliable. Also marked among the Japanese is their dislike of revealing their own troubles to others, despite their strong dependency need. Their sense of shame is still strong.

Fumiko's language difficulty prevented her from having a close association with Americans, whether Caucasian or Japanese. She was geographically and socially isolated from other Japanese. Such isolation implies difficulty in releasing tension and in learning about social resources. Fumiko lived in an area where few Japanese lived. There might have been other Japanese living in the general area of her residence. As it is in Japan, however, the Japanese community in the United States is socially segregated. One's informal associations are generally limited to same-status people. For example, employees of large Japanese firms, who are for the most part well-educated, and their family members do not associate with people who are less educated and who hold lower-status jobs. Fumiko's husband was a co-owner of a small Japanese restaurant, and she had very little intimate association with other Japanese.

In addition to the sociocultural factors contributing to Fumiko's attempted suicide, together with the accepting attitude of death and suicide, there is another cultural factor to be taken into account in her killing of her children — prejudice against orphans. Without parental love, protection, and supervision, orphans are regarded as unreliable, especially where money is concerned. (The fatherless family is usually associated with financial insecurity in Japan, where sexual prejudice is very strong in employment.) Orphans are not usually hired by such institutions as banks. Employers screen out such undesirable applicants through preemployment investigation conducted by private detective firms (kōshinsho) (Hayashida 1975). Knowing that the children will suffer from prejudice, the mother believes it is best for her to take the children with her in death. The mother who leaves her children behind in a suicide attempt is viewed as a "demon-like person" (oni no yōna hito) (Ohara 1965, p. 284).

The expected prejudice against orphans intensified Fumiko's emotional identification with her children. The Japanese mother generally experiences strong emotional identification with her child. It is often the most symbiotic mother–child relationship, stemming from their frequent physical contact and from the usual absence of the father from the home. The relationship is further strengthened by the formal, often cold relationship between Japanese husband and wife. When a man with strong dependence upon his generally indulgent mother becomes a husband and father, he may become a rival of his child, competing for his wife's attention and care. Since Japanese women have little opportunity for satisfying their desire for self-development, mothering is often the only channel available for this purpose. The extremely strong identification between mother and child is intensified by the general mistrust of outsiders — the idea that the child is safe only under maternal protection.

Personality

In addition to the expected loss of security following divorce and the perceived lack of social resources, the third factor in the Japanese murder-suicide is the mother's personality. Dr. Inamura found *oyako shinju* to be associated with schizophrenia, epilepsy, hysteria, and depression. According to the information I gathered from Fumiko's friends and social workers, she probably would not have scored particularly higher than most Japanese women on any of these items, with the possible exception of depression. Depression in times of severe difficulty is expected among normal Japanese women, who generally are socialized not to be self-confident, as Mahler's studies show. The extreme attractiveness of Japanese women, which many American males idolize, seems to be largely rooted in their strong dependency need. Depression, thus, seems to be a natural product of the situation rather than of Fumiko's personality.

A suicidal definition of the situation is made, according to Shneidman, by people whose personality tends toward inimicality and constriction (attitudes), perturbation (sentiment), and the idea of death (internalized value). Inimicality is an important factor in Japanese suicide—for example, nonconforming behavior, including argumentativeness, in a woman may become inimical to her adjustment-adaptation. Fumiko did not, however, show any nonconforming trait, except in her self-destructive action itself. Her suicide seems to have been caused by a misfortune of being married to a man who had an extramarital affair and who wished to divorce her.

There is another case in which misfortune played an important role in a suicide. A young lecturer at a Tokyo university killed his student mistress who had become pregnant. After the murder, he told a friend that the body, which he had buried deep in a mountain, would never be discovered.

He confided further that the young woman would have been happy to be killed by him because she loved him. When the body was found and he was discharged from the university, his wife begged him to commit *shinju* (family suicides). He complied, and the couple killed their two children before committing their double suicide. Why did the wife beg for *shinju?* One explanation is that Japanese people are harsh to the family members of a criminal. They are, in general, more concerned with their own honor and security than with the needs of others. Thus, we can say that the wife's suicide was caused not by inimicality but by her desire for "honor of her post-self" or for the avoidance of the sufferings she expected would befall her and her children.

Returning to Fumiko, a more important cause of her decision to choose suicide was constriction or tunnel vision. The adjustment to a new culture depends, at least partly, on intellectual curiosity. The Japanese as a whole lack such curiosity, and this lack is a product of their education. They are not eager to learn foreign ideas even if they are living in a new culture. Like many Japanese who have moved from Japan to the United States, Fumiko did not learn much about the American attitude toward life, including social welfare services, even though she had lived in this country for more than 14 years before her suicide attempt.

This lack is due to a basic attitude among Japanese toward socialization, as an American woman who is married to a Japanese farmer says:

It would not be what you want to do but what you have to do and what's expected
of you. What you're expected to do at this time, what you're expected to say at this
time, how far you're supposed to bow. Sometimes I feel sorry for the Japanese in
a way, because they can't express themselves, they can't say things they really want
to say. [Interviewed by Judy Woodruff, "Frontline," PBS, 1988, #611]

The lack of intellectual curiosity is shown even by university students.
Considering that intellectual curiosity is associated with reading, it is not
surprising to learn that Japanese people usually do not read. According to a
survey conducted by the All Japan University Students Life Cooperative Union
of 7,468 students nationwide in 1990, "the average reading time dropped from
44 minutes a day in 1987 to 33 minutes a day. A third of the students said they
hardly spent any time reading at all" (Survey in *Kashu Mainichi,* March 11, 1991).
The "33 minutes" reading may include the reading of comics, which seems to
dominates Japanese university students' life.

The stifling of the individual's wishes and feelings characterizes the
socialization of Japanese women, even those who are highly educated. The
psychiatric services of Dr. Yasuhiko Taketomo, a professor at Albert Einstein
Medical School, were sought by a 27-year-old Japanese woman who was a
graduate of an elite university in Tokyo (1986). She had married an American
and followed him to New York where they had lived for the past two and a half
years. The young woman's complaint was that she had no self-consciousness *(jiko
no ishiki),* by which she meant that she could not understand her own feelings and
act according to her own thinking.

After one hundred treatment sessions, she told Dr. Taketomo, "Now I know
rather clearly how I feel, think, and wish. I can communicate with other people,
although I still cannot express my opinion in public." She also became aware that
she "had been too concerned with how others looked at me or how I should have
behaved as a daughter of F Family. Recently, however, I came to cease changing
my action according to my judgment of how other people would think of me."
Japanese often seem to lose their human potentials in an attempt to fulfill the
roles assigned to them by their "paper" identity (e.g., "as a daughter of F
Family"). The patient was aware of her tendency to change her behavior in order
to adjust to the immediate situation for the purpose of maintaining the honor of
her family rather than of her self as an individual.

This young woman suffered from an identity crisis because of cultural
conflict, and the treatment she received allowed her to react more flexibly to
external stimuli. Through her struggle under the doctor's supervision, she came
to appreciate her own identity as a human being and to understand the idea of
freedom and responsibility, social relations, and the conflict of values. In short,
she matured, growing out of the shackles that had been imposed upon her by
Japanese culture. As Allan Bloom writes, "Man cannot remain content with what
is given them by their culture if they are to be fully human. A culture is a cave"
(1987, p. 38).

The stifling of the individual's wishes and feelings is accomplished through
education. While the objective of Western education is self-actualization, the

goal of Japanese education is to produce bureaucrats and their faithful followers. This aim is today indicated by *kanri kyōiku* (managed education) *seikatsu shidō* (life guidance), and textbook censorship.

Kanri kyōiku is the strict control of students' behavior inside and outside school. Even matters that would seem very trivial to Americans — for example, the color of socks that students wear — are important in Japan, because Japanese leaders believe that every aspect of behavior indicates an individual's personality. Textbooks are aimed primarily at preparing students to become loyal conformers and/or to pass the entrance examination. Although severe entrance examinations are not unique to Japan, the emphasis on rote memorization at the expense of questioning and discussion seems to be. "The shocking ignorance of the recent past" among young Japanese, as mentioned earlier, is due, in part, to governmental censorship of textbooks and, in part, to the omitting of undesirable information by teachers (e.g., detailed information about World War II). The excuse given for the omissions is that there is no time for them, since such information is not required for entrance examinations.

The stress on rote memorization sacrifices the student's ability to relate learning to both a worldview and daily problems, and it encourages intuitive knowledge rather than rational analysis. Scientific attitudes are emphasized in the physical sciences but not as much in the social sciences because of the many taboos, including the emperor system, minority group relations, and others. Nonconforming students are punished physically or otherwise by their peers (called *ijime*) and by teachers. Sometimes physical punishment results in suicide, murder, or mental disorders.

Such an education inevitably produces constriction, particularly in females, who are objects of strong sexual prejudice. The primary virtue of Japanese people is *propriety,* or playing the proper roles, and female roles center around the principle of service to males. A female graduate from an elite university must start her employment by serving tea to male co-workers; her primary role is to make working conditions more comfortable for males. It is commonly believed in Japan that when the woman speaks out the family disintegrates and the nation declines. Although Japanese women appear to behave more freely nowadays, their thinking does not seem to have changed as rapidly as their appearance has.

Constriction produces perturbation because it prevents the development of self-confidence, adequate self-expression, and communication skills. When Japanese live abroad, social isolation is likely due to the general lack of intellectual curiosity and of adequate communication skills, as shown in Fumiko's *oyako shinju.* Dr. Hiroshi Inamura has observed the susceptibility of Japanese in foreign countries to mental disorders and suicide (1980).

CONCLUSION: THE FUTURE
OF SUICIDE PREVENTION IN JAPAN

My assumption is that the concern with suicide is humanistic, related to the belief in man's capability to develop his potential (e.g., reason, love, self-expression, health) by his own reasoning. Japanese tradition is authoritarian familism, with the primary concern being social order and international competition at the expense of individual welfare and development. Consequently, Japanese people traditionally showed little intellectual interest in suicide.

Since the defeat in World War II, the Japanese are changing their attitude toward suicide, primarily because of their democratization. They have absorbed American theories and practices of suicide prevention. A result is a surprisingly fast development of suicide prevention effort.

The further development of suicide prevention is necessary due to the high degree of anxiety and insecurity among Japanese people, a result of the accelerating intensity of the examination hell (shiken jigoku) for youths and work stress for middle-aged males.

An explanation of Japanese suicide needs deep understanding of their culture, as the case of parent–child deaths (oyako shinju) showed. Statistical correlational studies are necessary for comparative purposes, but, as Dr. Shneidman says, "sensing the nuances of nomothetic (statistical, behavioral, cognitive) data is necessary for studying suicide in foreign culture, and this is done only by ideographic, intuitive, psychological explanation." Social meanings attached to self-destructive behavior are understandable only by personolgical-contextualist approaches to suicide.

REFERENCES

Archambault, R. D., ed. (1964). John Dewey on Education: Selected Writings. Chicago: University of Chicago Press.

BenDasan, I. (1971). !Nihonjin to !Yudayajin (The Japanese and the Jew). Tokyo: Kodansha.

Benedict, R. (1946). The Chrysanthemum and the Sword. Boston: Houghton Mifflin.

Bloom, A. (1987). The Closing of the American Mind. New York: Simon and Schuster.

Doi, T. (1962). Amae: a key concept for understanding Japanese personality structure. In Japanese Culture: Its Development and Characteristics, ed. R. Smith and R. K. Beardsley, p. 132. Chicago: Aldine.

Edman, I. (1965). John Dewey. Indianapolis, IN: Bobbs-Merrill.

Eto, J. (1990). In Newsweek, April 2, p. 20.

Foster, G. M. (1965). Peasant society and the image of limited good. American Anthropologists 67:293–315.

Gluck, C. (1985). Japan's Modern Myth: Ideology in the Late Meiji Period. Princeton, NJ: Princeton University Press.

Hori, I. (1968). Folk Religion in Japan: Continuity and Change. Chicago: University of Chicago Press.

Iga, M. (1986). The Thorn in the Chrysanthemum: Suicide and Economic Success in Modern Japan. Berkeley: University of California Press.

Inamura, H. (1980). Nihonjin no Kaigai Futekio (Inadaptability of Japanese in Foreign Cultures). Tokyo: NHK.

_____ (1990). Chu-Kōnen no Jisatsu (Suicide of Middle- and Old-Age Japanese). Kyoto: Dohosha.

Kawashima, T. (1976). Nihonjin no Hō-Ishiki (Legal Consciousness of Japanese People). Tokyo: Iwanami Shinsho.

Kissinger, H. (1989). Opinion section. Los Angeles Times, April 30, p. 6.

Kosaka, M., and Usui, N. (1966). Nihonjin no Jisatsu (Suicide of Japanese People). Tokyo: Sobunsha.

Kurihara, A. (1981). Gendai Seinen Ron (On Contemporary Youth). Tokyo: Chikuma Shobo.

Mahler, I. (1974). A comparative study of locus of control. *Psychologia* September, pp. 135–149.

_____ (1976). What is self-concept in Japan? *Psychologia* September, pp. 127–133.

Murray, H. A. (1938). *Explorations in Personality*. New York: Oxford University Press.

Nakamura, H. (1964). *Ways of Thinking of Eastern Peoples: India-China-Tibet-Japan*. Honolulu: East–West Center Press.

Nishida, K. (1911). *Zen no Kenkyū (A Study of Good)*. Tokyo: Iwanami Shinsho, 1988.

Ohara, K. (1965). *Nihon no Jisatsu (Suicide in Japan)*. Tokyo: Seishin Shobo.

Pepper, S. (1961). *World Hypotheses*. Berkeley, CA: University of California Press.

Riesman, D., and Riesman, E. (1967). *Conversations in Japan*. New York: Basic Books.

Saeki, S. (1987). Nihonjin o Sasaeru Mono (What supports Japanese people). *Bungei Shunju*, February.

Sansom, G. B. (1943). *Japan: A Short Cultural History*. New York: Appleton-Century-Crofts.

Shneidman, E. S. (1980). *Voices of Death*. New York: Harper & Row.

_____ (1981). The psychological autopsy. *Suicide and Life-Threatening Behavior* 11:325–340.

_____ (1985). *Definitions of Suicide*. New York: Wiley.

Smith, P. (1991). Letters from Tokyo. *New Yorker,* January 21, 1991.

Sugimoto, Y., (1990). *Nihonjin o Yameru Hōhō* (Ways to Stop Being Japanese). Tokyo: Hon no Ki.

Survey (1991). *Kashu Mainichi,* March 11, 1991.

Taketomo, Y. (1986). Haji no Ba kara Hokori no Ba e (From the field of shame to the field of pride). *Kyoiku to Igaku (Education and Medicine)* 38:36–42.

"*Tensei Jingo*" (1987). Asahi Shimbun. Reprinted in *Kashu Mainichi,* April 25, 1987, p. 1.

Umehara, T. (1987). Shinto and Buddhism in Japanese culture. *The Japan Foundation Newsletter,* Vol. 17, July.

Van Wolferen, K. (1989). *The Enigma of Japanese Power*. New York: Alfred A. Knopf.

Wagatsuma, H. (1987). *Shakai Shinrigaku Nyuumon (An Introduction to Social Psychology)*. Tokyo: Kodansha Gakujitsu Shinsho.

Weisman, A. D. (1974). *The Realization of Death: A Guide for the Psychological Autopsy*. New York: Jason Aronson.

White, R., and Lippitt, R. (1953). Leader behavior and member reaction in three social climates: authoritarian, democratic, laissez-faire. In *Group Dynamics,* ed. D. Cartwright and A. Zander, White Plains, NY: Row Peterson.

Woodruff, J. (1988). Frontline interview. PBS, #611.

Yamamoto, S. (1987). *Nihonjin no Jinseikan* (World View among Japanese People). Tokyo: Kodansha.

_____ (1990). *Hikaku Bunka-ron no Kokoromi (An Attempt for a Comparative Theory of Cultures)*. Tokyo: Kodansha.

19: SUICIDE PREVENTION IN JAPAN

Yoshitomo Takahashi

In 1965, Edwin Shneidman was invited to the sixty-second Annual Meeting of the Japanese Association of Psychiatry and Neurology held in Hiroshima to give a special lecture on suicide prevention. At the time, he was co-director of the Los Angeles Suicide Prevention Center (LASPC) and Clinical Professor of Psychiatry at the University of Southern California School of Medicine. He was also invited to visit various places throughout Japan to give lectures on this subject.

His visit marked the passage of 20 years since the end of World War II, during which Japan had made an effort to reconstruct its economy from the ruins of the war. The public's concern about mental health had gradually begun to increase. In Japan, the suicide rate was 25.7 per 100,000 in 1958, the highest in the nation's recorded history and also one of the highest suicide rates in the world. Thus, suicide prevention was a very topical subject at that time.

Many Japanese mental-health professionals still recall Shneidman's lectures vividly because of the fact that they were delivered at an opportune time. LASPC had been established in 1958, and Shneidman tried very hard to share his seven years of experience at LASPC with Japanese audiences. However, the concept of suicide prevention was not widely accepted then in Japan. Among Japanese psychiatrists, the attitude used to be, "Just as patients in surgical wards die of cancer, psychiatric patients sometimes die of suicide. Suicide cannot really be prevented." This typified the passive and resigned attitude that was prevalent. Shneidman's visit to Japan was not only timely but also provided an incentive to recognize the necessity of research on suicide and its prevention.

As a quarter of a century has now passed since Dr. Shneidman's visit to Japan, further light should be shed on some aspects of the present situation and problems associated with suicide prevention activity in Japan.

CHANGE IN SUICIDE RATE

The National Police Agency (NPA) recently reported its annual statistics of suicide (1991). From my clinical experience, I have gained an impression that the actual number of suicides is much higher than that reported by the NPA; since there is still a strong stigma against suicide, people try to conceal it if possible. However, we have to depend on the NPA's statistics, which are the only ones available for nationwide investigation (Takahashi, 1992).

Figure 19-1 shows annual changes in the numbers of suicides in Japan, and Figure 19-2, those in the suicide rate. As these figures show, the first peak for both the number and rate occurred in the 1950s, followed by stabilization, and then a second peak was observed in the mid-1980s. After 1986, when both parameters were highest, there was a downward trend. In 1990, Japan had a suicide rate of 17.8 per 100,000, similar to that in the 1960s and 1970s. Figure 19-3 shows changes in the suicide rate according to age group, and a decrease in the rate among adolescents and young adults is evident from the 1950s to the 1990s.

Needless to say, suicidal Japanese people have as many risk factors for suicide as those in other countries, including prior suicide attempts, psychiatric disorders including alcohol or substance abuse and personality disorders, lack of social support system, older age, male gender, various types of loss, physical or sexual abuse in childhood, accident proneness, family history of suicide, and exposure to other people's suicide or tragically accidental death. Taking these factors into consideration, some characteristics of suicide in Japan will be described next.

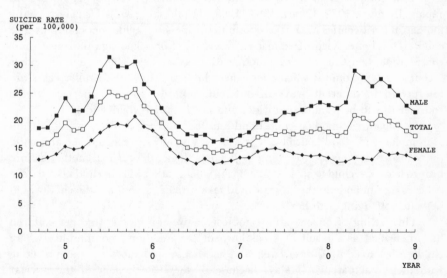

FIGURE 19-1.   Changes in Number of Suicides in Japan

NUMBER OF SUICIDES

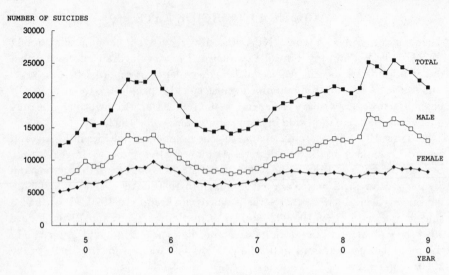

FIGURE 19-2.   Annual Changes in Suicide Rate in Japan

CHARACTERISTICS OF SUICIDE IN JAPAN

Oyako-shinju

One type of suicide in Japan, that often attracts public attention is *oyako-shinju,* or parent–child suicide, which accounts for about 5 percent of all suicides in Japan (Inamura 1977, Ohara 1963, 1965, Takahashi, 1992). Usually a young mother in her twenties or thirties commits suicide after killing her children. The children most often victimized in *oyako-shinju* are of preschool age. Japanese show considerable sympathy toward a mother who has not been able to find any other recourse but to commit suicide with her children. However, similar cases are interpreted in different ways in different cultures. Most Westerners would consider this to be a murder-suicide, and not a parent–child suicide.

In Japan, the mother–child bond and the mother's dedication to the child are emphasized. Paradoxically, it is this very bond between mother and child that causes *oyako-shinju.* According to Japanese logic, the suicidal mother cannot bear to leave the child to survive alone; she would rather kill the child because she believes that nobody in the world would take care of it, and that the child would be better off dying with her.

This feeling of oneness and symbiosis between a mother and her children has intensified as a result of breakdown of the traditional community, where children belonged to a wider circle and had fictive and substitute parents along with their real parents. Today, because of the development of the nuclear family, children, particularly those of preschool age, belong to their parents alone.

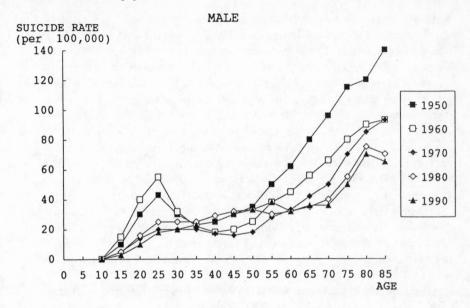

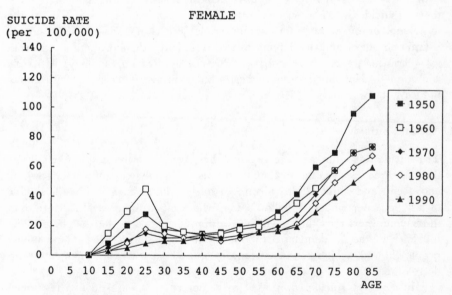

FIGURE 19-3. Changes in Suicide Rate According to Age

Inseki-jisatsu

Detailed statistics are not available for this phenomenon, and the following is my own impression.

When someone commits a crime, the people associated with him feel both shame and a desire to be protective. A good example is former Prime Minister

Kakuei Tanaka's chauffeur: he committed suicide rather than give testimony in court that might have been damaging to his boss, when Tanaka was indicted for taking bribes from the Lockheed Corporation in 1976. This type of suicide often happens in Japan (Fuse 1985, Takahashi 1991b). Although the mass media do not cover cases of suicide openly, this does not apply to this type of suicide; big articles often appear on the front pages of newspapers, reporting in detail how someone has committed suicide in order to take responsibility (*inseki-jisatsu*).

In 1991, there was a scandal involving seventeen Japanese leading securities companies, which secretly paid their most favored customers huge stock-loss paybacks. In the midst of this stock scandal, a man employed by Daichu Securities Co., who was allegedly involved in the issue of dubious accounts statements, shot himself to death (*Japan Times* 1991).

When there is an investigation for some wrongdoing, the person investigated often commits suicide, leaving a suicide note saying something like, "God knows that I did nothing wrong, but I have caused the company a great deal of trouble through this indictment. I take responsibility for it by committing suicide. I am sorry."

De Vos (1962) called this *role narcissism* or "intense identification of one's self with one's professional self" (p. 276). Role narcissism compels an individual toward suicide when a serious error in role performance is made by the individual or by another for whom the subject is responsible. The suicide committed out of guilt for having caused trouble to others through a failure in role performance combines intropunitive communication (apology) with role commitment. Not only a committed error but an anticipated error or failure may induce suicidal anxiety.

Age and Suicide

The suicide rate among young Japanese has shown a decreasing tendency over the past three decades, but in 1986 there was a sharp increase of suicides among adolescents and young adults, forming a suicide cluster triggered by the suicide of a famous pop singer, Yukiko Okada, who jumped to her death. More than thirty youngsters took their own lives within 2 weeks after her death, and the influence of the incident lasted about a year. The suicide rate among young people showed a high tendency only in this year, and since then has been decreasing.

In contrast, suicide committed by senior citizens was and is a big social problem. Although individuals aged 65 and older accounted for 12 percent of the total population of Japan in 1990, there were about 6,000 suicides in the same age group, constituting 29 percent of all suicides. According to estimates by the Ministry of Health and Welfare, the elderly population will grow to 24 percent of the total population by the year 2020, and Japanese society will become more advanced in age in the near future. Therefore, suicide by the elderly is and will be a big social problem (Takahashi 1991a, 1992, Takahashi et al. 1992).

As with parent–child suicides described earlier, the number of old couples' suicide pacts has been gradually increasing, and there were sixty such cases in 1990. Although the number is still not very high, it could become a serious problem in the near future. One such example is when an old spouse suffers from an incurable and chronically disabling disease such as senile dementia, and his or her partner also suffers from some form of illness due to advanced age. Because of the breakdown of the extended family system in Japan, such couples often do not get the support from their children or relatives that used to be the case. Neither do they want to be dependent on others. Such circumstances are made more difficult in that no adequate social system for supporting these lonely couples without recourse has yet been established. When a failing spouse with whom a partner has lived and shared his or her life can no longer function because of dementia, the other partner, usually the husband, unable to find any solution for this defeating struggle, becomes depressed and decides to kill his wife and then himself.

DEVELOPMENT OF TELEPHONE COUNSELING SERVICE

The telephone counseling service is one aspect of Japan's suicide prevention activities that has developed most over the last quarter of a century. Although the concept of volunteerism is not very popular among Japanese, the activities of telephone counseling are one of the fortunate exceptions.

Since Tokyo Inochi-no-Denwa (Life Line) was first established in 1971, such services have become available all over Japan (Inochi-no-Denwa 1991), and it has become a model for other telephone services in Japan. Tokyo Inochi-no-Denwa is a nonprofit private organization, conducting 24-hour telephone counseling. In 1990 alone, 30,545 calls were dealt with. There are 461 counselors 46 males (average age: 46.5), 415 females (average age: 50.8). Candidate counselors take a series of psychological aptitude tests and training. In addition, they have to take first-year and second-year training, about 120 hours total. After being accepted as counselors, they should undertake continuing training in supervision and post-counseling on a regular basis.

Tokyo Inochi-no-Denwa also has its own psychiatric clinic, psychological counseling service, and offers special telephone counseling by physicians about medical problems. As for legal problems, lawyers affiliated with the service offer advice.

It also accepts calls in non-Japanese languages. There are about 5,000 calls from persons of 75 nationalities besides Japanese every year. There are now plans to start a facsimile counseling service for those who are handicapped with hearing problems.

Education of lay-volunteers to become telephone counselors has several advantages. It utilizes human resources, provides up-to-date knowledge of mental illness and crisis intervention, and promotes mental health for the participants themselves. Even if the volunteers stop working as counselors, they remain core persons who can provide the general public with accurate information on mental health in the community.

PROBLEMS TO BE SOLVED IN THE FUTURE

Resistance Against Consulting a Mental Health Professional

Although the tendency has been changing gradually, there is still strong resistance among the general public against consulting a mental health professional. Japanese families are unwilling to accept the fact that one member may suffer from mental illness. They try to take care of the afflicted individual by themselves for as long as possible, and do not seek professional help until the condition has deteriorated.

People do not talk about mental illness openly, but tend to conceal the fact in the work place that someone may be suffering from a psychiatric disorder. If such a fact is known, it often becomes an obstacle to promotion or sometimes a reason for dismissal, either overtly or covertly. Because of this social stigma in general, people often miss a chance to seek professional help at an earlier stage. Therefore, more concerted efforts should be made to educate the public about mental health and the effectiveness of treatment in order to counter the stigma.

Necessity of Educational Programs Focusing on Suicide

Although a curriculum dealing with mental illness is provided at medical schools, specific education focusing on suicide risk or its prevention is inadequate. Only a few medical schools offer special lectures on suicide prevention and the treatment of the suicidal individual. But even these spare only a couple of hours for these topics in addition to other general subjects. It should be emphasized that medical students who will become core providers of accurate psychiatric knowledge should be offered proper educational programs on suicide and its prevention.

Education of General Practitioners

Murphy (1986) pointed out that the general practitioner can play an important role in detecting a patient's suicide risk at an early stage and initiating appropriate intervention for the crisis. This also applies to the present situation in Japan (Takahashi 1989). According to an unpublished survey in Japan, nearly 80 percent of depressive patients first go to general practitioners other than psychiatrists complaining of various physical symptoms, but only about a quarter of them are properly diagnosed as suffering from depression. This shows how important it is to provide the general practitioner with up-to-date knowledge of psychiatric disorders and suicide risk. Furthermore, active interaction between psychiatrists and other medical specialists should be encouraged in order to exchange opinions on suicide prevention.

School-based Suicide Prevention Program

In early 1986, a junior-high-school student who had been tormented by bullying committed suicide, triggering a suicide cluster all over Japan among other junior-high-school students with similar problems. This was followed in April of the same year by the above-mentioned jump-suicide of a pop-idol singer, prompting more than thirty young people to commit suicide within 2 weeks. When such suicide clusters occur, the mass media put out big articles about the tragedy, but no adequate countermeasures are considered, and the public's concern decreases after a couple of weeks.

School-based suicide prevention programs such as those conducted in the United States of America should be started in Japan as well, although some researchers have doubts about their efficacy (Shaffer et al. 1990). One fear in America was that talking about suicide with youngsters might prompt them to become suicidal, and this tendency is particularly strong among Japanese.

Given that there is strong resistance against a suicide prevention program for high-school students, the first step should be to educate parents or teachers on suicide risk and how to make contact with mental health professionals. Parents and teachers can play an important role as responsible adults in detecting suicide risk among children and adolescents. In addition, they can be aware of how to promote their own mental health by acquiring knowledge of suicide risk among youngsters.

Elderly Suicide

As touched upon briefly earlier, suicide by the elderly is a big problem. The proportion of the elderly population in Japan will grow by about 200 percent within the next 30 years. Japan will no longer be able to pride herself on having the longest average life span in the world if she leaves this problem unsolved.

Although the statistics show a high suicide rate among the elderly in Japan, clinicians have gained an impression that elderly patients rarely seek help from mental health professionals. The reasons for this are as follows (Takahashi 1991c, Takahashi et al. 1992).

Elderly persons often experience various forms of loss, such as unemployment, retirement, death of a friend or spouse, or physical illness. Any given elderly individual may experience multiple losses within a short period, or at the same time. Because of this, people tend to regard their depressive state as natural, especially considering the situation in which they are living. This erroneous psychological overinterpretation is made not only by persons associated with the elderly, but also the elderly themselves. Thus their depression is not considered a treatable condition so much as something that the elderly must endure.

In addition, elderly Japanese have strong resistance against seeing a psychiatrist and tend to put off asking for an appropriate psychiatric consultation.

Depressed aged patients complaining of various physical symptoms often consult doctors in disciplines other than psychiatry. However, these general physicians often lack knowledge about psychiatric disorders and tend to stick superficially to the patient's ill-defined physical symptoms. Depression, therefore, cannot be diagnosed and treated properly.

All of these circumstances lead to the tragedy that potentially temporary depression is left untreated, resulting in unnecessary suicide.

The most important aspect I would like to emphasize here is that educational programs should be started for the elderly, the general public, and physicians, providing up-to-date knowledge of psychiatric disorders and suicide risk. Opportunities should be provided for all those involved, with details of concrete warning signs of depression and suicide. We should also establish a system for identifying high-risk groups, and start treatment as soon as possible. This would also lead to elimination of the stigma associated with psychiatric disorders in the long run.

Psychological Help for Those Affected by Suicide

Ruth Benedict (1946) has called Japan a culture of shame. In such a culture the attitude of speaking about a relative's or a friend's suicide candidly cannot be recognized. If neighbors know that someone has committed suicide and his or her family or friends have difficulty in mourning, people try to avoid touching upon the subject and leave the persons concerned alone. It has been pointed out that at least five people are greatly influenced psychologically by someone's suicidal behavior. It is also reported that the suicide rate among those who have experienced the suicide of a family member or friend is much higher than that among the general public (Roy 1983). Therefore, those affected by suicide should be offered appropriate psychological help in Japan as well.

CONCLUSION

Since 1987, the suicide rate in Japan has been decreasing, but it is doubtful that this decreasing tendency will continue in the future since Japan is now going through rapid and unprecedented social changes.

The typical extended family system has been gradually collapsing and the number of nuclear families has been increasing. As women have made advances into various fields of society, the social system has been changing. The divorce rate has also been increasing. Too much emphasis is now being placed on academic performance, which accelerates the so-called examination hell. The competition for entry to prestigious universities is so keen that even elementary school pupils go to supplementary schools and study late into the night, and the rigorous examination system is now even being extended to competition for places at good grade schools or junior high schools. The gulf between the rich and the poor has also been increasing, and the incidence of substance abuse, including alcohol, stimulants, solvents, and even cocaine, has been increasing among young Japanese recently. Furthermore, with the advent of a highly aging society, suicide by the elderly is already a big problem and will become more serious in future society.

Considering these social changes, there is a great likelihood that Japan will show a rapid increase in the suicide rate in the near future. I think that the time has come for Japanese to consider once again what Shneidman advocated for suicide prevention a quarter century ago.

At the end of the symposium in 1965, the chairperson, Professor Tsuneaki Nomura of Jikei Medical University, concluded by making the following summary. His comments are still relevant and speak to the present situation regarding suicide and its prevention in Japan. I would like to conclude this chapter by citing Dr. Nomura's closing comments (Nomura 1965).

> Not much attention has been paid to suicide in Japan, compared with accidental death or death due to physical illnesses. In this symposium, all the participants have emphasized the importance of psychiatric studies on suicide.
>
> We need international cooperation in order to exchange research data and discuss suicide from the viewpoints of ethnicity, cultural background, and anthropology. . . . Today we have learned from Dr. Shneidman's lecture in particular that suicide research which has been done in the United States has not only focused on studies of suicide itself, but has also promoted practical activities aimed at suicide prevention. We must make rigorous efforts to promote interdisciplinary cooperation in order to elucidate the complicated aspects of suicide and develop practical prevention measures. . . .
>
> It is not rare for the psychiatrist to encounter a patient's suicide and experience self-guilt. We should not keep this personal guilt to ourselves, but share this painful experience with other psychiatrists, mental health professionals, and the public so that we will be able to learn from it and enlighten society in order to prevent suicide at the community level. [p. 926]

REFERENCES

Benedict, R. (1946). *The Chrysanthemum and the Sword: Patterns of Japanese Culture.* New York: New American Library.

De Vos, G. A. (1962). Suicide in cross-cultural perspective. In *Suicidal Behavior: Diagnosis and Management,* ed. H. L. P. Resnik, pp. 235–245. Boston: Little, Brown.

Fuse, T. (1985). *Suicide and Culture.* Tokyo: Shinchosha. (Written in Japanese.)

Inochi-no-Denwa (1991). *1990 Annual Report on Inochi-no-Denwa Activities.* (Written in Japanese.)

Japan Times (1991). Stock fraud suspect is found dead. July 31, p. 2.

Murphy, G. E. (1986). The physician's role in suicide prevention. In *Suicide,* ed. A. Roy, pp. 171–195. Baltimore: Williams & Wilkins.

National Police Agency (1991). *National Police Agency's 1990 Annual Report.* Tokyo: Printing Section of Ministry of Finance. (Written in Japanese.)

Nomura, T. (1965). Concluding remarks of the symposium "Suicide in Japan." *Psychiatria et Neurologia Japonica* 67:926. (Written in Japanese.)

Ohara, K. (1963). Characteristics of suicides in Japan: especially of parent–child double suicide. *American Journal of Psychiatry* 120:382–385.

_____ (1965). *Suicide in Japan*. Tokyo: Seishin-shobo. (Written in Japanese.)

Roy, A. (1983). Family history of suicide. *Archives of General Psychiatry* 40:971-974.

Shaffer, D., Vieland, V., Garland, A., et al. (1990). Adolescent suicide attempters: response to suicide-prevention programs. *Journal of the American Medical Association* 264:3151-3155.

Takahashi, Y. (1989). Suicide risk: principles of suicide prevention for general practitioners. *Medical Postgraduates* 27:164-171. (Written in Japanese.)

_____ (1991a). Seniors' suicide seen as special problem. *The Japan Times,* May 23, p. 17.

_____ (1991b). Patterns of depression and suicide in Japan. *BASH Magazine* 10:4-5.

_____ (1991c). Review: suicide in the elderly. *Suicide Prevention and Crisis Intervention* 15:122-134. (Written in Japanese.)

_____ (1992). *Clinical Evaluation of Suicide Risk and Crisis Intervention*. Tokyo: Kongo-Shuppan. (Written in Japanese)

_____ (in press). Depression and suicide. In *Affective Disorders: Perspective on Basic Research and Clinical Aspect*. ed. T. Kariya, and M. Nakagawara. New York: Brunner/Mazel.

Takahashi, Y., Onose, H., Terasaki, T., et al. (1992). Psychiatric study of suicide prevention for the elderly. *Daiwa Health Foundation Annual Report* 16:96-103. (Written in Japanese.)

SURVIVING SUICIDE
Part VIII

"Suicide is a personal and an interpersonal disaster. The moment of a disaster's happening is its most dramatic moment. But it is not its only moment."

— Edwin Shneidman

With the development of contemporary suicidology — especially during the last decade — survivors of suicide have begun to receive the professional concern and research attention that their difficult emotional experiences warrant. Part VIII presents two essays: a focus on what happens to the significant others who remain behind after the suicidal death, and a study of the lives of the survivors of suicide of ninety-three New York City policemen who killed themselves between 1934 and 1940.

20: BEREAVEMENT AFTER SUICIDE

Norman L. Farberow

The saga of suicide does not end with death; there is an aftermath. The focus of this chapter is on what happens after the death for the significant others who remain behind, engulfed in bereavement and mourning. We will focus on the significant others made up of: 1) the family, who may or may not be in treatment; 2) the therapist, in practice or in the hospital or clinic; and 3) other patients.

Webster states that bereavement is derived from *reave* or *rob* and defines it as, 1) to deprive, to rob as of life, hope, happiness; 2) to leave forlorn or destitute as by loss by death. Bereavement includes mourning, defined as the expression of grief at someone's death: to feel, or express sorrow, to lament. Mourning comes from memoir, to remember, think of, be mindful of.

It is a commonly held belief that the bereavement of a suicide is much more difficult than the bereavement after other forms of death — natural, accidental, and even by homicide. However, the comparatively few studies that have been done indicate there are relatively few differences, and that the differences that do exist may lie more in the area of intensity than kind. While problems exist in comparability of the results — in terms of methodology, kinship (loss of parents, spouses, siblings, children), time elapsed after death, use of control groups, and so forth — studies comparing suicide survivors with survivors of natural and accidental deaths have reported the same reactions of phases of shock (intense yearning and protest, disorganization and reorganization), feelings of guilt, disbelief, isolation, grief, psychological distress, depression, anger, and so forth. In addition, no differences have appeared in physical aspects, such as health effects, medication use, sleeping pill use, and so on.

PREVAILING CONCERNS

A number of accounts of survivorship of suicide have specified aspects which are significantly different, at least clinically. One of the most significant differences between suicide and other forms of death is that suicide is voluntary while the other deaths are, for the most part, involuntary (disregarding for the moment the vast array of indirect suicide behaviors). The fact that the decedent chose to die, to leave behind all loved ones, to sever irreparably all ties with family and friends, to deliver an unanswerable message, and to deprive the survivors of any opportunity to help or to change his mind, makes the fact of suicide very hard to reconcile. Some of the most frequent concerns found among survivors of all ages and all kinds of kinship are the following:

(1) *The search for "why."* This search may preoccupy the survivor to the exclusion of all other activities, driving him endlessly to explore and review, to probe and to seek, always looking for the one clue that will make the decision understandable and, hopefully, more bearable. The drive may have its roots in a need to deny the suicide or to prove it really was not a suicide, or at least to understand the rejection and to find some logic in the action so that it can be tolerated. On the one hand, the continual review of events may be positive if it helps to reach closure; but it is not helpful if it becomes an obsessional inability to let go and thus hinders the mourning.

(2) *Guilt.* These feelings are more likely to be exaggerated in suicide than in any other form of death. Thoughts ruminate in the form of "what if" and "if only," or, "Did I do everything possible to prevent the suicide?" Sometimes the survivor may project his own guilt by blaming others. When guilt does appear in a survivor in therapy, the therapist may be the one looked to for support, consolation, comfort, or even exoneration. Here, reassurance is important, but the therapist must be careful not to dismiss the guilt feelings too quickly or too lightly, for oftentimes it is a feeling that needs to be worked through. In some cases, the therapist may wonder why no guilt appears. One possible reason may be that the patient fears the therapist will agree and thus will end up feeling himself really to be blameworthy.

(3) *Stigma.* Perhaps because of religion, culture, social customs, mores, and traditions, stigma and shame are felt as a result of the suicide. Society, the survivor feels, views not only the suicide as a psychologically damaged person but also the survivor, making him feel different and frequently inferior. If the survivor is in treatment, such an attitude is of significance to the transference, for it empowers the therapist (who represents society) to sit in judgment, to forgive or to condemn, to confirm or to erase the stigma. Such power might discourage the patient from revealing his feelings, even hold him back from revealing his own personal thoughts of suicide.

(4) *Identification with the suicide, or modeling.* With the example of a suicide in front of him, especially if the suicide was an admired or prominent person, the possibility of suicide when problems become pressing or stresses become overwhelming presents itself more readily. Suicide is seen as an option for what feels, at the time, like unsolvable problems.

(5) *Trust.* The suicide affects the willingness of the survivor to trust. The resultant feelings of abandonment, unworthiness, and unlovability makes him

hesitant to commit himself to the full in any subsequent relationship, affecting not only the present but also future commitments as well. In therapy, it affects especially the transference.

(6) *Anger.* Anger may be much more frequent and more intense among the survivors of suicide than among the survivors of other forms of death, primarily because of the rejection and abandonment issues. The anger at the suicide may be intense, but may also be repressed because of the strong social mores that makes it unacceptable to be angry at the dead, or at someone who suffered so much, or at a member of the family (especially a parent or an ill spouse). Learning in therapy that such feelings are acceptable and expected allows the survivor to acknowledge the feelings, relieve his guilt over having them, and to move on in working through grief. Also, accepting the anger may allow the survivor to begin to accept and to understand better the suffering that must have led the loved one to suicide.

Marilyn Hauser (1987), a psychologist/registered nurse, lists additional special aspects of bereavement in suicide. Again, however, the reactions outlined are found in all other forms of death as well as in suicide, but not perhaps to the same degree. Hauser, drawing on her own experience after the suicide of her father, notes the following:

(1) *The death is frequently experienced as sudden and unexpected.* This may be so even when there have been repeated threats and even attempts, and is related to the need to deny and resist the fact of the suicide.

(2) *The suicide is sometimes especially violent.* Body damage, injury, and blood occur with many of the methods in suicide deaths, especially in males. Because the death occurs so often in the home, the disfigured body and gruesome scene is more often seen by family members, leaving anxiety, nightmares, intrusive memories, and other posttraumatic symptoms in the survivors.

(3) *Mourning.* The fact of a suicide death can distort the usual mourning rituals. Feelings of shame, embarrassment, and stigma among the survivors may lead to withdrawal and isolation. Friends, who otherwise would be comforting and supportive, react to the suicide with awkwardness and are less available for either emotional or practical support.

(4) *Communication.* Distorted communication patterns result from the rejection aspect. Unconscious anger can lead to blaming, scapegoating (especially in the family), separating, distancing, and causing rifts in the family. These may increase the feeling of being different and increase the feeling of shame.

Dunne (1987) has likened the symptoms found in children to those seen in children diagnosed as having PTSD. He lists the following:

(1) *Cognitive-perceptual difficulties.* These take the form of distortions, either misperception of what actually occurred or distortion of the event in the memory. There may be loss of memory for details, perceptual overgeneralizations and confusion of sequence of events (especially for children who witness the suicide or discover the body). It is worsened if the child is lied to about the nature of the death.

(2) *Foreshortened sense of the future.* The children may pessimistically believe they will die young, or will not live beyond a certain date.

(3) *Collapse of developmental accomplishments.* Regression has been related to a sense of shame, stigma, loss of sense of basic trust, withdrawal, and of being a loner. There are frequently disruptions of school performance.

(4) *Dreams and/or nightmares.* Terr (1981) describes posttraumatic play involving acting out of the traumatic events in games which include a copy of the act. Such behavior may be dangerous when carried out too realistically.

(5) *Contagion.* This may occur as the survivors become intensely caught up in suicidal ideas and fantasies.

Other symptoms listed included flashbacks of painful memories, preoccupation with death, reversal to either extremes of behavior — excessive clinging and fearfulness or growing up overnight and becoming a parent to the remaining parent.

Impact of Suicide on Caregivers

Survivors can be identified in relationships other than family, sweetheart, or lovers. Another area deserving of close attention is the special relationship that develops between caregivers and their patients or clients, whether in a hospital, clinic, or community practice. This relationship is often intense and complex in terms of therapeutic investment and personal commitment on the part of the therapist. When a suicide of patient does occur, it results in a mixed and often confused state, arousing as it does both professional and personal reactions. The feelings described by therapists who have experienced a suicide by one of their patients parallel those of kinship survivors, with grief, guilt, anger, anxiety, depression, worry, and rejection appearing in varying degrees. In addition, however, are the professional concerns of responsibility, control, self-esteem, fear of colleagues' opinions and censure, potential malpractice suits, worry about the effect on their professional reputation, and others. That the experience of a suicide by a therapist is not rare is indicated by studies reporting the frequency of patient suicides among caregivers, ranging from the prediction in an early study (Kahne 1968) that one out of every four psychiatrists will experience a suicide in his practice, through the estimate of 51 percent in a more recent study (Cherntob et al. 1988). In this survey the investigators found there was no relationship between years of practice and a suicide occurring. They also confirmed previous studies in reporting that those therapists who experience a suicide indicated symptoms similar in kind and intensity to those found in clinical groups seeking therapy. Many of the studies suggested ways in which help could be provided to the therapists, such as consultation, formal reviews, support through networking, individual or group meetings, psychological autopsies, therapist support groups and others. Unfortunately, none of these suggestions has been examined systematically to determine its effectiveness.

At the same time that the caregiver is dealing with his own reactions he must often address other responsibilities arising from the suicide. These responsibilities are similar whether the decedent has been treated in the hospital, clinic, or private practice. The therapist has the responsibility to help the family and other patients as they struggle with their feelings of loss even as he deals with his own.

Dunne (1987) discusses a number of these concerns in relationship to the family. The family needs to be notified immediately and given not only the details of how it happened, but an explanation of why at this particular time. Often, a first reaction is to blame the caregiver, who needs to understand the feelings behind the behavior and not react defensively, nor counterattack with blaming of the family. He may have to handle accusations of incompetence, of failing in his responsibility for keeping the patient alive, along with threats of a suit for malpractice. He faces the task of trying to help the family to assess their expectations realistically and, at the same time, acknowledge the limitations of therapy nondefensively. Dunne emphasizes that the therapist needs to avoid a natural tendency to be a therapist for the family as well. He should share his own personal grief. If he wishes to attend the funeral of the patient, he should do so only if the family agrees and gives permission. At the same time, in all his conversations with the family, he has to be aware of the possibility of legal actions and make no statements that can be used against him, or his hospital, or his agency. The therapist also needs to keep in mind the possibility the family will need help for their grief and be ready to recommend those deemed most suitable. These might include survivor groups as well as family or individual therapy.

Dunne also discusses the concerns when the suicide is a patient in a hospital or clinic. The reactions of other patients will be determined by the degree and kind of psychopathology, intensity, and duration of contact with the deceased, and the presence or absence of suicidal behavior in any of the other patients. Along with typical grief reactions, a patient with prior suicidal behavior tends to react much more severely and intensely than other patients with none, with greater tendency toward identification with the deceased and more suicidal ideation. There may be fear that other caregivers cannot handle their (the patient's) suicidal impulses. There may be anger toward the deceased, the staff, and the hospital or clinic. In general, the response to such feelings is to be open about the event and not try to cover up or deny it, for other patients are quick to sense the protective falseness and to react with growing distrust. Accurate information about the suicide should be given as quickly as possible to avoid the proliferation of rumors. This may be accomplished through meetings held for patients and staff, or with posted notices. Efforts should be made to anticipate the expression of emotional responses, perhaps by small meetings led by nondefensive staff. Special precautions may need to be taken with previously identified suicidal patients to avoid similar suicide acts, perhaps by intensifying staff observation during the day and decreasing the period between staff rounds at night, as well as more frequent therapy sessions for a short while. In the hospital there should be provisions to return to routine as quickly as possible.

Each patient's status should be reviewed individually to determine the impact of the suicide on the patient, with critical evaluation of passes and privileges for a while.

The staff also needs time to mourn, with staff meetings planned to discuss the death to see what can be learned, and not to fix blame. Opportunities for individual discussion and consultations should be provided. It is useful to provide supervision and consultation for the rest of the caseload to avoid loss of confidence, withdrawal, excessive anxiety, and countertransference reactions toward other patients.

Suicide of the Therapist

When a therapist commits suicide it profoundly affects the patients whom he had been treating and frequently confounds their further therapy. Frequently there is an unrealistic assumption of responsibility for the death with feelings of guilt for having burdened the therapist with his problems on top of the therapist's own. Other reactions include strong feelings of anger at being betrayed by a therapy that had held out hope for help but that was not enough to help the provider, thus challenging the usefulness of such treatment. Some of the patient-survivors develop severe somatic symptoms and present considerable suicidal risk through identification with the therapist. Feelings of abandonment and rejection may increase the risk sharply for those whose entry into therapy had been prompted by suicidal feelings.

In subsequent treatment, the therapist has to reassure the patient that most therapists are able to resolve their own difficulties and to seek consultation for their problems. He has to help the patient distinguish between the problems the therapist was experiencing and the patient's problems so that he can resolve any feelings of having caused the death.

TREATMENT CONCERNS

Treatment of the Survivor

Some general comments and suggestions for the therapist who has undertaken treatment of a suicide survivor follow. Before initiating such treatment, the therapist needs to know and understand his own feelings about suicide to make sure no prejudicial attitudes color or affect his work with the survivor. He must be nonjudgmental, nonscapegoating, nonblaming — refraining from pointing the finger at the deceased's therapist or the treatment received, the family, or the suicide. He must be knowledgeable about the grief process and what occurs in bereavement so he can evaluate the reactions presented by the survivor. He must be able to determine whether the survivor's reactions are attributable to grief, or whether they might have their origin in other problems and conflicts of the survivor.

Needs differ, often on the basis of time. Some survivors react to the death immediately by seeking therapy to help get through the shock and disorganization of the recent death. Others mourn for a long time and seem to recover slowly. Zisook and Schuchter (1986) have noted continued mourning in their nonclinical subjects after 4 years. The pace of recovery varies widely with each survivor regardless of the mode of death. Some react to the death with pathological grief, that is, intensely and excessively — their lives become consumed with it. Such cases may require long-term treatment, perhaps even hospitalization. Some adjust but develop all kinds of other conditions, frequently somatic, some of which are directly or consciously attributed to the loss. When the symptoms are enduring, unusual, or unrelieved, treatment is indicated. The emotional symptoms may take the form of severe depression, either or both emotional or physiological, intense guilt and self-blame, suicidal feelings and behavior and protracted withdrawal from customary social networks.

Treatment may be offered to the individual only, or it may be considered best for the family to enter as a unit. Treatment for the family together is indicated when the mourning produces scapegoating, blaming, isolation, and disturbed behavior, especially in children. Suicide of a family member affects the family severely, disrupting its functioning, requiring reorganization of relationships and development of new roles at the same time that it deals with implied and overtly stated blame and rejection. The approach can include family therapy, group therapy, and couples therapy. The choice will depend on the type of loss (kinship), time lapsed since the loss, whether other kinds of losses have occurred in the interim, and the background and training of the leaders.

Not every survivor needs therapy. The group process, whether in group therapy or short-term grief counseling, has seen widespread application over the past decade. Formats have varied considerably in terms of length of time the group is conducted, open-ended or predetermined number of meetings, open or closed membership, kinship, leadership, use of professionals, use of nonprofessional survivor-facilitators, and other factors. Relatively little evaluation of effectiveness of the different kinds of formats has been done. Rogers and colleagues (1982) used trained volunteers to lead groups in a time-limited format of eight weekly meetings. The results were considered useful and positive by the survivors, the program perceived as helpful, and a symptom scale reported as much lower at follow-up. Battle (1984) conducted an open-ended group with no time limit. Most of the survivors (67 percent) reported feeling helped while the rest indicated either that the group could not help them further or it did not help at all.

Evaluation of the Survivors After Suicide Program conducted at the Los Angeles Suicide Prevention Center (Farberow, 1992) also indicated positive results. The format used a closed-end approach, once-a-week sessions, with survivors mixed in kinship, and the sessions led by a professional and a survivor-facilitator. Reading material and suggested discussion topics were distributed at each meeting. A comparison group was obtained from persons applying for the program who did not follow through when their group was started. In addition to obtaining demographic data and reactions to the format, subjects were asked to rate a set of nine feelings at three points in time, immediately after the death, at the time the program began and after the program was concluded. Controls completed their questionnaires 2 months after their group would have started. Feelings rated were depression, grief, anxiety, shame or stigma, guilt, anger at self or others, anger at the decedent, puzzlement, and suicidal feelings. Results indicated that the intensity decreased for all feelings in all subjects, participants and controls, over the two time periods, immediate postdeath to entry into the program, and start to end of the program. Grief and anxiety decreased for both groups in the first time period; depression and grief also went down significantly for the participants and anger at self and others went down for the controls. Further significant decreases occurred for the participants in grief, depression and guilt in the second time period, covering the time the program was in operation; no changes appeared for the controls. Apparently the group experience in the SAS program helped some survivors to move through some of the difficult feelings of bereavement more quickly. Guilt feelings, which had been much stronger among the participants than in the controls at the time the program was started, had diminished so that there was no longer any significant difference when the sessions ended. Perhaps the sharing and the learning about the ubiquity of such feelings during the sessions had lessened their intensity. It is of interest to note that a 2 year follow-up of about one third of the subjects indicated that all the feelings were rated low by almost half of the members of both groups, with the lone exception of grief, which was rated low by only 20 percent of the subjects. Some affects, like feeling suicidal, shame, and guilt had almost completely subsided, but a few, like depression, anger, and grief (especially among the participants) were noticeably persistent.

For most participants, the time format (one and one-half hours, once a week for 8 weeks, with voluntary monthly meetings afterward if desired) seemed to have worked well. Most participants reported they had been helped in facing the reality of their loss, felt reassured their feelings were acceptable, and felt they had regained better control of their lives.

A strong impression was that the combination of professional and survivor as co-leaders worked out very well. They saw the survivor-facilitator as one who "had been there" and had successfully gone through the painful experience. For many it meant it would be possible to function again even though they felt at the time they would never recover. The professional, on the other hand, gave a sense of security to the occasional evidence of emotional disturbance, suicidal feelings, or severe depression that arose in the sessions. The therapist was present to evaluate the need for traditional therapy when indicated by any of the participants, as well as the need for direct intervention when suicidal impulses emerged. Twenty-two percent of the participants reported suicidal feelings, mostly in the first few weeks after the death.

Perhaps the major contribution of the program was to provide support at a time when many of the participants were reporting difficulties because their usual sources of support were absent, apparently as a result of the fact that the death was a suicide. Sometimes friends, ordinarily available at times of crisis or loss, were too uncomfortable with their own feelings about the suicide. Many times this was reported occurring within families as well.

When possible, group treatment seems to be the treatment of choice. Sharing is the predominant benefit, with participants discussing their individual feelings in a nonjudgmental atmosphere, finding that their feelings are typical and normal, lessening the stigma, and feeling cared for and supported. They exchange experiences including a variety of coping strategies, some of which they may be able to adopt or at least adapt. They learn about suicide from each other and from the leaders and frequently become involved in advocacy, such as educating the public and professionals and helping to remove the stigma. The feeling of helping each other often relieves the strong feelings of anger and frustration from not being allowed or able to help their loved one. Some participants go on to receive training and become survivor-facilitators, where they, in turn, can become models and help others through the tragedy of their loss.

REFERENCES

Battle, A. (1987). Group therapy for survivors. *Crisis* 5:48–58.

Cherntob, C. M., Hamada, R. S., Bauer, G., and Torigue, R. Y. (1988). Patients' suicides: frequency and impact on psychiatrists. *American Journal of Psychiatry* 145:224–228.

Dunne, E. J. (1987). Surviving the suicide of a therapist. In *Suicide and Its Aftermath: Understanding and Counseling the Survivors*. ed. E. J. Dunne, J. McIntosh, and K. Dunne-Maxim, pp. 142–150. New York: W. W. Norton.

Farberow, N. L. (1992). The Los Angeles Survivors After Suicide program: an evaluation. *Crisis* 13:23–34.

Hauser, M. J. (1987). Special aspects of grief after a suicide. In *Suicide and Its Aftermath: Understanding and Counseling the Survivors,* ed. E. J. Dunne, J. L. McIntosh, and K. Dunne-Maxim, pp. 57–70. New York: W. W. Norton.

Kahne, M. J. (1968). Suicide among patients in mental hospitals: a study of psychiatrists who conducted their psychotherapy. *Psychiatry* 31:32–43.

Rogers, J., Sheldon, A., Barwick, C., et al. (1982). Help for families of suicide: survivors support program. *Canadian Journal of Psychiatry* 27:444–449.

Terr, L. C. (1981). Forbidden games. *Journal of the American Academy of Child Psychiatry.* 138:14–19.

Zisook, S., and Schuchter, S. R. (1986). The first four years of widowhood. *Psychiatric Annals* 16:288–294.

21: THE ILLEGACY OF SUICIDE

Jack Kamerman

I believe that the person who commits suicide puts his psychological skeleton in the survivor's emotional closet . . .

—Edwin S. Shneidman

Thus, then, though Time be the mightiest of Alarics, yet is he the mightiest mason of all. And a tutor and a physician and a scribe and a poet and a sage and a king.

—Herman Melville, *Mardi* LXXV

INTRODUCTION[1]

It may seem presumptuous of a mortal to think he needs to come to the defense of time. But, in social scientific study, time has fared worse than geography, generation worse than culture. Perhaps this is so because, in a period of self-defined rapid social change, people assume that anyone who came before must have been very different (and consequently have nothing to teach us) and, in the same way, that only contemporaries obey the same rules as we do. So, ironically, to be temporocentric in this case is to minimize the importance of time.

To be fully understood, psychological and social events must be situated in relation to time in at least two senses: historical time and biographical time. People revolve on an axis in relation to their daily lives and, in a larger sense, in an orbit in relation to historical events. Biographical time has been framed in terms of the life cycle (Leenaars 1991). Historical time, when it was acknowledged at all, was more often seen as a history of suicide rather than as a history in which a phenomenon like suicide was embedded.

---

[1]Shneidman (1972), recognizing the character of the aftermath of many suicides, suggests the term *illegacy* be used rather than *legacy* for "the tragedies that continue after the self-destructive deed" (p. xi).

Historical time may be defined not simply sequentially, but conceptually. George Herbert Mead (1932) cautioned that every history is written from a particular present, that is, from a particular temporal point of view and that, in this sense, as any one present appears and recedes, history changes. This applies to biography (personal history) as well as to what we usually call history.

Within a given generation, there are generation units (Mannheim 1952), groups which work up the events of a generation in particular ways. The bases of these particular views of the times may be socioeconomic class, ethnicity, occupation, and so on — the sociologist's stock in trade.

If one of the key tasks in understanding suicidal motivation is to understand the meaning the act has for the suicidal person (see, for example, Douglas 1967, Shneidman 1963, 1985), it is equally true that to understand the experience of suicide survivors, we must understand the meaning the act has for the survivors and their social circles.

THE STUDY OF NEW YORK CITY
POLICE OFFICER SUICIDES, 1934–1940

Between 1934 and 1940, over ninety New York City police officers committed suicide, more than double the rate of the previous 6 years. The cumulation of these suicides became the concern of Mayor Fiorello La Guardia, who approached the Committee for the Study of Suicide headed by Gregory Zilboorg for help as well as that of the philanthropist Marshall Field, who was also the committee's treasurer, and of Lewis Valentine, the city's police commissioner. They provided, respectively, the clout, the expertise, the money, and the day-to-day cooperation to undertake a study of these suicides. In a research artifact characteristic of a bygone age (prelitigious America), permission for the study was granted in a letter dated 15 June 1939, from La Guardia to Valentine, which reads in part:

> For some years past a Committee for the Study of Suicide has been in existence, making a study along scientific lines. It is properly financed and properly sponsored.
> I have been in touch with this committee and talked our situation over and you will soon receive a letter or a call from Dr. Gregory Zilboorg. Please arrange to see him at once and also to have him meet any one of the department you or he may deem necessary.
> . . . Please get the work going as soon as you can and give it your full cooperation.

During the period of the study, 1939–1940, the work records of the dead officers were examined and summarized and their families and colleagues were interviewed. In sum, an enormous amount of data was collected. For several reasons, the data of the study were never analyzed or published. The Committee had been in existence since 1935. Zilboorg's plan was to publish the cumulative findings of their research in four volumes (Friedman 1967a). However, because of his wish to publish all four volumes at the same time, because of the outbreak of World War II, and because of Zilboorg's poor health, nothing was published.

In 1967, Paul Friedman (1967b), at Shneidman's request, published a paper analyzing the findings of the 1940 study. He concluded that police officers, many hired under the rather lax standards that existed in the period before La Guardia came to office, could give free rein to their aggressive impulses. However, La Guardia's attempt to clean house in the agencies of New York City government at the very least placed constraints on the aggressive style of these marginal figures and at most put their employment in jeopardy. Fettered and threatened, and, in some cases, beset by psychological and behavioral problems ignited by precipitating biographical troubles, and with lethal means almost always at hand, they committed suicide at an alarming rate.

In a reanalysis of these suicides, Michael Heiman (1975a, 1975b) questioned Friedman's thesis that the policies of the La Guardia administration were particularly significant in setting the causal engine in motion. He pointed out that other police departments in the United States (at least among those few that kept such records) had similar rates without the presence of a crusading mayor. He also suggested that "one would expect that a majority of these suicides would have occurred in the 1931–1935 period when the Seabury Investigation and the reformist movement neutralized Tammany's influence and posed the greatest threat to the delinquent behaviors of marginal policemen" (p. 18).

However, when you are dealing with numbers that are so small (for example, the actual number of police suicides in San Francisco from 1934 to 1939 was four!), the notion of comparable *rates* loses its meaning. In addition, whatever handwriting was on the wall after the Seabury Investigation, La Guardia did not in fact take office until 1 January 1934. Although La Guardia had worked through him before his appointment as Police Commissioner in August 1934, it was not until that appointment that Lewis Valentine could begin to have a real effect on the day-to-day workings of the department and, perhaps more important, on the perceptions of its officers.

An examination of the New York City Police Department's Annual Reports reveals precisely how this moral fervor was translated into threat. In 1933, twenty officers were dismissed from the force on departmental charges (as opposed to conviction in court); in 1934, the number was thirty-six (New York City Police Department 1934). In 1935, the number jumped to ninety-six (New York City Police Department 1935). The personnel levels of the department were virtually identical in those 3 years.

The history of the 1930s is also the history of the Great Depression. In its first few years, many people, having never experienced a depression of the duration of this one, believed it would soon end. By 1934, the faith of many that "prosperity was just around the corner" had been undermined. To have a steady job in such unsettled and unsettling times, especially one that paid reasonably well, was particularly precious. Because the cost of living was going down, the same salary was worth a lot more (Garraty 1987). Add to this the fact that a police officer in this period generally commanded great respect in his family and his neighborhood, that Department hiring quotas were stagnant, and that standards for hiring were higher than in previous years, and you get some sense of what was at stake when a cop was threatened with the loss of his job.

It wasn't simply for corruption that a cop could be dismissed. Disciplinary action for being drunk on duty became more common. Formal charges and informal accusations of drinking on the job were involved in a number of these police suicides.

The Legacy and Illegacy of Police Suicides

For the past several years, at Shneidman's suggestion and with his advice, I have been studying the families of those police officers, the survivors who have lived with the legacies and illegacies of their deaths. These suicides have by now tracked through their families for over 50 years. They have affected the lives of wives, sons and daughters, grandchildren, and great-grandchildren. The study is still in progress. What follows is based on data collected so far.

To understand the effect these suicides had on these widows, we need to understand, among other things, what widowhood meant in the 1930s. That is related to the widows' statuses as wives, policemen's wives, daughters, daughters-in-law, mothers, women, and policemen's widows.

For some, the suicide became the central organizing event of their lives. For others, it became a temporary hardship, requiring readjustment but leaving their lives in most ways no different or even better than before. However, even in these cases the suicide became a sort of family legend.

In addition to the importance of psychological factors, bereavement in the case of suicide becomes a central life-organizing condition to the extent to which:

1. The status affected, for example, "wife," is an important one as defined by culture and historical period—for example, to be an Irish cop's wife in New York in the 1930s.
2. The death changes a survivor's lifestyle for the worse, that is, the degree of economic privation that the death causes;
3. The death causes a survivor to lose prestige in his or her community—for example, by being burdened with the stigmas attached to the suicide's being a Catholic, a police officer, a husband and father in the 1930s and so forth;
4. Available statuses do not compensate for the one lost (in this case, "wife"); and,
5. Support systems do not exist to cushion (in some cases neutralize) the above-mentioned effects.

To these women in the period 1934–1940, their two major statuses were wife and mother. If a woman wasn't married, it was something that needed to be explained. Similarly, if she was married, but had no children, that was also something that needed to be explained. After her husband died, the importance of being a wife was simply transferred to the importance of being a widow, that is, having been a wife. As a widow, her husband's status still defined hers. To be a police widow meant not simply a pension, but continued social contact with her husband's friends, many of whom were police officers, and, to a lesser extent, the continued participation, albeit in an altered way, in departmental activities.

> They took the kids [children of deceased officers] to Coney Island every year, and they sent us gift certificates for clothes, at Klein's, which was sort of degrading, actually, in a way. . . . Mama didn't like charity, but we went, and we collected twenty-five dollars; you wouldn't believe what we came back with. . . . She didn't like the word charity, but we took it anyway. And she figured why not? Because they gave money for her and the two boys. . . . I mean the only bad part about the clothes was waiting until the clothes arrived from all the floors at once. That was the only degrading thing. But the clothes were fine. My God, twenty-five dollars in those days. My lord, two suits . . . you know it was just unreal. And they took us once to the Waldorf, and to the Hotel Astor. We had a captain sitting at the table. Turkey dinner. And the parents — my mother had to sit up on the balcony and watch us eat [Interview with son, 31 October 1989].

Most of the widows of the original group were eligible for police pensions, usually $50 per month. That amount was not nearly the amount of their husbands' salaries (for example, in the case of a patrolman, $37.50 per week), and in many, if not all cases, had to be supplemented by working or by help from families. Police widows were eligible for jobs as bedmakers, women who came to police precinct stations and did housekeeping chores like making beds.

> I wrote to the station house on Staten Island and asked them if I could have a job, a position, I don't know. I understood I could get fifty dollars a month by making beds in the station house. And I went down for an interview, and — I guess he was a lieutenant — he said, "How many children have you got?" I said, "Two." He said, "You're lucky you haven't got six." That's all I got. I didn't get the job. That was the answer. And in those days, there was no insurance for the health, no insurance for policemen, no life insurance, and no Social Security. . . . So everything was down. . . . Well, if I hadn't had my mother and father, I couldn't have done it [Interview with widow, 21 November 1989].

For Catholic widows, the suicides of their husbands presented both symbolic and practical problems. Funeral arrangements had to be made, but suicides could not be buried in Catholic cemeteries unless they "were not of sound mind." Death certificates sometimes gave license for burial in Catholic cemeteries, by including phrases like, "suicidal during mental depression," "mental unbalance," "mentally deranged," and "depressive psychosis" as contributing causes. Sometimes the circumstances of death were covered up by sympathetic priests or undertakers. "He was given a big funeral, and if it were a wrong thing, he never would have been buried in St. Peter's Cemetery [a Catholic cemetery]" (Interview with widow, 21 November 1989). In a few cases, Catholics were simply buried in Protestant cemeteries.

Police officers, who see themselves as the pillars on whom others lean, view suicide and its antecedent problems as signs of weakness. At the same time, they are sympathetic to those problems because to one degree or another they are recognizable and often defined as endemic to police work. But no matter what personal sympathy may be involved, a suicidal death is not a hero's death, as line-of-duty deaths are. There may have been ceremonial funerals for some of these officers, but there were no medals.

For these women, having been wives meant automatically moving into the status of widow. Since few if any of these women worked after they were married, being a wife became each one's primary self. If one was a wife *and* a mother, motherhood became the more important status, particularly given the etiology of her widowhood. To remarry meant to lose one's pension. ("Once is enough for me. And then, not only that, I'd lose my pension also if I remarried" [Interview with widow, 3 March 1991].)

The ones who didn't remarry had a great stake in canonizing their dead husbands, both to justify their decision not to remarry and to provide their children with untarnished fathers. A widow who in the 1940 interview described her husband as uncommunicative, sexually demanding, and distant from their children, when asked in 1989 why she didn't remarry, said, "When you have one good man, you don't want to try another." She went on to say that they had a "very good marriage" and that, as a father, he was "very good. Very good. Very patient."

Finally, support systems—for example, friends and family—can help to soften the aftereffects of a suicide. The difficulty for some widows, and this is certainly not specific to suicide although it tends to be greater in that case, is that their husbands' families may blame them for the death.

> I'm sure they, on my father's side of the family, they probably assumed that something—my mother did something wrong for him to do that. I'm sure that's what they . . . they never came out and said it, but they didn't come to visit us until 2 years after he died. [Interview with son, 31 October 1989]

In some cases, they may be willing to sustain contact with the widow only insofar as it is necessary to see their grandchildren.

Children as Legatees: Mythology and Reality in Families

In addition to so many other problems, widows had to contend with the image their children would carry of their fathers. Even in cases where children were beyond infancy at the time of the suicide, the real cause of death was often masked. The 1930s, it must be remembered, was still an era in which an attempt was made to insulate children from the psychological and economic realities of the adult world. "Don't discuss that in front of the children" was an operating assumption, not, as it is today, a charming reminder of a bygone age of innocence. Even in cases where the suicides were reported in newspapers, some children didn't know that their father had been a suicide until much later. In cases where the children were infants at the time of their fathers' death, hiding the real cause of death was easier, but still not without consequences.

Finally, when I was 16, she [his mother] told me. Up to 16 she only mentioned that . . . she said it was pneumonia. And it was more or less . . . she didn't want to talk about it too much. But then she sat me down at age 16, and I said to her . . . well, I knew something because I never believed it was pneumonia. I took it very well. I wasn't traumatized at all. . . . I knew something was wrong right from the beginning. Because what's so bad about talking about pneumonia? That's how I felt. So it was actually no surprise whatsoever. And I think, well, of course, she was crying when she was telling me, but I just didn't. . . . Well, I wasn't shocked at all. Because I knew something was wrong. . . . I was annoyed that he did it that way that she had to find him. If he wanted to do it, do it, but not like that. That's how I felt. I just . . . I was a little angry about that. I *was* angry about that, that he did it so she found him. [Interview with son, 31 October 1989]

This son became an alcoholic a year or so after finding out the true cause of his father's death. His older brother, who looked exactly like his father and who was 4½ when his father died, also found out only at 16 that his father was a suicide. The older son died in a boating accident in his mid-forties. He had had a previous boating accident and had been warned by his wife not to go out on the boat again. He had also told his brother that "the best way for him [the older brother], that *he* would want to go, would be to drown. And that's exactly how he went. Very strange."

In the case of older children, their images of their fathers are to a greater extent their own, that is, based to a lesser extent on their mother's view. In a striking case, an officer in the original group committed suicide about 4 years after his policeman father, after whom he was named, had committed suicide, firing the bullet into his head at exactly the same point that his father had fired a bullet into his.

It is possible that some children are never told of the circumstances of their father's death. In the only case so far in my interviewing where a child told me that her father died of natural causes, she fumbled for that answer. It seemed more a frequently repeated lie than her real belief about his death. (Her mother also told me that her husband had died of a heart attack, and then she immediately changed the subject.) That particular case may have involved deception on the daughter's part or simply suspicion. In any case, it is likely that a suicide still has some effect on children no matter what they have been told.

When children were told that their fathers had committed suicide, they were also provided with explanations of why their fathers had done it, explanations which they embellished and refined.

I know he didn't confide about the job, according to my aunt. . . . He kept things to himself. The job got to him because he was like in the, I think it was the emergency squad. He was the first one on the scene of the crime. He'd probably seen a lot that he didn't want to discuss with his wife or anyone. He kept a lot of things to himself which was, I'm sure, bad. And I know the last few weeks of his life, he had . . . he had an old nose injury, and sinus trouble, but this time it was very severe, and his father was dying at the same time, of pneumonia. He kept on visiting with this horrible cold, and he was getting migraine headaches, and he said to my aunt, and I'm quoting her, ". . . He thinks he's losing his mind because of the headaches." To me, he wasn't losing his mind because I don't think an insane person would realize something is wrong. I feel that he probably had a nervous breakdown. And so he said to her, "I wouldn't want to be burden to my mother, . . . to my wife and children." And a few weeks later, he shot himself. [Interview with son, 31 October 1989]

In all cases of children interviewed so far, they maintained, from their own memories or on the basis of what they had been told (as in the above quote from an interview with a son who was an infant when his father died), that their fathers loved them very much, treated them well, and were in general model parents.

Just as with the romanticization of their marriages, widows tended to rework over time the circumstances leading up to their husbands' suicides. Of course, if professionals sometimes puzzle over the causes of a suicide, widows also might have trouble understanding it. Every widow I spoke to had a theory as to why her husband had killed himself. In only one of my interviews with widows did the widow see herself involved in the causative chain, and then not really in a way that would likely be construed as blameworthy.

I never really found out the true story. I never really found out the truth because, I don't know what it was, there seemed to be such a blockage in my head, and I didn't want to . . . the things I was thinking of, I didn't want to hear, anyhow. And it was never brought up. . . . The only thing I was afraid of was, maybe he had a drink, going in [to work]. And maybe they smelled liquor on him. And then he was so afraid of me hearing, or that I'd be annoyed about it or something, and this is what he'd done. I don't *know*. That's only *my thoughts*. I don't know. Other than that I don't know. [Interview with widow, 2 November 1989]

In other cases, problems related to the job or to things going on in the husband's psyche constituted their explanations of their husbands' suicides.

Well, it was a shock, that is all. And I mean, nothing to explain it, you know. The only thing—this is a very, very personal thing—the only thing I can think of is he became . . . incompetent? Incontinent? No—the sex business . . . What is the word? [Interviewer: Impotent.] Impotent, yes, isn't that awful—Yes. That's the only thing. And that was only in the last couple of weeks before he died. Now, whether that affected him or not, I don't know. He didn't go to a doctor. He went to the . . . the . . . oh, what is the big thing the police give at Christmas time? When they go to . . . the Holy Name Society. He went to that, and he was dead on the twentieth [of December]. [Interview with widow, 21 November 1989]

According to records from the 1940 study, in the first case there had been no drinking, but the officer had had a disciplinary charge brought against him for being off his post. In the second case, the officer had been brought up on a disciplinary charge that had been resolved the day before his suicide with an apology to the offended citizen. In the 1940 interview, his widow had mentioned the suspension of sexual activities shortly before the suicide, but didn't see it as related to the suicide. Instead she pointed to the disciplinary hearing and the fact that he had become nervous and had experienced a buzzing in his head, which had led to an appointment with a police physician, as the only things that might have had a connection with his suicide.

It is difficult to decide from the interviews done so far the extent to which the suicide has become part of family lore passed down from generation to generation. Elizabeth Stone (1988) suggests that a suicide in a family may be followed by another suicide as a covert form of family loyalty. This may be so because in some cases the suicides, rather than being an object of shame, may receive a rather flattering characterization in the family's oral history (Stone 1988). Certainly, it would be interesting to know what the granddaughter of one of the officers in the original sample, who died at nine after being hit by a train while walking down a railroad track, knew about her grandfather.

GRIEF AFTER SUICIDE AND OTHER KINDS OF DEATH

Until recently, the theme of much of the work on grief after suicide was that suicide survivors have different experiences from those left behind by deaths from natural causes. Certainly, a suicidal death is different from a natural death in important respects. Guilt is a likely element in all grief, and so, too, is blame. But in the case of a death by suicide, guilt and finger-pointing are particularly strong.

Recent studies of bereaved college students seem to suggest that, particularly after a period of time has passed, the grief experience, no matter what the cause of death, tends to be similar. (See, for example, McIntosh and Kelly 1988, McIntosh and Milne 1986, Range and Niss 1990.) However, to understand the experiences of those left behind it is first necessary to situate them generationally. If young people are more accepting of suicide than their elders (see, for example, Boldt 1982–1983), then studies of college students may have more to do with stage of life and historical location than with some universal experience of survivorship. That may also be true of people widowed recently, that is, in the era of relative acceptance (Farberow et al. 1987). Certainly, one task of anyone examining these studies is to situate them both chronologically and by the age of the group studied, that is, by the two dimensions of generation. It is incumbent on those trying to understand the experience of women widowed in the 1930s to understand widowhood in the terms of the 1930s rather than in the terms of the present. One widow told me that it took her 2 years before she wanted to socialize with friends again. She added that she used to go on outings in the country with her husband, but had not done that since his death:

> No, there's no way to go to the country anymore. Those days are over. The only thing to look forward to now is the good Almighty. I don't know why he's leaving me around so long. Sometimes I get so disgusted and think, Why? Everybody is . . . even my brother is five years younger than I am, and he's gone. So here I am, all by myself. [Interview with widow, 2 November 1989]

Well, even now [55 years after her husband's death] I don't think I'm over it. I mean, you still think of it, especially at night. . . . [Interview with widow, 21 November 1989]

These widows are women caught in a time warp, stuck in the 1930s like needles on a phonograph record replaying the same groove over and over again, each life frozen at the point of her husband's death. That is why widowhood became the flagship experience of their lives.

REFERENCES

Boldt, M. (1982-1983). Normative evaluations of suicide and death: a cross-generational study. *Omega* 13:45-57.

Douglas, J. D. (1967). *The Social Meanings of Suicide.* Princeton, NJ: Princeton University Press.

Farberow, N. L., Gallagher, D. D., Gilewski, M. J., and Thompson, L. W. (1987). An examination of the early impact of bereavement on psychological distress in survivors of suicide. *Gerontologist* 27:592-598.

Friedman, P. (1967a). A history of the Zilboorg Archives. In *Proceedings, Fourth International Conference for Suicide Prevention,* pp. 307-315. Los Angeles: International Association for Suicide Prevention.

———— (1967b). Suicide among police: a study of 93 suicides among New York City policemen, 1934-1940. In *Essays in Self-Destruction* ed. E. S. Shneidman, pp. 414-449. New York: Science House.

Garraty, J. A. (1987). *The Great Depression.* New York: Anchor.

Heiman, M. F. (1975a). Police suicides revisited. *Suicide* 5:5-20.

———— (1975b). The police suicide. *Journal of Police Science and Administration* 3:267-273.

Leenaars, A., ed. (1991). *Life Span Perspectives of Suicide: Time-lines in the Suicide Process.* New York: Plenum.

Mannheim, K. (1952). *Essays in the Sociology of Knowledge,* ed. P. Kecskemeti. London: Routledge and Kegan Paul.

McIntosh, J. L., and Kelly, L. D. (1988). Survivors' reactions: suicide vs. other causes. In *Proceedings, 21st Annual Meeting, American Association of Suicidology,* ed. D. Lester, pp. 89-90. Washington, DC.

McIntosh, J. L., and Milne, K. L. (1986). Survivors' reactions: suicide vs. other causes. In *Proceedings, Nineteenth Annual Meeting, American Association of Suicidology,* ed. R. Cohen-Sandler, pp. 136-138. Atlanta, GA.

Mead, G. H. (1932). *The Philosophy of the Present.* Chicago: University of Chicago Press.

New York City Police Department. (1934) *Annual Report: 1934.* New York: New York City Police Department.

———— (1935). *Annual Report: 1935.* New York: New York City Police Department.

Range, L. M., and Niss, N. M. (1990). Long-term bereavement from suicide, homicide, accidents, and natural deaths. *Death Studies* 14:423-433.

Shneidman, E. S. (1963). Orientations toward death: a vital aspect of the study of lives. In *The Study of Lives: Essays on Personality in Honor of Henry A. Murray,* ed. R. W. White, pp. 200-227. New York: Atherton.

———— (1972). Foreword. In *Survivors of Suicide,* ed. A. C. Cain, pp. ix-xi. Springfield, IL: Charles C Thomas.

———— (1985). *Definition of Suicide.* New York: Wiley.

Stone, E. (1988). *Black Sheep and Kissing Cousins: How Our Family Stories Shape Us.* New York: Times Books.

THE RIGHT TO DIE
Part IX

"Pain is what the suicidal person is seeking to escape. It is meta-pain, the pain of feeling pain" (Edwin Shneidman).

Yet, what about suicide of the terminally ill? Is this death the same as other suicides? "Rational" suicide, euthanasia, assisted suicide, planned death, medical withdrawal, all are terms that describe such a death. Issues of suicide must be seen in the context of larger issues of how we die. Substantial cultural differences exist in how we think about dying and, in particular, the dying of the terminally ill. The right-to-die concept is one of the most controversial and elusive issues facing suicidology today. Part IX consists of two chapters: some reflections on the right to die, and a consideration of suicidology and the right to die from the different cultural perspectives of the Netherlands, Germany, and the United States.

Louis Jolyon West

In 1972, a debate on the ethics of suicide prevention sponsored by the University of California Extension at San Francisco featured Edwin Shneidman arguing in favor of suicide intervention. His opponent was Thomas Szasz, a psychiatrist notorious for unorthodox beliefs: he holds that mental illness is a myth, and suicide is a civil right. Shneidman eloquently expressed his beliefs that the doctor-patient relationship should include a sense of responsibility for a life at risk; and that suicidal ideation is usually a symptom of an illness, and thus treatable. Shneidman went on to point out that when the patient chooses to talk about a possible suicide it suggests that he or she is ambivalent. A suicidal patient who is ambivalent can often be dissuaded. It should be the psychotherapist's duty to help a patient recognize this fact, and guide him in navigating through emotionally troubled waters. Szasz, on the other hand, defined the therapist-patient relationship in terms of a contract between equals. Unless it is implicit in the contract that the therapist will intervene on behalf of the patient, the therapist is not obligated to act, and indeed should not do so. For Shneidman, it is the healer's duty to treat the suicidal patient, while Szasz considers unethical any treatment that is not specifically contracted for. While Shneidman's view has the potential for meddling, the error is on the side of preventing an unnecessary death. The consequence of Szasz's noninterference, when fatal, is irreversible (Shneidman and Szasz 1972).

Since that landmark debate, a number of highly publicized cases have challenged medical and legal professionals, as well as the public, to examine their understanding of the quality of life and to question the proposition that individuals have the *right* to die when they (or designated others) decide that life's quality has significantly and irreversibly diminished. Does an individual have the right—legally, morally, or both—to take his own life, or to expect others to do it for him, and if so under what circumstances?

Recently the Shneidman–Szasz debate has taken on added dimensions. It now includes suicide committed by an individual who has a terminal illness or is in severe pain. Death with dignity, euthanasia, planned death, all are terms that describe such a suicide. It may be committed actively (by ingesting a fatal dose of sedatives) or passively (by refusing life-sustaining treatments when faced with an irreversible illness). It may be an independent act, or it may require the assistance of a physician. The latter's involvement may be either direct (as in administering a fatal dose of potassium chloride) or indirect (as in prescribing sedatives for sleep, knowing that the patient plans to take an overdose; or as in deliberately discontinuing life-sustaining medical care).

REFUSING VITAL MEDICAL CARE

The first type of planned death involves the right of individuals to refuse life-extending medical treatment. Many competent patients, even those with potentially curable diseases, die because they decline to undergo appropriate medical or surgical procedures. Usually, when physicians and families respect those wishes, such deaths occur privately, a matter between doctor and patient. This right is based on the belief of self-determination and of bodily integrity. It should require that patients be fully informed about their condition and about treatment alternatives.

However, there have been numerous cases in which a patient's refusal of life-saving treatment has been challenged, when physicians or family or friends disagreed with the individual's decision. This has occurred most prominently when the proposed treatment would be clearly life saving. In every such case that has gone to court, and the patient's competency has been established, the patient's right to refuse treatment has been upheld. This right has been confirmed for Jehovah's Witnesses who reject potentially life-saving blood transfusions for themselves (although not for their children), and for many others including terminally ill cancer patients who ask to be removed from respirators, diabetic patients who refuse amputation, cancer patients who refuse chemotherapy, other severely impaired people who would rather die than be kept alive by artificial means, and many who are just tired of being sick or for some other reason don't want to go on living. In Hungary, with the highest known suicide rate in the world, physical illness is the largest single cause of self-destruction (Furedi, personal communication, 1989).

In the past, the physician's occasional decision to prolong life contrary to a patient's wishes reflected a long tradition of paternalism in medicine. But much has changed with the advent of informed consent, the decline of the family doctor, the emergence of health maintenance organizations, the development of technologies that save lives but also prolong the process of dying, and the increasing number of medical malpractice suits. By confirming the right of fully-informed, competent patients to refuse medical intervention, the courts have also been redefining the doctor–patient relationship.

TERMINATING LIFE-SUSTAINING MEDICAL CARE

Another way to die results from the withdrawal of life-sustaining treatment from patients who may be considered already dead because they have lost all higher brain functions. Persons with overwhelming damage to the cerebral hemispheres (such as from trauma or organic disease) commonly pass into a state of unconsciousness often called *cerebral death,* a comatose, vegetative state wherein the body nevertheless retains the vital pulmonary and cardiovascular functions. (This condition differs from *brain death,* in which the EEG shows only the most primitive electrical activity, and only spinal reflexes remain.) When the coma lasts for more than a few weeks, the condition is called a persistent vegetative state. In such a state patients can live for months or years if nutritional and other supportive measures are provided. The chance and degree of recovery depend upon the cause and severity of cerebral damage. Complete recovery from deep coma caused by depressant drug poisoning is possible if the patient receives prompt medical attention to restore and maintain respiration and blood pressure and to prevent complications. However, if the cause of coma is severe brain disease or trauma, only about 15 percent of patients who recover — even within a few hours — are likely to do so without permanent neurologic impairment (Wyngaarden and Smith 1985). There are no recorded cases of recovery from persistent vegetative states after more than 3 months.

Because people in such vegetative states can be kept alive for months or years by respirators and artificial feedings, unaware of their circumstances, decisions about their treatment are frequently left to their families and physicians. If doctors and families agree to withhold treatment, doctors may quietly practice what some have called *judicious neglect* to let the people die. However, disagreements are not infrequent, and may end noisily in court.

A landmark case, that sparked great public debate and finally forced a judicial decision in New Jersey, was that of 21-year-old Karen Ann Quinlan. The case involved the withdrawal of a respirator from a permanently comatose adult. In April 1975, Karen lapsed into a deep coma after ingesting a mixture of tranquilizers and alcohol. Within 3 days she was respirator dependent and in a decorticate position, receiving nutrition by nasogastric tube. After 3 months, when there was no hope of her recovery, Karen's parents consulted with a priest and then requested that the respirator be removed. However Karen's attending physician, viewing this as a violation of medical ethics, refused. The local prosecutor and the New Jersey state attorney general agreed with the physician and threatened criminal proceedings if the respirator was removed. The case was then referred to the New Jersey Supreme Court, which decided in 1976 that an individual's right to privacy included a right to refuse medical care, and recognized that right for incompetent patients. The respirator was finally turned off. To everyone's surprise Karen remained alive for 9 years, breathing slowly on her own, sustained year after year by artificial feedings, until June 1985 when she finally succumbed to pneumonia. The New Jersey decision, although not binding in other states, did set a precedent for allowing the removal of a respirator from incompetent and comatose patients who have no chance of recovery. It did not address the question of discontinuing the tube feedings of food and water without which Karen could have survived only a few days.

Subsequent disputes have been based on different understandings of what constitutes medical treatment. Most physicians, patients, medical ethicists, and legal advisors agree that a person who is in a chronic vegetative state, unable to breathe except with a respirator, is terminally ill. For such patients a respirator is seen as a medical procedure that prolongs the dying process. However, there are different opinions about hydration and the use of feeding tubes. Some believe that if the patient is dependent only upon artificial nutrition, his condition may be considered stable and not terminal, and he should continue to receive basic supportive care. For example, Rosner (1988) believes that nutrition and hydration by feeding tubes or intravenous lines are not medical treatments but supportive care no different from washing, turning, or grooming a dying patient. He argues that even if the courts legally sanction the withdrawal or withholding of fluids and nutrition in some instances, it should not be done; legal permissibility is not synonymous with moral license. Similarly, Rosenblum and Forsythe (1990) distinguish the situation in which a patient is terminally ill and dying from one in which a patient is not terminally ill or imminently dying. They suggest that by withdrawing nutrition and hydration it is the physician who thereby sets in motion the course that will inevitably and directly cause the patient's death. Because the patient's death is not due to any underlying illness, the physician's role will change fundamentally from healer to killer.

In contrast, Oboler (1986) states that if the brain is dead, the patient is dead, regardless of the state of his spinal reflexes, and he should be declared dead and removed from the life-support system. However, if the patient has lost higher cortical function but brainstem function is preserved, he may live for years with apparent sleep-wake cycles but no awareness of any external or internal stimuli. Since the prognosis for recovery from the persistent vegetative state is nil, according to Oboler, there is no ethical responsibility to continue treatment other than providing basic nursing care to maintain the dignity of the patient.

Similarly, Cantor (1989) contends that the withdrawal of artificial nutrition is fully consistent with traditional medico-legal doctrines and does not represent the intentional killing of a helpless human being. He offers a standard—respect for human dignity—to justify the withdrawal of artificial nutrition from a permanently unconscious patient. That standard could also be applied to situations involving other incompetent patients who face a protracted coma, or in which medical interventions would sustain a patient in a status regarded by a clear majority of people as demeaning. Knox (1989) considers the provision of nutrition through artificial means to be an invasive medical intervention which, while providing benefits, also imposes burdens and may ethically be stopped.

Several court decisions in the 1980s *have* equated hydration and artificial feeding with other forms of life-sustaining treatments and have allowed their withdrawal. In 1986, when Elizabeth Bouvia, a fully competent quadriplegic, demanded that a California hospital stop tube-feeding her and allow her to starve, a state appeals court backed her. The court said Ms. Bouvia had the right to refuse medical treatment — even life-sustaining treatment such as food. (However, having won her case, Ms. Bouvia changed her mind about starving herself and is still alive. See p. 373.) In 1987, a New Jersey court allowed the family of 32-year-old Nancy Ellen Jobes, who had fallen into a vegetative state after an auto accident, to have her feeding tube removed. She died a short time later.

On 25 June 1990, the United States Supreme Court gave a decision in its first right-to-die case, which involved the removal of a feeding tube from Nancy Cruzan. Ms. Cruzan was 25 years old in 1983, when she was severely injured in an automobile accident from which she never regained consciousness. A feeding tube was surgically implanted in her stomach. She was not on a respirator. In July 1988, a Jasper County (Missouri) Circuit Court granted her parents permission to have the feeding tube removed, but the Missouri Supreme Court decided there was no legal authority to grant the Cruzans' request. The family then appealed to the U.S. Supreme Court. The Court ruled that Missouri officials could block the removal of Ms. Cruzan's feeding tube unless there was "clear and convincing" evidence that she wouldn't want to be kept alive. The Court held that, while the Constitution protects the refusal of life-sustaining treatment by *competent* patients, states may require "clear and convincing" evidence of refusal of treatment by *incompetent* patients before tube feedings could be withdrawn from a person in a persistent vegetative state. The State of Missouri subsequently withdrew from the case. Nancy Cruzan's parents then provided the necessary evidence that Nancy would not want to be kept alive by tube feeding. This evidence was in the form of testimony by three former friends of Ms. Cruzan who claimed they had heard her express wishes to this effect, in conversations regarding the forced feeding of severely handicapped children, and also regarding the Quinlan case. Ms. Cruzan's feeding tube was removed, and she died 26 December 1990, at age 33.

Who should decide when treatment is to be withdrawn from a permanently incompetent patient? Is it the family, the physician, the hospital administration, or the State? The Cruzan decision established that, in the absence of "clear and convincing" evidence of the patient's wishes, the State (which has an interest in preserving life) can deny a family's request to terminate treatment. Lo and Steinbrook (1991) believe that this ruling leaves many clinical questions unanswered, such as what constitutes clear and convincing evidence of refusal. Furthermore, they say that the Cruzan ruling may undermine family decision making, encourage cynicism and disregard of the law, and promote defensive medicine. Veatch (1989) would allow great flexibility to families and surrogate decision makers chosen in advance by the patient. In those cases in which a patient is unconscious or otherwise unable to make choices regarding treatment, and has no family or designated agent, he believes an outsider should decide. However, this outsider should not be a doctor but rather an objective observer appointed by a court. According to Veatch, it is wrong for physicians, in their clinical role, to decide to withhold any medical treatment.

There are other controversial medical interventions that in some cases save lives, but in others merely prolong dying. One is cardiopulmonary resuscitation (CPR), which can be a traumatic and painful procedure. Although it often represents the definitive treatment for patients who have suffered a catastrophic event, there have been numerous reports of patients who received CPR despite the presence of an irreversible, terminal disease and arguably against their wishes. To prevent this, a "do not resuscitate" order can be put in a patient's chart at the patient's written request, or it may be initiated by the primary physician. Goodman (1987) recommends that physicians should distinguish between acts which save lives and those which prolong death. He submits that a "do not resuscitate" order is appropriate when a patient already has medically proven, irreversible, untreatable, and terminal disease of a major organ such as the brain, heart, lungs, kidney, or liver, or an untreatable or irreversible systemic neoplastic or metabolic disease. Schneiderman and colleagues (1990) advise physicians to distinguish between an interventive effect, which is limited to some part of the patient's body, and a benefit, which appreciably improves the person as a whole. They classify treatment that fails to provide the latter, whether or not it achieves the former, as futile. Another treatment that some may consider futile is the administration of antibiotics to cure a life-threatening infection, such as pneumonia, in a patient who is already near death from other causes. Pneumonia was once considered to be "the old man's friend" because it provided a swift and relatively painless death. Now, antibiotics can cure the infection while prolonging the patient's process of dying from some other illness, such as cancer or AIDS.

There are several methods available to insure that patients' wishes regarding their medical care are respected in the event they may one day be unable to express those wishes. A proxy can be appointed who is familiar with an individual's attitudes about life-sustaining medical treatment. Through a durable power of attorney, the breadth of decisions may be stipulated. For example, a person could appoint a spouse, child, friend, or sibling to make all health-care decisions, or might choose to limit the appointee's power in certain ways (e.g., with regard to the removal of artificial hydration and nutrition). The durable power of attorney differs from an ordinary power of attorney, which ceases when the principal is no longer competent. All states and the District of Columbia have statutes that recognize the durable power of attorney.

The *living will* allows individuals to specify the conditions under which they wish to be allowed to die without medical intervention or heroic measures in the event of a terminal illness. More than forty states have enacted legislation that recognizes living wills. Such legislation varies from state to state, but has in common the recognition of a legal instrument whereby citizens can declare in advance certain directives concerning medical care in the event of terminal illness. In most states, a living will is only effective when the principal becomes terminally ill, while the durable power of attorney extends treatment decisions to the appointee whenever the patient is unable to express his or her desires. A living will must be executed (and not revoked) by the individual before he or she becomes incompetent. Some states exclude tube feeding from the treatments that may be refused. Some will not honor a living will executed in a state other than the one in which the individual is located when he or she becomes incompetent, and some even put strict stipulations on such issues as who may act as a witness to the living will. Thus it is important that interested persons check the regulations governing living wills in their state. To be most effective, a copy of the durable power of attorney should be carried by the concerned individual at all times, and should provide clear and current directions for reaching the appointed individual.

A number of recent studies have evaluated the attitudes of the highest risk group—the elderly—regarding living wills, proxies, and their preferences for treatment. Cohen-Mansfield and colleagues (1991) asked 103 nursing home residents about their preferences for the choice of an agent for health-care decision making and about their preferences regarding the use of four types of life-support treatment under hypothetical levels of future cognitive functioning. Participants tended to choose a son or daughter as the agent for future health-care decision making. They generally preferred not to receive life-sustaining treatment, especially if their perceived level of future cognitive functioning had declined, or if the life-sustaining treatment involved permanent rather than temporary procedures. Gamble and colleagues (1991) surveyed seventy-five ambulatory elderly persons in a rural county in eastern North Carolina. When asked about preferences for medical care in the setting of a terminal illness, 86 percent (sixty-five persons) stated a desire to receive basic medical care or comfort care only. Seventy (93 percent) wanted their family or spouse to make decisions about terminal care if they themselves were unable to participate, but discussions on this topic between these persons and their chosen proxies had actually occurred in only thirty-four (45 percent) of the seventy-five subjects.

Despite the availability of living wills and durable powers of attorney, a number of studies have demonstrated that as yet elderly persons do not often take advantage of them. In their survey, Gamble and colleagues (1991) found that although the preferences of their subjects were consistent with the provisions of a living will, none had signed the living will document provided by the State of North Carolina, and only two of seventy-five (3 percent) had discussed a living will with their physicians. Eighty-one percent (sixty-one persons) stated a desire to discuss end-of-life care with their physicians, but only a small minority (eight [11 percent]) had actually done so. These discussions were usually initiated by the patient (five of eight). The authors conclude that living-will legislation is congruent with the desire of many elderly persons to limit medical care in terminal illness. They recommend that physician–patient and patient–proxy communication should be improved regarding living wills and preferences for medical care at the end of life.

Hare and Nelson (1991) compared two interventions in Minnesota designed to increase the percentage of adult clinic patients who completed living wills and placed them on file with their physicians. The first intervention relied solely on a booklet that described the Minnesota Living Will Act, general information concerning advance directives, and medical interventions that could be considered extraordinary if used for a patient in a terminal condition. The second intervention relied on both the booklet and on repeated physician-initiated discussions with the patient about the probable value of a living will. The booklet/physician intervention was found to be significantly more effective within a 4-month period than either the booklet-only intervention or no intervention. The authors conclude that time spent by physicians in early discussion with their patients—before a crisis—may be both shorter and qualitatively better than time spent later in discussion with family members facing the need to make decisions during a crisis.

Both the public and the medical profession appear to favor the voluntary withdrawal of life-sustaining intervention. A 1990 Times Mirror Poll found that 80 percent of those polled believed there are some circumstances in which a patient should be allowed to die. Only 15 percent thought doctors and nurses should always do everything possible to save a patient's life. In 1988, a survey conducted by the American Medical Association demonstrated that 80 percent of the responding physicians favored ending life support for the terminally ill if that's what the patients and their families wanted (Cooke 1989).

EUTHANASIA

Euthanasia literally means an easy or good death or the means of inducing one. In common parlance it refers to a merciful death caused by an intervention rather than (as above) by the withdrawal or withholding of a procedure. Sometimes the distinction is defined as active vs. passive euthanasia. Smith (1989) considers the difference to be between helping to die versus letting die. For Heifetz and Mangel (1975), euthanasia is death through commission rather than omission (withdrawal or refusal) of medical intervention. The term is often used interchangeably with *mercy killing,* or the deliberate taking of life to prevent or to end suffering.

In the United States, there have been a number of highly publicized cases of mercy killing by family members (see Heifetz and Mangel 1975, Thomasma and Graber 1990, and Veatch 1989). In 1973, Lester Zygmaniak, aged 23, shot and killed his 23-year-old brother George three days after George had been left paralyzed from the neck down in a motorcycle accident. The brothers were apparently very close, and the paralyzed brother begged to be killed. Lester was acquitted of murder on grounds of temporary insanity. In 1983, Hans Florian shot his wife, who was suffering from Alzheimer's disease; he was older than she, and he did not want to leave her alone when he died. A grand jury refused to indict him. In contrast to these is the case of Roswell Gilbert, who, in 1985, shot and killed his wife of 51 years to end her suffering from Alzheimer's disease and osteoporosis. He was convicted of murder by a Florida court, although he was later granted clemency by Governor Bob Martinez.

There have been a number of cases of the mercy killing of patients by physicians. In 1949, Dr. Hermann Sander, a New Hampshire physician, administered an intravenous bolus of air to his patient, Abbie Borroto, who was dying of incurable cancer and could neither eat nor drink. He noted in her hospital record that she died within 10 minutes. Sander was charged with first-degree murder. In a highly publicized trial, he was acquitted on the grounds that the patient might have been dead when he injected the air. A similar verdict was reached in the 1973 trial of Dr. Vincent Montemorano, a surgical resident who was indicted for murdering Eugene Bauer at a Long Island hospital with an injection of potassium chloride. Bauer was dying of cancer of the pharynx and was in a coma at the time. Montemorano, who denied the charge, was acquitted on the grounds that the cause of Bauer's death was unclear. In neither of these cases was it brought out that the patient wanted to die.

In 1988, the *Journal of the American Medical Association* (JAMA) printed an anonymous letter by a gynecology resident who claimed to have carried out voluntary euthanasia on a 20-year-old woman suffering from ovarian cancer. In the middle of the night the doctor was summoned to see "Debbie," who had not eaten or slept in 2 days, had not responded to chemotherapy, and was having unrelenting vomiting and difficulty in breathing. Her request to die was expressed in one sentence: "Let's get this over with." The doctor wrote that he could not give her health, but he could give her rest, which he did within 4 minutes by administering 20 mg. of morphine. (It's over Debbie 1988). After the letter's publication, there followed a shower of correspondence to the *JAMA* by physicians about euthanasia, both pro and con. Although the facts about "Debbie" were murky (e.g., Did she want to be relieved of pain or released from suffering? Was 20 mg. of morphine a fatal dose?), the ensuing debate exposed a wide variety of professional opinion.

Proponents view euthanasia as the most humane intervention possible for patients whose suffering cannot be alleviated through other medical means. Vaux (1988) suggests the case of "Debbie" may represent *double-effect euthanasia,* in which the patient's death is the result of medication given to relieve pain but with the knowledge that it will hasten death. Because death is not the intent, but rather a side effect of treatment, such euthanasia is considered by many to be morally acceptable. In fact, double-effect euthanasia (or agathanasia, a better death) probably occurs fairly often. Physicians may prescribe large quantities of analgesics for patients suffering from end-stage cancer pain with the full knowledge that such doses may depress respiration and hasten death (Thomasma and Graber 1990). A recent University of Colorado poll of roughly two thousand physicians revealed that more than half believed euthanasia would have been justified for some of their patients. Another third said they had actually given pain medication they knew would hasten a patient's death (Cooke 1989).

Opponents of euthanasia see its use as representing an erosion of respect for life, and fear that it could become a quick fix. Veatch (1989) believes the legalization of euthanasia could all too easily evolve into a mandate to murder for the good of society as defined by the government. If doctors are allowed to put to death patients who want it, then they might do so to patients who do not want it. Critics claim that there is historical precedent for mercy killing getting out of control. In the 1930s, German doctors began killing psychiatric and medical patients for "compassionate" reasons. Smith (1989) and others have noted that, in fact, putative mercy killing really was not for the benefit of the patients in Nazi Germany. They were killed because they were seen as having no value to society. The Third Reich's euthanasia campaigns began with the involuntary sterilization of "genetic undesirables" (i.e., the mentally retarded, the mentally ill, the chronically ill, the handicapped, and the "racially undesirable") and culminated within a few years in their extermination.

Nearly two decades ago, the Netherlands became the first country in modern society to tolerate active physician involvement in the death of patients. Officially in that country, euthanasia is still illegal: the penalty is 12 years in prison. However, few cases are prosecuted if doctors follow certain guidelines set by the court after a trial in 1972. In that case a Dutch physician was prosecuted for giving a patient, who happened to be his mother, a fatal dose of morphine at her request. The physician was convicted and given a suspended sentence of one week in jail and one year's probation. The court said that euthanasia would be acceptable if (among other things) the patient were incurably ill, the patient's suffering were intolerable, the patient requested that his or her life be terminated, and the patient's physician performed the euthanasia. At about the same time, the Royal Dutch Medical Association issued a statement that although euthanasia should remain a crime, courts would have to determine whether the physician's act was justified by his "conflict of duties" to his patient. A patient's "justifiable" wish to die could outweigh the doctor's desire to prolong life.

Through subsequent court decisions in the Netherlands, including those of the Supreme Court, the criteria for tolerating euthanasia have been refined. The most important criteria remain these: (1.) there must be an explicit and repeated request by the patient to be killed; (2.) the physical or mental pain must be severe and without hope of relief; (3.) all other options must be either exhausted or refused by the patient; and (4.) the doctor must consult another physician to verify the diagnosis and prognosis. Dutch physicians who do not want to participate in voluntary euthanasia are free to refuse (de Wachter 1989). Estimates of the number of deaths resulting from euthanasia in the Netherlands range from two thousand to ten thousand per year. It is frequently performed in hospitals, but patients may choose to die at home with the physician in attendance (Newman 1990). The majority of euthanasia deaths involve consenting adults, but some reports indicate that the option has been offered to children, with and without parental consent (Pellegrino 1991). Patients who are near to death account for most cases, but people with chronic bronchitis, multiple sclerosis, and debilitating rheumatism have also been granted their wish to die. An unspecified number of cases go unreported to avoid the inconveniences of prosecution. In any event, few cases have been prosecuted, and acquittal is the rule (Cooke 1989). The Dutch Parliament is currently considering legalizing euthanasia.

In Los Angeles in 1980, Derek Humphry founded the Hemlock Society, based roughly on the system then operating in the Netherlands. (The Hemlock Society's model proposes that a patient with a fatal illness should be able to obtain a lethal chemical that can be drunk or injected. If two doctors certify that the patient is dying and in pain, such chemicals should be legally supplied. Any doctor would be free to refuse to participate.) In 1975, before he moved to the United States from Great Britain, Humphry helped his wife Jean, who had terminal cancer and allegedly could not tolerate the pain and suffering, ingest a lethal potion given them by a doctor friend. Humphry wrote a book, *In Jean's Way*, about the experience. Ironically, Humphry's next wife, Ann, recently committed suicide, blaming him for ruining her life and for having killed her parents who were ill but not terminal. She had come to reject euthanasia and to denounce the Hemlock Society of which she was cofounder ("A bitter legacy." *Los Angeles Times*, October 23, 1991). Humphry's latest book, *Final Exit: The Practicalities of Self-Deliverance and Assisted Suicide for the Dying*, is essentially a do-it-yourself manual for suicide. It was on best-seller lists for months following publication in March 1991, and stirred up considerable controversy. For example, one scathing review (Kass 1991) calls the book "evil" and cites particularly the rising inclination toward suicide by adolescents. Of the nearly 276,000 high-school students who attempted suicide in 1990, 25 percent sustained serious injuries. Kass declares, "Thanks to Derek Humphry's book, our youth (in attempting suicide) need no longer fail."

Recent public-opinion surveys reveal that the majority of Americans believe terminally ill patients should have the right to ask their doctors to put them out of their misery, and that doctors should be allowed to do so. A 1985 Lou Harris Poll asked whether a patient who was terminally ill, with no hope in sight, had the right to ask a doctor to be put to death; 61 percent said yes, 31 percent said no. A poll for the Hemlock Society, conducted in 1988 by the Roper Organization of New York City, demonstrated that most people believe doctors should be allowed to end the lives of terminally ill patients who request it. Fifty-eight percent believed doctors should be thus authorized; 27 percent did not; the remainder had no opinion.

In the Netherlands, euthanasia is often a matter between two people — doctor and patient — who have known one another for many years. However, the American health care system often does not provide such a prolonged doctor-patient relationship, or an intimate setting in which patients and doctors might comfortably discuss euthanasia. The Hemlock Society's legal arm, Americans Against Human Suffering, fought for passage in 1988 of the California Humane and Dignified Death Act. The law would have allowed patients to request euthanasia if it was determined by two doctors that they would die within 6 months. Unlike in the Netherlands, mercy killing would also have been possible by proxy: a friend or relative with power of attorney could authorize it if a terminal patient became unable to. Failure to obtain sufficient signatures for the initiative prevented the referendum from appearing on the California ballot in 1988. When it did appear in 1992, it was defeated.

Most courts in the United States have recognized a limited right to passive euthanasia (the right to refuse necessary medical treatment). But state legislatures have effectively forbidden active euthanasia by implicitly characterizing it in criminal law as first degree murder. Lacewell (1987) recommends reforming the American criminal law to take account of the motive of the actor and any consent and request expressed by the victim. Veatch (1989) opposes, on principle, any move to legalize active killing (as opposed to discontinuing or not initiating treatment) lest even isolated examples of such mercy killing should undermine the value we attach to human life. He believes that mercy killings will still take place but, being outside the law, each instance will receive careful scrutiny in court, where a judge and jury can evaluate the victim's condition and the killer's motives. He sees great danger that mercifully killing the intractably suffering for their own good, will as a matter of psychology, lead to killing the undesirable, the useless, or the unconscious. Rosenblum and Forsythe (1990) call for physicians to say that they will not deliberately kill, and to say to the lay community that if it insists on tolerating or legalizing active euthanasia, it will have to find nonphysicians to do its killing.

ASSISTED SUICIDE

Pellegrino (1991) defines assisted suicide as the provision by a physician of the means by which patients can end their own lives. It is a long reach from believing that a patient has a right to refuse treatment to believing that a patient has a right to commit suicide. Nevertheless, a number of factors are apparently influencing public opinion to challenge the traditional opposition to suicide in Anglo-American law, medicine, and culture. Such factors include the rising incidence of suicide; the activities of suicide advocacy groups such as the Hemlock Society, the Society for the Right to Die, and Americans Against Suffering; and conflicting legal decisions in some cases involving the rights of handicapped individuals, mercy killing, and murder-suicide attempts by elderly couples. In a March 1988 issue of the *New England Journal of Medicine,* ten prominent doctors acknowledged that many of their colleagues were already giving patients the means with which to end their lives. They do so privately, without publicity, by writing a prescription for sleeping pills and telling the patient who is in the final stage of an illness, "Take only one pill for sleep. If you take all of them you will die" (Cooke 1989).

A recent, much-publicized case of assisted suicide was that of Janet Adkins. A resident of Portland, Oregon, and a member of the Hemlock Society, she was diagnosed as having Alzheimer's disease in June 1989. In January 1990, when medication failed to relieve her progressive memory loss, Mrs. Adkins began planning the suicide that she carried out in Detroit on Monday, 4 June 1990, with Dr. Jack Kevorkian's suicide machine. Dr. Kevorkian had invented a device for assisted suicide that the Hemlock Society publicized. The device requires an intravenous needle to be inserted into the subject's arm. A saline solution starts to flow; then the subject pushes a button that releases two substances into the intravenous drip: first thiopental sodium to induce unconsciousness, then potassium chloride to stop the heart.

Michigan has no laws against assisted suicide. Murder charges against Kevorkian were dismissed, but he was ordered not to use his machine again. However, on 23 October 1991, two female suicides were discovered in Michigan, one hooked to Kevorkian's i.v. machine, the other to another of his devices. His medical license was suspended. New murder charges were filed, but later dropped. Since then, five additional female suicides in Michigan have been attributed to Kevorkian and other of his devices. Already a controversial figure, Kevorkian (1988) had earlier written that physician involvement should extend far beyond mere termination of life. He proposed the establishment of well-staffed and well-organized medical clinics, called *obitoria,* where terminally ill patients could opt for death under controlled circumstances of compassion and decorum. He would also permit exploitation of the related benefits that could accrue from the acquisition of organs for transplantation, and the performance of daring and otherwise impossible human experiments under irreversible general anesthesia.

While Janet Adkins was not typical of the older suicide victim, nor would she have qualified under any of the proposed new laws that require certification of a terminal illness with less than 6 years to live, her death focused attention on the rising rate of suicide among the elderly. Americans aged 65 and older are twice as likely as the rest of the population to take their own lives. Since 1981, the rate has increased by 25 percent. Such statistics probably do not reflect the true rate of suicide because autopsies are rarely performed on elderly victims. Furthermore, statistics do not reflect such passive forms of suicide as refusal to eat or to take medication. A recent study of nursing-home residents suggested that when such methods are taken into account, the suicide rate in that group is eight times higher than that of the general population (Osgood and Brant 1990).

A recent case of physician-assisted suicide was described in the 7 March 1991 *New England Journal of Medicine.* Dr. Timothy E. Quill of Rochester, New York, wrote that he helped a 45-year-old leukemia patient identified as "Diane" by prescribing a quantity of barbiturates sufficient to cause death. Quill wrote that the woman chose suicide rather than to undergo a painful and prolonged treatment with chemotherapy that offered only a 25 percent chance of recovery. A grand jury subsequently cleared him of criminal wrongdoing, even though he could have been charged with second-degree manslaughter (punishable by up to 15 years in prison, or with assisting a suicide, punishable by up to 4 years imprisonment). The State Board for Professional Medical Conduct also ruled that no misconduct charges would be filed against Quill. The three-member panel decided that a physician cannot know with certainty what use a patient might make of the drugs he prescribes, nor is it within a physician's power or authority to compel a patient to do one thing or another with any prescription. The Board members made it clear that they were not condoning assisted suicide, and emphasized that Quill's situation was substantially different from Kevorkian's and from "Debbie's" anonymous physician. Unlike the doctors in those two cases, Quill had a longstanding relationship with his patient, and he didn't participate directly in ending her life. If the Board had determined that professional misconduct charges should be filed, Quill could have faced penalties ranging from a warning letter to fines, suspension, or even the revocation of his medical license.

State laws vary with respect to assisted suicide. Michigan has no laws proscribing such acts. In Washington, an initiative (#119) reached the November 1991 ballot (but failed to pass) that would have legalized physician-assisted killing for mentally competent adults with less than 6 months to live who voluntarily chose the procedure. At present, California considers assisting a suicide to be a felony punishable by up to 5 years in prison plus all of the other disadvantages of being convicted of a felony such as the loss of the right to vote. For a physician, the penalties would include also the loss of the license to practice medicine. However, public support for suicide has been growing. In a 1975 Gallup Poll, 40 percent of respondents said a person with an incurable disease has the moral right to commit suicide; by 1990, 55 percent expressed such a view.

DISCUSSION

One problem with both euthanasia and assisted suicide is that the rights may not be the same for everyone: some people may be viewed as having a greater right to die than others. For example, discouraged victims of AIDS may ask their doctors, members of their families, or their friends, to help them end their lives. But these would-be helpers may not realize that there are other ways to deal with depressive feelings, and that such a patient, properly treated, might well be glad to find himself still alive and able to use his remaining time of life—like the rest of us—as he chooses. There are some people within our society who would be only too happy to help AIDS patients to die—in other words, to exterminate them. It would be tragic if this attitude were reinforced by the friends and families of AIDS patients, or by the patients themselves.

Even the most suicidal patient is often ambivalent about wanting to die.

Suicidal ideation may be a symptom of a psychiatric illness, or of the depression that can accompany severe illness, physical disability, bereavement, or even giving birth to a child. It may be not be a positive desire to die but rather a desire for relief from physical or psychological suffering. If communicated, it may be a cry for help or reassurance. The desire by patients to end their dependence on life-sustaining medical care in order to regain a sense of control over their lives and their bodies may be expressed in terms of a wish for death. However, the desire to die, as every psychiatrist well knows, can be — and often is — reversed. People may change their minds and decide to live if they are provided compassionate intervention which may include anti-depressant medication. Ms. Bouvia, paralyzed from cerebral palsy and also suffering from arthritis, won the right to refuse artificial feedings but changed her mind after also winning a suit to prevent doctors in the public facility that housed her from discontinuing or reducing the morphine which she needed to control pain, and to which she had become addicted.

Another who reconsidered was Larry McAfee, a 34-year-old Georgia man paralyzed below the neck after a motorcycle accident and respirator dependent. He decided that a life that depended on a machine was not worth living and asked a judge for permission to turn off his breathing system. The judge ruled in McAfee's favor in September 1990, and the Georgia Supreme Court upheld the decision in November. The court's unanimous opinion was that McAfee's right to discontinue treatment fell under privacy rights guaranteed by the state and federal constitutions. Those rights were held to outweigh whatever interest the state might have in preserving McAfee's life. However, having won the case, McAfee decided to postpone his death after doctors and health care workers introduced him to new computerized machines that provide greater autonomy even to severely paralyzed persons. McAfee's immediate problem was a health-care funding system that would pay to house him in a hospital, but wouldn't pay for his care in a less-expensive, but better-suited, nursing home. Three months after he won his right-to-die suit, he addressed the Georgia State Senate urging it to revise the state's "archaic" method of caring for the severely disabled (Quadriplegic pleads for dignified life. Chicago Tribune, February 22, 1990).

In fact, many patients who refuse life-sustaining treatment do so not because they seek relief from intolerable pain and suffering, but because they see no other way to end their total dependence on others. Thomasma and Graber (1990) discuss the case of Donald C., a young man who was severely burned and disabled and refused further life-sustaining treatment. However, the psychiatrist who examined Donald determined that what he really wanted was to end his sense of helplessness and, by choosing death, to gain personal control over his life. After winning the right to refuse further therapy, and finding that the power of decision was now in his own hands, Donald C. chose life and gave permission for the next stage of treatment. In this case a thoughtful and sympathetic psychiatrist recognized that the patient did not really want to die, suggesting that anyone who is asked to help a patient end his life should enlist the aid of a skilled mental-health professional.

With regard to terminally ill patients, greater attention should be paid to their physical and psychological comfort. Guyther (1973) notes that in days gone by people died at home in familiar settings, among familiar faces. Now more than 80 percent of Americans die in hospitals or nursing homes, where they are surrounded by assorted monitors, respirators, strange gadgets, and unfamiliar people. Rarely does the patient have any choice about the institutional environment. An alternative to hospitals and nursing homes is hospice care, which has emerged out of an awareness that the needs of the dying patient often are not adequately met by most modern medical institutions. The hospice gives to the patient and the family more responsibility in making decisions regarding life and death. As pointed out by Mathew and Scully (1986), society should ensure that its dying members have access to care directed specifically to their needs. Hospice care in the United States has yet to find its proper place, and to be widely accepted as an essential facet of the health-care delivery system. When it is, requests for assisted suicides by terminal patients are likely to decline.

Shneidman (1978) notes that when competent, well-functioning people are asked to name what they would consider to be most important if they were dying, they usually place control over their own treatment and management at the top of the list, followed by relief from pain. But what actually happens is that there are conflicting agendas between the dying person's fight for dignity and the hospital staff's interest in having a good patient, that is, one who doesn't die too soon or linger too long. In discussing the treatment of elderly cancer patients, Thomasma (1987) advises physicians to construct a treatment-decision contract, which recognizes that incompetence and death may occur in the near future. Through dialogue about probable outcomes of various interventions, both patients and physicians can explore fundamental values to be respected in the course of treatment. In this way, physicians can preserve their traditional role of championing the value of life while at the same time respecting the considered judgments of elderly patients about their care.

It is especially important to distinguish the theoretical exercise of the right to die from the clinical understanding of how powerful the desire to live really is in people if they are mentally well. If someone really wants to die, it is not that hard to kill oneself. Every year many people jump off buildings, blow out their brains, or take an overdose of sedatives. Modern suicide prevention enterprises try to prevent such suicides, and many can be prevented. Therefore, when a patient comes to his or her doctor, asking for help to die, it is the doctor's chance to intervene. Physicians should reassure their patients that they will not allow them to endure pain or discomfort beyond their tolerance. Currently available machines such as the Bard-Harvard device allow patients safely to administer their own intravenous analgesics. Patient-controlled analgesia, or *demand analgesia,* (as an alternative to traditional dosing techniques in which nurses administer scheduled intramuscular injections) enables patients to control their own pain medication. Control over pain also decreases patients' levels of fear that, should the pain worsen, they will have to wait for someone else to provide relief. As a result, the patient who controls his own blood levels of analgesics usually requires significantly less medication to remain comfortable.

More doctors should learn how to help people live with dignity and serenity right up to the final moment. Kaye (1988) urges physicians to maintain open and honest communications among themselves, their patients, and the patients' families. No matter how often the physician treats a dying patient, he or she should never be casual or matter-of-fact about death. Death should always command respect. Those who care for the terminally ill can become enriched by observing the courage of many dying patients, and marvel at how most people want to live their lives to the natural end, which nature and modern medicine can make easy. Again it is Shneidman (1978) who reminds us that working intensively with the terminally ill, sitting unhurriedly by the bedside, and coming to know the dying patient as a person, can be a rewarding experience that will illuminate the rest of one's practice. Indeed, it can give one the wisdom and perspective to face one's own end with nobility of spirit when the time comes as it must to us all.

REFERENCES

Abrams, G. A bitter legacy (1991). *Los Angeles Times,* October 23, E1, E3.

Cantor, N. L. (1989). The permanently unconscious patient, non-feeding and euthanasia. *American Journal of Law and Medicine* 15:381–437.

Cohen-Mansfield, J., Rabinovich, B. A., Lipson, S., et al. (1991). The decision to execute a durable power of attorney for health care and preferences regarding the utilization of life-sustaining treatments in nursing home residents. *Archives of Internal Medicine* 151:289–294.

Cooke, P. (1989). The gentle death. *Hippocrates* 3:50–60.

de Wachter, M. A. H. (1989). Active euthanasia in the Netherlands. *Journal of the American Medical Association* 262:3316–3319.

Furedi, J. Personal communication, 1989.

Gamble, E. R., McDonald, P. J., and Lichstein, P. R. (1991). Knowledge, attitudes, and behavior of elderly persons regarding living wills. *Archives of Internal Medicine* 151:277–280.

Goodman, R. S. (1987). "Do not resuscitate." *Medicine and Law* 6:479–486.

Guyther, J. R. (1973). The right to die. *Maryland State Medical Journal* 22:44–45.

Hare, J., and Nelson, C. (1991). Will outpatients complete living wills? A comparison of two interventions. *Journal of General Internal Medicine* 6:41–46.

Heifetz, M. C., and Mangel, C. (1975). *The Right to Die.* New York: Berkley Medallion.

Humphry, D. (1991) *Final Exit: The Practicalities of Self-Deliverance and Assisted Suicide for the Dying.* Portland, OR: Hemlock Society.

It's over Debbie. (1988). *Journal of the American Medical Association* 259:272.

Kass, L. R. (1991). Suicide made easy: the evil of "rational" humaneness. *Commentary* 92:19–24.

Kaye, J. M. (1988). The physician's role with the terminally ill patient. *Clinics in Geriatric Medicine* 4:13–27.

Kevorkian, J. (1988). The last fearsome taboo: medical aspects of planned death. *Medicine and Law* 7:1–14.

Knox, L. S. (1989). Ethical issues in nutritional support nursing. Withholding and withdrawing nutritional support. *Nursing Clinics of North America* 24:427–436.

Lacewell, L. A. (1987). A comparative view of the roles of motive and consent in the response of the criminal justice system to active euthanasia. *Medicine and Law* 6:449–463.

Lo, B., and Steinbrook, R. (1991). Beyond the Cruzan case: the U.S. Supreme Court and medical practice. *Annals of Internal Medicine* 114:895–901.

Mathew, L. M., and Scully, J. H. (1986). Hospice care. *Clinics in Geriatric Medicine* 2:617–634.

Newman, M. E. (1990). Active euthanasia in the Netherlands. In *To Die or Not To Die,* ed. A. S. Berger and J. Berger, pp. 117–128. New York: Prager.

Oboler, S. K. (1986). Brain death and persistent vegetative states. *Clinics in Geriatric Medicine* 2:547–576.

Osgood, N. J., and Brant B. A. (1990). Suicidal behavior in long-term care facilities. *Suicide and Life-Threatening Behavior* 20:113–122.

Pellegrino, E. D. (1991). Ethics. *Journal of the American Medical Association* 265:3118–3119.

Quadriplegic pleads for dignified life. (1990). *Chicago Tribune,* February 22, p. 18.

Quill, T. E. (1991). A case of individualized decision making (Sounding Board). *New England Journal of Medicine* 324:691–694.

Rosenblum, V. G., and Forsythe, C. D. (1990). The right to assisted suicide: protection of autonomy or an open door to social killing? *Issues in Law and Medicine* 6:3–31.

Rosner, F. (1988). Withdrawing fluids and nutrition: an alternate way. *Bulletin of the New York Academy of Medicine* 64:363–375.

Schneiderman, L. J., Jecker, N. S., and Jonsen, A. R. (1990). Medical futility: its meaning and ethical implications. *Annals of Internal Medicine* 112:949–954.

Shneidman, E. (1978). Some aspects of psychotherapy with dying persons. In *Psychosocial Aspects of Terminal Patient Care,* ed. C. A. Garfield, pp. 272–283. New York: McGraw-Hill.

Shneidman, E. S., and Szasz, T. S. (1972). The ethics of suicide prevention. *Audio-Digest Psychiatry* 1 (2) July 24, cassette. (Debate sponsored by the University of California, San Francisco, Continuing Education in Health Sciences, April 29, 1972).

Smith, G. P. (1989). *Final Choices: Autonomy in Health Care Decisions.* Springfield, IL: Charles C Thomas.

Thomasma, D. C. (1987). Ethical and legal issues in the care of the elderly cancer patient. *Clinics in Geriatric Medicine* 3:541–547.

Thomasma, D. C., and Graber, G. C. (1990). *Euthanasia: Toward an Ethical Social Policy.* New York: Continuum.

Vaux, K. L. (1988). Debbie's dying: mercy killing and the good death. *Journal of the American Medical Association* 259:2140–2141.

Veatch, R. M. (1989). *Death, Dying, & the Biological Revolution: Our Last Quest for Responsibility.* New Haven, CT: Yale University Press.

Wyngaarden, J. B., and Smith, L. H., Jr. (1985). *Cecil Textbook of Medicine.* Vol. 2. Philadelphia: W.B. Saunders.

23: SUICIDOLOGY AND THE RIGHT TO DIE

Margaret P. Battin

As suicidology reflects on the issue of the right to die, it can make no bigger mistake than by seeing suicide and suicidal behavior in short-sighted isolation, without reference to the cultural context within which it occurs. Two kinds of myopia currently afflict us in particularly constricting ways: the refusal to see issues of suicide in the context of larger issues about how we die, and the failure to notice substantial cultural differences in how we think about dying and the choices we make about dying. I think suicidology can profit considerably from examining different end-of-life practices in cultures otherwise closely related to our own, and it is for this reason that I'd like to look here at differences in end-of-life practices and their conceptual backgrounds in three otherwise rather similar countries: the Netherlands, Germany, and the United States. Much of what we say about suicide and suicidal behavior in our own culture may look very different in the light of such contrasts, and much of what we do in studying and preventing suicide may be called into question in this way.

DEALING WITH DYING IN THREE ADVANCED NATIONS

The Netherlands, Germany, and the United States are all advanced industrial democracies. They all have sophisticated medical establishments and life expectancies over 70 years of age; their populations are all characterized by an

Author's Note: This chapter incorporates extensive material from two of my previous papers: "The Way We Do It, The Way They Do It," from *Journal of Pain and Symptom Management* 6:1–8 (July 1991), copyright © 1991 by the U.S. Cancer Pain Relief Committee, reprinted by permission of Elsevier Science Publishing Co. Inc., and "Assisted Suicide: What Can We Learn from Germany?," from the *Hastings Center Report* 22:45–51 (March–April 1992), copyright © 1992, reprinted by permission of the Hastings Center, as well as some material from my forthcoming paper, "Is There a Place for Euthanasia in America's Care for the Elderly?" to be published in *Rationing Health Care: Ethics and Aging,* edited by J. Walters and D. Covig.

increasing proportion of older persons. They are all in what has been called the fourth stage of the epidemiologic transition (Olshansky and Ault 1986)—that stage of societal development in which it is no longer the case that most people die of acute parasitic or infectious diseases. In this stage, most people do not die of diseases with rapid, unpredictable onsets and sharp fatality curves; rather, the majority of the population—as much as perhaps 70–80 percent—dies of degenerative diseases, especially delayed degenerative diseases, that are characterized by late, slow onset and extended decline. Most people in highly industrialized countries die from cancer, atherosclerosis, heart disease (by no means always suddenly fatal), chronic obstructive pulmonary disease, liver, kidney or other organ disease, or degenerative neurological disorders. Thus, all three of these countries are alike in facing a common problem: how to deal with the characteristic new ways in which we die.

DEALING WITH DYING IN THE UNITED STATES

In the United States, we have come to recognize that the maximal extension of life-prolonging treatment in these late-life degenerative conditions is often inappropriate. Although we could keep the machines and tubes—the respirators, intravenous lines, feeding tubes—hooked up for extended periods, we recognize that this is inhumane, pointless, and financially impossible. Instead, as a society we have developed a number of mechanisms for dealing with these hopeless situations, all of which involve withholding or withdrawing various forms of treatment.

Some mechanisms for withholding or withdrawing treatment are exercised by the patient who is confronted by such a situation or who anticipates it; these include refusal of treatment, the patient-executed DNR order, the living will, and the durable power of attorney. Others are mechanisms for decision by second parties about a patient who is no longer competent or never was competent. The latter are reflected in a long series of court cases. These are cases that attempt to delineate the precise circumstances under which it is appropriate to withhold or withdraw various forms of therapy, including respiratory support, chemotherapy, antibiotics in intercurrent infections, and artificial nutrition and hydration. Thus, during the past 15 years or so, we have developed an impressive body of case law and state statute that protects, permits, and facilitates our characteristic American strategy of dealing with end-of-life situations. These cases provide a framework for withholding or withdrawing treatment when we believe there is no medical or moral point in going on. This is sometimes termed passive euthanasia; more often, it is simply called allowing to die, and is ubiquitous in the United States.

For example, a recent study by Miles and Gomez (1988) indicates that some 85 percent of deaths in the United States occur in health-care institutions, including hospitals, nursing homes, and other facilities, and of these, about 70 percent involve electively withholding some form of life-sustaining treatment. A

1989 study cited in the *Journal of the American Medical Association* claims that 85–90 percent of critical care professionals state that they are withholding and withdrawing life-sustaining treatments from patients who are "deemed to have irreversible disease and are terminally ill" (Sprung 1990 p. 2213). Still another study identified some 115 patients in two intensive-care units from whom care was withheld or withdrawn; 110 were already incompetent by the time the decision to limit care was made. The 89 who died while still in the intensive care unit accounted for 45 percent of all deaths there (Smedira 1990). It is estimated that 1.3 million American deaths a year follow decisions to withhold life support; this is a majority of the just over two million American deaths per year. Withholding and withdrawing treatment is the way we in the USA go about dealing with dying, and indeed "allowing to die" is the only legally protected alternative to maximal treatment recognized in the United States. We do not legally permit ourselves actively to cause death.

DEALING WITH DYING IN HOLLAND

In the Netherlands, voluntary active euthanasia is also an available response to end-of-life situations. Although active euthanasia remains prohibited by statutory law, it is protected by a series of lower and supreme court decisions and is widely regarded as legal, or, more precisely, *gedogen*, legally tolerated. These court decisions have the effect of protecting the physician who performs euthanasia from prosecution, provided the physician meets a rigorous set of guidelines.

These guidelines, variously stated, contain five central provisions:

1. that the patient's request be voluntary;
2. that the patient be undergoing intolerable suffering;
3. that all alternatives acceptable to the patient for relieving the suffering have been tried;
4. that the patient have full information;
5. that the physician have consulted with a second physician whose judgment can be expected to be independent.

Of these criteria, it is the first which is central: euthanasia may be performed only at the voluntary request of the patient. This criterion is also understood to require that the patient's request be a stable, enduring, reflective one — not the product of a transitory impulse. Every attempt is to be made to rule out depression, psychopathology, pressures from family members, unrealistic fears, and other factors compromising voluntariness. In general, pain is not the principal basis for euthanasia, since pain can, in most cases, be effectively treated; "intolerable suffering," understood to mean suffering that is in the patient's (rather than the physician's) view intolerable, may also include fear of or unwillingness to endure *entluisterung*, or that gradual effacement and loss of personal identity that characterizes the end stages of many terminal illnesses. It is also required that euthanasia be performed only by a physician; it may not be performed by a nurse, family member, or other party.

Putting an end to years of inflammatory discussion in which speculation about the frequency of euthanasia had run as high as twenty thousand cases a year, a comprehensive study requested by the Dutch government was published in 1991.[1] This study, popularly known as the Remmelink Commission report, showed that about 1.8 percent of deaths in the Netherlands are the result of euthanasia at the explicit request of the patient with some form of physician involvement and about 0.3 percent of deaths involve physician-assisted suicide. The report of another 0.8 percent of cases of life-terminating acts without the explicit and persistent request of the patient has stirred enormous controversy in the United States, where it is often claimed that this shows that one thousand patients were put to death against their wishes; but what the Remmelink Commission in fact reports is that in these cases, although the strict criteria for euthanasia were not fulfilled, in more than half, euthanasia had been previously discussed with the patient or the patient had expressed in a previous phase of the disease a wish for euthanasia if his or her suffering became unbearable, and in virtually all the remaining cases the patients were near to death and clearly suffering grievously, yet verbal contact had become impossible. Of the total deaths in the Netherlands, the Remmelink Commission found that about 17.5 percent involved decisions to withhold or withdraw treatment although continuing treatment would probably have prolonged life, another 17.5 percent involved the use of opioids to relieve pain but in dosages probably sufficient to shorten life (a practice ubiquitous in the U.S.), and a total of approximately 2.9 percent involved euthanasia and related practices.

Thus, euthanasia is comparatively rare in the Netherlands, even in a medical climate in which, as in the U.S., medical decisions about dying are common; physician-assisted suicide is even rarer. Nevertheless, euthanasia is a conspicuous alternative to terminal illness well known to both physicians and the general public. Surveys of public opinion in the Netherlands show growing public support for a liberal euthanasia policy (increasing from 40 percent in 1966 to 81 percent in 1988) (Borst-Eilers 1991), and whereas there is a vocal minority opposed to the practice (including a group of about one thousand physicians), it is apparent that both the majority of the population in Holland and the majority of Holland's physicians support it. The Remmelink Commission found that 54 percent of physicians had performed euthanasia or assisted in suicide (though the percentage is highest [62 percent] among general practitioners and lowest [12 percent] among nursing home physicians), and an additional 34 percent said that although they had not practiced euthanasia or assisted in suicide, they could conceive of situations in which they would be prepared to do so. The

---

[1] A summary of the findings is available in English in P. J. van der Maas, J. J. M. van Delden, L. Pijnenborg, and C. W. N. Looman, "Euthanasia and Other Medical Decisions Concerning the End of Life," *The Lancet* 338 (14 September 1991): pp. 669–74.

Commission commented, "a large majority of physicians in the Netherlands see euthanasia as an accepted element of medical practice under certain circumstances," (van der Maas et al. 1991) though these circumstances are comparatively rare.

In Holland, many hospitals now have protocols for the performance of euthanasia; these serve to ensure that the court-established guidelines have been met. However, it is believed that most euthanasia is practiced in the patient's home, typically by the *huisarts,* or general practitioner, who is the patient's long-term family physician. Euthanasia is usually performed after aggressive hospital treatment has failed to arrest the patient's terminal illness; the patient has come home to die, and the family physician is prepared to ease this passing. Whether practiced at home or in the hospital, it is believed that euthanasia usually takes place in the presence of the family members, perhaps the visiting nurse, and often, the patient's pastor or priest. Many doctors say that performing euthanasia is never easy, but that it is something they believe a doctor ought to do for his or her patient when nothing else can help.

Thus, in Holland, a patient facing the end of life has an option not openly practiced in the United States: to ask the physician to bring his or her life to an end. Although not everyone does so—indeed, of people who die in a given year, at least 97 percent do not—it is a choice widely understood as available.

FACING DEATH IN GERMANY

In part because of its very painful history of Nazism, Germany appears to believe that doctors should have no role in causing death. Although societal generalizations are always risky, it is fair, I think, to say that there is vigorous and nearly universal opposition in Germany to the notion of active euthanasia. Euthanasia is viewed as always wrong, and the Germans view the Dutch as stepping out on a dangerously slippery slope.

However, it is an artifact of German law that, whereas killing on request (including voluntary euthanasia) is prohibited, assisting suicide—where the person committing suicide is determined to do so—is not a violation of the law. Taking advantage of this situation, there has developed a private organization, the *Deutsche Gesellschaft für Humanes Sterben* (DGHS), or German Society for Humane Dying, which provides support to its very extensive membership in choosing suicide as an alternative to terminal illness.

Founded in 1980, by September 1991 the DGHS had grown to some fifty thousand members, and has been adding new members at the rate of one thousand per month. Many of its members are already elderly or terminally ill. After a person has been a member of the organization for at least a year, he or she may request a copy of DGHS's booklet *Menschenwürdiges und selbstverantwortliches Sterben,* or "Dignified and Responsible Death," which is not commercially available. The DGHS does not charge for this booklet. The booklet itself includes a statement of the conditions under which it is obtainable—including the requirement that the member has not received medical or psychotherapeutic treatment for depression or other psychiatric illness during the last 2 years. Each copy is numbered; the member is urged to keep track of it, not to give it to third parties, and not to make public its contents in any other way. The booklet is to be returned to DGHS after the member's death. The DGHS reports approximately two thousand to three thousand suicides per year among its members.

The specific advice provided in the DGHS's booklet contains, among other things, a list of ten drugs available by prescription in Germany, mostly barbiturates and chloroquines, together with the specific dosages necessary for producing a painless, nonviolent death. (Although the DGHS was originally associated with the provision of cyanide, it no longer publicly recommends this.) In addition to the drugs that will produce death, the booklet lists companion drugs for preventing vomiting and for inducing sedation. It also lists drugs available without prescription in other European countries (some just a few hours drive from parts of Germany), including France, Italy, Spain, Portugal, and Greece. DGHS recommends that the member approach a physician for a prescription for the drug of choice, asking, for example, for a barbiturate to help with sleeping or chloroquine for protection against malaria on a trip to India. Where this deception is difficult or impossible, the DGHS may also arrange for someone to obtain drugs from a country where they are available without prescription. In unusual cases, it will also provide what it calls *Sterbebegleitung,* or accompaniment in dying: this is provided by a companion who will remain with the person during the time that is required for the lethal drug to take full effect, often as much as 10 to 12 hours or longer. However, the DGHS now urges that family members or friends, rather than DGHS staff or members, provide accompaniment, and has recently inaugurated an *Akademie der Sterbebegleitung,* or Academy of Accompaniment in Dying, to train such persons in what to expect and how to be supportive.

DGHS also supports refusal of treatment, where that is what the patient wishes, and in general attempts to protect a broad range of patients' rights. It provides members with a series of forms, including copies of Germany's version of the living will and durable power of attorney. In the format provided by the DGHS, both of these forms not only stipulate health care choices or persons empowered to make them on behalf of a no-longer-competent patient, but they also include provisions authorizing the DGHS to take legal action against any person or organization (that is, any physician or hospital) that refuses to honor the patient's antecedently stipulated wishes. For those who choose suicide as a way of bringing their lives to an end, the DGHS also provides a form intended to provide clear evidence both of the considered nature of that choice and to dispel any suspicion of foul play. The form—printed on a single sheet of distinctive pink paper—is to be signed once when the person joins the DGHS, asserting that he or she is a member of the organization and that he or she wishes to exercise the right to determine the time of his or her death; the same form is to be signed again at the time of the suicide — presumably, at least a year later — and to be left beside the body.

DGHS also relies heavily on its network of regional bureaus to encourage and facilitate feedback. Since assisting suicide is not illegal in Germany, there is no legal risk for an individual in soliciting information about suicide or in that person's family reporting back information about methods of suicide attempted or used. DGHS attempts to keep very careful track of its members' experiences with the information it provides, and uses this feedback to revise and update its drug recommendations. To facilitate this, the drug information provided in its booklet is printed on a separate sheet inserted in a slip pocket inside the back cover, and this list of current recommendations is revised and updated on a monthly basis. DGHS thus claims to be able to do what is much riskier in countries where assisting suicide is illegal: to make extensive use of feedback about actual methods of suicide. In mid-1991, when the Hemlock Society's president Derek Humphry's book *Final Exit* (1991) hit the top of the *New York Times* how-to best-seller list, DGHS president Hans Henning Atrott complained that the American book's information wasn't fully reliable: it was based, Atrott claimed, on published toxicological information, or information about what drug doses might prove sufficiently toxic to cause death, and not on empirical information about what drug doses would be certain to cause death. Because of the quite different legal situation in Germany, DGHS is able to collect reports about its own members' suicides and thus to adjust its drug recommendations on the basis of actual experience. Humphry replied that he gets just as much information from the forty seven thousand members of the Hemlock Society, including explicit information about suicide deaths from patients' families, from doctors, and even occasionally from patients whose suicide attempts were not fatal, but it is clear that such information is collected in a very different climate in the U.S. Fearing that they would be subpoenaed, the Hemlock Society was forced several years ago to burn first-person reports from a sizable number of physicians of cases of euthanasia they had performed or suicide in which they had assisted.

Even though assistance in suicide is not illegal in Germany, the DGHS remains controversial, though criticism is often directed against the person of its founder and not against the principle of assistance in suicide itself. Late in 1991, Hans Henning Atrott was accused of selling cyanide to an attorney hospitalized for mental illness, and in May 1992 police raided his office, finding capsules of cyanide, barbiturates, and a large amount of cash. What the outcome of this scandal will be remains, at this writing, to be seen, though the point of criticism clearly has to do with Atrott's alleged profiteering and assisting a mentally ill person, rather than with the DGHS's practice of assisting competent terminally ill individuals in suicide.

The existence of the DGHS is made possible by a distinctive feature of German law, a feature in which German law differs from that of England, the

U.S., the Netherlands, and most of Europe. During the Middle Ages in most of Europe suicide was a felony punishable by desecration of the corpse, burial at a crossroads, forfeiture of the decedent's estate to the crown, and, in some instances, execution if the suicide attempt was not fatal. Suicide was decriminalized in England and Wales only in 1961, primarily for the purpose of permitting medical and psychiatric treatment without criminal onus for those who had attempted suicide. In contrast, suicide was decriminalized in Germany by Frederick the Great in 1751. Assisting suicide is not a crime in Germany either, provided that the person about to commit suicide is *tatherrschaftsfähig,* that is, capable of exercising control over his or her actions, and also that he or she acts out of *freiverantwortliche Wille,* or freely responsible choice.[2] Thus, while assisting the suicide of a disturbed, depressed, or demented person, or a person coerced by external forces, would not be permitted under German law, it is permitted to aid an informed, voluntary suicide, including what we might be tempted to call a rational suicide. However, killing upon request — the act involved in euthanasia — is prohibited under German law.

To be sure, the details of German law on these points have been receiving extended discussion, especially with respect to the apparent conflict between the fact that assisted suicide is not illegal but that there may be a duty to rescue a suicide in progress. Like U.S. law, German law imposes an obligation to rescue upon specific parties standing in certain professional or personal relationships to other persons; this is the basis of the physician's legal duty to rescue his or her patient. Thus, as one widely prevalent interpretation of the legal situation holds, although the physician is not prohibited from giving a lethal drug to a patient, once that patient has taken the drug and becomes unconscious, the physician incurs a duty to resuscitate him or her.[3]

These provisions of German law — all currently highly controversial — have the effect of curtailing the role of German physicians in suicide, and tend to insulate the patient from physician aid. Thus, German law reinforces a posture that might also seem to be a product of fear of euthanasia and suspicion of authoritarian physicians: in Germany, taking death into one's own hands in these contexts is an individual, private matter, to be conducted outside the medical establishment and largely without its help. This is not to say that the provisions of German law are the product of studied judicial deliberation or current political consensus; they are often viewed as an artifact of earlier times. In any case, although it apparently would not be illegal for physicians to assist in the

---

[2]See Volker Krey, "Tötung durch Zulassen eines Selbstmordes" [Killing by allowing a suicide to occur], *Strafrecht Besonderer Teil,* vol. 1, 7th edition (Stuttgart: Verlag W. Kohlhammer, 1972, 1989), pp. 35-37.

[3]See Volker Krey, "Euthanasie nach deutschem Strafrecht — Strafrechtlich Probleme der Sterbehilfe für unheilbar Erkrankte" [Euthanasia according to the German criminal law: the problem of aid-in-dying for the terminally ill], in 5. Europäischer Kongress für humanes Sterben, (Augsburg: Deutsche Gesellschaft für humanes Sterben e.V., 1985), pp. 145-50, and also the previously cited work.

initiation of their patients' suicides, as a matter of practice they do not do so. There is some move to suggest that the obligation to rescue extends beyond the physician to a spouse, friend, or any person with knowledge of a suicide in progress, but this is currently an extremely controversial issue in German law.

That neither suicide nor assisted suicide are illegal under German law does not mean that there can be no attempts to prevent suicide. Indeed, Germany has an active organization for suicide prevention, the *Deutsche Gesellschaft für Suizidprävention* (the German Society for Suicide Prevention), which directs its attention in particular to recognizing suicidal tendencies in disturbed, depressed, or demented persons — that is, persons who cannot be said to be in control of their actions and who are not exhibiting freely responsible choice. Since, of course, it is not always possible to determine in advance whether a given person's suicide might count as in control or not in control, or as the product or not the product of freely responsible choice, in practice Germany's suicide prevention efforts look very much like those elsewhere, and are generally directed across the board at preventing suicide.[4]

To be sure, assisted suicide is not the only option open to the terminally ill in Germany; nor is it, apparently, particularly frequent. There is increasing emphasis on help in dying that does not involve direct termination, and organizations like Omega, offering hospice-style care and an extensive program of companionship, are attracting increasing attention. Nevertheless, the DGHS is a conspicuous organization, and many Germans appear to be aware that this alternative is available even if they do not use it.

OBJECTIONS TO THE THREE MODELS OF DYING

In response to the dilemmas raised by the new circumstances of death, in which the majority of the population in each of the advanced industrial nations dies of degenerative diseases after an extended period of terminal deterioration, different countries develop different practices. The United States legally permits only withholding and withdrawal of treatment, though of course active euthanasia and assisted suicide do occur. Holland also permits voluntary active euthanasia, and although Germany rejects euthanasia, it tolerates assisted suicide. But there are serious moral objections to be made to each of these practices, objections to be considered before resolving the issue of which practice our own culture ought to adopt.

Objections to the German Practice

German law does not prohibit assisting suicide, but postwar German culture discourages physicians from taking any active role in death. This gives rise to

---

[4]See, however, Hermann Pohlmeier, *Selbstmord und Selbstmordverhütung* [Suicide and suicide prevention] (Munich: Urban & Schwartzenberg, 1983) for a discussion of suicide and suicide prevention that also considers the relationship of suicide prevention to issues about freedom to choose suicide; a briefer statement can be found in his editorial, "Suicide and Euthanasia — Special Types of Partner Relationships," *Suicide and Life-Threatening Behavior*, 15, no. 2(1985):117–123.

distinctive moral problems in Germany's practices. For one thing, it appears that there is little professional help or review provided for patients' choices about suicide; because the patient makes this choice essentially outside the medical establishment, medical professionals are not in a position to detect or treat impaired judgment on the part of the patient, especially judgment impaired by depression. Similarly, if the patient must commit suicide assisted only by persons outside the medical profession, there are risks that the patient's diagnosis and prognosis are inadequately confirmed, that the means chosen for suicide will be unreliable or inappropriately used, that the means used for suicide will fall into the hands of other persons, and that the patient will fail to recognize or be able to resist intrafamilial pressures and manipulation. The DGHS policy for providing assistance requires that the patient be terminally ill and have been a member of the DGHS for at least one year in order to make use of its services, the latter requirement apparently intended to provide evidence of the stability of such a choice, but these minimal requirements are hardly sufficient to answer the charge that suicide decisions, which are made for medical reasons but must be made without medical help, may be rendered under less than ideally informed and voluntary conditions.

Whether Germany's different cultural and linguistic climate, as we shall explore in a moment, protects these decisions in other ways remains to be seen.

Objections to the Dutch Practice

The Dutch practice of physician-performed active voluntary euthanasia also raises a number of ethical issues, many of which have been discussed vigorously both in the Dutch press and in commentary on the Dutch practices from abroad. For one thing, it is sometimes said that the availability of physician-performed euthanasia creates a disincentive for providing good terminal care. I have seen no evidence that this is the case; on the contrary, Peter Admiraal, the anesthesiologist who is perhaps Holland's most vocal proponent of voluntary active euthanasia, insists that pain should rarely or never be the case for euthanasia, since pain (in contrast to suffering) is comparatively easily treated (Admiraal 1990). Instead, it is a refusal to endure the final stages of deterioration, both mental and physical, that motivates requests.

It is also sometimes said that active euthanasia violates the Hippocratic Oath. Indeed, it is true that the original Greek version of the Oath prohibits the physician from giving a deadly drug, even when asked for it; but the original version also prohibits performing surgery and taking fees for teaching medicine, neither of which prohibitions has survived into contemporary medical practice. Dutch physicians often say that they see performing euthanasia—where it is genuinely requested by the patient and nothing else can be done to relieve the patient's suffering—as part of their duty to the patient, not as a violation of it.

The Dutch are also often said to be at risk of starting down the slippery slope, that is, that the practice of voluntary active euthanasia for patients who meet the criteria will erode into practicing less-than-voluntary euthanasia on patients whose problems are not irremediable, and perhaps by gradual degrees develop into terminating the lives of people who are elderly, chronically ill, handicapped, mentally retarded, or otherwise regarded as undesirable. This risk is often expressed in vivid claims of widespread fear and wholesale slaughter, claims that are repeated in the right-to-life press in both Holland and the USA; however, these claims are simply not true and as we have seen, the vast majority of the Dutch favor current practices. However, it is true that the Dutch are now beginning to agonize over the problems of the incompetent patient, the mentally ill patient, the newborn with serious deficits, and other patients who cannot make voluntary choices, though these are largely understood as issues about withholding or withdrawing treatment, not about direct termination (Ten Have 1990). In the rare cases where direct termination is practiced, these are not understood as euthanasia, but as a distinct form of *levensbeëindigend handelen*, or life-ending treatment.

What is not often understood is that this new and acutely painful area of reflection for the Dutch—withholding and withdrawing treatment from incompetent patients—has already led in the United States to the development of a vast, highly developed body of law: the series of cases beginning with *Quinlan* and culminating in *Cruzan*. Americans have been discussing these issues for a long time, and have developed a broad set of practices that are regarded as routine in withholding and withdrawing treatment. The Dutch see Americans as much further out on the slippery slope than they are, because Americans have already become accustomed to second-party choices. Issues involving second-party choices are painful to the Dutch in a way they are not to us precisely because voluntariness is so central in the Dutch understanding of choices about dying. Concomitantly, the Dutch see the Americans' squeamishness about first-party choices—voluntary euthanasia, assisted suicide—as evidence that we are not genuinely committed to recognizing voluntary choice after all. For this reason, many Dutch commentators believe that the Americans are at a much greater risk of sliding down the slippery slope into involuntary killing than they are. I fear, I must add, that they are right about this.

Objections to the American Practice

There may be moral problems raised by the German and the Dutch practices, but there are also moral problems raised by the American practice of relying on withholding and withdrawal of treatment in end-of-life situations. The German, Dutch, and American practices all occur within similar conditions—in industrialized nations with highly developed medical systems, where a majority of the population dies of illnesses exhibiting characteristically extended downhill courses—but the issues raised by our own response to this situation may be even more disturbing than those of the Dutch or the Germans. We often assume that our approach is safer because it involves only letting someone die, not killing him or her; but it too raises very troubling questions.

The first of these issues is a function of the fact that withdrawing and especially withholding treatment are typically less conspicuous, less pronounced, less evident kinds of actions than direct killing, even though they can equally well lead to death. Decisions about nontreatment have an invisibility that decisions about directly causing death do not have, even though they may have the same result, and hence there is a much wider range of occasions in which such decisions can be made. One can decline to treat a patient in many different ways, at many different times — by not providing oxygen, by not instituting dialysis, by not correcting electrolyte imbalances, and so on — all of which will cause the patient's death; open medical killing also brings about death, but is a much more overt, conspicuous procedure. Consequently, letting die also invites many fewer protections. In contrast to the earlier slippery slope argument, which sees killing as riskier than letting die, the slippery slope argument here warns that because our culture relies primarily on decisions about nontreatment, grave decisions about living or dying are not as open to scrutiny as they are under more direct life-terminating practices, and hence, are more open to abuse.

Second, and closely related, reliance on withholding and withdrawal of treatment invites rationing in an extremely strong way, in part because of the comparative invisibility of these decisions. When a health-care provider does not offer a specific sort of care, it is not always possible to discern the motivation; the line between believing that it would not provide benefit to the patient and that it would not provide benefit worth the investment of resources in the patient can be very thin. This is a particular problem where health-care financing is highly decentralized, as in the United States, and where rationing decisions without benefit of principle are not always available for easy review.

Third, relying on withholding and withdrawal of treatment can often be cruel. It requires that the patient who is dying from one of the diseases that exhibits a characteristic extended, downhill course (as the majority of patients in Holland, Germany, and the U.S. do) must in effect wait to die until the absence of a certain treatment will cause death. For instance, the cancer patient who forgoes chemotherapy or surgery does not simply die from this choice; he or she continues to endure the downhill course of the cancer until the tumor finally destroys some crucial bodily function or organ. The patient with amyotrophic lateral sclerosis who decides in advance to decline respiratory support does not die at the time this choice is made, but continues to endure increasing paralysis until breathing is impaired and suffocation occurs. We often try to ameliorate these situations by administering pain medication or symptom control at the same time we are withholding treatment, but these are all ways of disguising the fact that we are letting the disease kill the patient rather than directly bringing about death. But the ways diseases kill people are far more cruel than the ways physicians kill patients when performing euthanasia or assisting in suicide.

LANGUAGE AND CONCEPTUAL DIFFERENCES
IN THE WAY WE DIE

But to describe difference in end-of-life practices in three otherwise similar cultures is not yet to show why these differences are possible. To understand how these cultures can variously accept or reject active euthanasia, assistance in suicide, and withdrawing and withholding of treatment, it is necessary to see several conceptual distinctions at the root of these practices.

Differing Senses of the Term Euthanasia

In attempting to disentangle disagreement about the issues in euthanasia, and to explain how it can be so broadly accepted in one European culture, the Netherlands, so strongly rejected in an immediately neighboring one, Germany, and viewed with such ambivalence in American culture, it is essential to see that the term is used in two quite different senses. On the one hand, there is the sense, based heavily on the Greek etymology, *eu-thanatos,* or good death, that euthanasia is in the interests of the person whose death it is; it is better than the death this person would otherwise meet. In the Netherlands, euthanasia is understood in this way, but there is an additional component: it is understood that the wish of the patient is central, and that a death cannot be a good one which is not in concert with the wish of the patient. Hence, in the Netherlands, euthanasia is understood to mean, by definition, *voluntary* euthanasia—or, as the authors of the Remmelink Commission report put it, "the intentional termination of life by somebody other than the person concerned at his or her request" (p. 669).

In Germany, in contrast, the term euthanasia is characteristically understood in a way associated with the abuses by the Nazis: here, euthanasia has nothing to do with good death or death that is in the interests of the person concerned and preferable in that person's eyes to the death he or she might otherwise meet, but an ostensibly medical procedure performed for ulterior, nonmedical ends. The corruption of the term euthanasia began with the infamous T4 program, begun by Hitler in 1939, in which chronically ill, retarded, and handicapped Aryans were selected for this "benefit" though they were neither already dying nor had made any request to die (Lifton 1986). The T4 program increasingly moved to the involuntary selection of those determined unfit for work or who failed other tests of function. The T4 program was discontinued at the protests of both the Catholic and Protestant churches in 1941, but the personnel from this program were reassigned to the newly opened concentration camps, where they continued to perform killings of persons deemed unfit for various reasons. With the T4 personnel went not only their technology but the term "euthanasia," and it became firmly associated with Nazi medical experimentation and genocide. In Germany today, the term still retains this association with Nazi brutality and the involuntary killing of people for wholly nonmedical reasons. Indeed, so strong is the stink of the word "euthanasia" that protest groups have organized to suppress the discussion of it even in settings like academic bioethics conferences.[5]

Thus, we can identify two distinct, wholly different senses of the term euthanasia, and note that they are used in these quite opposite ways in two adjoining European countries. While the Dutch accept euthanasia in the voluntary, self-benefitting sense they have in mind, the Germans reject euthanasia in the involuntary, politically motivated, essentially Nazi sense they have in mind. Meanwhile, in the United States, discussions of the issues in euthanasia shift back and forth between these two quite distinct senses. The result is a general failure to communicate and, consequently, continuing political friction.

Multiple Senses of Suicide

Background conceptual issues are even more apparent in the matter of the language we use for self-caused death, and failure to understand the differences among different cultures may produce even more confusion.

In current usage, English provides one principal term to denote self-caused death: suicide. In contrast to English's primary reliance on a single term, German employs several distinct ones: the traditional terms *Selbstmord* and *Selbsttötung*, the scientific term *Suizid*, and the literary *Freitod*. *Selbstmord* and *Selbsttötung* are the analogues of the English terms *self-murder* (also *self-murther*) and *self-killing*, which were in widespread use in English during the seventeenth and eighteenth centuries; in English these terms were eventually supplanted by the Latinate *suicide* and have virtually disappeared from contemporary use. The German terms both remain current. The German *Selbstmord*, the term most frequently used in ordinary spoken and written discourse, carries extremely negative connotations, no doubt associated with its literal meaning, self-murder, including the implication of moral wrong. In partial contrast, *Selbsttötung*, literally self-killing, has connotations that are comparatively neutral in their factual quality but still decidedly negative, just as *killing* is neutral in English compared to murder but still decidedly negative. *Selbsttötung* is used primarily in bureaucratic and legal contexts. The German term *Suizid*, linguistically analogous to the English term, also literally means self-killing, but is comparatively neutral in its moral connotations; it conveys an implication of psychiatric pathology and is the technical term characteristically used by clinicians and researchers. While these terms are primarily found in their conversational,

[5]See Peter Singer, "On Being Silenced in Germany," *The New York Review of Books*, 15 August 1991, pp. 36–42, and Bettina Schöne-Seifert and Klaus-Peter Rippe, "Silencing the Singer: Antibioethics in Germany," *Hastings Center Report* 21 no. 6 (1991):20–27, for accounts of responses to discussion of euthanasia and other topics. Also see the more comprehensive volume *Zur Debatte über Euthanasie* [On the debate over euthanasia], ed. Rainer Hegselmann and Reinhard Merkel (Frankfurt: Suhrkamp Verlag 1991), containing much of the discussion as well as responses to it. An example of the opposition is to be found in Christian Stadler, *Sterbehilfe—gestern und heute* [Aid-in-dying: yesterday and today] (Bonn: Psychiatrie-Verlag, 1991).

bureaucratic, and clinical applications respectively, they are also sometimes used interchangeably.

German's fourth term for self-caused death, however, is quite another matter. *Freitod* (literally free death or voluntary death) is a positive term, free from connotations of either moral wrongness or pathology; it also avoids the drabness of bureaucratic facticity. It is associated with voluntary individual choice and the expression of basic, strongly held personal values or ideals, especially those running counter to conventional societal norms, and suggests the triumph of personal integrity in the face of threat or shame. *Freitod* has an archaic flavor, often associated with Romanticism, and would not generally be used in ordinary conversation; however, it is readily recognizable to most speakers. But while the most common term for suicide, *Selbstmord,* and the comparatively uncommon literary one, *Freitod,* both refer to the act of bringing about one's own death, they have very different connotations and describe what are understood to be quite different sorts of acts. *Selbstmord* is taken to involve a generally repugnant, tragic act, generally associated with despair, anger, or depression; *Freitod,* in contrast, is seen as expressing voluntary, idealistic choice. Even the verbs used with the different German terms for suicide reinforce their semantic differences: one "commits" *Selbstmord (man begeht Selbstmord),* but one "chooses" *Freitod (man wählt den Freitod).* It is not grammatically possible to speak either of "choosing" *Selbstmord* or of "committing" *Freitod.*

To be sure, both English and German also offer a variety of peripheral terms to refer to suicide—for example, English's *self-destruction* and the archaic *self-slaughter;* German's *Selbstentleibung* (literally, self-disembodiment), all terms with strong connotations of violence, as well as an assortment of verbal expressions, many of which appear in similar forms in both English and German, *sich das Leben nehmen* (take one's own life), and often make reference to the means of death employed: *sich erhängen* (hang oneself), *sich erschiessen* (shoot oneself), *sich ertränken* (drown oneself), and so on. But the central contrast lies in the difference between English's current reliance on a single principal term— suicide—and German's routine use of several different terms, especially *Selbstmord, Selbsttötung, Suizid,* and *Freitod.* Despite its comparative archaism and infrequent usage, this last term, *Freitod,* plays an especially significant role and is crucial to understanding the nature of institutionalized assisted-suicide practices in contemporary Germany.

The term *Freitod* is often thought by educated Germans to date from the eighteenth century, emerging around the same time that Frederick the Great was decriminalizing suicide. The term seems particularly associated with the *Sturm und Drang,* or storm and stress, movement in German literature, especially the plays of Goethe and Schiller—plays read, of course, by German students during their high-school years. Perhaps the most familiar, celebrated example of *Freitod* in German literature would be said to be the death of Goethe's character Werther, the hero of his 1774 novella *The Sorrows of Young Werther.* In this compelling tale, a projection of Goethe's own ill-fated love affair with Charlotte

Buff, Werther chooses to end his own life rather than sink from a condition of extraordinary sensitivity and sensibility into the respectable tedium of everyday life.[6]

Curiously, however, etymological sources do not actually trace the word *Freitod* as far back as Goethe; rather, they find that it originates with the title of Section 22 of Nietzsche's *Also Sprach Zarathustra* (1883), *Vom Freien Tode* (variously translated "On free death" or "On voluntary death").[7] In this work, Nietzsche develops the notion of *Übermensch*, or superman, a concept later misunderstood and appropriated by National Socialism, and asserts a central teaching of Zarathustra: "Die at the right time." *Meinen Tod lobe ich euch, den freien Tod, der mir kommt, weil ich will*, says Zarathustra — "My death, praise I unto me because *I* want it" (p. 75). The death to be avoided is the "common, withered, patient death" of those who are "like sour apples": their lot is to "wait until the last day of autumn: and at the same time they become ripe, yellow, and shrivelled" (p. 75). The death that Zarathustra preaches is an active, extra-ordinary, heroic death, an earlier, self-willed death of which the ordinary man is hardly capable.

Perhaps because of the association of Nietzsche's *Übermensch* with Nazism, *Freitod*, with its quite positive connotations, is rarely thought to originate there, and is instead attributed, erroneously, to the pre-Romantic ideal. But the term is not found in either Goethe or Schiller, and, indeed, the single term, *Freitod*, is not even found in Nietzsche, though it originates from Nietzsche's two-word phrase.[8] Yet, however problematic its actual origins, the term does have a distinctive, well-recognized sense in contemporary German: although it refers to the act of bringing about one's own death, it does not convey the very negative moral connotations associated with *Selbstmord*, the factual but still negative connotations of *Selbsttötung*, or the pathological ones associated with *Suizid*. On the contrary, the connotations of the term *Freitod* are wholly positive: achieving this kind of death is an admirable, heroic — if very difficult — thing to do.

There is no analogous term in English. While there have been recent attempts at coinages in English (for example, *self-deliverance*) to describe suicide

---

[6]Considerable critical discussion has been devoted to the issue of whether Werther's death — depicted as resulting a dozen hours after a self-inflicted gunshot wound to the head, clearly involving considerable suffering, is really intended by Goethe as a pure example of *Freitod*, or whether, on the contrary, it is a parody of it or warning against it. The publication of *The Sorrows of Young Werther* did lead to a rash of copycat suicides among young men, many of whom were dressed in clothing similar to Werther's — a blue waistcoat and a yellow vest.

[7]Friedrich Kluge, *Etymologisches Wörterbuch der deutschen Sprache* [Etymological dictionary of the German language], (Berlin: DeGruyter, 1989), p. 231. See also Karl Baumann's remarkable dissertation on the development of the terms Selbstmord and Freitod: *Selbstmord und Freitod in sprachlicher und geistesgeschichtlicher Beleuchtung* [suicide and free death as illuminated by linguistic and intellectual history] (Giessen: Dissertationsdruckerei und Verlag Konrad Triltsch, 1934), which includes extensive personal reflections from other linguists and over one hundred responses to a questionnaire about usage of these two terms.

[8]The first known occurrence of the single word *Freitod* is dated 1906, some 23 years after Nietzsche's *Zarathustra*. See Baumann, *Selbstmord und Freitod*, p. 13.

but avoid that term's negative connotations, there is no widely recognized, familiar English term with long historical resonances of the sort that *Freitod* seems to have. The only other English terms for suicide that do not have negative connotations carry either pronounced religious associations or the implication that the suicide serves the interest of some other person or cause: there are terms like *self-sacrifice* and *martyrdom*. The very concept of *Freitod*—a notion without religious, altruistic overtones and without negative moral or psychological implications, but which celebrates the voluntary choice of death as a personal expression of principled idealism—is, in short, linguistically unfamiliar to English speakers. Language is crucial in shaping attitudes about end-of-life practices, and because of the very different lexical resources of English and German, it is clear that English speakers cannot straightforwardly understand the very different German conception of these matters. Even in situations of terminal illness, the very concept of voluntary death resonates differently for the German speaker who conceives of it as *Freitod* than it does for the English-speaker who conceives of it as suicide.

Thus, while one sees in both Germany and the United States the development of notions of what is often called rational suicide and the conception that this may be a reasonable choice in terminal illness, they occur in very different cultural climates. In an English-speaking country like the United States, there is no tradition that recognizes a distinctive sort of suicide, different from immoral or pathological suicide, and no tradition of legal or other protection for it. Nor is there a similar tradition in the Netherlands. Not even among the English Romantics is there a literary model quite like Werther, whose death could readily be described as *Freitod*. The sense of the German term *Freitod* is simply not to be found in any single term in English, or in Dutch. Furthermore, it could be constructed in English only with comparatively clumsy circumlocutions: "suicide that is self-centered but without the negative connotations of either suicide or self-centered; "self-deliverance but with long, positive historical resonances," and so on, but these paraphrases would hardly capture the rich connotative field that has developed around the term *Freitod*. This is not to say that German speakers are always actively aware of the history and connotations of *Freitod*, but that the German language provides resources for thinking about, expressing, and experiencing choices about suicide in terminal illness in a way that English and Dutch do not.

Indeed, the DGHS deliberately exploits the conception of ending one's life in terminal illness as *Freitod* rather than *Selbstmord*. The distinctive pink form, mentioned earlier, to be signed when joining the DGHS and to be signed again at the time of one's final act, does not refer to that act as suicide, but as free death: it is labelled *Freitod-Verfügung*, or free death directive. On the line just prior to the space for the second signature, the form reads: *Ich habe heute meinen Freitod eingeleitet*—"I have brought about my free death today." This is the form that will be found beside the body. The terms *Selbstmord* and *Suizid* appear nowhere in this document, and the bureaucratic term *Selbsttötung* appears only in the reverse side in the language of quotations from German law about the legal status of suicide.

It is tempting to say, then, that choices about ending life may be rather different for the German speaker than for the English or the Dutch speaker. If so, it is also plausible to suppose that choices of suicide in terminal illness, protected not only by legal but also by linguistic and hence conceptual supports, may be much easier to make in Germany than they are in the United States, where legal, linguistic, and conceptual structures all militate against them, and perhaps easier than in the Netherlands, where euthanasia is widely accepted but suicide seems less so. Furthermore, presumably, not only may these choices to suicide be easier for the German speaker to make, they may also be easier for survivors to accept and for the culture as a whole to acknowledge. Of course, there are factors in German culture that militate against suicide as well— religious sanctions, for example; but the picture may nevertheless be rather different from the one we see in the Netherlands and the United States, and it may be a picture that is difficult for outsiders to perceive or understand.

THE PROBLEM: A CHOICE OF CULTURES

Thus we see three similar cultures and countries and three similar sets of circumstances, but three quite different basic practices in approaching death. All three of these practices generate moral problems; none of them, nor any others we might devise, is free of moral difficulty. But the questions that face us are this: which of these practices are best, and what consequences would they have for altering our attitudes as suicidologists?

It is not possible to answer this question in a less-than-ideal world without some attention to the specific characteristics and deficiencies of the society in question. In asking which of these practices is best, we must ask which is best *for us*. That we currently employ one set of these practices rather than others does not prove that it is best for us; the question is, would practices developed in other cultures or those not yet widespread in any be better for our own culture than that which has developed here? Thus, it is necessary to consider which differences between our own society and these European cultures have real bearing on the model of approach to dying we ought to adopt.

First, notice that different cultures exhibit different degrees of closeness between physicians and patients—different patterns of contact and involvement. The German physician is sometimes said to be more distant and more authoritarian than the American physician. For example, although empirical data have yet to be published, a large study currently in progress at the University of Göttingen is exploring a number of hypotheses that are often said to characterize medical decision making.[9] These center around the claim that

---

[9]Personal communication, Karl-Heinz Wehkamp, Director, Sozial-medizinisch-psychologisches Institute der Evangelisch-Lutherischen Landeskirche Hannovers. Dr. Wehkamp is currently involved with the study at the University of Göttingen, "Ärztliche Entscheidungen in Konfliktsitua-

decision making remains largely in the hands of the physician; while consent by the patient is legally required, and indeed consent forms for major procedures are routinely signed, neither patient understanding nor consent is much emphasized. In circumstances in which the patient faces oncoming death, according to the hypotheses of the Göttingen study, it is the physician who makes decisions about the initiation or withdrawal of life-sustaining therapy. In these decisions, the evaluations and views of nurses and other caregivers play a considerable role and consent is for the most part sought from the patient's relatives; however, in most cases the patient, who is often no longer competent, is not included in decision making. For the most part, patients in the system of hospital care do not demand or achieve self-determination in matters of dying.

On the other hand, the Dutch physician is sometimes said to be closer to his or her patients than either the American or the German is. In the Netherlands, basic primary care is provided by the *huisarts,* the general practitioner or family physician, who typically lives in the neighborhood, makes house calls frequently, and maintains an office in his or her own home. The *huisarts* is usually the physician for the other members of the patient's family, and will remain the family's physician throughout his or her practice. Thus, the patient for whom euthanasia becomes an issue — say, the terminal cancer patient who has been hospitalized in the past but who has returned home to die — will be cared for by the trusted family physician on a regular basis. Indeed, for a patient in severe distress, the physician, supported by the visiting nurse, may make house calls as often as once or twice a day, or more (after all, it is right in the neighborhood), and is in continuous contact with the family. In contrast, the traditional American institution of the family doctor who makes house calls is rapidly becoming a thing of the past, and whereas some patients who die at home have access to hospice services and house calls from their long-term physician, many have no such long-term care and receive most of it from staff at a clinic or housestaff rotating through the services of a hospital. The degree of continuing contact the patient can have with a familiar, trusted physician clearly influences the nature of his or her dying, and also plays a role in whether physician-performed active euthanasia, assisted suicide, and/or withholding and withdrawing treatment is appropriate.

Second, the United States has a much more volatile legal climate than either the Netherlands or Germany; our medical system is increasingly litigious, much more so than that of any other country in the world. Fears of malpractice action or criminal prosecution color much of what physicians do in managing the dying of their patients. We also tend to evolve public policy through court decisions, and to assume that the existence of a policy puts an end to any moral issue. A delicate legal and moral balance over the issue of euthanasia, as is the case in the Netherlands, would not be possible here.

---

tionen" [Physician decision-making in situations of conflict], which is directed by Hannes Friedrich, Eva Hampel, Klaus Held, Bettina Schöne-Seifert, and Jürgen Wilhelm.

Third, we in the United States have a very different financial climate in which to do our dying. Both the Netherlands and Germany, as well as every other industrialized nation except South Africa, have systems of national health insurance or national health care. Thus the patient is not directly responsible for the costs of treatment, and consequently the patient's choices about terminal care and/or euthanasia need not take personal financial considerations into account. Even for the patient who does have health insurance in the United States, many kinds of services are not covered, whereas the national health care or health insurance programs of many other countries variously provide many sorts of relevant services, including at-home physician care, home-nursing care, home-respite care, care in a nursing-home or other long-term facility, dietician care, rehabilitation care, physical therapy, psychological counseling, and so on. The patient in the United States needs to attend to the financial aspects of dying in a way that patients in many other countries do not, and in this country both the patient's choices and the recommendations of the physician are very often shaped by financial considerations.

There are many other differences between the United States on the one hand and the Netherlands and Germany, with their different models of dying, on the other. There are differences in degrees of paternalism in the medical establishment and in racism, sexism, and ageism in the general culture, as well as awareness of a problematic historical past, especially Nazism. All of these and the previous factors influence the appropriateness or inappropriateness of practices such as active euthanasia and assisted suicide. For instance, the Netherlands' tradition of close physician–patient contact, its absence of malpractice-motivated medicine, and its provision of comprehensive health insurance, together with its comparative lack of racism and ageism and its experience in resistance to Nazism, suggest that this culture is able to permit the practice of voluntary active euthanasia, performed by physicians without risking abuse. On the other hand, it is sometimes said that Germany still does not trust its physicians, remembering the example of Nazi experimentation, and given a comparatively authoritarian medical climate in which the contact between physician and patient is quite distanced, the population could not be comfortable with the practice of active euthanasia. There, only a wholly patient-controlled response to terminal situations, as in non-physician-assisted suicide, is a reasonable and prudent practice.

But what about the United States? This is a country where 1) sustained contact with a personal physician is decreasing, 2) the risk of malpractice action is increasing, 3) much medical care is not insured, 4) many medical decisions are financial decisions as well, 5) racism is on the rise, and 6) the public is naive about direct contact with Nazism or similar totalitarian movements. Thus, the United States is in many respects an untrustworthy candidate for practicing active euthanasia. Given the pressures on individuals in an often atomized society, encouraging solo suicide, assisted if at all only by nonprofessionals, might well be open to considerable abuse, too.

What, then, is appropriate for our own cultural situation? Physician-performed euthanasia, though not in itself morally wrong, is morally jeopardized where the legal, time allotment, and especially financial pressures on both patients and physicians are severe; thus, it is morally problematic in our culture in a way that it is not in the Netherlands. Solo suicide outside the institution of medicine (as in Germany) is problematic in a culture (like the United States) that is increasingly alienated, offers deteriorating and uneven social services, is increasingly racist, and in other ways imposes unusual pressures on individuals. Reliance only on withholding and withdrawing treatment (as in the United States) can be, as we've seen, cruel, and its comparative invisibility invites erosion under cost containment and other pressures. These are the three principal alternatives we've considered; but none of them seems wholly suited to our actual situation for dealing with the new fact that most of us die of extended-decline, deteriorative diseases. However, permitting physicians to supply patients with the means for ending their own lives still grants physicians some control over the circumstances in which this can happen—only, for example, when the prognosis is genuinely grim and the alternatives for symptom control are poor—but leaves the fundamental decision about whether to use these means to the patient alone. It is up to the patient then, and his or her advisors, including family, clergy, physician, other health-care providers, and perhaps a raft of self-counseling books, to be clear about whether he or she really wants to use these means or not. Thus, the physician is involved, but not directly; and it is the patient's choice, but the patient is not alone in making it. We live in a quite imperfect world, but, of the alternatives for facing death—which we all eventually must—I think that the practice of permitting physician-assisted suicide is the one most nearly suited to the current state of our own quite flawed society. This is a model not yet central in any of the three countries examined here—the Netherlands, Germany, or the United States—but it is the one I think suits us best.

Contemporary suicidology must, I think, come to terms with these realities. It must observe that different choices and background assumptions about dying characterize different cultures, and it must use these facts to reexamine the background assumptions of our own culture and the choices we permit and reject. The question of one's own role in one's own death will become, I think, *the* major social issue of the next decade, as we consider legalizing assisted suicide, physician-assisted suicide, and physician-performed voluntary active euthanasia; and if contemporary suicidology is to remain the enormously important field it has become, it must be capable of responding openly to these issues.

REFERENCES

Admiraal, P. (1990). Euthanasia in general hospitals. Paper presented at the Eighth World Congress of the International Federation of the Right-to-Die Societies. Maastricht, Holland, June.

Baumann, K. (1934). *Selbstmord und Freitod in sprachlicher und geschichtlicher Beleuchtung.* Giessen: Dissertationsdruckerie und Verlag Konrad Triltsch.

Borst-Eilers, E. (1991). Controversies in the care of dying patients. Paper presented at University of Florida conference, Orlando, Florida, February.

Hegselmann, R., and Merkel, R., eds. (1991). *Zur Debatte über Euthanasie.* Frankfurt: Suhrkamp Verlag.

Humphry, D. (1991). *Final Exit: The Practicalities of Self-deliverance and Assisted Suicide for the Dying.* Eugene, OR: The Hemlock Society.

Kluge, F. (1989). *Etymologisches Wörterbuch der deutschen Sprache.* Berlin: De Gruyter.

Krey, V. (1989). Tötung durch Zulassen eines Selbstmordes. In *Strafrecht Besonderer Teil,* vol. 1, 7th. ed., pp. 35–37. Stuttgart: Verlag W. Kohlhammer.

Lifton, R. (1986). *The Nazi Doctors: Medical Killing and the Psychology of Genocide.* New York: Basic Books.

Miles, S., and Gomez, C. (1988). *Protocols for Elective Use of Life-sustaining Treatment.* New York: Springer-Verlag.

Nietzsche, F. (1883). *Thus Spake Zarathustra.* Trans. T. Cannon. New York: Modern Library.

Olshansky, S. and Ault, A. (1986). The fourth stage of the epidemiological transition: the age of delayed degenerative diseases. *Milbank Memorial Fund Quarterly/Health and Society* 64:355–391.

Pohlmeier, H. (1983). *Selbstmord und Selbstmordverhütung.* Munich: Urban & Schwartzenberg.

———— (1985). Suicide and euthanasia—special types of partner relationships. *Suicide and Life-Threatening Behavior* 15:117–23.

Singer, P. (1991). On being silenced in Germany. *The New York Review of Books* 15:36–42, August.

Smedira, N. (1990). Withholding and withdrawal of life support from the critically ill. *New England Journal of Medicine* 322:309–315.

Sprung, C. (1990). Changing attitudes and practices in foregoing life-sustaining treatments. Journal of the American Medical Association. 263:2213.

Stadler, C. (1991). Sterbehilfe—gestern und heute. Bonn: Psychiatrie Verlag.

Ten Have, H. (1990). Coma: controversy and consensus. *Newsletter of the European Society for Philosophy of Medicine and Health Care* 8 (May):19–20.

van der Maas, P., van Delden, J., Pijnenburg, L., and Looman, C. (1991). Euthanasia and other medical decisions concerning the end of life. (Summary of the report to the Remmelink Commission.) *The Lancet* 338:669–674, September.

CHRONOLOGY

1918   Born in York, Pennsylvania.

1938   Received A.B. in Psychology from UCLA.

1940   Received M.A. from UCLA. Employed as civil service examiner by city of Los Angeles. Published "An Experimental Study of the Appraisal Interview."

1942–1945   Military Service (Private to Captain).

1944   Married Jeanne Keplinger.

1947   Became a father; first of four sons born.

1948   Received Ph.D. in Psychology from University of Southern California. Published "Schizophrenia and the MAPS Test."

1948–1955   Worked as clinical psychologist at VA Hospital in Los Angeles. Published *Thematic Test Analysis*.

1949   Discovered suicide notes in office of Los Angeles County Coroner.

1951   Met Henry A. Murray.

1955–1966   Co-founded and co-directed the Los Angeles Suicide Prevention Center. Published *Clues to Suicide* and *The Cry for Help* with N. L. Farberow. Also published *Essays in Self-Destruction*.

1961   USPHS Special Research Fellow, Harvard University. Published "Orientations toward Death."

1966–1969   Became Chief, Center for Studies of Suicide Prevention, National Institute of Mental Health. Published *Bulletin of Suicidology*.

1966   Invited by Melville Society to Williams College as Speaker. Published "The Deaths of Herman Melville."

1968   Founded The American Association of Suicidology. Published *On the Nature of Suicide.*

1969   Visiting Professor at Harvard University. Published *Death and the College Student.*

1969-1970   Fellow, Center for Advanced Studies of the Behavioral Sciences, Stanford. Published *Aspects of Depression and Suicide among the Gifted.*

1970-1988   Professor of Thanatology, UCLA. Published *Deaths of Man, Voices of Death, Definition of Suicide, Contemporary Developments, Death: Current Perspectives, Suicide Thoughts and Reflections,* and *Endeavors in Psychology: Selections from the Personology of Henry A. Murray.*

1978   On leave from UCLA. Research Associate at Karolinska Hospital in Stockholm, Sweden. Published "Clinical Thanatology and Psychotherapy" with Loma Feigenberg. First grandchild (of four) is born.

1982   On leave from UCLA. Visiting Professor of Thanatology at Ben Gurion University of the Negev, Beersheva, Israel. Published "Some Aphorisms of Suicide and Some Implications for Psychotherapy."

1987   Received APA award for Distinguished Professional Contributions to the Public Service. Published "A Psychological Approach to Suicide" and "The Indian Summer of Life."

1988   Retired from UCLA as Professor of Thanatology Emeritus. Published "Dying, Denying and Willing the Obligatory."

1991   Donated, with eldest son David, Melville collection to UCLA on the centennial of Melville's death.

1993   Reconceptualizing suicide and contemplating death. Published *Suicide as Psychache: A Clinical Approach to Self-Destructive Behavior.*

APPENDIX:
A Shneidman Bibliography

1943

The experimental study of the appraisal interview. *Journal of Applied Psychology* 27:186–205.

1946

Information form useful in vocational counseling. *Occupations,* 25:108–109.

A short method of scoring the Minnesota multiphasic personality inventory. *Journal of Consulting Psychology* 10:143–145.

1947

The Make A Picture Story Projective Personality Test: a preliminary report. *Journal of Consulting Psychology* 11:315–325.

Psychodrama and the MAPS test. *Journal of Projective Techniques* 11:1–26. (With Ernest Fantel).

1948

Schizophrenia and the MAPS Test. *Genetic Psychology Monographs* 38:145–223.

1949

The Make-A-Picture-Story (MAPS) Test. New York: Psychological Corporation.

The Guilford-Shneidman-Zimmerman Interest Survey. Beverly Hills, CA: Sheridan Supply. (With J. P. Guilford and W. W. Zimmerman).

Some comparisons among the Four Picture Test, Thematic Apperception Test, and Make a Picture Story Test. *Journal of Projective Techniques* 13:150–154.

1951

Thematic Test Analysis. (Ed.). New York: Grune & Stratton.

1952

The case of Jay: psychological test and anamnestic data. *Journal of Projective Techniques* 16:297–345, 444–475.

Manual for the MAPS test. *Projective Techniques* 17:1–92.

1954

Validity of MMPI interpretations. *Journal of Consulting Psychology* 18:425–428. Reprinted in *Research in Clinical Assessment,* ed. E. I. Megargee. New York: Harper and Row. Also in *Basic Readings on the MMPI in Psychology and Medicine,* ed. G. S. Welshe and W. G. Dahlstrom, Minneapolis: University of Minnesota Press, 1956. (With Kenneth B. Little).

1955

Acute paranoid schizophrenia in a veteran. In *Clinical Studies in Personality,* ed. A. Burton and R. E. Harris, pp. 86–116. New York: Harper and Brothers.

The validity of thematic projective techniques interpretations. *Journal of Personality* 23:286–294. Reprinted in *Research in Clinical Assessment,* ed. E. I. Megargee. New York: Harper & Row, 1968. (With Kenneth B. Little).

Attempted, threatened and completed suicide. *Journal of Abnormal and Social Psychology* 50:230. (With N. L. Farberow).

1956

Clues to suicide. *Public Health Reports* 71:109–114. (With N. L. Farberow).

Some relationships between the Rorschach technique and other psychodiagnostic tests. In *Developments in the Rorschach Technique,* vol. 2, B. Klopfer, pp. 595–642. New York: World Book.

1957

Some comparisons between genuine and simulated suicide notes. *Journal of General Psychology* 56:251–256. (With N. L. Farberow).

A method for educing the present correlates of perception: an introduction to the method of successive co-variation. *Journal of General Psychology* 57:113–120.

Clues to Suicide. (Editor). New York: McGraw-Hill. (With N. L. Farberow). Translated into Japanese.

1958

Some relationships between thematic and drawing materials. In *The Clinical Application of Projective Drawings,* ed. E. F. Hammer. Springfield, IL: Charles C Thomas.

A Nisei woman attacks by suicide. In *Clinical Studies in Culture Conflicts,* ed. G. Seward, pp. 335–338. New York: Ronald. (With N. L. Farberow).

Suicide and the police officer. *Police* 2:51–55. (With N. L. Farberow).

Some relationships among thematic projective tests of various degrees of structuredness and behavior in a group situation. *Journal of Projective Techniques* 22:3–12. (With C. L. Edgar).

TAT heroes of suicidal and non-suicidal subjects. *Journal of Projective Techniques* 22:211–228. (With N. L. Farberow).

1959

Congruencies among interpretations of psychological test and anamnestic data. *Psychological Monographs* 73:1–42. Reprinted in *Research in Clinical Assessment,* ed. E. I. Megargee. New York: Harper & Row, 1969. (With Kenneth B. Little).

Suicide and death. In *The Meaning of Death,* ed. H. Feifel, pp. 284–301. New York: McGraw-Hill. (With N. L. Farberow).

Conversations about suicide: a review of Bosselman's *Self-Destruction. Contemporary Psychology* 3:329–330.

Current aspects of the problem of validity: suggestions for the delineation of validational studies. *Journal of Projective Techniques* 23:259–262.

1960

Suicide of the aged. *Report to the U.S. Senate Sub-Committee on Problems of the Aged and Aging,* part 4, pp. 970–980.

A socio-psychological study of suicide. In *Perspectives in Personality Research,* ed. H. David and J. D. Brengelmann, pp. 270–293. New York: Ronald. (With N. L. Farberow).

The MAPS Test with children. In *Projective Techniques for Children,* ed. A. I. Rabin, pp. 130–148. New York: Grune & Stratton.

Psycho-logic: a personality approach to patterns of thinking. In *Current Issues in Thematic Apperceptive Fantasy,* ed. J. Kagan and G. Lesser, pp. 153–195. Springfield, IL: Charles C Thomas.

The Travis Projective Pictures. In *Fifth Mental Measurement Yearbook,* ed. O. Buros. New Brunswick, NJ: Rutgers University Press.

The logical, psychological and ecological environments of suicide. *California's Health* 17:193–196.

The clergy's responsibility in suicide prevention. In *Preventive Mental Hygiene and the Clergy,* ed. Oakland, CA: Alameda County Mental Health Service.

1961

Suicide: the problem and its magnitude. V. A. Medical Bulletin no. 7. Washington, DC: U.S. Government Printing Office. (With N. L. Farberow).

Some facts about suicide: causes and prevention. (P.H.S. Publication, no. 852.) Washington, DC: U.S. Government Printing Office. (With N. L. Farberow and C. V. Leonard).

The Cry for Help. (Editor). New York: McGraw–Hill. (With N. L. Farberow). Translated into Japanese and Spanish.

A suicide prevention center. In *Current Psychiatric Therapies,* ed. J. H. Masserman. New York: Grune & Stratton. (With R. E. Litman and N. L. Farberow).

The case of El. *Journal of Projective Techniques* 25:131-154.

A suicide prevention center. *American Journal of Psychiatry* 117:1084-1087. (With R. E. Litman and N. L. Farberow).

1962

Suicide: evaluation and treatment of suicidal risk among schizophrenic patients in psychiatric hospitals. V.A. Medical Bulletin no. 8. Washington, DC: U.S. Government Printing Office. (With N. L. Farberow).

Suicide: some classificatory considerations. In *Special Treatment Situations,* ed. Des Plaines, IL: Forest Hospital Publications.

Projections on a triptych; or a hagiology for our time. *Journal of Projective Techniques* 26:379-387.

1963

Suicide among general medical and surgical hospital patients with malignant neoplasms. V.A. Medical Bulletin No. 9. Washington, DC: U.S. Government Printing Office. (With N. L. Farberow).

The logic of politics. In *Television and Human Behavior,* ed. M. A. May and L. Arons, pp. 178-199. New York: Appleton-Century-Crofts.

Suicide: trauma and taboo. In *Taboo Topics,* ed. N. L. Farberow, pp. 33-43. New York: Atherton.

Orientations toward death: a vital aspect of the study of lives. In *The Study of Lives,* ed. R. W. White, pp. 200-227. New York: Atherton Press. Reprinted in *International Journal of Psychiatry* 2:167-188 and in *Suicidal Behaviors,* ed. H. Resnik, pp. 19-48. Boston: Little, Brown. Translated into Japanese.

A look into the dark: a review of Meerloo's *Suicide and Mass Suicide. Contemporary Psychology* 8:178-180.

Investigations of equivocal suicides. *Journal of the American Medical Association* 184:924-929. (With R. E. Litman, T. J. Curphey, N. L. Farberow, and N. D. Tabachnik).

The suicidal patient and the physician. *Mind* 1:69-75. (With N. L. Farberow and R. E. Litman).

1964

Pioneer in suicidology: a review of Louis I. Dublin's *Suicide: A Sociological and Statistical Study. Contemporary Psychology* 9:370-371.

Some reflections of personality explorers, 1938-1963. *Journal of Projective Techniques* 28:156-160.

Suicide, sleep and death: some possible intercorrelations among cessation, interruption and continuation phenomena. *Journal of Consulting Psychology* 28:95–106.

Tranquilizers and suicide in the schizophrenic patient. *Archives of General Psychiatry* 11:312–321. (With S. Cohen, C. V. Leonard, and N. L. Farberow).

Premiers secours lors de crises suicidairées. *Medicine et Hygiene* 22:637–633. (With R. E. Litman and N. L. Farberow).

1965

Projective techniques. In *Handbook of Clinical Psychology,* ed. B. Wolman, pp. 498–521. New York: McGraw-Hill.

The Los Angeles Suicide Prevention Center: a demonstration of public health feasibilities. *American Public Health Journal* 55:21–26. (With N. L. Farberow).

Suicide prevention telephone service. *Journal of the American Medical Association* 192:21–25. (With R. E. Litman, N. L. Farberow, S. M. Heilig, and J. Kramer).

Some reflections on death and suicide. *Folia Psychiatrica et Neurologica Japonica* 19:317–325.

1966

The Logics of Communication: A Manual for Analysis. China Lake, CA: U.S. Naval Ordnance Test Station. (With P. Tripodes).

Review of D. J. West's *Murder Followed by Suicide. American Journal of Psychiatry* 123:501–502.

Suicide prevention around the clock. *American Journal of Orthopsychiatry* 36:551–558. (With N. L. Farberow, R. E. Litman, C. Wold, S. M. Heilig, and J. Kramer).

Foreword to Japanese edition of *Clues to Suicide.* Translated by K. Ohara and M. Shimizu.

Case history and hospitalization factors in suicides of neuropsychiatric hospital patients. *Journal of Nervous and Mental Disease* 142:32–44. (With N. L. Farberow and C. Neuringer).

Suicide among adolescents. *California School Health* 2:1–5.

Suicides of children and adolescents: a national problem. *Technical Assistance Project Proceedings of a Conference on Depression and Suicide in Adolescents and Young Adults.* Montpelier, VT: Department of Mental Health.

1967

How the family physician can prevent suicide. *Physicians Panorama* 5:5–10. (With L. H. Dizmang).

Multiple MMPI profiles of suicidal persons. *Psychological Reports* 21:401–404. (With A. Devries).

A major cause of death among the young: self-destruction. *Social Service Outlook* 7:13–14.

Description of the NIMH Center for Studies of Suicide Prevention. *Bulletin of Suicidology* 1:2–7.

Some current developments in suicide prevention. *Bulletin of Suicidology* 1:31–34.

Essays in Self Destruction. (Editor). New York: Science House. Translated into Japanese.

Sleep and self-destruction: a phenomenological approach. In *Essays in Self Destruction,* ed. E. S. Shneidman, pp. 510–539. New York: Science House.

How to prevent suicide. *Public Health Pamphlet,* no. 406. New York: Public Health Pamphlets. (With Philip Mandelkorn).

1968

Suicide: psychological aspects. In *International Encyclopaedia of the Social Sciences,* pp. 385–389. New York: Crowell-Collier.

Suicidal phenomena: their definition and classification. *International Encyclopaedia of the Social Sciences.* New York: Crowell-Collier.

First Training Record in Suicidology. Chevy Chase, MD: National Institute of Mental Health.

The Suicide Prevention Center of Los Angeles. In *Suicidal Behaviors,* ed. H. Resnik, pp. 367–380. Boston: Little, Brown. (With N. L. Farberow).

Suicide prevention: a current national view. In *Proceedings: Fourth International Conference for Suicide Prevention,* ed. N. L. Farberow. Los Angeles: Del Mar.

The deaths of Herman Melville. In *Melville and Hawthorne in the Berkshires,* ed. H. P. Vincent, pp. 118–143. Kent, OH: Kent State University Press.

Preventing suicide. *American Journal of Nursing* 65:111–116. Reprinted in *Readings in Public Health Nursing,* ed. D. Mereness Dubuque, IA: W. C. Brown. Also reprinted in *Suicide,* ed. J. P. Gibbs. New York: Harper & Row.

The role of nonprofessional volunteers in a suicide prevention center. *Community Mental Health Journal* 4:287–295. (With S. M. Heilig, N. L. Farberow, and R. E. Litman).

Orientations toward cessation: a reexamination of current modes of deaths. *Journal of Forensic Sciences* 13:33–46.

Suicide prevention: the hospital's role. *Hospital Practice* 3:56–61.

Classifications of suicidal phenomena. *Bulletin of Suicidology* 2:1–10.

1969

Aspects of Depression. (Editor) Boston: Little, Brown. (With M. Ortega).

Suicide, lethality and the psychological autopsy. In *Aspects of Depression,* ed. E. S. Shneidman and M. Ortega, pp. 225–250. Boston: Little, Brown.

On the Nature of Suicide. (Editor). San Francisco: Jossey-Bass.

The suicidal death. In *But Not to Lose,* ed. A. H. Kutscher. New York: McGraw-Hill.

Logical content analysis: an explication of styles of concludifying. In *The Analysis of Communication Content,* ed. G. Gerbner, O. R. Holsti, K. Krippendorss, et al, pp. 261–279. New York: Wiley.

Some characteristics of genuine versus simulated suicide notes. In *The General Inquirer: A Computer Approach to Content Analysis,* ed. P. J. Stone, D. C. Dunphy, M. S. Smith, and D. M. Ogilvie., pp. 527–535. New York: Wiley. (With N. L. Farberow).

1970

The Psychology of Suicide. New York: Science House. (With N. L. Farberow and R. E. Litman).

1971

The National Suicide Program. In *Organizing the Community to Prevent Suicide,* ed. J. Zusman and D. Davidson, Springfield, IL: Charles C Thomas.

"Suicide" and "suicidology": a brief etymological note. *Life-Threatening Behavior* 1:260–264.

On the deromanticization of death. *American Journal of Psychotherapy* 25:4–17.

Prevention, intervention and postvention of suicide. *Annals of Internal Medicine* 75:453–457.

Perturbation and lethality as precursors of suicide in a gifted group. *Life-Threatening Behavior* 1:23–45.

1972

Prevention of suicide: a challenge for community service. In *Handbook of Community Psychology and Mental Health,* ed. S. E. Golann and C. Eisdorfer, pp. 449–460. New York: Appelton-Century-Crofts.

Death and the College Student. (Editor). New York: Behavioral Publications. Reprinted in *New Meanings of Death.* ed. H. Feifel. New York: McGraw-Hill.

The creative artist and the savage god: a review of A. Alvarez's *The Savage God. Psychotherapy and Social Science Review* 6:19–22.

Can a young person write his own obituary? *Life-Threatening Behavior* 2:262–267.

1973

Deaths of Man. New York: Quadrangle/New York Times Book Company. New York: Penguin Books, 1974. Translated into Japanese. Nominated for the National Book Award in Science, 1973.

Suicide. In *Encyclopaedia of Psychology.* Port Washington, NY: Dushkin.

Suicide. In *Encyclopaedia Britannica,* vol. 21:383–385. Chicago: William Benton.

Who owns the patient? In *Critical Incidents in Nursing,* ed. L. S. Bermosk and R. J. Corsini. Philadelphia: W. B. Saunders.

Suicide notes reconsidered. *Psychiatry* 36:379–395.

1974

Community programs in suicidology. In *American Handbook of Psychiatry,* ed. S. Arieti. New York: Basic Books.

1975

Psychiatric emergencies: suicide. In *Comprehensive Textbook of Psychiatry,* revised edition, ed. A. Freedman, H. Kaplan, and B. Sadock, vol. II, pp. 1774–1784. Baltimore: Williams & Wilkins.

Postvention: care of the bereaved. In *Consultation-Liaison Psychiatry,* ed. R. O. Pasnau, pp. 245–256. New York: Grune & Stratton.

1976

Suicide: an overview. a psychological theory and recent developments. *Psychiatric Annals* 6:9–121 (not inclusive).

Some psychological reflections on the death of Malcolm Melville. *Suicide and Life-Threatening Behavior* 6:231–242.

Death: Current Perspectives. (Editor). Palo Alto, CA: Mayfield.

Suicidology: Contemporary Developments. (Editor). New York: Grune & Stratton.

1977

The psychological autopsy. In *Guide to the Investigation and Reporting of Drug Abuse Deaths,* ed. L. I. Gottschalk, S. L. McGuire, E. C. Dinoro, et al. Washington, DC: USDHEW, U.S. Government Printing Office.

Aspects of the Dying Process. *Psychiatric Annals* 7:25–40.

Foreword to *Suicide: Assessment and Intervention,* by C. Hatton, S. Valente, and A. Rink. New York: Appleton-Century-Crofts.

1978

Some aspects of psychotherapy with dying persons. In *Psychosocial Aspects of Terminal Patient Care,* ed. C. A. Garfield, pp. 201–218. New York: McGraw-Hill.

1979

Clinical thanatology and psychotherapy: some reflections on caring for the dying person. *Omega* 10:1–8. (With L. Feigenberg).

Risk writing: a special note about Cesare Pavese and Joseph Conrad. *Journal of the American Academy of Psychoanalysis* 7:575–592.

A bibliography of suicide notes, 1856–1979. *Suicide and Life-Threatening Behavior* 9:57–59.

1980

Voices of Death. New York: Harper & Row. New York: Bantam, 1981. Translated into Japanese, Swedish, and German.

Death Current: Perspectives. 2nd Ed. (Editor). Palo Alto, CA: Mayfield.

A genuine classic in suicidology: review of Jean Baechler's *Suicides. Contemporary Psychology* 25:108–109.

Foreword to *Terminal Care,* by L. Feigenberg. New York: Brunner/Mazel.

Psychotherapy with suicidal patients. In *Specialized Techniques in Individual Psychotherapy,* ed. T. B. Karasu and L. Bellak, pp. 305–313. New York: Brunner/Mazel.

A possible classification of suicidal acts based on Murray's need system. *Suicide and Life-Threatening Behavior* 10:175–181.

1981

Suicide Thoughts and Reflections, 1960–1980. (Editor). New York: Human Sciences.

Endeavors in Psychology: Selections from the Personology of Henry A. Murray. (Editor). New York: Harper & Row.

Suicidal Behaviors. In *Prognosis: Contemporary Outcomes of Disease,* ed. J. F. Fries and G. E. Ehrlich, pp. 478–480. Bowie, MD: Charles.

Commentary. In *The Endless, Winding Way in Melville: New Charts by Kring and Carey,* ed. D. Yannella and H. Parker, pp. 38–41. Glassboro, NJ: The Melville Society.

1982

On "Therefore I Must Kill Myself." *Suicide and Life-Threatening Behavior* 12:52–55.

The suicidal logic of Cesare Pavese. *Journal of the American Academy of Psychoanalysis* 10:547–563.

Aspects of the Personological System of Henry A. Murray. *Personality and Social Psychology* 8:604, 617–619.

1983

On abolishing death: An etymological note. *Suicide and Life-Threatening Behavior* 13:176–178.

Review of *Lifelines: Clinical Perspective on Suicide,* by E. L. Bussak, S. C. Schoonover, and A. D. Gill. *New England Journal of Medicine* (January 13) 308:108–109.

1984

Death: Current Perspectives. 3rd Ed. (Editor). Palo Alto, CA: Mayfield.

Aphorisms of suicide and some implications for psychotherapy. *American Journal of Psychotherapy* 38:319–328.

Personality and "Success" among a selected group of lawyers. *Journal of Personality Assessment* 48:609–616.

Suicide prevention. In *Encyclopaedia of Psychology,* vol. 3, pp. 383–386. New York: Wiley.

Make-A-Picture-Story (MAPS) test. In *Encyclopaedia of Psychology,* vol. 2, p. 328. New York: Wiley.

Henry A. Murray. In *Encyclopaedia of Psychology,* vol. 2, p. 412. New York: Wiley.

Epilogue in *Cancer Treatment,* 2nd ed, ed. C. Haskell. Philadelphia: W. B. Saunders.

Remembrance of Mort Meyer. *Journal of Personality Assessment* 48:558–559.

1985

Definition of Suicide. New York: Wiley. Translated into Japanese.

Some thoughts on grief and mourning. *Suicide and Life-Threatening Behavior* 15:51–55.

Forem des Sterbens und Thanato-Therapie. In *Die Begeitung Sterbender: Theorie und Praxis der Thanato-Therapie,* ed. I. Spiegel-Rosing and H. Petzold. Paderborn, Germany: Junfermann Verlag.

Some psychological reflections of Herman Melville. *Melville Society Extracts* 64:(November) 7–9.

1986

Some essentials of suicide and some implications for response. In *Suicide,* ed. A. Roy, pp. 1–16. Baltimore: Williams & Wilkins.

Melville's cognitive style: the logic of *Moby-Dick.* In *A Companion to Melville Studies,* ed. J. Bryant, pp. 543–564. Westport, CT: Greenwood.

MAPS of the Harvard Yard. *Journal of Personality Assessment* 50:436–447.

Foreword to *The Thorn in the Chrysanthemum: Economic Success and Suicide In Contemporary Japan,* by Mamoru Iga. Berkeley, CA: University of California Press.

Review of new perspectives in schizophrenia, ed. M. N. Menuck and M. V. Seeman. *New England Journal of Medicine* 20:(March) 314, 795.

1987

At the point of no return. *Psychology Today* March, pp. 54–58.

Dying, denying and willing the obligatory. In *Social Change and Personality: Essays in Honor of Nevitt Sanford,* ed. M. B. Freeman. New York: Brunner/Mazel.

A Psychological Approach to Suicide. In *Cataclysms, Crises and Catastrophes: Psychology in Action,* ed. G. R. VanderBos and B. K. Bryant, pp. 147–183. Washington, DC: American Psychological Association.

Approaches and commonalities of suicide. In *Attitudinal Factors in Suicidal Behavior and Its Prevention,* ed. R. F. W. Diekstra. Leiden: Swets & Zeitlinger/Brill.

Suicide and suicide prevention. In *Concise Encyclopaedia of Psychology,* ed. R. Corsini, pp. 1093–1094. New York: Wiley.

1988

Foreword to *Suicide Notes,* by A. Leenaars. New York: Human Sciences.

Reflections of a founder. *Suicide and Life-Threatening Behavior* 18:1–12. Also in *Understanding and Preventing Suicide,* ed. R. Maris, pp. 1–12. New York: Guilford.

1989

A multidisciplinary approach to suicide. In *Suicide: Understanding and Responding,* ed. D. Jacobs and H. Brown, pp. 1–30. Madison, CT: International Universities Press.

The indian summer of life: a preliminary study of septuagenarians. *American Psychologist* 44:(April) 684–694.

The suicidal psychologics of *Moby-Dick.* In *Youth Suicide Prevention: Lessons from Literature,* ed. S. M. Deats and L. T. Lenker, pp. 15–47. New York: Plenum.

1991

A life in death: Notes of a committed suicidologist. In *The History of Clinical Psychology in Autobiography,* ed. C. E. Walker, pp. 225–292. Pacific Grove, CA: Brooks/Cole.

The commonalities of suicide across the life span. In *Life Span Perspectives in Suicide,* ed. A. Leenaars, pp. 39–52. New York: Plenum.

Key psychological factors in understanding and managing suicidal risk. *Journal of Geriatric Psychiatry* 24:153–174.

Foreword to *Adolescent Suicide: Assessment and Intervention,* ed. A. Berman and D. Jobes. Washington, DC: American Psychological Association.

Foreword to *The Suicidal Patient: Clinical and Legal Standards for Professional Psychological Practice,* ed. B. Bongar and E. Harris. Washington, DC: American Psychological Association.

1992

A conspectus of the suicidal scenario. In *Assessment and Prediction of Suicide,* ed. R. Maris, A. Berman, J. T. Maltsberger, and R. Yufit, pp. 50–64. New York: Guilford.

What do suicides have in common? a summary of the psychological approach. In *Suicide: Guidelines for Assessment, Management and Treatment,* ed. B. Bongar, pp. 3–15. New York: Oxford University Press.

A comment on "Rational Suicide and the Right to Die." *New England Journal of Medicine* 326:(March 26) 889.

1993

Suicide as psychache. *Journal of Nervous and Mental Disease* Vol. 181, No. 2.

Suicide as Psychache: A Clinical Approach to Self-Destructive Behavior. Northvale, NJ: Jason Aronson.

The Psychology of Suicide, Revised Edition. (Ed.) Northvale, NJ: Jason Aronson. (With N. L. Farberow and R. E. Litman).